The Global Emerging Market
in Transition

THE GLOBAL EMERGING MARKET IN TRANSITION

Articles, Forecasts and Studies 1973–1998

VLADIMIR L. KVINT

FORDHAM UNIVERSITY PRESS
New York • 1999

Copyright © 1999 by Fordham University Press
All rights reserved.
LC 98–54126
ISBN 0–8232–1902–X

Library of Congress Cataloging-in-Publication Data

Kvint, V. L. (Vladimir L'vovich)
    The global emerging market in transition : articles, forecasts.
and studies / Vladimir L. Kvint.
        p.   cm.
    Includes bibliographical references.
    ISBN 0-8232-1902-X (alk. paper)
    1. Russia (Federation)—Economic conditions—1991–
2. Investments, Foreign—Russia (Federation)   3. Economic
history—1990–   4. Investments, Foreign.   I. Title.
HC340.12.K96   1999
332.6'73'0947—dc21   98-54126
                                                        CIP

Printed in the United States of America

To
my mother, Lydia

CONTENTS

PART III
THE EMERGING MARKET OF RUSSIA

PART IV
MANAGEMENT SYSTEMS AND SCIENTIFIC
TECHNICAL PROGRESS

PREFACE

This is not a typical book. It was not written all at once—it contains articles, forecasts, and studies made over the last 25 years. Life passes so quickly one can hardly remember how old one is . . . having just written that phrase, I remembered my age.

I did not know how many pages in this book I should dedicate to those individuals who have helped me. So I decided to thank first those who inspired me with the idea to prepare this collection. Secondly, I need to thank those people who helped me with the actual preparation of the book.

Before all else, however, I am grateful to my mother for her unconditional support in all my life's endeavors and to my father for, during my childhood, introducing me to business. I am grateful to my older brother Pavel, a talented engineer who, instead of dating girls, often stayed home to explain the fundamentals of modern technology. I am also grateful to my daughters, Liza and Valeria, for forcing me, after a long day's work, to sit down behind my desk and write many of the articles that are collected here. It was also crucial to have the support of my Dina, her son, Danny, and her family who provided an encouraging and warm environment during the preparation of this book.

We all have different periods in our lives. My American period was particularly difficult because I arrived here without any knowledge of the English language. I'm reminded of my cat, Benji, who understands everything, but can say nothing. It was under these circumstances that I came to *Forbes* magazine and tried to explain the "strange" concept that the Soviet Union would soon disappear. They ended up publishing this as a cover story. This was the beginning of my publishing career in the United States. Consequently, there is no limit to my gratitude to *Forbes*'s editors James Michaels and Lawrence Minard.

I thank Ann and Ken Bialkin, Evelyn Kenvin and Arthur Rosenbloom, Vicki and Ron Weiner, and Arthur and Kathryn Taylor, whose help was invaluable in helping me to understand American business life and culture.

Of course, I am very grateful to Lawrence Weinbach, Donald Hanson, and Peter Berger, who were my leaders—my guiding forces—during my years at Arthur Andersen. I would like to express my gratitude to James Hatt, Dr. Olga Blinkova, Dr. Sergey Morozov, and all my colleagues at PLD Telecom (New York), ELBIM Bank (Moscow), Fordham University, the University of Bridgeport, and New York University.

Throughout my 30 years in the academic structures of various countries, I have never met a man with greater academic tact than the head of the Management Systems Department at Fordham University, Professor Robert Wharton. Dr. Wharton and Deans Ernst Scalberg and Sharon Smith created an environment that allowed me time to write and study. These are the people who, in my business and academic life, helped me to prepare this book.

I thank Andrew Claffey, Christopher Cox, Jacqueline Gallus, Theresa King, Peggy Weinberg, and Elena Suhir who worked with me during the last two years to prepare the manuscript of this book.

Finally, I thank Fordham University Press who encouraged my enthusiasm in putting this book together. Executive Editor Mary Beatrice Schulte and Production Manager Loomis Mayer were instrumental in bringing this project to completion. Of course, all potential success and any interest in this book will be shared with my relatives and friends, but should any dissatisfaction with its contents arise, all conclusions drawn here are solely my responsibility.

VLADIMIR L. KVINT

INTRODUCTION: THE FUTURE BEGINS TODAY

The business world of the 21st century and the new millennium will not arise out of nowhere; it will inherit the characteristics, from the last 15 years of the 20th century, of the world's business map. Specifically, there is no one event in the history of business at the end of 20th century that better predicts the business world of the next century than the birth of the Global Emerging Market.

Today, when only days remain before the new millennium, anyone who writes about the future will find it very difficult to convince his readers that his forecasts and predictions will materialize for the quite simple reason that everyone with access to a computer is a potential fortune teller, and even individuals unfamiliar with statistical and mathematical methods can draw their own reliable conclusions. At the same time, it is still very important to grasp the point of view of other experts and professionals in the field.

Before I proceed to offer ideas about the future, I would like to tell my readers that my past principal forecasts have become reality with almost total accuracy. I remember that sometime, in the period between 1979 and 1982, I concluded that the Soviet Union had no economic future, and, as early as 1988, I began to publish forecasts that the Soviet Union would disappear from the world political map in 1991–92. These forecasts were published in several major European and American newspapers and magazines.

Today, at the beginning of 1999, although many people are thinking about the future, very few try to get an understanding of it by looking backward. Despite the new methods that economists and mathematicians have developed, a true understanding of the past remains essential for any analysis of the future. When we properly apply the past's coefficients, we foster our analysis for a better understanding of the future. Thus, the articles I have chosen to include here reflect the results of forecasts I have made in the past. I hope that readers can accept these forecasts as feasible as well as useful and, as a result, can reach similar conclusions on their own.

At the same time, in analyzing business opportunities, it is not enough to think of the present as an indicator of the future, because in business the present is always the past. Just imagine a businessman who is involved in an international trade transaction trying to make business plans based on his information about the current business world. The Global Business World today is completely different from what it was just 10 to 15 years ago. Fifteen years ago the world was divided into 17 developed countries and 125 developing countries. Today, of those 125 developing countries, approximately 45 have become rapidly growing emerging markets, representing 25 percent of the global GDP (the U.S., for example, represents only 21 percent). Thus, it should be clear that without an understanding of changes this businessman could miss many major profitable opportunities.

In the next 10 years, the Global Emerging Market will continue to evolve along two vectors of growth. On the one hand, emerging markets will continue to grow from 80 developing and underdeveloped countries, and, on the other, the top emerging market countries will acquire characteristics of developed ones. Of course, such major global trends as political disintegration, economic re-integration, regional decentralization, privatization, demilitarization and the conversion of military economies to civilian, and globalization will continue to affect the business world in the 21st century.

Rationale for Article Selection

This volume contains articles, chapters from various books, and other types of research that can help the reader understand three major requirements of the future Global Business World. The pieces focus on development trends in the Global Market and several of its major emerging regions, primarily the former Soviet Union, processes of privatization, dynamics of management systems, and technological progress. Several articles that describe different characteristics of international joint ventures representing major business and legal successes in the forum of cross-border transactions are also included.

I believe that this selection of articles will provide readers with a better understanding of the past and, therefore, a better vision of the future. International politics during the 1980s was marked by the collapse of communism, the end of the Cold War, the break-down of dictatorships in Latin America, Pacific Asia, and the Indian subcontinent, and the end of apartheid in South Africa. These changes, together with the technological revolution of our era—telecommunications, in particular—have enhanced the globalization of business. The increase in the gross domestic product (GDP) of leading countries during the 1970s and 1980s was largely the result of the globalization of business. More than 50% of the industrial products in the developed countries are the result of the cooperation among developed countries with one another and with the emerging market countries in particular.

Articles describing international business and political processes and economic policies cannot be separated effectively, because these subjects are inherently interrelated. Given the influence of modern political, social, and economic processes in a particular region, international business may also affect the foreign policy of a particular country, and vice versa. As a result, this book accents political and economic factors, because these factors almost always determine the risk involved in international investments. Any entrepreneur or executive will confront the problem of determining whether the country in which he or she is considering investing is in fact an emerging market. The answer to this question is more difficult than it appears, simply because currently no agreeable definition of what is meant by an emerging market currently exists.

Structure of the Volume

The book's structure will help readers understand the implementation of the practical decision-making process with respect to global trends. In general, the book's structure is in a chronologically reverse order in each of the Parts; although my first publications appeared in 1967, the earliest included here were written in 1974. This book excludes not only the first seven years of my research, but of my approximately 300 articles and 18 books, I have included only those I found to be useful for understanding future business with or within emerging markets. Nonetheless, for the convenience of the readers, I have added a partial bibliography, listing not only my own publications but also interviews I have given, as well as opinions and reviews of my publications, including personal critiques by journalists who, as one may imagine, offered "thorned roses" in evaluating the different aspects of my life and studies.

Part I: Understanding the Global Emerging Market

Developing and implementing practical strategy and tactics toward emerging markets is a practical, day-to-day responsibility and goal of any executive, whether in a multinational company or a small and/ or family business, or in multilateral institutions and research centers. Thus this book starts with explanations and definitions of global trends, classifications of different perspectives of emerging markets, and a general understanding of the nature of the modern Global Emerging Market.

In Part I, Section A, I offer several tables where I have combined the opinions of five major publications covering the economic and business issues of emerging markets. These are *The Emerging Markets Monitor, J. P. Morgan Emerging Markets Economic Indicators, Standard & Poor's Emerging Markets,* and *Emerging Market Investor. The Economist,* as well, was included, because the final pages of each issue of the magazine exhibit special emerging market indicators.

In this section, I placed the opinions of these magazines regarding nine European countries, ten Latin American countries, six African countries, and four Middle Eastern countries. Though these publications agree that three European countries, four Latin American countries, and eight Asia Pacific countries are Emerging Markets, no single common opinion exists on African or Middle Eastern countries. This suggests that each executive must rely totally on his own judgment as to whether whether a country has emerged with regard to a particular business that relates to his company. To arrive at this decision, he must evaluate the risk of his investment in a particular market.

Fifteen years ago, in the mid-1980s, when an international decision-maker heard about the possibility of risk, he immediately tried to avoid the deal in its entirety. Today the situation is totally different. Every multinational company, even middle-size companies and small-size manufacturing and financial service firms, have either an Emerging Markets or a Risk Management division. A risk management system typically inolves *identification of risk aversion, develop-*

ment of risk management strategy, method of managing risk, means of measuring risk levels, evaluation of system and ability to make adjustments. All these issues are covered in Part 1, Section A.

This section will allow readers to understand how to incorporate global risk management in their practical activities. The achievements and problems of the modern world have changed the goals of existing multilateral institutions such as the World Bank and International Monetary Fund (IMF). New demands are placed and new approaches are required in the decision-making processes of national and regional governments as well as of companies and their branches. This new situation in the investing process is illustrated by my articles published in the *Harvard Business Review* and in those describing the initial stages of the transitional period in Russia. This first part of the book highlights the processes of creation, registration, and functioning of international joint ventures. International joint ventures are the main legal and economic form of cross-border functions.

An international joint venture (IJV) is one of the major forms for implementation of internationalization and globalization of business. A joint venture (JV) may take the form either of a partnership or some other type of business cooperation. Regardless of the type chosen, the resulting entity is a joint venture if it represents the collaborative effort of two or more existing companies united for short- or long-term economic purposes. A JV is an IJV when the parties are from different countries.

The underlying nature of IJVs is the mutual interest of domestic and foreign companies in cooperating in business deals. Typically, foreigners contribute know-how, brand names, and managerial skills. Locals contribute production facilities, established marketing networks, cheap natural resources, and efficient labor resources.

Project financing, which is an increasing financial trend in the 1990s, allows companies with limited resources to participate in deals through the use of mutual resources. IJVs also present opportunities to receive project assistance from multilateral and national agencies. Companies from different countries involved in project financing, focusing on managing risk and profits, are likely to create an IJV. Because of this, new forms of IJVs (accommodative and conventional) have appeared. An *accommodative* IJV helps partners reallocate risks associated with the project and establish more efficient ties between suppliers and consumers. A *conventional* IJV usually has limited contract support between partners, who share full market risk. This form may cause the IJV to be less leveraged.

Other contributors to the establishment of IJVs have been multi-lateral institutions like the World Bank, the International Monetary Fund, and others. The globalization of business and involvement of multilateral institutions (e.g., setting regulations on economic and business activities, offering financial services and loans) creates a favorable climate for establishing and operating IJVs. As an example, the objective of the World Trade Organization (WTO) is to eliminate trade barriers. By bringing down those barriers, the WTO enhances expansion of international business and the creation of IJVs capable of producing goods and services abroad for import-export purposes. Product standards set by the WTO make products more desirable for other organizations.

In this volume, IJVs are described in several articles, two of which were originally published by the *Harvard Business Review*. In these articles, there are explanations of the business and legal natures of international joint ventures and strategy for the creation and location of international joint ventures. You will gain an understanding of how to choose the right partner and how to negotiate the establishment of a joint-venture, as well as some operational issues of setting up IJVs. For the successful creation of an IJV it is necessary to have one non-binding document—letter of intent—and three official legal documents: the joint-venture agreement, joint venture bylaw (statute), and a document of approval from the countries participating in the venture. All these issues are covered in Part I, section B: Investing in the Emerging Markets.

Part II: The Top Emerging Markets of Europe, Central Asia, and Latin America

The second Part of the book is dedicated to the emerging markets in Europe, Central Asia, and Latin America. From the European countries, I have chosen the top six Emerging Markets. This Part describes business conditions in the leading European emerging markets—the Czech Republic, Greece, Hungary, Poland, Portugal, and Turkey—as well as in some of the outsiders, such as Bulgaria and Ukraine. A parallel can be drawn with the business conditions of the

Central Asian and Latin American emerging markets and those in Kazakstan and Brazil. Additionally, on the regional level, I have focused specifically on the Balkan region, which, though relatively new and one of the last European Emerging Markets, has yet to attract a strong interest of the international business community. I zero in on the Balkan country of Bulgaria. Among the former Soviet-bloc countries it is the most interesting one, with unique geopolitical characteristics—on the coast of the Black Sea and on the route from the Balkans to the rest of Europe. On the one hand, this country is already an associate member of the European Union and is credited with adhering to the Currency Board of the IMF; on the other, it is still rarely viewed as on par with the European Emerging Markets in many respects.

The birth of the initial emerging markets occurred in the "old world" of Europe. The timing of their appearance determined the differences among them and created broad gaps in their development trends. Though some of these countries, such as Portugal and Greece, are today full members of the European Union and NATO, by several indicators they are still classified as emerging market countries. Some may be pre-emerging markets, such as Albania. Some, like Bulgaria, Romania, and Ukraine, are on the cusp of being emerging markets.

Because of the strong interest many investors have shown in high-growth European emerging markets, in 1996 I completed a study of Europe's Top Six emerging markets. I classified them not only according to the opportunities they present, but also by their level of development. Some of these include the Czech Republic, Greece, Hungary, Poland, Portugal, and Turkey. In this I also tried to describe the Ukrainian market. Ukraine is the largest European country in territory, with the exception of the European part of Russia and Turkey with its Asian part. Home to 53 million inhabitants, it is also one of the most populated European countries. Ukraine was always in Russia's shadow, but now it has great economic potential and plays a key political role between Russia and NATO member-countries.

The Central Asian countries—which contain approximately 60 million people, largely Muslim—will substantially influence the future of Russia in particular and Eurasia overall. Moreover, the Muslim-populated Russian regions like the Tatar Republic, Bashkirtastan, and republics in the Caucasus mountains like Dagestan, contribute to the significant role Islam is playing in the emerging markets in this part of the world.

In this book I highlight two specific areas: the largest Central Asian country both by territory and population, Kazakstan, and one of the most beautiful autonomous republics in the Caucasus mountains, Dagestan. Several of the articles I wrote in cooperation with Dr. Z. Uzbekov, Dagestan's Minister of Privatization from the early years of that country's privatization process, are included here.

Part III: The Emerging Market of Russia

Part III covers the largest emerging market in the global business world—Russia. No executive can overlook this country, regardless of whether or not he plans to be directly involved in this market, because it directly or indirectly influences the political, social, cultural, economic, and business life of the entire planet. Peace and prosperity in Russia enable all other countries to reduce their military expansion and advance the notion that the territory of this country, the largest in the world, does not divide East and West, North and South, but brings them closer to one another. Peace and prosperity in Russia provide a new market of raw materials and an enormous consumption capacity. The most important part of this section is the account of Russia's transition from a communist dictatorship to a free-market economy. Russia's privatization and the internationalization trends of its economy are granted particular attention.

After the Soviet Union crumbled in December 1991, Russia, without the other 14 former Soviet republics, became the largest country in the world by territory. Siberia alone, while a part of Russia, is larger than the world's second largest country, Canada. By the way, I have quite often been surprised to discover that in spite of the fact that Canada is the U.S.'s next-door neighbor, few Americans have an understanding of the vastness of Canada's territory and the real population. Among the world's first five largest countries by territory are the U.S., China, and Brazil. Siberia, only a part of Russia, is slightly larger than Canada, but Siberia and Canada are also almost equal in population—both have around 30 million people.

Though Russia's participation in the Global Market began just before the disintegration of the Soviet Union in the late 1980s, it will take at least another 20 years for it to become a full player in the global business community. In 1989 a very difficult transitional period in Russia began. At that time the direction of Russia's advances were assumed to be obvious: it was a transition to a market-oriented economy. Those who considered capitalism to be perfect spoke not of a "market economy," but rather of a bright, instantaneous capitalist future for Russia. I was one of these naïve people. As a result, one of my articles, published in Vienna, in January 1990, was called "Capitalism Immediately."

We in the Soviet Union were so accustomed to the pressures of the communist propaganda machine that we fell into the habit of interpreting every piece of official information with an exactly opposite meaning. Every article on capitalism described its evils, yet I was convinced capitalism was perfect. When I was finally allowed to travel abroad in December 1988, and, in particular, on my first trip to the United States, to New York City, in May 1989, I gained a more realistic perspective. I was surprised to see homeless people and lots of uncollected garbage in the street, and the wastefulness, in my opinion, of streetlights in operation in broad daylight.

Everyone understood that Russia must move to a market economy, yet few understood the economic abyss from which Russia must rise. Because all information was either simply wrong or was deliberate "misinformation" the so-called Sovietologists and Western experts had little idea of how damaged and imbalanced the Russian economy was. They knew that the military expenses exceeded official figures, but few were aware that in reality more than 50% of the USSR budget was oriented toward the military-industrial complex.

Even today, many Western businessmen don't seem to grasp the realities of the Russian economy. In 1990 I began to publish articles in *Forbes* and *The New York Times* and in publications in Austria, Great Britain, Belgium, Germany, and Italy about political and economic crises in the USSR and possible scenarios of transitional outcomes. These articles are concentrated in the first section of Part III: Transition to a Free Market. They began by covering Gorbachev's experiments of perestroika and glastnost. My major goal, as an insider at that time, was to deliver the main point to Western political, economic, and business leaders: regardless who holds the office of "dictator" of the Soviet Union, whether it is former KGB Head Yuri Andropov, brainless Konstantin Chernenko or Mikhail Gorbachev, this country had no future as a market economy. Major elements of perestroika were developed in the early 1980s by Andropov's and Chernenko's economic advisers, but the health of these dictators did not give them the opportunity to implement these programs. They were in office less than two years. When the two years of extravagant funerals and fanfare were over, Gorbachev had no choice but to proceed to introduce these programs. At that time, I published several articles intended to give a portrait of the real Gorbachev. The names of the articles speak for themselves. For example, I wrote in *Forbes* that "The Best Way to Help Gorbachev Is to Make Life Difficult for Him" (June 1990), in which I mentioned that the stronger the pressure from the West, the higher the military expansion, the sooner the Soviet Union would collapse and disintegrate. The real success of glastnost in Russia was not only Gorbachev's desert, but more so that of the tough policy of its true authors—Ronald Reagan, Margaret Thatcher, and Helmut Kohl.

When Gorbachev received the Nobel Peace Prize, I had no choice but to publish in *Forbes* "The Myth of Good Czar Gorbachev" (February 1991). Here I emphasized that it was he who instituted the repressions in the Baltics, in Georgia, Armenia, Azerbaijan, and Moldova. He behaved like a master manipulator of Western opinion, a despot like any other, who blamed his "wicked" ministers for the evils around him. When he took office, the country was already on the brink of disaster. Responding to the force of popular anger he moved toward democracy. To his credit, he did so in a positive manner. Nonetheless, to his last day in office he objected to removing the provision that makes the Communist Party the leading policy-making fixture in the country. This is not to say that Gorbachev was not an admirable figure—he was; but he was a follower, not the initiator, as many Westerners wrongly believe.

Other political factors of the transitional period were described in several of my articles. Special attention was given to the failed coup d'état in August 1991, and prior to that many times my readers heard my predictions of the impending complete and irretractable disintegration of the Soviet Union. I recall my *Forbes* cover story "A Soviet Economist's Revolutionary Proposal: Russia Should Quit the Soviet Union" (February 1990). At that time it was indeed a revolutionary proposal. Vivid in my mind even today is my meeting with Henry Kissinger in early January 1990 in his New York office. I told him the

Soviet Union had only months, not years, left to exist. He disagreed, convinced that the Communist Party, the Red Army, and the KGB would keep the country together and strong. The same happened during a panel discussion in Basel, Switzerland, in March 1990 with Zbigniew Brzezinski. He didn't share my opinion either. My forecast was published also in *The New York Times*, where I predicted the exact date of the disintegration of the Soviet Union. In "Opportunities in Soviet Disintegration" (October 1990) I mentioned explicitly that "By 1992, there will be no country called the Soviet Union."

At approximately the same time I published several articles in *Forbes*, *The New York Times*, and *The Chicago Tribune* with a straight prediction that Yeltsin, not Gorbachev, would be the key political figure. Remember, this was while Gorbachev was still president of the USSR and General Secretary of the Communist Party of the Soviet Union. This was one year before Yeltsin was elected president of the Russian Federation, at that time only one of the republics of the Soviet Union.

I must to mention one of my current forecasts, still in progress—the probability of the restoration of the monarchy. I believe that in some countries undergoing transition the restoration of a monarchy can be a very positive step. It is of particular importance in those countries with a small middle class where society is polarized. A monarch traditionally represents neither communists nor anti-communists, neither the rich nor the poor. The monarch represents the nation as a whole, and this concept of unity is very important for a nation in transition. Particularly this has possible applicability, in such countries as Bulgaria, Albania, Russia, Romania, and Serbia. Greece might be added to the list, but Greece does not need a monarchy (see my articles "Restoring the Romanovs" [*Forbes*, December 1994] and "Bulgaria is the Last Klondike in Eastern Europe [*The Kvint Newsletter*: February 1995). Finally, I would like readers to understand that "The Last Days of President Yeltsin" I wrote when the crisis of 1998 had not yet happened in Russia. Nevertheless I had a strong feeling that, without change in the political leadership of Russia and the retirement of Yeltsin, the political and economic collapse which started in August 1998, would continue.

It is not as important for my readers to read my forecasts that have become reality as to be given the opportunity to make their own correct forecast. And each of you is capable of doing this. For the

last eight years I have been teaching both graduate and undergradu-
ate courses in the School of Business at Fordham University on how
to make correct political and economic forecasts in emerging markets. I have also given courses of lectures on these matters at New
York University's Stern School of Business, at UCLA's Anderson
Graduate School of Business, at Babson College in Massachusetts,
and individual lectures at universities in Austria, Belgium, Bulgaria,
Germany, Great Britain, and Poland, among others.

So, then, how does one make correct political and economic forecasts? Any of you who will be involved in the decision-making process, whether initiating or ceasing business ventures in the "new
emerging market countries," must begin your analysis with basic
economic factors and major economic indicators. You cannot begin
to make a decision to participate in processes of privatization in any
country worldwide without a quick, but sharp, analysis of these factors. This is covered thoroughly in the sections on Processes of Privatization, Regionalization, and Industrial Analysis.

We definitely live in the Information Age. One tap of a computer
button will access the Internet, Lexis-Nexis, Reuters, Dun & Bradstreet, where volumes of pages of information on any country are
readily available. But for your decision-making methods you need
only several clear and concise pieces of information on the country
in question. To do so, your analysis need consist of only five basic
economic factors:

(1) natural resources, including land
(2) labor resources
(3) domestic and foreign capital
(4) existing production facilities and infrastructure, such as like tele-
    communication and transportation, and, finally,
(5) the factor that influences the previous four factors: scientific and
    technological advances.

Among major economic indicators that must be analyzed are
GDP, GDP per capita, and rate of GDP growth over the last 20 years
in the country. One must focus closely on the statistics of industrial
development, standard of living, and consumption capacity, dynamics of foreign direct and portfolio investment in the country, and
other economic indicators. No single indicator will offer the right
answer; only a combination of information pieces will point in the

right direction, though including more of them than necessary should be avoided.

Since information on emerging markets is often either flat wrong or deliberately flawed, conclusions should never be based on only one a single source. The best way to obtain information is, first, from the country of your potential investment itself, that is, secondly from the central government of the country, secondly, from the regional authorities, and, finally, from the companies of your potential partners or companies you would like or intend to privatize. Only when you identify the differences in the sources and in the information you have obtained and are able to account for the existence of these differences will you be ready to make a decision.

The vast majority of the emerging market countries are not homogeneous in their geographic, economic, and political characteristics. As a result, regionalization is one of the most important contemporary trends. Part III offers a description of several regions of Russia and a thorough analyses of their industry.

Part IV: Management Systems and Scientific Technological Progress

To be successful in any emerging market, the ability to evaluate the management systems is no less important than the ability to understand the economic development of each region. In order to take advantage of the privatization process or the creation of IJVs, when one negotiates trade transactions or weighs investment opportunities, one must first understand the management systems on federal, regional, and corporate levels. My studies show that. in the initial stages of internationalization of any emerging market, 16% of all the failures by foreign executives are the result of bureaucracy. An increased understanding of Emerging Markets in general does not necessary imply that the management system directly corresponds to the knowledge of the specific markets. One will eventually realize that the role of this factor declines in importance gradually, not immediately, as some might expect, because even experienced foreigners fail to evaluate fully all the elements the management systems of the Emerging Markets comprise.

Any analysis of the management system of a country must be assessed via five critical elements present in the country's system: *orga-*

nizational structure of the management system; qualifications of executives, managers, and staff of the management system (excluding engineers and blue-collar workers); specifics of the decision-making process; management system technology, computerization and office supplies; and finally a thorough evaluation of information.

In Part III of the book, I also speak of information, but not as it pertains to the management system. In this case, one should understand information from a different perspective—as only a "raw material" of the decision-making process and as the only by-product of this process. All these issues are covered in Part IV. Specific attention is given to the compensation of executives and the board of directors; the bureaucratic problems; management system functioning processes; forecast development strategy and tactics; long-term preparation, current operational plans; and employee motivation. Control of the decisions' implementation is illustrated in this part of the book mostly from the aspect of scientific and technological development, though regional programs and technological improvements on the corporate level are also described.

The Global Emerging Market is not homogeneous. The main differences among emerging markets are in their technological and industrial levels of development. We can discuss instances, such as some northern African and Latin American countries, that technologically are far behind developed countries in North America and Western Europe. At the same time, countries like Russia, Hungary, the Czech Republic, and even Bulgaria possess technological levels that are not greatly inferior to those in the Western countries. In particular, Russia has had some very well-known scientific and technological achievements: the first artificial satellite of the earth— Sputnik; the first human being in space—Yuri Gagarin; the first nuclear power station; and, what may be a surprise for many, in 1965 the first two Nobel Prize winners for laser technology—Basov and Prokhorov. The Soviet Union had no modern economy as we understand it today, but it was a Soviet economist who received the Nobel Prize in Economics in 1975—Leonid Kantorovich.

Practically all Russia's achievements were reached within its military-industrial complex. Today, the trend of converting military industries to civilian purposes is widespread in Russia. This affords foreigners the optimal opportunity to understand both Russian scientific technological progress and the regional and federal programs that helped Russia achieve its success in many areas of technology and science.

In Part IV I have selected articles describing scientific and technical policies. Part IV contains two chapters of my main research book *The Management of Scientific-Technical Progress: A Regional Aspect,"* which outlines the primary methods Russians employed to accelerate the country's technological development. I selected only two chapters of this book to include here: "Economic Entity of Regional Scientific Technical Policy" and "Process of Formation of This Policy." In my opinion, one of the most important building blocks of Russia's technological success was a system for technological preparation of production. This system was initially developed in the early 1970s and I was one of those who developed the economic aspects of this system.

Finally, automatization and robotization techniques in the Soviet Union and Russia were far behind those of the U.S. and Western Europe. Nonetheless, the automatization of mining and nonferrous metals industries in Russia proved to be successful. I participated in the development of economic preparation of many of these systems and you can find my articles about this in Part IV. These articles will help readers understand how to conduct economic analyses of some Russian technologies. My research from the early 1970s until the present has focused on management systems of technological development. I believe that Part IV of this book will be functionally useful for my readers.

Overall, all the articles in this volume represent the last 25 years of my research and studies. It is always difficult for people to combine two seemingly uncombinable abstractions—space and time. When I was putting this volume together, I came to understand that time serves as the space of human growth and change. It is clear that the last quarter-century was not a time of evolution, but revolution in mankind's history. In retrospect, as if I were glancing at these 25 years in the rearview mirror, it became apparent to me that, as a result of all the political and economic difficulties we have witnessed, future generations will have a chance to live in a more perfect world. Throughout the 1970s, 1980s, and 1990s we have created solid grounds for the future of our descendants. I hope that the readers of this book will turn its last page with the same conclusion of optimism and feeling of confidence.

Part I

UNDERSTANDING THE GLOBAL EMERGING MARKET

Classification of
Emerging Markets

INCORPORATING GLOBAL RISK MANAGEMENT IN THE STRATEGIC DECISION MAKING PROCESS

Introduction

Ten years ago, the global business world was totally different from what it is today. While this is not surprising, the scope of the changes is virtually unprecedented. In 1986, the world was divided into 18 Developed Countries and 125 Developing Countries; 98% of all international transactions were between the 18 developed countries, while only 2% were with the 125 developing countries.

Since 1987, approximately 40 of the developing countries have become Emerging Market Countries. Currently, these Emerging Market Countries account for approximately 70% of the world population, 15% of all international transactions, and 25% of the global GDP, which is more than the U.S.'s 21% contribution to global GDP. These Emerging Markets Countries exert a strong influence on the remaining 85 developing countries, for whom they serve as a beacon, and on the developed countries as well, as new markets and competitors.

Investing in Emerging Market Countries

During the last ten years, the annual growth rate of foreign and domestic investment in emerging markets increased from 15% to 25%. In 1987, only one-half of one percent of the total assets of western pension funds, hedge funds, and mutual funds were invested in Emerging Markets. In 1994, the percentage of these funds invested

In *Executive Summaries*, an official publication of the World Economic Development Congress, September 25–26, 1996, Published by the World Markets Research Center, February 1997.

in emerging markets increased to 16%, and in 1995 to around 21%. The growth rate of private American investments in Emerging Market Countries was 37% in 1993, 41% in 1994, and 47% in 1995.

Between 1995 and 2005, multilateral institutions will invest over $300 billion in Emerging Market Countries. Naturally, the surge in investment has also had an enormous influence on employment, with the growth in the number of new jobs in emerging markets at 20% per annum—ten times greater than in developed countries.

Emerging Market Countries have also become major markets for exports from developed countries. Japan, one of the first Emerging Market Countries during the 1960s, ships 50% of its exports to Emerging Market Countries. Likewise, 40% of U.S. exports and 32% of EU exports are shipped to Emerging Market Countries (1995).

Global Trends

Global business today is influenced by 5 major trends—political disintegration, economic re-integration, regional decentralization, privatization, and internationalization of global and national business. Because of the rapid increase in the number of Emerging Market Countries, especially during the last six years, two more trends have developed which affect global business—deficit of investment and shortage of capital. These new trends have forced Emerging Market Countries and even regions within the same country to compete for foreign investment.

Emerging Market Classification

There is no common approach to using specific economic indicators in classifying countries as pre-emerging or emerging markets. Nor is there agreement on criteria used for this classification among major publications specifically covering emerging markets.

Tables 1 through 4 contain the results of a study of major worldwide publications specifically covering emerging markets (*The Emerging Markets Monitor, J. P. Morgan Emerging Markets Economic Outlook, Standard & Poor's Emerging Markets, Emerging Markets Investor,* and *The Economist*). The study summarizes the classifications designated by the publications for a total of 43 countries on five continents. Of the 43 countries considered, only 15 are designated as emerging markets by all the publications, and 12 of the 43 are designated as emerging markets by only one of the publications. These discrepancies exist because each publication has its own approach for classifying emerging markets. The only significant similarity in the approaches used by each of the publications is the use of fundamental economic and financial indicators.

Kvint's Emerging Market Classification

Table 5 includes the results of a recent evaluation I conducted to determine a list of Emerging Market Countries. It is important to note the differences between my evaluation and the above study. There are many countries that my analysis determines to be emerging markets, which are not considered to be emerging markets by the publications listed in Tables 1 through 4. These include the following countries:

Europe

- the Baltic States of Latvia, Lithuania, and Estonia. These countries have stable, developed democracies, all with higher GDPs per capita than several countries in Tables 1 through 4
- Slovenia, which is the most economically stable country among all of the former Soviet-bloc countries

Asia/Pacific Region

- four out of five Central Asian Republics (all but Tajikistan)
- Kazakstan, which has much lower country risk than Bangladesh
- Pakistan
- Vietnam

South America

- Guatemala

Africa

- Tunisia and Zimbabwe.

In addition, the *J. P. Morgan Emerging Market Outlook* and *Emerging Market Investor* consider Iran and the Ivory Coast, respectively, as Emerging Market Countries, while my analysis does not.

Table 1: Emerging Market Classification, European Countries

Europe	a	b	c	d	e	Total
Bulgaria	x	x				2
Czech Republic	x	x	x	x	x	5
Greece	x	x	x	x	x	4
Hungary	x	x	x	x	x	5
Poland	x	x	x	x	x	4
Portugal	x	x	x		x	4
Russia	x	x		x	x	4
Turkey	x	x	x	x	x	5
Romania	x					1
Slovakia	x		x			2

a *The Emerging Markets Monitor*

b *J.P. Morgan Emerging Markets Economic Outlook*

c *Standard & Poor's Emerging Markets*

d *Emerging Markets Investor*

e *The Economist*

Table 2: Emerging Market Classification, Latin American Countries

Latin America	a	b	c	d	e	Total		
Argentina	x	x	x	x	x	5	a	The Emerging Markets Monitor
Brazil	x	x		x	x	4		
Chile	x	x	x	x	x	5	b	J.P. Morgan Emerging Markets Economic Outlook
Colombia	x	x	x	x		4		
Equador		x		x		2		
Mexico	x	x	x	x	x	5	c	Standard & Poor's Emerging Markets
Peru	x	x		x		3		
Panama			x			1	d	Emerging Markets Investor
Uruguay			x			1		
Venezuela	x	x	x	x	x	5	e	The Economist

Copyright Vladimir Kvint

Table 3: Emerging Market Classification, Asia/Pacific Countries

Asia/Pacific	a	b	c	d	e	Total
Bangladesh	x			x		1
China	x	x	x	x	x	5
Hong Kong	x	x		x	x	4
India	x	x	x	x	x	5
Indonesia	x	x	x	x	x	5
Korea	x	x	x	x	x	5
Malaysia	x	x	x	x	x	5
Pakistan				x		1
Philippines	x	x	x	x	x	5
Singapore	x	x	x	x	x	4
Taiwan	x	x	x	x	x	5
Thailand	x	x	x	x	x	5
Vietnam	x					1

a The Emerging Markets Monitor
b J.P. Morgan Emerging Markets Economic Outlook
c Standard & Poor's Emerging Markets
d Emerging Markets Investor
e The Economist

Table 4: Emerging Market Classification, African and Middle Eastern Countries

Africa	a	b	c	d	e	Total
Algeria					x	1
Cote d'Ivoire		x				1
Egypt	x					1
Morocco		x		x		2
Nigeria		x		x		2
South Africa	x	x		x	x	4

Middle East	a	b	c	d	e	Total
Israel		x			x	2
Saudi Arabia				x		1
Kuwait				x		1
Iran				x		1

a — *The Emerging Markets Monitor*
b — *J.P. Morgan Emerging Markets Economic Outlook*
c — *Standard & Poor's Emerging Markets*
d — *Emerging Markets Investor*
e — *The Economist*

Copyright Vladimir Kvint

Evaluation of National Credit Risk

There are also evident differences in analytical methods used to determine national credit risk by emerging market professionals. The significance of these differences is amplified when institutional and even public investors use this information to make investment decisions. Publishing the results of these analyses can mislead members of the business community who are not very knowledgeable about emerging markets. In addition, for professionals working with the emerging markets, the results of different analyses often lead to more questions than answers.

For example, the results of my national credit risk analysis of emerging markets are very different from *The Economist* Intelligence Unit's credit risk ratings, which are based on economic and political factors. The EIU's results are questionable for several reasons. The following paragraphs cite some examples where my evaluation of national credit risk differs from EIU's.

Colombia vs. Argentina, Brazil, and Venezuela

EIU considers Colombia to be the safest country in Latin American. This is difficult to understand when its president is *persona non grata* because of allegations of business dealings with drug cartels. EIU considers Argentina, Brazil, and Venezuela as riskier countries than Colombia, although there is greater political and economic stability and numerous economic reforms are taking place in both Argentina and Brazil. My analysis concludes that primarily because of political issues the national credit risk associated with Colombia is higher than the risks associated with Argentina, Brazil, and Venezuela.

Turkey vs. China and Indonesia

EIU considers Turkey to be riskier than both China and Indonesia (currently governed by a form of dictatorship). Primarily because of Turkey's strong orientation toward democracy, my analysis considers Turkey to be less risky than either China or Indonesia. Turkey is a member of NATO, and an associate member of the EU with a special customs agreement, not to mention a stable democracy and economic system.

Table 5: Kvint's Emerging Market Classification

Europe	Asia/Pacific	South America
Albania	Bangladesh	Argentina
Bulgaria	India	Brazil
Croatia	Indonesia	Chile
Czech Republic	Kazakstan	Guatemala
Estonia	Kyrgyzstan	Uruguay
Hungary	Malaysia	Venezuela
Greece	Pakistan	
Latvia	Philippines	
Lithuania	Turkmenistan	**Africa**
Moldova	Uzbekistan	Algeria
Poland	Vietnam	Egypt
Romania	Sri Lanka	Morocco
Russia		Nigeria
Slovak Republic	**North America**	South Africa
Slovenia	Mexico	Tunesia
Turkey	Panama	Zimbabwe
Ukraine		

Copyright Vladimir Kvint

Greece and Hungary vs. Poland and South Africa

EIU considers Greece to be riskier than both Poland and South Africa. Greece is a country with a stable democracy that has an unquestionable orientation toward capitalism, is a member of the EU and NATO, and has a much higher GDP per capita than either Poland or South Africa. In addition, EIU considers Hungary to be riskier than Poland. This is questionable when one considers that Hungary is slightly ahead of Poland in terms of market reforms, and has a higher GDP per capita and standard of living than Poland.

Malaysia vs. Taiwan, Poland, and Chile

EIU considers Malaysia to be riskier than Taiwan, which currently has many political problems. In addition, Malaysia is considered by this publication to be riskier than both Poland and Chile, both of which are in the middle of economic reforms (which are successful even though the country still has a difficult business environment).

Global Risk Management

During the 1990s, global business risk management has become an important aspect of strategic and tactical business practices. In the past, risk was something to be avoided. However, the explosion of Emerging Market Countries during the 1990s has resulted in a fundamental change in the way that international business considers risk. Emerging Markets have become one of the most important parts of global business. Today, risk is, to some degree, inherent in every emerging market. But rather than avoiding it, investors are looking closely, measuring, and taking steps to adjust and cover risk.

A very important step in risk evaluation is the selection of indicators of political, economic, and technological risks of investment. In order to manage risk, one must understand the modern meaning of global business risk. Global refers to "worldwide," but also to "thorough or entire"; thus, global business risk refers to the risks associated with conducting all areas of business, from production to finance to post-sales service worldwide. During the last three years, all leading investment companies, commercial banks, insurance companies, mutual and pension funds, and accounting firms have created risk management departments.

Global risk is broken down into two components, systematic risk and unsystematic risk.

Unsystematic risk includes: product risk (raw materials/parts risk, human resource risk, credit risk, operating risk, regulatory risk, legal risk, after-sales liability risk) and financial risk (currency risk, interest rate risk, liquidity risk, settlement risk, derivative risk, fraud risk). National (OPIC), regional (MERCOSUR), and multilateral (MIGA) institutions and organizations play an important role in global risk management. These organizations are critical in helping companies to manage unsystematic risk.

While investors feel that they can evaluate, manage, and adjust for unsystematic risk, such as product and financial risk, systematic (market) risk is outside their control. Market risk, however, can be managed on a limited basis by those who have influence in the market—the central, regional, and city governments. Now is the time for governments to create risk management systems to identify, evaluate, and adjust for various types of risk. During the process of developing a government risk management system, it is important to consider the requirements of worldwide investors. To attract international investors, regional and central governments from emerging markets need to meet the demands of international investors. This includes reducing political, economic, and business risk to a level acceptable to investors.

In addition to considering the risks involved with a particular emerging market as a whole, it is important to consider separately the risks associated with various economic sectors of the emerging market. For example, by my evaluation, there is a low level of economic risk associated with investing in Argentina. However, in Argentina there are high levels of risk associated with investing in the mining and pharmaceutical industries. Another good example is Liberia. Many investors are afraid of the high level of risk associated with this country. However, it is easy to obtain financing for Liberian shipping companies that are backed by Panamanian assets and operated by third-world countries.

The Risk Management System

"Global risk" for any country must take into account a comprehensive evaluation of political, economic, business, and technological risks. This is true for countries that are pre-emerging or emerging, developing or developed, for any global regional organization such as the EU, MERCOSUR, ANDEAN Pact, ASEAN, APEC, etc., or for any rural or metropolitan area or economic region within a country. Of course, these risks are not separate; they overlap. However, for the purpose of analysis, it is necessary to consider these risks separately and then identify any correlation or areas of mutual influence. Based on these interactions, it is possible to determine the overall risk level associated with a specific country, region, or investment project.

After analyzing many risk management systems, I tried to pinpoint the major elements of the systems agreed on by the majority of industry. The elements included in my analysis are equally important for industrial, financial, and consulting firms. A global risk management system should include the following major elements:

Identification of risks
Determination of risk aversion
Development of risk management strategy
Method of managing risk
Means of measuring risk levels
Evaluation of system
Ability to make adjustments.

Risk management is truly a dynamic field. At the Fifth Annual World Economic Development Congress I served as the chairman of the Global Risk Management Summit. After discussing the definition of risk and methods of risk management with politicians, economists, and business leaders at the Congress, I concluded that there is no single, agreed-upon definition of risk with respect to international business. Without an agreed definition of *risk*, it is difficult to agree on a single method for *managing* risk. The general view is that global risk management systems are formed as a result of combining the expanding focus of technical specialists with firm executives, managers, and political leaders.

The reliability of all risk management systems currently in use is still questionable. The following characteristics are commonly associated with reliable risk management systems: top-down structure, formal policy setting, flexibility, frequent review/evaluation, accountability in the system, i.e., the importance of addressing risk exposure. Practically all experts agree on the following fundamental steps in the development of risk management systems: (1) identification of risk, (2) determination of appropriate system for managing risk, and (3) continued measurement of risk.

There is also not one generally accepted statistical or optimization method for managing and measuring risk that has proven better than any other. However, credit was given to several companies' risk management practices including those at ABB, Canadian Imperial Bank of Commerce, Arthur Andersen, Walt Disney Co., Stanley Works, Inc., and Walmart. These companies were noted for their use of extensive modeling and sensitivity analysis in the practice of risk management.

During the 1990s, under the influence of new political and economic trends, and especially with the appearance of the global emerging markets, risk management has become a natural, yet critical element of the strategic decision-making process.

EMERGING OR DEVELOPED, WHAT'S THE DIFFERENCE?

Securities Operations Letter: You have developed three approaches to identifying emerging markets. Why did you develop these approaches, and what are they?

Vladimir Kvint: They were needed because there is no general agreement on the definition of an emerging market among market participants, academics, and economists. The three approaches to developing a definition are the financial approach, the political approach, and the business approach. The financial approach was actually created by IFC, the International Finance Corporation.

Q: What is the financial approach?

Kvint: It says that countries with average per capita income of $8,625 are considered developed countries. Countries below this figure are considered as emerging market countries.

Q: Does the $8,625 per capita income level place several countries of the European Union in the emerging country category?

Kvint: Yes, several emerging EU countries have not reached that level. Many financial companies go strictly by the $8,625 level. They would consider Greece or Portugal as an emerging market country because neither has now reached this level, but I consider Greece and Portugal as developed countries.

Q: What about the political approach?

Kvint: The political approach involves the newly achieved political stability and orientation of government in some countries. Russia, for example, is an emerging market because for the first time they are enforcing a constitution, elections are scheduled, and they have moved toward a democratic form of government.

Securities Operations Letter, International Edition, August 2, 1998, pp. 1, 3, and 8.

Q: What about the business approach?

Kvint: The business approach considers the level of development of capitalist institutions, such as insurance companies, commercial and investment banks, and accounting firms.

Q: What has caused emerging markets to grow so rapidly?

Kvint: Back in 1985, there were almost no emerging markets. But after dictatorships failed in Latin America, as well as military dictatorships in Southern Europe and Southeast and Pacific Asia, and the collapse of communism in the former Soviet Union, emerging markets began to appear. They have totally changed the nature of global finance.

Q: How so?

Kvint: They created a shortage of capital, for one thing. Prior to 1984–85, the number of emerging markets was minimal. Countries like Japan had excess capital, and they did not know where to invest. Now 70 countries have reached the level of emerging markets, and they are competing with each other for capital.

Q: Would you consider a country that limits foreign investment to be an emerging market?

Kvint: If a country does not allow foreign investors to operate, it is not an emerging country. In Bulgaria or Ukraine, for example, insurance firms cannot operate independently. They can only create joint ventures in which they own no more than 39% of the business.

Q: You've written that emerging countries should allow third-party auditors to be used. What is the impact of not using auditors?

Kvint: If a Big Six firm cannot issue a valuation opinion, investors will not invest on a large scale. The firms cannot issue a valuation without a third-party auditor.

Q: Let's talk about the Soviet Union. Have the Soviets priced their companies on the basis of market value or book value?

Kvint: Unfortunately, privatization in the Soviet Union has been based not on market value, but on book value. It means companies are sold for about 10% of their market price. Anyone will pay 10% of the value of a company, and they will pay substantially more under the table. This is the relationship between corruption and privatization.

Q: What percentage of the Russian economy was in private hands?

Kvint: In 1990, only 4% of the economy was in private hands; today 70% is in private hands.

Q: How many stock exchanges does Russian have?

Kvint: During 1992–93, they created five stock exchanges, but there is not one settlement and trust organization, so you have to deliver all certificates physically. As a result, many trades never settle, and people have turned to the Mafia to settle and clear trades.

Q: What's being done about this problem?

Kvint: In November 1994, Yeltsin signed legislation covering the exchanges and the creation of settlement organizations. Several international companies are improving the markets, but it will take at least three years.

Q: What is the state of the South American markets?

Kvint: The South American countries have not been homogeneous in their development of capitalistic institutions. Chile is the most advanced, followed by Argentina and Brazil.

Q: What are the major problems in Ukraine?

Kvint: Ukraine started its economic reform without understanding what to do first. They started with the liberation of price, prior to privatization. The result was a dramatic increase in inflation. Ninety-five percent of the people fell below the poverty line and a crisis occurred. Instead of a nationalized currency, "dollarization" occurred. Then they realized which steps they needed to take. Inflation is now less than 3% a month as opposed to the 200% a month before. Private banks and all the Big Six accounting firms have opened offices, and three stock exchanges have been opened.

Q: Can foreigners buy shares in these markets?

Kvint: Through March of this year there was no legal procedure for trading shares. As a result, foreigners were not allowed to purchase shares on the primary market. They could not buy shares directly. Foreigners could buy only through a secondary market.

A DIFFERENT PERSPECTIVE ON EMERGING MARKETS

The Investment Appeal of Emerging Markets

It is no surprise that the Fourth World Economic Development Congress, which took place in October in Washington, D.C., had "emerging markets" at the top of its agenda. It is the single most important issue for the world business community. As an investment class, its status is on the agenda of international business executives and entrepreneurs alike. Emerging markets play an integral role in the international financial markets, in particular derivative instruments, pension reform, pension, mutual funds, and currency markets.

A new world order is emerging. The collapse of communism is almost complete, and with it a whole global economy has been set into motion. More than 25 new emerging markets have appeared since the disintegration of the former Soviet Union, bringing the total to 60. The newly independent countries that are opening up their borders both politically and economically are creating numerous opportunities for both the world and themselves. The question is how quickly the rest of the world will be able to follow. It is only natural that available investment dollars will be spread thin. In addition, there is the inherent uncertainty and risk involved in plunging capital in a volatile environment—as most emerging market countries are.

The key is for these countries to show a positive commitment toward establishing and sustaining a continuous and growing GNP, fueled by an increasing stream of net exports. This will help their financial markets develop, make the markets less volatile, and attract into these markets more investors with highly sophisticated investments and financial instruments.

The term "emerging markets" has become a buzzword popular

In *The Fourth Annual World Economic Development Congress*, Addendum: A Special Summit Briefing of Some of the Speakers' Addresses, October 1995, pp. 50–54.

with the press and first appeared in relation to the stock market in the early 1970s. It did not refer to markets in newly democratic or semi-democratic countries like those in the Middle East, Latin America, and the Pacific Rim. Instead, it was purely a financial term that focused on emerging equities, debt securities, and stock markets in developing countries. The term has evolved substantially from those days. Today, when viewing emerging markets, it is necessary to consider the social, political, and business perspectives as well as the purely financial ones.

It is clear, however, that there is a big difference in what people mean when they refer to emerging markets. The lack of one agreed-upon definition stems from the fact that there are several approaches to identifying and analyzing emerging markets that do not necessarily correlate to one another. This makes it difficult to assess the risk of investment. In this article I analyze the various approaches used and then make my recommendations.

IFC Sets the Standard

The first institution to become vocal on emerging markets was the International Finance Corporation (IFC), a multilateral subsidiary of the World Bank, created in 1956. Its approach to identifying emerging markets relies heavily on GDP per capita: once a country's GDP per capita is $8,625, the figure as of 1993, it is considered a developed country. Below that it could be an emerging market. But since the IFC did not establish a minimum GDP per capita, by this approach it is impossible to differentiate between an emerging and a developing country.

Therefore, relying on this approach too much can be misleading. Some countries, such as South Korea and Israel, which are considered developed, have a GDP per capita lower than the IFC figure. Thus, someone might mistake these for emerging markets. Even Greece, a member of the European Union, is sometimes categorized as an emerging market because of these standards.

Institutions that follow and invest in emerging markets have adopted a variety of their own standards. This further complicates the matter. Several institutions continue to categorize Portugal as an emerging market, yet it is a member of the European Union. These contradictory classifications would never occur if a multi-pronged approach was used to evaluate the countries for emerging market status.

A Diversified View to Emerging Markets

The current method by the IFC does not recognize the different standards of living in each country. For example, in North America and Russia, climate and transportation costs increase the amount of income necessary to live, compared with a smaller country of mild temperature like Israel.

If a country has a strong and stable democratic government but lacks market economy, such as Poland, Bulgaria, and Slovenia, should it be an emerging market? At the same time even if Mainland China reaches the required level of income per capita, it will not be an emerging market in my estimation because it is not a democratic country. Countries like China must remain classified as developing countries because the political risk for business is very high. The same is true for countries such as Colombia and Ecuador where democratically elected governments are in place but the political situation is nevertheless very unstable.

Equally, countries with a stable regime, but no democracy are not emerging markets as yet. Their structure is not good for the entrepreneurial spirit or for foreign investment. Most modern international businesses are sophisticated enough to recognize that the handshake of a dictator is not a guarantee against political risk. I believe people have already learned this from the former president of the USSR and the last General Secretary of the Communist party, Comrade Gorbachev.

Capitalist Institutions Are Key

In deciding on what an emerging market country is, it is not sufficient to appraise the country strictly from a financial or political point of view. Nor is a combined approach enough. It is also critically important to evaluate the level of development of capitalist institutions and business activity. The capitalist institutions to which I refer are insurance companies (to guard against political and regular business risks), commercial and investment banks (especially international banks that appear in countries with new markets), internationally recognized law firms, and, of course, capital market institutions themselves (currency commissions, stock markets and commodities exchanges, and settlement and depository organizations). Finally, a country needs a well-developed telecommunications and transportation infrastructure that will allow international corporations to do business with fewer obstacles.

The Kvint Approach

My approach to identifying emerging markets is based on an integrated point of view, so my list differs substantially from those of the major publications. As I mentioned, China is a country that I feel cannot be considered an emerging market.

Of course, one can say that China is industrialized enough to be considered an emerging market. To me this is definitely the wrong approach. Using that standard, the USSR and all the former Soviet-bloc countries would have been classified as emerging markets due to the high-technology, military-industrial complex that existed. Though highly industrialized, clearly those were not countries where one should have invested money. The political risk was substantial, with no protection for international investment.

From a political point of view, Bulgaria and Romania have created important links with the rest of the industrialized world. Both are associate members of the European Union and have signed free trade agreements. Financially, they are also improving. Both solved their problems with the London and Paris Clubs, and have a strong orientation toward a market economy. That, in turn, has resulted in a GDP higher than that of Chile or Argentina. Also in these countries, the necessary major capital institutions are on the track to becoming fully developed.

The final illustration of my point is Albania. Until 1991, Albania was one of the most isolated countries in the world. For many years it had no connections with the communist and capitalist countries alike. Before the 1980s, Albania had connections with China, but cut those off as well when China started to implement some market economic reforms. Then, in 1991, Albania had its first legal democratic election, won by the Democrats. After a short period of a declining economy, in 1994, it became the most rapidly growing economy on a market-oriented platform. At the moment, Albania has the lowest rate of foreign debt in relation to GDP among all emerging markets worldwide. Inflation has declined to 4.5% this year, and production is growing by approximately 15% annually. Albania became a member of the Council of Europe, and has developed a legal system to protect foreign and domestic private investment. Still, the GDP per capita is only $700.

It seems to me that Albania is still not an emerging market but rather what I would term a pre-emerging one. From this point of view, I would classify many countries as such markets: Algeria, Egypt, Vietnam, India, Bangladesh, Pakistan, Chile, and Ukraine.

It Is Time to Refocus

For those who are still weighing the business, economic, and political risks in Russia and the former Soviet republics, it is a diverse picture. The social and political climate in Russia is definitely receptive to a market economy with all the necessary capitalist institutions.

Even GDP per capita is closer to the IFC requirement for a developed country, and 75% of the economy has been privatized. Russia, therefore, is an emerging market. So, too, are the Baltic states. Ukraine probably will become an emerging market in the next year. Pre-emerging republics include Moldova, Kazakstan, Kyrgyzstan, Uzbekistan, and Turkmenistan.

For international businesses, the various classifications of what constitutes an emerging market may be a moot issue. Most of the major corporations and financial players are already well established in those countries. What their new goal should be is to look for those countries that are in the pre-emerging market phase. Given the right circumstances (political, social, and economic), they should look for opportunities to begin to tap the potential of these markets. There are plenty of such countries that fall into this category. The most noted are Egypt, India, Bangladesh, Pakistan, Vietnam, Albania, FYRO Macedonia, Yugoslavia (Serbia and Montenegro), the republics of the former Soviet Union, Colombia, Ecuador, Panama, Uruguay, and Jordan.

Investment Interest Is Rapidly Rising

The emerging marketplace is already succeeding in drawing investors. The "developed" markets are fairly well tapped and as such offer few major growth opportunities. Why invest in the U.S. which grows at a rate of 2%–3% a year when you can invest in China which is growing at a rate of 15%–25%?

The International Monetary Fund estimates that major Western pension, mutual, and hedge funds invested 16% of their assets in emerging markets in 1994, compared with 0.5% in 1987. With the dissemination of technology and the consolidation of financial assets in these funds, investing has become less speculative. Without globalization, derivatives might never have assumed the importance they have today. They initially originated as instruments to hedge against currency and interest-rate fluctuations, but with globalization they literally took off. We also saw, in 1994, how risky they can be.

The following statistics will provide a more comprehensive understanding of the potential of emerging markets: more than 50% of Japanese exports, more than 40% of U.S. exports, and more than 30% of European Union exports were earmarked for emerging markets in 1994. To put the phrase "emerging markets" in context, it is important to remember that 75% of the world's population lives in emerging markets, and this market produces 21% of the world's GNP. Over the next ten years, multilateral institutions such as the World Bank, International Monetary Fund, the European Bank for Reconstruction and Development, and the Asian and African Multidevelopment Banks will give a combined total of over $300 billion to emerging markets.

In 1993, foreign direct investment in emerging markets grew by 37%. U.S. companies, in 1994 alone, exported more than $2.7 billion of U.S. products through the multilateral development banks, serving Asia, Latin America, Africa, and former Soviet-bloc countries. These numbers are only the direct effect of multilateral institutions.

According to the Bretton Woods Committee, the indirect effects are even greater: "U.S. exports are on the order of $5 billion higher each year because developing countries, with multi-development banks, have been opening their markets and expanding their capacity to import goods."

Templeton Russia Fund on the New York Stock Exchange

Direct investment by developed countries in the commercial and industrial activities of emerging market countries during the last five years reached $2.50 billion. The resulting development of capitalist institutions in this part of the world creates new possibilities for the international investment community. This new stage was marked by a milestone event on September 15, 1995. On that day, the first publicly trade Russian fund on the New York Stock Exchange was created, the Templeton Russia Fund, Inc. During 1993–94, I was a consultant for the Russian State Investment Corporation in its deal with PaineWebber to create the first Russian closed-end fund for $105 million. Ultimately, $135 million was raised in 1994. The Paine-Webber fund became the first closed-end venture capital Russia fund. The Templeton Russia Fund is classified as a non-diversified closed-end publicly traded fund.

The fund's objective is long-term capital appreciation. The managers will mainly invest in equity securities of Russian companies. They plan to sell a total of 4,600,000 shares at $15 per share, making the maximum $619 million. This fund was made possible by the leadership of Dr. J. Mark Mobius, president of Templeton Emerging Markets Fund. He lives in Singapore and has two experts in Moscow. Of course, this staff is not enough to understand the trends and changes in the huge emerging market in Russia. I hope he will increase the number of experts there.

The underwriters that participated in the Templeton Russia Fund include Merrill Lynch, A. G. Edwards & Sons, Inc., C. J. Lawrence/Deutsche Bank, Nomura Securities International, Inc., and Prudential Securities, Inc. As part of the fund's policy, the managers will invest at least 65% of the total assets in the securities of Russian issues. The fund wants to have the option of investing the remaining 35% in other countries should the investment climate in Russia become volatile. The fund will primarily invest in Russia's most visible businesses and companies. The risk with this strategy is lessened, but so will the gains be. As they begin to know the Russian landscape better, the fund will invest in debt securities of less visible companies so that higher returns can be achieved.

Another of the fund's restriction is not to invest more than 25% of its assets in any one industry, and no more than 10% in more than one issuer. In addition, the fund is limiting its investment in debt securities to no more than 20% of its total assets.

The Templeton Fund is the next important step for Russia. A series of events have occurred, each one making Russia more and more attractive as an investment in the emerging marketplace: first came the Moscow International Currency Exchange in 1992. Next, in February 1993, was the creation of the first publicly traded company on NASDAQ, the telecommunications company Petersburg Long Distance, Inc.; then came the PaineWebber Russian country venture capital fund, followed by the introduction of derivative instruments in the Russian market. The Templeton Fund is the latest milestone. It is paving the way for more funds if its kind.

Emerging markets have become a global market where major financial instruments can be used. The creation of all major capitalist institutions is a stamp of approval for any emerging market as a stable capitalist market.

HOW EMERGING IS EMERGING?

One question to consider in preparation for what lies ahead is how to define what an emerging market really is? How many institutional investment funds use a written policy to determine which countries qualify as emerging markets? How familiar are plan sponsors with their managers' definition of the term? The World Bank's International Finance Corporation defines emerging markets to be those with a GDP per capita below $8,625, but it does not indicate a minimum GDP per capita, points out Vladimir L. Kvint, Director, Emerging Markets, at Arthur Andersen Economic Consulting, New York, and Professor of Management Systems and International Business at Fordham University's Graduate School of Business.

Kvint's approach to the issue, which he outlines in a recent edition of his newsletter, *Inside Russia*, includes considering the level of development of capitalist institutions, meaning insurance companies, commercial and investment banks, international law firms, and such institutions as exchanges, depositories, and clearing facilities. Additionally, a market needs a transportation and telecommunications infrastructure that can support the business activities of international corporations. "If these factors are in place, then it does not matter what the GDP per capita is," asserts Kvint. "If the capitalistic institutions appear, it means there is a business interest in these markets."

Some of Kvint's classifications might take some seasoned global investors by surprise, among them: Chile, long considered a Latin American success story, is better as a pre-emerging market, due to a lack of "major, recognized international business institutions there, and it is very difficult to obtain insurance against political risk," not to mention "under-developed telecommunications and transportation services. You cannot go anywhere—the framework is not yet ready." But it is very close to emerging market status, Kvint adds, as is Albania, which in 1994, he points out, became the most rapidly growing economy on a market-oriented platform. Inflation in Albania is just 4.5%, and production is growing about 15% annually.

Global Investment, 2, No. 1 (December 1995), 43–44.

Other "pre-emerging markets" on Kvint's list include India, Pakistan, Egypt, and several Newly Independent States in Central Asia. China, by the way, doesn't even make the pre-emerging market list. "For me, it is a very simple issue," says Kvint. "Would a businessman or entrepreneur want to go or not to go? The major issues for him are the business approach, not the financial approach."

However one defines emerging markets, the characteristics that they share—higher economic growth rates, evolving legal and physical infrastructures, and a desire for foreign investment—are reason enough to be optimistic about their prudent inclusion in future asset allocation strategies. Throwing good money after bad doesn't achieve satisfactory returns in any asset class, and emerging markets are no different. The provision of keen global market insights will, therefore, be the basis of investment success stories even more in the year ahead than they are today.

Investing in the
Emerging Markets

INTERNATIONAL MONETARY FUND AND THE WORLD BANK: THE ADVANTAGES AND SHORTCOMINGS

In 1944, the Soviet Union had the opportunity to become a founding member of the IMF and World Bank. Joseph Stalin sent representatives (including the father of Victor Gerashenko, the current head of the Central Bank) to several meetings. Stalin ultimately decided that these institutions were too imperialistic for USSR participation. So, for the next 48 years, the Soviet Union remained outside the circle of legal, international, economic, and financial institutions. But when the Soviet Union was near collapse, the Soviet and then Russian leaders rediscovered the IMF and World Bank. They saw them as two of the major sources for additional out-of-pocket expense money, and these institutions began to look more attractive.

Russia Joins International Business Institutions

For Russia, an historic event occurred in 1992: it became a member of the IMF and World Bank. This membership was important not only for monetary reasons, but also because it was a major indication of Russia's movement toward supporting civilized, modern, international business. In April 1992, leaders of the Western countries, including President George Bush and Prime Minister Helmut Kohl, initiated action to provide Russia with $24 billion in aid. In July 1992 the IMF met to decide whether to issue this money to Russia. Although the aid was approved, the bureaucratic mechanisms of these institutions were not much better than the communist bureaucratic mechanisms, and so a substantial portion of the money, as of August 1994, has still not been issued.

In *The Kvint Newsletter*, 1, No. 1 (August 1994).

The major problem of any large organization, like this multilateral institution, is its mechanisms for implementing its programs. As expected, they are oriented toward working only with governments, not with private companies and entrepreneurial institutions in recipient countries. As a result, the money often flows to inexperienced governments in which there are few people who understand a capitalist economy.

Unique Problems, Standard Approach

An important role of the IMF and the World Bank was in developing an economic and business information system in Russia. For example, these institutions created a system for calculating economic indicators. In addition, membership in the IMF and World Bank gave Russia access to many advisers who had tremendous influence on the activity of the Russian government. Unfortunately, these organizations had only a primitive understanding of the way business is conducted in Russia, especially during the initial transition years, 1991–93. Thus, their recommendations did not provide the desired results and, in some cases, were counter-productive. One dramatic example is the policy recommendations the IMF advisers gave to Acting Prime Minister Gaidar. As expected, the initiatives of Gaidar and Jeffery Sachs of Harvard "liberalized" prices prematurely, before the demonopolization of the economy, conversion of the military industry, and privatization. Prices for all basic needs such as meat, milk, and clothes jumped sky-high. People lost the ability to feed their families. IMF "experts" exacerbated the situation by recommending that the Russian treasury not print new ruble bills. As a result, companies had no currency to pay salaries, and serious deflation occurred. Later the government had to issue, on a monthly basis, more money than was ever in circulation.

A serious problem with organizations such as the IMF and World Bank is that they attempt to remedy a country's specific problems with a generic set of recommendations and solutions. Ideas that might work well in Poland, for example, will not necessarily produce results in Russia. The Poles, in contrast with the Russians, have a memory of capitalism. Communism was instituted in Poland 45 years ago, compared to 73 years ago in Russia. But the biggest difference is that in Russia there was no private economy at all, while in Poland about 40% of the economy was private. This advantage enables capitalist systems to take root more in Poland than in Russia, a subtle distinction that has been lost on the IMF and World Bank.

New Solutions Are Needed

Past experience has proved that the world business community needs a new mechanism to solve large-scale economic and business problems. This mechanism must be more flexible, and have a shorter lead time between political decision making and implementation. In addition, it must be oriented toward private capital and entrepreneurs, and not just toward governments. Global institutions of this kind are developing, such as the regularly scheduled G-7 meetings of the leading industrial countries: Canada, France, Germany, Great Britain, Italy, Japan, the United States, and now Russia. G-7 meeting members are generally making good political decisions, but not all of the decisions are being implemented.

Economic decisions are usually made without the input of economists, and are not as sound. It is necessary to convert these meetings into real institutions and create the mechanism for implementation.

The difference between institutions with 50 years' experience such as the IMF and World Bank and new institutions is their emphasis. The older institutions are geared more toward long-term macroeconomic decisions, while the newer ones address shorter-term tactical goals. In order to be most effective, plans to solve global-scale problems must be put into practice on a regional level. Several new regional institutions have appeared, such as EBRD (European Bank for Reconstruction and Development), which was opened in April 1992. I participated in the recommendations for the creation of this institution in 1989 and early 1990. The Soviets finally realized that, for this institution to be successful, it was necessary to invest amounts comparable to what other leading countries were investing. As a result, EBRD became one of the first institutions where the former Soviet Union, and later Russia, played a role not only as a recipient but also as a decision maker. Unfortunately, the EBRD did not focus its activity, and is therefore not visible in post-Communist countries.

Central Asian Republics Are Neglected

By overlooking the important Central Asian republics, these world organizations have left that part of the world without a stabilizing influence. Countries such as Iran and Iraq have not hesitated to increase their business activities in these regions, and, therefore, their political influence has grown. Likewise, Turkey has become very active in Turkmenistan and Azerbaijan. For the first time in history, Central Asia is established into independent countries. Therefore, it is vital to create a Central Asian institution to work with these republics. While they do not yet play a geopolitical role, and while they are not yet a major target of the world business community, both will occur within the next ten years.

Business people must also understand that multilateral institutions are not world institutions—even the World Bank, despite its name. Many countries, even with formal participation in this institution, do not receive any money. Of the Eastern European countries, Poland, Hungary and Romania have the best relationships with multilateral institutions, but Bulgaria is neglected by these groups. As a result, international business is only slowly focusing on this country. And Western business people have not recognized that this country offers wonderful opportunities for business.

Follow the Money Trail

International investors should closely follow the activities of the major multilateral institutions. If countries are receiving funding from multilateral organizations, it is a signal that these economies are worthwhile for investment. Once a government receives money, private entrepreneurs within the country can revive a flagging economy. This leads to better business opportunities, as well as stabilization. For example, the fact that Russia joined G-7 and the Paris Club is a positive indication that the economy is stabilizing. Individuals should read news regarding such international organizations for clues that could lead them to potential investments. Private entrepreneurs and investors can obtain guarantees for investment in these countries.

DON'T GIVE UP ON RUSSIA

The Russians love their dictators, I've heard American say. I suppose one could argue the point. But Westerners who think Russians are hostile to a free economy are just plain wrong. The 25% of the population that voted for the nationalists in the last parliamentary election were not voting against capitalism; they were protesting the hardship caused by "shock therapy," the ill-conceived economic policy that resulted in skyrocketing inflation, high unemployment, a fuel shortage, and a decrease in food consumption, all of which have left 90% of Russians living below the poverty level. Still, if the 1991 coup plotters—the Communist Party, the KGB, and the army—couldn't squelch the beginnings of democracy and a free economy, neither can the lack of bread.

This is no time for U.S. investors to retreat from Russia. The climate for international joint ventures has never been better. Russians know that without cooperation with the West, the country cannot survive, let alone prosper. Not one elected leader has called for government control of foreign property. Russia has become a member of the International Monetary Fund and the World Bank, and some 18,000 foreign companies have already invested in the country. According to a study I conducted of joint ventures attempted between 1989 and 1993, between 35% and 38% of consummated joint ventures are already profitable or well on the way. That's the highest success rate for new businesses in the world.

It's true that the country still needs modern insurance and banking systems and more firms to handle accounting and auditing. Industry must be fully demonopolized and state property privatized. Russia also needs more laws governing business; too many Russian entrepreneurs see the black market as the seat of modern industry. Nevertheless, the country offers foreigners advantages available nowhere else: a cheap labor force more highly educated than the United States's, inexpensive factories and land, and a plethora of natural resources. Despite the lack of maintenance in the oil fields,

Harvard Business Review, March–April 1994, pp. 62–74.

Russia produces more oil and gas each day than Saudi Arabia and more natural gas, steel, and cement than any other country.

Russia is on sale now, and those who arrive late will have to pay more. The price of land will undoubtedly rise, and the country is developing protectionist stances as it comes to appreciate the full value of its resources. Still, many Americans remain reluctant to invest, understandably deterred by the fact that most joint ventures attempted in Russia never get off the ground. But their failure is less a function of business conditions in Russia than poor planning on the part of foreign investors. Western partners of joint ventures in Russia have usually neglected to scout out the best locations, negotiate fair deals, and verify the information that companies provide.

Potential investors who want to beat the trend can begin by learning from the mistakes of the first wave of joint ventures. My own history may offer some insight into the beginnings of these ventures, the mind-set of the Soviet leaders who allowed them, and the emergence of Russian capitalism decades before the Soviet Union's collapse.

My capitalist education began early. I was born in 1949 in the city of Krasnoyarsk, the industrial heart of Siberia. Most Westerners imagine Siberia as a permafrost wasteland with few people and no businesses. In reality, there are 28 million people living in an area a little larger than Canada. Krasnoyarsk has warm summers—for two months, anyway—and beautiful rivers in which I swam as a boy.

At 15, I got my first job as a metal-worker in Krasnoyarsk. Later, I spent a year mining for nonferrous metals in Norilsk, the northernmost city on earth, with a climate that makes Anchorage seem tropical. Eager to stay warm and above ground, I enrolled in graduate school to study electrical engineering in the mining department at the Krasnoyarsk Institute of Nonferrous Metals. During my studies there, I came across one of the first Russian translations of Paul Samuelson's work and became fascinated by the potential of economic theory to shape human behavior. At 23 I competed to earn a place at the Moscow Institute of National Economy.

Going to this institute after working in Siberia was like moving from the bottom of society to the top. For the first time, I met the scholars who had written the textbooks I had been reading. It was 1972, and already the first wave of new management theory was sweeping the school. We studied organizational structure and management systems based on U.S. models and read translations of U.S., British, and Japanese texts. Even then, almost everyone knew that communism was a stupid idea. People didn't say this in public—it was much too dangerous—but we talked among ourselves. Anyone who had ever worked at a company even briefly knew there was absolutely no connection between real life and communism. People needed incentives to work, and companies needed incentives to produce.

After I earned my Ph.D. in 1975, I took a job as head of organizational management at the Norilsk Mining Metallurgical Concern, the largest Soviet enterprise, with 150,000 employees in a single location. I introduced a matrix structure to encourage cooperation between divisions the size of companies. For the first time, the bosses, who ran these divisions like fiefdoms, were forced to share employees and resources. Productivity increased, and the matrix structure remains to this day. The following year, I accepted a position as chief economist and deputy chairman of the Siberian Nonferrous Metallurgy Automation Company (SibAuto), a technology company that automated the nonferrous metals industry and one of the first Soviet businesses to base its production on actual customer orders rather than subsidies from the state.

At SibAuto, I learned more about the importance of motivating workers than I could have in any school. All workers in Soviet companies earned nearly the same salaries, no matter how much or how efficiently they produced. The state did not allow us to pay our best workers more than 30% above the average salary; so I had to find other ways to raise our employees' standard of living. First, I sent a portion of our profit to the trade union, which gave money to the company canteen. The canteen used the money to prepare sumptuous lunches to be sold for just a few kopecks. Our trade union chairman helped out by securing free passes to various spas so that we could reward our best workers with vacations. People started to pay more attention to their work because they knew that their managers would recognize excellence with more than communist medals.

In 1978, I was invited to join the Siberian School of Economists, part of the Academy of Sciences. The leaders of the Siberian School included Nobel Prize-winning economist Leonid Kantorovich and Abel Aganbegian. While I came from the region, most members had exiled themselves to Siberia to be as far as possible from Moscow's communist bureaucrats. In the subfreezing temperature, we could discuss our passions: the free market, and new management methods. Members even sent the general secretary of the Communist Party a letter saying that there was no future in the Soviet economic system. A risky move, but where could the secretary send people who were already in Siberia?

During this time, I developed methods of studying natural resources and business opportunities in various regions of Russia. I organized the first economic expedition through the Arctic Seaway to evaluate its natural resources and local enterprises. Bundled in snowsuits, our group of 15 traveled for 63 days by ship, helicopter, and jeep through the icy terrain, often going for days without meeting anyone. We observed mile after mile of oil and gas fields; plants that produced nickel, cobalt, copper, and timber; fish factories; and transportation and construction companies. I knew that with the development of the right infrastructure for mining and transportation, the economic potential of this region was enormous.

In 1981, when I arrived at the Institute of Economics of the Academy of Sciences in Moscow to study for a second doctorate in regional management and economics, in some respects it was like going back in time. The institute was the official consulting arm of the central government. (Our director would become deputy prime minister for economic reform under Mikhail Gorbachev.) Using Marxist analysis, people studied why communism was more productive than other economic systems. I asked my new colleagues, "If the Soviet economy is so much better, why are you buying foreign cars and shoes? Why are Russian companies using so much foreign equipment?" When I asked one scholar when he'd last spent time inside an industrial company, he said, "In 1953."

The institute, nevertheless, had a fine department of political economy, and I wanted to improve my understanding of the connection between public policy and economics. We had special access to government statistics—the ones not available to the public—which were much more detailed and accurate. Based on these numbers, I prepared a study in 1988 analyzing the political and economic situation in the Soviet Union. I concluded that the Soviet Union could not support its military and political apparatus beyond 1991 or 1992 and was headed for a collapse. I was not psychic; the statistics and political environment had simply swayed me. The economic basis of communism had been deteriorating since 1970. From 1970 to 1985, the gross national product's rate of growth declined 300%.

The mounting economic crisis forced the communist leadership to open markets and court foreign investment. I had already begun to study how international joint ventures in Europe increased the level of technology and production. Foreign companies could produce the equipment, technology, and management systems Russia desperately needed as well as the money to develop oil and gas fields and nonferrous metal and diamond pits. International cooperation, I believed, was critical to Russia's survival.

By the mid-1980s, even Gorbachev realized that Russia did not have enough investment capacity, equipment, and workers to advance Soviet industry. In 1987, he opened the doors to direct cooperation between Soviet and foreign enterprise. The Soviet government invited other market-oriented economists and me to consult on the draft of a joint-venture regulation.

Some Russians called Soviet bureaucrats pen pushers; they were actually more like erasers. They deleted 95% of our draft of progressive legislation from the text. The final agreement limited the rights of foreign partners to 49% and made it impossible for foreigners to hold the post of chairman or director general. The doctrinaire bureaucrats were afraid that without these restrictions fat, cigar-smoking capitalists would take control of the motherland. Of course, they did no such thing. Only 23 joint ventures were created in 1987 under the poorly formed regulation. But this was good news to me: when the second joint-venture regulation was drafted in 1988, the bureaucrats no longer feared a mad rush to buy Moscow. They heeded our calls to abolish restrictions.

The most successful joint-venture partners were German, Finnish, and Austrian companies, whose members knew the country well and had good relationships with Soviet bureaucrats. Most Americans didn't understand the market, so they weren't in any rush to invest. Dialogue, the second U.S.-Soviet joint venture, was an exception. It began as a modest company that assembled computers from U.S. parts. Although Soviet companies had little hard currency, they could usually scrape together enough to buy a couple of Dialogue's computers. The venture grew rapidly and was one of the few to see immediate profits.

Today there are more than 18,000 joint ventures in Russia and

more than $10 billion in foreign investment. The number of U.S.–
Russian joint ventures has increased from 625 in January 1992 to
2,800 in January 1994. The numbers vary, but, according to my research, around $1 billion in U.S. investments flowed into Russia
from October 1992 through December 1993. Large U.S. industrialists are on the scene, including IBM, General Electric, Ford, Hewlett-
Packard, Eastman Kodak, Playtex, Chevron, and AT&T. In 1993,
PepsiCo signed a $3 billion multiyear trade pact, and in 1989 and
1990, McDonald's invested $50 million in a food-processing plant
and a restaurant in Moscow. Thousands of small and midsize ventures have also arrived. Most of the joint ventures have been in software, heavy industrial production, tourism, and hotels. There has
also been an explosion in the growth of research and development.
Companies like Bell Labs are working with Russian scientists to
study space, electronics, optics, lasers, and nuclear energy.

I applaud Gorbachev for opening the door enough to let in these
foreign investments. He deserves much credit for glasnost and the
liberalization of daily life. But while he talked about economic reform and political freedom, he never came out against communism.
Gorbachev was not a real revolutionary; he was a reformer who supported small reforms, and he bungled even those. Gorbachev never
came out in favor of private property.

Boris Yeltsin, on the other hand, is the first modern Russian revolutionary and the first true anti-communist. He destroyed the last
Russian empire in front of our eyes. Yeltsin understands the importance of creating a political climate that encourages investment. But
revolutionaries can only destroy old systems; they cannot create new
ones.

Yeltsin does not understand capitalism. He has relied on Russian
advisers who have never lived and worked in capitalist countries and
on Western consultants who do not understand the Russian economy and have recommended standard measures to move the country
toward capitalism. Yeltsin's decision to liberalize prices in January
1992, before the decentralization of management systems, before
demonopolization, and before the privatization of state property, resulted in a pseudoliberalization of price. Because state monopolies
owned all property, they raised prices. Inflation rose from 15% to
159% per month. This kind of shock therapy was a mistake on the
part of an inexperienced government. The resulting economic hard-

ship gave Russians the impression that life would be even worse under capitalism.

Soon Russia will need new leaders who can help the country understand the function of capitalist institutions. These leaders will have to take steps to prevent hyperinflation, lift restrictions on the activities of foreign banks and insurance companies in Russia, and create jobs programs and systems of social protection for elderly veterans, students, and the poor, particularly during the worsening meat shortage. (There are as many cows now as in 1954, but the human population has increased since then by 35 million.) I'm not calling for a return to socialism, but for a dose of compassion as Russia moves toward capitalism.

Russia desperately needs investment from the West to ease this difficult transition. Recent regulations allow foreigners to form wholly owned companies and subsidiaries, but joint ventures are still the best investment option. Americans can benefit from reliable Russian partners with good connections and access to raw materials and equipment. Deciding where to invest and how to structure a deal, however, can be fraught with problems. Americans would do well to learn from their predecessors' mistakes.

Choosing the Right Location

The first question I hear from U.S. managers considering joint ventures is, "How far from the Kremlin can our headquarters be?" They overestimate the power of government bureaucrats, who no longer make all the decisions, and underestimate the power of regional leaders—the heads of various political and administrative subdivisions—and executives, who now have much more autonomy. During the first two years of joint-venture activity, 85% of all foreign joint ventures were located in Moscow and 10% in St. Petersburg. Only 5% were scattered over the rest of the former Soviet Union. Americans who favor high-risk ventures might consider locating in Moscow, the hot seat of political turmoil. I suggest heading north instead.

In general, the political risk of investments in Russia decreases from south to north and west to east, meaning that investments in

Siberia and along the Pacific Coast are more reliable than those in the many European regions of the country. Most people in Siberia, or their ancestors, went there as exiles. They don't like communism and stay far away from the centers of power. All political violence has been in the European parts of Russia, where unemployment is higher than in Siberia or the Russian Far East. More corruption, especially bribery, and higher levels of crime exist in Moscow.

I am partial to my home, Siberia. Each of Siberia's 13 regions has a university and excellent graduate schools. Most important, Siberia has abundant resources. According to recent studies undertaken by geologists at the Academy of Sciences, the oil reserves of eastern Siberia are larger than those controlled by all OPEC nations combined. Krasnoyarsk produces more platinum, nickel, and timber than any country in the world—with old machinery and without foreign investment. Privatization has resulted in the conversion of military plants to civilian products; a potentially lucrative plant for optical equipment for submarines, for example, is now manufacturing sewing machines.

Equally attractive to investors is the Russian Far East, a secret the Japanese have known for years because of their proximity. One hundred and fifty Japanese companies have already established direct ties to various Russian enterprises in the Russian Far East. The area is rich in oil and gas, diamonds, gold, nonferrous and rare metals, coal, timber, and fish from Siberian rivers and the Pacific and Arctic oceans. The Sakhalin, Primorskiy, and Khabarovsk regions have already developed the infrastructure necessary for industry.

Given that nearly a quarter of the Pacific region's lumber resources are in the Russian Far East, the timber industry should attract numerous foreign investors. What the area needs now is foreign technology for furniture, paper, and cardboard manufacturing. Fortunately, people in this area do not view trees purely for their lumber potential. After many decades of ecological devastation, environmentalism is a growing force in Russia. The population in the Russian Far East will welcome any foreign company that can reduce waste and still make money.

Companies would also benefit by locating in any of Russia's 15 free economic zones. Four years ago, I was involved in creating Russia's first FEZs, which offer special privileges, such as tax holidays, to encourage the investment of foreign capital. Unfortunately, from

1989 to 1993, the government didn't draw up plans for developing these zones; as a result, progress is slow.

When foreign investors consider a specific area, they should get a copy of the regional program, usually available through the regional government. Each lists which foreign technologies are considered vital to the area and the region's preferences for imports. Regional programs also indicate the availability of state-owned property that foreigners may purchase. Consultants or local economists can help potential investors explore regions, track down programs, determine transportation options, and calculate the cost of developing infrastructure. Investors must keep in mind that a portion of any investment made in eastern Siberia will need to go into transportation and basic services.

Choosing the Right Partner

The importance of picking the right partner is obvious, but I've lost count of how many U.S. businesses I've watched make disastrous mistakes. According to my joint-venture study, 28% of potential joint ventures failed because they lacked a reliable Russian partner.

During the initial negotiations, Americans should gather as much documentation about a company as possible, including: records of outstanding obligations to the state, such as loans; recommendations from banks; and the company's registration numbers and licenses, which can be found in regional government offices. Some companies may have a license to produce a product, for example, but not to export it. I've seen numerous Americans and other Westerners neglect to ask about licensing and even more who fall for the line, "Our license will be arriving any day." Too often the next day turns into the next month, which usually means never.

I came across one U.S. company that signed an agreement with the Krasnoyarsk Oil and Gas Geological Company without knowing that the company had the right to do geological research but no license to develop oil fields. To make matters worse, the U.S. company also failed to consult the Ministry of Geology before signing the deal. When the company finally approached the ministry to obtain a license, the ministers were furious that they hadn't been contacted prior to the signing. Naturally, they denied the request.

An Austrian company had a similar experience when the second largest Soviet publishing house, Molodaya Gvardiya, approached the Austrians because it needed computer equipment for its publishing facilities. The Russian publisher had no hard currency, so it agreed to pay the Austrians in waste paper, which can be sold to newspaper companies at good prices. The Austrian partner, however, had neglected to check one detail: Had the state supplies committee granted the publisher permission to sell its waste? (The Austrians had no idea that the state even regulated waste!) Not only had the company failed to obtain this license, but also it had neglected to get permission from the Ministry of Foreign Economic Ties to sell *any* goods abroad. The deal was over before it had even begun.

Unfortunately, too many U.S. companies spend considerable money on trips and negotiations only to discover that their Russian partners have lied. I've seen Russian companies claim to earn $100 million in profits when they have absolutely nothing. And I've seen too many Americans neglect to ask for documentation. Foreigners who are the victims of fraud can take legal action, but the settlement will probably not justify the expense, and such action could hurt a company's reputation in the Russian business community. Consequently, it is essential to verify all information the company supplies, using an independent auditing company that meets Western standards.

Occasionally, Russian companies hire such auditing firms. In most cases, both partners need to agree on an auditor and decide who will pay for the service. Foreigners should also compare and contrast information from several sources in the company. In general, foreigners are more likely to receive accurate information from lower level managers than from senior executives. One important fact to keep in mind when assessing financial information is that the Russian accounting system—a relic of the communist era—does not allow for a realistic appraisal of products or assets. Concepts like "current market value" do not exist.

Foreign businesses should also be skeptical of figures offered by government officials, who are masters of the "double lie squared." Any information channeled to them has already been doctored by the so-called First Department, the group responsible for classified information, which still operates within almost every state-owned enterprise as well as in many private ones. The difficulty of obtaining accurate figures makes the case for independent auditors much more compelling.

Understanding Cultural Differences

When Americans go to Japan, most attempt to learn about Japanese customs. But too many Americans don't bother to learn about Russians and their extremely diverse cultures. Each region has its own economic and labor histories and ethnic and religious traditions. One American accountant wanted to negotiate a contract in Tataria. Because he had heard that meat was in short supply, he brought plenty of first-rate bacon as a goodwill gesture. But the Tatars are Moslem. They don't eat pork.

The possibilities for miscommunication are endless. If someone asks two Russians how they met, the Russians will be embarrassed. Russians are generally secretive, especially with foreigners. This attitude comes from years of living under a repressive regime. In general, Russians have an inferiority/superiority complex about Americans. On one hand, they see all Americans as millionaires who look down on their poor Russian neighbors. One the other, Russians refer to Americans as *burdocks*, simpletons who crumble in the face of hardship.

Americans who want to transcend these stereotypes should stress to their Russian colleagues that their success took years of hard work. I remember a negotiation in Miami between a Russian and a wealthy American that was going well until the American began reminiscing about his first foray into business. At the age of 14, he told us, he hired ten people to clean the bathrooms along Miami Beach. He described in detail how he would sit in a beach chair and sun himself while his workers cleaned the stalls. The story revealed more to the Russian than the American imagined. It told the Russian that the American never got his hands dirty; he let other people do his work.

To make a good impression, Americans should spend time socializing with potential Russian partners. Many deals have been hatched in a sauna between discussions of life, family, and philosophy. But politics, a sensitive subject that is becoming more sensitive every day, should be avoided at all cost. Foreigners don't want to lambaste

Vladimir Zhirinovsky only to discover that their potential Russian partners are among the 25% of the population that votes for him.

Americans should not try to be mentors for Russians. Rather than pontificating, they should rely on stories from their experience to convey information. Most important, Americans should not assume they know more than their Russian colleagues. I spoke to a potential investor who asked if the Russians would understand him when he talked about laser technology. I reminded him that the Russians earned a Nobel Prize in laser technology in 1964.

Designing the Deal

Many Americans mistakenly treat the problem of the quasi-convertible ruble as the most important aspect of their negotiations. After July 15, 1992, when the Russian banks began to hold exchange auctions, inconvertibility became less of a problem. Through banks and financial companies, Americans can buy dollars with rubles at these auctions, invest rubles in dollar-producing businesses, or opt for a barter or collateral deal instead.

The most important point during the negotiations is the share of initial capital investment each party contributes to the joint venture. This division and ownership last for the life of the joint venture, and parties will divide all profits according to the percentages of initial capital investment. Americans should not underestimate the purchasing power of the ruble during these negotiations, and they must realize the value of any property. Too often Americans ask Russians to contribute more than their fair share.

Befriending Local Leaders

Before 1987, befriending Russian bureaucrats meant shaking hands with the right people or offering bribes. The situation has changed dramatically; keeping up relationships with despots doesn't work anymore. Even state-owned companies have gained more independence from the central government. So have regional leaders, as I mentioned earlier, many of whom are now more powerful than U.S. mayors.

To form strong personal connections with regional leaders, Americans can work with them to solve regional problems. This level of involvement will help convince these leaders that the company's intent is not only to take from Russia, but also to improve life in the community. One U.S. oil company won over regional leaders when it donated equipment to start a small factory to produce sausage. Many other companies, however, have neglected to foster goodwill.

Consider the owners of an oil refinery on the West Coast of the United States. In 1988, the executives managed to meet Gorbachev and former Prime Minister Nikolai Ryzhkov, who gave the company permission to build a plant in western Siberia. I warned lawyers representing the company that the proposed site was in an ecological disaster area. I told them to speak with members of the regional government, who would undoubtedly have reservations, as would the local people, who could barely breathe because of the pollution. But the lawyers went ahead with the project without consulting anyone. Soon the local citizens were holding rallies, and the regional government was doing everything it could to block the refinery. After the company had invested $17 million, the deal fell through.

To sell ministers and regional leaders on a proposed joint venture, U.S. and Russian partners should write a strong project summary that discusses how the venture corresponds to national, regional, and local goals and concerns. Recommendations from members of institutions like the Academy of Sciences will strengthen the proposal. Every Russian ministry has from 5 to 50 research institutes that can supply information and analysis. Foreign businesspeople should also make themselves available to both the local and the national Russian press for interviews. Good public relations is more important now than ever before.

Compensating Employees

Average Russians are better educated than average Americans, and given the proper conditions, they can be excellent employees. Still, the average salary of Russian employees in international companies is only $55 per month. A lot of small foreign businesses have paid even less, treating Russian workers little better than slaves.

Most Russians subsist on cabbage, bread, and potatoes. They live in crowded apartments and share bedrooms and bathrooms with other families. Thirty percent of Russians still live in communal conditions—generally squalid ones. My work at SibAuto, the company that automated the nonferrous metal industry, taught me that if you take care of employees' social problems, you'll have the best workers. Given the high inflation rate, rubles are of little value to Russian workers. So companies need to pay workers with something besides money, such as apartments, health care, and medical and food products, which are in short supply. Russia has a strong tradition of bartering. It's an excellent way to motivate workers and strengthen relationships between employers and employees.

Anticipating Shortages in Materials

The last point I want to stress is that failure to anticipate shortages can destroy a business before it gets off the ground. One of the first and most highly touted joint ventures with the West was a women's fashion magazine, *Burda Moden Russia*. Raïssa Gorbachev supported the project in 1987 but arranged only hard currency financing, which left the project undercapitalized. By 1991, a dire paper shortage and the diminishing influence of the Gorbachev name with suppliers spelled trouble for the magazine. Paper mills began selling to the highest bidder, and *Burda Moden Russia* lacked the capital to compete. In hindsight, one of the partners should have been a paper supplier, but the venture had too much debt to make this switch. The magazine folded that year.

McDonald's, in contrast, prepared for shortages before it opened the first of three restaurants. The company established its own farm, where it grew potatoes for french fries and kept livestock for burgers. By the time the first golden arches went up in Pushkin Square, the venture was self-sufficient. Companies with this kind of foresight have the greatest chance of success. By avoiding the common mistakes that plague their predecessors, they position themselves to enjoy large profits later.

Some experts are counseling U.S. companies to move slowly as they develop joint ventures in Russia. My advice: Invest early and move as fast as you can. Companies can minimize the risk of bureaucratic entanglements and benefit from the fire-sale prices in the largest market in the world.

THE RUSSIAN INVESTMENT DILEMMA

Do the risks of starting joint ventures in Russia outweigh the benefits?

Some experts are counseling U.S. companies to move slowly as they develop joint ventures in Russia. In "Don't Give Up on Russia," Siberian-born Vladimir Kvint advises Americans to invest early and move fast. Despite sky-rocketing inflation and other economic hardships, the climate for international joint ventures has never been better, he argues. Russia has a cheap and highly educated workforce, inexpensive land, and abundant natural resources. According to a study Kvint conducted of joint ventures attempted, between 35% and 38% of those consummated are already profitable or well on the way. That's the highest success rate in the world for new businesses.

Still, Americans are deterred by the fact that most of Russia's joint ventures never get off the ground. But their failure is less a function of business conditions in Russia than of poor planning on the part of foreign investors, Kvint argues. And potential investors can learn from their predecessors' mistakes.

Russians know that without cooperation with the West, the country can't survive, let alone prosper. Russia is on sale how, Kvint writes, and those who arrive late will miss the bargain-basement prices in the largest market in the world.

Seven experts consider their pros and cons of investing in Russia.

Marshall I. Goldman, Kathryn W. Davis Professor of Russian Economics, Wellesley College, Wellesley, Massachusetts; Associate Director, Russian Research Center, Harvard University, Cambridge, Massachusetts

Vladimir Kvint's article is a perfect illustration of the hazards and uncertainties of dealing with Russia. Kvint wrote the piece before the dismissal of two of the most outspoken supporters of economic reform: Yegor Gaidar, the deputy prime minister, and Boris Fyodorov, the minister of finance. Their removal from the government is hardly an encouraging sign for foreign investors because it probably heralds an increase in inflation and less resistance to the protectionist calls of Russian nationalists and communists. Kvint reassures us that the 25% of the Russian population who voted for the nationalists (he neglects to mention the 20% who voted for the communists) did not vote against capitalism. True, but they did not vote *for* capitalism and reform, either.

No elected leader, Kvint says, has called for government control of foreign property. That is certainly reassuring, but at the same time the existing government has become more protectionist. One U.S. company, for example, spent several months preparing bids on a project after it had been assured that foreign bids would be considered. When the time came for the authorities to make a decision, however, they reversed themselves and said that only Russian companies could bid.

Nor does it help that Russia does not yet have a commercial code that governs in practice as well as in theory. As those involved in the profitable Radisson-Slavyanskaya Hotel joint venture discovered, even favored ventures (President Bill Clinton stayed there during the summit in Moscow) are at risk. The hotel's account has been frozen, and it is being sued for several million dollars by two maids because they were not given permanent employment.

In arguing that there is no better time for international joint ventures, Kvint apparently disagrees with the mayor of St. Petersburg, who warned that, with ever-increasing crime and corruption, it is now more difficult to start a joint venture than it was in 1990. In the past, the Russian Mafia focused on domestic businesses because attacks on foreigners were certain to provoke a response by the KGB. But as government authority has weakened, these gangs of thugs and racketeers have penetrated the previously immune foreign sector.

Thinking themselves beyond the reach of the Mafia, most Western companies, especially the multinational ones, at first refused to pay them off. In retaliation, the Mafia launched a bazooka attack on the bottling plant that Coca-Cola was building in Moscow and has intimidated many of its distributors. Showing its impartiality, another Mafia group regularly hijacks PepsiCo trucks and, as in the days of Al Capone, sells the soda itself. Fear of the Mafia has made it more difficult to recruit new managers, especially those who have families.

Obviously, paying off the Mafia (which is illegal under the U.S. Foreign Corrupt Practices Act) or hiring others to provide protection (sometimes the protectors are the would-be firebombers) adds significantly to the cost of doing business—something Kvint neglects to discuss. Most Western companies, for example, estimate that it costs $300,000 to $400,000 a year to maintain an expatriate in Russia. No wonder so few Western ventures are making a profit and so many are losing money.

Kvint would be much more convincing if he gave us more extended examples of joint ventures that have gone well. While he does mention a few companies, the bulk of his analysis tells us why so many joint ventures have lost money—not a very reassuring argument. Nor is it reassuring that the outflow of capital from Russia of about a billion dollars a month far exceeds the inflow of private capital. It is also noteworthy that Japanese business people, who are very active in China, have a diminishing presence in Russia. In part that is because of the political dispute over the Kuril Islands, but it is also a reaction to the hundreds of millions of dollars that the Russians owe to Japanese companies. The Japanese are good at taking a long view toward investment, but they have apparently decided that investing in Russia is too long-term.

Despite the many horror stories, which Kvint seems to regard as the exception rather than the rule, there are no doubt opportunities for resourceful investors. However, there is no easy or guaranteed way to succeed, and usually there are corners to cut and pockets to pad. Because Russia is so rich in raw material and human capital, many will want a share of what someday could be a very profitable market. But that someday will have to bring with it a return to commercial law and order and a willingness to participate in the international business community.

Jean-Pierre von Rooy, President, Otis Elevator Company, Framington, Connecticut

Otis Elevator took Kvint's advice: we invested early in Russia and moved as quickly as we could. Based on our experience, I couldn't agree more with Kvint's assessment.

Between 1990 and the end of 1992, Otis Elevator formed four joint ventures in Russia and one in Ukraine to manufacture, install, and maintain elevators. Our company has invested $50 million already, and discussions are continuing on possible additional ventures. The first shipments of Otis elevators produced in Russia—which are manufactured using Western technologies and are designed for Russian offices and apartment buildings—were made last September.

We expect strong business growth because of the urgent need for new housing in Russia. Nearly all of the half million elevators in the country are in desperate need of refurbishment or replacement.

Although our new Russian employees may lack expertise in sales, marketing, and accounting, their engineering skills are terrific. For example, they have already identified mistakes in some of our drawings. The transfer of Western technology into the ventures is going relatively smoothly for that reason. Of course, we would love to see better commercial banking facilities and improvements in communication and transportation. And we wouldn't object if networks of small supplier businesses were developed and import regulations simplified. Being realistic, however, we do not expect to make a quick profit on our investment.

As the former Soviet republics struggle with the transformation to free-market economies, we will continue to be patient. We fully expect that our strategy in Russia will pay off, and we are confident in Russia's long-term future.

Ruth Harkin, President and CEO, Overseas Private Investment Corporation, Washington, D.C.

While Kvint is correct in arguing that the Russian investment climate is better than the U.S. press reports and in advising Westerners to pay closer attention to the particulars of Russia's culture and economy, he should have placed the onus on Russia to put its house in order before it courts further foreign investment.

Although the parliamentary crisis in October and the December elections have exacerbated Russia's political instability, a number of other impediments to international investment have existed for a much longer time. For example, hyperinflation and the declining ruble tend to cause capital to flow to ventures that generate hard currency—oil, gas, mining, natural-resource production, and the like—rather than to the production of consumer goods. But because the Russians consider natural-resource production a strategic area, they are ambivalent about whether they want foreigners to invest in it. This presents an economic catch-22: a poor economy in precisely those areas where the Russians are uncertain they want it.

Other problems continue to discourage investors. Russia's decision-making structure remains haphazard, without clear legal protection for investments, contracts, or mineral rights. Often there is no clear delineation of responsibilities between agencies or between central and regional authorities. Federal and local authorities continually amend old levies and add new ones, leaving Russia's tax and fee structure unstable. For some projects, exported oil may be subject to as many as six or more taxes totaling 60%. For other projects, the total tax bite may be smaller. Both the size of the levies and their variations among projects are generally greater in Russia than in emerging economies outside the former Soviet Union.

International lenders thus see Russia as risky and are unwilling to make loans without the protection of guarantees and insurance from Western governments. Further, the Western nations as a whole have failed to provide much of the funding promised by the G-7 at last year's Tokyo summit. Even so, the United States has unilaterally moved to back much-needed investment.

A significant portion of that backing has been provided by the Overseas Private Investment Corporation, the Clinton administration agency charged with supporting U.S. investment in the developing world and emerging economies. To free up critically needed capital, the agency is offering U.S. investors $2.5 billion in loan guarantees and political risk insurance for joint ventures in the newly independent states of the former Soviet Union. That level of support will leverage an even greater amount of investment—perhaps as much as $8 billion—for the economies of all the former Soviet republics. It will have the added benefit of generating billions of dollars in U.S. exports and creating tens of thousands of U.S. jobs.

As Kvint argues, Westerners must do more to understand and adapt to the Russian way of doing things. The converse is also true. In the meantime, support from Western governments can be an important catalyst for taking joint ventures from conception to completion.

Constantine S. Nicandros, President and CEO, Conoco, Inc., Houston, Texas

My advice to companies investing in Russia is different from Kvint's Full steam ahead. I urge instead, Proceed with caution. Western investment in Russia does indeed offer great potential both for investors and for Russia. Realizing the potential, however, requires major steps by the Russian government to improve the investment climate. As president and CEO of Conoco, an integrated international oil company and a subsidiary of DuPont, I have seen firsthand both the potential that exists in Russia and the problems that the country needs to overcome.

Kvint points out that there are major opportunities for Western companies to invest in Russia's petroleum industry. On the one hand, Russia has the largest oil and gas reserves in the world. On the other, the country's oil production is declining in the face of severe capital constraints and less-than-current technology. Attracted by those opportunities, Conoco decided in late 1991 to participate in the first U.S.–Russian joint venture to develop a new oil field. The field is in the Arkhangel'sk region, north of the Arctic Circle and a thousand miles northeast of Moscow. Our partner is the Russian geologic enterprise Arkangelskgeologia, and the joint venture is called Polar Lights.

We chose to participate in developing this relatively small oil field with two goals in mind: to use the project as a test case to learn whether or not we could successfully do business in Russia and, if we could, to use it as a platform for future investments. As a learning experience, it has been very successful.

For one thing, we have found the technical capabilities of the Russian workforce to be superior. Any doubts we might have had about the Russian's welding skills, for example, were put to rest when 25 of 26 welders passed American Petroleum Institute after very little training. Their subsequent performance in building the 37-mile pipeline required by the project has been outstanding. We also have discovered that the existing infrastructure can be used effectively with much less upgrading than once thought necessary. In most instances, the Russian rail system, barges, trucks, and heavy construction equipment such as cranes and bulldozers have performed well.

Because of those two advantages, the project is coming in on schedule and very close to the original budget, even though the oil field is in a remote location. We have, of course, encountered logistical, efficiency, and managerial shortcomings—inevitable considering the years of neglect under the old communist system and the lack of market discipline. But those deficiencies do not reflect the capabilities of our Russian colleagues. I am convinced that once they are given the tools and the opportunity to use them in a rewarding environment, their successes will rapidly rival those found in the OECD countries.

The most important problem our project continues to face is the Russian investment climate, which can be characterized only as one of complete disarray.

First, although current Russian law allows Western joint venture companies to export oil, actual joint venture exports have been significantly curtailed as a result of the government's bureaucratic efforts to allocate export rights. The ability to export is a critical one, given that internal market prices for crude oil are substantially lower than world prices. Second, Russia has no defined tax code. Various taxes are being invented by different entities; if actually imposed, they would exceed the total income that investments would generate.

The Russian government is the only player that can guarantee export rights and replace the present legislative and tax nightmare with rational and efficient structures. It must be able to assure investors that their products can be exported and that taxes will be at levels that allow adequate returns on investments. Until those steps are taken, Russia will not be able to attract Western investment on the scale necessary to bring about a real improvement in its economy.

Karl M. Topp, President and CEO, Die Welt Development Company, Inc., Woodside, New York

Nothing would be more foolish than giving up on Russia, especially at a time when, as Kvint points out, Russia is on sale.

Simply knowing all the facts about this giant country, however, is not enough to persuade the average U.S. businessperson to invest there. Only a few emotionally and financially committed people with staying power will succeed. Nothing good has ever happened quickly in Russia. Likewise, no one has ever built a successful enterprise there without a great deal of patience.

Die Welt Development Company (DWDC) is one of the few U.S.–Russian joint ventures in Kaliningrad, a city that is suffering a severe energy shortage, among other hardships. More than half the city has no heat in the coldest weather. Stories of global warming do not help the people living there, but U.S. business creating new enterprises can.

When I consider the energy problems in Kaliningrad, I think of the people I know in the city and *oblast* who were forcibly shipped there by Stalin after 1945. Until then, Koningsberg, as it was known, never lacked the organization it takes to supply a million people with energy to heat their homes and to live. I believe it is up to U.S. citizens to share their knowledge with the Russians so that they can help themselves.

In Kaliningrad, DWDC is currently promoting the rebuilding of four hydroelectric power plants that today do not produce anything but fish in their lakes. Those plants had their guts dismantled and used as raw materials. As things stand now, no factories or hotels can be built in the *oblast* unless they generate their own power.

Kaliningrad's transportation system is also on the verge of collapse, but not one bicycle in the completely flat territory is for sale. DWDC is trying to change that situation. Why? Bicycles were the vehicles that helped Germany rebuild after World War II. Many German bicycle shops went on to sell mopeds, then scooters, then motorcycles, then minicars, and, finally, Volkswagens. As utopian as it may sound, companies can actually make money in the process of helping the Russians.

Finally, Kaliningrad boasts 500 kilometers of boatable waterways, but thanks to Stalin and his successors, no one owns a boat. DWDC has done research to demonstrate the viability of a boating business and will proceed with plans to populate the waters of Kaliningrad.

My most recent interest is the insurance business. Here, too, it will be an uphill battle—not because of the Russian but because of the U.S. insurance industry. The representatives I spoke with wanted to know only who was backing the effort and who would insure their policies. The U.S. insurance industry is apparently no longer in the risk business. Well, in 1993 the Chinese sold 350 million policies to someone, but surely not to a timid partner.

Working with the local people, staying in fourth-class hotels, and bringing my own food and water, I have witnessed firsthand the great potential for doing business in Russia. The needs of its huge population are enormous, and those considering investing in Russia have a good chance of success if they make an emotional commitment and take the time to build a sound business foundation.

Arthur H. Rosenbloom, Chairman, Patricof & Company Capital Corporation, New York, New York

I am fully prepared to yield to Kvint's expertise on the subject of finding attractive business opportunities in Russia and identifying local players best positioned to exploit them. However, as an investment banker charged with responsibility for recommending pricing and negotiating strategies to clients, I believe that his otherwise exemplary piece glides over some of the most intractable issues involved in making deals happen in Russia, Central Europe, or any other place where legal and financial norms are ill adapted to late-twentieth-century deal transacting. While Kvint allows that "the country still needs . . . more firms to handle accounting and auditing" and that Russia "needs more laws governing business," a closer look at these issues demonstrates their magnitude. I will illustrate them with examples drawn from my own experience.

Absence of Modern Commercial Law. Last year, Patricof & Company acted for a non–U.S. buyer acquiring control of a large heavy-equipment dealer in Central Europe. In the United States, a considerable portion of the purchase price could be financed by a pledge of the perfectly good equipment to which the target company had clear title. But how exactly does a lending institution perfect a lien on those assets in the absence of a Uniform Commercial Code or its equivalent? Assuming a bonded-warehouse-type solution, in which the lender essentially advances funds as assets leave the warehouse under its control, would a claim of title by the lender in the event of default be enforceable under a local law otherwise silent on the subject? Our client could get no comfort in this issue from local council and was forced to borrow in the West on its local credit lines (the Western lender would not lend on Central European assets), thereby diminishing the credit available for its existing operations.

Lack of Sophistication in Determining Corporate Values. In the fall of 1992, I chaired a seminar in Eastern Europe for CEOs and CFOs of companies slated for privatization. When I asked these otherwise sophisticated managers how much they believed their businesses were worth, they invariably directed me to the statement of net assets on their companies' balance sheets. It will take a while before such managers, raised in command economies, fully embrace the notion of corporate values determined by discounted cash flows or multiples of revenues or earnings.

Absence of Western-type Accounting. While accepted European accounting standards have reached central and Eastern Europe, historical (and to some degree current) accounting statements are notoriously unreliable because of volatile price swings, uncertainties about inflation, translation errors, arbitrary assignments of asset values, and a lack of true independence by former state-run agencies.

None of the problems I have described (to which I could add considerably more) are intended to suggest that companies shouldn't undertake transactions in Russia or in Central or Eastern Europe generally. But it's important, I believe, to go in with eyes wide open to some of the stumbling blocks to deals, beyond the obvious ones of political risk, problems created by time and distance, and the inevitable delays resulting from bureaucratic hassles.

It's my guess that some of the enterprises likely to show the largest internal rates of return are start-up investments with modest capital input, such as the *Polish TV Guide*-like publication owned by a businessman I know from Pennsylvania, or coin-operated U.S.-made washer/dryers in high-rise apartment buildings in Hungary. As in the case in merger-and-acquisition transactions, in which most deals (many of them extraordinarily successful) are made between small private companies and pass below Wall Street's radar screen because of their size and the absence of public-disclosure requirements, we'll never get to hear about many of the best deals that will be made in Russia.

Daniel Yergin, President, Thane Gustafson; Director, Cambridge Energy Research Associates, Cambridge, Massachusetts

Russia is trying to make a triple transition: from communist dictatorship to democracy, from centrally planned command economy to market economy, and from empire to national-state. Any one of those moves would be immensely taxing, and no one can know how it will turn out. The biggest part of economic reform—winding down the overwhelming military-industrial sector, with the consequent rise in unemployment—has not yet begun. Because of the uncertainties, we find scenario planning to be very valuable in our work with companies that are considering investments in Russia.

In light of all the gloomy news from Russia, the scenario that would seem the most implausible is what, in our new book, *Russia 2010 and What It Means for the World*, we call *chudo*—the Russian, economic miracle. "Miracle," of course, should be in quotes, as we're talking about something that would be hard wrought over a decade or more. Yet that scenario is no less plausible than the darker ones, and it is consistent with Kvint's perspective.

Circumstances are very harsh in Russia today. Yet we see five elements that could converge to create a *chudo*. The first is the human material: people in Russia are highly skilled and educated and also have great technological competence. Under communism they were unable to convey that competence into commercial innovation, which was one of the undoings of the Soviet economy. Now technology and the market can be joined.

Second, there is a huge pent-up demand for goods and services. Whether it is housing, appliances, or services, the Russians have been enormously deprived. That demand provides incentives for entrepreneurs to fill the need and also for people to work so they can buy those goods and services. A housing boom has already begun on the outskirts of Moscow.

Third, a great deal of potential can be achieved from the very fact of the transition. Previously, the economy was organized to produce the goods that the leaders wanted. Now the very act of rearranging those same elements of production to make the goods that the people want will contribute to prosperity. Two of the things that were repressed under communism were entrepreneurial energy and managerial talent. As they are liberated, they will act as a driving force for economic growth.

Fourth, Russia has physical resources that can be measured, including immense reserves of oil and gas, which can generate earnings on the world market.

Fifth, ironically, Russia has the same advantage it had a century ago, at the time of its last economic miracle. It was a late starter then, meaning that it was able to introduce advanced technologies. Today, being a late starter means that it can skip over copper-wire phone systems and go right to fiber optics and the latest generation of radio-based telecommunications. Integration with the world economy will itself be a driver. Enabling technologies like computers and communicators will spur economic growth. Information, instead of being rigidly controlled, will be easily available and widely disseminated. Business people in the Urals will plug instantaneously into the world economy.

But a *chudo* will require investment. Much of that will have to come from the Russians themselves. The process of what some Russians call the "primary accumulation of capital" has already begun. Russians hold perhaps as much as $25 billion in Swiss back accounts and elsewhere abroad. As the economy starts to grow again, they will bring that money home and invest it. Currently, foreign direct investment in Russia is very small. But when the issues that matter to foreign investors, such as property rights, become clarified, that will change.

In spite of the awesome challenges that Russia faces in its transition, a decade from now it could be a country of economic growth, its exports seeking entry into markets of other industrialized nations. And Russian may be heard in the financial markets, in the business hotels, and on the ski slopes of the world. By then, we will know much more about the character of something we see as virtually inevitable: capitalism, Russian-style.

Vladimir Kvint responds:

There is no question that doing business in Russia is very difficult, as all the commentators point out. The communications industry is underdeveloped, the transportation infrastructure is inefficient, and the railroads are in terrible condition. In addition, although Russia is the world's largest producer of oil and gas, the second-largest producer of electrical energy, and the third-largest producer of coal, the problems of supply and distribution of fuel and energy are enormous.

The Russian business infrastructure presents additional problems. First, the country does not have a modern banking system. It is almost impossible to expect a Russian buyer to insure a letter of credit. Currently, the Export-Import Bank of the United States recognizes only four Russian banks, and only one of them is private. Second, foreign investors face many problems even when using their own insurance companies, because Russian insurance law does not recognize foreign insurers on Russian territory. Third, as Arthur Rosenbloom underlines, accounting systems need to be improved. Fully 80% of the companies open for investment do not have balance sheets or auditing practices that meet Western standards.

Nevertheless, of the seven commentators on my article, six are executives in government or industry who see the glass as at least half full when it comes to investing in Russia, whereas only one, Marshall Goldman, who works in academia, sees it as half empty. Although the former know firsthand the difficulties of doing business in Russia, that practical experience has made them realize that there is nowhere in the world where business is problem-free; the problems elsewhere are simply different. Moreover, they understand that because Russia made the switch to capitalism only recently, some patience is in order.

If one looks at the changes made so far, it is clear that they are all positive. Business conditions in Russia are indeed developing and improving rapidly. The telecommunications industry is much better than it was in 1989. All cities and towns now have airports. Almost 2,000 private banks and 12 foreign banks are operational. All of the Big Six accounting firms have opened offices. And now, at least some executives of large industrial companies are able to give more reasonable assessments of how much their businesses are worth.

Goldman is correct in saying that I wrote the article when Yegor Gaidar and Boris Fyodorov were still in office. But I suggested that Gaidar's ill-prepared pseudoforms only caused trouble and oriented the people against market reforms. Indeed, I would argue that after the resignations of Gaidar and Fyodorov, the situation has improved.

Gaidar and Fydorov are children of the Soviet system. Gaidar worked for the main magazine of the Communist Party, and Fyodorov worked on the Central Committee. With the failure of communism, they began to create their own image, which proved unfortunate for the millions of people whom they brought into poverty and for the thousands of foreigners who tried to work with Russia. They succeeded in convincing the Russian people of their knowledge and capitalist expertise, but they actually had no experience with capitalism and made all the predictable mistakes. When

Gaidar came into office, Russia's inflation rate was 10%–12% per month. After his primitive pseudoliberalization of prices, it jumped to 150%–180% per month and even higher.

It is therefore understandable why, in the absence of a strong moderate candidate at the time of the election, so many people voted for Vladimir Zhirinovsky. They voted for change and for an alternative to Boris Yeltsin. Zhirinovsky promised to stop shock therapy with social protection and slow reform. Today several moderate alternatives to Zhirinovsky have emerged in the Russian political arena, the two most prominent being current prime minister Victor Chernomyrdin and Alexander Rutskoi, who was vice president until October.

Although I agree with Ruth Harkin and Constantine Nicadros that Russia has no defined tax code, this problem has not discouraged foreign buyers of oil. I am certain that any large foreign company would agree to buy crude oil and even to give Russian companies the additional benefit of refining it in foreign refineries.

Harkin is correct in saying that the Russians are imposing too many restrictions on foreigners who would like to invest in the natural-resources industry and participate in the process of privatization. That strategy was a mistake made by Gaidar's cabinet. And Goldman's mention of the frozen bank account of the Radisson-Slavyanskaya Hotel is a good example of the absence of a commercial code. Freezing foreign accounts was one of the Gaidar government's ways of stabilizing Russia's hard currency situation. On the subject of corruption and crime, Goldman has fallen victim to the mass media in likening today's Russia to the days of Al Capone. That comparison is a far cry from reality.

It is true that crime has grown rapidly in Russia since the disintegration of the communist system. Obviously, democratically oriented individuals were not the only people who lived under communist control; many criminals did too. As a result, the number of registered crimes increased 52% from 1990 to 1993. And, although the Mafia lives primarily in newspaper headlines, it is true that protection payments are being made. Extortion from large companies, however, is limited, and it is mostly small businesses that are preyed upon.

Fortunately, domestic and foreign investors realize that the crime rate in Russia is far below that in most large cities worldwide. It would probably be a pleasure for a New York City policeman to work in Russia. Not one foreign nation has decreased investment, not even the Japanese, as Goldman suggests. In fact, Japanese investment has increased from $1 million in 1987 to $51 million in 1991 to more than $100 million in 1993. And, while it is true that previous Japanese governments did not increase their investments significantly because of the dispute over the Kuril Islands, the only thing that has decreased is the rate of those investments relative to other foreign investments, not the actual amount.

Goldman says that my argument would have been more convincing if I had given more examples of joint ventures that have gone well. There are hundreds. PepsiCo, for example, already has three joint ventures in Russia and will have four by the end of the year, with a total investment of about $55 million. The Coca-Cola Company has two joint ventures and continues to implement a $34 million project. And Caterpillar has two joint ventures with sales of $200 million in 1993. Caterpillar is very pleased with the results and has created a third joint venture, which will start production this July.

The use of the word *chudo* by Daniel Yergin and Thane Gustafson brings to mind the European and Japanese economic miracles after World War II. They were based not only on the principles of a free-market economy but also on price controls, nationalization of inefficient industries, and hugh state investments in those industries. And, like Russia today, neither Japan nor the European nations followed all the recommendations of the International Monetary Fund.

It is clear that now is the time to do business in Russia. No one can lead Russia astray from the road to market-oriented reforms, for the simple reason that there is no alternative to that path.

RUSSIA IS CREATING A SYSTEM TO ENSURE FOREIGN INVESTMENT: $1.5 BILLION COLLATERAL FUND ESTABLISHED TO SAFEGUARD FOREIGN VENTURES

The recent political fights should be taken in their proper context. After 70 years of communism, the road to democracy is anything but straight. What is clear is that there is no longer any turning back; nothing can strangle democracy in Russia.

As sure as there is political infighting now, there will also be fights between President Yeltsin and the new parliament a year from now; it is an unavoidable part of their mentality. In spite of these political struggles, Russia is moving quickly to a free market economy. The business climate remains stable.

To pursue this burgeoning marketplace, it is important to stay well-informed. Using a law firm that is firmly established in Russia, like Baker & McKenzie or Coudert Brothers, is not enough. One must also understand the economic mechanisms that impact government decision-making and implementation, along with the power structure in each industry.

Yeltsin gave an enormous boost to the development of a free-market economy with a decree issued on February 2, 1993, that authorized the formation of the State Investment Corporation (SIC). This new company insures foreign investments against political risk, and could act as a guarantor for foreign investment on the basis of collateral operations with foreign banks and companies. The Russian government has allocated over $1 billion liquid state property, plus U.S. $50 million cash and 200 billion rubles, to establish the initial fund of this Corporation.

The Kvint Newsletter, 1, No. 1 (October 1991).

What does this mean to foreign investors? In theory, it means that if the SIC evaluates a project as viable and potentially profitable, it can allocate a substantial amount of Russian treasures (precious metals and stones) as collateral guarantees for these investors.

If nothing bad befalls the foreign investment (from a political point of view), and the investor is successful and generates enough revenue to cover the investment and even turn a profit, the SIC will gradually take back the collateral.

Old Problems and New Possibilities

Previously, the guarantee of the Soviet government, or the hand-shake of Brezhnev or Gorbachev, would have sufficed. Even in 1990–91, when such arrangements ceased to provide protection, foreigners continued to rely on them. Only after losing large sums of money will they come to understand that in this new situation, it is essential to act carefully, evaluate all guarantees, letters, and agreements with Russians.

Of course, one could not sue any Russian company that reneged on a written agreement, but that isn't so simple; if the contract is not written according to Russian law, it is void. And even if it is written properly, and the litigant wins the suit, what type of compensation or remuneration can be obtained from a company that may have no hard currency or not enough rubles?

Many professionals know that during the wonderful years of perestroika, Gorbachev spent most of Russia's gold reserves. According to my estimate, Russia has no more than 750 tons of gold left. However, Russia not only produces gold, but is also one of the world's largest producers of precious metals like platinum and palladium, and precious stones such as diamonds. Without revealing any state secrets, I would say (based on my experience with the nonferrous and precious metals industries) that the current Russian state reserves of these treasures is the greatest in the world. So, the SIC collateral would probably take the form of platinum, palladium, and diamonds, and much smaller amounts of gold. The collateral-building activity of this Corporation is creating a real system of protection of investments and interests.

The Corporation's importance to Yeltsin is illustrated not only by these indications of financial commitment, but also by personal commitment. Russian business is conducted on a very personal basis. If a Russian doesn't like you, he won't do business with you, even if it's in his best financial interest to do so. Yeltsin appointed Ambassador Yuri Petrov, his personal friend and former chief of his presidential staff (1991–93), as chairman of the SIC.

SIC is not the only institution foreign investors can work with. For many years, world insurers have known Ingostrach, the state insurer for foreign activity. It is recognized by many foreign insurers, and has representatives in several countries, international experience, and connections.

It appears that this company could be a good insurer for investments of up to $200 million by my estimate, but not more. Since 1993, some foreign insurers have also become active in the Russian market. I would not be surprised if the American Insurance Group (AIG) soon creates a joint venture with a reliable Russian company.

In 1991–92, it was almost impossible to believe any letters of guarantee from Russian institutions. Even VnesheconomBank (VNB), the Russian state bank for foreign debt, frequently did not support its guarantees in 1992. In 1993, the situation finally came to a head. VNB began to recognize its obligations, particularly irrevocable letters of credit. It seems to me that VNB, VneshtorgBank (Russian state bank for foreign trade), and some private banks will work according to banking norms, especially those Russian banks that have correspondent accounts with foreign banks. For example, Moscow-based Incombank now has 130 correspondent accounts with the Bank of New York.

Earlier this year, it became possible and legal for foreign banks to open branches in Russia, or to create joint banks with at least $3 million in foreign investment. At present, however, there are no American banks with Russian partners who are active in Russia. Most large American banks have representatives (plus a secretary and driver), but do not have operational branches. French banks Credit Lyonnais and BNP, and Germany's Dresden Bank, are among the first few to have operational branches in Russia.

By 1994, some American banks will be forced to come to the Russian market, or their clients will work without them and do their banking elsewhere. These pioneers will have to be tough, sturdy banks—the government is stingy about giving out licenses, and it's a rigorous process. I believe that one of the first American banks to become fully operational in Russia will be Chase Manhattan Overseas Corp., as they have opened an office in Prague, and are active in Eastern Europe.

Now, there is not only the legal climate, but also the business environment and first capitalist institutions to help foreigners who wish to discover this new mecca of international activity.

DEVELOPMENT OF INTERNATIONAL JOINT VENTURES IN RUSSIA: RISKS AND OPPORTUNITIES

For 74 years of Soviet history, foreign economic activity was a monopoly of the state. Even state enterprises and industrial ministers were not authorized to have direct business relationships with foreigners. All foreign trade and foreign business cooperation belonged exclusively to two state executive bodies, the Ministry of Foreign Trade and the State Committee for Foreign Economic Ties. The former was responsible for all export and import activities, while the State Committee was responsible for Soviet investment abroad, such as construction of a cement plant in Iraq, a ferrous metallurgical facility in India, and a nickel plant in Cuba. The great majority of this activity is now in the form of unpaid debt to Russia from these countries. The total amount of debt to Russia is $64 billion, while Russian debt to foreigners is $80 billion. All activity of the state, however, was the result of political, not economic, decisions. Thus, in terms of economic implications, it was not until 1986 that foreign bodies were permitted to own property within the Soviet Union, with the exception of embassies and some foreign government trade representative offices. When foreign investors like FIAT went to Russia between 1966 and 1970, this was not a true form of foreign investment, but rather a trade transaction, as the USSR government bought the plant.

Inefficient economic mechanisms virtually exhausted all the natural resources which were easily extractable or harvestable. More and more input was required to extract the same output, which led to diminishing returns. In the USSR and its satellite countries, it was necessary to garner resources from an ever-expanding geographic area; to exploit the East and North; to dig deeper to try to maintain

In *Creating and Managing International Joint Ventures*, ed. Arch G. Woodside and Robert E. Pitts (Westport, Connecticut: Quorum Books, 1996).

output. The industrial structure of the USSR was based on the extensive economic model. Even Western European countries came to this meadow; Germany, France, and Italy started to drink from the river of natural gas flowing through the Siberian pipeline. Finland continued to receive its energy blood from Russia. But the natural surface resources were depleted. The development of new oil and gas fields and new nonferrous metal and diamond pits required more investment and more resources, which Russia did not have. It required more workers and more equipment, neither of which Russia had. As a result, the growth of GNP in Russia declined every year, from 1970 through 1985. The cumulative decline was more than 250%. Moreover, this economic mechanism did not stimulate the introduction of Russian scholars', scientists', and technologists' discoveries and innovations into practice. Russian achievements were more widely and more quickly put into practice in other countries. For example, the Russian invention of the continuous steel casting method for steel production is used for 90% of steel production in Japan and the United States, while in Russia it is for used only 30%. Seventy percent of steel production in Russia is based on older, outdated methods. The same happened with Russian laser technology, for which they won the 1964 Nobel Prize, as well as with other technologies.

By the end of the '70s, Soviet non-military plants had a technological base which was 15 to 20 years behind that of developed countries. While President Reagan encouraged modernization of equipment by decreasing the amortization schedule from 7 to 5 years, the rate at which Russia upgraded its own equipment was only 2% per year. As a result, the gap in levels of technical modernization between Russia and the United States and other developed countries continued to grow. The situation continued through the mid-'80s, and continues even today.

Computerization of industry in Russia began on a wide scale only in the '80s, and is still essentially in the introductory stage, especially in services. It became clear that without industrial and technical cooperation with the world business community and the world market, the USSR would continue to regress, compared to the rest of the developed world. This became obvious even to the bureaucrats from the Central Committee of the Communist Party, and these factors combined to bring about the birth of perestroika and the new winds of freedom. As a result, 1986 was the first time that the two state monopolies for foreign economic activity were destroyed. Industrial ministries like the Ministry of Machinery Building, the Ministry of Nonferrous Metals, and the Ministry of Communication and Post won the right to create foreign trading companies. Through these companies, they were authorized to sell part of their output abroad and to keep part of the export proceeds for technology development. Also, they were authorized to buy new equipment abroad.

In 1987, the 500 largest state industrial companies were accorded the same right. Finally, on January 13, 1987, an historical decision was made to permit joint ventures with the participation of foreign companies. But ideology was so central to this decision that Gorbachev signed two decrees that day; one concerning joint ventures with participation of organizations from *socialist* countries, and one concerning joint ventures with participation of organizations from *capitalist* countries. The decrees said that up to 49% of the joint venture could belong to the foreign partner, but the foreign partner could not have its representative as the chairman or director general of the joint venture. The result was that *during all of 1987, only 23 joint ventures were created, 2 of which were U.S.–Russian.*

The disappointing outcome of all the changes in the USSR, and the rapid disintegration of the national economy, made it possible for market-oriented economists to prepare a draft of a new, more liberal joint-venture regulation, which became law on December 2, 1988. The Communist Party bosses were kind enough to sign this decree, because they were faced with the reality that by the end of 1988 only 192 joint ventures had been established. The party bosses were amazed that more foreign companies had not come to take advantage of the socialist paradise. From that point forward, foreigners could occupy any position in the joint venture, and the percentage of investment was not limited. The liberalized regulations immediately gave rise to an increase in joint ventures—1,274 by the end of 1989. Companies from Germany, Austria, and Finland, countries that had long experience and long-time economic relationships with the Soviet government, led the way.

The year 1990 saw continued growth in joint ventures, which reached 2,905 by the end of the year. I started my analysis of joint venture experiences in 1988. These seven years showed trends and problems in the creation of joint ventures. It was important to me because in 1988 I had participated in drafting the joint-venture regulations that still form the basis of current regulations in all the former Soviet republics. Of course, as usual, all the drafts developed by scientists, scholars, and lawyers from academic institutions were duly changed by the bureaucrats from the Central Committee of the Communist Party and the USSR Council of Ministers. Nonetheless, the final decision in December 1988 was a substantial improvement, and I felt some responsibility for it. Following are the initial conclusions of this study.

Location of Joint Ventures with Foreign Companies' Participation (Particularly from Capitalist Countries)

These firms were strongly influenced by their understanding of the risk of investing in Russia, especially the political risks. During 1989, 85% of all joint ventures created were located in Moscow, 10% were in St. Petersburg, and only 5% were scattered over all the other territory of the former USSR! This results from foreigners' perception that the highly centralized Soviet government structure was still very much in place; that the iron curtain was not just an image, but a virtual reality. Companies tried to be close to the government, and, as a result, most of the offices were set up in central Moscow. However, there was no economic reason or basis for this decision. Lack of information on other locations prohibited the joint ventures from being set up elsewhere. Foreigners only knew of Moscow as the center for all activity, and did not want to be far from it.

At the same time, joint ventures in the Russian Far East and Siberia (a territory larger than the U.S. or Canada) accounted for only 1% of all joint-venture activity (12 of more than 1200 ventures). This showed that foreigners had no information regarding the social and economic processes that were taking place in the ruined Soviet Union, as it approached its end. The political risk of investment is much lower in the Far East and Siberia than in Moscow and St. Petersburg. The Far East population is very involved in the political struggle and there nationalists and pseudo-patriots have created centers of activity.

The disintegration of the Soviet Union seriously changed the whole process of the creation of joint ventures. By 1992, 34% of the joint ventures created were in Moscow. During the same period, the percentage of joint ventures in other regions of Russia increased by only 4%. Serious changes in the Baltic States, however, caused the number of joint ventures created there to increase markedly. The Lithuanian parliament's Declaration of Independence in March 1990 showed the world community that the Baltic States were on their way to a market economy. Investors found that joint ventures in the Baltic States enjoyed a more stable environment. But the Baltic States lack sufficient economic factors to contribute to the high degree of profitability possible with Russian joint ventures. The Baltic States have no natural resources, the process of privatization is behind Russia's, and the economic conditions are not oriented toward attracting foreign investment, but toward development of domestic entrepreneurial business. This became especially clear at the end of 1991, when almost 68% of joint ventures in the Baltic States worked as intermediaries for exporting Russian raw materials or products such as nonferrous metals, although the Baltic States do not produce nonferrous metals. However, for foreigners, it was the easiest way to receive nonferrous metals without export licenses from the Russian government. But in 1993, this type of business with Russia decreased greatly because (1) the Russian government established borders with the Baltic States, (2) the Russian government created customs posts with the Baltic States, and (3) it became easier to receive export licenses from the Russian government to sell products in countries *outside* the former Soviet republics than to sell in the former Soviet republics. It has at last been understood by Russia that going directly to the world market with their products eliminates the middle man, and higher profits can be had. In 1993, the Baltic States's participation in this type of business decreased to 5% of the total amount of joint ventures.

The growth in the number of joint ventures has been very stable in Ukraine, Kazakstan, Turkmenistan, and Kyrgyzstan. This will continue from 1995 to 1997, particularly in Kyrgyzstan, Turkmenistan, Kazakstan, and Belarus. Regulations in these states have stimulated foreign investment much more effectively than in the other republics. Kyrgyzstan is the first of the former republics to permit foreigners to buy land, and the political situation there is more stable than in the European part of Russia.

The number of joint ventures in Moldova, Azerbaijan, Armenia, and Georgia has been insubstantial until now, and will, in fact, decrease because of the civil war in Moldova, and the strife between Azerbaijan and Armenia, and between Georgia and the Abkhaz Republic. Armenian business leaders living abroad tried to create joint ventures in Armenia, but the war and energy shortage (almost a complete lack of energy) halted any joint-venture activity.

Now, in November 1994 in the former USSR, 28,000 joint ventures with foreign participation or wholly owned foreign companies have been established, with 17,000 of these in Russia. Creating joint ventures is more difficult (only 8% of efforts were successful from 1988 to 1992, and in 1993 only 17% of efforts were successful) than reaching profitability (32%–35% of joint ventures, once created, are profitable, which is much higher than the rate of companies that reach profitability in the U.S.).

Industries

When Russian joint ventures began, the majority were concentrated in a few industries.

Intermediaries

These joint ventures do what the state can't. They buy raw materials and industrial waste from Russia and sell it abroad. The first legal Russian millionaires came from this business. Companies have played a very serious role in this industry because they receive money from foreign companies for disposing of industrial waste. Moreover, Russian industrial waste can very valuable. For example, one U.S. company extracted 60 pounds of gold from 10 tons of microelectronics scrap. In 1992, this type of joint-venture activity increased considerably. In 1993, 43% of all joint ventures attempted to play an intermediary role as a part of their activities.

Software

Another very profitable area for joint ventures, especially between 1987 and 1991, has been software. All the giants, such as IBM, Microsoft, and Lotus, came to Russia and created distribution companies. These companies utilized Russian engineers' and scientists' achievements. Software has been customized and translated for the Russian market. In addition, joint-venture activity in the computer industry, particularly with firms from the U.S., Japan, Taiwan, and South Korea, has increased substantially in Russia, focusing mainly on final assembly of computers. The shortage of computers in Russia created an interesting phenomenon regarding payment terms; Russian customers (state, private sector, and cooperatives) agreed to buy computers for hard currency because the locally assembled computers utilized inexpensive Russian labor, and so were slightly cheaper than imported computers. However, once the initial urgent need for computers had been satisfied, computers and software were then sold for rubles. In addition, the July 1992 introduction of the currency exchange market enabled the vendors to convert their ruble earnings rather easily.

Heavy Industrial Production

There was a great increase in the number of joint ventures involved in heavy industrial production, particularly in Russia, then in Kazakstan. In Russia, the majority of industrial joint ventures are connected with the enrichment of natural resources from raw materials and from industrial waste, and with the conversion of military plants. Instead of building tanks in Saratov, they now build buses. Likewise, facilities for building military electronics have been converted to TV production, while facilities that produced precision equipment for submarines now produce sewing machines.

Travel and Tourism

More and more joint ventures are appearing in the tourism and hotel industry. Prior to 1991, most of this activity was in the European part of Russia, the Baltic States, Ukraine, and even Georgia. Now, northern Russia, Siberia, and the Russian Far East see a great deal of activity.

Research and Development

In 1992 and 1993, an explosion of growth in R&D occurred. Foreigners began to understand and take advantage of the great resources to be found in Russian scientists' and scholars' achievements, inventions, and knowledge. The number of joint ventures in this area skyrocketed. Firms, like Bell Labs, are working with Russian scientists to study space, electronics, optics, lasers, and nuclear energy. Some of the joint ventures concentrate solely on the transfer of Russian technology and patents.

Telecommunications

Telecommunications problems were a major barrier to the development and internationalization of Russian business. But because telecom is a very profitable business, because it is easy to develop this business, and because many military communication systems have been and continue to be converted to civilian use, telecommunications has become one of the most internationalized industries.

Others

There has been a significant growth in the development of the insurance, banking, accounting and auditing, and social services industries. For example, many large insurance companies are in the process of creating joint ventures. AIG was the first; it created a joint venture with the Russian military pension fund in October 1994. Only 12 foreign banks, including Credit Lyonnais, Chase Manhattan, and Citibank, have been awarded domestic licenses to take deposits. The creation of joint ventures is just beginning in the health industry. Construction is a very attractive industry, with heavy participation from Turkish, Finnish, Austrian, and Polish companies.

Size

At the same time, the number of joint ventures with capital of more than $10 million has decreased, as more and more small businesses go to Russia. Because of the limitation on foreign insurance firms' activities in Russia and in all other republics except Belarus and Kyrgyzstan, President Yeltsin signed a decree in February 1993 regarding the creation of the State Investment Company. This company will insure foreign investment in Russia from political risk. It seems to me that this will increase the size of foreign investments in joint ventures in Russia.

Countries

Currently, companies from two nations dominate Russian joint venture business, Germany and the U.S. The growth in the number of German companies has been smooth and steady, while the U.S. growth was spurred on in 1992 by the failure of the 1991 coup. But Germany was strongly involved with investment in East Germany, and with new opportunities given to Germany by the creation of the European Union. As a result, the activity of Germany in Russia has slowed somewhat. They continue to build joint ventures in Russia, but the rate of growth has declined.

The failed coup attempt also gave U.S. firms more confidence that democracy would reign, and the market would open now, and U.S. capital became the leading investor in Russia. Italy has also been very active in the European parts of Russia and in Ukraine. Great Britain is a very strong player in Russia and Azerbaijan. But Americans and Europeans, because of new opportunities afforded by NAFTA and the creation of the European Union, will face a shortage of capital for investing in Russia.

When the joint-venture process first began, Japan was very involved, especially in the Russian Far East. The majority of Japanese companies that came to the Russian market were oriented toward working with their old government contacts and groups with which they had had contracts. However, the Japanese suffered the same setback as Occidental Petroleum, an American firm. Their approach did not work because most of the old bureaucrats and bribe takers had retired or lost power, something for which the Japanese were unprepared. Then, the Japanese government started to link investment with political decisions regarding the Kurile Islands. This has combined to substantially lower the influence of Japan and Japanese firms on joint venture activity in Russia. It was not a surprise when, under this pressure, Yeltsin canceled his planned trip to Japan in autumn 1992. Japan also recognizes now that it faces strong competition in Russia, and especially in the Russian Far East, from South Korea, Singapore, Taiwan, and, beginning in 1993, from China. After Yeltsin's 1993 visit to China, a Russian–Chinese business relationship quickly developed. South Korea's position in the Russian Far East and in Kazakhstan, where many ethnically Korean people live, is also quite strong. South Korean firms are building good relationships with the Korean community in Russia, using them as a source of market knowledge and assistance. As a result, in 1993 Japanese leaders revised their policy regarding Russia, and reduced the pressure over the Kurile Islands, resulting in new opportunities for Russian/Japanese business relations. This will enable Japanese to come to the Kurile Islands, at least as joint-venture partners. The Kurile Islands became a free economic zone, and I hope some Japanese companies will have special privileges there.

An interesting process began in the Caucuses and in the Russian Central Asian republics, where 50 million Muslims live. One could say that the Muslim business connection grew very quickly. Companies from Iran, Saudi Arabia, Kuwait, and the United Arab Emirates, as well as from Turkey, are fiercely competing in this area. These business relationships also have a political side, and it is clearly very important for the world community to protect this region from strong Islamic Fundamentalists' influence. It is, therefore, important to help companies who are in this region for economic reasons, not because of political or religious agendas. From that point of view, the Turkish government plays a very important role.

Role of Multilateral Institutions for Foreign Investors in Russia

In 1992, an historic event occurred for Russia: it became a member of the IMF and World Bank. This was important not only for monetary reasons, but also because it was a major indication of Russia's movement toward supporting civilized, modern international business and of Russia's readiness to abide by international economic and business conditions. The IMF and the World Bank were created in July 1944, according to an agreement signed at Bretton Woods, New Hampshire. (Later, the International Finance Corporation and Multilateral Investment Guarantee Agency were created.) For 50 years these institutions have been working to coordinate and create cooperation between developed countries and emerging democracies. Of course, conditions are different than they were 50 years ago, but these institutions continue their goal of helping to create a free, market-based economy and a stable economic foundation in Third World countries, developing countries, and post-communist countries. In 1944, the Soviet Union had the opportunity to become a founding member of this organization, and Stalin sent his representatives to several meetings. But then he decided that these institutions were "too imperialist" for USSR participation, and for 48 years the Soviet Union remained outside the circle of legal international economic and financial institutions. But at the end of the Soviet Union, Soviet and then Russian leaders found that the IMF and World Bank were two of the major resources for additional out-of-pocket expense money, and they started to use these institutions. In April 1992, leaders of the Western countries, especially Bush and Kohl, initiated a proposal to provide $24 billion in aid. In July 1992, the IMF met to make a decision whether to issue this money to Russia. But the bureaucratic mechanisms of these institutions were not much better than those of the communist bureaucracy, and so as of November 1994, the money still has not been issued or delivered in full.

Of course, the major problem of these multilateral institutions is their mechanisms. They are oriented toward working only with the governments of countries, not with private companies and entrepreneurial institutions in recipient countries. As a result, money flows to inexperienced governments who have very few people or no one who understands a capitalist economy. It is like sending money "down a rat hole," as I called my August 1992 *Forbes* article. Membership in the IMF and World Bank, however, delivered a lot of advisers and new conditions to Russia, which had a tremendous influence on the activity of the government there. Especially important has been the IMF's and the World Bank's role in developing an economic and business information system in Russia. They have created a system for calculating economic indicators. Russians representatives and a Russian Executive Director were appointed to work with the agencies, in what was basically an educational experience. Unfortunately, the IMF and the World Bank, especially during their initial involvement from 1991 to 1993, had a long-standing, primitive understanding of the processes in Russia. As a result, their recommendations led to negative results along with the positive. One dramatic example occurred in 1992. The inexperienced Mr. Gaidar was appointed as Acting Prime Minister, and inexperienced IMF advisers gave him recommendations. At the urging of Gaidar, with his ignorance of Russian business and economy, the Russian government made a decision to liberalize prices before demonopolization of the economy, before conversion of the military industry to civilian production, and before privatization. Immediately this policy led not to the liberalization of prices, but to a dramatic increase in prices. Prices for meat, milk, clothes, and all basic needs jumped sky-high. People were no longer able to feed their own families on their salaries. Executives, including joint-venture executives, *had* to increase salaries.

At this moment, IMF "experts" recommended that the Russian treasury NOT print new ruble bills. As a result, they exacerbated the situation. In addition to inflation, Russia was also hit by deflation. Due to the IMF recommendations, banks simply didn't have enough currency. For many companies, salaries went unpaid for 6 to 8 months, leading to civilian disobedience. Companies issued billions of rubles of IOUs instead of salaries to employees, and people lost all incentive to work. Finally, the Gaidar government understood that they had to print money, contrary to all the recommendations of the IMF and World Bank. They started to put into circulation new money each month, in amounts far exceeding what was already in circulation. This had a very negative influence for foreign companies which went, or tried to go, to Russia.

This illustrates that not all recommendations pertinent to, for example, Latin America will also be pertinent to former Soviet-bloc countries. Moreover, if a recommendation leads to good results in Poland, one cannot assume it will work well in Russia. For example, in Poland, the so-called "shock therapy" has produced results which were bad, but not as bad as the results in Russia. Why? Because in Poland, even in communist times, almost all agriculture, and almost 40% of the economy, were in private hands, unlike in the former Soviet Union, where less than 4% of agriculture was in private hands.

In general, in Poland all generations remember capitalism, because communism was installed only 45 years ago. In Russia, communism reigned for 74 years.

This is one of the examples of the dangerous activity of the IMF and World Bank, because they go to each country with standard methods and procedures, without an understanding of how to make recommendations that are specific to the situation at hand. And western advisers who have spent not even a year or two in Russia, but perhaps only a few weeks on business trips, put in their own two cents, which can be dangerous because their understanding of the circumstances is likely to be insufficient. At this point, the situation speaks for itself; it is necessary to change the mechanism of activity of these multilateral institutions.

Time has shown that the world business community needs a new mechanism to solve large-scale economic and business problems. First, this mechanism must be much more flexible. Second, the time between making political decisions and putting the decisions into practice must be shorter. Third, the mechanism must be oriented toward private capital and entrepreneurs, not toward governments.

The world is giving birth to many institutions that work for a time and then die. Some of the organizations, especially regional groups, are functioning well. But, a global institution is evolving—the regularly scheduled meeting of the leading seven industrial countries of Canada, France, Germany, Great Britain, Italy, Japan, and, of course, the United States. Of course, now the G-7 meeting is a great world political event that commands the attention of mass media and warrants front-page headlines. In most cases, during the meetings the G-7 leaders are making good political decisions, but not all of the decisions are implemented. Economic decisions are usually made without input from economists, and are not as sound. It would be smart to evaluate the price of the politicians' economic decisions. Unfortunately, most think that they are just as qualified to make economic decisions as to make decisions about soccer or football games, where they also are not professional. But naturally, this attitude lays the ground for mistakes to be made, and is part of the reason why decisions are not implemented. At the same time, the world may be fortunate that the decisions are not implemented.

How might the G-7 meetings be made into a workable global institution? These meetings of the greatest powers in the world have tremendous potential. It is necessary to convert these meetings to a real institution and create a mechanism for implementing the resulting decisions. The leaders allocate money, but it is usually not delivered to the intended recipient countries. Why? Because the meeting is a good forum for political decisions, but not for economic decisions. By developing the G-7 meetings into an institution, the resulting decisions will benefit from economic input and implementation will be improved. Just as an army has a strategic branch and an operational branch, I could say the difference between institutions with 50 years of experience, like the IMF and World Bank, and the new institutions will be their time frame. G-7, as an institution, should be oriented toward short-term goals. But, G-7 will try to protect its strategic role, and so the answer to the dilemma of an appropriate mechanism for implementing strategic decisions is simple and already exists; the traditional Bretton Woods institutions.

Many plans to attack global problems must now be implemented on a regional level. Several new regional institutions have appeared, such as EBRD, the European Bank for Reconstruction and Development. I remember my participation in the initial steps, when the Soviet Union, in 1989 and early 1990, participated in negotiations with other leading countries to create this institution. Initially, the Soviet leaders tried to create just one more source of loans. But, then some Party bureaucrats understood that in order to play an important role in this bank, and not just act as a country with its hand out, it was necessary to invest amounts comparable to what other leading countries were investing. And, they finally did it. As a result, EBRD became one of the first institutions where the former Soviet Union, and now Russia, plays a role not only as a recipient, but also as a decision maker. Unfortunately, this institution did not properly focus its activity. As a result, EBRD is not terribly visible in post-Communist countries. In addition, the fact that they are also active in Asia, which is certainly not part of Europe, is a mistake not only of a geographic nature. Multilateral institutions, global and regional, do not give any special attention to the Central Asian republics, and so a very dangerous situation has evolved—because countries like Iran and Iraq *do* give these republics special attention. As a result, through business activities, the political influence of Iran and Iraq has increased in this part of the world. It seems it is necessary to create a Central Asian institution to work with these republics, and perhaps also to work with the southern part of Siberia and the Russian Far East. Now, for the first time in history, Central Asia comprises established, independent countries. They do not yet play a geopolitical role, nor are they yet a major target of the world business community, but both will happen within the next ten years. In addition, large multinational corporations are not wasting time. They are already investing in activities in this part of the world.

Another very important point for business people is to understand that multilateral institutions—even the World Bank, in spite of its name—are not world institutions,. Many countries, even with formal participation in this institution, are not recipients of funding. For example, of the Eastern European countries, Poland has the best connections with the multilateral institutions, followed by perhaps Hungary and Romania. But Bulgaria definitely lies outside the vista of these agencies. To them, Bulgaria is like a forgotten land in Central Europe. As a result, international business is only very slowly focusing on this country. And, business people have not yet benefited from this country, which offers a relatively stable political environment and significant opportunities for business. Of course, it is possible to find reasons for this: that they did not have lobbyists (which are very important), or that they had to pay more attention to settling debt with the Paris and London Clubs. But these are not the reasons. The main reason Bulgaria has been all but forgotten is that the Bretton Woods Institution does not have a sound strategy. If we are to speak about the immediate future, an ironic picture could take shape. One or two of the biggest beggars and recipients, Russia and China, will also be key players among country donors. The G-7 could soon be G-8 or even G-9, with Russia and China as participants. In the Paris Club, Russia will be a full member, in spite of Russian debt. This new reality has to be in the forefront of the minds of business leaders. It is very important to understand that any political decision made by the G-7 is not like news of a football game, but can provide an opportunity to earn money.

Conclusion

Foreigners have gained experience. More and more information is available to the world regarding this market, from newspapers, newsletters, and magazines that sprout like mushrooms after the spring rains. Regulations in the former USSR are developing more and more quickly. The limits put on foreigners are diminishing. Foreign business people have become the darlings of the Russian, Kazakstan, and Kyrgyzstan business communities.

The form of joint ventures has changed from simple incorporated firms to firms that are privately and publicly held by shareholders. In 1993–94, the process of transforming joint ventures to wholly owned subsidiaries of foreign firms began. Also, 1993–94 saw the flight of mining companies to Siberia and the Russian Far East to mine non-ferrous and precious metals, oil, and gas. Russia, Ukraine, Kazakstan, Turkmenistan, and Kyrgyzstan have many small foreign businesses investing in the food processing and services industry, as it becomes easier to convert rubles to hard currency.

The failure of the coup in 1991 and the formal disbanding of the Communist Party also played a catalytic role in the future of foreign investment and especially regarding American joint ventures. Americans believed that the political risk in Russia was now lower than before. Between 1992 and 1994, there was a marked increase in the creation of American joint ventures, with America having invested more than any other country. In terms of capital invested, Germany tied with the U.S. By the end of 1994, the number of American joint ventures or wholly owned American companies in the former Soviet Union will exceed 4,000.

There are many misconceptions about foreign investment in Russia. One of them is that while all joint ventures are registered entities on paper, none of them are actually in operation. This is a fallacy. While both exports and imports were fairly low and consistent (below $1,000,000) through 1992, both skyrocketed thereafter. By June 1993, imports had jumped to nearly six billion, while exports increased nearly three times to three billion.

One may wonder how it is possible that imports of joint ventures are three times higher than exports. Where are they getting the hard currency to make this possible? The answer is that executives of joint ventures are afraid to take money from their exports and put it in Russian banks because of prior negative experiences (for example, when Vnesheconombank froze accounts in 1991–92).

Money for imports is generally held by the joint venture in foreign banks abroad. As a result, officially, import is higher than export.

According to my estimate, Russian joint ventures have approximately $8 billion in foreign banks abroad.

The period of 1994–95 will also be a time for transportation firms and telecom giants like US West, AT&T, Cable and Wireless, MCI, Sprint, Alcatel and Italtel, to create a new infrastructure and business environment, enabling the next phase of internationalization of business in the former Soviet Union.

The Soviet Union is dead, and in its place are newly emerging markets which have just started to be really open for foreign investment. Competition in these markets is a new occurrence. One form of a successful firm is a joint venture which is properly prepared and whose operations management is appropriate to the conditions in this new business world.

"TO CAPITAL MARKETS, WITH LOVE," SAYS RUSSIA

With a carrying cost of roughly 65% on the latest auction of its outstanding government debt, Russia is keen on opening its government bond markets to the world's yield-hungry investors. Up to now, the country's treasury bill market has been dominated by Russian banks. However, one of the steps necessary to attract investors made wary by past sins (i.e., revoking the visa of an outspoken American investor) is restructuring past-due Soviet-era notes into more liquid bonds, which the government managed to do this summer.

Bank Reform Equals Open Markets

It's a given that the Russian government needs to increase the flow of foreign capital. "Russia needs more portfolio and direct investment," explains Dr. Vladimir Kvint, director of emerging markets at Arthur Andersen Economics in New York City, "since it is falling behind other emerging markets."

In order to attract foreign investment, Russia announced it will open its capital markets on August 15, by ending the near-exclusive access that Russian banks have had to the country's high-yielding government bonds and bills. Until now, foreigners have been officially able to buy Russian T-bills only on the secondary market, from Russian banks acting as primary dealers. With yields of 65% at auction (down from a peak of 125% prior to the elections) and a mandated cap on the maximum interest rate paid to foreigners of only 25%, the franchise is a money-spinner for the teetering banking system.

The first step was allowing non-nationals to purchase up to 10% of a Russian bond issue earlier this year, enabling the Central Bank to bring in $2 billion over a three-month time span. Those issues featured a special capping of currency risks and maximum yields.

Financial Trader, 3, No. 6 (1996), 16.

The newly available T-bills will continue to carry a currency hedge, to protect against ruble devaluations, and thus will offer a current 19% annualized yield, whereas domestic investors still get up to an 80% yield. In addition, Russia's central bank has moved to stop "back door" access to the market by foreigners, insisting they now use the rather narrow "front door."

The ultimate goal may be to reduce Russia's overall interest costs to as low as 2.5% over the inflation rate, which is expected to drop to 25% on an annualized basis by the end of this year. Kvint predicts, "since foreign investments into Russia fell by 20% this year, we could see a further opening of the debt market in the coming months."

"Not-Quite" Brady Bonds

In order to convince global investors that the country is serious about its financial health, Russia worked with the London Club of Creditors, a loose conglomeration of around 600 banks holding debt from Vnesheconombank, to restructure past-due notes. This state-owned bank, the only entity allowed to trade with the outside world during communist rule, agreed to restructure into bonds $25.5 billion in principal and $7 billion in interest arrears. On July 1, those bonds started trading on a "when and if issued" basis.

There were reports that the bonds were recast under the Brady program, but there is no forgiveness included in the deal, as is often the case under a Brady restructuring for countries overwhelmed with debt. Rather, the principal will have a 25-year payback period and interest arrears will be paid within 20 years, and both instruments carry a seven-year grace period. In the mean time, interest will be paid at Libor plus 13/16. As a down payment on back interest, the Russians have paid $1.38 billion out of a promised $2 billion.

New bonds will be issued to creditor banks this December, at which time those banks will be able to sell off the bonds for more money than they could hope for from the illiquid notes. The London Club of Creditors is similar in concept to the Paris Club, but made up of private banks instead of governmental and quasi-governmental entities.

RUSSIA IS LOSING THE BATTLE FOR FOREIGN INVESTMENT

Although the present worldwide shortage of capital diminishes the interest of Western investors in Russia, in the future, this country is seen as an emerging capitalist market.

A year or two ago, Russia was placed high on investors' priority lists. The government established the foundations of main capitalist institutions; however Russian bureaucracy strictly regimented their rights. The old control mechanisms of the Central Committee of the Communist Party and of the Control Commission vanished without any effective replacement, thus allowing rampant corruption and crime to emerge.

Russian government must realize that the competition for capital among emerging markets is extremely intense. Many economic indicators, including those released by the World Bank, suggest that Russia should be considered a developing country. Arthur Andersen takes a practical approach to the Russian market by emphasizing the importance of capitalist institutions. Today, various insurance companies, private banks, all of the Big Six accounting firms, and many large law firms have representatives in Russia. Furthermore, this country is currently going through a telecommunications revolution overlooked by most analysts. All these factors force us to consider Russia as an emerging market comparable to that of Latin America, South Africa, or China. According to different sources, there are 34 to 40 emerging markets in the world today. Most of them are characterized by stable political structure and active capitalist institutions which allow them to attract significant foreign investment. Last year U.S. exports to Mexico were approximately $47.6 billion, to Taiwan, $19.6 billion, and to China, $12 billion. Direct U.S. investment to China is projected to amount to $250 billion over the next five years.

Russia, on the other hand, is not properly utilizing the existing capitalist institutions. Moreover, the Russian government, influ-

ITAR-TASS-Business World (Moscow), August 2, 1995, pp. 1–2.

enced by domestic lobbyists involved in a continuous power struggle, makes inconsistent and rushed decisions impeding this country's affinity for capital investment. The privatization process is a good example of very poor decision making. In all civilized countries, companies are privatized based on their fair market values. The Russian president, on the other hand, issued a decree commanding privatization in Moscow to be based on companies' book values, thus leading to significantly understated enterprise valuations. Today, approximately 75% of the state property has been sold at these deflated prices, creating a criminal business climate where the best properties are given away for bribes.

Another example of this disadvantageous action undertaken by Russia is the recent presidential decision to limit activities of foreign law firms in the country. It would be hard to think of a more counterproductive move. Many Western companies terminated their activities in Russia because they were unable to continue working with their trusted legal advisers. Even Baker & McKenzie, the largest international law firm operating in Russia, has to struggle with bureaucratic setbacks.

Russia is making a big mistake in yielding to lobbyists calling for restrictions on operations of Western insurance companies. According to the current regulations issued by the illiterate cabinet of Mr. Gaidar in 1992, foreign insurance companies cannot own more than 49% of their Russian subsidiaries—a move leading to a protected monopoly of domestic insurance companies.

Starting in 1988, the government began the laborious process of establishing free economic zones to create additional incentives for foreign investment. Of the twenty such zones planned, only two—in Kaliningrad and Nahodka—came into reality. The U.S., which has never suffered from a lack of investment capital, has 129 various free trade, technological, and economic zones. These were created by state governments to bolster regional development. Arthur Andersen has been using its credibility in the business world to encourage several Western companies to set up operations within Russian free economic zones. However, the recent presidential decree abolished all tax advantages and privileges of joint ventures operating in these special zones, thus effectively eliminating the special judicial status of free economic zones altogether.

As an enthusiastic promoter of investment in Russia who has been able to steer several large corporations toward the Russian market, what should I tell my clients now? How can the investment community trust a cabinet made of uneducated politicians that is easily swayed by lobbyists? How can Russia hope to attract capital under these circumstances? Last year's temporary increase in capital inflow has promptly disappeared because of political and economic instabilities. One of the sources of this unreliability lies in the Chechen conflict, which I approve in principal since I believe that Russia should preserve its unity. The entire situation was poorly handled by the government, allowing a small discord to escalate into a civil war that has tarnished Russia's world image. Once again, the main problem in Russia is the fact that many of the country's economic and military decisions are made by uneducated people.

Another problem is that many Russian politicians follow primitive recommendations of Western consultants who do not have a thorough understanding of the local market. People like Jeffrey Sachs rushed to offer free advice, creating a name for themselves at the expense of Russia's stability. He advised Gaidar's government to liberalize prices before privatizing the economy. These unacceptable recommendations, including the World Bank's suggestion of stopping government subsidies for agriculture and heavy industry, are continuing to be made. The Russian government should turn to the economic history of other countries instead of blindly following such recommendations. As an example of effective decision making, after the Second World War, Japan and Germany supported industrial development through state subsidies. Likewise, I am a strong advocate of Mr. Chernomyrdin's stance on this issue and believe that terminating state aid at this time would entail catastrophic consequences. Instead of covertly taking partial steps, the government should publicly accept the need to support heavy industry and agriculture as well as redirect its investment initiatives from retail and social infrastructure to these key economic areas.

To obtain the multi-billion-dollar investments it needs, Russia must first create incentives for foreign companies. Instead of forcing cooperation in insurance and legal services, where collaboration is an inevitable economic necessity, the government must encourage cooperation between domestic and foreign businesses in industry and agriculture.

DESPITE ROUGH WATERS, MARKET ECONOMY CRUISES AHEAD: OPPORTUNITIES ABOUND IN NIS FOR INTREPID INVESTORS

Recent political events in Moscow and their coverage in the media have been misleading about the situation in Russia. The battles of October have had no real impact on the development of a free market economy. As practically all Russian leaders (except a few stupid Fascists) understand, without the cooperation of the West it will be impossible to revive Russia and the other countries of the Newly Independent States (NIS). Even the recently dissolved Russian parliament was not opposed to foreign investment; rather, it was, in its own time and manner, enacting legislation necessary to create a favorable business environment insulated from changing political winds.

While the media devoted its attention to the political fighting, it completely forgot about Russia's far more serious economic crisis. The crisis began not after the 1991 coup, not even during Gorbachev's time, but actually around 1969–70. Back then, the annual growth rate of the USSR's GNP was 7.5%. When Gorbachev came to power in 1985, annual GNP growth had dropped to 3.5%. In 1991 when he left office, it was down to negative 2%. It seems to me that the newly independent Russian government mistakenly "liberalized" prices before decentralization, demonopolization, and privatization could take hold. This increased prices, pushing 85% of the Russian people below the poverty line and perpetuating an inflationary environment.

As a result, during 1992 the rate of industrial output in Russia decreased by more than 24%. Even more dangerous, food production has decreased to 1988 levels, and meat production has decreased by

The Kvint Newsletter, 1, No. 2 (November 1993).

60%. This situation continues in 1993; the decrease in industrial output will be about 15%–17% for this year. However, the process of economic stabilization will begin in 1994, when the decrease in industrial output will drop to 10%–12%.

How does this economic situation impact the interests of foreign investors? Make no mistake: as the necessary business infrastructure is rapidly created, sizable profits and plentiful growth can be achieved by joint ventures and foreign investments that capitalize on the current economic situation; this, in turn, will help build a free market economy. The level of profitability can be quite high once joint ventures are created—between 35% and 38%—which is higher than that of businesses in Manhattan or Zurich. But the path is filled with land mines, and one must have a good guide.

All You Need Is Parts

For example, about 20% of all industrial companies and 35% of all infrastructure companies in Russia are not profitable. Many, however, once were profitable and could be so again. These firms desperately need components that Russia doesn't produce, particularly those used in light industry. Most got into trouble because the fall of the centralized Soviet Union destroyed all their internal (and often, ineffective) connections with suppliers from other former Soviet republics. New market connections are just beginning to develop.

Small investments into these companies' unfinished products can provide the basis for very profitable businesses. The products of these joint ventures will be competitive in terms of quality and price due to a cheaper, educated labor force, inexpensive natural resources, very inexpensive energy for intra-Russian use, and inexpensive production and office facilities A similar situation is also found in other NIS markets.

Catalysts of Foreign Investment

The pace of investment has been slow in virtually all countries of the NIS, but some regions have created special programs to attract foreign investment. Thirteen free economic zones (FEZs) have been established in Russia, and one each in Ukraine and Belarus.

Not all regions present the same political risks for investment. For example, Azerbaijan and Georgia have quite favorable regulations regarding foreign investment, but I would not recommend investing in these regions at this time. Georgia is practically in a state of civil war, while more than 20% of the former Azerbaijan is under control of Armenian forces.

Hard currency in private hands totals $13–$15 billion; NIS governments hold about $38–$45 billion, most of which they are spending on emergency needs such as food, pharmaceuticals, chemicals, and some military industries.

Prices Rise, Along with Dollar's Value

The price of consumer goods and food continues to rise faster than the rate of inflation. I forecast that the rate of growth of the price of consumer goods will stabilize at around 8%–10% per month during the next 12 months, and then drop to about 5% per month. Prices for the same products also vary in different areas by as much as 150 times. For example, flour in the Kamchatka region of Russia costs 150 rubles/kg., while in Chechen republic it costs only 12 rubles/kg. In the Tyumen oil region, sugar costs 720 rubles/kg., while in the Orel region, sugar costs 160 rubles/kg. The price of chicken has risen by about 30% per month, and in some regions such as eastern Siberia and near the Volga River, by more than 200% per month.

Yeltsin's October decision to liberalize the price of bread will again broaden these regional differences, as well as seriously increase both inflation and the cost of transportation.

The NIS is practically the only market in the world where the strength of the dollar is steadily increasing. In June 1992, US $1 = 128 rubles. By August 23, 1993, US $1 = 987.5 rubles, and I predict it will rise to US $1 = 1,300 rubles by the end of 1993. While the purchasing power of the ruble slowly declines, the value of a roll of dollar bills will significantly increase, making the NIS a very good market for U.S. investment. Companies with foreign capital participation will become more and more successful.

Finally, some analysts have concluded that Yeltsin's September decree, which seriously limited the circulation of dollars in Russia, will make doing business more difficult. My opinion is different. Now foreigners can officially operate with both dollars and rubles. (See *The Kvint Newsletter*, October 1993, p. 3). This law may limit the activity of Russian companies, but not foreign companies in Russia. Unfortunately, the black market for money will once again work well.

KVINT'S FORECAST: BEYOND THE POLITICAL FOG, THE BUSINESS HORIZON LOOKS CLEAR

What has happened in the former Soviet Union in the past three years has no analogy in history. The world's biggest and last empire has collapsed. When I wrote in *The New York Times* on October 28, 1990, that by 1992 there would no longer be a Soviet Union, very few people shared this idea. Now it is an historical fact.

Sometimes, the business community acts as if the collapse occurred a decade ago; in fact, it was not even two years ago. Now, Russia, Ukraine, Kazakstan, and other former Soviet republics hold the attention of the world's investors and traders. Of course, politicians still keep the score in these countries. And the creation of a democratic government and market economy is a long, arduous process with ups and downs. But no serious person is arguing about the direction of change—only about the velocity and methods. Considering how far we have yet to go, the business climate is robust.

In Russia alone, there are about 3,300 private banks, thousands of brokerage and trading houses, one stock exchange, and approximately 480 commodity exchanges which are already operational. To date, some 11,580 joint ventures have been formed. I estimate that more than 25% of the Russian economy has been privatized, because freedom is working.

As a result, market-oriented leaders and foreign entrepreneurs are now forging ahead, despite the many difficulties and restrictions of Russian law. The legal codes of the Newly Independent States (NIS) are being legislated from scratch, while the people are desperate for a greatly improved economic outlook. Here are some notes on legislation and other developments that will impact foreign trade with the NIS.

The Kvint Newsletter, 1, No. 1 (October 1993).

First in Russia

When the Russian parliament reconvenes in December, there will be lots to do. And President Yeltsin will be eager to push through many of his laws to enhance the foreign investment environment.

Among the first will be the Law on Investment in Equity and Debt Securities, which will regulate all securities including bonds and notes. Another is the Law on Free Economic Zones. In 1989–90, I participated in the process to create the first free economic zones, regions that offer business privileges such as tax holidays. (The government is only now getting around to legislating their existence!) Also expected is a decree from President Yeltsin on the liberalization of foreign investors' activity in the Russian marketplace.

Upcoming decrees of the Government will include:

- Decision on the state investment program for 1993 (the year is almost finished, but the decision has not yet been made);

- Decree on stimulation of foreign investments in priority industries of the national economy, i.e., food processing, pharmaceuticals, and waste processing; and
- Decree on either abolishing or decreasing export quotas, and also decreasing the Russian Federation Government's regulation of export.

Outlook on Ruble Exchange Rate

During the summer and prior to the political fights of late September, the exchange rate between the ruble and the U.S. dollar had been stable at 985–1,080 rubles to the U.S. dollar, higher than it was last spring, when it fell to 1,200 rubles to the U.S. dollar. This was the result of hard currency interventions at the Russian currency auctions in Moscow, as well as artificial measures to keep the ruble high and encourage spending. The State Bank sold almost $4 billion in hard currency at these auctions in 1993. With the recent dissolution of the Russian parliament, the ruble rose above 1,250, a high it last held in March 1993. The political situation vis-à-vis the lack of a straight economic course will devalue the ruble to 1,700 or more by the end of this year, and especially in the first quarter of 1994.

Foreigners Receive the Right to Open Ruble Accounts

For the first time since 1917, foreigners have been granted the right to open ruble bank accounts in Russia. These accounts will be of two types:

- Account T, for import-export; and
- Account E, for participation of foreign investors in privatization, and also, I expect, for currency speculations.

These accounts will enable foreigners who are trading for rubles in Russia to repatriate their profits abroad in hard currency. This would eliminate the need for intermediate steps such as barter or hard currency auctions.

I would like to recommend that interested parties open these accounts immediately. Later, it is very possible that there will be a limit on the number of Accounts E that can be opened. There is already a limit of one Account E per foreigner.

Eastern European Trade with Russia

Trade between Russia and the former Soviet bloc of Eastern European countries decreased from $31 billion in 1990 to $12 billion in 1992. The drop is the result of the shift in trade from direct product exchange to the use of hard currency as the only means of payment. Formerly, Soviet-bloc countries and Russia would trade buses for oil, for example, without involving any exchange of hard currency.

The lack of hard currency has halted production in many companies whose products were once competitive on the world market. One might conclude that small investments in such companies would give them the boost in production necessary for them to sell again on the world market (and at low prices because of the lower costs of their production).

For example, from 1991 to 1993, the high-quality Hungarian bus plant Icarus decreased its production from 14,000 buses per year to 3,500. It could present a promising joint-venture opportunity for the right company.

Also, New York City–based Standard Trade and Investment Co. has signed an agreement with the Russian state-owned foreign trade company Vneshintorg, establishing a mutually exclusive and reciprocal purchasing and sales relationship. The companies agreed to represent each other in North and South America, and in the Commonwealth of Independent States (CIS is the Newly Independent States plus the Baltics), respectively.

Part II

THE TOP EMERGING MARKETS OF EUROPE, CENTRAL ASIA, AND LATIN AMERICA

EUROPE'S SIX TOP EMERGING MARKETS

Overview

In the early 1990s, the global business world changed entirely, due to the ascendancy of the emerging market countries. In comparison with the previous decade, emerging market nations as a group increased in land mass, population, and industrial production. Due to a complete lack of local capital and investment, these developing nations needed foreign assistance, although they still tried to maintain some elements of centrally planned, inefficient economic structures. They soon realized that they needed to attract foreign investment by reforming market policies. The processes of privatization, demonopolization, and demilitarization of the economies of these states in transition and countries with dictatorships caught the attention of the global investment community. Nevertheless, the shortage of investment in the world business community still restrains the desired growth and development that would elevate these countries to developed nation status. Today, by our estimates, there are 69 countries that qualify for emerging market status. Among these, certain European countries are playing vital roles. Portugal, Greece, Turkey, Hungary, the Czech Republic, and Poland are among the economic pacesetters of the emerging market world. They are ahead of other emerging markets in terms of their development of capitalist institutions and capital markets, as well as their level of cooperation with developed nations.

These six countries have many similarities. They all have membership in the European Union (at least as an associate member), have constitutionally elected presidents or prime ministers and parliaments, maintain positive relationships with their neighbors (excluding Turkish and Greek tensions), boast nuclear-free status, and have special regulations prohibiting the expropriation of property, includ-

Business Briefing—Emerging Market Investments, London, World Markets Research Center, July 23, 1996, pp. 34–38.

ing foreign capital. In terms of exchange rate regimes, Turkey, Greece, and Portugal allow their national currencies to float on world markets. The remaining three nations offer only limited convertibility, but the Czech currency could be convertible within one year.

Political risk varies among the six nations. Turkey poses the greatest risk to potential foreign investors, as the political arena is the most unstable. No one party has a substantial majority; hence, a coalition government is required. There are ethnic problems present as well, and all these factors discourage foreign investors. Within the former Soviet-bloc satellite countries, the communists have returned to power through democratic elections. Although these new governments have distanced themselves from the former rulers and claim to be social democrats of the new order, nationalization of industries and a protectionist environment is not completely unimaginable.

Economic risk in these countries can be gauged by membership in international lending institutions, the nature of their respective relationships with the Paris and London Clubs, the amount of total foreign debt outstanding, and the ratio of foreign debt to GDP. The six nations under discussion are all members of the WTO (the successor to GATT), IMF, World Bank Group institutions, and EBRD, among other institutions. In December 1995, the Czech Republic became the first former Soviet-bloc country to become a member of the OECD (Organization for Economic Cooperation and Development), followed by Hungary in spring 1996. Poland was formally asked to join the OECD in July 1996, and must ratify the accession treaty this fall. Overall, the group enjoys good relations with the Paris and London Clubs and offers encouraging signs to bankers. One such sign is the Czech Republic's recent payment in full of its IMF loan, ahead of schedule. As of 1994, foreign debt to GDP ratios among the six ranged from 19% (Portugal) to 55% (Poland), which indicates that the six nations' economic expansion is funded, to a significant degree, by foreign debt. When compared to developed nations such as the United Kingdom, whose foreign debt to GDP ratio is only 2%, it would appear that these six nations must make considerable improvements to reduce their reliance on foreign capital.

In five of the six nations, foreign investors may freely repatriate capital, with no restrictions. Turkey is the lone exception, with some minor restrictions. Poland is the only country of the six that does not allow free remittance of dividends and profits. Some restrictions on foreign direct investment (FDI) appear in all but two of these nations, Portugal and Greece. For instance, Turkey mandates that nonresident investors bring at least $50,000 per person into the country, and Hungary retains majority control of the energy sector and outright control of the aluminum, automobile, and pharmaceutical industries. In Poland, agricultural tariffs still exist. As countries apply to and pursue membership in the EU and OECD, most quotas fall to EU levels. Lower tariffs and the elimination of quotas within the EU can be considered positive signs for these economies, and they are poised to continue in this vein.

Foreign direct investment is crucial to the future success of these nations. Hungary's FDI cash flows have steadily increased over the past two years, by 24% in 1995, and by 27% in 1994. Hungary had nearly $6.9 billion in total inflows last year alone, and has become the darling of the international investment community. The other five, while not replicating the dramatic performance of Hungary, are also attracting investment. However, Turkey and Greece suffered a net decrease in FDI earlier in 1996, which could have resulted from the substantially heightened tensions between the two neighbors. But, both nations realize that this hostility discourages foreign investors, and have begun to back away from their previous threats. The three former Soviet-bloc nations, at close inspection, have too many restrictions on foreign capital, which puts them at a disadvantage when compared to the South American and Asian emerging markets. Of the other three countries, Turkey, Greece, and Portugal, Turkey has the most restrictive policies on foreign capital investment.

Portugal does not offer any special economic development zones, but the other five nations all have various types of free trade or free economic zones which offer grants, tax allowances, and other financial incentives.

Turkey

Because of geographical considerations, Turkey plays an important role in the surrounding region. If one includes the Asian portion of the country, Turkey ranks as the largest country in Europe (except, of course, for the European part of Russia). It has strong Western ties, which have been solidified with the completion of the Ankara Agreement with the European Union earlier this year. Its proximity to Central Asia (including the republics of Kazakstan, Turkmenistan, Tajikistan, Kyrgyzstan, and Uzbekistan) and the Caucasus region (Armenia, Georgia, and Azerbaijan) ensures that the nation will play a significant role in the development of the Newly Independent States.

Turkey's importance soared after the Soviet Union collapsed, for a number of reasons. Most significant is the issue of religion. Turkey has been a secular state dominated by Muslim traditions since its inception in 1923. The rise of the Islamic political party Refah and its recent dominance in national elections raised concerns about the direction of the nation, but these fears have not been realized. Refah has toned down much of its leftist, pro-Islamic platform and seeks to govern in a legitimate, moderate coalition.

The significance of Islam cannot be overstated. There are autonomous republics such as Tatarstan, Daghestan, and Bashkortostan within Russia, and former Soviet republics in the Caucasus region and Central Asia with predominantly Muslim populations. There are also Muslim populations living inside Ukraine on the Crimea Peninsula.

Nascent economies have begun to search for a suitable model on which to base their respective market economies and international relationships. One possible model is offered by Iran, an Islamic fundamentalist nation that espouses anti-Western rhetoric and has militaristic tendencies. Significantly, all rulers of the Central Asian republics have visited Iran, with the president of Turkmenistan the last to do so, in July 1996. It is obviously in the best interest of the world investment community that Turkey becomes the economic template for these new developing nations.

Turkey's geopolitical role is also significant. Its signing of the Black Sea Cooperation Agreement and its bilateral trade accord with Bulgaria (almost 9% of this Balkan nation is Turkish) ensure that Turkish people have a special role in southern Europe. For centuries, Turkey guarded the straits from the Dardenelles through the Bosporus, and controlled the flow of commerce between East and West, North and South. This unique location will continue to make Turkey the crossroads of international trade in the area and a focal point for international investors for years to come.

From a financial perspective, Turkey remains categorized as an emerging market nation. While capitalist institutions are entrenched in the economy, Turkey continues to struggle to become a fully developed country. This is reflected in its relatively low literacy rate of 81%, one of the lowest in Europe. Furthermore, the nation's standard of living, defined by GDP per capita, is adding to the difficulty of placing this nation outside the emerging market category. Turkey should still remain interesting to investors due to its cheap labor resources and potential in several sectors of its economy, particularly in industries such as iron and steel, seaports, construction and construction materials, and tourism. Turkey needs further infrastructure development. But, with its membership in all the main multicultural economic institutions and a population of 60 million, Turkey represents a major market for exporters and importers alike.

Greece

Greece is a country that also deserves closer inspection. On an economic level, Greece claims the highest GDP per capita of these six selected nations, and has only one-sixth the population of Turkey. Of course, one must realize that this high level of GDP is also the result of subsidies from the European Union, of which Greece is a full member. Full members in the European Union must have a minimum standard of living. It is the subsidies of the EU that ensure that Greece maintains the level of the other full members.

The main industry of Greece is the service sector, with tourism and shipping being the largest components. Industrial development is severely limited by the nation's mountainous terrain, which makes up nearly 90% of Greece's total land mass.

Greece has less geographic importance than Turkey, but its location is, nevertheless, quite significant. Greece has historically faced the backyard of communist-bloc countries, as it borders Bulgaria, the former Yugoslav Republic of Macedonia, and Albania. In terms of investment potential, this was a lifeless region. However, with the fall of the Berlin Wall in 1989 and the demise of the Soviet Union, economic cooperation between Greece and its neighbors could open up countless possibilities for Greece. From 1992 through 1995, the Greek government, for political reasons, refused to recognize the independence (and even the flag) of the former Yugoslav Republic of Macedonia. Developing an economic relationship with this nation was, therefore, impossible. However, relations have vastly improved of late, and Greece will now be able to capitalize on its location.

On the border of Turkey, Bulgaria, and Greece is a territory known as Thrace. This territory has an interesting historical location, as well as fine sites for spas and resorts. It also has tremendous agricultural potential. However, capitalizing on this to the utmost degree requires the cooperation of all these nations. No single nation would be capable of developing the region of Thrace on its own. Current tension between Greece and Turkey could make cooperation somewhat difficult, and the initiative could fall to Bulgaria, which has a positive relationship with both these nations. Furthermore, it is important for Greece to solidify its transportation network and develop ground transportation links with Northern and Western Europe in order to expedite trade in the region. The most likely route for transporting products would be through the Greek seaport of Alexandroupolis, through Bulgaria, and then on to Northern and Eastern Europe.

Greece is unique in that it is the only member of the European Union that does not share a border with another European Union nation. Greek sentiment toward the European Monetary Union (EMU) is positive, but whether the government begins to impose the requisite austerity measures is still far from clear. If the Greek government can deregulate more rapidly, the insurance industry and other capital market service firms can expand into the Balkans quickly.

Portugal

Another emerging market nation with vast potential is Portugal. In the last three years, Portugal has made great strides in developing its economy and is approaching industrial nation status. The Portuguese market is largely open to foreign investment. Pharmaceutical industry investment is one factor that has significantly contributed to the economy's growth. Foreign investors are attracted to Portugal because of the relatively low cost of labor, and because the Portuguese currency, the escudo, has become much more stable in recent years—a sign that it is becoming more respected internationally. However, because of high export volumes, and the similarity of Portuguese and Spanish exports, the escudo is identified with the Spanish peseta, and when Spain devalues its currency, Portugal inevitably follows.

The growth of the Portuguese economy in recent years has brought it to a level of development somewhere between the less-developed Central and Eastern European countries and the highly developed Western European countries. Among full members of the European Union, Portugal has the lowest GDP per capita. However, its GDP has grown to a level high enough to include it among developed nations. The IFC's criteria for a developed nation is $8,625 GDP per capita. Portugal already meets this criteria. While the rise in Portugal's GDP per capita results at least partially from direct European Union subsidies, another significant contributing factor has been the vast technological development that has occurred in recent years. However, Portugal is in need of a new development and growth strategy, as the economy's emphasis shifts from industry to the service sector. Developing and implementing such a strategy takes time, and as a result, the Portuguese economy has recently suffered some stagnation. Despite the cooling economy, Portugal has been able to attract a great deal of foreign investment, and is ahead of the Czech Republic, Greece, and even Poland, although it is still behind Hungary and Turkey. The recent creation of the Community of Portuguese-Speaking Countries (CPLD), consisting of Portugal, Brazil, Cape Verde, Guinea-Bissau, São Tome and Principe, Angola, and Mozambique will certainly raise the profile of Portugal in the world. Furthermore, Portugal has not yet taken advantage of its geographical position in terms of Euro-African development. Several African countries, such as Tunisia, Morocco, Egypt, and even Israel to some extent, are on the rise, and being located on the corner of the Atlantic Ocean and the Mediterranean Sea, Portugal is in a perfect position to take advantage of these emerging markets.

Poland

If we shift our attention to Poland, we can see a nation where the former Communist Party regained national power in recent elections. With its application to the OECD just accepted, Poland seems poised to regain its economic footing. FDI growth rates have been increasing, and exceeded 75% in 1995. The Mass Privatization Program (MPP) has been successful in selling off hundreds of state-owned enterprises to the Polish public, though this process has slowed considerably. In order to make its application to the OECD appear more attractive, Poland plans to allow its citizens to buy foreign stocks, and to lower its curbs on portfolio investment.

There is a noticeable anti-foreign sentiment among Poland's population, as local opinion polls show almost three-quarters of Poles against unrestricted land sales to foreigners. This feeling is aptly demonstrated by the government's insistence that foreign investors be allowed to purchase only small plots of land in city areas. Polish farmers support this policy, and have been rewarded for their efforts with protective quotas. However, this is a natural reaction, as all nations embarking on a course for a market economy feel that their natural resources, land being the most precious, should not be monopolized by foreigners. This reaction should not be considered a major obstacle to foreign investors. Even in the most developed countries, this sentiment can be found. One need just recall the popular uproar in the U.S. when a Japanese corporation bought Rockefeller Center. However, a foreign company cannot take land back to its home country. For example, Belgium reached this conclusion many years ago, and foreigners currently control 35% of the state's economy. Belgians do not see this as a threat, since foreign investment stimulates their economy.

Czech Republic

Among our group of nations, the Czech Republic has several characteristics that are rather unique. As part of the former Austro-Hungarian Empire, the Czech Republic has a special role in reintegrating the economies of the nations of the former Empire. Of course, this role involves only economic reintegration and is not related to political reunification.

Of the former Soviet-bloc countries, the Czech Republic is the most westernized. This results from its geographical location as well as from its history. The nation is, literally, on the border between

East and West, and therefore, Western influence was inevitable. Prior to World War II, the Czech Republic was one of the top six industrialized nations in Europe. During Soviet rule, the country advanced technologically, but not to its full potential. Now, with the return to capitalism, the nation has the opportunity to capitalize on its unique location as well on the entrepreneurial spirit of its people, some of whom remember what it was like to live in a thriving capitalist society fifty years ago.

Among former Soviet-bloc countries, the Czech Republic has the strongest democratic tradition. In fact, it is the only country whose executive leader, President Vaclav Havel, is a former dissident. Bulgarian President Zhelyu Zhelev is also a dissident, but has no real political power.

The privatization process in the Czech Republic has been the smoothest of the six nations. The transformation of property from the state to the private sector has been very efficient. Moreover, although the Czech Republic has about the same population as Greece, Portugal, and Hungary, its territory is smaller, and the privatization has been more easily managed. Foreign capital has been attracted to the Czech Republic by the general availability of educated, low-cost labor. Furthermore, foreign investors are not overly concerned about the political risk, since the Czech lands have never had a history of political violence or terrorism. The present political climate leads one to believe that this will remain the case.

Foreign capital is also attracted by the efficiency, the innovative spirit, and the dedication of the Czech people. This attribute, coupled with the fact that Czech society is very westernized, makes investors more willing to put their money here. As a result of the foreign capital that has been invested, the Czech Republic's economy has developed several very strong sectors. High technology, machinery, and shipbuilding are all thriving industries. This nation also enjoys small but efficient agricultural, food processing, and beer production industries, as well as beautiful spas and resorts, including the world-famous Karlovy Vary.

Hungary

Finally, we will take a closer look at Hungary. Geopolitically, it has no special advantages, as Turkey, Portugal, or the Czech Republic has. But Hungary is also part of the former Austro-Hungarian Empire, and has a significant location. It borders nearly every Central European country, placing it at the door to the Balkans. Moreover, Hungary's role, from an international political perspective, is more important than its location. Of all the Soviet-bloc countries, Hungary was a pioneer of economic and market reforms in 1968. Unlike Czech communists in the 1960s, who tried to incorporate a human rights agenda into their reform and provide more basic social freedoms, Hungary sought to liberalize small businesses and provide them greater business freedoms, flexibility, and incentives. The Czech approach was unrealistic under communist conditions of the 1960s and therefore doomed from the start. However, both the Czech approach and the economic reforms that Hungary undertook, even in the '60s, prepared them for the later demise of communism and the opening of the Austrian-Hungarian border. This economic reform, begun 20 years earlier than in any other Soviet-bloc country, is the reason that Hungary later received the benefits of East–West cooperation and more foreign direct investment than any other East European nation, and more, even, than Russia itself.

Hungary has the highest FDI per capita of the six nations under discussion, with FDI totaling $6.9 billion (including in-kind investments) in 1995. Poland, Greece and the Czech Republic combined have slightly less foreign direct investment. Even in terms of cumulative investment over the last five years, the combined totals of Poland and the Czech Republic did not reach Hungary's. In reference to GDP per capita, Hungary ranks ahead of Poland and the Czech Republic.

But now, after six years of transition, Hungary has faltered in its position at the top of emerging market nations. Countries that are instituting capitalist changes and restructuring more quickly are becoming more attractive to global investors. This new elite includes Poland and the Czech Republic. In general, the strategy of deregulation and openness has better implementation and practice in the other five countries than in Hungary. Hungary seems to have become content with the rate of change while other nations have maintained comparatively frenetic paces.

Hungary continues to have the potential to be the leading country in this region of the world, but is not fully utilizing its capabilities. As an associate member of the EU, it has relatively positive relations with its neighbors, although there are instances of minor ethnic tensions with Slovakia and Romania. It boasts a highly educated workforce and a well-developed infrastructure, particularly in telecommunications and transportation. The social infrastructure and the relatively high level of cooperation with Western countries make the business climate in this country very appealing for international investors. Some of the most interesting industries in the Hungarian economy are hospitality and tourism, electronics, food processing, wine production, and exports for the Russian consumer market.

However, in terms of the efficiency and profitability of these investments, Hungary still lags behind the other five countries we have mentioned. One should not be surprised if the Czech Republic moves ahead of Hungary in the near future. Hungary's foreign trade balance is negative and has been so for some time. However, export–import business in Hungary is operating, and Hungary could become the home base for many foreign industrial firms who, following four years of war and international sanctions, are ready to enter the market of the former Republics of Yugoslavia, now more or less open for business.

Summary

The six countries we have been discussing have been selected for a specific reason: of the 22 emerging markets in Europe today, these six represent the most developed economies, and in as little as five to ten years, they will be among the leading European countries.

All these countries must further develop the major capitalist institutions, especially in the industries of banking, insurance, and auditing services. To date, such development has been insufficient, with relatively few insurers active, and only a few foreign insurance companies operational. Portugal is the most advanced in this regard, with Turkey, Greece, and Poland trailing behind. The presence of foreign banks is most noticeable in Turkey, Greece, and Portugal, but Poland and the Czech Republic have made substantial inroads in recruiting non-domestic banks. Of the six nations, the Czech Republic has the highest number of private, local banks, though their capitalization is small. There are only two wholly state-owned banks in the Czech Republic.

Poland and the Czech Republic lead the way in signing double-taxation treaties with their trading partners. The Czech Republic was the last to start the privatization process, but is now in the fore-front of former Soviet-bloc nations that have sold off state-owned enterprises.

These countries will continue to enjoy the majority of foreign di-rect investment in the emerging market countries of Europe for many years to come. In terms of economic power, Poland will emerge as the leader of this group. This is due to several factors apparent in the Polish economy: the strong industrial base, the burgeoning en-ergy sector, the potential for development in telecommunications and transportation networks, the solid social infrastructure, and the population's embrace of capitalism. Following Poland, Turkey could be considered the most vibrant economy. Its great location, however, has one negative aspect. Turkey borders some countries with unsta-ble and tyrannical regimes, such as in Iran and Iraq, which substan-tially decreases the interest of international investors. The remaining countries, measured by various criteria, have equal economic poten-tial, but the Czech Republic will likely more fully utilize its potential and pull ahead of Greece, Portugal, and even Hungary.

BALKANS: EMERGING MARKET FOR INTERNATIONAL BUSINESS

The fall of the Berlin Wall and the disintegration of the Soviet Union created not one but several new markets for the international investment community. Serious investors must view each market separately, both in terms of development opportunities and in terms of their level of readiness for working with international business. I believe that in 1995 former Soviet-bloc countries in the Balkans will become the new focus of activity.

Some Eastern European markets, such as the Czech Republic, Hungary, and Poland, after experiencing tumultuous economic, social, and political upheaval, have emerged with a high level of opportunity. Due to Russia's huge heterogeneous economic landscape, development has been uneven. But *oblasts* of Moscow, St. Petersburg, and the 15 Free Economic Zones, especially those on the Russian Pacific Coast, have already become areas of activity for international businesses. The remainder of the Russian territory has yet to emerge as an international market.

The dissolution of Czechoslovakia, in reality, was very peaceful, and the resulting Czech Republic is already a capitalist country with an emerging market. Slovakia, even with its economic and political problems, is a fairly stable market-oriented economy offering low risk for foreign business investments.

The Balkans, on the south of Europe, are a particularly attractive new region. Still, a combination of instability and political problems have deterred the international investment community from viewing the Balkan region with an opportunistic eye. The bloody disintegration of the former Yugoslavia and the political problems surrounding FYRO Macedonia are two examples of the types of disasters that have plagued the area in the past. This, however, is no longer the case. Moreover, for some countries in this region that by association have been painted with the same brush, this was never the case.

The territory of the former Yugoslavia is even more surprising.

The Kvint Newsletter, No. 5 (1995).

Rather than headlines proclaiming war, one can read about the fact that the majority of the countries on this territory have been at peace for almost two years and are ready for business. Slovenia, Croatia, FYRO Macedonia, and most parts of Serbia (currently named Yugoslavia) not only are peaceful but are working in cooperation with international business on a number of important projects. In fact, tourism is very strong in Croatia. In 1994, tourism was responsible for bringing a total of $1.3 billion into its economy. More important, those businesspeople who have recognized the changes and opportunity are currently profiting from doing business in this region.

One region that was always stable, yet is still recognized for its investment potential, is Bulgaria. Arthur Andersen & Co., SC, hosted a meeting for business leaders with President Zhelyu Zhelev of Bulgaria on his official visit to the U.S. on February 15. At that time, President Zhelev took the first concrete steps in the privatization process, encouraging Western investors to participate in Bulgaria in the first stages of privatization. Companies wishing to enter this market may want to consider investing in the enormous potential now while one can get considerable value for the dollar.

An Important Route to Europe

The stability of Bulgaria and its location on the Black Sea create a natural role for this country as a bridge between the Black Sea and the Adriatic Sea, to North, Central, and South Europe. It is, perhaps, the most stable entrance through the Black Sea to Russia's natural resources. All these factors will make Bulgaria more attractive for international business once transportation systems are developed. For example, the best way for Turkey, Greece, and Macedonia to be connected with central, western, and northern Europe is by railroad through Bulgaria and Romania. But between Romania and Bulgaria there is only one bridge, located over the Danube River.

A priority project will be to build a second bridge. It is clear that the IMF, the World Bank, and the European Bank for Reconstruction and Development will allocate the money for this, and international companies should think about competing for this project. The project would entail construction of not only the bridge but the infrastructure of the surrounding area as well. This bridge will satisfy the immediate need of building railroads between Romania and Hungary, Hungary and Austria, and Hungary and Slovakia.

Transportation Is the Key

Another major international project awaiting development is ground transportation between the Black Sea and the Adriatic Sea. This will facilitate direct access to Italy, via the Adriatic. It is important to remember that Italy is the fifth largest investor in Russia and an extremely active trading partner. For Italy it is critical to have a more direct route.

Currently, the sea route is through the Mediterranean Sea and Black Sea to Bulgaria, FYRO Macedonia, and Albania. Revising the sea route will create an extremely important role for FYRO Macedonia. It seems to me that the American State Department recognized this role two years ago when it started to pay attention to Macedonia. Today in Macedonia there are American peace-keeping troops. Through diplomatic channels, the U.S. State Department did much to help Macedonia maintain its independence.

All the Balkan countries, including southern Romania, offer many business opportunities. For example, unknown Albania, which shares a border with Greece and is very close to central Italy, has many natural resources. Albania is one of the largest oil producers per capita in Europe, and is a producer of copper, nickel, black metals, food, and vegetable oil. Albania also has a highly skilled workforce. Currently, it is the sixth largest source of legal foreign labor for Italy.

The business relationship between Albania and Greece improved dramatically at the end of 1994. This is a very important relationship for Greece since the only land route to Europe is through Bulgaria. Greece is now looking to create another route through Albania.

The Balkans are one of the biggest new emerging markets in Europe. This area has already forged close ties with the EEC, both economically and politically. For example, Bulgaria and Romania are now associate members of the European Union.

This market is actively seeking foreign investors. But investors will enter the market only if the capitalist institutions are in place to support the activities. I view this as an opportunity for institutions such as auditors, banks, law firms, and other service providers. The timing is right to be in the Balkans. They will deliver a service that in turn will bring clients. It is like the development of railroads. Many people think that it is time to build the railroad when the cargo is ready to be shipped. But in reality it is too late. If the railroad gets built, there will be cargo. It is the basic principle of supply and demand. Capital institutions likewise must be created early, and business activity will grow.

BULGARIA AS THE LAST KLONDIKE IN EASTERN EUROPE

During the four-year revolution of President Boris Yeltsin, Russia has sold, for almost nothing, about 75% of its economy. Most of the Eastern European countries have finished their process of mass privatization. Only one stable country has not yet begun a large-scale privatization program: Bulgaria. Two years from now in Bulgaria there will be little to buy. But for now, it is a country of great adventure for entrepreneurs who want to make a fortune. That was the reason for my recent visit to Bulgaria.

Not only is Bulgaria across the Atlantic Ocean, it is also in the United States at JFK airport. There you can find the small and unpleasant terminal of Balkan Airlines. The airline works on the Bulgarian time schedule. If a flight is scheduled for 6:30 P.M., boarding will definitely start two hours later. Likewise, the crew will not arrive until that time.

Bulgaria, unlike all the other post-communist countries of Eastern Europe, is not yet tired of Americans. In Bulgaria, I focused on the current economic policy and short-term prospects. I met with President Zhelyu Zhelev, Prime Minister Jean Videnov, and Speaker of the Parliament Blagovest Sendov. I also visited with the Chairman of the Committee for Mass Privatization, the head of the Agency for Privatization (cash privatization), ministers, private entrepreneurs, bankers, and people in the street. It is from these meetings that I have drawn the picture I will share with you.

Strategically Positioned and Politically Stable

Bulgaria is a typical Balkan country, and it is under the pressure of different political strategists of Russia, the European Union, the United States, and neighboring countries. Although Bulgaria's neighbor, the former Yugoslavia, has had terrible battles during all

The Kvint Newsletter, 3, No. 5 (February 1996).

these years of transformation, Bulgaria has remained a stable country. Notwithstanding political fights inside Bulgaria, there is no sign of civil war. From a practical point, the political fights are divided by a Chinese Wall from the day-to-day life of the Bulgarian people and from business activities.

The presidential office is held by former dissident and anti-communist Zhelyu Zhelev. However, the parliament and local executive bodies are populated overwhelmingly by the new communists who call themselves "socialists." New presidential elections are scheduled for October of this year. The democratic forces are divided without any reason between their only real leader, President Zhelev, and a variety of politicians. Without support from the party, he can lose the election to the new communists.

Zhelev's contenders are numerous, including the current Minister of Foreign Affairs, Pirinski, and the nonpartisan Speaker of the Parliament, Sendov. But this is not cause for alarm. All the current political leaders in Bulgaria are strong supporters of cooperation with the West. In what may seem ironic to someone in America, the new communists strongly believe that Bulgaria needs to be a member of NATO and a full member of the European Union.

In the offices of the President, Prime Minister and Speaker, I saw displayed not only the Bulgarian flag but the 12-star blue flag of the European Union. The Bulgarian leadership is highly appreciative of its associate membership in that Union. It is funny that a few days later when I visited the President of Greece, a full member of the EU, I could not find such a flag.

For neighboring countries, Bulgaria is a crossroads. Because of political relationships it is the only ground route for Turkey and Greece into Western Europe, and Bulgaria is practically the only country that has relationships with both countries. Even though Bulgaria has no mutual border with Russia, the two countries have had one of the strongest relationships in Eastern Europe over the past two centuries.

For America, its relationship with Bulgaria, as well as FYRO Macedonia, is quite important. It is interesting to note that Bulgaria was the first country to recognize the independence of FYRO Macedonia. Both Russia and the U.S. welcomed this decision. Bulgaria's strategic location on the coast of the Black Sea and in the heart of the Balkans, along with its friendly relations with neighboring countries, is key to diplomatic consensus-building. And a European Union without Bulgaria has no ground connections between two parts of the EU.

To understand the political climate in Bulgaria, I would like to underline one important characteristic of the Bulgarian nature: tolerance. Bulgaria and Denmark are the only two countries that, during Hitler's occupation in World War II, did not betray their Jewish population. Not one Bulgarian Jew was sent to a concentration camp. Now the Jewish population is being given back property that was nationalized during the communist regimes. Significantly, this decision has gained the support of all political leaders.

Timing Is Everything

Economically Bulgaria is an industrial country with strong potential in machinery building (particularly in the electro-technical industry), production of textiles and linens, and manufacturing for the fashion industry. Bulgaria also produces the best tobacco in Eastern Europe and fine red and white wines, vegetables, and fruits.

Even though residents of Bulgarian cities, including the capital, Sofia, dine in darkness, there is a great potential for development of the electrical energy sector. Other attractive areas for Western investment are the mass media, the hospitality industry, and small but potentially profitable products like rose oil (attar of roses) and carpets. The tourist industry is ripe for development. Bulgaria not only is on the coast but also has the beautiful Rila mountains, which are the highest in the Balkans.

Prior to 1996, foreigners were not allowed to participate in the privatization process. There were a few exceptions such as the hotel Vitosha, which is now managed by InterContinental and owned by a former Bulgarian-German citizen. Internal capital fought for influence, and the only companies that were available for privatization were small ones. Now that mass privatization using the voucher system is in the final stage, 1996 will mark the beginning of cash privatization.

The first 500 Bulgarian companies, large and medium-sized, from heavy industry to telecommunications to large manufacturing companies, will be for sale. This is the way that the foreign investor can participate directly, rather than in the secondary market.

However, this process will not be easy, due to the Mafia-style corruption on the part of government officials and private industrial commercial groups, which are mostly funded by illegal capital. Nevertheless, none of these groups have sufficient money, and Westerners with capital can win tenders officially and legally.

The Bulgarian agency that conducts cash privatization issued more that 11,000 licenses for private Bulgarian auditors to evaluate companies that are for sale. Unfortunately, these local auditors do not have experience in this area. Also, the local auditors are not respected outside the country.

Additionally, in what appears to be a strange decision, the auditors are not permitted to participate in the process of raising capital, once the value of the company has been established, as is done in the West.

On the other hand, the Big Six certified accounting firms have been excluded from the process. This is one of the biggest negatives for investors trying to determine the true value of companies on the block.

A positive side is that, due to a lack of capital and understanding, the market value of the companies will be extremely low. Westerners with capital will be able to complete very profitable transactions.

Sheraton, InterContinental, GE, May & Co., AT&T, and Cable and Wireless have already moved into the market. These companies, like many others, are looking for opportunities but have not yet made major investments. Unlike in other Eastern European countries, major banks have not received licenses for cooperation. The Bulgarian government will be making a big mistake if it does not change this situation.

BUILDING CAPITALISM IN BULGARIA BY DECREE

Q: Mr. Kvint, what are your impressions from your contacts with the Bulgarian Government?

A: The first thing that I noticed is that Bulgaria is steadily going toward a market economy. However, Bulgaria lags behind the rest of the former communist countries with respect to privatization. On the one hand, this is good because Bulgaria has not yet sold its plants and assets below value. The bad side, however, is that the people responsible for the privatization program do not know much about privatization. They still estimate the value of the plants on the basis of the historical cost principle. This is absolutely incorrect from an economic point of view.

Q: How do you think this should be done?

A: I will give you an example. Let us take a plant for wine production. It might be very old, with bad facilities, ugly bottles and labels, although the wine may be very good. Therefore, the product should be valued, not the plant. The market price of the plant could be a thousand times higher than the value of its basic assets. The privatization should be executed using the market value of the plant in mind, not the historical value of obsolete assets. It would be very sad if Bulgaria repeats the experience of Russia—selling its assets for nothing. Following this path, nothing will come into the national budget. I would say that somebody is trying to build capitalism with decrees in the same way as communism was built in the past.

Q: Do American executives show any interest in investing in Bulgaria?

A: I would say that there are 59 countries in the whole world awaiting foreign investment that are actually ready for it. These are the countries where markets are currently being formed. There is a large capital deficit because these countries are trying to attract investment. It

Trud (Bulgaria), December 14, 1995, pp. 1, 9.

seems that Bulgaria does not understand this. It is not enough simply to open doors for capital to flow into Bulgaria. It is necessary to create special privileges for contemporary Western capital, know-how, and technology if you want to attract investors. In my opinion, the potential of Bulgaria is not evaluated correctly at this moment. It is not true that this is an unstable country where there are high risks for Western executives. On one hand, Bulgaria is considered not stable enough for investment, and, on the other, it is felt that after the war in the former Yugoslavia ends, investment will be directed toward Yugoslavia, not toward Bulgaria.

Q: Do you have any advice for Bulgaria regarding the privatization process?

A: I have met many representatives. They listen but they understand only a portion of what we are talking about. I met with Kalin Mitrev in New York. He understands what the problem is, but I don't know if he has any influence on the privatization process. In my opinion, it will be better, if people have a choice, to start with cash privatization and then include mass privatization.

Q: What kind of business do you think would be the most lucrative for a foreigner in Bulgaria?

A: Bulgaria has unique natural resources and can develop best in the tourism industry. This industry can attract enormous investment. This should be your number one priority. In some regions, the ecological situation can be improved, and international resorts can be built for recreation, business, and large conferences. Bulgaria can become the center of Eastern Europe. It is a very stable country and has numerous advantages; with resorts as number one priority, the second priority should be the wine industry, and the third, conferences. You have always demonstrated high quality but you do not have contemporary models or processes. There is also potential for this industry. In your refineries there is a shortage of oil; this is the primary industry that will attract foreign investment.

Q: Do you think that the American model can be applied to Eastern European countries?

A: The American and Western European models are absolutely compatible with the Bulgarian lifestyle. It seems to me that the people here have no idea about application of contemporary methods for governing. The problem is that the major capital in Bulgaria, from a few of the financial groups here today, will have to go behind the scenes. The firms that use contemporary methods will make progress in the future.

Q: Why do you think that the primary capital in Bulgaria is speculative?

A: This is because you do not know how to carry out privatization and you do not know how to attract strategic, not financial partners. Nobody does a market valuation of the companies that should be privatized. Ninety percent of the firms do not have balance sheets in accordance with Western standards, and even fewer are audited in accordance with Western standards. Here is what happens. They go to a Western executive and tell him that in Bulgaria there is a nice plant that they want to privatize and ask him to buy it. He says: "Show me the financial statements of the plant." However, they are not prepared. Serious investors who invest long term will not invest in Bulgaria. Instead, the speculator will come. He will correct a few things and then sell it again.

Q: Why do you think the left parties came into power again in Eastern European countries?

A: This is understandable. The economists in these countries are few because the economy has been under the pressure of communist rules and regulations. However, there were several groups of economists. Two Russians received the Noble Prize in Economics, including Leonid Kantorovich, leader of Siberian economists. In practice though, literate economists are few. The political goal was only to bring freedom. The politicians, who set Eastern European countries free from the communist rule, did not know anything about economics and did not orient themselves at the right time. Besides freedom, people also need economical conditions suitable for living. The cost is a significant increase in prices in Russia and in the rest of the Eastern European countries. The volume of production did not increase, and the standard of living for 90% of the population dropped below the minimum. While people wanted freedom in the beginning, they were later forced to vote for those who promised to take care of their everyday needs. Therefore, ideology should not be separated from economics. The democrats who brought freedom to the Eastern European countries forgot about economics.

UKRAINE: LIVING IN RUSSIA'S SHADOW

Living in the shadow of the neighboring Russia, Ukraine, Europe's largest emerging country, but one of the least known, is making considerable strides in reforming its economy and attracting foreign investment.

Some of its effort is showing results. Ukraine now offers just as many investment opportunities as Russia does. It is attracting attention particularly in the United States, which, without much media attention, has become Ukraine's largest foreign investor.

With hardly anyone taking notice, earlier this month, Ukraine, once among the five strongest nuclear powers in the world, voluntarily gave up the last of its nuclear warheads.

Although invisible on anyone's radar screen, Ukraine, sitting in the middle of the former Eastern bloc, will play an enormous role in shaping the political future of Europe over the next 10 to 15 years. It currently holds the European security hot seat, and its role and behavior are crucial, particularly when considering the future of NATO in Europe. In a policy move that could prove strategically significant for the entire region, Ukrainian President Leonid D. Kuchma said his country is not looking for NATO membership now, but instead wants closer ties to the Western alliance.

Ukraine is experiencing the longest period of independence in its history—it was independent for only two years between 1918 and 1920—and is trying to make the most of it. Foreign investment, mostly from the West, has taken off. However, total cumulative foreign investment has remained quite small relative to Ukraine's size, totaling only about $1 billion. The country sees its obscurity as one of the key reasons why it does not attract more foreign capital.

There are other reasons, however, including the challenging economic environment. Although the government has succeeded in getting inflation under control, the economy and industrial production continue to decline. In 1995, the gross domestic product fell nearly

12%, industrial production was down 11.5%, and agricultural output was off 4%, all from the previous year. Capital investment (mostly domestic) fell 35% last year. Production in virtually all energy sectors (electricity, oil, gas, and coal) fell, although less steeply than in the previous years.

Another major problem for foreign investors is the lack of insurers in Ukraine. Western insurance companies are not allowed to establish wholly owned branches, and are limited to a 49% joint venture with a local company.

The same 49% restriction applies to the ownership of banks and savings institutions, which is hurting the development of financial services. Ukrainian banks haven't developed to a stage where they would inspire foreigners' confidence. The government's restrictive licensing policy in the financial sector is largely the result of effective lobbying by domestic banks, which have been paying huge bribes to keep their privileged position.

There is another area in which Ukraine is making a serious error. The Ukrainian government is repeating the mistake of Russia by using book value, rather than market value, to establish the price of privatized companies and their shares. As a result, the government receives only a fraction of the companies' real worth, and the enterprises often fall into the wrong hands.

However, the Ukrainian investment climate has seen a significant improvement since the beginning of spring when Mr. Kuchma signed a new decree giving potential foreign investors a direct route to the privatization process, instead of access only to the secondary markets, as previously was the case.

As a result, international investors are beginning to fight for the best investment opportunities in Ukraine's military-industrial complex (90% of which is under conversion), sugar and oil refineries, high-tech industries, food processing, and machinery building (especially agricultural equipment). There is also a growing interest in the Black Sea port facilities, which, although antiquated and inadequate, are the best in the former Soviet bloc.

In addition to U.S. investment, which accounts for 22.8% of the total, foreign capital comes from Germany, which holds 17.3%, Britain, 6.3%, and the Netherlands, 6%. Cyprus is next, with 5.1% of the total, and only then comes Russia, with 5%.

The level of Russian investment and commercial influence, however, is expected to grow once Moscow begins to recognize the tremendous value of having property and investment in the geographic center of Europe.

In spite of Russia's preoccupation with political battling and its lack of a clear policy on investment in neighboring countries, it is Ukraine's largest trading partner, accounting for more than 50% of Ukraine's two-way trade.

American business is not sleeping either. U.S. exports to Ukraine grew 25% last year, reaching $225 million. But, Ukraine's exports to the United States went up 60% to $550 million, giving Ukraine a substantial trade surplus.

An investment in Ukraine is an investment in a European country with the fifth largest population, a stable business environment, market-oriented reform, and a president and government that, to their credit, have been democratically installed and rule by law.

KAZAKSTAN: RICH IN HISTORY AND RESOURCES

Kazakstan is a very young nation and one of the ten largest countries, by territory, in the world. The first is Russia. The territory of Kazakstan equals approximately all the territory in Europe. Anyone who tries to conduct business in the former Soviet bloc knows Kazakstan. But very few know the opportunities that lie in this stable and rich environment.

Kazakstan became independent for the first time in its history in 1991. Its land mass occupies roughly 12% of all former Soviet Union territory. Because of its size, the country has the lowest population density of all the former Soviet states, 6.2 people per square kilometer.

Even the nationality of Kazakstan was questionable in this century. When the Soviet government decided to create Kazakstan as an autonomous territory in the 1920s, there were two different major nationalities in the land, the Kyrgyz and the Kazaks. Although the Kazaks were in the majority, the land was named Kyrgystan. All official maps carried this name for 16 years. In 1936 Stalin corrected the mistake and renamed the territory Kazakstan (Kyrgyzstan became a separate republic). Only in 1995 was the new English spelling of the name Kazakstan (without the h) finally established.

When the Soviet Union was established in December 30, 1922, it was formed by bringing together five republics: Russia, Ukraine, Beloruse, Caucasus (which included Georgia, Armenia, and Azerbaijan) and Turkestan. Turkestan was a territory on which 20 years later all five Central Asian republics appeared: Turkmenistan, Tadjikistan, Kyrgyzstan, Uzbekistan, and Kazakstan.

Ethnicity

The ethnic structure of this country is very interesting. Officially the Kazaks, as an ethnic group, constitute less than 50% of the popula-

The Kvint Newsletter, 3, No. 7 (1996).

tion. The second largest group is Russian. A study I conducted in 1989 showed that Russians constitute approximately 46% of the population; only 42% were Kazaks. Current statistics show the mix to remain close: about 43% Kazak and 36% Russian.

A surprise to many is the fact that another substantial component of the population is German. In fact, Germans have a long history in Russia dating back to the time of Peter the Great. In 1941 when Hitler invaded Russia, Stalin expelled all the Germans living in the Volga region to Kazakstan where they were under guard. They remained there until the past six years when approximately two million emigrated to Germany. Even with the mass exodus, Germans still comprise four to six percent of the Kazakstan population, depending on whose statistics you believe.

Politics and the Economy

Nursultan Nazarbaev, president of Kazakstan, is on good terms with Russia's President Yeltsin, a point that is important to both countries. Indeed, of all the other 14 former Soviet republics, and even among all former Soviet-bloc countries, Kazakstan has the best relationship with Russia. Moreover, Nazarbaev has been able to secure good relationships with countries in the region. He was the first leader of Kazakstan to make a state visit to China and was able to establish good relations with all major Muslim leaders. Although he is personally against Muslim fundamentalism, he has visited Iran, Saudi Arabia, and Egypt. Interestingly, President Nazarbaev is also the first leader from one of the former Muslim Soviet republics to make a state visit to Israel, in January 1996. Additionally, as a result of its German constituency, Nazarbaev has developed a special relationship with Germany.

It is, in fact, difficult to overestimate the importance of Nazarbaev's role as a political leader between the Christian and Muslim worlds, or, for that matter, the role of Kazakstan in Russian–Chinese relations.

Strategic Military Relationships

Because Kazakstan was a major site for underground nuclear tests, it had a unique role in the former USSR's nuclear program. After the disintegration of the USSR, Russia was faced with another very difficult situation, in view of the fact that its entire space program depended on Kazakstan's Baykanur, the equivalent to the U.S. NASA's Cape Canaveral. In response to this dilemma, Russia signed a special agreement with the Kazakstan government regarding Baykanur, and, as a result, the Russian space program continues to operate there.

Natural Resources

The Kazakstan territory is extremely rich in natural resources. Kazakstan is the third largest worldwide producer of copper, after Chile and Russia. Two of the largest mining-metallurgical plants are Djezkazgean and Balhash (copper production). Kazakstan is a leading producer of lead, more than Russia and Ukraine combined. It also is a significant producer of zinc, titanium, and magnesium, and is among the top five worldwide of steel, chromium, pig iron, radioactive materials, and stone coal.

Kazakstan is not yet among the leading producers of oil. But its untapped oil resources rank fifth among the leading nations. Some of its oil resources in the western part of the country are producing crude oil, in cooperation with Chevron. Other oil fields are being developed through a concession agreement with ELF of France.

U.S.–Kazakstan Trade

In 1993 Kazakstan had a trade deficit with the U.S. of about $28.6 million. Kazakstan exported almost $39 million of products to the U.S., which included radioactive metals, iron, copper, fish, precious and nonferrous metals. It imported from the U.S. more than $67 million of products which included equipment and supplies for data processing, agricultural machinery, mechanical handling equipment, and telecommunications equipment.

In 1994 the U.S. trade surplus with Kazakstan had grown to $70 million. But for the first six months of 1995, Kazakstan exports to the U.S. jumped to $58 million; close to all of 1994 exports. During this period, Kazakstan had a trade surplus with the U.S. of approximately $14 million. Some of the most significant export items were pig iron, iron and nonalloy steel, ferrochromium, uranium and other radioactive metals, nonferrous metals, zinc, inorganic chemical elements, metallic salts, and copper.

International and Multilateral Institutions

Key to Kazakstan's acceptance as a trading partner and a place for investment is its relationship with significant world financial institutions. Kazakstan has been a full member of the World Bank since 1992, and is a member of all of the World Bank groups. The World Bank provides capital financing for building the country's infrastructure, which includes telecommunications, roads, and ports. In 1994, the International Monetary Fund signed a $179 million standby arrangement for Kazakstan. During fiscal 1995, the World Bank approved three project loans in Kazakstan, totaling $283 million.

Since 1993, Kazakstan has been a member of the Asian Development Bank (ADB). It has received from the ADB a $100 million loan and more than $2 million in technical assistance grants for its agriculture sector, as well as $20 million in concessional loans for the country's educational system.

European Bank for Reconstruction and Development (EBRD) loans are available for foreign investors in Kazakstan. They are distributed through three commercial banks there: Centerbank, Kazkommertsbank, and Kramdsbank. By December 31, 1994, EBRD had committed ECU 111.9 million for two projects. Kazakstan has observer status in the World Trade Organization but, unlike Russia, has not yet requested full membership.

Foreign Investment

In 1992 Kazakstan passed a law permitting 100% foreign ownership of companies including 100% foreign ownership of banks. Foreign banks in Kazakstan can be fully operational with both foreign and domestic currency accounts. For example, Chase Manhattan Corporation established a 50/50 investment banking joint venture in Kazakstan in 1993.

In the same year, Kazakstan became the first former Soviet republic whose parliament passed a law permitting foreign concession. In January 1995, a new law on foreign investment was passed, which augmented the rights given to foreign investors in 1990. The new law allows for repatriation of profits, grandfathers all foreign investment for ten years, and protects foreign firms against expropriation. However, the same law eliminated all tax holidays.

Kazakstan has attracted more direct foreign private equity investment than any other country in the former Soviet Union, including Russia. Commitments for long-term private obligations for Kazakstan amount to $46 billion, compared to Russia's $36.5 billion. By the end of 1995, the Kazakstan press reported 2,025 foreign joint ventures in the country. Most of these joint ventures were in the mining, agriculture, energy, and telecommunications industries. Foreign investment is authorized in all industry sectors except for the military. Furthermore, foreign joint ventures are not subject to export performance requirements, local content requirements, or restrictions on foreign personnel.

New laws effecting subsurface rights (except for certain mineral resources) were also enacted on January 29, 1996. The law dictates that Kazakstan and foreign subsurface users have the same rights and obligations. Rights may be granted by a license or contract, or both, depending on the use.

The new constitution does not allow private ownership of land but does allow for both domestic and foreign businesses to have long-term leases on land, and for the leases to be inherited.

As of January 1, 1995, most of Kazakstan's double-taxation treaties, which were carryovers from the USSR, were repealed. Treaties with Canada, Germany, France, and Japan remained in effect until the end of 1995. Currently, Kazakstan has double-tax treaties with only two countries, Poland and Pakistan. New treaties with Hungary, Italy, Turkey, the U.K., and the U.S. are awaiting ratification.

Of major importance to American businesses is the Bilateral Investment Treaty between the U.S. and Kazakstan. It provides guarantees against discrimination, permits hard currency repatriation, compensation in the case of expropriation, and the ability to have company/government disputes arbitrated by a third party.

Privatization

In March 1993, Kazakstan approved a privatization program. Although implementation has been slow, there have been some notable successes. For example, Philip Morris successfully took over a state cigarette factory in 1993.

The first privatization auction took place on April 29, 1994. In the first six months of 1995, 1,526 companies were privatized, but this was 322 fewer than were privatized in the corresponding period of 1994. Of the 1,526 privatized companies, 74% were small businesses, and 21% were agricultural enterprises. The majority of businesses taken private are in the retail and service sectors.

In the next two to three years, 8,000 medium-sized firms are expected to be privatized via a voucher or coupon system. Citizens can invest the coupons through a licensed investment fund. Investment funds are expected to purchase about 49% of the shares of these firms, while the rest of the shares are to be split among workers' collectives (10%) and the government (41%). In addition, about 280 very large or special businesses are expected to be privatized, but this will take place only on a case-by-case basis.

More than a dozen of the largest enterprises in Kazakstan that are insolvent have been put under temporary management, which consists primarily of foreign investors. The government has decided to sell 10% of the stock of these enterprises. Half the shares would be sold at cash auctions, and the rest would be exchanged for the investment coupons.

A Stable Investment Climate

Politically, Kazakstan is a relatively stable country, ranking higher than average among emerging market countries. But the level of development of democracy is lower than the average in emerging markets.

The former First Secretary of the Communist Party of Kazakstan, President Nursultan A. Nazarbaev, while a supporter of market reform, is practically a dictator. Oddly enough, this is good for Western business and entrepreneurs. They are investing in a country with a relatively low level of uncertainty and investment risk compared to the average worldwide.

Initially, foreign capital was attracted to developing the resources of Kazakstan. Telecommunication and hospitality industries were the next areas to become hot for Western investors. Now that Kazak-stan has completed the initial steps of internationalization, its politi-cal, social, and economic environments are ripe for almost any type of investment. Special support is provided by the Kazakstan govern-ment to help establish companies in terms of capital market institu-tions and financial infrastructure: stock exchanges, commercial and investment banks, and settlement, trust, and custodian organiza-tions. Basically, Kazakstan is now open for global business.

BRAZIL: SOCIAL DEVELOPMENT AND TELECOMMUNICATIONS MARKET ANALYSIS

Foreword

In the contemporary world, a strong connection exists between the development of the telecommunication (telecom) system and the social and economic progress of the country. This relationship is multi-directional. On the one hand, a country whose telecom system is well developed can benefit from social progress and an increase in economic achievement. On the other, the telecom sector is strongly influenced by that country's cultural traditions and political factors, as well as its business and economic environments. Based on this point of view, in order to properly evaluate the market's full potential, we need to give priority not to the telecom system, but to the economic, social, and political systems of the country. This is the basis of our study of Brazil as a market for telecom and of Telebras itself.

Brazil Overview

On a global basis, Brazil is the fifth largest country in the world, with a land mass of over 8.5 million square kilometers. With a population of more than 161.8 million people, Brazil is also the fifth most populous country in the world. Our projections indicate that population size will increase to more than 184 million by the year 2010. Population density in Brazil is 18.1 persons per square kilometer, which is low compared to the world average of 38 persons per square kilometer. At the end of 1993, the Brazilian labor force consisted of 71 million people, or the equivalent of 61.1% of the country's economically active population. Of this total, 66.6 million persons were em-

This study was prepared with the assistance of N. Podbereasky and L. A. Novaes.

ployed. Currently, there are roughly 173.3 million illiterate people over the age of 14 in Brazil. Of this total, 53.2% are located in the Northeast region, 28.5% in the Southeast. From a regional perspective, Brazil is the largest country in South America, sharing common boundaries with every South American country except Chile and Ecuador. Despite this, Brazil is one of the world's largest untapped markets for telecommunications services and one of the last markets in Latin America to be fully liberalized.

Brazil's potential in becoming an economic force in the region, given its vast natural resources and its strong domination of the continent's Atlantic coastline, has yet to be fully recognized after years of stagnation. The Brazilian economy itself, with large agrarian, mining, and manufacturing sectors, entered the 1990s with declining real growth, hyperinflation, an unserviceable foreign debt of more than $120 billion, and a lack of policy direction. In addition, the economy remained highly regulated, inward looking, and protected by substantial trade and investment barriers. Ownership of major industrial and mining facilities was principally divided among private interests—including several multinationals—and the government. Most large agricultural holdings were private, with the government channeling financing to this sector.

The Collor administration, which assumed office in March 1990, launched an ambitious reform program that sought to modernize and reinvigorate the Brazilian economy by stabilizing prices, deregulating the economy, and opening it to increased foreign competition. Itamar Franco, who assumed the presidency following Collor's resignation in December 1992, was out of step with Collor's reform agenda; thus, initiatives to redress fiscal problems, privatize state enterprises, and liberalize trade and investment policies lost momentum. Runaway inflation—by June 1994 consumer prices on a monthly basis had risen to nearly 50%—had undermined economic stability. In response, then–Finance Minister Fernando Henrique Cardoso launched the third phase of his stabilization plan, known as the Real Plan—a bold monetary reform program that called for a new currency, the *real*, which was introduced on July 1, 1994. As a result of the plan, inflation dropped to under 3% per month through the end of 1994, and confidence in the Brazilian economy was once again restored.

Cardoso was inaugurated president on January 1, 1995, and has

since called for the implementation of sweeping market-oriented reform, including public sector and fiscal reform, privatization of several key sectors, deregulation, and elimination of barriers to
increased foreign investment. Indeed, all these factors have thus far
contributed to a stabilization of the economy and the financial system which has set the backdrop for a new stage of development in
the telecom sector.

Brazil: Economic and Political Analysis

The success of the Real Plan, introduced in July 1994, is unques-
tioned. Inflation was brought down from approximately 2,300% in
1994 to some 9.2% in 1996, with the monthly inflation figures thus
far in 1997 suggesting a current annualized rate of 5.8%. At the same
time, real GDP growth is expected to rise 3.4% this year following
growth of 4.2% and 2.9% in 1995 and 1996, respectively. Real GDP in
Brazil rose a stronger-than-expected 5% year-over-year in the second
quarter of 1997, driven by a continued strong increase in industrial
production, agriculture, and telecommunications.

Since its inception, the Real Plan has relied on a stable currency
(based on a "managed" floating-exchange rate regime) to anchor
prices. This is instrumental in the development of a successful telecommunications system. While the administration has had some
success in tightening fiscal policy (with respect to state governments
and state enterprises expenditures), it has primarily been committed
to retaining its current policy mix of high real interest rates and a
strong currency in order to restrain inflationary expectations. As a
result of this policy mix, the Real is currently considered by many
analysts to be overvalued by 15% to 20%. Indeed, currency appreciation has led to a serious deterioration in the trade and current account balances in recent months. A $10 billion trade deficit is
expected in 1997, double the $5.5 billion trade deficit in 1996. This
rise exacerbated the current account deficit, which is now projected
to account for 4.5% of GDP in 1997. However, the deterioration in
the external accounts is not just attributable to the appreciation of
the Real. An examination of Brazilian import composition indicates
a high percentage of capital goods imports versus consumer
goods—a trend that is seen in developing countries as they look to

rebuild their domestic economic infrastructure and expand their exporting capabilities.

In the case of Brazil, the country has also benefited from the liberalization of intra- and interregional trade policies particularly with respect to Mercosul (the Southern Cone customs union which covers as much as 63% of the South American territory). This agreement not only will increase the role of Brazil's international practice, but will also have a special impact on its telecommunication system. Thus, by the year 2000, when Mercosul and its associate members, which include Chile and Bolivia, are expected to form an agreement with the European Union, international call traffic will substantially increase.

In light of the growing shortfall in the external accounts—which reduces the availability of capital for technological upgrades and services such as telecom—the government enacted measures throughout 1997 designed to encourage exports, and imposed various restrictions in order to discourage imports. Government officials, nevertheless, are optimistic on the amount of external financing needed to fund this shortfall, given the strong portfolio investment flows into the equity market, expectations for future foreign direct investment (FDI) and privatization proceeds. In 1996, foreign direct investment was $9.5 billion, almost three times 1995's level, providing little doubt that this rise is attributed to recent government reforms. Besides inflation reduction and the assurance of a relatively stable currency (supported by high foreign exchange reserves of over $60 billion which provides 12 months of import coverage), the government has granted attractive tax advantages to encourage foreign investment and to entice foreign corporations to construct domestic manufacturing facilities.

After generating privatization revenues of approximately $10 billion in 1997, the aggressive schedule of privatization in the next three years ensures strong capital inflows during the period. Indeed, with the privatization process of infrastructure in Brazil finally under way this year (with the first phase of the CVRD privatization and the Cellular Band-B concession), the telecom and energy sectors are also expected to generate more than $80 billion over the next several years. Not only do these very significant privatization proceeds create a positive economic benefit and environment for Brazil, but the specific industries being privatized are unleashing enormous untapped revenue potential for themselves.

Despite its success in implementing structural reform, according to our analysis of the process of political development, the Brazilian government still has more work to do. Important fiscal policy measures submitted to Congress—which include the reining in of spending by the municipalities in order to reduce internal public debt, reforms to the social security system particularly with respect to employers' contributions, and new taxes, of which the most significant is a financial transactions tax (slated to raise $6 billion annually)—have lost momentum in Congress due to political debate. While progress on this front is expected to come to a halt as campaigning for the October 1998 presidential and congressional elections begins in earnest, several successes as of late must be acknowledged. First, the amendment to the constitution to allow President Cardoso to run for a second consecutive term was passed into law. This has increased the confidence level of the international financial community that, with a second term in office, Cardoso will have the time to enact the necessary structural reforms in the economy and stay the course of the Real Plan. Second, the administration won a narrow victory in the Chamber of Deputies in gaining congressional approval for continued administrative reform. Although it is uncertain whether these reforms will become constitutional amendments, any progress on this front would strengthen Cardoso's ability to carry out the additional structural reforms needed to produce sustained economic growth.

In conclusion, Brazil has the time, the resources, and increasing political will to rectify the economic imbalances currently restraining the economy from attaining its full growth potential in excess of 6% per year. Until the reform package is approved and implemented, the economy will be characterized by "go–stop–go" growth. We think the government realizes that its credibility and popularity rest solely on the success of the Real Plan; hence, we believe that maximum effort will be devoted to maintaining control over inflation and the exchange rate, and so a maxi-devaluation is highly improbable. Although the current account deficit is likely to be in excess of 4% of GDP over the next few years, we believe that continued strong inflows of portfolio and foreign direct investment will provide the necessary financing for the telecommunications sector. This is supported by an improving fiscal account, political progress on reforms, a stable international interest rate and liquidity environment, and a financial system that is reasonably healthy.

Risk

Investors may be right to point to a worrying rise in the government's internal debt, and to lack of control on spending by state governments and to the possibility that the political climate for continued reform may yet deteriorate. However, they may underestimate at their peril the Brazilian capacity for economic growth and stability. Under the direction of President Cardoso and the Mercosul trade agreement, Brazil is quickly becoming an attractive investment alternative for foreign investment.

In terms of the expectation of foreign direct investment to Brazil's telecom sector, it is important to evaluate the risk of investment, We suggest using the Multilateral Investment Guarantee Agency (MIGA), a division of the World Bank Group, or a national analogy to MIGA, the U.S.'s OPIC (Overseas Private Investment Corporation) as benchmarks. All of these organizations use the same integrated indicators for investment in industry and services of emerging market countries. These indicators include (1) nationalization or expropriation of foreign property, (2) physical violence to foreign property during civilian disobedience, (3) or inconvertibility of currency. From the point of view of these three major indicators, we can then conclude, based on previous experiences of foreign investment in Brazil between 1992 and 1997, that there is a relatively low risk of investment in telecommunication of Brazil.

In terms of the 75 typical indicators used in order to evaluate political, economic, business, and technological risk of investment in Brazil, only one is higher than the level of other emerging market countries. And that is the level of corruption. But even this indicator, on a relative scale, is lower than that of Russia.

The Brazilian Telecommunications Market

The Brazilian government's plan to privatize the telecommunications industry is expected to raise a substantial amount of revenues and provide a significant increase in telephone services throughout the country. However, the repressed demand for telecom services, including wireless, will ultimately be constrained by the consumer's ability to afford these services. Unlike the United States, where approximately 98% of households have telephones, Brazil has fewer than 10 telephones per 100 residents. While this statistic is 2.5 times higher than that of China, it is still 8 times lower than that of Russia and the majority of Eastern European countries. In addition, income inequality among Brazil's southern, northern, and western states is high, as the country is highly stratified by class. The resulting degree of Brazil's economic stratification is evident in the distribution of telephone lines across varying income levels. Based upon 1993 data, households with the highest income levels, representing just 16% of Brazil's population, accounted for 81% of telephone lines. According to the World Bank, 32 million people (20% of the total population) live in extreme poverty, while the richest fifth of the population has about 50 times as much wealth as the poorest fifth. The ratio is 27 for Mexico, 16 for Argentina, 12 for Chile, and 12 for the United States. And although income distribution continues to improve, given the current success of economic reform, these data continue to be representative of the current situation.

Brazil can be characterized as a nation in waiting for "plain old telephone service" (POTS). Indeed, Telebras's operating subsidiaries are far behind in meeting the demand for landline telephones, with consumers and businesses waiting twelve months on average for new installations. For example, Telesp, which serves the state of São Paulo, is reported to have a backlog of 3 million unfilled orders for new telephone lines. And as the population continues to grow, the gap between the population and the number of lines installed will continue to widen. As a whole, at the present time, Brazil's reported national POTS order backlog is estimated at 10 million lines. However, if we were also to include the number of people who do not apply for phone service, the actual backlog would be 20% greater, according to the emerging markets statistics. In general, not only is the Brazilian telecom infrastructure inadequate to satisfy existing demand for service, but much of the existing network is antiquated and expensive to operate. The liberalization of Brazil's telecom market is expected to promote strong growth, as new entrants look to satisfy a high degree of commercial demand for dependable telecom services.

A Summary of the General Telecommunications Law

In August 1995, the Brazilian government ended the monopoly of the state-controlled telecommunication operator, Telebras. After passing the initial amendment to the constitution, the government had to prepare legislation for the institutional model that would be used to carry out the privatization process. On December 12, 1996, Communications Minister Sergio Motta delivered the General Tele-communications Law to the Brazilian Congress for review. The beginning phase of a country's development occurs during the initial stages of capitalization and privatization of the market. As such, this plan provides the framework for the privatization of the Telebras system, opening up the telecommunication sector to competition, and the creation of a formal regulatory structure to oversee the sector.

The Telecommunications proposal to restructure the telecom sector, which was made into law on July 16, 1997, is divided into three main parts:

- creation of the independent regulatory body, ANATEL, to regulate the services, monitor the concessions, and ensure competition and univeral access to services;
- reorganization of the 27 Telebras subsidiaries into four regional companies and Embratel, the long distance carrier; and
- development of a competitive telecommunication sector by allow-ing other carriers to bid and gain entry to offer regional services.

Though the law has been made public and progress is being made, several key issues remain, including the structure of the new regulatory body, the process and timing of the dividing of the Telebras system, the timing and methodology for rebalancing the tariffs, and the timing on the introduction of competitors to the region. Considerable time and effort will be devoted to this issue over the next few years, but this law demonstrates the Brazilian government's strong support for the privatization of the telecommunication sector.

Telebras Overview

The Telecommunicaes Brasileirad, more commonly known as Telebras, as a system represents the largest operator in the Southern Hemisphere and is one of the 20 largest telecom companies in the world. Telebras was created in 1972 in an effort to streamline the Brazilian telecommunications infrastructure, replacing over 800 municipal and state companies. By late 1993, Brazil had 12.79 million lines installed, 92% of which belonged to the Telebras network and the balance to five independent companies that had received concessions before the 1988 Constitution that granted Telebras its current monopolistic status.

The Telebras system is composed of the Telebras holding company, 27 local operating subsidiaries, and the long distance subsidiary, Embratel, which provides international and inter-state long distance telephone services. Telebras is responsible for the operation of roughly 90% of the telephones installed throughout Brazil, and as a state company it plays a key role in operating the state's quasi-monopoly on telecom services. The Telebras system owns approximately 94% of all public telephone exchanges and 92% of local telephone lines. The Telebras local operating companies also comprise the majority of the incumbent Band-A Cellular providers.

Telebras is governed by the Ministry of Communications, in conjunction with the Ministry of Economy, and must receive congressional approval for its annual capital budget, which is part of the federal government's annual budget. The federal government retains exclusive rights to grant concessions to provide telecommunications services in Brazil. Centralized federal telecommunications regulation in Brazil contrasts sharply with the regulatory model in the United States, where individual state regulatory authorities dominate wireline regulation.

The federal government effectively controls Telebras by ownership of 22% of Telebras capital stock and 51% of the voting rights. The Telebras holding company's ownership of the publicly traded operating subsidiaries ranges from 75% to 95%. The holding company's interests in the non-public subsidiaries are higher than in the publicly traded subsidiaries.

Market Analysis and Forecast

A review of Telebras's domestic telephone network highlights an annual average growth rate of 10% over the past eight years, with lines in service per 100 inhabitants increasing to 8.8, as of December 1995, from 5.3 in 1988. Based on the aggregate growth rate in the GDP of 10.7% for the next 5 years, and 8.6% for the next two five-year periods, we project that the economic growth rate to be 3.9% through the year 2010. Given this average annual economic growth forecast, we estimate that Brazil can reach line penetration with an upper range of up to 184 lines per 100 inhabitants and the lower range of as little as 114 lines per 100 inhabitants, with a median penetration of 138 lines per 100. Because the actual outcome depends on so many factors (such as capital inflow, number of licenses awarded, growth in number of executives, etc.) and it is not possible to predict there the exact change in magnitude, the actual demand will fall somewhere in this spectrum. Based on the compounded weighted average of the two scenarios, the total number of lines in 2010 will equal 266 million lines, including mobile, public, and fixed lines; we refer to this as the median scenario. The highest possible outcome of our analysis is 338 million lines according to the optimistic scenario and 209 million lines based on the conservative projection. This type of growth will also be evident in the rural regions where agriculture continues to be dominant component of the economy. As such, the respectable growth in this sector is likely to attract more foreign investors to regions that were previously not involved in international business and have a strong influence on Brazilian telecom.

The Recovery and Expansion Program for Telecommunication and Postal Systems (PASTE) identified among its goals the potential for a significant increase in the number of telephone lines throughout Brazil. Specifically, PASTE estimates suggest that on a nationwide basis phone service installation for fixed lines will increase by 13.5% through the year 2003. We found these estimates somewhat conservative. Although our figures were based on the original PASTE estimates, in our projections we also incorporated the impact of (1) line growth as represented by all lines including land lines, public phone lines, and cellular phone lines, (2) domestic and foreign investment in the telecom sector, and (3) "subsidy" financing (i.e., varying installation fees per region based on GDP per capita levels). In forecasting line penetration, we also took into consideration all telephone services, including wire lines (fixed telephones and public phones) as well as wireless telephones. Installed lines include main lines in service, including residential and non-residential lines, as well as inoperative lines. Our projections for the *residential line* growth were based on:

- population growth
- GDP per capita
- housing growth
- education levels
- crime statistics.

Non-residential line projections were based on:

- GDP per capita
- capital inflow (local and foreign)
- population growth estimates
- labor force statistics
- education and illiteracy rates
- industrial output
- regional development statistics.

We estimate main lines in service to be made up of approximately 75% residential lines and 25% in non-residential lines. We also determined that, based on current GDP per capita levels, out of 100 million adults only one-fourth could currently afford phone service. Thus, a tariff restructuring is necessary in order to satisfy current demand.

For modeling purposes, based on the above-mentioned assumptions, we estimate that fixed line service installation, including residential and non-residential lines, will grow to as much as 18%, with public phone growth lagging by 6%, by the year 2010. The increase in growth of fixed line service is a result of privatization, technological improvements, and tariff restructuring, whereas public phone estimates are directly related to the number of licenses awarded for public phone installations.

Penetration of wireless lines in Brazil will be higher than can be expected in a country with a similar macroeconomic profile. Mobile phone estimates were based on:

- GDP per capital
- the number of executives
- income per family
- crime statistics.

Comparing Brazil's cellular phenomenon with the U.S. experience, Brazil's cellular population penetration is already considerably higher than per capita income would appear to support in several markets, such as the northern and middle-eastern regions. Although we propose no tariff "subsidy" financing to the cellular telephone sector, based on the above-mentioned criterion, we predict that the growth of mobile lines will far outpace that of fixed lines, with cellular phone service growth averaging about 35% per year. Cellular service should remain increasingly popular, as its costs decrease with technology advances and the expected onset of competition. To consumers and businesses accustomed to waiting for a single line installation, comparatively prompt cellular service is an attractive option. These circumstances may facilitate cellular demand rates disproportionately higher than in countries of similar economic and demographic development. Thus, by the year 2010, Brazil may have on the median more than 150 million with wireless service compared to slightly more than 3 million public phones.

As of 1995, Brazil had 150,450 *intra-production* lines (as indicated by the number of extensions). Intra-production line projections were based on:

- GDP per capital
- population growth
- industrial and services development
- inflow of foreign capital.

We estimate that intra-production line growth to be as much as 3 times the main fixed line growth due to an increase in foreign investment. Again, the actual outcome will depend on the magnitude of change of all the factors and will fall somewhere in the range between the optimistic and the conservative scenarios.

Sensitivity Analysis

Historically, the development of Brazil's telecom infrastructure has been hindered by the government's tariff policy. Past presidential administrations sought to keep tariffs for basic, local telephone service low in order to help suppress inflation. Notwithstanding cross-subsidizing of cheap basic monthly service rates with high tariffs for domestic and international long distance calls, Brazil's tariff structure has limited Telebras's ability to capitalize on building a world-class infrastructure to meet the demand for new service.

Telebras's fundamental problem has been that basic local telephone service rates have been set too low to support a massive investment in infrastructure to meet the demand for new service. In modeling the Brazilian telecom sector, we have assumed that tariffs will be rebalanced gradually (i.e., local tariffs increase and long distance tariffs decrease) to converge to regional and subsequently international levels. With new tariffs, basic local service rates will approach a level that would support the costs of service.

In addition to continuing to rebalance service rates, the new tariffs will reduce the cost of new phone installation and eliminate the required purchase of Telebras's stock by the Baby Brases. By altering the current Telebras structure to a program where each Baby bras would be compensated for long distance calls originated and terminated in their respective regions, the more profitable subsidiaries will have to contribute a higher percentage of their revenues, subsidizing the less profitable operators. One of the key components of this proposal is to ensure that cross-subsidies are eliminated to create a competitive environment.

In addition, it is important to focus greater attention on the impact of the international call traffic. With the increase of the international emphasis placed on trade and foreign investment, the role of international calls cannot be undermined. The United States alone contributed US$10,300 million in 1995, a 54.32% increase in relation to 1994. Argentina is the second largest, followed by Germany, Italy, and Saudi Arabia. Furthermore, Mercosul, and the trade opening that lies behind it, will demand significant adjustment in the infrastructure and the international call traffic. However, in terms of development of international traffic calls we need to focus on the market as a whole, not on a country-by-country basis. As such, the market may be represented by the European Union, U.S. Mercosul, Japan, Switzerland, Canada, and all others.

We began our analysis by determining elasticity of demand on a national level to changes in installation fees, in order to be able to determine the Brazilian sensitivity to installation fees. We found out that on a national basis, the Brazilian market has a fairly low elasticity of 39%. We then created three scenarios with varying fee proposals and were able to see that the Brazilian market on a national level is not responsive to changes in fees. However, this analysis gave us the understanding that we must look at market sensitivity on the regional level instead.

We analyzed the installation fee change impact on line demand across various regions by introducing fee reductions (for fixed line service only) whose levels were based on differences in the standard of living represented by (1) income per capita, (2) housing growth, and (3) educational level of the labor force, and (4) crime statistics. We assumed the average installation fee in Brazil to be R$300. In order to make up the difference in the standard of living levels, we applied a fee reduction of R$100 for poorer areas. The difference would, in effect, be subsidized by an increase in the tariff rates introduced in the higher income states such as Rio de Janeiro and São Paulo. We kept the fee at R$300 in the south because we felt that this region best mirrors the profile of the nation.

The outcome of this sensitivity analysis had been just as expected—much greater stimulated growth in demand for fixed lines as compared to demand generated without the ruse of varying the installation fee level. For instance, in the northeast where demand is highly elastic (we define elasticity as a unit change in line demand for a given unit change in price), we found that we were able to stimulate demand by as much as 22% by the time we dropped the installation fees to R$200. Meanwhile, in the southeast, where demand is less elastic, the demand for phone service dropped by less than 5% in total when we increased the installation fee by R$25, or 8%.

It is our opinion that changing the tariff structure in such a way makes it possible to decrease the social and economic gap of regions through the development of the telecom in the regions. Not only will the industry be able to create a more homogeneous country by the year 2010, but the Ministry of Communications will no longer have a need to look for subsidies.

We also analyzed the tariff impact on line demand across various regions. We found that the full impact of tariff change on line demand was apparent in the same month the change went into effect.

We also noticed that nationwide price elasticity of demand is higher on long distance services as compared with local calls, where we recommend dropping prices in incremental fashion to bring them more in line with local call rates. For example, the effect of a R$.02 drop per year took almost two years to take full effect. This stems from the low price elasticity ratio, which implies that Brazilians hesitate to make fewer local calls following price increases. We propose gradually increasing local tariff rates to bring them more in line with social and economic development goals as well as international levels. This will enable phone companies to cover more of the expenses incurred in providing local telephone service.

The impact of a change in the tariff rates on international calls showed a 12.38% increase in demand by the year 2000, at which time tariff rates (based on our recommendations) will have been reduced to R$1.50 per minute. This is an extremely encouraging result, indicating marginal price elasticity of demand.

Conclusion

Demand in the telecommunications market cannot be evaluated solely by the use of traditional methods. Instead, the government needs to examine social, economic, and political developments which influence the size and potential of the market. According to our study, the Telecom services market has excellent potential in terms of traffic growth and line-in-service penetration. Furthermore, Telecom has great potential to improve its operating efficiency. Without the old rigid rate requirements, Telebras will have not only the ability to generate higher revenues, but the tremendous opportunity to improve its network modernization and expansion. Global competitiveness of Brazil will be strongly determined by the development of the telecom services.

Part III
THE EMERGING MARKET OF RUSSIA

Transition to a Free Market

THE LAST DAYS OF BORIS YELTSIN

In February 1990, Forbes published an article by Vladimir Kvint predicting that the Soviet empire would fall apart and Russia would go it alone. Most of the experts scoffed: It couldn't happen. The accepted view was that the KGB, the Communist Party, and the Red Army would hold the empire together. They didn't. Two years later the USSR expired more or less peacefully into 15 republics. Again putting his neck out, Kvint predicts that the Yeltsin government will soon fall and be replaced by a much more authoritarian regime.

Eighty-one years ago this autumn, the October Revolution swept from power a weak and ineffectual democratic government in Russia and replaced it with totalitarian rule. As it turned out, this was a dark day in world history.

Today Russia is ripe for another revolution. Weak and utterly rotten, the current government came to power by democratic means but is anything but democratic. It is a little more than a cover under which a gang of kleptocrats impoverish the country. Under communism, people had rubles but nothing to buy. Things are reversed now, with shops full but most people's wallets empty. If this be capitalism, most Russians aren't sure they want it. The situation validates for them the old communist joke: Capitalism is man's exploitation of man, and communism is the other way around. If that weren't bad enough, tens of millions of Russians are not being paid even their miserable wages. In protest, unpaid coal miners block the Trans-Siberian railroad for weeks at a time. Unpaid soldiers sell weapons, uniforms, even tanks and aircraft to any willing buyer: a pretty frightening situation in a country that still possesses thousands of missiles and a large nuclear stockpile.

You can't judge Russian prosperity by what you see in Moscow. One hundred miles outside the capital, a mere 20 miles from regional centers, there is hunger, and people are wearing rags. Tattered clothes and bread-and-potato diets are more representative of Russia today than the relative prosperity of a few big cities.

In Siberia's frigid Krasnoyarsk region (population: 3 million) the average wage is less than $300 a month, and Krasnoyarsk is a hostile place to stay alive.

Not insignificantly, the elected governor of Krasnoyarsk is General Alexander Lebed, the tough and disciplined military man who became a popular hero for ending the war in Chechnya. Whether the Yeltsin government lasts a few more months or somehow staggers into 1999, Alexander Lebed is Yeltsin's probable successor.

Tossed out by the Yeltsin government because he was too popular, Lebed was elected governor of the Krasnoyarsk region, which covers 14% of the Russian territory, by a landslide. He is relatively untouched by corruption and has to his credit brought an end to the fighting in Chechnya. He has been brutally critical of the Yeltsin government and of the kleptocrats. Although he himself is not an extreme nationalist, he could well come to power with their support and in alliance with Viktor Chernomyrdin, Yeltsin's former prime minister, who is close to Russia's communist-era leaders.

What would it take to trigger a coup d'état? Asked that late last year, Gen. Lebed told *Forbes*: "Maybe it will be a woman whose child dies from hunger or cold, who will carry him out on the street, and the crowd will explode. It's an unpredictable situation" (*Forbes*, January 12, 1998).

In that sense the situation resembles that of October and November 1917. The democratic Kerensky government was not so much overthrown; it simply crumbled. Describing the Kerensky regime, the writer Alan Moorehead declared: "It was like a body with no bones in it, like a mind with no will." You could say much the same about the Yeltsin government. "Bolshevism," Moorehead writes, "succeded to an empty throne."

Less than two years ago (December 30, 1996) *Forbes* explained how a handful of Russian bureaucrats-turned-businessmen were able to grab control of Russia's prime assets at a small fraction of their true values. By my calculations, they and their hangers-on have taken over assets worth as much as $150 billion since Yeltsin's corrupt privatization program started in 1992.

The tycoons and their friends and retainers flaunt their new wealth in such places as Cannes and Nice on the French Riviera.

Last year, as poverty spread through much of Russia, those two Mediterranean resort cities were host to 100,000 Russian tourists, three times as many as in 1994. They come loaded with so much cash that almost every expensive shop posts the franc/ruble conversion rate and signs in Russian as well in French.

As a Russian, it hurts me to say this, but I think the new government, authoritarian though it will be, will govern better and prove a better partner for Western nations than the present so-called democracy. I once admired Yeltsin (see "Who's in Charge Around Here?" below) and put great faith in him. Unfortunately, Gorbachev was right when he predicted that Yeltsin would create widespread corruption.

In Soviet times, the state exploited the workers by paying barely subsistence wages and using the rest of the national product for its own purposes. But the profits from industry, which once help fund the government, now go into private pockets and are neither invested nor paid out in taxes, leaving the government seriously short. In past times a government faced with spending in excess of revenues would rev up the printing presses and use inflation as a hidden tax on the economy. But the Yeltsin government cannot use the printing press. Its sole financial accomplishment has been a stable ruble that stopped hyperinflation—and with the August 17 devaluation, even that achievement is history. Thus Yeltsin and his aides have to finance the deficit in the most primitive of ways: By not paying its bills. According to Washington, D.C.'s PlanEcon, a research outfit specializing in former Eastern-bloc economies, the Russian state owes its workers 77 billion rubles, equal to one-third of all rubles now in circulation. Private-sector industries owe their workers another 70 billion.

How do people live without paychecks? They subsist on dwindling savings and the food they and their relatives raise on tiny plots outside of town.

Most experts and, of course, the government claimed positive GDP growth for the economy in 1997. These claims were based more on wish than on reality. Had the growth occurred, living conditions for ordinary people might have gotten slightly better and they would have regained some hope. But it didn't happen. By my estimate, there was no growth in 1997, and 1998 will be even worse. I believe

Russia will suffer a 2% fall in both industrial output and GDP, thus continuing the downward trajectory of recent years.

Agriculture is a disaster: During the last five years, livestock production declined, in absolute terms, to the level of 1953, the year of Stalin's death. Why? Because while the cost of inputs had risen sharply in real terms, the price of food has not.

Russia has a trade deficit this year for the first time since the breakup of the USSR. Yeltsin apologists like to blame this shortfall on low world prices for oil and other raw materials, but this is only part of the picture.

In a situation like this, the IMF loan is useless. It may enable Russia to roll over its foreign currency obligations but will not do anything for the country's underlying economic problems. It will not close the gap between what the government takes in and what it pays out.

Almost alone among nations that privatized, Russia got close to zero for the assets it divested thanks to the privatization program carried out by Yeltsin and his two main aides—Anatoly Chubais and Yegor Gaidar—between 1992 and 1995. Instead of selling businesses in open bidding at fair prices, they basically gave state-owned monopolies to a small group of clever opportunists, without competitive bidding and usually without first breaking up the monopolies.

Once basic industries like fuel, fertilizer, and machinery were in private hands, the new owners were permitted to push prices as high as they wanted. It was shock therapy, but the shock didn't accomplish what it was intended to do: Scarcely a ruble of the monopoly profits were reinvested in the economy. Much more went to places like the French Riviera, Swiss banks, and expensive jewelry shops.

In early privatizations there was the legal fiction that the buyers were paying book value, but this was a joke. It was book value unadjusted for the inflation that at one point in the early post-communist days reached an annual rate of 2,200%. So-called book value often amounted to mere pennies on the dollar.

Abetting the opportunists were the bureaucrats. A few months ago I was in Toronto with a midlevel Russian government official. He wanted to buy a briefcase. I took him to a leather goods shop where he examined bags priced between $300 and $700. He turned up his nose. Then he saw one with a price tag of $3500. He bought it—with cash. That would have been ten months of his official salary.

When the October Revolution of 1917 snuffed out the weakling Kerensky government, it was a tragedy for Russia and for the world. The communist government that followed was one of the cruelest regimes in human history. The fall of Yeltsin need not end so badly for the world, though it may cost many of today's new rich dearly. A tough new government must expropriate the tycoons' assets and then resell their ill-gotten gains in competitive bidding at prices that reflect true economic values. By my calculations, this would raise upward of $30 billion, and create a tax-paying industrial base. It would be a first step toward creating a sound economy that might be able to support democracy.

Yeltsin? He is so badly tainted by association with the kleptocrafts he has just about lost his legitimacy in Russian eyes. For instance, last year Yeltsin's son-in-law Valvery Okulov was named chairman of Aeroflot—a holding of one of Russia's richest new capitalists, Boris Berezovsky. Okulov's qualifications for the job: He had been an Aeroflot navigator. But few were surprised at the appointment: Berezovsky had financed Yeltsin's re-election bid.

Yeltsin himself may or may not have any hidden assets. But Anatoly Chubais has come under strong suspicion in the press for the sources of his money.

Meanwhile, former acting prime minister Yegor Gaidar was so thoroughly discredited by the privatization and price reform fiascos that he lost his low-level seat in the Duma in the election in 1995.

How will the end come? This is Russia and anything can happen. A military coup is possible, but the end could come in other ways. Yeltsin might strike a deal to step down (he is not a well man) before the next elections, which are set for June 2000. In the event of his early retirement, power would go briefly to Sergi Kiriyenko, the 36-year-old prime minister, who has no political base. Within three months new elections would be called.

My understanding is that Boris Berezovsky, desperate to hold on to his newly gained millions, has tried to broker a deal between Yeltsin and Lebed. Such a deal would enable Lebed to come to power via the ballot box. For arranging such a deal Berezovsky apparently hopes to be allowed to keep most of his fortune. He may be kidding himself. Lebed is tough and cynical, and at any rate knows he can succeed only if he can recapture the assets the government gave away.

So, forget those IMF loans; they are almost irrelevant. Equally futile is the suggestion made by speculator George Soros that the IMF and G-7 countries impose a currency board on Russia. Forget it. Unlike Argentina, say, Russia is not a country with capitalist institutions; a currency board will change nothing because it will not address Russia's basic problems.

The August 17 devaluation will simply make matters worse. As London's *Financial Times* observes, devaluation will take another big chunk out of Russians' savings and make its foreign-debt burden even harder to service. And as *Forbes Global* publisher Domingo Cavallo observed (*Forbes*, April 6), currency boards and other reforms succeed only when introduced by local leaders—as in Argentina—not when imposed from outside.

The 90-day debt moratorium compounds the problems. Having stiffed the world's lenders, where does Yeltsin think he can turn for new money?

What about dollarizing the economy? This, too, would not help. Russia already has more than 40 billion U.S. dollars in circulation, more than any country save the U.S. But ownership of these dollars is concentrated in a relatively few number of hands. Dollarizing the economy would make life even harder for those without them.

Smelling the end, many lesser kleptocrats are scurrying for foreign passports—hundreds of Russians have bought themselves residency status in the Bahamas and other Caribbean places. Canada also gets lots of votes.

Whoever seizes the vacant throne, it will not be Bolsheviks this time because communism is discredited here as nowhere else in the world. It is conceivable that Yeltsin will resign and Lebed brought to power via elections. But however the government changes, it will try to force through the social and economic reforms that Yeltsin is unable or not prepared to carry out.

Unwilling to face these facts, the International Monetary Fund, under strong pressure from the U.S. government, is providing new multibillion dollar loans to the Yeltsin government, presumably to save Russian democracy and to keep its nuclear arms in relatively safe hands. They will do neither.

It is not even clear that IMF money can postpone the day of reckoning. Where did the $50 billion that Russia already borrowed go? (There is another $17 billion in IMF commitments plus $100 billion in now-frozen Soviet-era debt.) Will the new IMF money simply end up in the Swiss bank accounts of the kleptocrats and their friends? These people have already grabbed many of the best assets that belonged to the old Soviet State and diverted to their overseas bank accounts a large share of the foreign exchange Russia has earned from exports. One of the first priorities of any post-Yeltsin government would be to bring that money back home and undo the phony privatization that was tantamount to grand larceny.

In running away, the new rich may save their skins but not necessarily their fortunes. Any future government, whether it emerges from new elections or from a coup d'état, will most certainly press criminal charges against the big guns and demand repatriation of its capital. There's plenty of precedent—Switzerland has handed back money Ferdinand Marcos stole in the Philippines, and has frozen the Salinas drug money from Mexico.

Look, therefore, for a renationalization of much Russian industry and a reimposition of many controls, at least for a while. The future of post-Yeltsin Russia will not be the American model of capitalism. Assets genuinely owned by foreigners will probably avoid expropriation since any Russian government will need foreign capital and will go to great lengths not to offend its sources. Shares owned by small investors are also probably safe: The owners had no part in the looting and paid market prices for their holdings.

If things go well, Russia could go the way of Taiwan and Chile: a period of authoritarianism paving the way for the establishment of democracy. But don't grieve for Yeltsin government when it falls: It is neither democratic nor capitalistic, but simply kleptocratic.

FIXING RUSSIA

In his speech announcing his nomination of Viktor Chernomyrdin as prime minister, President Boris Yeltsin stated that no one could have expected the Russian financial crisis. Soldiers and workers aren't getting paid, export earnings end up in Swiss bank accounts, and no one could have foreseen a crisis? The man is clueless.

The crisis cannot be ended by IMF loans or half-hearted reforms. It can end only when the crooked privatizations of the early 1990s are reversed, some controls reestablished, and the crooks who stole the proceeds from Russia's exports forced to disgorge their foreign bank accounts. This Yeltsin cannot do: He is the creature of the kleptocrats.

When Yeltsin falls—whether via resignation or by a coup d'état—his successor will have to do things that may be seen abroad as a backsliding to communism, but that will be a misconception. I do believe that money honestly invested in shares and physical assets from abroad and by ordinary investors at home will not be confiscated. To attract foreign investors back into the economy and to persuade ordinary Russians to invest their savings, both groups will have to be made whole—although foreigners who bought those now-frozen government bonds (GKOs) are going to be stuck holding the paper for a long time. Voiding the crooked privatizations and doing it again honestly and openly could bring in more foreign exchange than all the money that would come right out from under Russian mattresses.

I think, therefore, that sound investments made now in Russia will pay off: in telecoms—but not in mass media—in oil exploration, public utilities in some regions, transportation, high-tech and software companies, the construction industry, and a few reliable banks.

But know what you are buying. There is a big difference between companies run by Western-style management and publicly traded in the U.S. and those that are run by the old-style bureaucrats and their kleptocratic masters. Which means that companies controlled by Russia's new magnates should be avoided. These companies are

Forbes, September 21, 1998, pp. 70–72.

likely to be renationalized and ultimately resold, perhaps in part to foreign interests, in open tenders organized by foreign and domestic accounting, law, and investment banking firms.

On the other hand, several of the mutual funds managed by foreign firms, such as Templeton Russia fund, could be promising investments once Yeltsin is out of the way and Russia starts afresh. With their prices down 87% and more, there are certain to be bargains among Russia stocks.

We had all better hope that the change comes quickly. For many years, when Westerners asked me about control of nuclear weapons in Russia, I laughed, because these weapons were always in strong hands: Brezhnev, Gorbachev, Yeltsin. These guys would never use nuclear weapons. They loved life and the privileges their rank brought them. They had no death wish.

It is different, though, with military men who have not been paid and whose families have no money for decent food. Discipline in the Russian army hasn't been at such a low level since the last days of the czar. Soldiers have been selling guns and tanks and aircraft. What's to stop them from selling nuclear and biological weapons? Terrorists do not need to buy a nuclear bomb as a whole; they can buy them in pieces from different places. Chechen guerrillas have already threatened Russian leaders with word that they possess biological weapons.

Americans worry about the possible coming to power in Russia of a nationalistic dictatorship that might turn aggressive to make the Russian people forget their troubles. Not to worry. Even a military dictatorship would have an enemy close at hand: the pseudocapitalists who hijacked the Russian economy and stole the bread from Russian mouths. As recently as 1992 these pseudocapitalists were as poor as most other Russians. They had no capital and no access to it but bribed and muscled their way to wealth by methods described in previous issue of *Forbes*. They then proceeded to send abroad the money earned from Russian exports, leaving Russian companies unable to pay their workers. These people, not foreign investors, will feel the wrath of Yeltsin's successors. Indeed, selling foreigners a stake in the economy will be seen as the only real hope of putting Russia on a more prosperous path.

YEAREND—BULL RUN IN RUSSIA, EAST EUROPE MAY SLOW

New York, Dec. 12 (Reuters)—More players, more issues but lower returns are expected for the fixed income markets in Russia and East Europe in 1997, U.S. experts said.

Investors expect 1997 to be less bountiful than 1996, which so far has seen Russian debt double in value while Poland has risen 35% and Bulgaria 28%, they said.

This year's heady ride, of course, followed the 1995 liquidity crunch brought by rising U.S. interest rates, while next year's performance will be compared to the much stronger baseline levels of 1996.

Vladimir Kvint, senior consultant at Arthur Andersen Economic Consulting, said Russia's political risk has diminished with a succession of free parliamentary and presidential elections, and portfolio investments have risen to reflect the changing perception.

Kvint estimated that foreign direct investment would touch $3 billion this year, up from $2 billion in 1995. Yet he said he thinks foreign investment remains paltry if one considers Russia's wealth of natural resources, educated labor force, and well-developed industrial infrastructure.

What is holding foreign investors back from directly participating in Russia's epochal transformation? Long-term foreign investors still fear Russia's financial instability, Kvint asserted. He said a financial crisis could erupt in five months, noting that Russian citizens have been putting $2 billion to $3 billion worth of rubles per month into foreign currencies. Their savings—estimated at 25% of the gross domestic product—are not deployed productively in the Russian economy, he added.

Kvint did not expect Russia's economic growth to turn positive, as Russian officials have projected. Instead, he expected a contraction of one percent in 1997. Faced with mounting wage arrears and social unrest, the central bank may not resist the temptation to print ru-

---

Reuters, Thursday, December 12, 1996, 14:13:09 (partial).

bles, leading to rising inflation and currency devaluation, he said. The specter of devaluation could speed capital flight from Russia and reverse the portfolio investment flow, he said. This could prompt investment in East Europe to spread between large markets of Poland and the Czech Republic and smaller new markets of Slovenia and Romania, he added.

But Jaroslaw Aranowicz, senior European analyst at Freimark, Blair, and Co., doubted a financial crisis would happen in Russia. He pointed to the economy's resilience and promising progress on tax collection by the government.

But he agreed with Kvint's assessment that under-investment would limit Russia's economic growth, predicting a flat growth rate for 1997, compared to the official forecast of a two-percent rise.

WATCHING RUSSIAN BUSINESS VENTURES

While the world waited for the first stage of Russia's presidential elections, Vladimir Kvint was watching commercial activity more closely than the balloting. Kvint had predicted the breakup of the Soviet Union two years before it disintegrated in 1991, and he expected Boris Yeltsin to be elected president. What he cannot forecast is when the new Russia will realize its promise as a global economic power.

Kvint is a professor at Fordham University and an emerging markets expert at Arthur Andersen & Co., S.C., in New York. His analysis of events in Russia starts with a basic point: No country this huge has ever tried to so totally change its economic system. So, it is remarkable that Russia has made as much progress in six years, despite the resulting problems of crime, poverty, and confusion, he said.

"My opinion of the future of Russia is very optimistic," he said. "In 1987, there were 23 foreign companies in Russia. After the rules were lifted that limited foreign investment, there are now 60,000. Now the situation is not drastically better than it was . . . in 1992 when inflation was 2,300%. But without capital flow a country cannot survive."

Of 100 U.S. firms trying to create joint ventures in Russia from 1988 to 1992, Kvint found only 8% were successful. Among the failures, 28% cited the absence of a reliable partner with financial resources; 20% blamed financial problems; and 15% said they were victims of a bureaucracy that was in turmoil. One example was a joint venture by Du Pont Co. drafted by a U.S. lawyer that fell apart in Russia simply because it was written on the wrong form, he said.

In the period 1992–94, Kvint's survey saw the success of joint ventures double to 17%. The top obstacle remained the absence of a reliable local partner, he said, but other factors have improved. Limited convertibility of the ruble, privatization of huge amounts of land

Interview with David Wallace, in *Philadelphia Business Journal*, August 30–September 5, 1996, p. 16.

and resources, and a stabilizing government have improved the business climate. "We are working with a totally different country than we had only four years ago," he said. "I don't want to paint a rosy picture, but it is not what the mass media says it is."

News accounts of organized crime and the cash-strapped local economy have scared away investors and business interests, except for those with the deepest pockets. Riding out the transition period hasn't been easy for Russians or anyone else, said Nikolai Tchoulkov, the deputy permanent representative of Russia to the United Nations. He pointed to disorder in the tax system that has impeded economic development and said efforts are under way to eliminate the double and triple taxation that have plagued start-up ventures. The number of different local and regional taxes and their definitions are to be changed, he said. Regional taxes can be as high as 25% and a value-added tax can quickly turn profits into losses.

"Russia will be moving from net losses of investment dollars to a slow gain in the next few years," he said confidently. "Russia's imports have increased and export duties on oil and timber have been cut, some by as much as one-half."

The tax initiatives came after Yeltsin gave local and regional officials unprecedented power to deal directly with foreign companies, Tchoulkov said. Local governments want tools to reduce unemployment, create economic development, and assist their residents. And most local officials are viewed completely separate from the presidential elections—the way a city's election for mayor may be isolated from the party politics of a national campaign.

U.S. exports to Russia could reach $3 billion this year, a new high, said Kvint. Last year's $2.8 billion in U.S. exports represented a 10% increase over 1994—so companies are finding ways to make deals, whether through cash sales, barter, deferred payments, or other methods. Russia remains a risky place for business but an important market in the long-term.

After all, he said, Russia and its former satellites represent 25% of the entire world population that has only opened for business since the early 1990s.

Russia controls vast quantities of natural resources as the third-largest oil producer and the largest supplier of natural gas, cobalt, and platinum.

So, instead of campaign promises and other election year hoopla, Kvint is watching the companies who wait on the sidelines. When they finally get the signal from Russian voters that they are ready to continue with economic reform, then the real competition will begin.

RUSSIA'S IMBALANCE OF POWER

On June 16, Russia will hold its most important election of this century as its people vote to retain or replace President Boris N. Yeltsin. But this political puzzle, like all puzzles, has a clear, finished picture: No matter who is elected, Mr. Yeltsin will remain in power. The only question is what title he will hold—or give himself.

I will not predict the mechanism by which Mr. Yeltsin will keep his power in the framework of the Russian constitution and political struggle. I can only draw analogies. In China, there is a president, a prime minister, even a general secretary of the Communist Party, but power is held by Deng Xiaoping, whose only title now is President of the Bridge Association. Or one can go back to the 1920s in Poland, where Jozef Pilsudski, a hero of World War I, created the title Boss of the State after he seized power from the parliamentary government.

Mr. Yeltsin will likewise remain Russia's ruler in some way after the election (which could not conceivably, by the way, be won by the undeclared candidate Mikhail S. Gorbachev, whose popularity in the West is not at all matched in Russia). The communists in parliament already know the rules of the game and the limits on their power. Mr. Yeltsin taught them much of this in 1993 when he had parliament shut down by a barrage of tank fire. Democracy? No. But it did provide three years of stability.

Today, the new communists are staging a comeback. And while this does not threaten Mr. Yeltsin's power, it will, like his overwhelming presence, help shape the nation through the rest of the decade. New communists won about 35% of the seats in the lower house in Russia's parliamentary elections on December 17, largely because voters had had enough hardships from the "shock therapy" employed to build a market economy.

The communist resurgence has needlessly worried many Western investors. The new communists are not against a market economy, only the method used to get there. In fact, it is too late for Russia to revert to the old-style communist system, as capitalist institutions, such as private banks and insurance companies, have already been established and the country cannot live without foreign cooperation, trade, and investment.

This story has been played out in almost all the former Soviet republics and the countries of Eastern Europe except the Czech Republic and Albania. Many anti-communists and dissidents who came to power on the wave of independence in 1990–91 have lost elections, and former communists have returned to power.

Perhaps the most prominent example is Poland, where the anti-communist Lech Walesa lost re-election as president last year to Aleksander Kwasniewski, a former communist. Even in Bulgaria, where the dissident Zhelyu Zhelev remains president, new communists have won parliamentary elections and the office of prime minister, who holds the economic power.

These events show that while the people would like to have a market economy as dessert, they prefer to retain as a main course some social protections of the communist era and, of course, to have adequate wages. The election results in Russia are not an indication that people want to live under communist dictatorships, but only that their best choice was to return to office those leaders with socialist and protectionist orientations. The vote also represented a protest against the business and government corruption that has swept the country.

All this should reassure Western investors. In addition, the Russian parliament, where the new communists largely reside, has no direct influence on business in Russia or on business cooperation with the West. Only Mr. Yeltsin has that power, both directly and through the government of Prime Minister Viktor S. Chernomyrdin.

Most Russians know that without cooperation with the West the nation cannot expect to survive. They and their former Soviet neighbors know they cannot rebuild businesses without Western technology, managerial skills, and capital market institutions.

Still, these countries' efforts are clumsy. Just as the Soviet Union tried unsuccessfully to build communism by decree, so the new leaders are making futile attempts to build capitalism by decree. They began privatizing companies at book value, not market value, thus raising minimal capital. Soon, nothing will remain to sell, and they will not have enough money to provide the social protections they promised.

And so in the elections after 2000, these new leaders will suffer the same fate as their predecessors: the people will reject them. In their place will be democratically elected leaders who will have an understanding of market economics and who will not need to rely on socialist-communist slogans. These elections will mark the end of the transition from communism to democracy in post-communist countries.

ELECTION RESULTS IN THE RUSSIAN DUMA

As usual, the American mass media is overestimating political changes in Russia and their implication for business. The conventional wisdom about the election results in Russia is that the communists have come back to parliament. The communists won approximately 22% of the vote, the party of the opportunist Vladimir V. Zhirinovsky won about 11%, and less than 9.5% was won by Viktor Chernomyrdin's party called "Our Home Is Russia."

According to Western popular opinion, Chernomyrdin's party is the one hope to protect freedom and the market economy in Russia. Don't be misled. Remember December 1992 and January 1993 when Yegor Gaidar was forced to resign as acting prime minister, and the American media was unified in its opinion that the then new Prime Minister Chernomyrdin, the "apparatchik" and communist, would cause Russia to revert back to the dark days of communism. When I published an article in *The New York Times* in January 1993, I received negative letters asking how I could support the apparatchik Chernomyrdin! It is interesting that today he is viewed as the only protector of freedom.

This is the image the press provides. But it is misleading for American business. What is the reality? In 1991 when the Soviet Union disappeared, and the people spoke about a "velvet" (bloodless) revolution, democrats in Russia had not yet come into power. The highest levels of communist apparatchiks were replaced by second-class apparatchiks (a younger generation from the provinces). The appointment of Gaidar was a move typical of the communist bureaucrats. Who was Gaidar? He worked for a magazine called *The Communist*, the party's main public relations machine. When, as acting prime minister, he made serious mistakes, throwing 90% of the people below the poverty line, President Yeltsin had no choice but to replace him. Yeltsin then appointed the much more experienced Chernomyrdin, who served in the Communist Party, but

The Kvint Newsletter, 3, No. 3 (1995).

whose executive experience was in heavy industry, mostly natural gas and oil.

Definition of Communism

The term "communism" in Russia also has varying meanings whose subtleties the West does not understand. In Russia there is another Communist Party, "Communists-Labor-Russia-for-the-Soviet-Union," that is trying to restore the former Soviet Union. This party did not attract enough votes to secure a party spot in parliament. The "Communist Party of the Russian Federation" received 22% of the vote. Together with its members who secured seats individually and its main ally, the Agricultural Party, they control 33% of the seats in the new Duma. This group is not against cooperation with the West. Nor is there an agenda to take military actions in the world. What is its position? It's a socialist democratic party. One interesting side note is that of the six members who organized the coup in August 1991, two are members of the Communist Party and were elected to the Duma: Anatoly Lukiynov, the speaker of the former USSR parliament, and General Varennikov, of the army.

Through personal experience, I strongly believe that after 70 years of communism in Russia very few people (with the possible exception of some old-timers and a few young extremists) would like to rebuild communism in Russia. The overwhelming majority know what Stalin's Communist Party accomplished; at least 20 million people were killed or died in prisons. Is it possible to believe that 22% of the population would like to revert to that?

Voting Against, Not For

What are they voting for? The public is not voting for a particular candidate or party; rather, it is voting against Yeltsin's government. They are the same 25% of the people who in 1993 voted for Zhirinovsky. However, in 1993 they had no choice. They did not want to vote for Yeltsin (they thought that he did not care about the day-to-day life of people). Because Yeltsin sent his political rivals to prison, they voted for the opportunist Zhirinovsky. This election was different. There were 43 parties on the ballot. People voted for the party that paid attention to their everyday needs. Because the Chernomyrdin party, created only this year, was viewed by many as the party of Yeltsin, it was a vote against Yeltsin. All the hundreds of millions of dollars spent by Chernomyrdin's Party of Government Power were not enough to make people believe in Yeltsin's vision for the country.

Tactically, it was a dramatic mistake for President Yeltsin two days before the election to make a speech on television against the Communist Party. Yeltsin tried to show people how to vote by speaking against the Communist Party.

In Russia it is usual that when a dictator proclaims he is "against" something or someone, the people become united in their feelings "for" it. During communist times, when the Communist Party propaganda machine wrote negative articles about the U.S., people drew opposite conclusions. Yeltsin, from some points of view, is a dictator, and he intends to survive as such in Russia.

What the Election Really Means

What are the positive and negative outcomes of this election? On the positive side, it is important to keep in mind that ultra-nationalist parties such as Communists-Labor Russia-for the Soviet Union received only 4.2% of the vote or less than the number required to be in parliament. Nor did the Russian communists get sufficient votes to take over parliament. It means that very few people are voting for ultra-nationalists. The party of Gaidar also did not win any seats. This signifies that people are not voting for those candidates trying to be populists, and who are not taking responsibility for their inflammatory slogans.

One more note: Chernomyrdin did not lose; he won, despite a less than 10% showing. He had no choice. He could not distance himself from Yeltsin, because, if he tried to do so, Yeltsin would have fired him. But he is still a powerful contender in Russian politics.

On the negative side, people with strong economic programs and with an understanding of the market economy do not have sufficient political experience. Rather, opportunists like Zhirinvosky and the leader of the Communist Party of the Russian Federation, Gennadi

Zyuganov, have learned how to manipulate public opinion. This is a very negative result of the elections.

There is one clear message for the presidential elections scheduled for June 16, 1996. President Yeltsin is very unpopular. Currently he has no strong competitor, and many view this as very dangerous, because any opportunist who could manipulate public opinion could become president. However, that is the wrong conclusion to draw from this. Yeltsin is not a Gorbachev. He will not give up power, and the bureaucrats around him will not give up their privileges. Elections will take place, and instead of receiving minimal support from the people (like 5%), Yeltsin will win. He knows how to handle the political process.

What does it mean for business leaders? Russia has arrived at the same stage as Italy. Politicians are fighting for power and privilege, but business is going on and the market economy is developing. More and more capitalist institutions have appeared in Russia.

There are 3,000 private insurance companies, more than 2,000 private banks, 75% of Russia's industrial companies are in private hands, as well as 90% of trade and 90% of the law firms. This is the real guarantee against communism. Communists who gained in the elections know they are there for the moment. It is also in their best interest to continue to privatize business. They are using the political arena for their private interest, looking out for their income.

PRIVILEGES OF THE DUMA AND BORIS YELTSIN'S POWER

On December 17 there will be a new political spectacle in Russia: election to the parliament. Some believe that this is an important election, one that will have an impact on business, or be a prognosticator for the presidential election on June 16, 1996. This election, however, is of no real importance. The parliament has no influence on business or the power structure in Russia.

Recently, at a business lunch with a very prominent Wall Street analyst, we discussed the upcoming parliamentary election. I gave my rational for saying that the parliament has no influence whatsoever on what happens in the business community. The analyst's reply is typical of those dealing with investors whose information comes predominantly from the Western media, "I believe your argument, and even your reasoning, but I cannot tell it to investors because they are taking this election seriously. I have to play the game, or they will think I do not understand the political situation."

I do not agree with the opinion in the popular press, which places importance on the parliament. The parliament (State Duma and Federal Council) has no importance. An example will make this point very clear. Earlier this year, the State Duma had a vote of no confidence in the government of Viktor Chernomyrdin. The act was a direct reflection on President Yeltsin, because every minister, including the prime minister himself, was appointed by President Yeltsin. The day following the negative vote, Yeltsin told the Duma that if it cast a no-confidence vote again, he would dissolve the Duma, divesting it of all its power. The next day, the Duma reversed itself and voted positively for the prime minister. The members of the Duma understood their mistake.

The fact that the State Duma has no power is fortunate for the country. The Duma is composed primarily of opportunists and former or current communists, who change their clothes depending on the situation or political weather. This has not been recognized by

The Kvint Newsletter, 3, No. 2 (1995).

the Western media, because they are not familiar with the backgrounds of the members, and do not track their American counterparts. The overwhelming number of Duma members are concerned only about their personal power or their privileges, or about both. In Russia these two concerns are very strongly connected.

The semi-democratic election to the last soviet parliament we saw in 1989 was the last election of romantics. Opportunists and bureaucrats understood the rules of the new political game. Today, the parliament definitely does not represent democracy. I do not know who is an advocate of the democratic cause in Russia. Perhaps its strongest protection is a result of the development of a market economy. Even the former communists and "apparatchiks" (functionaries) have a stake in the new game and understand that power is in the hands of the president and government.

Privileges Are a Key Motivator

One of the goals of the new parliament was to take away the special power and privileges the members had during Soviet times. The result has been quite different. Current parliament members have even more privileges than in former days. First of all, under Soviet rule, being a member of parliament was not a job in itself. Members met only twice a year for approximately two days. Now membership is a full-time job with a huge salary (which they could never get in business because the majority do not have the necessary skills to be employable in private industry). Each member has a free office in the center of Moscow, free assistants (a minimum of five), 24 days a year paid vacation in the best spas, a dacha, an apartment practically free in Moscow for those from the regions, free limousine service, and special prices for food. There are even special tailors for members of the Duma. Yeltsin, as a former associate member of the Politburo, understands the value of these privileges and how to mange the members. Yeltsin knows both how to give and how to take away if they are "bad boys."

In October 1993, he demonstrated vividly what he can and will do, by dissolving the parliament.

Members of the Cabinet

Unlike the system in the U.S. in which cabinet members do not also serve in Congress, in Russia members of the cabinet are often members of the Duma. In fact, the members of the Duma who wear those two hats do have power. Many in that position, having been appointed by Yeltsin, are most interested in maintaining the status quo.

Members of the government are individuals of a much higher quality than those in parliament. They are doing a good job of conducting business in a difficult transitional time.

Parties Vie for Power in Parliament

Among the leaders who are emerging for the December election is Yegor Gaidar. He is the "democratic," former communist, son and grandson of major players of Stalin's propagandist machine. His party is called Choice of Russia. They have no chance.

Other powers on the scene include the Communist Party, the Yabloko Party that presents itself as the party of reform, and several chauvinistic movements with charismatic leaders like General Lebed. Among the secondary group, there is the party led by former Vice President Rotskoi (Yeltsin abolished the position of vice president when drafting the current constitution), and the party of Vladimir Zhirinovsky.

All these parties, with the exception of Zhirinovsky's, favor cooperation with the West. In the previous election, when leaders of viable parties were in prison and could not participate, Zhirinovsky's party received 25% of the votes. There is no chance that will happen again. It is likely that the new parliament will include members of the Agricultural Party, Women's Party, and various other parties such as the Party of Economic Freedom.

High Stakes in June

The real test is in the presidential election that will take place on June 16, 1996, four days after President Yeltsin's presidential powers end. The outcome of that election is definite and positive. If he is alive, Yeltsin will continue to be president or head of state. It does not matter what his title is; he is Boris Yeltsin. Even if it is a different title, he will remain in power.

He could use many approaches in maintaining his power. He could use the traditional approach of scaring regional officers by helping them have a clear picture of what could happen if he is not reelected. Or he could use his control over the power structure (security services and the Ministry of Defense) to ensure his power. Unlike Gorbachev, Yeltsin has demonstrated that he knows how to manage his constituents in order to win. And they are just awaiting his orders on how to be useful.

I remember how many people discussed Chernomyrdin's comment that he was not going to run for the presidency. It was never an option. If something happens in the next three or four years, he could be a successor; after that time a new leader will emerge.

I have very simple advice for the many investors who are focusing on the political fights in Russia. There is going to be stability. Yeltsin will remain in power if he is alive, and the Duma will continue to fight for its privileges. For those doing business, it is best to work with the owners of privatized companies, with executives of state-owned companies, with local and federal authorities, and with the office of Yeltsin, for those are the people in whom the power resides.

RUSSIA'S CRUMBLING INFRASTRUCTURE

Russia needs investment in modern technology and more financial experience from the West if it hopes to make a difficult transition from socialism to capitalism. But Russia will have a hard time attracting foreign investment without a transportation system.

Certainly, the big international lending institutions, which are providing aid to Russia, are paying a great deal of attention to its economy. Yet they have given practically no thought to its woefully underdeveloped transportation infrastructure, especially to ground transportation. A modern transportation system is crucial to Russia's growth, to developing its vast stores of natural resources, and to playing a larger role in international business.

For example, ships sailing from the U.S. and Canadian west coasts to Western Europe require 14 days of transit if they use the Panama Canal. If this cargo traveled via the Russian Arctic Seaway, it would take half the time. But this option is foreclosed because there is no modern port on the Russian Seaway. To take advantage of this money-saving route, American and Western European shipping companies first must invest in developing navigation systems and ports for the Arctic Seaway.

Russia's government also must find funds to build and improve roads. Although money in Russia is in short supply, one source of funds could come from a reduction in the military budget. The Russian army continues to have funds to build railroads, and could cut this expense by transferring the activity to building civilian roads and railroads.

Russia's crumbling aviation infrastructure also presents real and growing problems. In 1994, the air transportation industry suffered 45 accidents, including 14 crashes in which 299 people were killed. This compares with 53 fatalities in 1993. Not surprisingly, the airline industry experienced a decrease in total miles flown and a 12% decline in passenger traffic.

The Journal of Commerce, Tuesday, September 12, 1995, p. 8A.

The former Soviet republics are trying to renovate airports and air traffic control systems, and are looking for foreign cooperation. But foreign investment is coming in only slowly.

One reason is that no one has tried to place a value on potential investment properties. Potential investors do not know the real worth of investment opportunities. Still, a few positive things are happening. Recently, the United Nations Economic Mission in Eastern Europe decided to invest in the construction of an international airport in the autonomous republic of Kalmykia, on the western coast of the Caspian Sea.

By and large, however, Russia's transportation problems are pervasive, and they have led to a reduction in the volume of goods being shipped. The total decline for all modes of transportation was 75% in 1994 compared with 1993. This includes transportation by railroads, trucks, ships, river boats, air carriers, and pipelines.

The transport picture for goods headed for export markets was somewhat better. Those deliveries actually were on schedule in 1994 more often than in 1993.

For some goods, such as oil, the improvement was dramatic. Average waiting time for oil deliveries in 1994 decreased by 37% over 1994. The average railcar turnaround time was seven days, which shows that Russians are starting to understand the penalties for late delivery.

Still, Russia has a long way to go before its transport system functions effectively. Most of its trucks do not meet international standards. During the first four months of 1995, the number of road accidents jumped by 17%, and about one-fourth of those accidents resulted from the poor conditions of the roads.

In addition, the sea merchant fleet has not recovered from mismanagement under Communism. Delivery of goods declined by 17% in 1994, even though much of the Russian fleet was rented by foreigners for export/import operations.

With the disintegration of the Soviet Union, Russia lost most of its important seaports on the Black Sea. Novorossiysk is an exception, but it needs substantial investment to become a modern port. Fully 60% of Russia's ports are too shallow for modern tankers.

Gas and pipelines, too, require repairs and modernization. They have a crucial function in Russia's economy. In 1994, they were used to deliver 397 million tons of natural gas, 250 million tons of crude oil, and 15 million tons of oil products.

What role can foreign industrial companies play in repairing Russia's infrastructure? Above all, they can pool their resources via consortia to improve the transportation system in the regions in which they operate.

That will require a substantial investment of funds; a rough estimate would be $60 billion over the next 15 years. Even with that level of investment, Russia will not have a transport system on a par with America's in the 1950s.

Still, it would be a vitally needed start. Russia's transport system is at least a century behind America's. But Russia's economy cannot begin to move forward without a substantial upgrade in the nation's transportation infrastructure.

RUSSIA'S CAPITALIST INSTITUTIONS

There is no single Russia; there are many, and they are intertwined. There is the Russia of great opportunity, the Russia of political upheaval, the Russia of crime and bribery, and the Russia of entrepreneurs and executives trying to conduct business despite uncertainty.

These differing faces confuse foreigners who want to invest in this emerging market. Considering the Western media's preoccupation with bad news from Russia, a sensible business executive would reasonably hold back. Still, there have been enormous changes for the better in Russia, and many of those changes specifically benefit investors.

Among the typical misconceptions about Russia is that Western commercial involvement there is extremely limited. There is no truth to that. In 1987, when it first became possible to establish joint ventures with foreign capital, there were only 23 companies registered in the entire Soviet Union. Today there are more than 40,000 firms in the former Soviet Union; companies wholly owned by foreigners account for nearly 25% of the total.

During the first half of 1994, imports by these companies alone reached $4 billion, and exports topped an estimated $12 billion. It is difficult to get exact figures because many companies deposit some of their revenue in foreign banks to protect themselves against unexpected adverse decisions by the Russion central bank.

Despite numerous obstacles, the number of American companies venturing into Russia has increased. Between 1988 and 1992, only eight out of every 100 American companies that tried to establish a joint venture succeeded.

But the situation has improved substantially in 1993 and 1994. The percentage of successful ventures with foreign participation more than doubled, from 8% to 17%. The main reason was a legal change in June 1992 freeing foreign investors from the requirement to find a Russian partner and allowing them to establish wholly

The Journal of Commerce, January 25, 1995, p. 8A.

owned companies in most industries. The exceptions were insurance companies, railroads, and defense manufacturers, which still had to find local partners.

Beyond restrictions on establishing subsidiaries, foreign direct investors must consider the quality of the infrastructure for conducting business. This requirement goes beyond roads, bridges, and telecommunications systems; it includes the services of an array of capitalist institutions and service providers, including banks, insurance companies, accounting firms, and stock and currency exchanges.

The U.S. government has stepped into the breach to offer political risk insurance. The U.S. Overseas Private Investment Corp. has guaranteed almost $1 billion in private U.S. investment in Russia and another $1 billion in other former Soviet republics.

Earlier this year, the Russian government stepped in, too, establishing its first insurance company abroad. The firm, registered in the Bahamas, insures U.S. investors against political risk in Russia.

Before 1989, there were no private insurers in Russia and only two USSR state insurance agencies. Now there are more than 3,000 insurance companies. While only about a dozen are reliable, their very existence shows the financial services industry is beginning to grow.

Other financial services also are expanding. Russian banking has gone through major reforms since the end of the Soviet era, when there were no private banks. Now there are more than 2,000 private domestic banks and 25 foreign ones, including Chase Manhattan, Citibank, and Credit Suisse.

Another vital step on the way to a market economy was the establishment of the Moscow Currency Exchange in July 1992. The exchange is open for business four days a week, and the ruble has become a limited convertible currency. Today, individuals can buy and sell rubles in banks and kiosks in any big city in Russia.

As interest grows in the Russian market, effective information exchange becomes all the more crucial. The Iron Curtain was not just a physical structure represented by the Berlin Wall. It was a state of mind maintained by a lack of information, business, and otherwise.

Now, little by little, that situation is being reversed. Hundreds of institutions have expanded their services to provide business data. Itar-Tass, Reuters, the Associated Press, and Dun & Bradstreet, to name just a few, respond to hundreds of requests from Russian and Western business people daily. The U.S. Chamber of Commerce also plays an important role in exchanging information. About 150 different private counsel and information services have developed both in Russia and abroad.

Physical infrastructure, particularly in transportation, also is improving, although more slowly. The breakup of the Soviet Union left Russia with fewer than half its seaports. The unstable political situation there and in other former Soviet states does not make transportation within the country any easier.

A strong economy cannot be developed without laws and regulations to govern it. As a totalitarian country, the former Soviet Union was not concerned with protecting investors and their property. Business law had to be created practically anew, and it will take a long time to bring it up to the level of sophistication enjoyed by most Western countries.

Many Russian statesmen and lawmakers understand the need for a regulatory environment favorable to investors. They are hampered by a totalitarian mentality that still prevails in the government bureaucracy. For example, while announcing a general strategy to encourage investment, the government approved a draft law that would essentially establish mandatory government participation on the board of directors of any company in which it owns stock.

Despite such setbacks, Russia has made impressive progress in a short time in building a capitalist infrastructure. Potential investors should not be deterred by sensationalist media coverage of Russia's problems. They should focus, instead, on Russia's real advantages—including abundant natural resources and an educated work force—and the progress that already has been made.

CRIMINAL ACTIVITY IN RUSSIA: FACT AND FICTION

The notion that criminal activity in Russia is rampant is quickly making the rounds of potential investors. Whether it is real or imagined, the issue of crime and the power of the "Russian Mafia" is taking a front seat in strategic decisions on investment, trade, operations, and capital markets. President Yeltsin issued a decree at the end of 1993 initiating a campaign against organized crime. But this new problem continues to be a topic in the newspapers and on TV programs. What is the reality? And what are the genuine risks for foreigners?

The answers to these questions are inextricably linked to the failure of communism and the disintegration of the Soviet Empire into 15 independent republics. The absence of a central totalitarian government gave much awaited freedoms to its citizens. Unfortunately it also gave greater freedom to criminals.

The connection between a police state and crime makes sense on many levels. One only has to think back to the Stalin era, when criminal leaders suffered the same fate as the political leaders whom Stalin secretly rounded up in the middle of the night to be sent to prison or killed without the benefit of a trial. More recently, the KGB was responsible for tracking foreigners in Russia. Almost every step of a foreigner was closely watched. When I heard the song by the Police, "Every Step You Take, Every Move You Make, I'll Be Watching You," it reminded me of the KGB. But then foreigners were protected, even from street criminals.

An Increase in Crime

As everywhere around the globe, the rate of growth in criminal activity in Russia has risen over the past few years. Official statistics suggest a 52% growth from 1990 to January of 1994. By my calculation,

The Kvint Newsletter, 1. No. 8 (May 1994).

however, the rate of growth has been approximately 30% per year. The basis for the government's figure is shown below.

Types of Criminal Acts		
	Rate of Growth 1990–1993	Actual Numbers 1993
Muggings	2.5	516,000
Robberies of private house and apartments	2.2	450,000
Murders and assassinations	1.9	29,900
Rapes	−4.0	14,400

In all probability, the real number of crimes was much higher, but victims are often afraid to go to the police (militia). My estimate is that there was a total of 2,800,000 crimes committed in Russia during 1993.

In 1992, the first government program to fight organized crime was created by Alexander Rutskoi, but the crime issue was put aside when he became involved in the political battle for power. Later, in 1993 and 1994, when mass media headlines reported the deaths of 11 heads of Russian commercial banks, including that of the second largest bank, Rosselhoz Bank (Russian Agricultural Bank), attention again focused on the problem.

The Issue of Crime in Perspective

The image with which we are left, that Russia is a land filled with reckless hoodlums, is very deceptive. In terms of the number and crimes per capita, crime continues on a relatively small scale. Additionally, organized crime controls relatively small amounts of money. Many of the foreigners who are becoming victims are those who enter into relationships with criminals, who do not exercise caution. The fact that many foreigners don't speak any Russian complicates the situation.

It is true that since the late 1980s and early 1990s, Russian streets have become more dangerous. There is no justice system to handle criminals under the new democratic laws. Many criminals who are arrested on the street are freed the next day. Today, Russian crime mirrors that of America, and Moscow rivals some of the most crime-ridden areas in the United States.

Republics with the Worst Records

Criminal activity is not homogeneous throughout the Republics. Places like Kazan, the capital of the Tatar Republic, Tbilisi, the capital of Georgia, and several Moscow suburbs have always been plagued with high levels of crime.

Republics with weak central control, such as Georgia, have become very dangerous. For example, in 1993, an employee of the U.S. State Department, traveling by Russian jeep with the chief bodyguard of Georgian President Schevardnadze, did not stop when signaled by a young Georgian soldier. One shot was fired, directly into the head of the U.S. government official, who immediately died.

In Tajikistan, many criminals, including rapists and muggers, became leading members of the government. One of the muggers was even called "Father of the Nation."

From 1991 onward, organized crime first appeared on the streets, then penetrated the militia, and finally became intertwined with local government structures in many of the republics.

Americans Stand a Greater Chance of Being a Victim of a Crime in America than in Russia

Russian Entrepreneurs: True Victims of Crime

The artificial exchange rate between rubles and dollars made foreigners the target of crime. In reality, the main targets of street organized crime are Russian entrepreneurs and leaders of the financial markets. The first to gain attention were the babushkas selling wares on the streets and young Russian merchants; then the process of privatization of stores and public catering created new potential victims.

Entrepreneurship Open to All

After the breakup of the former Soviet Union, two new industries were created. Former KGB agents and militia officers utilized their training by entering organized crime or becoming private body-guards. Militia officers retained special rights to use their uniforms and guns after official work hours. They worked as doormen in restaurants and hotels, which gave them the opportunity to supplement typically low police wages.

Some entrepreneurs, particularly those who were affiliated with the Communist Party, became leaders of white-collar crime. The tremendous amounts of money they received from the Communist Party opened the door to illegal activities. Other leaders of this new wave of white-collar crime became "black marketers." For them Market Economy equaled the "Black Economy." Such was the creation of organized crime in Russia and the republics.

The Black Market

I recently met with the leader of a large financial group whose powerful private empire includes banks in Russia and abroad, insurance and consulting companies, trade houses, and construction organizations. I asked him where he received his initial capital. He responded, "Black Money, but no one can prove it." The construction business provides him with about $1 million a month, and by laundering money through his other businesses he justifies his income.

The Closer One Is to Cash, the Greater the Likelihood of Becoming a Target

Usually, the first clue to participation in unsavory organizations is a fancy brand name watch, worth 410,000 rubles or more, and expensive Italian clothes. How any Russian could buy a Rolls Royce with honest money is a mystery.

The most dangerous situation occurs when government authorities and especially state-owned companies fall into the hands of bribe-giving criminals.

Criminals Participate in Privatization

The first signs of privatization appeared in 1987 and 1988, when entrepreneurs opened a few stores and cafeterias. Criminals were not ready to participate. Between 1989 and 1991, however, kiosks began to appear selling everything from underwear to pants and other goods that were in short supply. Criminal groups, for the first time, organized to control different markets. It was a time of violent, bloody street-fighting.

Today, the typical criminal has become more sophisticated. When privatization of small businesses became commonplace, a new area of activity, racketeering, opened to criminals. Its focus was almost exclusively on cash businesses. Kidnapping became a regular occurrence. The militia was not prepared for this new level of crime, as its weapons had become obsolete, and its cars were too slow. Further, because of the large sums of money involved, bribery of the police became a common practice.

The real big-money crime, however, is white-collar crime in connection with the privatization process. The criminals seek help from the officials in achieving two goals: to set the valuation of a particular factory that they would like to buy at as low a price as possible, and to complete the privatization without competition. At the federal level, only the scale is larger.

New Structure to Face Problems

In an effort to stem the tide of criminal activity, the militia was restructured in late 1992. For the first time, the militia joined Interpol. But Interpol was naïve and even gave commendations to individuals with criminal connections.

While the militia was restructuring, the first capitalist institutions appeared in Russia: private banks, trading houses, commodity and stock exchanges, and small insurance companies. But regulations to govern the operation of capital markets did not appear in any of the former Soviet-bloc countries until 1994. As a result, activities of capitalist institutions were often in conflict with normal Western business protocol, leaving the door open for white-collar crime.

White-Collar Crime

Also of great concern are the former bureaucrats with white-collar experience in Russia who left with large sums of black-market money. These people are engaging in international crime that is more difficult to detect and stop.

Special criminal investigations began in 1992 concerning former Communist Party funds. At that item, the Russian government hired several investigation companies including Manhattan-based Krill and Associates. Although public statements were made exposing large sums of communist money, I'm not sure how accurate they were. Recently, one such investigation company in Russia reported it has statistics on how many tons of gold and platinum the Communist Party sent abroad.

The Criminal Problem Is Overrated

While crime is a serious problem, it would be wrong, even absurd, to overestimate its influence. A vast majority of people are trying to build and operate businesses honestly, under difficult circumstances.

One way to reduce the risk of corruption is to heed the advice of Senator Howard Baker, Jr., former White House Chief of Staff. In a recent conversation, Mr. Baker, who created the merchant banking company Newstar, Inc., to invest in Russian projects, suggested investors stay away from high-profile projects, because they are under a high level of bureaucratic control and are often connected with bribes.

A substantial percentage of projects involving bribes are in hard currency materials such as oil and oil products, natural gas, fertilizer, nonferrous metals (especially aluminum, nickel, copper), and to a lesser extent precious metals. In these deals, bribes are given to bureaucrats to secure issuance of export licenses and an increase in export quotas. Trade negotiations are based on world prices. However, in order to justify the lower prices that are achieved through bribing officials, problems such as poor quality of products and shipping delays are raised. The result is a 30%–40% drop in prices.

Protecting Business Ventures

One of the ways to protect a venture is to exercise due diligence on the source of initial funding. This is particularly important when dealing with private companies, small banks, insurance, or industrial companies. Checking should also be done with the Russian banks and with government authorities.

Since cash is the target of organized crime, it is best to limit exposure. For example, employee salaries can be paid by direct transfer of funds. Today, all major credit cards are available in Russia, and more than $0.5 billion of credit card money was spent last year. Remember, not all public officials or police are corrupt. Problems should be reported not only to local officials but also directly to the Ministry of Internal Affairs. Foreigner complaints are given much quicker attention.

NEW RUBLE ZONE DOOMED, EXPERTS ON RUSSIA SAY

"Russian economic and financial policies are not stable or honest. Why should anybody want to follow Moscow's lead?"

The pact signed this month by Russia and five former Soviet republics to form a new ruble zone is doomed, Russian specialists and economists said.

The agreement to create an economic and monetary union with the ruble as a common currency would require the republics to bow to Russian demands on fiscal and monetary policy, they said.

"Russian economic and financial policies are not stable or honest," said Vladimir Kvint, Russia specialist, economist, and professor of management systems and international business at Fordham University in New York. "Why would anybody want to follow Moscow's lead?"

The new ruble zone will only be temporary because it will fall apart, said Mr. Kvint, who also is a senior consultant with Arthur Andersen & Co., which has 300 people in the former Soviet Union to provide consulting and accounting services.

The Commonwealth of Independent States "has no government and no president; it's just a piece of paper," he said.

The ruble-zone agreement signed September 7 includes Russia, Armenia, Belarus, Kazakstan, Tajikistan and Uzbekistan. The plan to unify banking, tax, and customs systems is designed to help the Russian Central Bank gain control of the supply of rubles in order to dampen inflation. In the past, the money supply of the member republics was determined by national actions that were not coordinated.

"Some of the republics with relatively good economic situations didn't sign the pact," Mr. Kvint said. He said that Turkmenistan, for example, has been successful with its own currency.

The Journal of Commerce, Tuesday, September 14, 1993 (partial article).

RUSSIAN EXPERT ADDRESSES COMMUNITY GROUP AND FACULTY: PROFESSOR, CONSULTANT, AND AUTHOR VLADIMIR KVINT ON CAMPUS

Vladimir Kvint is an internationally recognized specialist on the economy and natural resources of Russia and other former Soviet Republics. A professor at Fordham University and a senior consultant at Arthur Andersen Economic Consulting, Kvint spoke before the California–Russia Trade Association at Whittier Law School September 21, and addressed Whittier Law School faculty on September 22.

Kvint was on tour to support his new book, *The Barefoot Shoemaker: Capitalizing on the New Russia*, a contemporary examination of the Russian economy and the social, geographical, and historical forces that drive it.

Vladimir Kvint was the keynote speaker at Whittier's International Law Symposium in 1990 following a cover story he wrote for *Forbes* magazine in which he predicted the collapse of the Soviet Union and the rise of Boris Yeltsin to power. Since then he has become one of the most sought experts on trade with the former Soviet Republics.

On September 21, addressing the California–Russia Trade Association, Kvint brought to light the many advantages of trading with the new republics. For example, it is two and one-half-times more efficient to ship goods from American west coast seaports to Western Europe using the Russian Arctic Seaway than to cross the Atlantic via the Panama Canal. Also, many companies are taking advantage of the low cost of manufacturing in the new republics, including South Korea's Hyundai Corporation and Goldstar Corporation. Most important, according to Kvint, is that Russia is a new, untapped mar-

Law School News (Whittier Law School) 12, No. 1 (Fall 1993).

ket where goods can be manufactured and sold. Kvint contends that any government maneuvers will not affect foreign business interests in the long run. "It is inevitable that Russia will become part of the international business community," he said. "Political fights are absolutely not connected with business negotiations with the West."

As if to challenge this point, later that afternoon Russian President Boris Yeltsin abolished the parliament to gain more power. Parliament in turn impeached Yeltsin and promoted Vice President Aleksandr Rutskoi to President. Russia's Constitutional Court, which is in place to preserve the constitution and act as a check to the executive branch of the President, declared that Yeltsin's move to disband parliament was unconstitutional, and that parliament's impeachment of Yeltsin was valid.

The next morning Kvint spoke to law school faculty at a breakfast meeting, explaining the economic ramifications of these political moves. He said that violating the constitution in order to obtain power or privileges has many historical precedents. Peter the Great, for example, killed many people by his own hand and violated the constitution to expand Russian interests into Eastern Europe. Lenin and Stalin constantly violated the Russian constitution to achieve their ends.

"Stalin's motto was: 'Where there is a person, there is a problem,'" Kvint relayed. "Stalin eliminated 40 million problems." He perceived that Yeltsin dismissed parliament because they stood in the way of his reforms, but that a radical change in government was highly unlikely.

Although there is still great unrest in the former Soviet republics, Kvint perceives these kinds of constitutional crises as growing pains. In the Soviet Union, 97% of business was controlled by the government. Russia is now moving rapidly toward privatization, with, for example, over 300,000 private farms being sold to individual Russians. He concluded, "If the KGB, the Communist Party, and the Militia cannot stifle capitalization, it [political in-fighting] will not affect negotiations with the West."

Kvint has gained fame through his predictions, and he offered the following to the faculty: that Yeltsin will win the elections in the spring; that he will attempt to abolish the Constitutional Court; that Russia will continue to move toward a more open economy; and that personal freedoms will continue to grow in the former Soviet Union.

RUSSIAN DIAMONDS

Boris Yeltsin does not consider himself bound to deals made by Mikhail Gorbachev—as Harry Oppenheimer and De Beers are learning.

Harry Oppenheimer and his son Nicholas were in Moscow early last September. The Oppenheimers control De Beers Consolidated Mines Ltd. and were there for the opening of De Beers's first Moscow office.

De Beers, South Africa's giant mining company and marketer of diamonds, is the world's largest producer of diamonds. Through its Central Selling Organization cartel, De Beers has long controlled the prices and supply of raw diamonds to cutters and polishers around the world. Russia, the world's second-largest producer of diamonds (after South Africa), is important to De Beers.

According to top Russian officials, the Oppenheimers were scheduled to meet with Boris Yeltsin, the prime minister, and other top Russian officials, but at the last minute the appointments were canceled. The snub was apparently deliberate: It was a Russian way of telling De Beers it wanted more money for its diamonds than it had gotten in the past. (De Beers's spokeswoman denies appointments were scheduled but confirms that no top-level meetings took place.)

Not that De Beers needed reminding that it needs the Russians. Angola, one of the world's largest diamond producers, virtually stopped doing business with the Central Selling Organization in the late 1980s. De Beers's operatives have been scrambling to avoid losing the vital Russian diamond production.

In 1990 De Beers signed a five-year deal with Mikhail Gorbachev's government promising De Beers 95% of all Russia's raw diamond production. De Beers agreed to pay $5 billion over the life of the deal.

But Gorbachev is out, and Boris Yeltsin apparently wants more. Under the Gorbachev agreement, the Russians receive from De Beers an average price of approximately $68 per carat, Yeltsin figures he can do better. He knows that last year De Beers paid $205 per carat for uncut diamonds it purchased directly from Yakutia, the eastern Siberian region that accounts for most of Russia's diamonds. The Yakutian diamonds were of higher quality, but not three times better.

Yeltsin has an out. De Beers's 1990 deal cut with Gorbachev says only that Russia must sell 95% of its uncut diamonds to De Beers. It says nothing of cut and polished stones. What Russia will probably now do is start cutting and polishing more diamonds rather than delivering them raw to De Beers.

Russia already has several diamond-cutting and -polishing plants. Three of them—in Smolensk, Moscow, and the city of Barnaul, in western Siberia—have modern equipment and experienced cutters. Aware of the possibilities, several small Japanese, Israeli, Dutch, and American firms are trying to create joint ventures with the Russian cutting plants.

If the Russians are playing rough with De Beers, it's because they badly need foreign exchange. With their gold holdings dwindled, diamonds (together with platinum) remain Russia's major quick potential source of more hard currency. Squeezing more money out of De Beers is one way to get it. Adding value through cutting and polishing is another.

From the end of World War II until early 1990, the Soviet Union sold almost no diamonds in the 5-to-10–carat range, and no diamonds larger than 10 carats. When they were found, such treasures were kept in the Russian State Diamond Fund. Worth billions, the trove includes such mammoth stones as the 232-carat "Star of Yakutia" and the 332-carat "XXVI Congress of the CPSU."

As it begins to sell off its big stones, Russia will need to cooperate with Westerners. That's because the market is highly specialized, and customers want their diamonds rough or cut and polished to their specifications.

On the prowl for large uncut stones is Maurice Tempelsman. Working out of Paris and New York, Tempelsman lines up a buyer for a large stone, locates the stone in Russia, then gives the Russians the designs for cutting and polishing the stone.

With most uncut stones, however, De Beers is still in control. Last year Yeltsin's government signed an agreement with officials from Yakutia (now Sakha). It says employees and managers of Yakutia's diamond mines and factories will retain ownership of 23% of the proceeds; Sakha/Yakutia's regional government and local authorities get 40%; the Russian government, and government funds, such as the armed forces' social security fund, get 37%. De Beers figures it will end up as marketing agent for all three groups.

To further strengthen ties with the local government, De Beers agreed to help build a diamond-cutting plant in Sakha called Polar Star.

Clearly, De Beers is doing everything in its power to retain control over Russia's diamond output. But that big X in President Yeltsin's appointment book suggests that the Russians are going to be driving increasingly hard bargains.

A HEALTHY REALISM FOR THE RUSSIANS

For 40 years I lived in Russia, where communist propaganda bombarded people with images of the United States as the enemy. But this was largely ineffective, since most Russians distrusted such information. Only now that I am in the United States do I understand just how effective media propaganda can be.

A case in point: After Yegor T. Gaidar was replaced as Russian prime minister last year by Viktor S. Chernomyrdin, the American media routinely used negative labels like "former apparatchik" in referring to Mr. Chernomyrdin, while asserting that under Mr. Gaidar's leadership, a revolutionary shift to capitalism was taking place.

These views are incorrect. There is only one true revolutionary among Russian leaders, and that is Boris Yeltsin. But while revolution may bring down an old system, it does not create a market economy. Mr. Gaidar did not privatize a single large enterprise. People simply cannot be ordered to capitalism by executive fiat.

More to the point, Mr. Gaidar had no relevant experience. While Mr. Yeltsin is a great politician, he has at least one serious drawback—an inability to admit mistakes. And he made a mistake when he appointed Mr. Gaidar.

First, Mr. Gaidar had essentially worked in only one place, at the magazine *The Communist*. Still, the American media dubbed him "the progressive leader of economic reform in Russia."

In addition, Mr. Gaidar never worked in Russian industry and had no understanding of the Russian economy. He was educated at the Department of the Economic Geography of Foreign Countries at Moscow University, a privileged school mainly for children of high party officials and Politburo members. His doctoral thesis, about managers' workstyles, was not a dissertation on economics. He began his economic education only when he became prime minister. No country, especially Russia, can afford such on-the-job training.

Mr. Chernomyrdin also served the party machine for several years, but a critical difference is that he earned his position the hard way, advancing because of his achievements. Starting as a laborer in a petrochemical plant, he worked his way up to being minister of the Soviet gas industry. When the Russian economy was in a bad slide, Mr. Chernomyrdin bucked the tide by finding the means to increase production, not cut it.

Mr. Chernomyrdin and Mr. Gaidar do have much in common, including favoring a market economy. But only a few old-timers remain who fail to grasp that Russia has no alternative.

The essential difference between the two is that Mr. Chernomyrdin knows from experience what tough choices must be made, understands the economy, and has true managerial experience. His choice of executive deputy prime minister was excellent: the best and youngest Russian financial expert, Boris Fedorev. Unlike Mr. Gaidar. Mr. Fedorov has broad experience in Russian banking as well as with the European Bank for Reconstruction and Development and the World Bank. Mr. Chernomyrdin and his deputy know it is impossible to help Russia without broad involvement in the world economy.

Mr. Chernomyrdin inherits a catastrophic Russian economy, in far worse shape than when Mr. Gaidar became acting prime minister. Mr. Gaidar, following the advice of a Harvard professor, Jeffrey Sachs—also ignorant about the Russian economy but hired because of his American credentials—enacted disastrous reform policies.

Their reforms were based on liberalizing prices, but when property belongs to the state monopoly, that amounts to nothing more than the monopolization of price increases. Thanks to this "serious and deeply thought policy," about 95% of Russians now find themselves living below the poverty level and inflation is running wild.

I hasten to stress that it was necessary to start reforms, and affirm that I am no supporter of the hard-liners. But only after property belongs to workers can prices be liberalized. It was Mr. Gaidar and his supporters who brought devastation to Russia's first 200,000 private farmers, who faced bankruptcy when prices for industrial products rose well beyond their reach.

Now that Mr. Yeltsin has appointed Mr. Chernomyrdin, he is much stronger than when the unrealistic Mr. Gaidar was at his side.

WHY YELTSIN IS STYMIED

When President Boris N. Yeltsin of Russia failed to get his congress to approve his economic plan along with his choice for prime minister, Yegor Gaidar, he accused the legislative body of seeking to return the country to the dark days of communism. Then Mr. Yeltsin proposed holding a national referendum next month to determine who is the country's boss—the president or the congress. But not everyone agrees that congress is against reform; some say it's just Mr. Yeltsin's current plans. "Who gave Yeltsin special powers to conduct his economic reform? Congress," said Vladimir Kvint, a professor of international business at Fordham University. What annoys congress now is that Mr. Yeltsin's reforms have been badly executed, Mr. Kvint said. "When Gaidar started the reform process, inflation was 150%. Now it's 1,850% a year."

The New York Times, International Section, December 13, 1992.

GORBY TAKES THE FIFTH

Is Yeltsin persecuting Gorbachev? Or could it be that the deposed So-viet leader can't get used to a system where even the highest are ac-countable to the law?

Recently Mikhail Gorbachev has been complaining bitterly to West-ern correspondents that the Russian militia, acting on orders from the Russian government, seized not only the building housing his Gorbachev Foundation but his limousine as well. Poor Gorby. Is this any way to treat the man who brought about the end of Soviet tyr-anny?

The story, however, is not quite so simple as the Western media has made it out. The huge building has an interesting history. A showcase property built of marble and situated in central Moscow, it was built by the Communist Party with public money. It housed the institute where leaders of foreign communist parties studied how to topple their governments.

When Russia's president, Boris Yeltsin, abolished the Communist Party after the August 1991 coup, who became the true owner of the property? The Russian parliament gave Yeltsin the power to allocate former Party property. But by this time, Gorbachev had already taken up residence in the building and had also taken over a luxurious villa once reserved for Politburo members. Gorbachev declared all this the property of the Gorbachev Foundation.

Poor Gorby indeed.

On several occasions, the Russian government told Gorbachev that he could use the building but would have to pay rent. Gorba-chev not only ignored the government but rented out one-third of the space for a huge new restaurant and for various foreign joint-venture tenants. For this he had received at least $120,000 in hard currency during the past few months. The foundation also didn't pay taxes due on the property.

Obviously miffed, in early October Yeltsin declared the building the property of the Russian Finance Academy, and the militia took

Forbes, November 9, 1992, p. 48.

over the building. That's when Gorbachev began complaining resentfully to Western correspondents.

That's not Gorbachev's only woe. He has been summoned to appear as a witness—not as a defendant—before the new Constitutional Court, Russia's highest court, in a case involving the abolition of the Communist Party. Gorbachev has refused to appear. Why? Could it be because he is afraid of two questions: How much money did he send abroad as General Secretary of the U.S.S.R. Communist Party; and to what accounts did he send it? Educated as a lawyer, Gorbachev knows that if he makes a false statement under oath, he could be arrested.

He clearly does not want to explain to the Russian people why, at a time when they were suffering privations, Gorbachev sent money to foreign communist parties as well as to their leaders. In 1990, for example, $2 million went to the General Secretary of the U.S. Communist Party, Comrade Gus Hall. Receipts signed by Hall are on the desk of the General Prosecutor of Russia. When money is sent abroad, it leaves a paper trail. This trail haunts Gorbachev.

During Gorbachev's time, the gold in Russia's reserves fell from 983.5 tons in 1985 to 450 tons in 1991—at $350 an ounce, the difference amounts to almost $6 billion. And because additional gold was produced during that period, the amount shipped abroad was probably much higher. Much of this gold was used to buy food and other supplies from the West, but did some of it find its way into the Party higher-ups' numbered accounts in Switzerland, Liechtenstein, Panama, Hungary, and elsewhere? Most Russians think it did.

If he wanted to, Gorbachev could provide some answers. Only Gorbachev had the power to decide how much gold, platinum, palladium, diamonds, and other precious stones and metals should be sent abroad, especially those not officially for sale. A Politburo member who helped him with the Party's foreign financial dealings, Oleg Shenin (*Forbes*, October 28, 1991), is now in prison, charged with organizing the August coup.

Expect more bitter complaints about political persecution from the deposed Soviet leader. Gorbachev must find it most unfamiliar living under a system where even the highest of the high are subject to the rule of law.

DOWN THE RATHOLE

Doesn't anyone remember what happened to the loans to Latin America or to Mikhail Gorbachev's regime?

The recent political summit in Munich ended with only one concrete result. The leaders of the industrialized countries agreed to give the Russian government $1 billion through the International Monetary Fund. This amount will likely be followed by another $6 billion stabilization fund to support the ruble by year's end, with many more billions to follow. But anyone who thinks this money will improve the situation in Russia is in for a big disappointment. It will be money down a rathole, as people from the staff of the Russian government find ways to take part of the cash.

The IMF is working according to the following logic: Mr. Yeltsin is fighting with the Communist Party mafia to create a market economy in Russia, and he is decreasing the risk of nuclear conflict. To help this democrat, President Bush has urged giving Russia $24 billion as soon as possible.

The flaw in this humanitarian logic is this: The money would take the form of sovereign loans and be handed over to politicians and bureaucrats who haven't a clue as to how the money should be put to work. In this the Russian aid proposals remind one of the more than $100 billion in sovereign loans that were extended to Latin America in the 1970s and early 1980s.

Seventy years of Soviet history show that government in Russia can't manage money. During Gorbachev's six years in power, the Soviet government received $93 billion in Western loans and aid. Where is this money? Did it help the Russian economy? In June of this year production of meat and food products fell to 65% of the level of 1988's output and is now at a critically low level.

The $6 billion in funds for the stabilization of the Russian ruble will soon evaporate. How is it possible to hope that $6 billion will help a country where every month the government is printing 275 billion worthless rubles? The IMF experts urge the Russians to stop printing money. Unfortunately, this is impossible.

Forbes, August 3, 1992, pp. 40–41.

Hyperinflation has set in. Inflation jumped from an annual rate of 150% in 1991 to almost 1,400% during the first half of this year. In April the average salary was 1,000 rubles; in June, 2,500 rubles. In August, it will be 3,500. If the government tries to stabilize the currency by not printing new rubles for two months, the effect will be like slamming on the brakes of a speeding freight train. Deflation will be so strong that almost 70% of Russian industrial companies will not be able to pay salaries. Civil disobedience will soon follow.

But there is a way in which the IMF's money could help develop the competitive market economy Russia needs if democracy is to take root. Rather than send this money to the Russian government, the IMF and developed countries should make it available as nonsovereign loans for Russian entrepreneurs, private companies, and the first capitalist institutions that are more or less working in Russia— the 500 commercial and private banks, trading houses, 450 commodity exchanges and brokerage houses, and 2 stock exchanges. (Foreign stocks are now being traded in Moscow and St. Petersburg; the shares of American and German companies will be traded in seven other cities next year.)

Money should be sent to Russia through the Western companies that want to invest there. Far better than bureaucrats, these companies will produce the equipment, technology, and management systems Russia needs. This money is also necessary to hire foreign managers who will help to install and use this equipment in Russia; otherwise, much of the equipment will never be installed. In all former Soviet republics, approximately $10 billion worth of brand-new foreign equipment sits quietly in storage.

Like the IMF, the U.S. Export-Import Bank is trying to help Russia. But the people at Ex-Im are going about it the right way, by providing loans directly to Russian buyers of American exports. The IMF should follow the Ex-Im Bank's line, which will create U.S. jobs as well as help Russia.

An outstanding politician who has made a lot of economic mistakes, Yeltsin is now doing a good job of improving the business climate in Russia. In June Yeltsin appointed Vladimir Shumeiko as executive deputy prime minister and Georgy Hija and Victor Chernomerdin as deputy prime ministers; all three had previously occupied positions as chairmen of big industrial companies.

Under new business regulations passed earlier this year, foreign insurance companies, including American International Group and others, were finally allowed to enter the Russian market. Privatization is now on the fast track. Foreigners now not only can become partners in joint ventures in Russia but also own companies outright.

Another key reform was enacted June 14: Foreigners can now purchase land, but only if they agree to buy and improve the structures that are on the land. And in July Russian and American officials eliminated the double taxation of profits earned in Russia. I believe that by the end of the year five free economic zones will be operational, including Nakhodka (on the Russian Pacific Coast), Kaliningrad (formerly Konigsberg), St. Petersburg, Novgorod, and Kemerovo (a coal region in eastern Siberia), with perhaps free circulation of hard currency in each one.

Western business people are responding to the new business climate. Each month nearly 100 new joint ventures and enterprises are created by foreign investors. Since January of this year 75 Russian-American joint ventures have appeared.

To help Yeltsin & Co. keep things moving in the right direction, some Western aid is necessary. But the U.S., the IMF, and others waiting to help should remember that the purpose of aid is not to give handouts and create dependency, but to support the foreign and native entrepreneurs who will cultivate real long-term economic growth. Anything else is money down a rathole.

OPPORTUNITY IN A SHATTERED LAND

The business map of the future is being drawn in the old Soviet Union and in Eastern Europe. Most of the attention is going to the disintegration—the splitting apart—of the world we knew. But another process is at work, too, which could be significant for Western business. A reintegration—the creation of new alliances—is beginning.

The entities forming in the wake of the Soviet Union's breakup will develop nontraditional economic ties with each other, and there will be new opportunities for Western investors to profit. There are risks—risks that the new nations will develop protectionist stances as they come to understand their potential and risks that the political leaders on whom foreign investors bet will simply prove to be the wrong ones. Remember Mikhail Gorbachev.

But countries with common histories as former Soviet republics or allies will integrate into loose economic blocs of fully sovereign countries in the next few years. This will happen, I think, so economies can be linked and strengthened. These new alliances offer rare opportunities for Western businesses.

Already the Soviet Union has broken apart as a union, and something similar is likely to happen in the Russian federation because of ethnic divisions, economic and social problems, and territorial disputes over rich natural resources. At least three republics—Tatar, Bashkir, and Checheno-Ingush—will break away from Russia. For some of the same reasons, Georgia will probably lose the republic of Abkhasia and the autonomous territory of South Ossetia.

This is not to diminish Russia's importance—and potential. It produces more oil each day than Saudi Arabia, Iraq, and Kuwait together, and more natural gas, steel, cement, and tractors than any country in the world. Boris Yeltsin and other leaders know Western participation is necessary for economic revival, and have opened the market.

The New York Times, Sunday, Janaury 19, 1992, p. 11F.

Yet uncertainties remain. Russia is not homogeneous. The Russian Far East and Siberia are stable and have low political risks, so are excellent places to invest. But in the Caucasus region, in middle Asia, and in the new state of Moldova, ethnic conflicts are a possibility, increasing risk.

The process of reintegration is happening elsewhere, too. Austria, Hungary, Czechoslovakia, Croatia, and Slovenia, which have a common economic history and leaderships interested in such an alliance, are likely to form the next economic commonwealth in central Europe.

In Estonia, Latvia, and Lithuania, leaders have formed a Baltic Council, for economic and political ties, creating the Baltic Bridge Union to link Russia with Scandinavia and Poland. The three nations knew they could not make it, economically, without each other.

It is also possible that Moldova will unite with Romania. In the Near East, we will see a new economic and political role for Turkey, which could help former Soviet republics form economic ties to countries in Asia and the Middle East.

Taking advantage of reintegration requires know-how on the part of Western investors. For example, although the monetary systems of the newly sovereign countries are expected to be ruble-based, Western executives would probably be wise to consider the possibility of doing business in at least five to six new currencies in the new commonwealth. The independent states will probably adopt something similar to the existing Benelux monetary system, under which the currencies of Belgium and Luxembourg differ in appearance but are considered by central bankers to be equal.

Furthermore, the former Soviet republics are likely to become more protectionist. Executives interested in this market must establish a legal presence there soon so they will not be shut out later. Executives must build relationships with local and central authorities, and with business leaders, too.

The effort will be worth it. Real estate prices are unbelievably low, and, during impending privatizations, enterprises will be sold at low prices. The former Soviet market still does not know its own value. Purchases of enterprises at below-market prices is risk-justified. Watch the new maps. The opportunity is there.

COPYING THE COMMUNITY

While Western Europe was unifying, the Soviet Union was becoming unglued. Last week Russia's President, Boris N. Yeltsin, and the leaders of Ukraine and Byelorussia, replaced the union with a new commonwealth. The republics will use the ruble as their common currency, defend themselves jointly, and harmonize their economies. Five Asian republics joined the commonwealth last week. That leaves the Soviet President, Mikhail S. Gorbachev, "a king without a country," said Vladimir Kvint, a lecturer at Babson College. In the new commonwealth, "the relationships between the republics will be like the relationship between countries in the European Community," he said. That is a remarkable transformation. All that's needed now is a workable economic plan. Some things remain the same.

The New York Times, Business Section, Sunday, December 15, 1991.

POLITICAL, ECONOMIC, AND LEGAL REFORM IN THE SOVIET UNION

The development of Soviet-American relations has received much attention in the United States. Clearly, the development of such a relationship facilitates peace; for those who trade do not start wars with one another. Currently, the Soviet Union is undergoing the process of social revolution. Public forces are becoming polarized. This process has its own dynamics and logic.

When perestroika began in 1985, economic tasks were considered the most important. Prior attempts at economic reform were made, but they always occurred without a corresponding change in the political sphere. Political leaders of the USSR failed to understand that economic and political changes must occur simultaneously. However, the present leadership of the Soviet Union understands that without political change, economic change is bound to fail.

By the end of 1985, steps were taken toward the political democratization of the Soviet Union. For 70 years, Soviet propaganda described Soviet society as the best and most democratic. Suddenly, people realized that they were living in a tyrannical country. Gorbachev counseled that this was the moment when the Soviet people had to learn how to live under a democracy. For many Soviets that was a major breakthrough.

In the field of democratization of life, the Soviet Union has achieved a certain degree of success. But these achievements represent only the first steps toward democracy. The regime continues to suppress personality and the open market economy.

Economic changes in the Soviet Union have been very slow. Dramatic improvements have not occurred. To some degree, however, capital investments were reoriented to the needs of the people. In addition, the state's monopoly over foreign trade was slightly decreased, and the bureaucratic machine was to some extent dismantled.

Whittier Law Review, 12, No. 2 (1991), 143–146.

Before perestroika began, there were 106 all-Union ministries and approximately 800 different ministries in Union republics. During the years of perestroika, approximately 350 ministries were abolished. The upper echelon of the bureaucratic machine were reduced. However, there still are 19 million people working in this sphere. Three million out of these 19 million are just drivers of the official cars. The Soviet Union trained people not to make decisions. The bureaucratic machine does not have technology of management.

During the first years of perestroika, the bureaucratic machine experienced pressure from democratization. Bureaucrats looked to the General Secretary for support. However, the General Secretary was on the side of democratic change and provided no support.

The leaders of perestroika were much more decisive in the political sphere than in the economic sphere. The economic changes did not lead to an increase in the standard of living. The Council of Ministers tried to solve new tasks using old methods. As a result, economic changes that were introduced did not give birth to a new economic mechanism. The leaders of perestroika and the government progressed very little in these areas. This gave the opponents to perestroika enough time to organize and consolidate.

At the end of 1989, chauvinistic and negative forces joined the bureaucratic machine. Consequently, the pressure on economic and political reform became much stronger in all directions. In addition, opponents had enough influence to slow down changes in the legal sphere of democratization. Moreover, some new laws were openly aimed at preserving the economic interests of the central machine. As a result, the laws that were adopted go only half way toward the goal of complete reform, and do not protect the rights of enterprises to economic freedom. This crippled Soviet enterprises. These enterprises are currently unprotected from the willpower and dictate of the ministries. Furthermore, cooperatives, which were created during perestroika and had more freedom of action, came into conflict with state-run enterprises. The main producers of all goods and services are still state enterprises. The contribution of cooperatives is much smaller than that of state enterprises. While the countries' gross national product is 875 billion rubles, the contribution of cooperatives is only 2.8 billion rubles.

Drafts of new laws and regulations were prepared, but the process of adoption proved problematic. The law providing for private ownership was not included. The joint-venture regulation, the foreign trade law, and the laws concerning free economic zones were not introduced by the Supreme Soviet or the Supreme Council of the Soviet Union in 1989 or 1990. However, the parliaments of separate republics have begun to introduce such laws.

The political struggle between the center and the republics, to achieve widespread social reform, has become extremely heated over the last six months. In response to these problems, Gorbachev proposed the creation of a president's power. He has tried to strengthen his diminishing influence over the people.

The democratization process in the Soviet Union has slowed. The situation in the Baltic republics and Russia has severely hampered political and economic reform. This problem can largely be attributed to the decision-making process used by the Soviet leaders. Retroactive decision-making process predominates. Progressive remedial measures are rarely implemented. Consequently, when a destabilizing event occurs, the process of reform is severely disrupted, allowing time for other unexpected exigencies to arise, thereby delaying progress. Real economic and political reform is difficult to come by in this environment. This is frustrating when the vast majority of the Russian people want dramatic and far-reaching reforms to be instituted immediately. However, economic and legal reform will continue to erode the state machine. American lawyers should pay special attention to the latest regulatory developments within the various republics. Economics and law will become interrelated.

The regional unrest and political turmoil has frustrated the opportunities to integrate with Western businesses. This has adversely affected the Soviet Union's ability to obtain technology and investment from abroad. Nevertheless, joint ventures with the West have developed very quickly. While in 1988, only three joint ventures per month were created, in 1989, 85 joint ventures per month were established. These numbers have increased to 125 joint ventures per month in 1990. Currently, there are more than 2,300 joint ventures in the Soviet Union.

On December 11, 1989, a regulation was adopted making it necessary to obtain licenses for 80% of everything that is exported from the Soviet Union. The USSR became the first country in the world to require licenses for exports, not imports. This represents one more victory for the bureaucrats. Bureaucrats justify this regulation by pointing to their desire to satisfy the domestic market, to enable people to buy more, and to prohibit valuable goods from being exported. However, economic principles dictate that the more restrictions, the lower the level of optimization.

It is patently apparent that, during the past 70 years, nothing good was achieved. The market was never properly utilized. New restrictions will only bring similar results.

Today, the Soviet people can buy only 3% of their necessities on the open market. Recent elections to the Republican Supreme Councils and to local bodies of power have shown vividly that the populace supports the movement toward the market.

The hard currency situation in the Soviet Union has deteriorated, and international debt is growing dramatically. It has currently reached $58 billion. However, for a country the size of the Soviet Union, this is not a large debt. The Soviet Union should have little difficulty paying the interest.

What tasks will the lawyers face in 1991? The economic and political situation in the Soviet Union is consistently changing. The turmoil and chaos of the various republics has created an extremely unstable environment for reform. The question remains as to what extent the future confederation will retain the vestiges of the old legal system. It appears as though only ten or eleven of the current republics will join the confederation. It will be difficult for American lawyers to understand the legal framework that exists in the republics. Perhaps most important, American law firms will face the problems of protecting American investment in the USSR.

This widespread involvement of American lawyers will help create proper legal standards for the Soviet legal community. Furthermore, it will bring Soviet legal principles in line with modern legal standards, thus promoting continued political and economic reform.

THE NEW MAP OF EASTERN EUROPE

Vladimir Kvint, a Russian-born economist, has contributed forward-looking coverage for *Forbes* on the collapse of socialism. In "Russia as Cinderella" (February 1, 1990) he was perhaps the first writer to predict that the Soviet Union would come unglued. Now, he looks beyond the dissolution and sketches out the new economic and political groups he is convinced will emerge.

Forbes, September 16, 1991.

SIBERIA: A WARM PLACE FOR INVESTORS

The breakup of the Soviet Union presents great opportunities for U.S. investors and business people. But to grasp them they will have to recognize that there no longer is a Soviet Union.

Shortly before the failed coup took place, this joke came out of the Soviet Union: Mikhail Gorbachev sits in his office, musing on a huge portrait of himself. "Soon, my friend, the people will take us down," murmurs Gorbachev. "You are a fool," the portrait responds. "The people will unhang me. They will hang you." The joke was close to the mark. Leaders of the coup had counted on the Soviet people's being ready to dump Gorbachev. In that they were probably right. But the coup leaders, along with most foreign governments, ignored the fact that Gorbachev had become irrelevant. It was Boris Yeltsin and his Russian government, not Gorbachev and the Soviet government, that the people and large parts of the military defended against the coup.

Which is another way of saying that the Soviet Union is dead. In its place 15 sovereign nations are emerging— Russia, the largest by far. Some of these new nations, or old ones reborn, will gravitate economically toward Russia; others will move closer to Eastern Europe or the Balkans.

Each of these new nations will seek a seat in the United Nations, will establish its own diplomatic relations and create its own military forces. Most of them will be as independent of the old center as Poland or Hungary has become. What remains in the Kremlin will be something like the British Commonwealth of Nations: a ceremonial, consultative body based upon common interests whose commonality will fade over time.

A late August headline in *The Wall Street Journal* said that people "worry" that the Soviet Union may break up. Why this should worry anyone in Washington or anywhere else is beyond me. I suppose

Forbes, September 16, 1991, pp. 96–97.

some people simply cannot confront change. This fission is a wonderful development. Breaking the vast empire into more manageable pieces, grouped on economic rather than political lines, presents tremendous opportunities for foreign business.

The USSR will no longer be the Union of Soviet Socialist Republics. The terms "socialist" and "soviet" will disappear, just as the word "empire" disappeared with the emergence of the British Commonwealth. Its disappearance will be of more than formal significance because the breakup hastens the move toward market-based economies. All political maps, encyclopedias, political directories will become outdated.

The Baltic republics, Georgia, Moldavia, Armenia, Ukraine, Belorussia have called it quits. Others may follow. They will not even be part of the new, loose union. Altogether, more than 80 million people will secede entirely.

From now on, the republics remaining in the union will decide what rights, functions, and money to delegate to the center. The one who pays is the one who orders the music. Republics will finance the army, which will shrink because of that.

Civil war? Most unlikely, except for the small-scale continuing war between Armenia and Azerbaijan and some ethnic clashes in Georgia and Central Asia. Over the last 18 months the leaders of the republics proved that they can solve mutual political and economic problems directly.

What's the timetable for the new order? The treaty that will replace the one aborted by the coup will last for about three years as a progressive document of a transition period. It will take at least that long for the various republics to stand on their own feet economically. Except for Russia, Ukraine, Belorussia, and Georgia, none of the other, smaller new republics has an economic basis for independence. At least not yet.

Every historical epoch creates its markets out of a mixture of politics and economics, and this one will be no different. There was the European Hanseatic cities union in the 14th to 16th centuries. There were trade routes like the Silk Route. Now America, Canada, and Mexico are uniting in one market, as European countries were.

In place of one gigantic market created by force and maintained by force in the old Soviet Union, the new market groupings will follow more economic logic, which itself will lead to different political ties. While lecturing in Austria recently, I witnessed a similar process close up. Austrian, Hungarian, and Czechoslovakian businessmen were going back and forth, putting together an economic grouping not unlike that of the old Austro-Hungarian empire; this grouping will probably be the link between Western Europe and the countries farther east. Ukraine, having left the Soviet Union, will gravitate toward this grouping.

Siberia, though part of the Russian Republic, will get a certain independence. Because it faces the Pacific Ocean, it will become a Pacific Basin economy in good part. A federation of several Siberian cities has already been created. New air routes are connecting California and Alaska with Far Eastern Russia. In June Alaska Airlines began offering service three times a week from Anchorage to the city of Khabarovsk. And the Soviet carrier Aeroflot has had weekly flights to Khabarovsk from San Francisco via Anchorage since May. All this suggests American business should look at Siberia via the Pacific rather than via Moscow.

Kazakstan and the republics of Central Asia—Tadzhikistan, Uzbekistan, Turkmenistan, and Kirgizia—will soon establish a kind of union among themselves. But this union will not gravitate toward the Middle East, despite historical and religious ties. As a market, these republics will establish close economic relations with the Russian Republic, but as equals, not as colonies as under the communists.

All this turmoil, this breaking of old ties, presents a tremendous opportunity for U.S. business. This year more than 100 joint ventures a month have been created in the USSR. Since August 1990 the U.S. has been the leader in total capital invested.

But the Americans are not necessarily looking in the right places. Now 60% of Soviet-American joint ventures are situated in Moscow, focusing on the western part of the old Soviet Union. Small Estonia has as many joint ventures with Americans as Siberia does. Yet 75% of all Soviet natural resources are found to the east of the Ural Mountains. Western investment in Siberia and the Far East is very safe. But the U.S. will need to move fairly fast. The Japanese are already very active in Russia's Far East, and the South Koreans even more so. Investments in fisheries and timber will pay off fast in Siberia.

American investment in the reconstruction of the machine-building and metallurgical plants may be very profitable. Factories to recycle the rich mining, metallurgical, and agricultural waste that covers the former territory of the USSR are badly needed and can be highly profitable. The Japanese are already buying coal waste from Yakutia and other regions in the Russian republic to produce chemical elements for manufacturing.

The new order in the East will require huge investments in communications and transportation—and large doses of modern technology. The KGB has been artificially blocking cooperation in these spheres in efforts to keep the Soviet Union isolated. The KGB will have a diminished influence in the new republics. I think a fiberoptic cable will soon connect Europe and Japan through Soviet territory. The time has come to fully use the potential of the Arctic Seaway. I have studied it for many years and know that it is the shortest and the cheapest way from Europe to Asia as well as from Vancouver to Europe.

There is so much to be done that there is opportunity for everyone. But, first, Western governments and Western investors must learn from their own experience that aid and investment channeled through the central government is inefficiently used. Money spent to shore up Gorbachev is money wasted. Government loans should be channeled only to specific republics and for specific programs. Private investors should concentrate on projects, backed by reliable feasibility studies, that can pay back their investments in three to five years.

The Union of Soviet Socialist Republics is as dead as the Holy Roman Empire. The Russian people know this. Foreigners haven't yet gotten the full message.

GENNADI YANAYEV, OVERACHIEVER

The rise of a mediocre man like Gennadi Yanayev demonstrates how weak and desperate the Soviet Communist Party has become. Neither a smart reactionary nor a talented technocrat, he is gray, cynical, and pragmatic just like the party machine itself. As an economist, he is nonexistent.

I first met him in 1970 and since then I have watched his rise in the communist power structure. At the time, I was head of a students' construction unit and knew him when he was a mini-boss of the Komsomol, the young communists' organization that is a breeding ground for party bosses. Obedient and cautious from the beginning, he liked to tell off-color anecdotes but never the most innocuous political joke. Even then, however, he was cunning.

He never had any experience of real work at a factory or a research organization or as a manager. Instead, he rose from one meaningless job to another. In one position, his main expertise was hosting foreign delegations. In his next career leap he was in charge of building latter-day Potemkin villages, ensuring that Soviet reality was polished for foreigners. His next promotion was to a high job directing phony Soviet trade unions.

Then, an unseen mighty party hand moved him up, and last year he became a Politburo member, at a time when Mr. Gorbachev was trying to sit on two chairs—democracy and reaction—simultaneously.

But President Gorbachev fell from both chairs. He abandoned democratic goals and surrounded himself with men of the old breed like Gennadi Yanayev, and they finally crushed him.

Editorial, *The New York Times*, August 20, 1991, p. A21.

THE COUP'S AFTERMATH: WILL GORBACHEV BE THE LOSER?

The coup last week in the Soviet Union failed before most people outside of Russia could learn how to pronounce the plotters' names. But it demonstrated powerfully how deeply the Soviet Union has committed itself to reform. "Even the heads of the KGB and the military could not succeed with a coup," said Vladimir Kvint, a lecturer at Fordham University. "That means political risk has diminished. Investment in the Soviet Union is safe." But the Soviet Union still is likely to undergo more wrenching change. Boris N. Yeltsin's heroic stand elevated his status even more. He will no doubt use it to push harder for autonomy for the 15 republics. "Yeltsin already has agreed to recognize the Baltic states as independent," said Mr. Kvint. The real loser from the coup may turn out to be Soviet President Mikhail S. Gorbachev. Though he will stay on as president, he will become "a king without a kingdom," Mr. Kvint said.

Business, *The New York Times*, International Edition, August 25, 1991.

DEAD SOULS

Workers in the Soviet Union seem lazy and thieving, but the Soviet people are fundamentally honest and capable of hard work. It is the system that has made them bad—and the system is dying.

All the economic news from the Soviet Union is bad these days. But underneath the turmoil, and with unemployment heading for 30 million, change for the better takes hold slowly but irresistibly.

Under new laws Soviet citizens can work for foreign companies in the USSR and abroad, not as runaway serfs but legally. This is a tremendous step toward freedom. And foreigners, who have always been officially considered in the USSR to be capitalist spies working under cover, can now work at a Soviet enterprise and even manage a Soviet company on a contract basis.

This means Soviets can leave, though new travel laws still have not been passed. A brain drain is developing. It is still difficult to get out, but you can do so if you can land a contract from a foreign firm. Such contracts are highly coveted. The average monthly salary in the USSR is 290 rubles, about $2.40 a week at my estimate of the black-market rate of exchange. Though Gorbachev makes 12 times more than an average citizen, he makes less than $150 a month at an official rate set by himself. Of course, neither of these figures represents reality: Ordinary citizens get cheap rents and cheap bread, and Soviet bigwigs get nearly everything free. Still, these pitiful figures indicate how little disposable income Soviet citizens have.

So, people who can are leaving. Soviet biologists, mathematicians, economists, and financial specialists are welcome in a world labor market where there is an overall shortage of highly trained professionals.

Salomon Brothers, for example, invited a 30-year-old Soviet banker with ten years of experience in a Soviet bank to join a company's New York office.

The Soviet Union has brilliant computer specialists, especially in the software field. These too are trickling out and adapt quickly abroad. Soviet immigrants never ask for money in the subway; in a matter of several years they get their own houses, cars, things they could never have hoped to have at home. Most of these highly trained people swim well in the stormy waters of American business.

But the emigrants represent only a fraction of the Soviet Union's vast store of trained and educated people. Most of these will stay at home. They represent one of the Soviet Union's greatest resources. All these workers need to become productive is the introduction of capitalist incentives.

And that is why I say that, underneath the turmoil, a better way is developing. Forget what you have heard and read about lazy, thieving Soviet workers. It is the socialist system that is rotten, not the people. The old Soviet socialist system was unproductive because it was a mass of disincentives. Moscow dictated the salary of a Norilsk miner far in the North and of a cotton grower deep in the South. You got what some bureaucrat said you should get rather than a market-clearing wage. This led to bad labor discipline; the fired drunkard immediately crossed the street and went to another factory for the same small salary.

Yet factory managers fought to swell their payrolls. To squeeze more money out of the bureaucracy, each company tried to fake the number of working hands it needed. Unneeded workers were known as "dead souls"—after Nikolai Gogol. There were some 12 million of them in the Soviet Union.

In a way, this situation may be better than the American system of welfare, as far as the recipients are concerned; at least they do not get something for absolutely nothing. But the dead souls are a drag on productivity; why should Ivan work hard when Stefan is sleeping on the job and Ivan and Stefan both get the same wage?

In the Soviet system jobs were not so much for production as they were a means of regimenting people. Not to have a job was a crime, even though loafing on the job was not. A person out of work was called *tuneyadets*, "the one who eats in vain," a sponger. Laws against unemployment were also used as a political whip against dissidents.

The brilliant poet Joseph Brodsky, who later received a Nobel Prize, was sent to prison for doing nothing. "But I am a poet," he said to a judge. "Okay," argued the judge, "but I asked you about your job."

Finally, in January Gorbachev introduced the "Status of the Unemployed." Giving the jobless rights is a major step away from communism and toward a free society. It comes in the nick of time: Soon millions will need it. In East Germany, where the economy and productivity of labor was better than in the USSR, 4 million out of 8 million workers lost their jobs after reunification.

New, productive jobs aren't opening up as fast as the old, useless ones are being shed. But still they are opening up. Case in point: There are more than 7,000 new cooperative technical consulting and manufacturing firms, employing more than 300,000 people.

Making the situation worse, the whole system has been rife with the disease of stealing; lacking the bargaining power to get a living wage, workers are driven to theft. The so-called *nesuni*—the "carriers" or the "factory-lifters"—are everywhere: A worker at a meat factory carries away every day under his coat 3 kilos of meat; at the cable factory, a piece of cable. If somebody works at a rubber factory, he will take home "article #2"—the modest official name for condoms, which are always in great demand. Condoms are a kind of currency for such workers. Some workers say: "A day without a gift from the factory is a day lived in vain."

This happens not because Russian workers are any more dishonest than American workers or any others. The chief explanation is that in the USSR nothing belongs to anybody one knows. Some people think that it all belongs to the bosses in the Kremlin, and in a way they are right. Others say it has been declared that this property belongs to the nation. "And that means, to me, since I am a part of the nation. So, I am not stealing, I am just taking what belongs to me," a Soviet worker might reason.

It is, however, rather easy to stop the disease. Those who work in cooperatives, where part of the property really belongs to them, do not steal.

Many years of work among and with the Russian workers allow me to conclude that they are diligent, assiduous, and creative under the right circumstances.

When I was head of a construction team in Norilsk, we had to lift permafrost by shovel; there was a constant shortage of bulldozers.

To save my workers from this hellish job, I illegally hired a bulldozer driver. He agreed to work during the night, because by the morning he had to be back with his Caterpillar on his regular job.

How did I pay him? Vodka is hard currency in the Soviet Union.

Unlike rubles, vodka can buy everything, so I promised the bulldozer driver that he would be paid for his work with three bottles of vodka.

But I was young then and made a terrible mistake—I gave the vodka to the driver when he started work. So when I came at 2 in the morning to see what he had done, the first bottle was done indeed, and the driver was lovingly opening the second one.

Next time I knew better. Work first, vodka later.

Does this mean that Russians are bad workers, and that they drink too much? In the USSR private agricultural lots are tiny; they constitute only 3% of arable land. However, these tiny plots yield 30% of all the country's meat and milk production, 60% of potato crops. People work when they get paid properly.

Since 1989 the Chinese have leased a lot of land in Kirgizia. The local Soviet collective has a crop of 23 tons of tomatoes per hectare. The Chinese get 1,000 tons!

Of course, the American seeds that the Chinese use play their role. The seeds of the American management system, implanted into the Russian soil, will yield good crops, as well. The Soviet Union has everything it needs to improve its standard of living. Everything, that is, except proper management.

Seventy-five percent of the most important natural resources sit to the east of the Ural mountains—in Siberia and in the Far East. The regions suffer from significant labor shortages. A free market economy would offer financial incentives to attract workers where they are needed and would offer them goods and services to spend their wages on.

The mismanagement and waste of resources under the old regime were almost incredible. In the late 1960s the bureaucrats decided to introduce the Asian Tadzhiks, who knew only cattle breeding and trade, to heavy industry. It took 20 years and a vast fortune to build an aluminum plant in Tadzhikistan. Three hundred Tadzhiks were sent to the Krasnoyarsk aluminum plant in Siberia, the second biggest in the world, to study for nine months. When the brand-new specialists in metallurgy returned home, only a dozen of them went to work at the plant. The rest of the Tadzhiks went back to what they knew best—cattle herding.

Or take what happened to the nomadic Siberian nationalities, cattle breeding ethnic groups in Hakassia and Tuva. Soviet power forced them to be settled in towns. Their children were taken to the city orphanages, where both urban and rural lifestyles became alien to them. They found refuge in vodka.

Using politics rather than economics to dictate resource allocation, the Kremlin wasted billions of dollars and ruined lives. Uzbekistan, for example, has 30% unemployment and constant water shortages. Moscow created chemical plants in Uzbekistan that do not need a lot of people but demand a lot of water.

These things happen when you substitute central command planning for the free market.

At the same time, plants assembling agricultural combines, refrigerators, and TV sets were established in Siberia, where there weren't enough workers to man the plants.

You don't undo a mess like this without creating new problems. The sprouts of new growth first poke through the old asphalt. The millions of unnecessary jobs started to shrink.

State companies newly leased by the workers usually begin by eliminating unnecessary jobs. A better system evolves only slowly. During the past two years more than 3.5 million people have deserted the state enterprises to go to work for cooperatives. By my estimates, by 1993, 8 million to 10 million others will join them as a semicapitalist economy grows up alongside the socialist one. By 1996 the private sector will employ 20 million.

Don't be confused by the fact that the Kremlin first moves toward freer markets, then pulls back. Such ebbs and flows are inevitable, but they cannot salvage the old system. Socialism is dying in the Soviet Union. The nation is irrevocably, if hesitantly, embarked on the road to capitalism and economic freedom. Progress is slow, but the Kremlin cannot turn back the clock.

UNITED WE FALL

I would immediately abolish the Union treaty and offer all the republics absolute independence and the opportunity to consider entering a new union on mutually beneficial terms. This actually
should have been done two or more years ago, because the desire to
keep the Soviet Union together is a surrealistic task, one could even
say an unrealistic task.

My forecast is that by the end of 1991 or in 1992, the union will
cease to exist. Gorbachev's desire to keep the union in its present
shape using his police measures will unfortunately only lead the Soviet Union to a bloody civil war.

In the interest of peace, the West must stop all economic, political, and moral help to Gorbachev, and support, instead, the democratically elected republican parliaments. There is only one force in
the Soviet Union that can lead the country to civil war—and that is
Gorbachev.

Moscow Magazine. April 1991, p. 45.

CZAR GORBACHEV?

Vladimir Kvint's articles in *Forbes* on events in the Soviet Union have been close to prophetic: A year ago, when few thought the Soviet empire could ever break up, Kvint predicted and advocated the withdrawal of the Russian Republic from the USSR (February 19, 1990). Then, last June, he warned that the uncritical Western support for Mikhail Gorbachev would create the unintended consequence of strengthening the reactionary wing of the Communist Party. The bloody Soviet repression in Lithuania in January confirmed that prediction. What now?

THE MYTH OF GOOD CZAR GORBACHEV

The U.S. and Western Europe tried to help the cause of Soviet reform by pandering to Gorbachev's government. As the repression in the Baltics shows, the cause would have been better served had we been tougher with the Kremlin.

In failing to press Gorbachev on behalf of Lithuanian freedom, the "Western governments . . . unwittingly brought to a halt the further progress of perestroika. President Bush and his allies . . . have strengthened the hands of those in the Soviet Union who are trying to stop the movement of progress."

So wrote Vladimir Kvint in an almost prophetic Forbes *article. "The Best Way to Help Gorbachev Is to Make Life Difficult for Him" (June 11, 1990). Kvint's point was simple and blunt: By insisting that Gorbachev move toward reform and freedom we would strengthen his hand in the difficult job of curbing Communist extremists and centralists: by easing up we reduce his need to crack down on the hard-liners. The dire prophecy was redeemed in a shower of lead and a clanking of tank treads last month in Lithuania.*

What does Kvint see now?

In 1991 the name "USSR" will disappear from the political map of the world. It would be interesting to know what the Norwegian Nobel Committee now thinks of last year's winner, Mikhail Gorbachev.

Until January this revolution could have been peaceful. But unwavering Western support for Gorbachev and centralized Soviet power have strengthened the hard-liners and increased the chance of a bloody civil war.

Last spring Gorbachev imposed an economic blockade on Lithuania. In this way he tested the reaction that might come from the West were he to back down on reform. Then, at the summit in May, President Bush accepted several promises from Gorbachev. Gorbachev never fulfilled them. The law on freedom of travel and immigra-

Forbes, February 4, 1991, pp. 36–37.

tion, for example, was not passed, even though Gorbachev promised to adopt it in June, right after the summit. Thus, the green light for today's tanks appeared then, in May.

Gorbachev is a master manipulator of Western opinion. He will fire the generals who, he claims, gave the order to put down Lithuania behind his back.

In doing this, Gorbachev will be repeating an ancient Russian drama. For centuries, Russian serfs believed in the image of the "kind" czar. They believed that everything wicked was done by his evil ministers, acting behind his back. "If only the czar knew" was an emotion that helped countless Russians rationalize the state's irrational brutality against them. Many of those who knew about Stalin's atrocities believed that he was unaware of them. He was a "good czar." So is Gorbachev; only his generals and ministers are wicked.

Only this time the Western leaders behave like the Russian serfs. By making Gorbachev the beloved child, they allowed him to become a despot.

Yes, a despot. The latest news, ignored or not comprehended by the Western press, is that Gorbachev abolished the President's Council early in January. Now Aleksandr Yakovlev, the main promoter of democracy in Gorbachev's team, is out of a job. And in December Gorbachev fired Vadim Bakatin, the minister of the interior, who apparently disagreed with Gorbachev's plan of suppression for Lithuania and other rebellious republics. After Bakatin's sacking, Foreign Minister Eduard Shevardnadze broadcast to the world his fears about the coming dictatorship. The Western World regretted the resignation but pretended it didn't hear his warning.

There are now democratically elected parliaments in 7 out of 15 republics. In these parliaments lies big potential for democracy. But this potential cannot be realized in a despotic country, and that is why civil war is now almost inevitable.

While it may fool naïve Westerners, the image of the kind czar— Gorbachev in his latest incarnation—cannot deceive people in the USSR any longer. The real disintegration of the USSR will start sometime between March and October of this year, when hunger and economic crisis will reach their peaks. Lithuania, Azerbaijan, Armenia, Georgia, and Moldavia will be the fuses of the explosion.

By my estimate, approximately 12% of the country's territory could be enveloped in civil war. There is little hope that it won't be bloody.

At any rate, perestroika is dead. But perestroika was a naïve notion, anyway. It means "reconstruction," but reconstruction could not help socialism to survive. In any case, Gorbachev and his allies never forswore socialism or even communism.

Gorbachev's timing has been sophisticated. He made good use of the approaching war in the Persian Gulf. It is clear that President Bush is worried about retaining Gorbachev's support, but at this point there is no reason for Bush to worry. Gorbachev cannot back Saddam Hussein: He needs Western capital and technology; and by changing his position on the Persian Gulf, Gorbachev could incur the real wrath of the West. This is something he is truly afraid of.

For Western businessmen interested in doing business in the Soviet Union, now is a time for caution but not paralysis. Some of the new independent republics will voluntarily enter a new confederation. They will delegate to it some political responsibilities. The confederation will also deal with nuclear arms and military strategy. But Gorbachev and his crowd will probably end up as figureheads. Boris Yeltsin and the leaders of the other republics are the people to deal with in the USSR now—both for foreign governments and for business people hoping to get a foothold. Yeltsin now is popular in all the republics, not in Russia only. His main task is to revive Russia and to rebuild ties with the other republics, without the center. Yeltsin understands that revival is impossible without integration with the West. Under him the Russian parliament has already adopted the best legislation as to the protection of Western capital.

What should the U.S. do? Stop all economic aid and loans to the centralized USSR government; this aid is senseless. This would involve suspending the trade agreement signed at the spring summit until all Gorbachev's promises are fulfilled. Nor should there be any new meetings with Gorbachev until he provides a new union treaty—signed by the republics voluntarily, not with a tank muzzle at their heads. The U.S. and the other Western countries should loudly and firmly condemn the invasion of Lithuania and establish direct contacts with the democratic republics and their parliamentary governments. In continuing to back Comrade Gorbachev, the U.S. is—not for the first time in recent history—backing the wrong horse.

HARSH LOOK AT SOVIET PROSPECTS

A top Soviet economist now lecturing and consulting in the U.S. believes the Soviet Union will begin to break up over the next year, that a significant portion is likely to fall into civil war, and that by November the country will be swept by a food crisis of severe proportions.

Nonetheless, Vladimir L. Kvint, who lectured last week at Northwestern University's J. L. Kellogg Graduate School of Management, said now is the time for American and other Western businesses to invest in areas of the Soviet Union that can be identified as having a low risk of unrest and a high probability of a good return. Kvint holds the lifetime title of Soviet Professor of Political Economy, and currently is distinguished lecturer at Fordham University.

"The Soviet Union will cease to exist as a political unit in the next year, but the resources will stay," Kvint said in an interview at Northwestern. "A substantial number of the regions carry little investment risk."

For example, he said, areas in Siberia and the Far East used during Stalinist days for internal exile are alive with the entrepreneurial spirit and have few, if any, of the social conflicts apparent in many other regions. Some of those people were exiled for demonstrating entrepreneurial skills.

"It is no accident that the level of productivity [in such regions] is 30% higher than [in] other regions," Kvint said. "In some spots, it is 40% to 50% higher. They have a totally different attitude to work—they have pride in their work."

Kvint's positive assessment of business opportunity comes as American and Western firms are pulling back or retrenching in the Soviet Union in the face of mounting repression in the Baltic states and elsewhere, and in light of a host of difficulties and disappointments encountered in the past several years.

Kvint, who advises American businesses, said he was not of the

Article by John N. Maclean, *The Chicago Tribune*, Sunday, February 3, 1991.

opinion that firms should invest in the Soviet Union "no matter what." But if careful risk analysis shows profits can be made safely, "then why not?" he said.

Kvint makes some of the same arguments in an article in the February 4 edition of *Forbes* magazine, blaming excessive Western support for Soviet President Mikhail Gorbachev for helping bring on the current round of repression.

"Unwavering Western support for Gorbachev and centralized Soviet power have strengthened the hard-liners and increased the chance of a bloody civil war," Kvint wrote in *Forbes*. He said Gorbachev tested the West by imposing last spring's economic blockade on Lithuania.

When the West failed to react to that and other provocations, Kvint argues, Gorbachev saw a "green light for today's tanks."

Kvint, who was an advocate in the Soviet Union of market systems as long as a decade ago, said he has used a variety of criteria to do a risk analysis of the Soviet Union, combining historical, economic, and political approaches. The analysis is so specific, he said, that he can predict that about 12% of the country's territory will be in a state of deep unrest in the coming year, if not civil war.

In the long run, Kvint said, he believes at least some major areas of the Soviet Union will successfully pursue reform.

"Now is the right time to invest in a number of regions in the Soviet Union," Kvint said. "You should invest in separate producing regions where you know the local government has been democratically elected [7 of the 15 Soviet republics have elected parliaments].

"You should invest in those that have gained a significant independence from central controls such as where enterprises are leased from the state by employees," he said.

In hotel construction, for example, there are some businesses that have been leased back from the state. Building hotels raises the possibility of being paid in hard currency, as the concerns earn tourist and business cash. The Soviet ruble cannot be converted into other currencies.

The Russian Republic, containing 85% of the Soviet Union's natural resources, is so large it cannot be seen as a single unit, Kvint said. If the Soviet Union breaks up and Russia becomes a separate country, it would be the largest country in the world.

Kvint predicted the republic's president, Boris N. Yeltsin, may emerge as a head of a union of republic presidents and become a more powerful figure than Gorbachev.

Russia, like other republics, has claimed its natural resources for itself, but said it would cooperate with the state for a set price. Kvint said business has increased markedly in Russia, where in 1988 there were about 8 new joint ventures announced each month, and in 1990 there were about 125 joint ventures a month.

THE SOVIET UNION ON THE WAY TO THE MARKET: ONE STEP FORWARD, THEN TWO [STEPS BACKWARD]

Not only will the Soviets' way to a free market economy be long and hard for Gorbachev, but the population must also have some painful experiences. The past year is proof. Inflation and unemployment have increased markedly. According to my evaluations, in 1990 the rate of inflation was at 18%, the unemployment rate at about 3%, but on a trend to increase as 50 to 60 million people are still working in positions that are not actually productive.

The civil wars in the republics are bringing economic losses on the general order of 10% to 12%. Additionally, the concurrently uncertain political situation in the war regions has negative effects on foreign investment. Although in the past year total joint-venture international investments increased to more than $800 million, actually only a third of the joint ventures work according to plan. With half a billion dollars, American firms are the main investors.

The efforts at autonomy have borne fruit in at least one area. Since January 1 the registration of joint ventures is no longer centralized at the Ministry of Finance, but, rather, administered by the Ministries of the republics.

"Experts' Forum," *Neue Kronen-Zeitung Wirtschafts* (Vienna), January 26, 1991.

OPPORTUNITIES IN SOVIET DISINTEGRATION

Despite the Soviet parliament's approval of President Mikhail S. Gorbachev's plan to create a market economy, the Soviet Union will not live to celebrate its 70-year anniversary in 1992. The Soviet Union's political and economic crises are intensifying, and if the forces of disintegration continue—as I expect they will—the Union will come apart. By 1992, there will be no country called the Soviet Union.

In place of the old Soviet Union, new states will appear. These states will welcome foreign investment. For Europe and the United States, these resource-rich republics could become the new Klondike. But to take advantage of the opportunities that will arise as the Soviet Union disintegrates, investors will have to think in terms of several diverse markets—not one country.

My own assessment, as a regional economist, is that the safest place to invest will continue to be the Russian Republic. Even without its empire, Russia will remain the largest country in the world. Siberia alone, which is part of Russia, contains not only 92% of the Soviet Union's oil, but also 85% of its natural resources. According to my calculations, it would cost one-fifth to one-third as much to transport oil to the United States from Russia as from the Middle East.

But Russia is not homogeneous. That is why the degree of political and economic risk varies depending on the territory.

The region of Russia called Dagestan, on the Caspian Sea, is largely Muslim, but is also home to 36 other ethnic groups. Dagestan is very stable and open to foreign investment, unlike its neighbor Azerbaijan where ethnic fighting is rampant.

Moscow and Leningrad are attractive places to invest. In the Soviet Far East, the Sakhalin and Primorski territories near Japan are especially attractive as markets. Political risk there is minimal, and a basic infrastructure is already in place. The Pacific region in general

The New York Times, October 28, 1990, Section 3, p. 13.

is becoming the center of world business activity, and the Russian Far East, with its tremendous resources, can play a major role.

So far, the parliament of Russia is the most full-blooded and reliable in the Soviet Union. Next comes the government of Ukraine and then, with more reservations, the governments of Estonia and Latvia. Guarantees coming from the other republics are not worth much now.

The 1990s will see the reemergence of Russian companies, after nearly 70 years. The 1990s will also see these companies become integrated into the world economy through alliances with foreign companies. What will be created, as these changes unfold, is a new nation, devoid of empire, but with the potential for creating abundant wealth.

WHO'S IN CHARGE AROUND HERE?

In Russia, Boris Yeltsin, not Mikhail Gorbachev, is in charge. Bad news for the communist elite and for Saddam Hussein, Fidel Castro, and other scroungers. Good news for world oil supplies.

The fight for power between Mikhail Gorbachev and Boris Yeltsin is almost over. Yeltsin and his team will define the future of Russia. Gorbachev will end up in a largely ceremonial role.

Americans have been slow to understand this. They tend still to think of Boris Yeltsin, chairman of the Russian parliament, as simply the opposition to the Communist Party. No. Mikhail Gorbachev is president of the USSR, but Yeltsin has more real power in Russia.

In the long sweep of Russian history—from the 12th century, the time of Novgorod, the Free City, to today—Boris Yeltsin is the first leader, with the possible exception of Aleksandr Kerensky, ever elected by the people. By the people, not by some gang, not by birth or by the knife. Yeltsin started a real revolution, a breakthrough to the lost future, lost in October 1917 when Russia last had a chance for democracy and for real economic development.

Fourteen days after he had been elected chairman of the Russian parliament, he managed to unite the divided Russian parliament for the declaration of sovereignty. Today the USSR parliament, headed by Gorbachev, is powerless against the fine-tuned Russian parliament.

Gorbachev, afraid to antagonize extremist groups like Pamyat, has failed to speak out against anti-Semitism. Yeltsin has already talked of creating a special commission to safeguard the rights of Russian Jews.

With such moves, 76% of the USSR's territory has gone out of Gorbachev's control. Russia becomes the biggest new country in the world. It has 92% of the oil and gas condensate resources of the USSR, 85% of the coal, 78% of the gas, 92% of the lumber, the

Forbes, September 3, 1990, pp. 54–57.

majority of nonferrous metals. As for platinum and diamonds, Russia is the only producer in the Eastern European countries. Russia has powerful chemical, automotive, and machine-building production, and the productivity of its labor is higher than that elsewhere in the USSR.

In one and a half to two years Russia will achieve complete independence—quicker than Lithuania—because, unlike Lithuania, Russia has an economic basis for freedom; it can stand on its own.

Yeltsin is already acting to implement that freedom. He has cut the number of ministries from 51 to 28; in 8 of these ministries the staff numbers only 20 people, and their direct task is not to interfere in the economy but to cut back on the powers of the old ministries.

Aiming for financial sovereignty, the Russian parliament has authorized all Russian banks to withdraw from the USSR banking system, which would deprive the government of financial management levers. Yeltsin clearly intends, for the first time in USSR history, to break the monopoly of the central government on foreign trade and currency transactions. The Bank for Foreign Economic Affairs of Russia was created. He has created a TV network for Russia independent of the USSR network.

Russian oilfields pumped out 115 million tons of the oil that was exported by the USSR in 1989; 88 billion cubic meters of gas, 88,000 tons of copper, 17 million tons of pulp, 400,000 cars and trucks, and 17 million watches exported by the USSR were produced in Russia. Export of part of the petroleum production generates hard currency, all of which will go to this new bank, to remain in Russia, rather than to the government of the USSR.

Why is Yeltsin so popular? In part because he defied a basic rule for political careers in the Soviet system. The rule says there is no comeback for a fallen politician. This terrible totalitarian machine first produced bosses, then utilized them as fuel for itself to further its horrendous movement. At best, it just threw people away, reduced them to ashes, letting them live and die in obscurity. At its worst, it killed them.

But Yeltsin didn't disappear into obscurity. He came back and became so popular that it is in the best interests of Gorbachev to protect him rather than try to edge him out. For if anything were to happen to Yeltsin, it could cause a civil war. Yeltsin, however, has already freed himself from "protection" by the KGB: His personal guards—up to ten people—do not work in the KGB and are responsible to the parliament of Russia.

In reemerging from obscurity, not only did Yeltsin become immensely popular, he helped make obsolete the very notion of the USSR as a whole. This kind of makes Gorbachev a king without a kingdom. Soon Yeltsin may become the chairman of a Council of Presidents of Independent Republics, where there will be no place for Gorbachev. Remaining president of the USSR, Gorbachev will have purely nominal and ceremonial functions, not unlike those of the queen of England in the British Commonwealth.

Meanwhile, Gorbachev, although an historic and definitely positive figure, still tries to solder the old saucepan of socialism. His efforts are wasted, because this saucepan never did hold water. People in the USSR have a saying: "Soviet paralysis is the most progressive in the world."

Yeltsin's past shouldn't be idealized. He was the almighty party boss of the huge Sverdlovsk territory. I am quite sure than in 1985 Gorbachev was closer to understanding democracy than Yeltsin was, but in 1986, when Yeltsin was appointed Moscow party boss, he started to leave Gorbachev behind.

Yeltsin worked from 8 in the morning until 12 at night and slept in a small room next to his office. He really tried to improve the quality of life for people. Suddenly Moscow started to look more human, there were more vegetables in the shops, the ruined transportation system was improving. He kicked out the entrenched Moscow "apparatchiks." Corrupted and lazy, they tried to stop him. In 1987 he made a critical speech at the closed plenary meeting of the Party. Gorbachev had called for self-criticism within the Party, but this was going too far. Within the Politburo, Yeltsin was abandoned by everybody.

Badly hit by heart disease and "burnt out," Yeltsin was pushed out of the way, to the joy of bureaucrats. But Gorbachev did not destroy Yeltsin entirely, instead giving him an insignificant job. That was Gorbachev's way of getting rid of Yeltsin and at the same time persuading the West that people could dissent and still hold top jobs.

But at home it made Yeltsin a martyr. He was thrown from the top, he "suffered for truth," he became more human and, at the same time, a symbol. Sakharov was a bigger martyr, a real martyr, but for the bulk of the nation he was too much of an intellectual, too much a "citizen of the world," while Yeltsin is flesh of the flesh, blood of the blood.

Thus, whatever was said against him by Gorbachev immediately worked for Yeltsin. His modest "Moskvich" car, in which he used to drive to the meetings of parliament, contrasted sharply with the huge black party limousines, baptized by the people as "coffins." At the 19th party conference, when Yeltsin asked for political rehabilitation, Yegor Ligachev assailed Yeltsin with all the rhetoric at his command: "Thou are not right, Boris." After that, the cooperatives manufactured millions of badges with the words: "Thou are not right, Yegor." In 1989 92% of Moscovites elected Yeltsin to the USSR parliament.

In 1990, before leaving for the summit, Gorbachev gathered the Russian parliament deputies, asking them not to vote for Yeltsin. That virtually guaranteed Yeltsin's election.

Although power has moved from Gorbachev to Yeltsin, the critical moves still lie in the future. The first move will be the conversion of state enterprises into rented, private, stockholding companies. This process will start widely at the end of 1990. The second will be abolition of a centralized distribution and supply system. Here the first critical point will be reached sometime between February and June 1991, the second not earlier than the winter of 1991–92. These are problems, but the problems of growth, not stagnation.

What is the near future? The economic privatization program is already laid out—far ahead of Gorbachev's timid moves to allow private property. When the Russian paliament meets again on September 3, I'm sure foreign economic activity will be a top-priority question.

Some of the most far-reaching consequences of Yeltsin's accession to power will be in the area of foreign relations. This year the decisions will be made whether to cut supplies from Russia to such hot points as Cuba, Libya, and Syria. Can Yeltsin and the Russian parliament overrule the USSR government on foreign relations? Yes. And Russia will demand hard currency for its oil rather than almost giving it away to Cuba. Soldiers from Russia will no longer be sent to interfere in ethnic conflicts beyond Russia's border.

If Saddam Hussein has any hopes of help from Russia, he is only fooling himself. On the contrary, Russia can help relieve any shortages Saddam Hussein tries to create. It can do so by stepping up its own oil production. All it needs is Western geophysical technology and equipment. For this it will make its own deals, bypassing Gorbachev's government.

The question of Russia's participation in the United Nations and the European Community will soon be on the agenda. Membership won't come overnight, but things are moving in that direction.

In all this, for the real initiatives, look to Boris Yeltsin and not to Mikhail Gorbachev. Yeltsin is the leader. A poll of public opinion has shown that 84% of the USSR population supports Yeltsin, while only 12% supports Gorbachev.

And, for perhaps the first time in Russian history, what the population really wants really matters.

COLD WAR ON OIL MELTING WITH CHANGES IN RUSSIA

Iraq's invasion of Kuwait could be a blessing in disguise for the West, and for the Russians, whose firm support for sanctions against Baghdad reflects the new, still unfamiliar, face of Soviet politics.

The increasing assertiveness of the Russian Federation under Boris Yeltsin, its radical president, also promises to speed up the unlocking of untold energy riches in Siberia to Western oil companies.

This favorable scenario for both sides of the diminishing East–West divide is endorsed by Professor Vladimir Kvint, one of the young Siberian economists who are striding boldly toward a Soviet market economy. Currently lecturing at Fordham University in New York, he was last week feted by *Forbes*, the American magazine, as the man who accurately predicted the split between Russia and the Soviet Union.

In an interview with *The Times*, he made clear that he believes Mr. Yeltsin will by next year have created the right business climate for Western companies. Within two years, he sees this producing the boost in oil output vital to regenerating Russia and alleviating pressure on world oil prices.

The Germans have long recognized that the Russians' underdeveloped natural resources are a long-term answer to Western Europe's poverty in indigenous oil and gas. The battle Bonn fought against a fiercely anti-Soviet Washington, in the early 1980s, over the Siberia–West Europe gas pipeline demonstrated West German determination not to be caught out by over-reliance on Middle East energy. The two oil shocks of the previous decade were enough.

Appalling mismanagement, lower world oil prices, and cold war concern about military secrecy combined to discourage any oil rush to the remoter regions of the Soviet Union by Western companies. With hindsight, that would appear unfortunate.

Economic confusion and a lack of state-of-the-art oil technology combined to reduce Soviet oil output to about 11.8 million barrels

The Times (London), Friday, August 10, 1990, p. 23.

per day this year from 12.2 million per day two years ago. These severe cuts in supplies to its former Eastern European satellites have given a harsh reality to the statistics. But the picture for proven reserves is much brighter. At the end of 1989 these stood at 58.4 billion barrels, putting the Soviets on a par with producers like Venezuela and Mexico. American reserves, by comparison, were 34.1 billion.

Professor Kvint underlined it as the lack of financial, hard currency resources that is behind the under-development of Soviet oil.

The Russian Federation stretches from the Baltic Sea in the West, across Siberia, to the Pacific. Established resources are fabulous. The huge oilfield discovered between the Lena and Tungunska rivers in Siberia is just one of the many waiting to be tapped.

Professor Kvint cautions against investing hope in the traditional Soviet oil center on the Caspian. He is also highly critical of the poor quality of the equipment produced for the oil industry in Baku, the capital of Azerbaijan.

In Mr. Yeltsin, however, he sees change for the better. Economic policy in Russia, in his view, has undergone a decisive shift since June when Mr. Yeltsin proclaimed Russian sovereignty. "This drastically reduced the political risk of economic development, especially in Siberia and the [Soviet] Far East," Professor Kvint said.

The Yeltsin program allows only 500 days to reorient the Russian economy, a healthier pace than envisaged by Soviet President Gorbachev. Professor Kvint is convinced that this will allow 100% private ownership to Russians and foreigners alike within a year.

Though the ultimate goal of ruble convertibility will probably not be achievable in less than three years, he expects the republics to begin operating parallel currencies before then. The speed at which they are introduced will depend on the republics' relative economic performance.

"There are too many rubles without any backing," Professor Kvint says. Last year alone, some 8 billion [BP16.8 million] unbacked rubles were issued. The parallel convertible ruble, he anticipates, could only be issued on a limited scale, probably some 20 billion initially. This would be largely backed by hard currency earnings.

The market economy Mr. Yeltsin is going hell-for-leather toward will not mean any rape of the Russian Federation's resources. Professor Kvint expects it to put a real price on them. "Business will be only on an economic basis," Professor Kvint stressed. And that goes for oil too. "Russia has huge potential. And it does not even produce offshore yet. Joint enhancement of existing fields and development of new ones could drastically increase oil output." If he is right, Western companies could soon be treating Mr. Yeltsin like the governor of Alaska.

RESHUFFLING THE SOVIET DECK

Some people thought we sounded pretty farfetched when our cover story February 19 predicted Russia would quit the present Soviet Union, which would then re-form as a looser federation. That has partly come to pass. Boris Yeltsin proclaimed the sovereignty of Russia's laws over the Union's; the Ukraine and Uzbekistan have made similar moves. Our article was written by Vladimir Kvint, 41, a Siberian economist who is currently lecturing at Fordham University in New York and doing consulting work. What does Kvint see now? "The most influential figure is not Gorbachev but Yeltsin," he says, and adds, "American companies must now consider the different policies of the new governments of each of the republics." He says Siberia and the Soviet Far East are currently politically stable and thus the safest and most fertile fields for foreign investment.

Forbes, August 6, 1990, p. 8.

THE BEST WAY TO HELP GORBACHEV IS TO MAKE LIFE DIFFICULT FOR HIM

Reagan, Thatcher and Kohl pushed Gorbachev toward democracy. Until Americans understand this, they cannot deal intelligently with the Soviet Union.

In failing to press Gorbachev on behalf of Lithuanian freedom, the Western governments may have unwittingly brought to a halt the further progress of perestroika. President Bush and his allies wanted to avoid pushing Gorbachev into a corner. Instead they have strengthened the hands of those in the Soviet Union who are trying to stop the movement of progress.

The general attitude in the U.S. seems to be the following: Gorbachev has liberated the USSR and Eastern Europe, now he is in a difficult situation, and America should support him whatever he does.

I also think Gorbachev needs help. But a totally different kind of help.

Few Americans, even those who specialize in Soviet affairs, have any idea about the real processes of making decisions, about the methods of collecting reliable data in the USSR. It is not their fault. In Siberia, for example, only three or four cities are open to foreigners, and there they will definitely see nothing. It is almost impossible to understand the situation in the USSR having never spoken with the outlaws of society in Penza, or traveled to the Arctic zone, which occupies 40% of Soviet territory.

Without correct information, it is difficult to understand the forces moving Gorbachev to perestroika. These forces were partly domestic: the sick economy and increasing demands for democracy. But outside forces were at least as important. The outside forces were Ronald Reagan, Margaret Thatcher, and Helmut Kohl. Acting

Forbes, June 11, 1990, pp. 168–172.

together, these forces brought the USSR to the table of negotiations and led to the first historic agreements between Gorbachev and Reagan.

I do not mean to say that Mikhail Gorbachev is not a positive figure. He is. Other Soviet leaders would have tried to deal with festering problems with military force. However, he is not the initiator; he is the follower. When he took over five years ago, the country was already on the verge of disaster. The people had lost their faith in everything. Labor productivity stopped growing after 1978. In natural resources, each additional unit of output required increasing input; oil wells had to pump much deeper, mining and exploration went farther and farther east, farther and farther north. In 1985–86 oil production started to decrease by 4.2% a year. In every respect, the Soviet economy was at a dead end.

In 1985 Mikhail Gorbachev, in charge of agriculture, was the youngest member of the Politburo. Agriculture was proving to be the Bermuda Triangle of the Soviet economy; vast investments were poured into it, only to disappear without increasing output. He was the first Soviet leader to take seriously reports sent to him by Siberian economists on the disintegrating economy. Most other Soviet leaders tried to ignore the facts.

But remember this: Gorbachev did not appear from nowhere. He was not a total break with the past. He grew within the almighty party bureaucratic system. Gorbachev is an excellent tactician, and he obeyed all the laws of that dark and illogical system.

Theoretically, under communist ideology, the majority rules. In reality, a tiny elite minority suppresses the majority. The system creates lies upon cynical lies. For example, in 1964, when Khrushchev was in the south on vacation with his longtime colleague Mikoyan, the Politburo gathered in Moscow to overthrow Khrushchev. When Mikoyan saw the way the wind was blowing, he immediately sent to Moscow a "wise" telegram. "I side with the majority." This cynicism is typical of the Communist Party leaders. The "majority" Mikoyan sided with was in fact a tiny minority suppressing tens of millions of Soviet citizens.

So, while making Gorbachev a star, America should not forget that he is a leader of the same Communist Party that did all this. And Gorbachev always insists that perestroika is only an improvement of socialism.

By 1985 major forces outside the country were influencing Gorbachev. By escalating the arms race, Reagan and Bush pushed military expenses sky-high for the USSR. The weak economy of the USSR could not bear the burden any longer.

While Reagan, along with Margaret Thatcher and Helmut Kohl, was applying pressure, events within the Soviet Union were strengthening the position of the democratic forces there. People were becoming disgusted with the cruel, corrupted system and appalled by the coffins arriving every day from Afghanistan.

Gorbachev, responding to the strength of popular anger, moved toward democracy. For example, many people demanded the government confess Stalin's guilt for his crimes. But only when these demands became almost irresistible did Gorbachev accede to them. Gorbachev is and was part of that same reactive system, which does not initiate reform but grants it only reluctantly when the pressures become irresistible.

Up to the very last day Gorbachev spoke against the amendment to the constitution abolishing the provision for the leading role of the Communist Party. And only when members of the Supreme Council, supported by millions of people, voiced their protest did he agree.

To Gorbachev's credit, he responded to the demand for democracy in a positive manner. However, Gorbachev should not be called a liberator of Eastern Europe. What is happening there was not a matter of his wishes. At the end of 1988–89 the communist regimes there were in a state of clinical death. Hunger in Poland and Romania became a real danger. Economic war among the socialist countries was on the way. Democratic forces inside these countries were ready to take power. The economic basis of tyranny had collapsed—this, and not any special Gorbachev strategy, is what has liberated Eastern Europe.

In the beginning of perestroika, bureaucrats and other reactionary forces were thrown on the defensive. Political reforms in the country found such strong promoters as Alexander Yakovlev. But Prime Minister Ryzhkov dragged his heels and proposals by market-oriented economists were not implemented. The few elements of a market economy that were finally introduced were overwhelmed in the horrendous chaos of a so-called planned economy.

By the end of 1989 the foot-dragging had allowed the bureaucrats to consolidate with Russian nationalists and anti-Semites to create a powerful force against reform. This, combined with the West's weakening, less definite position, stopped social revolution in the USSR in March 1990. This was reflected in the people Gorbachev personally selected to join the President's Council. Out of 16 members, only 3 can be called progressive. The notorious anti-Semitic leader Valentin Rasputin is a member.

Hitler failed in his ambition to hold a parade in Red Square, but Pamyat, the Russian fascist, anti-Semitic organization, held a meeting in Red Square. Just as the czar's agents used anti-Semitism as a means of turning popular discontent away from the regime, so the KGB is using it today.

Lithuania came as a test of Gorbachev's new position. Toward the end of 1989 it was suggested to Gorbachev that he could abolish the Union Treaty (which was signed in 1922; Latvia, Estonia, and Lithuania were chained forcibly to the USSR in 1940) and allow the republics the opportunity to join the USSR under new, mutually beneficial, fair conditions. Gorbachev failed to do so. Lithuania and the other Baltic states went on to declare their independence.

As the anti-reform forces gained strength, Gorbachev dithered, in large part because the Western powers let up their pressure. Kohl seems willing to concede anything for the opportunity to unify Germany. Thatcher is loyal to her views, but her own position in Britain has become weaker. The While House has adopted a much softer line.

However, what Gorbachev badly needs is renewed pressure from the West, to help nudge the system back on to the path of reform and democratization. It is a general belief in the West that if the West supports Lithuania's demands for freedom, it is going to ruin Gorbachev. What about the supposed danger that Gorbachev will be overthrown if the West puts too much pressure on the USSR over Lithuania or any other matter? It's nonsense. Gorbachev is not in danger. What happened to Khrushchev cannot happen to Gorbachev. In Khrushchev's time there was only one decisive force—the Politburo, whose members decided to overthrow the leader. But today there are four forces: Comrade President, the KGB, the Central Committee of the Communist Party, and the Supreme Soviet (the parliament). But there is one main power: the President. He brings together other dispersed forces. They need him, if only as a symbol.

The KGB? It is as active as ever. But it is controlled by the president. The party? I am sure that the Communist Party, which is disintegrating now, in half a year will be abandoned by a lot of important people. After the next elections it will definitely lose its majority status.

The military? The USSR should not be mistaken for Chile or Nicaragua. The Soviet military has never been a powerful force in its own right. The rumors concerning the political role of "military discontent" are nothing but a political game. Soviet military people have always been nothing but pawns on the political chessboard. The military is an instrument, not a wielder, of power.

As for the KGB's overthrowing Gorbachev, that's out of the question. The KGB's people are counting on Gorbachev to rescue them from the people's wrath. They remember all too well what happened to the secret police after the democratic upsets in Eastern Europe.

So Gorbachev is not in danger, but his reforms are. If America is firm, Gorbachev will find arguments to resist the diehards in the USSR. He will be able to say to them: If we crush Lithuania, America will not sign arms control agreements or trade agreements, and we will not be able to feed the people. We must let Lithuania go.

The USSR is a prison of nations, and no republic, including the Russian Federation, wants this union anymore. The prisoner and the guard are both unhappy.

The anti-democratic forces in the USSR have no economic basis anymore, but they can flourish if the U.S. offers arms control, scientific-technical cooperation, and investments—without demanding important domestic political concessions in return.

The 1917 revolution, or rather counterrevolution, repressed the Russian spring of economic development for 72 years. Only the undoing of that revolution and its replacement with a democratic regime can get the country's economy moving to market. Shortsighted efforts to "save Gorbachev" will serve only to save a rotten regime from history's garbage heap for a few years longer.

FREE THE RUBLE!

Lacking an international currency, the people of the Soviet Union cannot speak the only language the free, international economy understands: money. So let currencies compete.

Vladimir Kvint is a member of the "Siberian School" of Soviet economists and an associate of economists Leonid Abalkin and Abel Aganbegyan, the godfathers of perestroika. Below, he rejects the idea of a gold standard for his country but urges that the ruble soon be made convertible into foreign currencies. He urges that the ruble be allowed to float by permitting foreign currencies to circulate freely in the Soviet Union, thus setting a natural exchange rate. Only that way can the Soviet Union be integrated into the world economy.

Is the ruble nothing but rubble, a weak substitute for money in the crisis-ridden country? Definitely, no. It is just a prisoner that is not allowed to go to the party of the world economy, for mostly political reasons. But it is not worthless.

The ruble is already convertible. Wise foreign businessmen know how to convert their rubles into hard currency, using not only old methods of barter and counter-trade but also some new ones. In the center of Vienna, you can convert your rubles into hard currency in a bank. The rate is funny and unfair to those holding Soviet currency: 6 U.S. cents for one ruble. This is far below what the ruble should be worth, but it's all foreigners will pay today for a currency they cannot easily use. The bank should not be blamed for this. The Soviet government should.

The Soviet Union's former leadership imprisoned the ruble the same way it imprisoned Soviet citizens. Things are now much better for citizens, but not for the ruble. It is still not freely convertible, not officially free to travel outside the homeland.

Nonconvertibility of the ruble is a malignant tumor that affects all aspects of the Soviet economy. It kills motivation of labor, it enlarges shortages, it stops the flow of foreign investment to the USSR.

Forbes, April 2, 1990, pp. 92–95.

Let's look at this problem. The Soviet Union is not a poor country. Statistics developed during Stalin's time naïvely conceal Soviet gold and diamond reserves, but a simple correlation analysis of Soviet data and the world gold and diamond markets shows that the USSR has one of the biggest gold reserves in the world. And since World War II, the USSR hasn't sold diamonds bigger than 10 carats and almost no diamonds bigger than 5 carats. It is clear that, being among the biggest diamond producers, the Soviet Union stores all these treasures in its diamond fund.

The USSR is the owner of huge natural resources. It is the biggest producer of oil, gas, steel, timber, and the majority of nonferrous metals: copper, nickel, cobalt, and platinum. All of this is not mythical but real backing for the ruble.

So much for those who say the Soviet Union lacks the reserves to back a truly international currency.

The USSR is known in all the banks of the world as one of the most reliable payers of interest. And though the international economic debt of the USSR has grown to more than $50 billion, and its hard currency debt today is 2.2 times its annual export revenues, for the USSR it is only a matter of several months' work to repay all the debt. By comparison, Hungary needs about ten years to do it. Poland, which has more than $40 billion in debt, does not even lend itself to comparison.

Yet the currency of the Soviet Union is close to worthless abroad because it lacks convertibility. Call it a wooden ruble. The wooden ruble is worsening the economic crisis under way in the USSR. People have 330 billion rubles in their savings accounts, and 120 billion rubles more, as we say, "in the stockings" at home. With inflation in the consumption sector at 15% in 1989, the holders of these rubles lose purchasing power month by month. Meanwhile, there is little to buy. Where they can, people resort to simple barter. For example, Soviet collective farms exchange 500 tons of grain for one 10-ton Kamaz truck, or 6 tons of grain for 1 ton of cement. This shows not only political but also economic nearness of our system to feudalism.

The American economist Thorstein Veblen (1857–1929) wrote about the formation of a money civilization in a negative sense. But I think that money civilization reflects a healthy economy. The USSR has not yet reached this level of health.

Not all the steps of the present government are incorrect, but the government is lagging behind the real tempo of perestroika. The steps are extremely, damagingly slow. Soviet enterprises are now allowed to keep 70% of their hard currency profits; the enterprises hold $3 billion. A hard currency auction has been held. The dollar/ruble rate for nontrade operations has been changed—since last November foreigners have been able to change $1 for 6.2 rubles, or 16 cents to the ruble, versus the silly official rate of $1.60 to the ruble. Collective farms are paid hard currency by the state for certain food products.

The exchange rate granted to foreigners, 16 cents, is barely one-tenth the official rate, but it is still nearly three times what I can get for my rubles in Vienna.

What we need, clearly, is a single realistic rate. This can be achieved only through a ruble that is freely convertible into other currencies. Based on my analysis of the current Soviet economic crisis, I will risk the following forecast: By 1991 a limitedly convertible ruble may already be available for joint ventures and in free economic zones; two or three such zones will become operational. One of them, near the Far Eastern port of Nakhodka (which means "discovery"), has already become a discovery for the Japanese businessmen who for over ten years have been pouring investments into this region.

The other forward station of entrepreneurial activity will be the city of Viborg, near the Soviet–Finnish border. My opinion is that in free economic zones all currencies will circulate, competing in terms of their "hardness." Currency auctions this year and especially in 1991 will become an everyday practice and not, as now, just a fashion show. Because of all this, the number of joint ventures will come up to 2,800 in 1990. In 1991, I think, a stock exchange will be established.

A serious problem remains. Whatever is the best in the USSR is exported, sold for hard currency. But the Soviet workers who produce these goods suffer burglaries by their own government worse than the ones described by Marx at the hands of the capitalists. They are completely separated from the hard currency profits they produce. (In a few small cases, hard currency salaries do exist. In 1988, for example, I went to the Latvian fishing collective farm Uzvara. There the fishermen get 25% of their salary in hard currency.)

In the USSR more than 15,000 enterprises export their goods to the West. All the workers of these enterprises and of the enterprises supplying them should get part of the enterprises' hard currency profits as some percentage of their salaries.

Will that be unfair to others? When I am called a proponent of capitalism in the USSR, I quote Marx. He said that total equality is a total inequality. Good labor should be motivated.

They should be allowed to spend their hard currency inside the USSR as well. This will also create a good market for foreign producers of consumer goods. This year the domestic hard currency consumer market will total about $2.5 billion. With such innovations the USSR can only benefit: The government will receive taxes on profits and customs duties for repatriation of hard currency profits by foreign businessmen.

It is necessary to abolish the stupid restriction that prohibits foreign companies from operating with rubles. Today, many of these companies already have rubles and many more would like to have them, but the former are prohibited from selling them to the latter. Last summer, walking along Lexington Avenue in New York, I tried to find out what I could buy for $1. Practically nothing. Even a hot dog is more expensive. In Moscow, with 1 ruble in your pocket, you can have, on Gorky Street, a tolerable lunch in a canteen. For 1 kopek (there are 100 kopeks to a ruble) you can buy a glass of mineral water or a box of matches. For 5 kopeks, less than 1 cent at the ruble/dollar rate I envision, you can travel all day long in the underground. For 20 kopeks you can buy a kilogram of good bread. So don't tell me the ruble is worth only 6 cents. But 6 cents is what it fetches abroad because of the current government policy of nonconvertibility.

So as not to create great inflation, the amount of convertible rubles issued into circulation should not exceed the value of Soviet exports and value of consumer goods and food products produced on the quality level of the world market. Moreover, the equivalent sum of wooden rubles should immediately be burned.

I do not think convertibility should be brought about by government fiat but rather by the market itself. I am proposing parallel circulation of wooden rubles—the nonconvertible money we now have—and limitedly convertible rubles. Hard currencies—dollars, for example, or deutsche marks—should circulate, too, because that will facilitate normalization and satisfaction of the market. We would have a system of competing currencies, with the market, rather than government fiat, setting the correct exchange rate among them. And the ruble would become real money in the international sense.

Speculations about putting the Soviet Union on a gold standard seem to me practically useless because, in 1971, the U.S. officially abolished the gold standard. And if the dollar has no gold standard, establishment of a gold standard for the currency of any other country would lead only to melting of its gold reserve. One should not violate the trend of internationalization of national economies—the replacement of gold as a form of money by credit money.

Political risk is never far from the international businessman's mind. Yet political instability or even crisis has not always hampered convertibility. In Yugoslavia, in the middle of bitter economic and political crisis and violent ethnic conflict, the government has declared the dinar convertible. What happened? Contrary to many predictions, Yugoslavia has enlarged its hard currency reserves significantly, just in one month.

In the Russia of the seventeenth century, all foreigners were called *nemtsy*—meaning "the dumb"—just because they didn't speak Russian. Money is the language of an economy. If the currency is nonconvertible, the language is untranslatable. Strictly speaking, we don't have real money in the Soviet Union. With a convertible currency we would have.

LENIN'S LEGACY

Whoever attempts to guide the Soviet Union over the coming years, he or she must confront the centuries-old nationalities problem. It is a daunting challenge. Lenin declared that Ukrainians, Balts, and other ethnic groups would, under communism, have the right to secede from the Soviet Union. Under Stalin and his successors, it was a meaningless right. But the Bolshevik promise has returned to haunt the Soviet Union's rulers in this time of glasnost and perestroika.

The author of our cover story argues that, economically, many of the Soviet Union's most independence-minded republics are better off inside the Soviet Union than outside it. The startling conclusion to the article: Russia herself should secede. "In order to unite," writes the author, "republics of the Soviet Union should separate."

The story was written by Vladimir Kvint. A pillar of the now-influential "Siberian School" of market-oriented Soviet economists since the early 1970s, Kvint has worked closely with deputy prime Minister Leonid Abalkin and Abel Aganbegyan, principal architects of perestroika. Kvint is currently honorable professor of economics in Vienna, and a consultant to Western businesses interested in Soviet ventures.

Forbes, February 19, 1990.

RUSSIA AS CINDERELLA

Instead of waiting for the outlying republics to secede, Russia itself should break away from the Soviet Union. So argues this influential Soviet economist.

Will the Baltic republics actually separate from the Soviet Union or not? If yes, will Moscow's response be military intervention, as it was in 1968 in Czechoslovakia? These are the questions that have been worrying many people for a long time. In the meanwhile, mutual reproaches within the Soviet Union are growing into real quarrels and may come to a dead end.

Is there no way out? Maybe a drastically new approach to this problem is necessary. Maybe Russia should be the first to separate from all the other republics and thereby give the others the freedom of choice, too.

For decades the official image was of a "unanimous family of nations" in the USSR, a friendly circle of people in national costumes, marching hand in hand toward progress and harmony. With glasnost, this fiction has given way to a more realistic picture. No more "hand-in-hand" circles.

Not so long ago my friends from Estonia were joking: Our republic is the most independent—just because nothing depends on it. Now that has changed: World peace, international stability itself, may depend on what happens in these Baltic republics and in Azerbaijan.

We are now accustomed to satellite photos of atmospheric masses, quickly moving and powerfully changing the global weather. The political and democratic will of people in the Soviet Union is changing the political atmosphere with the same power and speed. It goes without saying: People of any nation should have the right of self-determination.

At the same time there exist certain economic realities, and national feelings—no matter how passionately felt and how legitimate—cannot ignore these economic realities. Economists should have cool enough heads to give economic evaluation to political de-

Forbes, February 19, 1990, pp. 103–108.

cisions. The economic reality is that self-sufficiency is a two-way street. If Russia itself—as I suggest above—were to adopt the principles of self-sufficiency and take its own measure, the standard of living in the Baltic republics would inevitably and sharply decrease.

In this kind of divorce, the wife should not necessarily expect alimony. If Russia were to secede from the Soviet Union, it would not have to continue giving economic aid to its former fellow states.

In the beginning of our century an Italian economist, Vilfredo Pareto, formulated a principle of "economic well-being." As applied to the Soviet Union, Pareto's principle would be expressed in this way: The standard of living and effectiveness of the economies of any of the republics can be increased only up the point where it is not done at the expense of other republics. Otherwise, negative reaction, harmful to everybody, is inevitable.

There is a hope among Baltic nationalists that the Baltic republics have good prospects for developing industries connected with scientific progress—high tech, in the American phrase—as well as for the export of agricultural products. These hopes may not be realistic. Compare the cost structure in Estonia with that in Austria. Estonian costs for producing milk are 2.9 times higher than in Austria, and 2.8 times higher in the case of meat. The picture does not change in terms of others' products. In short, Estonian products simply cannot be sold in international markets at prices that would recover their costs.

Only 2.2% of Estonia's output is exported at present, well below the 6% figure for the Soviet Union as a whole. Lacking export income, where is Estonia going to get capital for the development of high technologies?

Other Union republics buy goods from Estonia at prices that are sometimes 10 to 20 times higher than prices on the world market. On the other hand, Estonia gets oil, gas, raw materials of the highest quality from Siberia at prices ranging from 50% down to 15% of the price on the international market. That means that under a system of regional self-sufficiency, the same Estonia will have to pay the real price for energy resources.

Were Siberia to reduce its deliveries of energy resources to the Baltic republics by 20%, it could cause a decrease of Baltic production output by 40%.

These concessional prices were part of the Soviet policy of aiming for equal economic development among the various republics. Instead of the full benefit of Siberian oil going to Siberia, some of it was shared with Estonia and other non–oil-producing republics.

The leveling of social-economic development of the republics for dozens of years has been carried out at the expense of "the older sister" in this "unanimous family." The older sister is, of course, Russia. Those republics that were "helped" in many parameters went far ahead of Russia. Instead of becoming the princess, Russia became Cinderella.

It is clear that the example of neighboring, highly developed Finland impresses the Estonians. They would like to be like Finland and hope that independence would do for them what it did for Finland. If the Baltic republics could return to the beginning of the century, maybe they could find their place in the economic system of the West, as Finland has. But today world markets are already divided; a system of world economic relations is formed already. It would be extremely difficult for Estonia, if at all possible, to break into this established system, where everyone fights for his place in the sun. Estonia can quit the Soviet Union, but it cannot roll back history.

The Baltic republics and other secessionist regions may hope for economic help from abroad. But it is highly unlikely that a whole region will be granted "refugee" status. As for loans, how can the Baltic republics repay them? With what? Overpriced milk?

It would be shortsighted and self-defeating for the Baltics and other secessionists to sacrifice economic well-being to the dream of political independence. For example, the idea of the introduction of new Baltic currency won't serve the purpose of creating a market system; it is at variance with the concept of a "common European home" and with the realities of today's life. The European Community is integrating; a unique currency; "ecu," has been created and is already functioning.

The secessionists tend to forget the sacrifices made on their behalf by the people of Russia and other areas. For example, in Sverdlovsk (Urals) and Donetsk (Ukraine) the basic industrial facilities are the oldest in the country, because much of the available capital has been sent to other parts of the Soviet Union. Yet the productivity of labor in Sverdlovsk and Donetsk is the highest in the country, and the standard of living is almost the lowest. It is not by accident that these regions became the sites of the biggest strikes of 1989.

Look deeper into some of the ethnic/nationalist tensions within the Soviet Union, and you find economic causes. Take the city of Uzen, in Kazakstan. The main reason for the hatred of the Kazaks toward the Caucasians working in Kazakstan is not a national one. In the Caucasian republic of Daghestan there is severe unemployment—up to 35%. Many people there moved to take jobs in the enterprises of Kazakstan. But there are no normal transport connections between Daghestan and Kazakstan. Because of that, many Caucasians, instead of commuting to Kazakstan, had to settle there with their families. Every thousand workers there manufacture production worth 3.5 million to 4 million rubles more than the equivalent production in Daghestan.

Several years ago I predicted that the economic disparities between these two regions would lead to conflict. They were unable to become one economic unity without transport communication.

I proposed to improve the situation immediately by building transport lines, but this proposal was not carried out. Unsolved economic problem, forecast in 1986, turned into bloody conflict in 1989.

So, I think it is criminal to pretend that there are no conflicts between the republics. The immediate result of such head-in-the-sand behavior is the war within the USSR between its republics of Armenia and Azerbaijan.

What is happening to the Baltic republics, therefore, has meaning for the entire Soviet Union. The notion of regional self-sufficiency is a child of perestroika. At the same time, it is one of the great dangers for perestroika. It can sharpen the contradictions and conflicts.

True self-sufficiency can be attained only by viable economic units, not by purely political or nationalist regions. The effectiveness of regional economies now depends first and foremost on interregional connections. One should take into account existing reality. Out of 150 Estonian industries, as few as 18 are oriented only to Estonian inner necessities. The same goes for other republics. Whether the people of the various republics like it or not, their economic destinies are bound together. The European Community is transcending national differences at least as great as those within the Soviet Union. This must be our model rather than anachronistic dreams of ethnic sovereignty. Autarchic development is impossible today, under the conditions of internationalization of the modern world.

Even a rather short railway blockade of Armenia showed what the results of a forced autarchy can be.

According to my evaluation, out of all Union republics only the Russian Federation, Ukraine, and Belorussia can independently solve their problems. They alone could make a viable economic entity. In Russia the ruble can be backed by gold, diamonds, mineral resources. If Baltic republics create their own money, how can they be backed, especially with the existing level of industrial and economic development?

This is not to denigrate nationalist sentiment. Indignation of any Estonian—or any Russian, or Tadzhik—can be easily understood, when an all-Union enterprise operates on their land having almost extra-territorial rights, like a foreign embassy. It is also very clear that no economic calculations can kill the eternal desire for freedom.

Hence my proposal for a Russian secession from the Soviet Union. In order to unite, republics of the Soviet Union should separate.

The Russian Federation should be the first to put forward the ideas of breaking the old Union treaty. This will give opportunity to all the republics to regard all pros and cons and decide voluntarily whether they want or don't want a new Union.

Only under the condition of liberty and voluntary unification can economic considerations be given full play. The quicker Moscow, the Supreme Soviet of the country, cancels the old Union treaty, the more probability there is that the Soviet Union will remain a union. Cancellation of the old treaty would be not a destruction of the country, but its revival. It is interesting that Russia possibly may be the first to profit from that, because it can also enter the new treaty, securing its interests.

Which of the republics is going to enter this new Union? I think, almost all. But this is not what is important. Who has lost after the end of the British Empire and creation of the British Commonwealth? England? Its role in the world of today shows that it has only profited by the new structure.

Has Austria lost after the disintegration of Austro-Hungary eight decades ago? I think the answer is even more clear—Austria has lost nothing; the standard of living of the Austrian population has increased.

As I see it, the USSR's future is one of politically and economically independent states, united in a federation or a confederation. Everything depends on conditions, written in the future Union treaty. Mutual benefit—not only mutual help—is the key to a strong Union of independent states.

Such a Union, based on a market economy, will facilitate integration of economies of independent republic states. For the Baltic republics, formation of a Baltic market is of essential importance, but it should be an open market, without obstacles in the way of effective cooperation with Russia and other republics on the one side and with the countries of the European Association of Free Trade and the European Community on the other.

But speed is necessary. It is impossible to solve the Soviet Union's nationalism problems by using force. But dithering is almost equally dangerous. If Moscow contemplates any longer, the results may be extremely negative. From the point of view of economy, this is a situation of dynamic balance. Whoever wants more in this situation may lose everything.

In Antwerp, I have seen a small statue of a worker, and the inscription on it, which consisted of only two words, was "Liberty works." It works for the people of Russia, though, as well as for those of the Baltic republics.

"WE ARE BOGGED DOWN"

The Soviet Union is burdened with an energy crisis, tight food supplies, and poverty. Vladimir L. Kvint, economist in Moscow, is now looking for solutions in the West.

Soviet economists want to learn from the West to overcome the crisis at home. Professor Vladimir L. Kvint, 40, a staff member at the Institute of Economics of the Academy of Sciences in Moscow, serves on the consulting staff of the Head of State and Party Chairman Mikhail Gorbachev. Recently he visited the Federal Republic of Germany.

Quick: Professor Kvint, the Soviet Union is experiencing a harsh winter. Have supply shortages already surfaced as a result?

Kvint: This is the cold season of the great economic crisis. Within the next few months the old system will self-destruct. On the other hand, this is an opportunity for renewal.

Quick: What areas present the biggest problems?

Kvint: Last year the government cut back on investments in heavy industry. This is a very dangerous step, because it results in lower energy supplies, while we haven't seen a concurrent increase in retail food supplies.

Quick: How is it that the economic crisis has worsened since the beginning of perestroika?

Kvint: It started long before perestroika. Economic growth has been on the decline since 1966. This means more and more labor, natural resources, and energy were thrown into the economy, but no actual gains were realized. By the early 1980s we had exhausted our resources. Today, each ton of oil, for example, costs us more than it is worth. When Gorbachev came to power, we had no idea just how

Interview by Wilhelm Dietl and Wolfgang Stockklausner, *Quick* (Munich), 4 (January 1990), 52–53.

much trouble we were in. Continued economic growth is simply impossible under the present conditions.

Quick: Does it have anything to do with the fact that hard work doesn't pay off?

Kvint: No, the problem lies elsewhere. As soon as people get serious about perestroika, they will realize that the old system has exhausted itself. But there isn't a new mechanism, yet. On the other hand, economic reforms that aren't preceded by political democratization are useless. We tried before to implement one without the other. It was dead before it was born. What we need is a fundamentally new mechanism. People won't work efficiently unless they are really free. So far, they haven't achieved an inner freedom. This is a difficult process. That which can lead to democracy can also lead to anarchy.

Quick: One phenomenon that wasn't discovered until the era of perestroika is unemployment. How is it dealt with among the population?

Kvint: Of the Soviet working population a total of 8% are unemployed. A regional problem. In areas with high birth rates there aren't enough jobs. In mountainous Daghestan, as much as 40% are registered as unemployed. Part of the reason is that people don't want to work.

Quick: Forty million Soviet citizens maintain an existence below the poverty level. How do you want to restore hope to them?

Kvint: An absolute minimum of 77 rubles per month is required to make a living. However, 46 million of my fellow countrymen have less. Retirees are hit the hardest. They have an average of 54 rubles. We are in the process of designing a law that helps the poorest among the poor. But everything depends on the economy. We need an economy that is independent and functions without control and as few subsidies as possible.

Quick: So, back to capitalism?

Kvint: Not at all. So far we haven't had a sound model of socialism. But this is where we are headed.

Quick: Have you found a role model, yet?

Kvint: I suppose a sound model of socialism exists in Sweden and Austria.

Quick: We would rather call it free enterprise. Your system has failed for 70 years. To realize this must be painful.

Kvint: It isn't for me. There are good shepherds and bad shepherds. A good shepherd doesn't pull the skin off his sheep but only shears their wool. For many decades we have had bad shepherds.

CRISIS AND RECOVERY IN SOVIET ECONOMY

The Soviet Union is only just beginning to understand the sheer scale of its economic problems, according to Professor Vladimir Kvint, a young Kremlin economic expert. In Kvint's view, the USSR will scarcely have enough time to fully introduce the perestroika process this century and it could soon face serious inter-regional economic competition, a threatening energy shortage, and soaring raw material costs. Despite the difficulties he feels sure that the way to a foreign trade boom has already been opened up and that the introduction of market elements in the economy cannot now be avoided. Professor Kvint, 40, a member of the Siberian School of Economics has had a successful career as an academic and a practical manager in Siberia. He moved to Moscow at the start of perestroika on the staff of Mikhail Gorbachev's economic adviser Abel Agenbegyan.

The character of the Soviet economy is becoming more and more open. Contacts between Soviet business circles and foreign firms, official and unofficial, are extending rapidly as a result of economic reform. But the present economic reforms in the USSR are not the first in its history. There were attempts at reform in 1956 and 1979, but these were limited to theoretical rights. The basic idea was that everything was in good order ideologically, but that the economy required the benefit of a little economic reform. Only naïve people can believe that economic reform is possible without significant political change.

Siberia Ignored

Many leading economists took part in earlier reform attempts, but without sufficient criticism. The real achievements of the Soviet economy were too little used; for example, the Siberian economic

East–West Forum (Vienna), No. 4 (December 1989), pp. 76–77.

school was very critical in the Brezhnev period, but no one listened—even though the achievements of the school were well known. The reform process is like learning to swim, and we are not quite able to keep afloat yet. Political change has been relatively swift and has now overtaken economic reform. It would not be a good thing if political change were slower than economic reform, as has been the case in China.

It would naturally be false to assume that there are no problems with groups and classes—there is an element, the size of which we cannot measure, that is opposed to reform. There is also a large passive section of society who are waiting for developments before they throw in their lot with either side. But in my personal view, there is no way back.

Quality Problem

When reform began in 1985 with a concept for acceleration, hardly anyone knew about the depth of the problems we faced. In 20 years the pace of our economic development had declined two and a half times: between 1966 and 1970 national income grew 7.3%; from 1971 to 1975 income grew 5.8%; between 1976 and 80 growth was 3.8%; and between 1981 and 1985 some 3.2%. This pace of growth has meant there have not been sufficient means available to fund social requirements of the USSR. Three percent income-growth is insufficient to cope with social growth.

I can give concrete examples of detailed problems in our economy. We produce more shoes per person than most other countries. Unfortunately, the quality is in many cases so poor that the shoes remain unbought on the shelf and are returned to the factories to be reused as raw materials. The mechanization of Soviet agriculture is on a greater scale than in the U.S.A., but production is only 20% of U.S. production. In future, we will not need to produce more tractors, but to improve their quality and learn to use them more effectively.

Attempts have been made to increase national income growth from 3.2% to 3.8%. This does not sound like an ambitious plan, but many possibilities for expansion appear to be exhausted.

Energy Problems

In the 1970s the USSR broke many world records in the use of water power and exploitation of oil resources—in 15 years oil production in Siberia increased from 1 million tons to 350. The tempo has stabilized and declined. Oil wells are having to pump ever deeper to maintain production. In my view, the plan for oil production will not be fulfilled this year. Every third barrel of Soviet oil goes for export, and this will bring increasing energy problems. My fear is a serious energy deficit.

There are similar problems with raw materials and in mining. Many metals are mined now at depths greater than 2 km, which involves immense and ever greater investment costs.

We also face enormous interregional problems in a fairer distribution of resources and raw materials. Some 70% of production is in the European part of the USSR, 75% of the energy is east of the Urals, and the biggest area of population growth is in Azerbaijan and the south. It is quite clear what the difficulties are between the regions.

Important Events

All these problems should be taken into consideration in a reform acceleration plan, but the unfortunate thing was that old mechanisms, in management, etc., were used. Perestroika had not made the success of these mechanisms possible; things could no longer function the old way, but this is not so negative. It is one of the most important events in perestroika.

The whole process involves the fate of thousands of people, and the one way to success lies in the destruction of old mechanisms and the introduction of market mechanisms.

Plan Not Fulfilled

This is a difficult process, and our 1990 plan will not be fulfilled. In 1985 it was said we would need two or three years to make perestroika work. The same thing has been said in every year since then. I said in an interview with *Novi Vremi* magazine that there would not be enough time to complete the process in this century. My view caused a scandal, but now many people would agree with me.

There is a virtually complete absence of a banking system in the USSR, and we have reached the limit of our strength with our foreign department. We plan further credits of 16 billion rubles, but these will be sufficient only for the most essential purchases and for debt servicing, although I also feel we will be able to maintain our position as the most reliable international creditor.

"European House"

New steps in internationalization have been taken. The concept of a "European House" presents us with good prospects. The speed of development of joint ventures, which will have a positive effect on the further development of our foreign trade, has increased 20-fold in two years. The Decree of May 18, 1989, has also made possible the establishment of joint ventures abroad, using Soviet capital and resources. This will be important with the establishment of the single European market in 1992, and will also have important effects on our trade with Austria before Austrian entry into the EEC. A first Soviet joint venture on Austrian territory has already been established.

Much will depend on the initiatives of local authorities in the future. The special economic areas will be a main support of this drive for foreign trade. Three zones are planned, and two more are likely in the Kola peninsula and at Ilitchovsk. The first firms who make their mark in these areas will be in a strong position for the future.

AUSTRIAN MACHINES FOR THE SOVIET UNION: IN 1990 THE ECONOMIC CRISIS WILL WORSEN

Professor Vladimir Lwowitsch Kvint was born in 1949 in Krasnoyarsk (Siberia). At 28 he became the Vice-General Director of the Unification of Companies of Nonferrous Metallurgy of Siberia. In 1978 the economic expert Abel Aganbegjan appointed him to the Siberian Division of the Academy of Sciences of the U.S.S.R. in Krasnojarsk. With the beginning of perestroika, he moved to Moscow with Aganbegjan, who is the economic adviser to Party leader Mikhail Gorbachev. In Moscow Kvint worked in the Academy of Sciences. He is the representative of the USSR Academy of Sciences on two common consulting projects that function as joint projects. He is also the leader of the non-profit organization East–West Business Circle in Moscow. In conjunction with the Ludwig Boltzmann Institute of the Economic University in Vienna and the State Academy of Lower Austria, Kvint is developing manager training.

Austria's interconnection with the Comecon Countries is still too small, asserted Professor Vladimir Lwowitsch Kvint, leading researcher of the Economic Institute of the Academy of Sciences in the USSR, in an interview with *Die Presse*. The Eastern countries have less than 10% of Austrian exports, of which the USSR has 6%. One has to consider that the Soviet Union has enormous deposits of energy and raw materials that Austria needs. Yet Moscow does not want to sell more oil, natural gas, and coal, but, rather, process them first.

In this area Austrian firms could form joint ventures with the USSR. Through this, the share of machinery and equipment exports could be raised. The share of exports is only at 32%, half as high as in Japan, and two and a half times as few as in the U.S. Austria could

Interview by Erich Von Hoorn in *Die Presse*: Independent Austrian Daily Newspaper, Monday, November 13, 1989.

also increase equipment delivery for the Soviet food and consumer goods industries. In addition to this there could be good chances for electronics exports.

Until now USSR companies have founded about 1,200 joint ventures with Western firms. In both September and October 130 joint business undertakings were formed. In relation to the total number of joint ventures formed, Austria places in fourth or fifth place.

Plenty of Free Enterprise, and Just a Little Planning

The professor and Doctor of the Economic Sciences judges the economic situation of his country as "complicated." He estimates inflation at about 8%. The decline in oil prices has had a negative effect, such that little is available for import. Debt, however, remains low.

In the coming year the economic crisis can only worsen. This will lead to the downfall of the old commando system, and free enterprise will break through, albeit with Soviet characteristics.

Kvint points out that the USSR had and still has good economists. As an example he reminds us of the Nobel Prize winner Leontieff, who now lives in the U.S. The USSR should not completely abandon planning, because of the enormous size of the country, but should concentrate on linking individual departments. At the same time, regional planning should be developed. Everything else must be left to the free market.

The economist is proud that Western companies use Soviet-style planning in their businesses. In the USSR, on the other hand, such planning has been used in absurd excess. Not just the economy but all of human life is completely planned.

Now new markets must be formed. For example, the workings of the market for means of production, which currently is still controlled by the State. Also, different stock exchanges must be established. Only when this is all introduced will the ruble be convertible. "Only an open country can have a convertible currency" is Kvint's slogan.

He points out the contradiction that developing countries like India and Bangladesh have limited convertible currencies, while the USSR does not, in spite of the fact that the USSR has enormous natural resources and large gold reserves. He expects a limited convertibility of the ruble within two years; in five years the ruble could be completely convertible.

The opening of free enterprise, which many Soviet citizens favor, also has its opponents. They claim that many want to sell the country to the foreigners. Yet interest in the Soviet Union is always increasing: "Our hotels are full."

During his visits to the U.S. Kvint has determined that the American economy is much healthier than the Soviet economy. U.S. President Ronald Reagan has been successful in strengthening the economy and reducing unemployment. At the same time, however, he has cut social security. For that reason, Kvint sees the proper economic development in Sweden and Austria. Austro-Marxism appears especially current to him.

One must view capitalism through modern eyes. Marx and Engels analyzed capitalism in the nineteenth century. Lenin analyzed it in the beginning of the twentieth. "Capitalism has reached a new stage."

Development in China Is the Opposite

There are great differences between development in China and development in the USSR. In the People's Republic, there have been economic reforms, and the country has opened Special Economic Zones; still, the political system has not been democratized. This leads to the tension which ultimately resulted in the June 4th massacre in Tiananmen Square.

In the USSR, everything is just the opposite: Democratization is going forward in leaps and bounds, but the economy lags behind. One can no longer speak of a single party. The People's Front in Latvia or the Ukrainian Movement Ruch are, however, de facto single parties.

Kvint supposes that perestroika will first show its success at the end of the millennium. He judges the development in Hungary as especially positive, and praised their elimination of barriers to private property rights. Even in Latvia there has been progress in this area. There is currently preparation for similar legislation for the entire USSR. This is necessary, as Western firms have already invested half a billion dollars in joint ventures.

RUSSIA CHARTS NEW ISLAND OF CAPITALISM

Murmansk brings to mind wartime arctic convoys, but a free economic zone the Russians are planning for the region could provide a major opportunity for injecting dynamism into Anglo-Soviet trade.

This is the view of Professor Vladimir Kvint, vice chairman of the Soviet Export Association and one of the fast-moving, market-oriented Siberian economists who have risen to prominence during the Gorbachev era.

Though one of the experts advising the Kremlin on how to put perestroika into practice, this leading economic researcher at the Soviet Academy of Sciences, made clear to *The Times* that he is far from convinced that the Soviet government is going about reform in the right way.

Failure to reorganize the economy in response to the political changes of recent years has meant that it is entering an economic and social crisis which will be at its worst at the end of next year, or early 1991, he said.

He sees this crisis as helping to destroy the old economic order, allowing a new one to be created more quickly. "There is only one way—the market economy—but it will have a specific Russian flavor."

But Professor Kvint, who has a background in heavy industry, is critical of the "guns-into-butter" policies now being pursued, switching defense plants to the production of much-needed consumer goods.

He says the policy is an "important mistake," arguing that the decrease in capital investment in the power and heavy industries which has resulted could cause an energy crisis.

The attempts to reduce the vast central bureaucracy have also proved a mistake, Professor Kvint said, pointing out that a 900,000 cut in administrative jobs failed to put more people into production industries. Instead, they mainly took generous state pensions.

Article by Colin Narbrough, *The Times* (London), Business and Finance Section, Wednesday, October 18, 1989.

Having seen its plan for standardized regional development fail miserably for the past 60 years, Professor Kvint thinks the Soviet Union must now adopt a policy of "investing at the best place," especially where it produces quick returns. Improvement would feed through to the regions later. In this context, he sees the free economic zones playing a key role. Current plans are for zones to be established next year at Vyborg, at the gateway to Leningrad on the Gulf of Finland, Novgorod, to the south of Leningrad, and Nahodka in the Soviet Far East. A zone on the Kola peninsula in the Murmansk region should be of particular interest to British industry, he suggested.

The offshore oil and natural gas potential of the Barents Sea, plus minerals, timber, and fish, could make the region attractive to hard currency investors from Britain. A free economic zone would allow Western industry to operate unfettered by Soviet costs.

Though Professor Kvint favors early steps towards ruble convertibility, all the indications from Moscow are that exposing the ruble to market forces is a long way off.

Free economic zones, built on Soviet and Western investment, would provide a solution to the currency problem, as they would be islands of Western technology and productivity levels well located to supply both foreign and Soviet markets.

The horrendous infrastructure problems of the Soviet Union would also be overcome, as the zones would have access to the sea lanes and the roads, railways, and services of their free market neighbors.

BEST LAID PLANS

There may be a different sort of crisis coming up, according to one of the Soviet Union's top economists. Professor Vladimir Kvint, one of the small brood of free marketers who followed Mr. Gorbachev's adviser Abel Aganbegjan back from Siberia to top policy positions, is now adviser to the Soviet Prime Minister, Mr. Nikolai Ryzhkov.

In a conversation with *The Guardian*, he said that the 28% fall in industrial investment in the Soviet Union this year is a sign that matters are coming to a head. Next year, he expects a showdown over the future of central planning, conducted by the ministries and by GOSPLAN.

The reformers, who have gained ground in Moscow infighting, will then be able to push through the abolition of the influence of the ministries altogether. GOSPLAN will become merely an organization for planning big state infrastructure projects. State enterprises will then become genuinely self-governing, responding to price signals from the marketplace.

There is no risk, he says, of the momentum of economic reforms being lost because no substantial part of Soviet society wants to go back to the old system. A Chinese-style reversal is just not in the cards.

Nevertheless, the Soviet economy has a long way to go before it can be rated a mixed economy even on Austrian or Swedish lines, examples of which Mr. Kvint approves.

The Guardian, Financial News, October, 18, 1989, p. 11.

DOING BUSINESS IN MOSCOW

Perestroika's financial face is trying to make the Soviet Union more accessible to foreign investment. But at this tentative stage it is a moot point whether greater accessibility is more than a modification of autarky. Foreign trade is a very modest part of the Soviet gross national product, and the logic and effectiveness of applying a diluted International Monetary Fund regime to the currency is questionable.

The aim seems to be to narrow the Soviet Union's $25 billion balance-of-payments deficit and exploit Soviet technological advances commercially. Professor Vladimir Kvint, vice chairman of the Soviet Export Association and a member of the USSR Academy of Sciences, puts it another way, however.

Western business can deal directly with Soviet enterprises, and it is no longer necessary to knock on ministry doors. Foreigners can hold majority shareholdings in joint ventures, control their boards, and repatriate their share of any hard currency profits. Joint ventures with Soviet partners can be based overseas, and Soviet enterprises have $2.5 billion to invest. There are 344 military plants being converted to peaceful uses.

Professor Kvint believes that joint ventures will get a shot in the arm from the creation of free economic zones. Indeed, with joint ventures being created at the rate of 130 a month, there has already been some success.

But the problem is how to pay foreigners. Professor Kvint is pressing for the first step toward convertibility by the end of next year. By then it may be possible to establish a limited convertible ruble in parallel with the non-convertible variety. Westerners will have the right to buy convertible rubles and Soviet enterprises will be able to pay a portion of workers' salaries in this currency to encourage productivity.

Taking a leaf from the IMF's book, the volume of new rubles would be limited to the growth of exports. Full convertibility could follow in three to five years. In principle, such a scheme would en-

The Independent (London), Thursday, October 12, 1989, p. 31.

courage efficient use of scarce hard currency resources and avoid such abuses as the $10 billion worth of equipment bought by ministries and now lying idle.

Yet the experience of developing countries—which, in a sense, the Soviet Union is—is that parallel exchange rates are an invitation to corruption. In any case, how will the convertible ruble convert? Will it be fixed, floating, or pegged? And will the joint ventures become islands of relative efficiency with little impact on the vast ocean of the Soviet economy? It would be a mistake if perestroika meant one thing to foreigners and another to the Soviet people.

POWER TO PERESTROIKA

Strikes, local civil wars, growing dissatisfaction in the population in the Soviet Union. The great rebuilding of the economy is only stumbling along. The politicians have had their circus, according to the citizens; now we want bread. Cash flow *asked the Soviet managers, economists, and strategists how they want to stop the growing threat of the bankruptcy of* perestroika.

Strategy
THE THEORISTS

A Squad of Unconventional Economists Lean on Effort and Individual Responsibility

The uproar in the little store in Moscow's Kalinin Prospekt is overwhelming: The foreigners are coming to fill their traveling cash boxes through the sale of jeans, radios, and sport shoes; then come the Moscow inhabitants, to snap up the much-desired and otherwise unattainable Western wares. The legalized black market belongs to the many new private Russian cooperatives, where demand creates an offer.

In the USSR in these weeks, much is possible: For the first time in Soviet soccer, two teams are bidding with large sums for a player; a Swiss advertising salesman has created advertising space on the "Sojus" spaceships; and the Italian media businessman Berlasconi is offering advertising time on Russian TV.

For the West, Mikhail Gorbachev's perestroika is the most interesting experiment of the decade. For people like Vladimir Kvint, Jurij Ponomarjov, and Tatjana Zaslawskaja it is more: Gorbachev's new guard of economists have to help the transition of the economy to success. Or they will go down with it.

Professor Kvint is a born and bred Siberian. He becomes noticeably livelier when he talks of his home. He came to Moscow at the invitation of the Academy of Sciences, in which the 39-year-old

---

Article by Arne Johannsen and Karl Wendl, *Cash Flow* (September 1989).

economics professor works as an expert on regional economics. Kvint, who comes from the ranks of the prominent Gorbachev adviser Abel Aganbegjan, is part of the "Siberian Mafia," as the many economic freethinkers from Siberia were called by the Kremlin.

Kvint gathered his experience in the far North, in Norilsk, the northernmost city in the world, as the representative leader of a Kombinat with 140,000 employees. His vision of a Russian economic reform comes from his experience as a manager.

Without exception, the new economic policy of the USSR is oriented more toward the practical avoidance of former pitfalls than toward a new theory. That which is possible will be tried. Each week a dogma falls. Even in the universities. "In the colleges, there is no great radical change," knows Professor Kvint.

The old houses of knowledge have caved in, there are not yet new ones—in all schools, therefore, history tests have been removed from the lesson plans.

The decree for a new land-lease system, which makes possible 50-year tenancies for private individuals and organizations over fields and farms, as well as farm equipment and factory buildings, is termed by the official news agency *Tass* as an "experimental document." With many experiments there is money to be earned. A lot of money. Already in Moscow there are stores like the boutique of Marina Osadchuk, in which hand-tailored suits and dresses are offered for three times an average Soviet salary—and they are being sold. Six hundred patients are on the waiting list of dentist Joseph Bochkovsky, even though treatment is his private practice is four times as expensive as in the state-run Polyklinik. Moscow's "YUCCIES"—Young Upwardly Mobile Communists—are slowly competing with the party secretaries for the privileged class.

Interview with Vladimir Kvint:
25 Million Price Changes

Cash Flow: Do you see examples of a new generation of economic theorists coming to power now in the USSR?

Kvint: What do you mean by "theorists"? I was already working in heavy industry at 14.

Cash Flow: Were you that bad in school?

Kvint: No, but I didn't want to study anymore. After fourth grade I already wanted to leave school, but my mother was afraid I would become a hairstylist and so she kept sending me.

Cash Flow: And so out of desperation you became a professor?

Kvint: It didn't go quite that fast. Next I really did work in house industry and only then did I decide to continue my studies. Next I graduated from a technical college for nonferrous metal, then I studied economics at the Plechanow College in Moscow.

Cash Flow: In Austria many academic careers generally develop differently . . .

Kvint: In the USSR as well: People go from school to college, then become assistants, and sometime later they become docents. They read a lot, but the real work world is a completely isolated region from this reality.

Cash Flow: What has to change in the practice of Soviet economics?

Kvint: Everything. We have to rebuild the entire economy.

Cash Flow: That sounds violent. But how does one begin such a thing?

Kvint: The most critical factor is that the companies gain more economic independence.

Cash Flow: But greater independence does not exactly guarantee higher production rates.

Kvint: No, but when the company has to make its own economic decisions—from material purchases up to selling their product— then the productivity as well as the quality of the products will increase. Actually this is our essential problem: quality. For example, we are the largest shoe producer in the world, but many shoes do not even leave the factory, but rather go directly from production to the reworking department.

In order to really change anything in its essence here, we have to offer the individual more incentive for his or her efforts.

Cash Flow: Thus payment according to the principle of effort?

Kvint: Until now, almost every person received the same wages, independent of individual effort. In many companies that led to a great number of employees receiving wages simply for attendance, or—especially in administrative departments—simply showing up once a month to pick up their pay. What that means for worker productivity I don't have to explain to you.

Cash Flow: The citizens ultimately judge the success of General Secretary Gorbachev by what there is to buy in the stores. And that does not exactly look rosy for the reformers right now. The production of fruit and potatoes is declining, and not even in Moscow can you find tea, toothpaste, and sugar.

Kvint: The production of potatoes and fruit is not sinking, but also not increasing. But especially in this sector is the increase in productivity so incredibly important. And that is just it, using agriculture as an example: only through privatization is this possible. It was for this reason that the building of private agricultural cooperatives was allowed. And the number of such organizations is constantly growing. Every farmer can come out of his *kolkhoz* and receive a piece of land; for machines, animals, and seeds he can request state credit.

Cash Flow: Privatization also means free trade. And in the USSR many goods are so scarce that just about any price can be demanded for them. Who should pay for the goods, when they even exist?

Kvint: A price reform is long overdue.

Cash Flow: There you imagine a lot.

Kvint: Of course: About 25 million price changes will be necessary. Additionally the entire system of price structure needs correction. The prices of certain basic grocery items haven't been raised in 25 years, independent of production costs. But naturally a price adjustment must not decrease the standard of living of the people. And finally, the quantity of products will not simply increase due to higher prices.

Cash Flow: At the movies many in the audience laugh when someone on the screen says, "In our country we only have one goal: Communism!" The ancient capitalist "Monopoly" is now produced in Russia. Is socialism at its end?

Kvint: One thing is clear: Without democratization and an increase in the standard of living there is no socialism. There were attempts at economic reform in 1964 and in 1979. But they failed, because there was no simultaneous change in the political spheres. There is a tight connection between the two. For three years now we have been experiencing a reform of the political system, but a fundamental economic reform will last even longer. By the end of this year nearly all companies should be functioning independently. With that, we will be fast on the way to our goals.

THE EXPERIMENT OF GORBACHEV: THE FREE-TRADE ZONES FOR THE RELEASE OF THE ECONOMY

Moscow—In the Soviet Laboratory, a new experiment is growing: the creation of free economic zones, true and proper areas of development, and accelerated industrialization, that, at the sign of deregulation and de-taxation, should attract foreign capital and render more agile and profound the intervention of the National Enterprises. The circulation of goods and services in these zones, both from and to the USSR, will be free of duties. Foreign exchange will have free rates of exchange. The doors will be open for anyone, to the Soviets first of all, in the quest for a small "El Dorado," to come to work.

In this way, the economists hope, new industries will be born in the selected zones. The old industries will be more easily restructured. The standard of living will improve for the population. Exports will increase, but, above all, the internal market will be enriched with new products. In sum, the "free economic zones" can be locomotives that are able to pull the Soviet economy out of the swamp of stagnation.

However, avers Vladimir Kvint, an academician and Vice President of the Scientific Council for Regional Economies, as well as one of the brains of the Siberian group raised by Abel Aganbegjan, "the Soviet economy is a convoy, too long and heavy for only three locomotives. We also need helicopters, and powerful motors. The zones must contribute to an effective economy in the entire country."

Even though the economist of perestroika would have perhaps wanted more, there are found, until now, three experimental free zones, with differing scope and objectives, according to the economic and geopolitical characteristics of the regions in which they

La Republica, August 18, 1989 (translation).

are situated. But, they share a common philosophy: to allow the best utilization of the resources in which the Soviet Union is rich, but which the bureaucratic economic management didn't know how to adequately utilize.

The first area, according to the map indicated by the Vice President of the Commission for the State for Foreign Commerce, Ivan Ivanov, will be established around Vyborg, northeast of Leningrad, almost on the border with Finland, and will have as a propeller the lumber-processing industry. The reasons for this choice are clear; the USSR, Kvint reminds, ranks first in the world in production of lumber, and 42nd in the production of paper.

A Jewel in Danger

The second free zone will be installed in the Siberian Far East, near Nahodka, not far from the large port of Vostochnyy. Here, plants should be established for the enrichment of carbon (of which Siberia is a large producer, with 30% of what is extracted from the entire Soviet Union), for wood processing, and for the production of fertilizer derived from minerals that could find natural markets in China and Japan.

Finally, the third free zone will have a completely different aim. It should be born in Novgorod, city of art, one of the historical and architectural jewels of the Soviet Union, 600 kilometers from Moscow, and 250 from Leningrad—a jewel put brutally in danger, like the health of its inhabitants, contaminated and polluted by the many industries nearby. "But to return Novgorod to its ancient splendors," explains Kvint "will take Western experience in restoring large centers." Thus, the creation of the free zones seeks to put together the necessary resources to restructure the industries, to make Novgorad a large international tourist center.

If, for the Soviet Union, one can speak of an experiment without precedent, areas of free development don't constitute a sure novelty on the international scene. What strikes one, however, is the surprise of China in the phase of its economic liberalization before political liberalization, while the Soviet Union of Gorbachev searches for a way to exit its great depression and made and makes modifications, even in its experimental ways, to this "invention." Here, though, the analogies end. According to Kvint, in fact, the causes of the Chinese crisis are not to be sought in the economic liberalization model adopted and even less in the creation of the "free zones," but in the gap that was created between the economic development and the development of democracy. "The country," he says, "has started to develop economically and technologically, but the development of the democracy has remained braked. The major part of the ruling group was afraid of making the 'next step.'"

In the USSR, the situation is "exactly the opposite. Our political changes have surpassed the level of our economy. From stagnation, we passed into stagflation: stagnation plus inflation." Now there is not much more time. To start the upswing, it is necessary to move with determination. But exactly from this, one would say, political aspect of the problem arises some disappointment in the economist. And he points to "free zones" as "a decision only half made."

The Weight from the Past

"In Russia, they say, try to plow the ground looking backward"—a reference to the conditioning of a past that weighs all the time. The project of areas of free development, it would seem to be understood, was more ambitious, with respect to how much was *not* decided, even taking into account the experience of China, where 19 tax free zones were established, 14 for technological and industrial development and 5 for the development of commercial business and services.

But is there no risk, one could object, to creating, within the "free areas," islands of well-being, with respect to a population constrained to managing with a frightful lack of a consumer market? Kvint's answer is what a Western manager could give. "As an economist, I can say that money must be employed where it can generate the most profit. The more developed a zone is, the more need there is to invest in that zone. Only when the development of this region will be at the top will the rest of the country be able to pass through. If these 240 billion dollars had been invested in the other towns of China, instead of in the free zones, they would have been invested all over vast China; it would not even have been felt."

Regionalization of the Russian Economy

RESTORING THE ROMANOVS

Boris Yeltsin yearns for powers that his constitution denies him. Don't be surprised if he solves the problem with a typically Russian move.

Nearly five years ago Vladimir Kvint, a former Soviet economist, predicted in Forbes *(February 19, 1990) that the old Soviet Union would break apart. At the time most people scoffed. But come apart it did. Now a professor at Fordham University's Graduate School of Business and a consultant on emerging markets at Arthur Andersen LLP, New York, Kvint makes another contrarian prediction.*

This will be very hard for a non-Russian to understand, but do not be surprised if Russia restores the monarchy with a Romanov sitting on the refurbished throne. If this sounds outrageously far-fetched, it sounds that way simply because people do not understand how bad the situation in Russia has become. I never thought a regime could be as corrupt as the old communist system, but the present regime is giving it a close race.

Russia today is not entirely a democracy. It is more a system of soft-core totalitarianism. While it is more democratic than it was under Gorbachev's rule, it is less democratic and more totalitarian than Spain was under General Franco or Chile under General Pinochet. That is a fact. Boris Yeltsin of 1994 is not the Boris Yeltsin of 1991. He loves power and will do whatever it takes to hold on to it.

Russia's presidential election is scheduled for 1996, and the campaigning will start next year. But so unhappy are most Russians with their lot today that Yeltsin knows he cannot win an election; he would be lucky to get 15% of the vote. There is no party or group that could hope to do better.

That is why I predict a return to monarchy. It will prove to be the only way Yeltsin can hang on to power.

As market relationships have developed among private companies, Yeltsin's power to control the economy has weakened. That this should happen is not surprising to people in the West. Democracy is, after all, a system of decentralization, with power and decision making spread widely across society. But Russians are not comfortable with decentralization. The Russian tradition is to look for a leader, for a "father of the nation." Hence the surprising nostalgia for Stalin. Even now, when all Stalin's crimes against humanity are well known, many Russians, young and old, continue to display his portrait. This does not indicate nostalgia for communism. It is nostalgia for a strong leader.

The idea of communism did not kill the concept of adulating one leader. The communist myth was that collective rule was vested in the Politburo, but it was only a myth. There was always a strong man at the center of power. For 74 years of communism, there was a succession of dictators with tremendous personal power: Lenin, Stalin, Khrushchev, Brezhnev, then two grandfathers who, despite illness, controlled the country: Andropov and Chernenko. Then there was Gorbachev, a communist in liberal's clothes. Now it's Yeltsin's turn—a totalitarian in democratic clothing.

Yeltsin has learned well the lessons of Gorbachev. Gorbachev was the first leader who thought it was possible to democratize society a little—just a little—and still retain dictatorial power. Yeltsin has not wanted to make the same mistake. He will not let power slip away from him as it did from Gorbachev. The first indication that Yeltsin would ignore democratic ideas and statements was when he directed his artillery against the first democratically elected parliament in Russia in October 1993—the same parliament that restricted the activity of the Communist Party in 1991.

To protect his position, Yeltsin has placed under his control the former KGB, the ministry of the interior (militia), border guards, and the army.

There remains a formidable barrier to Yeltsin's ambitions to recentralize power in his hands: the Russian constitution. He has continually invoked and promoted the constitution as a way of destroying his political enemies, most notably Vice President Aleksandr Rutskoi and former parliament leader Ruslan Khasbulatov. During the October 1993 elections he attacked the old constitution as undemocratic, which was true. He initiated the writing of a new one that was almost equally undemocratic, giving all power to the presidency.

Only one problem remained for Yeltsin: The constitution calls for elections. Set for June 12, 1996, presidential elections are just 18 months away. Yeltsin is now at the lowest level of his popularity. Only 10% to 12% of the population supports him, about the same level of support that Gorbachev had when he was forced out of office. At the same time, several political rivals have reappeared, including former Vice President Rutskoi; the current speaker of the Duma, Ivan Rybkin; Prime Minister Viktor Chernomyrdin; Aleksandr Nemtsov, who is one of the young, market-oriented regional leaders; and the infamous Vladimir Zhirinovsky. Even though the loudmouthed Zhirinovsky has no chance of winning, he is more popular than Yeltsin.

I do not think the election will take place as scheduled. That is a flat prediction. How can Yeltsin avoid an election? He has several options.

1. He could try to use his power in the upper house of the Russian parliament to postpone an election. This would be a direct violation of the constitution and would be opposed tooth and nail by the lower houses of parliament, and Yeltsin lacks the strength there to pull it off.

2. He could call for an immediate election. In this case no candidate would get more than 25% of the votes, Yeltsin included, and he could use that as an excuse to stay in power as a stabilizing force. On his most recent trip to the U.S., Yeltsin promised he would not do this, but I am not convinced. Yeltsin is truly the owner of his words: He gives them and takes them back.

3. Yeltsin could restore the Russian monarchy with himself as regent-for-life. He will never be able to create an absolute monarchy, but he can create a constitutional one that will allow him to hold the reins of power.

This is the most likely option he will take, because, unlikely as it may sound, it is less unlikely than the other two options, and Yeltsin will not go quietly from power.

This would not be the first time in Russian history that a regent would become a real monarch. The most famous regent in Russian history was Boris Godunov, a central character of Russian history as well as of grand opera. Czar Fyodor Ivanovich was not a statesman by nature, and therefore turned all his power over to his brother-in-law, Boris Godunov. After Fyodor Ivanovich died in 1958, Boris

Godunov was crowned Czar Boris I. Now another Boris yearns for absolute power in the Russian tradition.

Restoration of the monarchy would take people's attention away from the tribulations of their daily lives. But is there a groundswell for monarchy? Eleven centuries of Russian monarchy were not wiped out by less than a century of communism. After the disintegration of the Soviet Union, members of Russia's Romanov royal family who visited Russia from Europe and the U.S. were given a very warm reception. When the Great Princess Maria, first in line to the Russian throne, came to Russia for the first time last year, bringing along her young son Georgiy, she was met officially by the mayor of Moscow, Yun Louzkov, who presented her with roses and housed her in an official residence where the communist leaders used to put their most respected guests. This could not have happened without Yeltsin's okay. This is in stark contrast to the cold and rude reception that the former king of Romania received when he went to visit Romania in October.

Yeltsin has encouraged a regular flow of royalty to Russia. Queen Elizabeth II of Britain, a distant cousin to the Romanovs, was one. Other royalty have come from Belgium and Japan recently. It is almost as if Yeltsin were getting the people accustomed to royalty again. I would not be surprised if there were a deal between Yeltsin and Princess Maria. Yeltsin would agree to put her 13-year-old son Georgiy on the throne, with Yeltsin becoming a sort of regent. It is interesting to note that the other claimant to the Romanov throne, Great Prince Alexiy, who lives in Madrid, has not been invited to Russia, further evidence of a Yeltsin–Princess Maria deal.

I have no statistics but a great deal of anecdotal evidence supporting my belief that the ideal of a royal restoration would not be laughed at. In 1991, at the height of Yeltsin's popularity, one of the leaders of the Society of Nobility gave Yeltsin the title of "Great Prince." He did not decline the "honor."

It attracted little attention, but the former nobility has already received at least a smidgen of its privileges back. Descendants of those whose properties were expropriated by the communists have been granted preference in buying some of these properties, provided they are willing to at least match the other bidders. This isn't a big concession to the old nobility, but it's a start.

Imagine this scenario: Georgiy could be crowned as the new Russian czar. But because he is young and inexperienced, Yeltsin would rule on his behalf. As regent, Yeltsin could appoint himself or a stooge prime minister, and run the government.

Events could take the following turn: Parliament would vote for the restoration of the monarchy, or Yeltsin could organize a referendum, and the people, who are tired of the political fighting among current leaders, would agree. The Russian monarchy would not be absolute, but it would be much stronger than Japan's, Great Britain's, Spain's, or Sweden's.

The next step would be revival of pan-Slavism. At first, Russia will insist that it won't take over Ukraine, Moldova, or Poland, but the denials will grow weaker. A re-creation of the old empire isn't as unlikely as it may sound. As an example of Russia's power, in September the prime ministers of all former Soviet republics (except Turkmenistan and the Baltic states) signed an agreement creating an Intergovernmental Economic Committee with executive power over national governments of ten former Soviet Republics. This committee, situated in Moscow, gave Russia 50% of the voting power and other states a combined 50%. So Russia is already first among equals.

Yeltsin yearns for dictatorial powers. The Russian people like a strong leader. All that is needed to enable Yeltsin to fill this role is a semblance of legitimacy, which a restored monarchy could provide.

What does this mean for foreign business people and investors? It means they can expect a more stable Russia, if a nondemocratic one. Under a restored monarchy and a strong central government, Russia will continue down the road to a market economy and market reform. Borders between the former Soviet republics will become more porous, an important element for foreign investors.

It won't be easy for Americans and West Europeans to accept such an outcome, but it could in the long run be a force for stability and best for all concerned.

RUSSIAN HISTORY SHAPES TODAY'S BUSINESS LEADERS

For Americans to successfully do business in Russia they need to understand the complex relationship between the country and its leaders. This article provides an introduction to a topic that could fill volumes. It is excerpted from Dr. Kvint's upcoming book Management Strategy of International Business in Russia and Central Eurasia.

Russia boasts a huge expanse of land, abundant natural resources, and an educated workforce. These objective political and economic factors make Russia into a world power. Despite this, Russia has an inefficient economy and underdeveloped business capabilities. One reason for this is that subjective factors also play a major role in determining the success of an economy, especially the role of its leader.

Certainly, the ill effects of communism are the most obvious cause of Russia's problems. But on a more subtle level, it has been because there have been few true leaders to effectively manage both the human and the natural resources.

What does the word "leader" mean to Russians? What is the role of a leader in Russian history? What is the Russian approach to leadership for business development, for political leaders, executives, and entrepreneurs? The concept of leader in these many forms must be examined in the context of its history.

Role of Leaders in Russian History

Leadership in Russia is rooted in its totalitarian political history, and is shaped by that experience. Despite the fact that in its thousand years of history Russia was never a democratic country, there are a few notable exceptions where local democratic societies did exist (for example, the free city of Novgorod). During the 13th and 15th

The Kvint Newsletter, 1, No. 1 (June 1994).

centuries, Russia consisted of several principalities each competing with one another, although they were all dependents of the Tatar-Mongol empire. It is during this period that Russia gave birth to one of its first great leaders. One of the smallest and poorest principalities emerged as the most powerful: its name was Moscow.

The Prince of Moscow, Ivan Kalita, demonstrated his political prowess early on. He assuaged the ruling Tatars and in return was awarded the title of Great Prince. With this authority he was able to become the first leader and to begin the unification of Russia. The first lesson of Russian leadership became clear. Russians always try to find peaceful solutions with powerful neighbors. Power is the language they understand.

In a more modern example, even the tyrant Stalin followed this precedent. Stalin was happy when Hitler agreed to sign a peace treaty in 1939. He ignored the reports of Soviet intelligence indicating that Hitler was preparing for war, and preferred a peaceful resolution, no matter how tenuous. And just a decade ago, after Ronald Reagan taunted the Soviets with rhetoric of an "Evil Empire," and vastly increased the U.S. military budget, the Russians recognized that it was in their best interest to sit down with the Americans and negotiate.

Lessons for Business

Just as Ivan Kalita placated the Tatars and was rewarded for his good behavior, the same, unfortunately, is true of Russian business leaders. The goal of a Russian executive is to look good in the boss's eyes, even at the expense of sound business policy. This is a result of years of Russian tyranny that forced people to think one way, act in another, and document everything yet a third way. An old Russian proverb shows that an obedient child will accept milk from two mothers. Therefore, it is essential that foreigners working in Russia learn the opinions of the top policy makers.

In America, leadership is valued. Americans want recognition. Networking is an important part of business. This is not so in Russia. For years, people tried to remain innocuous and invisible. Under the totalitarian system, standing out could get one in trouble. The consequences of making a mistake were substantial. One mistake could ruin a person, and it often did. This is a revealing difference in how Westerners and Russians view leadership. Russians do not want to stand in the spotlight; they tend to shy away from leadership.

The goal of a Russian worker is to look good. How one presents oneself on a superficial level becomes more important than performance. For example, while most workers make every effort to be on time, that is where the responsibility for many may end. Managers must earn the respect of workers in order to get them to produce. The old Russian saying, "Servant to the czar and father of your soldiers," takes on important business meaning. Managers end up protecting the workers from the boss. A good team leader never tells the boss who on the team is bad but announces all successes loudly by name.

Another widespread tradition among Russian executives and managers is falsifying reports. The reason for this, again, is that looking good in front of superiors is more important than achieving positive results. Because it was impossible to continually check every plant all the time, this practice was commonplace, and still is. Thus, the first function of any venture is financial control. In ordinary management systems, controls are implemented at the end of the decisionmaking process, after strategic planning, gathering of resources, etc. In Russia, however, it's necessary that they happen first. Investors must check initial information and reports; otherwise decision making may be based on information that is false or misleading. The cost of such decision making can be very high.

The Power of Territory

The second lesson of Ivan Kalita that Russian rulers have since emulated is to focus on territory. For Russian political leaders, one of the best indicators of strength is the size of the land. All political leaders, like Ivan the Terrible, Peter the Great, and Stalin, concentrated on increasing the sheer size of the country. The belief was that any agreement should be signed if it created a chance of gaining more territory from a weaker partner.

Yeltsin has been the one exception to this rule, and this has earned him the reputation of a truly visionary leader. Rather than acquiring more land, Yeltsin gave independence to 14 of the former Soviet republics. His place in history is secure, because he was the first of the leaders to understand that the death of the Soviet Union was inevitable.

Nonetheless, he has worked to find common ground between the republics inside Russia and to form a central federation. For example, since he has become the leader of independent Russia, he has done everything to keep the Chechen and Tatar autonomous republics as part of Russia, and not cede them independence. Even for Yeltsin, size of territory continues to be central.

It is interesting that the importance of territory carries over to Russian business managers. Emphasis is placed on the size of the facility and land, number of employees, number of cars, and size of machines and equipment, rather than the level of efficiency and production. Most don't even know their own rate of return on equity. Russian managers will tend to bury income statements, and provide balance sheets instead.

As a result, foreigners need to be aware of the fact that when a Russian executive makes a business decision, productivity enters into the Russian's equation only long after size. The end result of dealing with such a manager can be a big white elephant.

RUSSIAN PACIFIC COAST: EXCITING OPPORTUNITY

When Americans think of the territory east of the Ural Mountains they tend to think only of Siberia. In reality, the region in the Pacific Coast is vast, both in terms of size and in terms of opportunity. The 6.2 million-square-kilometer region, abundant in natural resources and only 50 sea miles from Alaska, now has the independence and power to establish international relationships. Today, dollars are more important to the region than rubles. Rush hour has just begun.

The key to this shift in policy lies in the continuing decentralization of Russia, and the strengthening political muscle of local governments. Under Soviet domination, these regions had no economic independence. Today entrepreneurs and local government authorities focus more and more on international cooperation in the Pacific Rim. Between 1987 and 1993, 400 joint ventures with foreign capital were created in this region; now there are more than 2,000.

The single most important areas strategically on the Russian Pacific Coast are the four large seaports, connected to two major railroads. These seaports, open all year round, are the gateway to Russia from the Pacific Rim. Whoever controls the seaport controls an invaluable trading post.

Primed for International Business

Of the seven administrative regions on the Pacific Coast: Primorsky, Khabarovsk, Sahalin, Magadan, Kamchatka, Amur, and the Republic of Sakha-Yakutia, each has a local government. In six of these regions the leader is a governor. In Sakha-Yakutia there is a president. After three years of political fighting with the federal government in Moscow, the local governments have obtained legal control over business relations. Today, international companies can register to do business

The Kvint Newsletter, 1, No. 7 (1994).

directly in the region, and enjoy special tax privileges for international capital.

China is currently the most active trading partner with this area. While Japan at one time used to be the most important partner, countries such as South Korea, Singapore, Malaysia, Indonesia, and Thailand have increased the levels of their investment. But the effects of Japanese investment are still felt through Japanese equipment and products that are used extensively in Russian industry. In the 1980s, cooperation between regions existed primarily via barter trade. Today, countries like South Korea and Malaysia, and some American companies, are working primarily through consignment and collateral trade agreements.

A good indication of the area's attractiveness for investment is the fact that it has become the seat of intense competition between the major communication companies. US West, Cable and Wireless, AT&T, and Sprint have all created subsidiaries to service the region.

Investment Opportunities

The process of privatization, which accelerated in this region in 1993 and 1994, desperately needs financial institutions, insurance services, and other business institutions to support enterprises. There are too few banks and commodity exchanges, and not a single large insurance company. Those institutions that do exist do not have the expertise to meet the needs of business.

American companies with financial expertise will find a ready market for their services. The fact that 35% of trading companies have already been privatized is a sign that this area is ready to participate in international business. In addition, daily flights will soon take place between San Francisco, Seattle, and Anchorage and Magadan, Khabarovsk and Vladivostok, and major cities on the Russian Pacific Coast.

The Pacific Coast has goods and products that would be inexpensive and efficient to export to the west coast of the U.S. For example, the Pacific Coast exports 50% of Russian timber, 38% of its fish, 27% of its canned fish, and 15% of its cement. Compared to the other regions, the Russian Pacific is selling twice as many goods internally as it exports.

Opportunity for American Food Industry

Traditionally, the Pacific Region has imported 37% of its food supply, the principle portion coming from Kazakstan, and other former central Soviet Asian republics, such as Uzebekistan and Turkmenistan. The food produced in this region is of very low quality, however, and contains many chemicals.

Therefore, there is a tremendous opportunity for American food-processing companies to export to this region. American plants could deliver these products to the Russian coast from the west coast of the U.S. and Alaska. For both Americans and Russians, this will be a mutually beneficial arrangement.

Natural Resources

The economy of this area is strongly oriented toward the development of natural resources. This region is very rich, particularly in nonferrous metals, minerals, wood, and fish. The fish industry, nonferrous metals, and timber industries together occupy 50% of regional products. (The fish industry constitutes 19% of this figure.) In the past, most of these products—for example, 92% of nonferrous metals and 38% of timber—were sent into the internal regions of Russia.

The Pacific Coast is responsible for mining 98% of all Russian diamonds, 80% of its tin, 50% of its wood, 10% of its pulp wood, 6% of Russian black ore, and 5.2% of its coal. Because of its waterways, the region supplies 40% of the fish of Russia. In addition, it grows 85% of Russian soybeans and produces 13% of its honey.

The geological forecast of oil reserves for this area is 10 billion tons. This is more than 10% of all of Russia's oil reserves. It is reported that there are 14 trillion cubic liters of natural gas and 30 billion tons of oil and liquid natural gas. Because the shortage of capital for geological research limits exploration, the resources that are registered document only 302 million tons, and 1.7 trillion cubic meters of natural gas.

Perhaps the most abundant of the administrative regions is Sakha-Yakutia, which has diamonds, gold, coal, and natural gas. The Sahalin region is known for its rich deposits of coal, pulp wood, and fish.

Industrial Structure

While rich in resources, the region lacks many of the production capabilities necessary to capitalize on its bounty. Just to maintain the level of industrial activity of the past few years, many goods are required that the region itself does not produce. For example, 35% of the machines and equipment in this region's plants were delivered from Russia or imported from abroad. In addition, 40% of the products for light industry were also imported. The region is also desperately in need of chemical products for its industry. This does not take into account the goods necessary if the region is to develop its yet untapped resources.

GO EAST, YOUNG MAN

American businessmen and journalists by the planeload are landing in Moscow. If they are interested in profitable opportunities in Russia's future, they should be landing nine time zones away, in Magadan.

America was discovered because Columbus and his backers were looking for new business opportunities. With similar motives, American businessmen are now pouring into Moscow. But Moscow is not the only place where the Russian action is. For the real opportunities, Americans must look east of Moscow—and east of the Lena River—to the Soviet Far East. There they and other Westerners can make attractive investments with the fewest dangers, in terms of political risk.

Russia's Far East is developing as a new Klondike. Under the radical economic reforms of Boris Yeltsin, 11 free economic zones have been opened since the Russian parliament approved them on July 14. Five of them are in the Soviet Far East.

In a free economic zone, Westerners are granted tax holidays for five years. They can own a company, rent land, even use dollars, and take on Soviet entrepreneurs as partners. Free zones are free not only for the foreigners but also for the Soviets, who can now own brokerage firms, factories, newspapers. Stalin was not able to liquidate the entrepreneurial drive. This fact can be readily confirmed by anyone with some knowledge of the miracles of entrepreneurship Soviet women pull off every day simply to feed their families.

Speaking of potential partners, new Russian legislation is exploring the possibility of restoring, mainly to former Russian citizens, some of the property that was taken from their families during the October (1917) revolution. An example is the family of Yul Brynner, the late actor, whose father was one of the founders of nonferrous metallurgy in the Far East and who owned big plants there in the pre-Lenin days. The Brynners may now claim the property back. The state is unlikely to give it back, but, as a compromise, it may at least lease the enterprises to these families indefinitely. This possibility is

Forbes, November 26, 1990, pp. 234–238.

specifically provided for in the Russian Republic's new Law on Property, enacted on August 1, 1990.

When they think of investing in Russia, many American businessmen have a common concern: what to do with their rubles. The free economic zones solve the ruble problem. There you can use your rubles to buy construction materials, pay wages, rent land, and so on. You produce for rubles, and export for hard currency, which can now be paid into your account outside the country. If you want to be paid inside a free economic zone, the new law allows you to hold hard currency accounts, and to take your hard currency out of the country at any time.

It is unbelievable the bargains business people can get for their money in Russia. If a realistic ruble/dollar exchange rate of 3 rubles to 1 dollar is used, Russian labor costs are 5% or less what they are in America. And they may get cheaper. North Korea owes the USSR about $7 billion. To repay the debt, North Korea may send to the Far East free economic zones thousands of workers. They are even cheaper than the Soviet workers.

I think by the year 2000 foreign companies will invest in these regions no less than $10 billion. Russia plans to invest 3.7 billion rubles ($1.2 billion at realistic exchange rates) there over ten years; 1.5 billion rubles before 1995. These sums will be used to develop communications, roads, and other infrastructure.

The Soviet Far East is most attractive to foreign business because of its unique combination of natural resources and an advantageous geographical position. The Far East provides the shortest route from Europe to Asia, via the Arctic Seaway. It costs less than half as much to deliver cargo from Antwerp to Japan using the Arctic Seaway than it does using the Suez Canal. Rail? One ton of cargo delivered from Munich to Japan costs about $215 using the European and Trans-Siberian Railway, and just $110 by ship along the Arctic Seaway.

In 1984 the Canadians used the Arctic Seaway to ship cargo from Vancouver to Lithuania. The trip took seven days less than it usually takes through the Panama Canal.

In 1985 the trip was repeated, this time in winter. Navigation in the Arctic Ocean throughout the year has become the key to the real exploitation of the Arctic. The USSR has the world's largest fleet of icebreakers. There are about 25 of them, including 3 nuclear vessels.

There is a need for more icebreakers of different classes, as well as for specialized transport ships.

While the opportunities in the Soviet Far East are almost unknown to Americans, the Japanese have been quietly pumping investments into the region for the last few years. They are aware of the area's treasures: The Soviet Union provides 40% of Japan's imports of precious and rare metals, and 70% of the Soviet Far East exports go to Japan.

One hundred and fifty Japanese companies have already established direct ties with Soviet Far East enterprises to conduct barter exchange without hard currency, and they are completely ready to enter the free economic zones.

The Americans are timidly testing the waters. Alaska is in almost direct physical contact with the northern region of the Soviet Far East, Chukotskiy. Among the few concrete business results of the last colorless summit between Bush and Gorbachev was the opening of several new airports for flights between the U.S. and the Far East. As part of the negotiations, some Soviet airplanes can now bring 30 tons of cargo per flight to Alaska. There are no regularly scheduled flights from the West into the new airports, but there soon will be.

One of the new airports is in the major city called "Sunny" Magadan, on the shore of the Okhotskoye Sea.

The city's name is ironic. In Russian, the word "zone" is indelibly associated with prison camps, especially those of Stalin's time. Magadan was the capital of the prison zone, better known as the terrible "gulag." That is why the Soviets painfully call it "Sunny" Magadan. With a population of 570,000, Sunny Magadan may become the capital of a zone of a much more preferable kind, a free economic zone.

One immediate opportunity for earning hard currency lies with the region's huge but underutilized ship repair facilities. The ship construction market is not very active, but repairs are always necessary. The facilities already exist in the modern port cities of Vladivostok, Vostochnyy, Slavyanka, Soviet Gavan, and Nakhodka, which handle the bulk of trade between the USSR and its Pacific partners. This can bring immediate hard currency revenues. It is possible to lease port space for 50 years. Japan's Mitsubishi Corp. has already proposed to lease space and equipment, and pay hard currency.

Proximity to the Pacific Ocean also means fish and tremendous biological resources. The Far East accounts for 40% of the Soviet Union's fish harvest. By our estimates, $1 invested in fish farming—there are more than 20 such fish factories in the Far East—brings about $12 of profit.

Or consider logging. Thirty percent of Soviet forests accounts for 40% of Soviet lumber exports to such markets as Japan, Australia, and South Korea. The lumber industry of the Far East cries for Western capital and know-how. The waste is sickening. Forty percent of Soviet timber remains in the forest, rotting on the forest floor. Workers fell timber and raft it down the rivers. Ten percent of the timber they put into the water is lost during this trip. A Norwegian company has been catching this lost timber and selling it for hard currency, illegally, for years.

In the Soviet lumber mills, 55% of the raw logs processed are scrap. This scrap is uselessly burned. As a whole, only 15% or so of the cut trees are really used in the timber industry of the Soviet Far East. The other 85% is wasted.

Confronted with evidence of such waste, many Westerners believe that Russians, like Brazilians, would rather decimate their forests today and worry about nature tomorrow. This is not true. A huge national preserve, Terney, has been set aside in the Far East; larger than some of the smaller European countries, it is recognized by the United Nations as a symbol of purity. Hunting, fishing, even drinking from the river is prohibited there. When I got permission to enter this territory, I had to bring my own drinking water. Precautions are such that to enter this heavily guarded land, I received special plastic shoes and a disinfected coat.

My point is that responsible environmentalism is a force inside the Soviet Union today, and Western companies that can reduce waste while still making money will find a warm welcome.

Most Soviet gold and precious stones are mined in the Far East, in the basins of the Kolyma, Indigirka, and upper Amur rivers. While I was studying the mines of the Far East, I held in my hands heavy pieces of greenish gold and pale unpolished diamonds. This wealth contrasted terribly with the poor living and working conditions there. Gold is mined using the most archaic methods.

More than 90% of Soviet diamonds—the USSR is the world's fifth-largest diamond producer—are mined in the Far East, in Yakutia. Diamond mining is a good area for joint ventures. By my calculations, if $2 billion is invested in modern mining technologies, diamond production will increase by about 20% to 25%.

I have written before about prospects for Western investment in Soviet oil and natural gas exploration and production (*Forbes*, September 17). I should add that in the Soviet Far East significant gas and oilfields are being discovered between the Lena and Vilyuy rivers. Offshore Kamchatka, on the Pacific, is also very rich in oil, as is the eastern coast of the Okhotskoye.

The coal mining industry, too, has a big future. The Far East, which equals more than 60% of the territory of the U.S., has 30% of Soviet coal. Its proven coal stocks are estimated at almost 13 billion tons. Soviet geologists believe probable recoverable reserves are at least 15 times the official proven figure. Half these immense stocks can be mined by the open pit method, the cheapest and most efficient way.

Another important task of the Far East is building its own iron and steel industry. Vast deposits of iron ore have been discovered there, quite enough to develop an integrated steel works with an annual capacity of up to 10 million tons for almost 90 years.

Shikotan Island, one of the closest islands to Japan, now belongs to the Soviet Union, but sooner or later it will become a free economic zone for joint investments with Japan. I expect a big tourism industry to develop in the south of the Soviet Far East. The waters are wonderful—clear and pure. Today, on the shores of this island facing Japan is a Soviet military base. South Kuril Islands is called "The Emperor's Beach," because Japanese emperors used to come to the unit; even the Soviets have to obtain special permission to go there. But as the area's economy develops, economic interest will make Soviet leaders move the military out and open the island to tourists.

No one comes away with the impression that the Far East is a virgin land. It already has powerful, if not very efficient, industry. There is significant infrastructure, especially railroads. The industrial products of the Far East territory are exported to 50 countries, including 15 along the states of the Pacific Rim. The area's main partner is Japan. Altogether, the Far East territory accounts for 50% of all Soviet trade with the Pacific Rim countries. As trade among Asia's rapidly growing countries increases, the Soviet Far East's economy will become more and more active.

In the Far East there is only one person per square kilometer. Will there be a lack of labor resources? No. The overmanned factories of western Russia will soon have to slash their payrolls if the economy is to be made competitive, or simply productive. Large-scale unemployment is on the threshold. For jobs and for freedom, the best Russians will move east.

In the USSR's territory there are 11 time zones: The Far East is 11 hours ahead of Moscow. Economically, too, the Far East, not only Moscow, is Russia's future.

FAR EAST: A LOOK INTO THE FUTURE

The Far Eastern economic region takes up more than a quarter of the USSR territory or more than four percent of all the land on earth. It has five time zones; the pole of cold of the Northern Hemisphere; the Pacific coast; such great rivers as the Amur, Lena, Kolyma, and Indigirka; volcanoes; geysers; nonferrous, rare, and precious metals; diamonds; carbohydrates; forests; tundra; an ocean of wealth; and a sea of problems.

To Control the Situation Rather than Follow in Its Wake

Correspondent: A large group of prominent scientists, who are obviously rather busy, spent a month and a half working on the expedition. You spent nearly half that time traveling on the sea. Would it not be simpler to generalize and analyze the results of the research already done on many problems without traveling there altogether?

Kvint: We were not the first to invent economic expeditions. Russian scientists resorted to them already at the beginning of the century. The Academy of Sciences arranged many of them in the '30s and the '50s. Development needs made us resort to them once again. It is not only the comparatively poorly studied regions that need such expeditions. Judging by everything, very soon we shall apply such a research method to one of the oldest industrialized regions in the country—the Don-Dnieper area. It will be radically reconstructed.

What Are Hindrances?

Correspondent: What has hindered the industrial development of the Far East?

Interview in *Moscow News*, Weekly edition, 1 (1983).

Kvint: The scarcity of transport means that can operate without roads; the relative weakness of the social infrastructure; the departmental disunity that hasn't yet been completely overcome; and the scarcity of manpower. Roughly, there is one person per square kilometer in the region.

Kamchatka—The Black Sea and Back

Correspondent: We were talking about labor-saving machinery and processes. Which industry does it involve first of all?

Kvint: All of them, without exception. This is especially true of the areas where the natural conditions are extremely harsh. Minerals have to be mined where they are found. But if life conditions there are unfavorable, then there should be a minimum number of people working there. There is no reason to develop enterprises there that would be able to operate in more favorable climatic conditions. Therefore, in these areas people should do only whatever it is absolutely necessary to do there and, while doing this, use the technology that calls for the least possible amount of human participation.

Expenditures and Results

Correspondent: How interested is the entire country in the accelerated development of the Far East, where literally each and every step calls for heavier spending than in other regions?

Kvint: As I see it, we should put agricultural land and timber resources into the same category in, for example, the Amur Region and some areas of the Khabarovsk Territory, which very well could become the most important source for our country's raising soybeans and other valuable crops.

SIBERIA: EXPERIMENT WITHOUT COUNTERPART

History knows quite a few cases of barren expanses being transformed into blooming oases. However, the tremendous scale on which this is being done today in Siberia is awesome.

While on a tour of Siberia in 1913, the Norwegian explorer Fridtjof Nansen observed: "The day will come when Siberia will awaken, display its natural potential, and say its word." In those days, with the exception of a narrow strip running alongside the Trans-Siberian Railway in the south, the entire boundless territory, with incalculable natural wealth, was literally a blank spot on the economic map of Russia.

The great Norwegian made a realistic assessment of the difficulties involved in the development of Siberia. This led him to believe that it would not happen for a long time to come. But 20 years later Siberia had the Russian Federation's largest centers of coal mining (the Kuzbas) and ferrous metal industry (the Kuznetsk Integrated Metallurgical Plant). And on the 70th latitude the Norilsk Integrating Mining and Metallurgical Plant sprang up smelting nickel, cobalt, and copper from ores which were mined out of the permafrost ground of the Taymyr Peninsula.

Many people abroad at first thought it was a "prestige" project. However, when the problem of raw materials became acute in the rest of the world and the Soviet Union remained the sole industrial country to depend exclusively on its own resources, the attitude to tapping hard-to-reach areas abruptly changed. While on a visit to Norilsk, Pierre Elliott Trudeau, the prime minister of Canada, noted that the Soviet experience was of a planetwide significance.

Particularly impressive growth has been registered by oil and gas-mining (including gas condensate) in Western Siberia. In the 1965–80 period the output of crude oil increased more than 300-fold and that of the gas more than 150-fold. In 1985, according to plan, it will reach 390 million tons and 350 cubic meters, respectively.

Sputnik (Digest of the Soviet Press) (Moscow), 11 (1982), 42–51.

The Riches and Problems of the Yenisei Area

In terms of climate, landscape, and the presence of various natural resources, Siberia is not uniform. Nor have its different parts been developed to an equal extent. However, in the very center there is a territory which can safely be called "Siberia in microcosm." Claiming one-seventh of the surface area of the Russian Federation, it embraces parts of the Arctic tundra, the taiga, and fertile land with a moderate climate. The territory shares with the rest of Siberia almost everything to which it owes its fame, but it shares its problems as well. Because its main city is Krasnoyarsk, this part of Siberia is called the Krasnoyarsk Territory.

The Yenisei, one of the largest rivers in the world, has bound this immense, multifaceted expanse into a single administrative whole. Until recently the river, with its tributaries, was the only traffic artery along which civilization could reach into the virgin taiga and the wild tundra.

In Siberia laying a road is a greater challenge than, for instance, in the Pamirs or in the Amazon Valley. Apart from the forbidding mountains and swamplands, the work is compounded by the caprices of the soil, which has been almost forever bound by ice, and by notorious Siberian cold, which makes steel as brittle as glass and freezes machine oil. This is why, per unit of area, the network of roads in the Krasnoyarsk Territory is one-eighth of that in the Russian Federation as a whole.

Help comes from Aeroflot, although the delivery of freight and passengers by air requires expenditures from the state a hundred times greater than for motor transport and almost a thousand times greater than transport by rail. But what is to be done if the Yenisei area contains resources which have either become depleted or are simply nonexistent in old areas?

Siberian scientists believe that the Krasnoyarsk Territory will someday share the fame of the 18th-century Urals as the mineral treasure-house of Russia, the pioneer of the Russian industry in the 19th century and the leading center of the heavy and manufacturing industries in our day. In fact, this day is already dawning. True, the Krasnoyarsk people are introducing corrections in the Ural experience and intend to traverse the three-centuries-long path of "Russia's smithy" in two or three decades. While shipping various raw materials to other parts of the country, they at the same time are developing their heavy and manufacturing industries, producing everything from the highly efficient harvester combine Sibiryak and container-trucks, to the domestic refrigerator Biryusa.

The abundance of raw materials in the Urals has never been matched by the presence of its own energy base. The industrial development of the Yenisei area began with the creation of the power industry. The Krasnoyarsk hydropower station, the world's largest, of six million kilowatts, and the future still larger Sayan-Shushenskoye hydropower station, of 6.5 million kilowatts, which has already partly become operational, are located here. In the vicinity of the Kansk-Achinsk Fuel and Energy Complex (KAFEC) project, two thermal electric power stations of 10 million kilowatts each are being built.

In the per capita generation of electric energy the Krasnoyarsk Territory is already 50% ahead of the United States, although the Soviet Union as a whole still lags behind it in this indicator. Nevertheless, electricity cannot wholly replace man, even in highly automated production. The Krasnoyarsk people know this from their own experience: a shortage of labor slows the territory's development.

The problem of settling areas with people from the mid-latitudes, unaccustomed to such hard conditions, is a global one. In addition to the differences presented by the harsh climate, there are economic and social factors. The cash nexus, which has driven people north at all times, in the final analysis, does not solve the problem. A case in point is Alaska, which witnessed the "gold rush" of the early 20th century and a recent "oil boom," but, despite this, has remained one of the most sparsely populated areas of the world. In contrast, Siberia is being settled for good. It seems as if the key to the problem of peopling the northern latitudes has been found here.

Experiment Within Experiment

In the early 1970s in a plant of low-voltage electrical equipment in the town of Divnogorsk near Krasnoyarsk, at best one-fifth of the machine-tools functioned; the rest awaited operators.

The terrain here is extremely scenic, with a mild—by Siberian standards—climate, cedar forests, and rich hunting and fishing grounds. However, the people left—paradoxically enough, for the northern city of Norilsk, where the population has been steadily growing since the mid-1960s. Between 1965 and 1980 it almost doubled.

"The secret is simple," explained Boris Kolesnikov, manager of the Norilsk Integrated Mining and Metallurgical Plant. "In the given period the floor space of well-appointed flats specially adapted to northern conditions expanded more than twofold and dozens of general and vocational/technical schools and medical and childcare institutions have sprung up. The city has six sport complexes, and the plant has its own sanatorium near Moscow and a children's holiday center in the south of the Krasnoyarsk Territory."

Meanwhile, in Divnogorsk and several other industrial centers of the territory, where there was a constant shortage of workers, civil engineering projects lagged far behind industrial. Workers did not stay long in spite of high wages, longer holidays than the country's average, and advantages in pension schemes. The conclusion was obvious: man can be attracted to Siberia by various benefits, but he can be kept only by good conditions.

The development of Siberia is an experiment without counterpart anywhere in the world, either in the scale of allocations or in that of construction. Incidentally, this explains some miscalculations in economic and social planning.

Without an integral economic and social program there is no way to avoid miscalculations in the future when seeking optimum interlinked solutions to hundreds of problems. The choice for evolving and testing it fell to the Krasnoyarsk Territory. Why? Because it was the focus of the fuel, power, nonferrous and ferrous metal, timber, chemical, electrical, and transport-engineering industries.

The program was scheduled to cover a period of 10 years. The program was compiled by more than 30 organizations, leading Soviet scientists, and economic managers. What has been shown by these 10 years in the Krasnoyarsk Territory?

Of the many figures that characterize the results of the experiment, I will single out the most important ones. From 1971 to 1980 the territory's industrial output rose 2.3-fold. Labor productivity increased by 170%. In the per capita output of coal, nonferrous metals, and timber materials, the territory is now in advance of any developed country. In that of fabrics it is next only to the United States and Japan.

New towns—Lesosibirsk, Sayanogorsk, Sosnovoborsk, Svetlo-gorsk—have appeared on the map, and, like Divnogorsk, already have more arrivals than leavers. Almost 350,000 families have moved to new flats in these 10 years. Krasnlyarsk has opened its eighth higher educational institution.

Today, its people work under the Second Integral 10-year Program, which has been compiled for the period ending in 1990. It provides for completion of the Sayan-Shushenskoye hydropower project and for the launching of Turukhansk, whose capacity—20 million kilo-watts—will exceed the total energy potential of all the hydropower projects currently in operation or under construction in the territory. In Krasnoyarsk a plant of heavy excavators, which in terms of techni-cal equipment will be as good as the famous Kamatsu and Caterpillar plants, will go on line. The KAFEC will increase its contribution to the country's fuel and energy balance severalfold.

Siberia breeds in its people courage, stamina, and purposefulness. The only thing they cannot tolerate is an absence of prospects. How-ever, according to all indications, this does not threaten people in Krasnoyarsk or anywhere else in Siberia.

SIBERIA SAYS NO TO CASTRO

Russian economist Vladimir Kvint visited Siberian coal mines some years ago. He and his associates were questioned by coal miners annoyed that their government was lavishing money on foreign adventures when its own people lacked essentials. "Who needs that hairy fellow, Fidel?" was the way one miner put it. Now that the authorities in Russia are starting to listen to ordinary folk, we'd say Fidel Castro's days are numbered.

Who would have thought that a Soviet economist would be a contributor to The Capitalist Tool?

Forbes, September 17, 1990.

EASTERN SIBERIA COULD BECOME ANOTHER SAUDI ARABIA

Those who interpreted invasion of Kuwait as the start of a new era of high oil prices weren't paying attention to events in Russia.

When Saddam Hussein brutally annexed Kuwait, the price of oil took off. Here was an Arab ruler who was threatening to hold the industrial world hostage for its oil. It was not so much Saddam Hussein's tanks and his missiles and poison gas that frightened the West as his possible use of the oil weapon.

In fact, the Kuwait invasion was a sign of weakness on Saddam's part, not strength. Saddam could not finance his imperial ambitions on $17 oil, so he sought to drive prices higher at the point of a gun. A primitive man's primitive solution to a complex modern problem.

It won't work. What's more, most of the other Arabs know it won't work. That's one reason they are not backing Saddam.

Demand and supply will set the price of oil, not guns and embargoes. Demand is growing, but supply may be growing faster. By the beginning of the next century, Russia may be exporting more oil than Saudi Arabia is today.

Time is running out on the use of oil as a political weapon. Those who have tried to wield the weapon, Saddam Hussein and his predecessors, have counted on the fact that the Middle East sits on the world's largest proven reserves of oil. But we now know that there are even bigger reserves in Russia's Siberia.

Not tomorrow, but in the years ahead, more and more of this oil will reach world markets, ensuring that world oil prices will remain under pressure and making it virtually impossible for any Arab ruler to hold the world for ransom.

So, whatever happens to Saddam Hussein, the current level of world oil prices will prove to be unsustainable.

Forbes, September 17, 1990, pp. 130–133.

The Japanese seem to understand this better than the Americans do. Without doubt, their understanding of Siberia's potential helped persuade the cautious Japanese that they could afford to antagonize Iraq by participating in the blockade. As far back as 1975, Japanese interests launched their exploration for oil and gas off Sakhalin, the Pacific island just north of Japan.

Even now, with its economy in tatters, the USSR remains the world's absolute leader in oil production. Last year, production, according to official Moscow sources, was 12 million barrels a day. My own evaluation for the USSR is somewhat higher—12.5 million barrels. By comparison, Iraq and Kuwait combined produce just over 4 million barrels a day; Saudi Arabia produces 5 million barrels; all of OPEC produces 24 million.

Yes, the Russians need a lot of that oil at home—less than 20% of their production goes for export. Russia also desperately needs foreign exchange to buy other things, and their easiest way of getting that exchange is by boosting oil exports. With Western help, eastern Siberia could become another Saudi Arabia—although not, of course, with Saudi Arabia's low recovery costs.

A whole new source of oil is about to burst upon the world scene: eastern Siberia and the Arctic zone of the USSR.

From their magazines and newspapers, most Americans have gotten the idea that the Soviet Union's oil production is centered in the republics of Kazakstan and Azerbaijan—in the oilfields of Baku, Astrakhan, and Shevchenko along the Caspian Sea—and in the fields of western Siberia, which are fast being depleted. This is misleading. The Central Asia republics' reserves have been running out for decades; they now account for just 6% of Soviet production.

Nearly all the rest of Soviet production comes from the Russian Socialist Republic, primarily from the western Siberian fields tapped in the 1960s and 1970s. They are closer to population centers and enjoy milder climate conditions than the eastern areas. But thanks to mismanagement and abysmally low worker incentives and productivity, yields from western Siberia have been steadily falling.

These are old fields. To get the same amount of oil, one must now drill six times as many wells. And the cost of the ecological damage in these regions is bigger than the costs of the facilities for waste processing.

Yet with help from capitalist countries, western Siberia can significantly increase its oil exports based on its northern and deeper oilfields: On average in the USSR, only 7% of oil is extracted from the oilfield, about a fifth the level in U.S. fields. Especially promising are the Sea of Okhotsk shelf and formations near the Pechora River region, 1,000 miles northeast of Moscow.

But all this is small change compared with the exciting prospects for eastern Siberia. According to geologists of the Soviet Union's Academy of Sciences, the oil reserves of eastern Siberia are even bigger than those forecast for OPEC.

As long ago as 1978 it was clear to Siberian geologists and economists that western Siberia's oil production peak was rapidly approaching and that new fields must be sought farther east. By this time very promising geological forecasts had appeared, announcing secretly, as always, unheard-of oil and gas fields in eastern Siberia, in the Arctic offshore, and in the Pacific coastal regions of the Soviet Far East.

As the economic knowledge of these regions was practically nonexistent, I proposed a series of economic expeditions to evaluate the treasures locked beyond the Urals. These missions, similar in some ways to America's Lewis and Clark expeditions, included geologists, engineers, and physicians. I was one of them.

In 1979–81 we explored the Arctic regions of the USSR, the Far East, and various territories of Siberia. The geologists discovered tremendous potential between the eastern shore of the Yenisey River and the Lena, especially the oil belt dividing the Taymyr peninsula from the mainland.

A slow start has been made on development. East Siberian fields will produce only around 20 million barrels this year. Not much in global terms. But I think we'll see the same kind of growth in east Siberia as we saw in west Siberia: from 7 million barrels a year in 1965, to 7 million barrels of oil *every day*. By the year 2000, eastern Siberia will be yielding more than 140 million barrels of oil each year, as well as billions of cubic feet of natural gas.

But these are minimal figures for the year 2000. They assume little help from abroad in either technology or capital. If the capital and expertise of companies like Exxon, Royal Dutch/Shell, and British Petroleum could be turned loose on the region, there is no telling how high production might go. Straw in the wind: Chevron Corp.

has announced it is beginning exploration in Kazakstan, prologue, perhaps, to the oil fever to come.

Eastern Siberia may sound like another planet to Americans. In fact it is America's next-door neighbor, four hours' flying time from Anchorage and about seven hours' from Seattle. Harsh as it is, it is a much pleasanter place to live and work than the barren deserts of Arabia.

Alaska, until 1867 a Russian province, is separated from some Siberian oilfields by only several dozens of miles across the Bering Strait. There are some oilfields in the far eastern USSR—principally off Sakhalin Island and the Kamchatka Peninsula, for example— from which an overnight oil delivery to Alaska could be organized.

U.S. consumers would benefit directly from this proximity. I have calculated that total transportation costs to the U.S. west coast from eastern Siberian oilfields would be a fraction of the costs of importing oil from the Middle East. Russian oil may even be pumped from tankers into the Aleyeska pipeline. Within ten years this natural geographic proximity will become a new factor in economic growth.

The world's energy transportation routes and economics are going to be changed. The Arctic Seaway, linking all the northern USSR to the warm-water Pacific, is to become a very busy route indeed. And an extremely efficient one. Foreign companies began experimenting with this route back in 1980. I watched the unloading of the Mannesmann pipes from West Germany sent for the gas pipeline to the icy, unequipped shore of the northern point of the Yamal Peninsula.

In addition, the great eastern Siberian rivers, including the Yenisey, the Indigirka, and the Lena, create a natural transportation system for oil and other resources. And the 2,000-mile–long Baykal–Amur railroad, begun in the 1970s, runs through the middle north of Siberia and the Far East, connecting the oilfields with the already existing ports on the Pacific Ocean. From there, it is a one-day tanker run to Japan, and another day or two to Alaska.

Beyond oil and gas there are other Siberian treasures to harvest— nonferrous metals, coal (next door to one oilfield is the world's biggest brown coal field, estimated at more than a trillion tons), gold, and lumber. And while extracting oil you do not want to throw away diamonds, just because they are in the way.

Development in eastern Siberia will be somewhat slowed by environmental concerns. While Soviet environmentalists are not as anticapitalistic as their American counterparts and do not enjoy the weapons provided by the U.S. legal system, Soviet environmentalists will put pressure on the authorities to make sure that the eastern Siberian wilderness is not ravaged. In former years many big Siberian projects were facilitated by bribes to Soviet bureaucrats.

But Siberians will not allow the rape of nature and their lives anymore. Eastern Siberia is a beautiful wasteland, with huge forests and severe mountains. It has cold winters, but hot and bright summers. Several attractive cities exist in these regions, such as Norilsk and Krasnoyarsk and Irkutsk.

Under Soviet rule, development in Siberia has been tremendously damaging to the environment. With exploitation comes the same sad picture. All the trees are cut. Near the mines and oilfields, workers endure terribly shabby housing—one room for four people in a hostel, furnished with an old wardrobe, table, and TV set. For 4,000 to 5,000 oil workers, there is one club, usually painted Party red, where the entertainment is amateurish. No wonder the workers drink so much. The fatigue gradually accumulates; the productivity of labor falls.

If Western companies are to go to the USSR, they'll have to invest something. But at an estimated $8,000 per worker, it will still cost less for these companies to upgrade Siberian facilities than it now costs to house and feed workers in Alaska or on North Sea oil rigs. Employers will also have to invest in social infrastructure, and pay decent wages.

But to whom should interested foreign businesses apply? The USSR, led by Mikhail Gorbachev? Or the Russian Republic, led by Boris Yeltsin? The parliament of the Russian Socialist Republic has already declared its property rights for all of Russia's natural resources, including areas that currently produce 92% of the USSR's oil. Foreign oil entrepreneurs should find a willing ear in the new Russian government, which would far prefer to sell oil for hard currency than to other Soviet republics.

It is clear that the Russian Republic's market-oriented young economists will try to sell not just the crude oil but also higher, value-added refined petroleum products. That is why eastern Siberia may be of the greatest interest to petrochemical processors; the former will certainly be favored over those seeking purely extractive investments.

It is time for American business people to start thinking in terms of the Pacific Century, and of America and Russia as neighbors across that shrinking pond. It is also time to stop worrying about Arab oil embargoes and start thinking about how to bring all that Russian oil to world markets. Some Arab nations may be able to withhold their oil for a while to punish the West, but Russia, hungry for development, cannot.

THE ARCTIC COMES NEXT

With every year the "accent" on Siberia is being felt with increasing strength in the Soviet Union's economy.

The realization in Siberia of programs of nationwide importance have led to the establishment of its first economic belt, which has taken shape in the south, along the Trans-Siberian Railway. It accounts for the major share of the industrial output and more than 90% of the area's population.

At the end of the 11th five-year period (1981–1985) the lines will open on the Balkal-Amur Railway, which will pass across the Near North territory. The area of the BAM reclamation zone is comparable in size to Western Europe. Siberia's second economic belt is beginning to take shape there. The full implementation of the BAM Program will take more than just one decade and is projected into the 21st century.

Stage-by-stage development of the economy of the Soviet Union's eastern regions envisages a further advance northward. To this end investigations are carried out by more than 700 research and design organizations, as well as by institutes of higher learning.

A special place is held among them by the economic expedition of the Siberian branch of the USSR Academy of Sciences, under the scientific direction of Academician Abel Aganbegyan. The coming summer will be their fourth summer in the polar regions.

A Moscow News *correspondent interviewed the chief of the expedition, Vladimir Kvint, Cand. Sc. (Econ.).*

"The North zone occupies nearly half the territory of the Soviet Union and in area is comparable to the United States," he said. "Today it accounts for half the Soviet oil production, more than a third of our natural gas and timber, and a large share of nonferrous, rare, and precious metal ores. But a great proportion of this comes from the so-called Near North, where the habitat and climate are quite suitable for human life.

"However, it is already clear that we have to advance farther, to the high latitudes. In the opinion of the director of our expedition,

Interview by Georgi Bogdanovsky, *Moscow News Weekly*, No. 6 (1982).

Academician Abel Aganbegyan, the development of the Arctic wealth, which depends on navigation along the Northern Sea Route all the year round, is the greatest economic program for the future. That is why it is so important to lay the scientific foundations for it."

Correspondent: At the mere mention of the Arctic a person with no first-hand knowledge of it tends to feel uncomfortable, to say the least.

Kvint: Let us be frank: many of those who do know it at first hand feel the same. These are very severe parts. One criterion for checking an area's harshness is the index of climatic severity. In Moscow, for instance, it is 1.9, but on Dickson Island in the Kara Sea it is 7.

Correspondent: One doesn't often hear economists saying that they're actually going on an expedition.

Kvint: That is true. But although ours is called an economic expedition, its composition is closer to that of those scientific centers that conduct research into global problems affecting the whole of mankind.

Our expedition includes leading Soviet specialists in diverse branches of the economy, geology, ecology, medicine, modern technological systems, and agriculture.

Besides which, at different stages of the research we are joined by other scientists, officials of the USSR State Planning Committee, local economic executives, state and party functionaries.

This enables us to examine the strategic problems in developing the polar regions, and make a comprehensive assessment of both the benefits for the country and what expenditure of resources this will require.

Correspondent: What parts has the expedition visited?

Kvint: We began by studying the basins of the Yenisei and the Angara. Then we went along the Northern Sea Route and the Pacific coast of the country. This summer we shall head toward the lower reaches of the Irtysh and the Ob. In the future we'll study the economic areas along the Lena, the Northern Dvina, and the Pechora.

The Northern Sea Route was certainly the most difficult and the most important one. That expedition lasted nearly two months. Our ships travelled 4,100 miles. We flew 11,000 kilometers in planes and helicopters, visiting nearly 60 population centers and studying the work of more than 20 enterprises and organizations.

Correspondent: There is an axiom that fits the situation in Siberia perfectly: "natural wealth is within the reach of those who have reduced distances."

Kvint: In the area beyond the polar circle this demand is even more rigid. Transport expenditures here amount to 60%–70% of all the costs.

Navigation in the Arctic Ocean throughout the year has become the key to the real discovery of the Arctic. The Soviet Union possesses the world's largest fleet of marine icebreakers. There are about 25 of them, including three nuclear-powered vessels. But even they are already finding it hard to cope with the increasing number of assignments. There is a need for more icebreakers of different classes, as well as for specialized transport ships. It is also necessary to develop port facilities. Shipments along the Northern Sea Route even now can compete with other kinds of cargo transportation. Despite the considerable transport expenses, northern products prove highly valuable, provided their production is properly organized. The nickel and copper of Norilsk, for instance, are the cheapest in the country.

Work is under way to increase the navigability of the Siberian rivers. Railway tracks and pipelines are being extended into the Far North. The air fleet there is waiting for dirigibles and similar items. There is a considerable need of transport vehicles that can negotiate any sort of terrain.

Correspondent: Doesn't this, in turn, form part of another problem: creating special machinery and technology for the North?

Kvint: Indeed, the regional technical policy determines many things here. Any kind of work in the Arctic is at least three times more expensive. Losses caused by the inadaptability of the machinery to the harsh conditions exceed its initial cost by between three and seven times. On the other hand, one ruble of additional expense for manufacturing machines in a northern variant saves seven to eight rubles on their operation.

Adaptability, however, is only part of the regional technical policy. The main thing, to put it in the classical language of economics, is the correlation between live and materialized labor. We need to achieve maximum productivity with the minimum number of workers. This is done, for example, by using the prefab method in construction, widely applied when developing oil and gas deposits in Western Siberia. Industrial and other installations of any type are assembled from units which have already been "stuffed" with all necessary outfits at the factories.

About 40 organizations deal with developing technology for the North. So far demand is ahead of supply. However, it can be hoped that this problem will be gradually resolved, although for complexity it is similar to designing space systems. For instance, the working parts of the extracting mechanisms, used in the underwater tin mines on the shelf of the Laptev Sea, had to be created on the principles of bionics.

Correspondent: What will bring life into the future enterprises and towns beyond the polar circle?

Kvint: The North is by no means short of energy resources. The whole of the Arctic is highly promising as far as oil and gas are concerned, and its coal and hydropower reserves are large. Most of the methods for obtaining energy are already being utilized there. There are atomic, tidal, and geothermal power plants, and plans are under way to use wind power.

Correspondent: Could you say a few words about the ecological aspect of the situation?

Kvint: Today we do not always realize the meaning of environmental protection for the Far North. Nature is easily injured there. Even the reindeer, that embodiment of the tundra, can inflict tangible damage on it unless pasturage rules are observed. The ecosystem of our planet cannot be conceived without the Arctic, which is why the actual task must be to reduce to the minimum any harm inflicted on its nature.

Correspondent: To all appearances, the old notion that we shall go to the Arctic only to work is being reconsidered, isn't it?

Kvint: Indeed, the strategy of shift and site development is gradually losing ground. The rapid growth of the prices of raw materials and fuel everywhere inclines us to the trend of extracting and processing everything we can from beneath the earth's surface, wholly and utterly. This is only possible provided large territorial–industrial complexes are formed, in which enterprises of different branches make up a consecutive technological chain. In this case the expenses are cut by 10%–15% and the social issues are easier to solve.

On the whole, the projected Arktika Program considerably surpasses the BAM Program in volume of work and investment. Five large territorial–industrial complexes are already discernible in the Far North: the Timano-Pechorsky, North Ob, North Krasnoyarsk, North Yakutsk, and Chukotsky complexes. They will include dozens of production enterprises. And, as we know, leading enterprises in the east of the country each have a capacity as great as, and often greater than, that of entire industries in developed West European countries—for instance, the mining-and-smelting combine in Norilsk, or the Angara hydrocascade in the Near North, or the aluminium works in Bratsk.

Correspondent: Who is to implement the Arktika Program?

Kvint: During Soviet years the population of the North has increased sixfold. However, on the scale of the whole country its share amounts to a mere three percent. As to the Arctic, its population is about two million.

The high latitudes have always attracted enthusiasts. And enthusiasts are still there. But let us be objective: such spiritual élan is, as a rule, of a short duration and quickly comes into conflict with reality.

Today we know something about the human organism's capability to adjust to life in the North. First, not everyone, not even a perfectly healthy person, can adapt to the Arctic. Some people can live there for years; others, for only months. Second, northerners are in special need of a well-thought-out recreation system.

Correspondent: How can the impact of the severe climate be alleviated?

Kvint: First and foremost, by the provision of comfortable living conditions. An example of this is Norilsk, on the 69th parallel. In the past ten years its population has grown by 80,000—to the present 240,000 plus. For the level of public services and amenities Norilsk is in no way inferior to any of the best cities on the planet.

Big problems will also have to be solved in the field of labor in the North. There is a need for professional selection. Working schedules must be determined and controlled by medical personnel, with special attention to disease prevention.

All this is being done in Norilsk. Along with the economic five-year plan, there is also a health five-year plan there. The time is approaching when data on the state of health of every inhabitant of the city will be fed into a computer, and it will be possible to control man's health from day to day.

"THE POLAR STAR ABOVE US"

The Exploit—Long as a Life

Mankind is meant to attempt to solve the secrets and puzzles of the Unknown.

There were, and always will be, explorers and prospectors whose deeds, at first, seem reckless, but then make the whole world admire them.

Journeys to unknown countries have always been believed to be dangerous. Therefore, it was the destiny of a few courageous people to paint over the white spots on the pictures with new colors; and the pictures of distant countries came out as if from a brush of a painter.

One of these courageous people was William Barents, who made three journeys on the Arctic Ocean from 1594 to 1597 with the purpose of finding the northeastern pass from the Atlantic Ocean to the Pacific Ocean. The expedition of 1596–1597 for the second time discovered Medvegiy and Shpitsbergen islands. The impassable ice forced the expedition to spend a winter on the northeastern coast of the island called Novaya Zemlya.

On the basis of his observations, Barents designed the map of Novaya Zemlya, conducted an annual cycle of meteorological observations for the first time, and measured the depths along the course of a ship in the sea which soon afterward would be called by his name. The island in the archipelago Spitsbergen and the colony in the seaport Barentsburg on the islands of Western Spitsbergen were also named in Barents's honor.

William Barents died on June 20, 1597, near the northern end of Novaya Zemlya. He was buried on Novaya Zemlya.

Different things were said about northern lands. In 1246, Plano Karpiny, an envoy of Pope Innocent IV, went to the capital of the Tatar-Mongol kingdom for the purpose of exploration. On his way, Karpiny reported to the pope very "accurate" and "precise" facts:

Excerpt from V. L. Kvint and N. M. Syngur's *The Polar Star Above Us* (Moscow: Soviet Russia Publishing House, 1984).

beyond the country of self-eating people, he wrote, there is an ocean; across the ocean, there is a land where people-beasts live. The inhabitants of this land have a human look, but their extremities resemble those of bulls. They say two words in a human language, and they bark the third word like dogs. . . .

Of course, contemporaries had every reason to believe the report of the pope's honorable messenger; however, such reports did not deter the courageous. The courageous did not succeed very often; many of them did not see their homes again; but, year after year, more and more ships left moorings, going to the north, to the severe embraces of icy winds, snowstorms, and the everlasting darkness of polar nights. Sometimes it is hard to understand what force drove them there, and what tempted them to risk their lives every minute. Twenty-two-year-old Fritjof Nantsen wrote to his father: "I feel bored; and a hunger to experience something new does not leave me in peace. This hunger thrills me, and it is so difficult to restrain."

Perhaps each of the early polar explorers had his own beckoning dream and desire to conquer nature and help people.

Grateful mankind forever remembers the names sketched on a geographic map: Barents Sea, Laptev Sea, Bering Strait, Vilkits Strait, Shokalskiy Strait, Dejznev Cape, Litke Island, Ushakov Island, Vrangel Island, Sedov Archipelagos, Nantsen Island, Siberyak Island, Cheluskin Cape, Toll Bay, and Rusanov Bay.

The designations on geographic maps reveal a lot of things. The triumph of discovery resounds in such now-familiar words as Novaya Zemlya (New Land); the name of Nadejzda (Hope) Island speaks of faith and expectation; Slojzniy (Difficult) Island recalls the difficulties and dangers of the northern roads; humor, the reliable help in any journey, is reflected in the name of Domashniy (Home) Island, the severe span of the Arctic desert.

The famous polar explorer Fritjof Nantsen wrote: "One who wants to see human genius in its noble struggle against superstitions and darkness should read the history of Arctic journeys, should read about seas, and about the sailors who, when spending a winter during the polar night terrified with inevitable death, were going toward the unknown with streaming banners. Nowhere, perhaps, has knowledge cost more difficulties, troubles, and sufferings than there. But man's curiosity does not rest until there is no span where there is no man's footprint even in those areas, and until all mysteries are uncovered in the North."

Mankind has been proud of the polar explorers for a very long time. But there are people, entire ethnic groups, who live all their lives in the Far North, in the highest latitudes!

Century after century, generation after generation, the Saams, the Nents, the Nganasans, the Selkups, the Hunts, the Kets, the Evenks, the Nanayts, and the Dolgans were appearing in the world in the built-from-deer-hide chumes and yarangs and under the snowstorm's howl. Together with the adults, the young ones were learning how to find food; then, they were forming their own families, and were having children; however, while closing their eyes forever, they knew that the frozen land would let them in at the end and would give them the final shelter from the snowstorms. . . .

What is it like, not to come here for a year or two, but to always live here from birth to death? The exploit long as a life?

One may not necessarily agree, because everything is learned in comparison: if all one's life one sleeps on the floor, the floor does not seem that rough; if one has never seen bananas in his life, he does not lack them.

However, the northern nations knew that there are southern lands where the sun shines, where the cold is not as severe, and where the night does not last for half a year. They knew, and, yet, did not go to the South.

When, many thousands of years ago, in the beginning of the quaternion period in the geologic history of our planet, the ice was moving from the North, people rushed to retreat to the South as if they were running away from enemy forces. The majority left, but some stayed. And who knows, maybe the most courageous ones, those who did not want to abandon the land of their fathers, stayed in the North. . . .

Jack London called the northern lands a dominion of white silence. It is a poetic, accurate, and beautiful name; but only an outsider, in whose heart the memory of a little too clamorous motley of the southern nature is still alive, and in whose ears the din of the narrow streets of loud and fussy cities still sounds, could have chosen this name.

However, for a native inhabitant of the North, his land is not an icy desert, but an immense world that is, given the multitude of various flowers, senses, traces, and signs, a world where life overflows as in a big city. Regardless of how severe the North is, it is the motherland for the northern nations.

Yes, the North is the motherland for the northern nations, and life there is full of worries, events, and nuances which an outsider's eye sometimes is not able to see.

For the majority, the North is a synonym of the poverty of colors, and of severe and uninventive simplicity. However, many people forget that during its short summer the tundra flourishes with thousands of colors and jingles with running brooks and birds' voices. Butterflies are flitting; bumblebees are buzzing industriously; the mild greenish and grayish lichen, the yagel, which is the favorite dainty of the northern deer, is covering the land, which is tired of winter cold. Green leaves, like bright touches on a painting, are appearing on the thin branches of the dwarfish birches; polar poppies are reddening; and delicate flowers of the blueberries are softening the poppies' haughty beauty.

Even in wintertime, there are flowers in the North—the icy flowers. They grow on the surface of the sea ice from the crystals of salt and water, forming sophisticated and elegant, fragile and light twigs, which can be taken only by a delicate hand—they shatter from a crude touch.

However, the northern nature has always been a severe mother to its children. Constantly fighting nature's whims, the northern nations have been perfecting numerous skills.

The closeness to nature and constant dependence on it allowed the northern nations to accumulate a rich reserve of knowledge about the life of tundra and taiga, of northern rivers and seas. The experience was handed down from one generation to another. The northern nations unsurpassingy know the vegetative and animal worlds of their area. They can predict the weather, and can precisely orient themselves by the sun and the stars. It is amazing how deer guides faultlessly find the right direction during snowstorms in the plain and boundless tundra. The guides also know the taiga perfectly. Many researchers asked the native population to help gather information about the geography of the regions of study.

Practical knowledge of the nature and great creative potentials helped the northern nations to accustom themselves to the severe conditions while forming their material culture. They were very sharp-witted in assembling their dwellings and clothing. The dwelling of the nomads is easy to assemble and to transport on deer. Its conic shape withstands the wind pressure; deer hides preserve the heat; and warm clothing, soft and impenetrable by wind, and moist footwear protect against any frost. The Eskimos learned how to use even snow as a construction material. Everything needed for hunting and fishing was made innovatively from available materials—wood, deer hides, animal bones, and stones. In fact, the different methods of fishing were always adjusted according to the season, type of reservoir, and type of fish. Constructing clever traps for animals and birds was also strictly adjusted to their types and behaviors, to the conditions and landscape of the area.

Men, generally, worked with wood, bones, and metal, and manufactured tools; women worked with hides, sewed clothing, footwear, and covers for dwellings, and knitted. They loved to decorate clothing with glass beads, embroidery, and pieces of metal. They decorated their dwellings, kitchenware, and hunting tools with strange carvings as well. The northern wood- and bone-carvers and engravers are famous throughout the world.

The northern nations created their own fine writing. In their scheme-sketches the hunters relayed different information about their area, destinations, and the closest dwelling, and warned about nearby falling rocks or scattered poison.

All these amazing skills and talents were necessary conditions, the surviving conditions, for the northern nations. Their lives were passed in constant struggle with nature. Dangers and diseases awaited them at every step.

For example, the frequent use of raw meat or fish that was not sufficiently preserved—or, sometimes, even rotten—and the absence of vegetables caused a large number of gastric and intestinal diseases. There were neither doctors nor medicines; and sometimes whole communities perished.

Even the food supply was not always sufficient. In the years of successful hunting people would eat to satiety. However, by the end of the year, the reserves would be exhausted; and starvation would follow. People then would eat bark and grass, and soaked animal hides.

In 1581 Siberia was incorporated into Russia. Explorers of the North and industrialists not once reported to the czar's government about the difficult life of the northern nations, about the troubles of which theft and violence from the traders, not only domestic, but foreign as well, had added. Explorers spoke of the difficulties and conditions of the northern nations; but they spoke even more about the resources of the Siberian and northern lands awaiting exploitation.

Fearless explorers of the North, relying on the centuries-old experience of the northern nations and using their knowledge and skills, created a basis for steadily conquering the North. What does "to conquer the North" mean? It means to manage to make the North the home that it has always been for the northern nations; but it also means to live in the North in a new way and to raise the North to the level of more developed regions of the world.

The Soviet North is about 50% of the territory of the country. There are many arguments even now about the borders of the North and Arctic regions. Some restrict it to the Polar circle; others, to the line of zero-degree temperature; still others, to the presence of perpetual freezes (in our country, by the Amur River it goes down to the southern borders). We are not entering this argument, but we are talking about regions of the settlements of the nations of the Soviet North. In Russia, there are 108 such administrative regions and 7 such autonomous areas.

In the West, for a long time, the Soviet North has been called "the eastern Eldorado"—flattering, perhaps, not the North, but Eldorado.

The North is the richest reserve of natural resources and an ideal place to apply human potential and talents.

The Caucasians are proud of their land. They say: "Stab a stick into the land, and a vineyard will grow."

The northern land, unlike the Caucasian, is cheap and severe; however, dig a hole there, and, almost certainly, either a fountain of dark and thick oil or a blue stream of gas will escape the land, or grains of gold will appear. . . .

However, the northern nature hides its wealth well. The higher the latitude, the more severe the climate; the farther to the north from the Polar Circle, the greater the natural resources held by the frozen land.

It is obvious now that Timano-Pechorskiy oil province, located in the shore area of Barents and Pechorsliy seas, not only will become the fuel and energy source of the European part of the USSR, but also will actively influence the development of the entire Soviet mining industry for a significantly long time.

The oil and gas provinces of north Siberia and the Far East extend for many miles. These are Leno-Tungusskiy province, almost the whole of west Siberia, the Anadirskiy oil and gas region, East Arctic region, and Chukotka.

Explorers progress farther and farther north. One after another, like genies from bottles, blue torches explode and hit the sky with their powerful streams. While the whole is not bound with compliance with all the standards, the gas escaping from the land ought to be burned; and the bright stream of fire rises to the northern sky as if it wants to compete with the northern radiance. . . .

Science is not unchanging. In the 21st century, one of the main sources of energy will be various sorts of artificial fuel that will be developed from coal. Today, the northern regions give the country about 44 million tons of coal. The whole world knows the Taimirskiy, Tungusskiy, Lenskiy, and Pechorskiy coal regions. Many of the northern fields are so close to the northern sea path that they can be used for open mining and opening up from the sea.

Various uses of oil and gas began only relatively recently. Gold was appreciated a long time ago. Now, however, it is used not only as a basis of currency and financial system or, say, as a raw material for jewelry. Scientists are finding more and more uses for it. Today, some electric and technical manufacturers and the contemporary chemical industry cannot operate without this valuable metal.

There is also gold in the north of our country. There is fundamental and scattered gold in Kolima, Chukotka, and Yakutia.

The North is also rich in copper, mercury, wolframite, and tin.

The salt resources in Taymyr are practically unlimited; the presence of salt in one economic region and of apatits in the Maimecha-Koituiskiy region, commingled with the waste of the mining industry in Norilsk, creates a marvelous material basis for the development of enterprises in the chemical industry and in fertilizer production.

In the 20th century, people look at many things differently. Thus, what were rivers and lakes in the past have now become the sources of water, the hydro resources.

Unpolluted fresh water is needed not only by people, but also by plants and fabrics. In order to bring life to thousands of machines, water is needed. Hence, on the mighty northern rivers, one hydroelectric station after another—Irkutskiy, Bratskiy, Ust-Ilimskiy, Kras-noyarskiy, Ust-Hantaiskiy, and Kolimskiy—grows. The construction of Boguchaiskiy HES has begun; the stations on the guileful Kureika River are under way; and preparatory works are being conducted on the Low Tungusskiy River.

Timber resources are enormous in the North; the northern regions now produce more than one-third of all timber in the country.

There is also a large amount of gypsum, limestone, sand, and gravel there—all very important for construction, which, year after year, develops in wider and wider areas in the North.

Like a crown, the Yakutia's diamonds wreathe the northern treasure.

The North is full of paradoxes. In most of its territory, there is almost nothing for the normal living of a contemporary person; at the same time, however, the North is enormously rich in everything necessary for the normal living of a contemporary person.

How can we eliminate the paradox? A contemporary person is not self-sufficient enough. Inhabiting and mastering the North is today's task.

A lot has been already accomplished.

All means of transportation—by river, by sea, by air, by cars, and by trains—are rapidly developing. New industrial centers have been created in regions said to be unfit for economic development. The emergence of new colonies on the Kolskiy Peninsula is connected with the building of a seaport, developing the sea industry in Murmansk, and mining apatits in the Hibinskiy Mountains. In the Far North, Komy Autonomous Republic has acquired new cities of miners and oil miners. In Enisey's North, seaports such as Igarka, Dudinka, and Dikson, and, in the area of mining copper and nickel metals, a seaport such as Norilsk, have appeared. In the northeast, on the shore of the Kolima River, colonies of gold miners and the city of Magadan and, in Chulkotka and Kamchatka, industrial plants and others have emerged.

If, in 1939, in these vast territories, there were only three cities with a total population of about 50,000 people, at the beginning of 1983 there were now 28 cities. As if by magic, Norilsk has grown to a population of 200,000; Bratsk and Severodvinsk have arisen to a population of 200,000, and Vorkuta and Magadan, to a population of 100,000. Nizjnevartovsk and Surgut are developing rapidly. Murmansk, Petropavlovsk-Kamchatskiy, Yakutsk, and Anadir have changed significantly. In total, there are 90 cities and 358 colonies of a city-type in the Far North of Russia.

Since 1961, the population of the northern cities has doubled. In 1980, the average annual growth rate of the northern population surpassed this measure of population in Russia as a whole by 2%. Today, 8.2 million of our country's residents live in the North; 158,000 of them are members of northern nations.

The severe North continues to attract more and more people every year. Not only do the adventurous ones, the enthusiasts who like it more when it's more difficult and more interesting, go there, but also those who, with their families and with all their possessions, go there in the hope that the North will become their home.

A lot has been and will be accomplished by these people. However, it is impossible to overestimate the role of the northern nations in conquering their territories, the role of the northern nations who not only have lived there for many years, but also know and love their land, feel the special living rhythm of its nature, and know how sensitive it is and how much more should be accomplished for its safety.

Since long ago, there have been 26 nations in the North of our country: the Saams, Nents, Ents, Inganasans, Selkups, Hunts, Mancy, Kets, Evenks, Evens, Nanaits, Nivhs, Itelmens, Chukchs, Koriaks, Ulchs, Udegeits, Oroks, Orochs, Yukagirs, Chuvans, Dolgans, Negidalts, Eskimos, Aleuts, and Tofalars.

Russian chronicles, in the 11th century, already noted that the Nents lived in tundra and engaged in deer breeding and hunting. Not only did people from Novgorod at one time go to the North to trade with "self-eating people"; attracted by valuable furs, Novgorod's merchants, along with other trading people, progressed to the North, to the areas of the Nents' settlements. In the 16th century, the Nents were taxed with yasac; and, for successful collecting of furs, from the Mezen River to the Enisey River, a number of colonies were created: Okladnikov, Pustozersk, Ust-Tzilma, Berezov, Obdorsk, and others. A little to the south, in the Berezov region, along the Sosve River and its tributaries—Lianinu and Small Sosve—along the Obb River and in the Kondinskiy region, the Hunts and the Mancy live. Nowadays, these nations include almost 30,000 people. Some Mancy have settled in the annually growing Salehard and

Hanti-Manciysk cities. The Hunts mostly live along the middle part of the Obb River and along the Irtish River.

Moving toward the east, in the vast territories of the Enisey North, in Tuhanskiy county of the Krasnoyarskiy region, along the left bank of the Enisey River, and in the lowlands of the Podkamennaya Tungusska River, the Kets live. The Dolgans constitute the main population of Taymyr, which is located far above the Polar Circle, in the frozen region of Siberian land. In the bosom of the eternal freezes of Taymyr, which extends for 1,000 kilometers of latitude and 1,000 kilometers of longitude, the richest fields of nonferrous metals, coal, and other natural resources are hidden.

The Evenks and Evens have settled in the vast territory from the Enisey River to the Ohotskiy Sea: in the Tomskiy, Irkutskiy, Chitinskiy, Amurskiy, Sahalinskiy, and Krasnoyarskiy regions, in Yakutia, and in the Magadanskiy and Kamchatskiy regions.

In the northeast regions of the Yakut Autonomous Republic, the Yukagirs live.

In Chukotka—in Ust-Beliy, Anadir, in the region of the upper course of the Anuy and Yablonia rivers, in Kamchatka, and in Koriakskiy autonomous region—the Chuvans, Chukchs, Eskimos, Koriaks, and Itelmens live.

The Saams and the Chukchs inhabit two continents. Each of the northern nations has its own history, culture, traditions, rites, and national costumes.

THE ROLE OF THE BUDGET IN THE INTENSIFICATION OF THE ECONOMY OF THE AUTONOMOUS REPUBLIC

(with Z. Uzbekov)

The major changes under way, including the transition of the economy toward large-scale, intensive production, can hardly be conceived without a radical and general democratization of management and an enhanced role for and involvement of Soviet agencies in economic districts, republics, territories and regions.

The study of the methods and means to accelerate socioeconomic development in any region (whether an economic area, Union or Autonomous Republic, territory, region, or big city) must be based on a general analysis and estimate of the initial and achieved level of economic development. Regional programs, among them "Siberia," "Far East," "Donbass," and the like, reflect the achieved level, and provide indices of the region's specialization and the effectiveness of its production, the existing proportions and rates of its economic development, and the state of its natural resources. To bring out the key problems in regional development for a specified period, particular attention is concentrated in these programs on the nature of the existing social and economic disproportions.

In past analyses of these disproportions in the process of developing and implementing programs, little consideration has been given to regional financial balances, and poor use made of their potentials. The intensification of the economy, with the growing deficit of resources, highlights the importance of a region's financial system in achieving the distribution and redistribution of resources. In turn, the monetary aspects of the regional economy have an increasing influence on the social demands for economic and scientific-techno-

In *Economic Sciences* (Moscow) 11 (1987), 27–34.

logical progress. The studies of these problems are well known in several republics, among them Latvia. There, methods have been worked out for using a multisectoral industrial-financial model; along with methodological provisions for forecasting economic and social development in a union republic, a full outline has been made of industrial proportions, distribution, exchange, and consumption in interaction with the republic's system of finances and credit.

It would be expedient, in our view, to regard Autonomous Soviet Socialist Republics and administrative-territorial units of a regional level—territories, regions—as basic regional objects of financial planning in the development of the current economic program. Although the value and material structures of the reproductive cycle viewed within a single economic region are still to be worked out, and there is a discrepancy between the volumes of the produced and realized turnover tax and the volumes of capital and market turnovers, comprehensive long-term economic planning in any territorial-administrative unit acquires exceptional political, social, and economic significance.

Here, the objects of study are the Autonomous Soviet Socialist Republics (ASSR). The specifics of an autonomous republic which distinguish it from a territory or region are that it (a) has the status of a state and (b) enjoys a somewhat autonomous position within the framework of a single national-economic complex as far as economic management and the guidance of social and political activity in its territory is concerned. The decisions of the ASSR government are binding on all facilities located in its territory.

Analysis of both the financial resources and the financial situation in a regional economic complex is necessary in order to maintain its comprehensive, balanced, and dynamic development, providing local government bodies with information on the implementation of the State budget (with the objective of controlling the growth of fixed sources of income, making regular and correct payments to the budget, using properly allocations from the budget and the funds of economic units located in the given territory).

The absence of regional financial-industrial models of balances and plans accounts for the lack of scientific justification and balance in the territory's planning system, and for the disparity between the forecasted and the actual indices of economic growth. This lack affects in particular the imbalance between forecasted and achieved volumes of financing capital investments. The gap between the latter volumes is always larger than between the respective volumes of regional production. The higher volumes of the expected capital investments stem from the fact that forecasts do not take into consideration the impact of all external and internal factors affecting the formation of allocations for the region's economic development. Analyses of forecasts of the socioeconomic development for separate republics, territories, regions, and economic regions for 1959–1970, 1971–1980, 1981–1990, carried out by the Institute of Economic Studies of the Far Eastern Scientific Center of the USSR Academy of Sciences confirm this. In territorial planning this results in an unbalanced budget for the specific republic. To maintain the balance, benefits and additional allocations from the Union Budget are often envisaged, the share of these allocations going up to 10%. Considerable funding is singled out for this purpose to autonomous republics from the Union and Union Republic budgets, and this will be discussed below.

At different stages of developing its potential, socialist society made effective use of levers of mutual assistance in order to even out (whenever it was necessary) the levels of economic development in the republics. This is clear from USSR State Plans and Budgets, the system of territorial allocations to the budgets of Union and Autonomous Republics, and allocations from the Union Budget of significant sums to regions with a relatively low level of economic development. In the Russian Federation (RSFSR), areas of this kind, characterized by the respective social and economic indices, included the Tuva, Daghestan, and Kalmyk Autonomous Republics.

In 1984 there were allocated from the Russian budget for the financing of planned measures: more than 31 million rubles for Kalmyk ASSR; 24 million rubles for Tuva ASSR (in 1985 the figures were, respectively, 39.2 million and 39.7 million rubles). In 1985 there were allocated from the Russian budget to the state budget of Yakut ASSR 31.9 million rubles; to the budget of Kamchatka Region, 22.1 million rubles; to Magadan Region 53.2 million rubles. To help finance measures outlined in the State Plan for the Economic and Social Development of Russia in 1985, these regions were allocated receipts from income taxes. In Daghestan ASSR for many years the share of allocations from collective farm tax revenues to the local budget stood at 100%. In 1986 allocations from income tax revenues were envisaged at 100% and from turnover taxes, at 63.9%; that is, they stood above allocations to the budgets of other autonomous republics, territories, and regions of the North Caucasus economic region (60% and 32.6%, respectively, for Kabardino-Balkar ASSR; 50% and 18.4%, respectively, for North Ossetiyan ASSR; and 55% and 30.5% for Chechen-Ingush ASSR.).

All this is conducive to the further evening out of certain negative discrepancies in the levels of economic and, particularly, social development in various parts of the country, more rational interregional ties, and the optimization and balancing of the single national economic complex.

With the transition to new methods of economic management and the use of specifications in the system of economic relations, the forms of sources of income for local budgets will become more flexible and diversified. This calls for a general in-depth analysis of all the sources and reserves that go into the making of the state budget of an autonomous republic and a system of target funds for major regional socioeconomic and scientific-technological programs. This accounts for the substantiated and up-to-date character of the proposals from the Research Institute of Finances of the USSR Ministry of Finances on employing the target principle in drawing up long-term consolidated balance sheets which single out data from the basic comprehensive programs envisaged for realization in the planned period.

It is also expedient to discuss budget revenues in connection with comprehensive regional STP programs, due to the fact that in some regions with excessive manpower there is a trend to boost local budget expenditures while decreasing the rates of growth of fixed sources of income and a general lag with regard to per capita budget revenues. Thus, in Daghestan ASSR the latter is 180 rubles against 190 rubles in Kabardino-Balkar ASSR, with 220 rubles for Northern Ossetian ASSR and 312 rubles for Kalmyk ASSR. The composition and level of expenditure for the social infrastructure need to be improved. The planned scope of new industrial construction in these republics, which puts additional pressure on the social and industrial infrastructure, demands that the State Planning Committees of ASSR establish strict territorial control to ensure that ministries and departments observe the balance between capital investments in production and capital investments in the infrastructure (specification of funds earmarked for the development of the latter stands at 35 to 40 kopeks per ruble of production investments).

Due to the acute need for a radical renewal of the production apparatus along the lines of updated technology, improving the investment structure, and the scientific-technological policy, nearly all regions of the country have been almost simultaneously confronted with immediate tasks demanding considerable funding. It can be expected that under these conditions the share of additional allocations and financial aid from centralized funds and other regions is liable to decrease. As experience with large-scale economic experiments shows, regional development will be boosted by internal sources of capital accumulation, more fixed sources of revenue for local budgets, observing a regime of economy while making a rational use of all resources, and raising the effectiveness of economic management. It becomes an objective necessity to achieve greater independence in managing the resources of local budgets. The point here is the development of a system of *regional self-financing*. This raises the question of introducing full cost-accounting in the region, ensuring its essential independence from the single national economy. The results of our studies indicate a need to develop specific cost-accounting relations.

Working out plans and programs in keeping with the needs of regional development should be the priority of territorial departments in the planning bodies of autonomous republics, territories, and regions. Under the new conditions, major interaction between budgets at different levels will be achieved not so much by the system of annual allocations of funds as by the balancing of local budgets through long-term allocation programs.

The diversity and dynamics of factors having an impact on the effectiveness of regional production account for the complex character and inexperience in shaping the local budgets along centralized lines. It is necessary to expand considerably the financial and economic independence of the local Soviets of Peoples Deputies.

However, the scope of territorial financial planning is much broader and needs to balance the entire regional mullet-branch system.The plan embraces not only structures under the jurisdiction of local Soviets but the territory's entire economy, including economies with both Union and Union–Republic significance. For that reason, a scientifically substantiated regional financial-distribution program is possible only with consideration for all the above-mentioned factors.

Radical changes in economic management methods call for an increase in the revenues of local budgets through the establishment of more flexible links between the local budgets and the financial systems of enterprises under Union and Union–Republic jurisdiction. Studies show the expediency of transfering to local budgets not only the revenues from gains and turnover tax from enterprises under local and republican jurisdiction, but also a part of the pure profit of enterprises under Union jurisdiction and their payments for the attraction of manpower and introduction of new natural resources. Different forms are suggested for connecting the local budgets with the economic results obtained by enterprises under higher jurisdiction. In several experimental regions, it has been decided to transfer to the local budgets 10% of pure profit from facilities under Union jurisdiction—chiefly, profit from implementation of STP.

The importance of expanding the role of local Soviets in regulating financial-economic relations of industries under higher jurisdiction can be gathered from the example of Poti (Georgia). The interbranch association established there collected in its 1984–1985 account 10% of the envisaged gains in the balances of enterprises and 50% of those over and above the respective planned figures, 50% of payments for the use of water supplies from the Rioni River, and 10% of surplus gains from the realization of new, highly effective production.[1] The experiment studying the use of funds of enterprises under Union jurisdiction by local budgets in several regions of the RSFSR has been modeled in many urban and rural areas in other republics.

To ensure the overall, integral development of a region, it is necessary to enhance the territorial approach and the influence of planning, financial, and statistics bodies in the Autonomous Republics both on current and long-term development and on the management of economic and financial operations of enterprises and organizations under higher jurisdiction. This obviously calls for a large-scale regional experiment whose concept is now being developed at the Institute of Economics of the USSR Academy of Sciences, along with the USSR State Planning Committee and other interested organizations.

Turnover tax plays an important part in the formation of the local budget. Under this taxation system, financial bodies deal only with that portion which comes from sales in the territory under their jurisdiction. Meanwhile, there can be a wide margin between sales taxes and taxes from the sales of goods produced in the region. Although, for objective reasons, these figures can never coincide, a wide gap between them leads to unaccounted-for growth of national income in some regions at the expense of others, as well as to distortion of the actual part regions play in the system of enlarged reproduction.

Today, the prevailing trend is for the total volume of turnover tax to decrease. In regard to this, it is necessary to *first* raise the responsibility of managers of trade and other ministries and departments for the fulfillment of exacting plans for turnover taxes. The implementation of these plans is facilitated by the interbranch and intrabranch structural changes in production and turnover.

Second, to mitigate the negative impact of the failure by a number of enterprises to fulfill the plan for gains and turnover taxes, ministries and departments should, in our view, compensate the difference along central lines. This would promote the development of cost-accounting relations between ministries and their facilities and the region. However, the enterprises have the task of introducing, during the term of compensation through bank credit and by other funding, scientific-technological measures aimed at renovating, updating, and technologically reequipping the production apparatus, and of developing nomenclature and production quality that would provide conditions for profitable operation.

The trend toward enhancing the part played by turnover tax is in keeping with increased production in autonomous republics, the formation and use of interregional accumulations, and the development of relations between state-owned companies and budgets under the existing system of distribution. This trend does not contradict that of the diminishing share of turnover tax in accumulations of statewide significance, which should eliminate factors dampening the reflection of labor expenditure in prices. The point here is the diverse functional manifestations of the economic content of turnover tax as a form of the states' centralized net income.

The territorial aspect of improving the use of turnover tax is displayed not through pricing but through interaction with the budget to use a part of the net income primarily in areas of its production and realization. The provision on introducing, as of 1988, the channeling of allocations from turnover tax to the local budgets in fixed amounts to the volume of retail trade turnover in state and cooperative trade.

An essentially new and positive element of regional significance is the decentralized order of making allocations to the budget, ensuring systematic control by local bodies over the financial-economic activities of associations (enterprises).

The decentralized order is of interest when branches of large-scale industrial associations and enterprises are set up, among them those outside the bounds of autonomous republics. Were the branches to have independent balances, with the practice of decentralized payments (through budgets of local Soviets in whose territories the enterprises are situated), the republics' budgets could be receiving incomes. In these conditions it is necessary for the head enterprise (association) to issue orders to banks to transfer the required funds to the budgets of the local Soviets. The size of these allocations can be fixed at between 5% and 6% of the branches' pure profit, or be in proportion to the share of the branches' gains in the total volume of the association's gains or in the association's production plan.

The new conditions of industrial management have opened up broad vistas for the comprehensive development of regions. The effect of using specifications in distribution of gains is enhanced and extended. Previously, the gains of advanced enterprises made up for its shortages in their low-profit counterparts in the same industry, with no regard for the regional factor as such.

It would be expedient to give regional pricing bodies the right to set wholesale and retail prices not only on commodities but also on semi-finished goods and items for engineering needs inside the region in relation to demand and consumption, as well as the right to authorize additional charges to wholesale prices for export products manufactured by industries under local jurisdiction. This will help turn pricing into a flexible regional lever of the economic mechanism and ensure the quickest and most interested participation of the consumer in its coordination and approval. The aforesaid measures would ensure unity of prices for standard production and would put an end to unlawful overcharging by the producer and, thus, on their growth.

Price determination for exports would benefit from the proposal by the Institute of Economics of the USSR Academy of Sciences on the need, in calculating the surcharges to prices, to foresee not only the reimbursement of additional costs but also the size of additional gains earmarked as material incentive for cost-accounting teams, and to single out, along with wholesale prices for the domestic market, the surcharge on exports.

Payments for funds is a promising source for ensuring stable income for the local budget and attracting the interest of local Soviets in achieving a timely and most complete realization of capital investments. Under the new conditions of economic management local budgets will receive payments from the gains of enterprises under higher jurisdiction located in the region. However, until now the financial activities of ASSR have been insufficiently reflected in statistical data, and this hinders the rational use of the financial possibilities now available to the region. For instance, the "Finances" section of the monthly bulletins of the ASSR Statistics Board is represented by a single table. In its turn, the summary report of the ASSR Ministry of Finances on the fulfillment of plans on state incomes aggregates payments from gains in a form with no breakdowns according to enterprises and industrial branches or the national economy as a whole.

The financial, planning, and statistical bodies in the various autonomous republics have no unity in their methods of determining payments from gains (or in calculating turnover taxes). The result is that many of the auditing and planning forms from statistics boards and ministries of finances are difficult to use and compare. Different readings often stem from the fact that statistical materials do not always single out enterprises and organizations under local jurisdiction whose payments from gains make up a considerable part of the local budget's fixed income. Statistical audits mainly indicate enterprises of local food and forestry industries whose share of gains in the total balance of industrial gains of in, for example, Daghestan ASSR is in our estimate only 3% for 1985.

At present, money circulation in ASSR depends on the work of enterprises under higher jurisdiction, and those mainly concerned with producer goods. Under the new conditions enterprises under Union and Union–republic jurisdiction will determine the effective demand of the population for consumer goods. A balance between effective demand (including that for specific types of products classified as Subdivision 1 consumed inside the region) and the actual possibilities of achieving this balance in conditions of self-financing can be attained only along the lines of developing cost-accounting relations between the region and the enterprises under higher jurisdiction.

Starting in 1988 the development of social infrastructure will, to a greater extent, be carried out at the expense of the local budget. In keeping with the USSR Law on State Enterprises, taxes from the gains of enterprises under higher jurisdiction will constitute a significant share of this budget. In our view, its income should depend not only on the net income of the regional economy and the gains of enterprises under higher jurisdiction. With regard to the radical distinctions in the economic development of regions, it would be expedient to make it binding on enterprises to allocate to the local budget funds in direct proportion to the numerical size of employment in industry and the extent to which natural and technological resources are used in the region. At the same time regional bodies should take into consideration the fact that economic benefits are envisaged for enterprises located in promising areas. In this connection regional management bodies will be able to influence many key aspects of the regional economy.

Notes

1. For details see Vladimir Kvint, "The Harmony of National, Regional and Industrial Management in the Economy," *Voprosy Ekonomiky* [The problems of economics] (Moscow, 1985), No. 7, pp. 68–77.

DAGHESTAN–MANGYSHLAK: THE EFFECTIVENESS OF INTERREGIONAL COLLABORATION

(with Z. Uzbekov)

The Caspian Sea has a substantial ecological and economic impact on the social and economic development of the Northern Caucasus and western regions of Kazakstan. This is due to the mineral resources in the pre-Caspian zone which are of countrywide significance. Suffice it to say that the oil and gas deposits in Mangyshlak, and the development of the mineral resources in the pre-Caspian mining areas in Zhetybai and Uzen in Kazakstan, the greater part of which is already under way, and others will be industrially mined. This zone supplies most of the country's needs for sulfate sodium, potassium, magnesium, table salt, and other valuable raw materials. Here one finds virtually boundless reserves of limes and brines.

The planned, consistent development of the area's mineral resources has led to the emergence of a regional industrial area around the Caspian Sea. Its centers are Shevchenko and Guryev in Kazakstan, Astrakhan and Makhachkala in RSFSR (Russian Federation), Baku, and Krasnovodsk in Turkmenia. Daghestan and Chechen-Ingush, the western regions of this area, with a population of more than 5 million, have a relatively abundant workforce, something extremely unusual for the country. But these regions are far from the main centers of intensive economic development in the Caspian Sea area. The Caspian separates these regions from the rich Astrakhan condensed gas deposits. On its eastern shores are the starting points of such large infrastructure connections as the Uzen–Kulsary–Guryev–Kuibyshev oil main and the Uzen–Beinau gas main. The

In *The Socioeconomic Regional Development on the Basis of Increased Scientific and Technological Progress (STP)* (Moscow: The Institute of the Economy of the USSR Academy of Sciences, 1987), pp. 75–82.

latter brings natural gas to the oil main linking Central Asia with the central areas.

Nevertheless, the key economic benefit of the Caspian Sea, its transport potential, is inadequately exploited. Currently, only ferry services exist, and these are much located more to the south, away from the mutually attractive regions: Daghestan with its excessive workforce and western Kazakstan where manpower is at a deficit. Running parallel to the Baku–Krasnovodsk ferry line is another line linking Baku with the Turkmen town of Bektash, which is only a short way from Krasnovodsk. Investment in this transport complex was, in our opinion, unjustified.

As a result, the development of mineral deposits in the area has declined. According to scientists and other specialists, these and other processes are irreversible, and this poses a threat to the very existence of "Karabogazsulfat" and Bektash, the town of chemical workers. Given the present economic situation in the area and the prospects for the development of its industry, the Krasnovodsk–Baku ferry line has no future. This is due, no doubt, to the surplus of railway transportation in Central Asia. At present, there is a risk that less than fully loaded high-capacity ships will be used on a regular basis. In the first half of 1985 alone, 43 runs from Krasnovodsk were made without a single car on board, and 27 runs were made with only half a load. Nevertheless, new, well-equipped ferries were delivered to the area. The ineffective Baku–Bektash ferry line mirrors a larger countrywide economic problem, namely, the inadequate justification for large-scale economic projects and decisions.

Estimates show that, from the point of view of regional effectiveness and national economic significance, this ferry line should yield to a line linking Makhachkala with Aktau, the seaport of Shevchenko. In the next five-year period the importance of the Schevchenko–Makhachkala ferry line will increase dramatically. Moreover, the construction of a railway line from Krasnovodsk to Nizhny Uzen is a vital need, ensuring a link with Shevchenko along the eastern coast of the Caspian. This ferry line would provide the shortest route for trains hauling coal and other freight from Karaganda to Siberia and the industrial centers in Trans-Caucasia and the south of European Russia. Hence, economic priorities demand it. The sooner the line finds its way onto the country's national economic plan, the greater the economic effect for the country, and the greater the passenger comfort. To organize the work of regular ferry transport for railway freight cars, construction of a pier in Makhachkala is essential. This would permit the transportation of vegetables and fruit from the Northern Caucasus to residents of Mangyshlak Region in Kazakstan. Even more important is the opportunity offered those in Daghestan ASSR, the area with the largest workforce and closest to Mangyshlak Region, to live and work in Kazakstan. Currently, airlines linking Makhachkala with Shevchenko and Makhachkala with Novy Uzen serve these people, though the number of passengers accommodated falls well below the demand. Such is the situation in the proximity of two large seaport cities, Shevchenko and Makhachkala, located across from each other and separated by less than 300 kilometers.

At the same time, the ferry line cannot be viewed solely as a transport system. Its role should be estimated only in the context of the overall economic development of Daghestan ASSR and the Mangyshlak Region. Unfortunately, little attention has been paid to scientific investigation of the problem, particularly by the economic institutes of the Academy of Sciences of Kazakstan.

The Comprehensive Program for the scientific and technological progress of Kazak SSR foresees the development of transportation facilities in these ports, high-tech transportation processes that would substantially increase the volume of freight delivered from Kazak ports along the Caspian. To ensure uninterrupted and direct transportation of crude oil and oil products, tankers of the "river-sea" type will be introduced, and a second oil-loading pier, with two wharves, will be built in the port of Aktau. To carry fish products, vegetables, and fruit from the Northern Caucasus, the construction of new refrigerators is being planned. But to achieve all this, the preparation of an industrial base for receiving centers and ports in Mangyshlak region and Kazakstan alone is insufficient. Equally important are the more extensive infrastructure and industrial projects in Daghestan ASSR, particularly in the port of Makhachkala. It is obvious that local efforts in the autonomous republic to deal with these problems are also insufficient, given the lack of proper financing, capacities, and equipment.

Northern Caucasus in general, and Daghestan ASSR in particular, can be a reliable and promising provider for Mangyshlak Region, the entire pre-Caspian zone, and the regional economic area emerging here. Within this area the functions of Daghestan will not be restricted to delivery of fruits and vegetables to the cities in Mangyshlak Region. Given the steadily growing population, Daghestan's interregional functions must be linked with its reserves of drinking water, great recreational potential, and, in particular, the workforce in the autonomous republic. Daghestan is 6 to 7 times closer to Mangyshlak than the more heavily populated areas of Kazakstan. Hence, in the event that a ferry line is established, the activating of these factors only through the transport factor will provide the national economy with annual savings of almost 10 million rubles.

There are a host of other favorable conditions conducive to the emergence of an integrated area: Mangyshlak–Daghestan–Northern Caucasus, First, the concentration of increased regional transportation facilities in Daghestan, with the accompanying reduction in their growth in the northern part of the pre-Caspian zone. This is heightened by the factor of natural conditions and resources characterizing the ever more complex nature of mining, increasing costs, and the labor-intensive nature of raw materials in Mangyshlak. Second, the transportation factor and the proximity of processing capacities, among them the oil-processing complexes in Grozny. Third, the rational use of capital investments in Mangyshlak emerges as a condition and source of investing resources in the development of interregional entities (construction of a ferry pier in Makhachkala).

There is no single answer to this problem. The transport line in question is a bottleneck in the region, the cause of distinct imbalances: disproportionate money circulation plans in Daghestan and other autonomous republics as people are relocated to the eastern Caspian coast. In Daghestan ASSR, for instance, this leads to instability in forming the local income base, with all the attendant consequences. There are tens of thousands of skilled workers and specialists from Daghestan working in Mangyshlak Region. For every thousand workers, the annual production is 3.5 to 4 million rubles above that produced in the republic. A part of this returns in the form of wages.

This gives rise to a situation in which the growth of consumers and services in the republic breaks away from the monetary incomes at the expense of money migrating from Kazakstan. On the other hand, given certain types of merchandise, building materials, and turnover funds, there are reserves over and above fixed norms.

The social consequences of isolated formation of money income are well known. Here, it should be noted, intensification of passenger and freight sea transportation in the defined area in general, and between Makhachkala and Shevchenko in particular, is a major factor for leveling out baneful trends in the economy of a North Caucasus region with excess manpower resources.

The fourth prerequisite for the formation of the pre-Caspian industrial area is the high effectiveness of joint nature conservation undertakings, and the problems of rational use of natural resources in the northern part of the Caspian Sea in raising its fish yields.

The time has long past for the interregional social and economic integration of Daghestan and Mangyshlak, both in setting up a network of vocational and technical schools, secondary schools, and in the development of science and technology.

To achieve effective results in the proposed interregional interaction, it is necessary to develop the respective organizational and management structures. In the vertical management structures, overloaded by industrial functions, the interregional aspect of management is not fully reflected. This fact underlies the importance of horizontal economic relations and contacts between the interested parties, and characterizes the significance of the interregional economic mechanism of regulating production relations and relations of exchange between Daghestan ASSR and Mangyshlak Region on an equal self-supporting basis. In this respect, highly expedient is the issue of payment for labor resources in the form of demographic investments in the region serving as a base for the migrating population. In our case, Daghestan ASSR.

It is also expedient to work out a decision on the regional program "Daghestan–Mangyshlak." At present, narrow departmental and local-rule trends can be observed in the work of ministries and territorial organizations in the region. Evidence of this is the situation around the laying of the ferry line Makhachkala–Aktau.

The line Aktau–Makhachkala–Aktau is more attractive for passenger transportation and more expedient for freight transportation, reducing the distance covered by trucks, automobiles, and freight cars between Baku–Makhachkala and Makhachkala–Baku by more than

800 kilometers. Considering the shortening of the ferry line (158 x 2), there will be a total economy of over 1116 kilometers.

Now yearly tens of thousands of freight cars and trucks cover the extra distance of more than 1000 kilometers, inasmuch as they are ferried 468 kilometers from Aktau south to Baku, and, from there, 375 kilometers north to Makhachkala.

The Caspian shipping company had long disregarded the fact that Aktau and Makhachkala have the same latitude and the distance between them is the shortest, that Makhachkala is 375 kilometers closer to the country's economic regions where freight is dispatched to the republics of Central Asia, its volume making up the bulk of the freight channeled through the Baku ferry line.

An identical situation obtains with the other ferry ports on the Caspian. A national economic approach shows that neither the Baku nor the Sumgait ferry line can compete with their Makhachkala counterpart as regards economic expediency in transporting freight along the Caspian.

According to assessments of the functioning ferry lines, between 1962 and 1983 freight turnover went up threefold, but in the years that followed it fell to the 1970 level. This was due to the fact that there had been no increase in the number of ferries and freight cars were conveyed by railroad, bypassing the ferry, around the northern Caspian coast with excess runs increasing 1.5–2-fold.

In our estimates the economic and geographical location of Makhachkala port calls for the extensive transportation ties running from east to west and back through the Caspian Sea.

Regions adjacent to Makhachkala port are: Northern Caucasus, Donetsk-Dniepr economic areas from the west, the Central Asian republics and southern part of Kazakstan, and Siberia.

The envisaged pattern for transporting freight and passengers along the lines: Baku–Aktau–Makhachkala and Makhachkala–Aktau–Baku, is inexpedient economically, given the high balance costs of the ferry, and is far from realistic, because it does not take care of return transportation of freight in cars and aboard ferries.

The construction in the 12th five-year period (1986–1990) of a ferry line in Makhachkala would comply with national economic interests and ensure a high economic effect by

- eliminating the artificially created system of return deliveries of national economic freight shipments thereby vacating more than 300,000 cars;

- achieving a balance between the transportation load on western and eastern ferry lines;
- bringing down the load on the Makhachkala-Baku railway line and increasing its flexibility, raising maneuverability and optimization of ferry lines in the Caspian basin, ensuring self-supporting effectiveness of the Caspian shipping company and its profitability.

REGION AND INDUSTRY: MODES OF INTERACTION

Routes of Technical Progress

The electrotechnical complex in Minusinsk, Siberia, is growing rapidly. One of its plants produces automatic lathes for the plasma cutting of metal as well as components for warehouse technologies. Both automatic lathes and warehouse components are labor-saving. The costs of manufacturing this equipment are higher in this region than they would be, for example, in Ukraine. But there is a consumer is nearby, namely, a Siberian manufacturing plant. Nonetheless, most of the product is being shipped to the European parts of the country because industrial concerns prevail over economic reasoning.

In the current period of qualitative changes in the country's productive forces, a unified policy in science and technology is gaining in importance. The main goals of this policy are to determine the directions and priorities in the development of science and technology and initiate the large-scale introduction of the latest achievements in this area.

Experience has proven that solving these problems requires the joint efforts of experts in economics, sociology, technology, political science, and law. At the same time, a unified policy in science and technology is most effective when it is thoroughly worked out from the perspective both of the state and of specific industries and regions. Scientific and technological policy should be integrated into the overall management mechanism of the national economy.

The management of the national economy is being improved in all respects. As the search for new forms and structures of economic activity continues, it is very important to rationalize not only the state's and industries' management systems but also regional systems. The management of scientific and technical progress should take into account differences in the levels of economic progress in

Pravda, October 22, 1984, p. 3.

various regions and their social and climatic character, among other factors.

The system of planned and projected indicators of efficiency of scientific and technological progress should also take into consideration the use of new technologies and the exploitation of machinery in various regions of the country. That will promote the growth of the actual (instead of conditional) efficiency of new technologies and create an economic shield against those technologies that threaten the region's environment.

As is well known, the USSR is conducting large-scale experiments aimed at increasing the possibilities for plants and production associations to plan and manage their economic activities and strengthen their responsibility for the results. Such an approach offers new possibilities for cooperation between plants in different industries located at the same industrial center. Under such conditions, the role of regional bodies in coordinating the activities of these companies is expected to grow significantly.

In this regard, the activity of regional scientific centers of the Academy of Sciences of Ukraine is of growing interest. These centers coordinate activities not only of the Academy's institutes but also of industrial R & D centers in the region.

The same approach has been used by the Leningrad Scientific Center of the Academy of Sciences of the USSR. The Leningrad Scientific Center is responsible for scientific leadership over the territorial and industrial program for the intensification of economic development in 1985 and for the Twelfth 5-year plan. The government has approved an initiative by Leningrad to launch a program called Intensification '90. This initiative was recommended for consideration and support by a number of the State committees and ministries.

Several years ago, the Siberian division of the Academy of Sciences of the USSR prepared a large-scale regional R & D program entitled "Siberia." This year the program has been qualitatively changed. Its assignments were approved by the State Committee for Planning, the Cabinet of Ministers, sixty ministries, and 350 R & D organizations participating in the program. Following that series of approvals, the State Committee for Science and Technology, together with the Presidium of the Academy of Sciences of the USSR, adopted a provision that gave the "Siberia" program the status of law.

However, not every Center of the Academy of Sciences has become a regional scientific center coordinating and integratng the work of all R & D institutions in its region. regardless of their industrial subordination. In Lithuania, for example, a substantial share of the scientific and technical potential belongs to the R & D institutes of a number of industrial ministries. In some instances, even when institutes are located on the same street, they are poorly informed about each other's activities, sometimes conducting the same research. Obviously, in such cases there is not enough cooperation between them. Also, reliable contacts with corresponding institutes of the All-Union Academy of Sciences are lacking.

The Soviets play an important role in economic development and in achieving the goals of 5-year plans. This presupposes strengthening the role of regional authorities in the management of scientific and technical progress. However, the issues of management in science and technology are missing from the list of functions of regional authorities, a list that has been prepared by the State Committee for Planning. In the meantime, the need for such provisions empowering regional authorities with responsibility for management in science and technology is urgent.

For example, in Krasnoyarsk there are two neighboring companies that are subordinates of the same ministry, namely, the Ministry of Nonferrous Metals. The first one is Sibtsvetmetavtomatika; the second is a branch of Soyuztsvetmetavtomatika. As a result, the complete use of production capacities is not being utilized There simply are too many administrative and management personnel. This would be the right time for regional authorities to intervene. However, they do not have the proper tools to influence the situation.

In our opinion, it would be prudent to complement the economic experiments that are currently taking place throughout the USSR with the following practices:

- to estimate and analyze the advantages and disadvantages of establishing structures for management in science and technology in the regions
- to elaborate their rational organizational structure
- to outline their economic functions and responsibilities.

Later, by relying on the results of such assessments, it would be possible to prepare recommendations aimed at a more efficient combination of territorial and industrial approaches to the management of the national economy as a whole.

The state policy in science and technology is dynamic. Changes and improvement of its individual components and their shape reflect its permanent evolution, which is a result of the progressive development of socioeconomic relations in a mature socialist society.

REGIONALISM AS THE KEY TREND IN SCIENTIFIC AND TECHNOLOGICAL PROGRESS

The scientific and technological revolution of our time has led to radical structural shifts in the world economy and its industrialization, and to a growth of GNP in individual countries and groups of countries that could not be provided for by the available raw material and power resources in those parts of the developed world that were already at a high level of economic maturity. The radically new economic and technological level of development of the production forces called for a new territorial division of social labor. There began a large-scale transfer of natural resources from areas undergoing industrialization, leading to a new form of interaction between scientific progress and technology, society, and the natural environment.

Mankind is now faced with problems whose traditional solution in these areas has proved ineffective and, more often than not, unrealizable. The extraction of hydrocarbon raw materials in the deserts of the Arabian peninsula and Central Asia and from the shelf of the world's oceans, the development of deposits of nonferrous metals, diamonds, and coal in the North, the forests in the tropical zone and the arctic taiga, and the development of fallow and virgin lands in the zone of experimental agriculture has required new machinery and technologies, suitable for areas with extremes in natural and climatic conditions. The fact that these processes are occurring in the newly developing territories, with their insufficient transportation systems, poorly studied geological features, low population density, and shortage of skilled workers, has led to the development of a specific approach, namely, the regionalization of the scientific and technological solutions implemented there.

The extent of the extracting and primary processing industries operating in these areas has essentially changed the nature of applied

In *Economic Problems of Regional Scientific-Technical Complexes* (Moscow: Institute of the Economy of the USSR Academy of Sciences, 1983), pp. 41–66.

technologies. The gigantic growth of mining operations, ore concentration, and metallurgy has brought about regionalization of technologies. Those developed for these areas are usually ineffective when applied in the "old" areas.

For instance, coal deposits in the eastern part of Russia—in the Kansko-Achinsky and Ekibastuz basins—are worked on the basis of radically new line technologies that ensure labor productivity that is 25 to 35 times above the average for the industry. However, if the rotary extraction complexes, with an hourly yield of 12,500 tons (a freight-train load), were to be used at any mine in the European part of the country or abroad, they would not be working at their full capacity. Thus, geological conditions in the area—the reserves of natural resources, especially mineral, timber, and power resources—have a decided impact on the regionalization of scientific and technological progress. In areas of new development, the processes for regenerating an environment affected by technological developments take a different turn.

Thus, while the technical division of labor brought about technologization, regionalization is the result of its territorial division.

Today, scientific economics deals primarily with the applied aspect of regionalization. Particular consideration is given to problems of regional land use, the designing of machinery for use in the northern areas, and the creating of technology for implementation in permafrost conditions. These problems are still insufficiently developed for other areas with extreme natural conditions.

It must be noted, however, that regionalization first surfaced in the development of science, not technology, and was connected with the step-by-step procedures in developing new areas. Industrialization there was preceded by pioneering expeditions by specialists in geography, botany, zoology, geology, and engineering surveying. Studies carried out in these areas provided new data and registered phenomena that did not fit into the existing theoretical patterns and were regarded initially as exceptions. A study of these "anomalies" has begun, but it has not been concentrated enough. The industrial development of natural resources in new areas has begun to outstrip scientific attention to regional problems, which has been lagging for some time.

The economic issues that came up in industry could not, in many cases, be solved by the existing technology, which had been oriented toward use in areas with moderate natural and climatic conditions. Thus, for a long time the demands that society put to science remained unrealized. But gradually scientific knowledge has begun to make headway in the study of regional problems.

These studies have showed that the peculiarities and exceptions noted not only were typical of a specific area but also had applications in different areas and in diverse parts of the world. The exceptions studied along single methodological lines often turned out to be previously unknown regularities responsible for the functioning of natural, simulated, and social systems in respective regional conditions.

In-depth studies of regional peculiarities, separate regions as a whole, and elements of their noosphere called for specific development of the already known methods of research and the development of new, original combinations. Theoretical systematization of the data obtained not only helped realize the basic function of all sciences—development and organization of information on the phenomenon studied—but also prompted the intensive study of the subject of the particular science. Research teams that were set up initially to study regional peculiarities of a particular respective science gradually led to the emergence of new, specialized sciences. Thus, geological science spawned regional geology and regional geomorphology (the study of the reliefs of sections of the land surface and the sea bottom); from geography there emerged regional geography; and economic sciences led to the emergence of regional economics. Medical sciences gave rise to a large group of new scientific trends: medical geography, recreational geography, nosogeography, physiology of the northern mountain regions—all the result of science regionalization.

One can say that, all in all, the regionalization of science initially adhered to the subject principle. This stage was noted for the transition of regional sciences from the analysis of practical data and observation results to synthesis, developing, new meaningful subjects—a transition of these sciences from the empirical to the theoretical.

Regional sciences dealing with the initial study and economic development of newly emerging areas were taking their first steps. Among these sciences were the aforementioned regional geology, regional geography, regional economics, and regional medicine.

Their relatively extended development period brought these sciences to high scientific levels. Among their researchers were full and associate members of the countries' Academies of Sciences, and their works received high scientific and government recognition. Thus, by decree of the Presidium of the USSR Academy of Sciences, the A. E. Fersman prize for 1979 was awarded to Dr. I. N. Govorov, Ph.D (Geology-Mineralogy), for a series of works on regional chemistry and the genetic mineralogy of hydrothermal sources.

The USSR State Prize for 1982 was awarded for achievements in the field of regional medicine to twelve medical researchers, all of them well-known specialists, for a series of works in geographical pathology and the epidemiology of cardiovascular, oncological, and nervous diseases.[1]

Technical sciences were regionalized much later, and the nature of the process was different. Inasmuch as the intensive development of natural resources in the new areas outstripped the process of regionalization in all sciences, among them the technical sciences, hands-on work brought significant results in the adapting of machinery and technology to regional conditions.

The problems uncovered in achieving interaction between machinery and the environment, and the quest for their solution led to regionalization of several sciences. This was attempted not by expanding the subject of a particular science but by changing the range of its problematic orientation. Thus, regional trends manifested themselves in engineering, construction mechanics, geophysics and the physics of metals, and geological sciences.

The regionalization of the technical sciences differed from the same process in the other sciences in its focus on dealing with problems of economic development; at the same time it was falling behind the demands of practical work, which were especially acute. From the mid-1960s large-scale construction work had been going on in the northern areas. The power plants of Vilyuiskaya, Ust-Khantayskaya, and Kolymskaya were built on permafrost soils, and their dams and roadways consumed hundreds of thousands of tons of hydrotechnical concrete; and oil and gas mains were laid in the Arctic and adjacent regions. Yet only recently were the scientific foundations created for developing durable, frost-resistant concrete for the construction of roads and hydroelectric facilities. This major achievement of regional technical sciences with huge economic prospects was honored with the USSR State Prize for 1982 in science.[2]

Guided by the needs of the economy, science expanded the scope of its work, making its way into new areas and developing new guidelines whose practical use would be obvious only in the future. An example of this type of specialization is regional biology. Its provisions are finding wholesale application only in our time, when biotechnology is achieving ever wider application, and its adaptability to the environment calls for in-depth studies of regional problems.

Professor V. G. Kirillov-Ugryumov, chairman of the Higher Certification Board of the USSR Council of Ministers, while emphasizing vital guidelines of research, quoted the opinion of the Council of Experts in Biological Sciences that "regional problems have been insufficiently reflected in the theses of recent years. . . ."[3]

It is obvious that not all sciences have a pronounced regional aspect, not all can be "regionalized." The fundamental sciences—mathematics and philosophy—do not have any regional applications. Similarly, regionalization is ill-suited to astronomy. Its regional aspect emerges in connection with the effect of the location of its facilities on its results. This factor, for example, was decisive in placing the special astrophysical observatory of the USSR Academy of Sciences in the remote township of Nyzhny Arkhyz in Karachayevo-Cherkessk Autyonomous Region.

On the rise are sciences whose subject of investigation is of a regional nature. Among these is glaciology, which is concerned with the spreading of ice on the earth's surface (glaciers, snow blanket, permafrost, etc.), and its structure and physical-chemical properties, the study of deserts, seismology, ethnography.

It is reasonable to classify sciences by the extent and factors of their regionalization. Among the primary factors one can single out are location, technical means of investigation, scientific potential, and research methodology. The extent of regionalization ranges from regional sciences to those that are easily, moderately, or poorly regionalized and those that are non-regionalized.[4]

Regionalization of another integral part of the productive forces—the means of production—emerged against a background of their growing technologization. Initially, regionalization embraced separate mechanical tools. This was a rather long period, but by the mid-1970s more than 100 models of machines and materials intended for use in the North were being produced in the country.[5] Machines were in operation for mountainous and arid areas. The level of technological and territorial industrial specialization attained at the time enhanced the emergence of the new trend toward scientific and technological progress (STP)—*regionalization.* The regionalization of STP, its technologization, and the need to increase the economic effectiveness in developing new areas and conducting intensive reconstruction of developed regions led to the emergence of regional technologies. Today, they are effective in the agro-industrial complex, in most industries—construction, transportation, and communications—and in other branches of the economy.

*Regional technologies, the result of the interaction of two components of STP—technologization and regionalization—*are multi-aspect phenomena. While reflecting current economic trends brought on by the new level of development of the productive forces, regional technologies are a supplement to all the elements of the "science–technology–society" and "science–technology–environment" systems. These technologies, being, as it were, the material element of the means of production, are also the subject of scientific research.

Regionalization and technologization of STP are worldwide trends, yet in analyzing the interaction of regional technologies, society, and the environment it is useful to study the influence of production relations on the nature of the process.

The political science and political economy theories of technological determinism that emerged in the early 1940s did their best to deny the importance of the relations between production and society's sociopolitical goals in developing science and technology, exaggerating their role in any existing socioeconomic system. By this they excluded production relations from the subject of STP economics. But one cannot accept this in determining the subject of economic studies dealing with regional technologies. Consideration should be given to the fact that "the objective laws of development of production relations and their interaction with the productive forces are the subject of all the economic sciences."[6] As L. M. Gatovsky notes, this should be the starting point for investigating the interaction between economics and technology.

This scientific trend, while developing its particular methodology, stems naturally from the general methodology of dialectical materialism underlying our knowledge of production relations and the productive forces of society. In conformity with the view of dialectical materialism on the interaction of STP and the regional economy, it is important both to study the impact of STP on the economy of a region and the impact of the economy on the emerging, implemented, and operating technologies and to bring out the main aspects of this interaction. The solution of these tasks is of an analytical character. It is also very important not to restrict oneself to methods of analysis, but to study in their integrity regional technologies, production relations, and the environment in which they function.

As Isaac Newton emphasized, ". . . the study of difficult subjects by the method of analysis must always precede the method of synthesis."[7] Analysis and synthesis, together with induction and deduction, the historical and the logical, are integral parts of the methodology of political economy, the theoretical foundation of all economic sciences.[8]

As already mentioned above, the study of the economics of regional technologies initially lagged behind hands-on experience. The problem was handled by beginning with a technical-economic analysis of the experience of implementing technology in extreme conditions, leading in the late 1970s to the first regional economic and scientific-technological programs, based on the general concepts of goal orientation but without sufficient links with the principles of territorial planning, management, and regional economics. "Yet, first of all, there must be a special registering and systematizing of phenomena already known to science, the facts that have already been given their place in science as its primary material."[9] The information obtained in the course of this work conformed to the first stage of cognition in Lenin's well-known formula: "From live visualization to abstract thought and from there on to practical work—such are the dialectics of cognizing the truth." Today, the basic task of studying regional technologies from the point of view of methodology is to cover the other two stages of the quoted formula.

This brings to the forefront the vital task of studying the basic trends in the interaction of STP with the regional economy and working out the key principles of economic influence on this interaction, with the objective of increasing the economic effectiveness of STP in the country as a whole.

By defining the methodological approaches to the development of this scientific line, its problems can be broken down into three groups. These studies should begin with analysis of the interaction of regional technologies and the economics of the region.

In each interaction there is a steering party. In the interaction under study, this party is STP, and, at repetitive stages, regional technology. That is why problems dealing with the study of the influence of STP on the economics of a region are concentrated in group one.

This process, in its turn, gives rise to a entire range of new problems.

Thus, the functioning of a branch in a certain region is determined by a system of indices that currently do not take into account the impact of STP on the criteria of the optimum. Under the new conditions, new methods are required to take into account the diverse influence of STP on a region's economy. This accounting calls for a more in-depth study of the political economy aspects in the interaction of natural and value indices of STP and the way its results materialize in production.

The mechanism of STP influence on the levels and forms of organization of social production on a regional basis still lacks requisite study. The mandatory decisions of the last few years bring up as a key task of economic development the policy of conserving fuel resources, raw materials, and manpower. Thus, a vital question is what part is to be played by STP in pursuing this policy on a regional scale.

Today, the scientific and technological policy of the State determines the policy of industrial branches and the country's regions. Yet, while it is possible to analyze a wide range of means and levers to realize statewide and branch technological policies, the mechanism for analyzing regional scientific and technological policies is only in the beginning stages.

This brings to center stage problems listed under group two, dealing with the study of the demands of a regional economy for the realization of STP. The economic, social, climatic, and ecological conditions in the various regions set the requirements for an increase in the effectiveness of STP. These terms can be either of a negative nature, calling for increasing expenditure (low temperatures, permafrost soils, etc.), or of a positive nature, reducing costs (concentration of rich natural resources in the area, convenient geological conditions for extraction of mineral deposits, an effective branch structure in the economy of a region, etc.). It is important to single out and classify the basic indices that affect the regional specifics of STP and give them consideration in drawing up regional scientific-technological policies.

In addition to the analysis of the interaction between STP and the regional economic system, a synthesis is necessary. In studying the questions in group three, the prime task is to investigate the general economic aspects of STP in the region, to see how the economic laws of social development are interpreted in the economics of regional technologies. The solution to these problems can be affected by the conditions of economic organization of production and the sociopolitical orientation of society. At the same time, it must be noted that, even within a single country, the specific natural and climatic conditions and socioeconomic factors introduce distinctions into the progress and effectiveness of STP in its different regions.

Attention must also be paid to the economic trends governing the development of regional technologies, so that the regional resources for increasing the effectiveness of STP can be effectively tapped. The degree to which new technologies and the region's scientific and technological potential are utilized depends basically on the degree of implementation given to regional scientific and technological policy. Due to the fact that, at the present moment, long-term, scientifically grounded regional scientific-technological policy is far from being implemented in all of the country's regions, the regional resources of STP are only on their way to being effectively utilized.

An effective scientific-technological policy requires making a choice in favor of the more effective lines of development for STP and planning for their implementation.

Regional engineering and technology emerge as proof of the region's readiness for STP and is a key factor in increasing the effectiveness of production. At present the cognitive apparatus of the economy of regional technologies is at its initial stage. This apparatus should be developed on the basis of theoretical studies and generalizations from accumulated practical materials. To this effect, it is important to make a classification of regions (from the standpoint of using and introducing new technologies) and the types of regional technologies. This will make it possible, eventually, to define optimal technological solutions and standardize them.

Of substantial methodological importance here is considering the structural changes in the territorial-production complexes (TPC) under the impact of progress in engineering and technology, as well as its influence on enhancing the complex nature of the emerging TPC.

As an integral element of a unified system of national economic planning, the planning of science and technology has its distinctive features. Unfortunately, these features are mostly of a negative character. While, on the whole, planning in the USSR is based on a combination of industrial and territorial approaches, the plans for developing science and technology have, until now, developed along industrial lines.

The interests of both regional and statewide development call for the planning of STP along regional lines. At the present moment, however, this question is not being developed to its full advantage along either theoretical or methodological lines.

The development of comprehensive economic forecasting and planning of regional technologies should encompass the following aspects: industrial, inter-branch, territorial, and regional, integrating the three preceding aspects on a regional basis. The comprehensive forecast and plan must embrace all stages, from scientific research to the final result: the fullest effect of the achievements of STP introduced in the region.

On this basis it is useful to regard the forms and methods that are molded by experience, in different areas, for accelerating the implementation and increasing the effectiveness of regional technologies: regional STP programs, governmental bodies for STP in regions, and industrial scientific-production complexes organized along the lines of functional specialization for regional technological development of regions. These questions are all influenced by the correlation between statewide and regional approaches to the management of STP, and in their turn should be solved with the ultimate economic effect in mind. Under the conditions of intensive development of new territories and the deficit of manpower, coupled with the effects of the other above-mentioned factors, greater significance is attached to the regional aspects of STP effectiveness, which have not been reflected in the operating methods in calculating economic effectiveness, new technology, and capital investments.

The insufficient development of this regional aspect is already affecting the rates of introduction of several progressive technologies, such as technology "for application in the North," automation systems, and industrial robots. One must decide in which region this technology will be produced, and which regions will benefit from its implementation through manpower reductions and raising output. This includes evaluating the substitution of automated labor for live labor on the basis of introducing regional technologies.

The Basic Guidelines for Economic and Social Development of the USSR for 1981–1985 and for the period up to 1990 formulate the task of developing and implementing comprehensive programs for the solution of key scientific-technological problems. The solution should be approached from the positions given in the section dealing with improvement of economic management. Above all, it is the necessary to achieve an effective combination of industrial and territorial management, which calls for the development of a respective legal and methodological apparatus.

Regional programs of STP, properly developed and consistently implemented, will serve as a reliable basis and a stage of realization for countrywide, industrial STP programs and a comprehensive plan for the economic and social development of the region.

Proceeding from the existing problems and the substantiated methodology, the methodological apparatus for studying the economics of the regional aspects of STP should include methods that have been worked out in detail and tested by economic science—methods of systems analysis, program/object planning and management, and economic-mathematical simulation modified to regional needs—and be supplemented by new private methods applicable to the specific scientific aspect. Estimates have been made primarily for methods of inter-branch balance with elements of optimization to determine the effect of regional technologies on the indices of reproduction in the region, and dynamic programming and network graphs for simulation of the interaction of organizations taking part in programs for developing and implementing regional technologies, distributing capital investments, labor, and material resources for effective realization of STP regional programs.

Methods are emerging for the regionalization of technical-economic and social indices of STP, working out a technological characteristic of the region, conducting expedition observations, classifications, and grouping, and their results, along with mathematical models of scientific and technological development of different regional combinations and evaluation units.

Regional economics, which emerged in the late 1960s for the study of economic problems in different areas and served, along with the economics of STP, as a concrete theoretical basis for the economics of regional technologies, "has its own methods of research some of which are still at a stage of quests and experimental testing."[10] There is a major need for the development of adequate research methods in the economics of regional technologies and their coordination.

The present-day realities of STP—regionalization and technologization and the formulated and systematized group of problems emerging under their impact and in relation to them—are evidence of the vital importance of the process now under way, in which economics is becoming concerned with studies dealing with regional problems of scientific and technological development. These studies have been necessitated by the objective requirements of the socialist socialization of production and its territorial organization, the fuller and more comprehensive implementation of economic factors, and the trends of developed socialism, the growing significance of STP, and the above-mentioned factors, along with the need for the further development of economic theory.

K. V. Ostrovityanov, examining the theory of the development of economic sciences, wrote, "One of the trends in the development of the natural and social sciences is their differentiation. With the growth of the social division of labor and technological progress, new branches of science emerge which concentrate on ever-more-narrow areas of nature and society."[11]

As regional problems of STP, with their major impact on the development of productive forces and production relations, become areas of special economic research with a specific methodology and emerging methods-apparatus for their study, one can speak of the emergence of a special scientific trend in economics which can be defined as the economics of regional technologies.

Inasmuch as the object of the economics of regional technologies is to develop economic problems dealing with the designing, functioning, and effectiveness of technological systems in their regional execution, and to substantiate regional scientific and technological policies, develop theory and methods for optimizing management, planning and economic programming of science and technology by integrating territorial and industrial approaches to STP in regions, this scientific trend may be classified as having an applied character.

In substantiation of the need for constant analysis of the system of economic sciences to single out the newly emergent industrial and specialized subject, one can quote A. M. Yeremin: "In science, the division of labor denotes growth of productive (cognitive, heuristic) force. However, the specifics of science, as compared with, for example, the sphere of direct material production, are that, as a form of peculiar intellectual production, it does not wait for a new stage of labor division to emerge spontaneously, but registers actively this aspect of its development, thereby applying conscious effort to multiply its productive capacity."[12]

The fact that the economics of regional technologies emerged at the stage when STP enhanced its impact on the territorial development of productive forces and production relations can be explained by reference to V. I. Lenin's idea that, "only when social relations were reduced to relations of production and the latter to the heights of productive forces did it become possible to regard the development of social systems as a natural historical process. It goes without saying that without this view there can be no social science"[13]

The economics of regional technologies encompasses all the economic aspects of STP regional problems. This stems from understanding technologization as a universal trend of present-day STP, a view shared by scientists in the USSR and abroad. Today, technologization influences virtually all the spheres of social development, and the concept of "technology," taken in its broad sense, incorporates any technical system as a whole, the genesis and functioning of any natural or simulated social system. In our opinion the concept of technology is best defined in the work of the American scientist E. Yanych: "Technology . . . denotes a broad sphere of purposeful application of the physical, life, and behavioral sciences. This includes the overall concept of engineering, as well as medicine, agriculture, organization of management and other spheres of knowledge with their material stock and theoretical principles."[14] Such an understanding of technology includes all the elements of STP, while their regionalization along with technologization makes it possible to develop regional economic problems of STP in their systematized form as the economics of regional technologies.

The technological approach to STP in regions promotes the practical application of this trend in economic sciences. Inasmuch as the "technological means of production is to the best of knowledge an essential form of existence of production forces,"[15] the degree of regionalization of technology reflects the extent to which society has managed to master the process of controlling natural forces, the processes of rational development of natural resources.

The emergence and development of the economics of regional technologies were prepared through the development of the systems of economic, engineering, and natural sciences and the intensification of their interaction.

The regionalization of economic sciences led to the development of new projects dealing with the territorial and regional aspects in fundamental economic theories, and to the emergence of regional economics. The interaction of the latter with STP economics and both of them with the system of technological sciences, regional natural sciences, against the background of the trends of present-day social development led to the *nascent economics of regional technologies*.

The formation process of economics of regional technologies is not unique to economic sciences. Only under the impact of regionalization (not to mention other present-day trends in economic sciences) are several new scientific trends emerging. An indicative example is urban economics which, "as a branch of science, should be oriented to the study of production development, the distribution and consumption of material wealth, and the social organization of labor in the urban community. . . . Urban economics is based on specialized and branch economics [and] uses research of many other sciences. . . ."[16]

A wide circle of Soviet scientists has dedicated its efforts to developing the theory of regionalizing science and its technological applications.[17] A noteworthy contribution to the study of regional problems of STP was made by a number of economists.[18] Considerable effort was applied to the study of these problems by foreign scientists.[19]

The development of regional scientific trends by scientists in many parts of the world has called for cooperation, including a regular exchange of ideas and opinions. With this objective in mind, in 1960 the International Association of Regional Sciences was established, incorporating 600 scientists from more than 30 countries. Among Soviet representatives who became members in 1967 were the economists E. F. Baranov, L. N. Karpov, V. A. Mash, N. N. Nekrasov, and E. N. Chetyrkin.[20] The Council for International Scientific Contacts in Regional Studies was established under the Presidium of the USSR Academy of Sciences.

Inasmuch as the economics of STP and regional economics have the greatest impact on the emergence of the new scientific trends, it was natural for representatives of these sciences to have a hand in developing research on regional economic problems of STP.

Economic science, adhering to Marxist premises, started an active study of regional problems only in the last 15 years. In this field the accumulated empirical material is way ahead of the progress made in theoretical research. Many scientists still view the economic problems of STP and their management without taking into account their regional components.[21]

Given its relatively low level of development, an increase in scientific research and the number of publications in this field is inevitable. Currently, of the almost 900 books published between 1976 and 1980 by Ekonomika, a publishing house responsible for producing the bulk of high-priority theoretical and practical economic problems, only 4.5% deal with STP to one extent or another. Until 1982, there was almost no publication of any in-depth study of the experience and problems of key STP aspects on a regional scale and the resolution of regional scientific-technological problems.

The country's economic development has brought up several previously discussed problems whose resolution will be significant for the progressive development of the economic mechanism of the national economy and that of other countries. What literature has made the greatest contribution to solving the problems of economics of regional technology?

In 1975 the prominent Soviet economist N. N. Nekrasov published a monograph[22] dealing with the methodological and methodical problems of accelerating STP by considering the regional specifics of economic development. This book, with a second edition in 1978, was one of the first to deal with these problems. Yet the need for more rational use of the country's huge resources, with the objective of accelerating STP, brings the economics of regional technologies to the forefront of vital problems integrally linked with their practical implementation. Among other things, this acceleration is called for by the ever-increasing part working people are playing in solving the problems of enhancing the effectiveness of and increasing STP, the ever-growing complexity of economic relations, and the ensuing need to forecast and take into account the socioeconomic consequences of STP in regions, setting up timely control over acceleration of STP plans by local territorial management authorities and doing away with departmental barriers in deciding technological policies, and the need to increase efforts to combat the negative effects of technological progress in regions, etc.[23]

A joint monograph written by specialists from the Council for the Study of Production Forces under The USSR State Planning Committee is dedicated to regional problems of STP in several industries, and its impact on the territorial structure of the national economy.[24] This may be the first book published by Nauka Publishers which is wholly dedicated to the development of the regional aspects of STP.

The different aspects of regional technological politics as applied to problems of developing the North are dealt with in the works of A. G. Aganbegyan, G. A. Agranat, V. F. Burkhanov, Y. M. Dogayev, and S. V. Slavin.

V. P. Loginov used the example of the Kansko-Achinsk power-fuel complex to carry out identical studies along these lines.

S. V. Slavin was among the first of the country's scientists to formulate the guiding principles of a regional approach to STP reflecting the peculiarities of economic activity in specific natural, geographical, and economic conditions of the North.[25]

The works of Y. M. Dogayev study STP problems with a view to the prospects of developing the country's northern regions, delving into the specific problems of improving the methodology for defining the effectiveness of new machinery.[26]

The shaping of regional technological policy and the reflection of its aspects in the development of certain elements of the mathematical formula for defining the effectiveness of new technology (after the example of the mining industry) is discussed in works by V. P. Loginov.[27]

In their work on political economy, A. I. Demenev and V. I. Chichkanov make an attempt to bring out the regional peculiarities of shaping the material and technological base of communism.[28] The authors single out, alongside the functional and industrial structures, the regional structure of the material and technological base.

Unfortunately, the systemic approach to STP is not yet employed to its full advantage. Indices used for analyzing STP within the regional framework fail to reflect the unity and organic interaction of all its aspects and problems.

As has been noted in several scientific works, solving STP problems on a regional scale calls for developing the scientific justification for organizing productive forces along territorial lines at all stages of planning and management: in pre-plan studies, and in developing plans and programs and guiding their realization. The monograph by R. I. Shniper[29] deals with priority problems of raising the scientific level of regional pre-planning studies. The author emphasizes the scientific and technological problems of the economic concept of regional economic development, among them that of forecasting technological progress for regional industries and developing the scientific and technological potential on a regional basis.

The further development of the economic mechanism envisages the development of the methodology of territorial planning of STP and its practical realization. In this connection significance attaches to singling out STP as an independent object of complex territorial socioeconomic planning and management, as realized in the Donetsk Scientific Center of the UkSSR Academy of Science under the guidance of N. G. Chumachenko and N. N. Yermoshenko.[30] The authors suggested a methodology for working out a complex territorial STP plan, the foundations for its programming, and the forecasting of socioeconomic effects of the STP on a regional basis. The work defines major tasks for developing science and technology, and the structure of the plan in general. However, plan indices give insufficient attention to regional peculiarities and the use of regional reserves to make STP more effective. Naturally, it is possible to define and influence the aforesaid indices only by actual methods of STP planning and management in a given region. Only the first steps have been taken as yet, and only according to economic experiments barely covered in the press.

In the monograph by V. Y. Budavey an in-depth study has been made of the shaping promising comprehensive STP programs and their economic management. Yet, for all this, the comprehensive nature of the study overlooks the regional aspect. The author quotes the experience of a program-oriented approach to scientific and technological problems on a regional scale,[31] yet he examines only the combination of industrial and inter-branch principles of planning, excluding its territorial aspect.

Individual problems of regional development are presented in the works of G. B. Tersh,[32] V. I. Duzhenkov,[33] Y. M. Kanygin,[34] and others.

The works by G. V. Tersh discuss the regional peculiarities of technological progress in the building construction and materials, which enable him to say that STP studies should be carried out as applied to concrete economic regions and subregions, thus making it possible to determine in full measure the national economic effectiveness of STP.

V. I. Duzhenkov studied the formation of the regional scientific potential in its interaction with the location of production and its structure and technological level in economic regions. His work defines the trends of STP impact on the siting of several industries involved in material production and the key scientific tasks stemming from the basic provisions of promising regional socioeconomic policy.

Republican and regional publishers are producing works that often deal with the regional aspects of STP, give systematized factors influencing its effectiveness, study questions of STP interaction, and develop the territorial organization of productive forces.[35]

The First Practical Science Conference devoted to the economic problems of regional technological policy,[36] held in the fall of 1980 in Krasnoyarsk, consolidated ten years of theoretical and practical experience in developing the economic mechanism for STP management along regional lines. The conference led to the development of a strategy for further studies of regional STP problems under the conditions of developed socialism: the economic mechanism of developing and implementing regional technological policy, and comprehensive planning and organizing the introduction of new technologies along regional lines. A special place in the materials of the conference went to the shaping and realization of regional scientific-technological programs.

The All-Union Scientific-Technological Conference, "Methodological Problems of Developing and Realizing Comprehensive Republican Scientific-Technological Programs," held in December

1981 in Minsk, was a reflection of the multi-aspect complex of regional STP programs. Its materials give a complex scale of regional STP programs and show the lack of a single methodology for their development and actualization, and the priority and significance of the subject in question. The conference named the growing number of scientists concerned with economic regional problems of STP.

The rather small number of books and monographs on economics of regional technology is a temporary phenomenon. Nevertheless, the number of other forms of publication on this subject (articles, theses, or reports) has doubled in the last five years. This rate of growth of publications is typical only of those dealing with the more intensively growing aspects of science.

Notes

1. *Pravda*, November 5, 1982.
2. Ibid.
3. V. G. Kirillov-Ugryumov, "VAK USSR: Facing New Tasks," in *Economics and the Organization of Industrial Production* (1982), No. 7, p. 60 (Russian edition).
4. The concept of "regional scientific and technological progress" one comes across in publications (see *Methodical Recommendations on the Economics of Regional Scientific-Technological Progress* [Moscow: SOPS, 1972]) is not very exact. STP cannot be regional, local, isolated from worldwide scientific and technological development. The concept of regional can be applied to scientific, scientific-technological potentials, a network of scientific organizations located in a specific area. V. I. Duzhenkov makes a point of noting that "one should single out in a country's scientific-technological potential not only the potential of an industrial branch (branch STP) but also regional scientific-technological potential" (*Problems of Organizing Science*, [Moscow: Nauka (Science), 1977], p. 30).
5. V. F. Burkhanov, *Economic Development of the Northern Zone in the USSR and Providing It with a Base Transport Network*, Problems of the North 20 (Moscow: Nauka, 1979), p. 15.
6. L. M. Gatovsky, "On Studies of Economics of Scientific and Technological Progress," *System of Economic Sciences* (Moscow: Nauka, 1968), p. 129.
7. Isaac Newton, *Opticks* (Russian edition) (Moscow and Leningrad, n.d.), p. 314.
8. L. I. Abalkin, "Method of Political Economy," in *Economic Encyclo-*

pedia/Political Economy (Russian edition) (Moscow: Sovetskaya Entsiklopedia, 1975), 2:478.

9. K. K. Valtukh, "Substantiation of Plans and Procedures for the Development of Economic Theory," *Economics and the Organization of Industrial Production* (1979), No. 3, p. 37.

10. N. N. Nekrasov, *Regional Economics: Theory, Problems, Methods* (Russian edition), 2nd ed, (Moscow: Ekonomika, 1978), p. 47.

11. K. V. Ostrovityanov, "Political Economy of Socialism: Special and Industrial Economies," in *System of Economic Sciences* (Moscow: Nauka, 1968), p. 9.

12. A. M. Yeremin, *The System of Economic Sciences* (Moscow: Znaiye, 1968), p. 6.

13. V. I. Lenin, *Collected Works*, 6.1:138.

14. Erich Yanch, *Prognostication of Scientific and Technological Progress*, 2nd ed. (Moscow: Progress, 1974), p. 19.

15. V. D. Komarov, *Scientific-Technological Revolution and Social Ecology* (Leningrad: Leningrad University Publishers, 1977), p. 79.

16. N. A. Ilyin, *Urban Economics: Regional Aspect of Development*, ed. D. M. Khodzhayev (Moscow: Nauka, 1982), pp. 5–6.

17. Among them, special note would be given to the encyclopedic scientist V. I. Vernadsky; the geologists Y. A. Kosygin, E. M. Sergeyeva, A. A. Trofimuk, N. A. Shilo, A. L. Yanshin, I. S. Gramberg, E. E. Milanovsky, A. V. Peive, Y. M. Puscharovsky; the geocryologist P. I. Melnikov; geochemist L. V. Tauson; geographers I. G. Aleksandrov, A. G. Babayev, N. N. Baransky, I. P. Gerasimov, A. F. Treshinikov, A. G. Agranat, V. V. Vorobyev; the biologists D. K. Belyaev, V. N. Sukachev, A. V. Zhirmunsky, A. S. Isayev, V. L. Kontrimavichius; physiologists and medical scientits A. P. Avtsin, G. G. Vinberg, G. P. Danishevsky, V. P. Kaznacheyev, P. G. Tsarfis, A. V. Chaklin; specialists in geology N. V. Chersky, E. I. Shemakin; in building mechanics, N. P. Melnikov, C. K. Negmatullayev; in physical chemistry of inorganic compounds, M. V. Mokhosoyev; and in power engineering, D. A. Melentiyev, Y. N. Rudenko.

18. A. G. Aganbegyan, N. N. Nekrasov, P. G. Bunich, V. F. Burkhanov, M. A. Vilensky, O. I. Volkov, A. G. Granberg, Y. M. Dogayev, V. I. Duzhenkov, E. G. Egorov, Y. M. Kanygin, L. N. K. Karpov, V. P. Loginov, B. P. Orlov, V. P. Podoplelov, A. E. Problst, M. A. Sergeyev, S. V. Slavin, I. K. Taksir, V. P. Chichkanov, N. G. Chumachenko, V. A. Shelest, R. I. Shniper.

19. I. Deliev, V. Iasyrova (Bulgaria), U. Izard, V. Leontyev, G. Cumberland, G. Meier, T. Rayner (USA), R. Dickinson (Great Britain), A. Piccei (Italy), N. Saoshita (Japan), R. Courbis (France).

20. S. G. Korneyev, *Soviet Scientists: Honorary Members of Scientific Organizations Abroad* (Russian edition) (Moscow: Nauka, 1981), pp. 266, 16, 62, 86, 93, 145.

21. A. G. Vendelin, *The Territorial and Industrial Aspects of Managing Social Production* (Russian edition) (Tallinn: Valgus, 1975); L. S. Bklyakhman, *Economics of Scientific and Technological Progress* (Russian edition) (Moscow: Vyshaya Shkola, 1979); V. E. Astafyev, et al., *Economic Mechanism of Accelerating Scientific-Technological Progress* (Russian edition) (Moscow: Ekonomika, 1977), etc.

22. See above, note 10.

23. *Scientific and Technological Revolution and Improving the Management of Socialist Production* (Kiev: Naukova Dumka, 1978), pp. 155–156.

24. *Regional Problems of Scientific-Technological Progress in Industry* (Moscow: Nauka, 1982).

25. S. V. Slavin, *Development of the North* (Moscow: Nauka, 1975).

26. Y. M. Dogayev, *Economic Effectiveness of New Technology in the North* (Moscow: Nauka, 1969) and *Economics of Scientific and Technological Progress* (Moscow: Nauka, 1975).

27. V. P. Loginov, *The Economic Effectiveness of Mechanization* (Moscow: Nauka. 1975).

28. A. I. Demenev and V. I. Chichkanov, *Regional Peculiarities of Shaping the Material* and *Technological Base of Communism* (Sverdlovsk, 1979).

29. R. I. Schniper, *The Economic Aspect of Regional Pre-Planning Studies* (Novosibirsk, Nauka, 1978).

30. *Improving the Management of Economic Regions* (Kiev: Naukova Dumka, 1980), pp. 58–167.

31. V. Y. Budavey, *Long-Term National Economic Programs: The Theory and Methodology of a Program Approach to Planning STP* (Moscow: Mysl, 1980), pp. 189–190.

32. G. V. Tersh, *The Material Basis of Construction: Problems of Regional Development* (Moscow: Ekonomika, 1979).

33. V. I. Dyzhenkov, *The Problems of Scientific Organization: Regional Aspects* (Moscow: Ekonomika, 1979).

34. Y. M. Kanygin, *Scientific and Technological Potential: The Problems of Accumulation and Use* (Novosibirsk: Nauka, 1975).

35. *The Influence of Scientific-Technological Progress on Increasing the Effectiveness of Production in Kirghizia* (Russian edition) (Frunze, 1979); R. M. Razakov, *Problems of Increasing the Effectiveness* of *Technical Progress and Main Assets* (Russian edition) (Tashkent, Uzbekistan, 1980); I. Y. Yakubov, *Accelerating Scientific-Technological Progress* (Tashkent, Uzbekistan, 1980); Y. G. Bendersky, V. L. Kvint, V. N. Semyonov, *Scientific and Technological Progress and the Economy of Krasnoyarsk Territory* (Krasnoyarsk, 1979).

KEY TO THE REGION: COMPLEX PROGRAMS

Regional technical and R & D programs were first launched in the USSR during the Tenth 5-year Plan (1976–1980). Among those programs were two well-known projects, "Siberia" and "Far East." These projects aimed at studying problems of the complex use of natural resources and the socioeconomic development in those regions. The following are just a few examples proving the efficiency of these programs.

"Siberia" aimed at the possibility of mining brown coal in the Kansko-Achinsky basin by open mining on a large scale was demonstrated. The productivity of labor in the open mines in the Kansko-Achinsky basin could exceed 25 to 35 times the average for the industry if a completely new mining technology were applied and loading and transportation equipment of a very high capacity used. It was also found that the seismic equipment for oil and gas prospecting used in Tyumen is not suitable for Siberian conditions.

We could give a long list of examples proving the advantages of equipment specifically designed for certain climatic and geographic conditions. Actual practice demonstrates the clear necessity of planning programs that take into account the specific conditions in the various regions.

Planning and management are necessary for maximum rational use of all the economic resources the country has. The same planned approach should be applied to science and technology, not only in terms of specific industries but in terms of specific regions as well.

However, the conceptual basis for the regional aspect of scientific and technological policy has not yet been created. There is no research conducted on a regular basis in this field. R & D economic institutes pay insufficient attention to the problems involved in the regional development of science and technology. The mechanism for the management of scientific and technical development in the regions is just forming, a fact that explains the reduction in its effi-

Pravda, March 22, 1983, p. 2.

ciency. If the general plans for economic development are based on a combination of industrial and territorial approaches, goals in science and technology are mainly designed only for industries. However, these goals must become an integral part of the overall system of economic planning.

In the Soviet republics, the planning for scientific and technological development is presented as a list of those set by ministries. The regional and district planning committees, as well as the planning committees of autonomous republics, include in their economic plans only the goals of the companies subject to the local Soviets. However, it should be noted that in Krasnoyarsk Territory, Tyumen, Chita and other districts in Siberia, complex plans also include goals of enterprises subject to the Republican and All-Union authorities.

Recently, in some areas—for example, Leningrad, Irkutsk, and other districts—regional plans for scientific and technological development have begun to evolve. These plans include measures drawn up by companies and institutes located in that area, but these measures are usually adjusted for other sections of a complex territorial plan. Nevertheless, such plans can be useful to authorities in implementing the process of introducing scientific and technological innovations into production.

The Institute of Industrial Economics of the Ukrainian Academy of Sciences has offered another approach to regional problems of scientific and technological development. It prepared recommendations for a complex plan for the Donetsk district, which contains major indicators for costs and the efficiency of companies, for strengthening scientific potential, and for resolving technical problems in R & D institutes. The plan covers 29 cities and 12 counties. During the Tenth 5-year Plan, because of scientific and technical innovations, industrial output increased by 55% and sales by 60% in the Donetsk district. This plan was therefore also recommended for Ukraine as well.

Under the Tenth 5-year Plan, several scientific and technical programs were created, and a regular upgrading of the Complex Program for Scientific and Technological Progress for the next 20 years was introduced. The program, including both its industrial and its regional aspects, should be revised every 5 years.

The program-and-target approach to planning is used in a number of Soviet republics. For example, in Byelorussia during the last 5-

year plan 50 industrial organizations and 21 universities participated in the realization of 20 complex programs coordinated by the Republic's Academy of Sciences. The efficiency of introducing results of research into production exceeded the funds spent on conducting them 4.3-fold.

There are similar examples in other places. Good results in accomplishing a complex program for increasing the productivity of labor on the basis of introducing scientific and technological achievements were achieved in the Sverdlovsky district. The same programs are under way in Moscow, Leningrad, Tomsk, the Lvov districts, and Krasnoyarsky region.

We are witnessing the formation of an entire system of regional programs, programs of different levels, scope, duration, and resources. In this connection, it would be worthwhile to secure by legislation their role in a national system of economic planning and management.

On the whole, the hierarchy of these programs could appear as a system of complex programs of the Soviet republics, large economic regions, districts, autonomous republics, cities, and territorial production complexes (TPKs). Regional programs should reflect the achievements of the regional science and the prospects for the technical reconstruction of local enterprises. Eventually, all these factors would benefit the development of productive forces in the regions.

In the Soviet republics, regional programs are created with the support of the republics' planning committees, which later provide specific recommendations. However, there are no such planning committees on the local level. Usually this function is performed as an additional duty by a department or an expert in charge of planning in the region. In actuality, this approach leads to the lack of proper attention to local planning. In this regard, I think, we are given a good example by the Donetsk district. There, a department of territorial production planning was established which, together with the Donetsk Scientific Center, coordinates activities in this field.

Of course, in some instances, successes in the realization of scientific and technical achievements have come as a result of volunteer efforts. But when we are dealing with long-term (5- to 10-year) programs, mere enthusiasm is not enough. It is necessary for public committees (a program's council) to cooperate with those organizations that are in charge of implementing those programs. This practice is spreading throughout the country, for example, in the Leningrad, Novosibirsk, and Nikolaev districts.

In the republics, economic regions, and districts, regional programs are being prepared. They will be included in the forthcoming All-Union Complex Program for Scientific and Technical Progress. Public committees are also participating in this preparatory work. For this reason, it is so important to create legislation concerning the methods and legal status of these public committees. The lack of a legislative basis for their activities brings misunderstanding of their rights, possibilities, and functions. As a result, not all of these state organizations respond to the requests of public committees.

It is necessary to define more clearly the role of the regional branches, centers of All-Union and republics' Academies of Sciences, in terms of their relation to industrial R & D institutes. It is a matter not only of the coordination of efforts of research and production entities but also of their cooperation in accomplishing regional programs. Until now, the power of the All-Union Academy of Sciences as well as the State Committee on Science and Technology has not been supported by legislation that would outline procedures for the review of their decisions by ministries and industrial departments. As mentioned above, however, this is very important.

It is urgent to make an obligatory list of indicators for regional programs and to prepare corresponding recommendations to them.

Results will follow shortly. For example, losses related to the use in the North, in mountains, or in deserts, of equipment that is not adjusted to specific climatic conditions are counted in billions of rubles annually. Meanwhile, each ruble invested in the production of regionally suitable equipment saves 5 to 8 rubles during its exploitation.

A unified state policy for science and technology must be formulated and must define corresponding policies in the regions. Future success will depend very much on what place the complex regional programs for scientific and technical progress take in a planning and management system.

Privatization and Industrial Development in Russia

PRIVATIZATION IN RUSSIA

Total Number of Privatized Companies—86,000

Total	1992 (39 thousand Companies)			1993 (47 thousand Companies)	
	100%	100%	100%	100%	100%
Industries				29.3	29.2
Industry of Construction Materials	1.5	2.2	2.1	2.0	2.0
Light Industries	7.3	8.2	8.2	8.5	8.3
Food Industry	3.7	4.9	5.5	5.1	5.0
Agriculture	1.8	1.6	1.4	1.6	1.7
Construction	6.6	7.9	8.9	9.0	9.1
Track Services	1.5	2.1	2.7	3.0	3.1
Whole Sale	1.3	1.1	1.2		
Retail Sale	39.4	34.8	33.2	34.9*	34.8*
Public Catering	8.0	7.7	7.1	7.0	7.0
From Total					
Social Services	23.1	20.6	18.2	18.1	17.8

* whole and retail sales combined

Privatization: Political and Economic Strategy for the Transition to Capitalism

Privatization in the former Soviet-bloc countries is the most important step toward social, political, and economic changes. Once privatization has taken place, the move to a market economy is irrevocable.

The reasons for this are quite simple. The process of privatization is destroying the economic base of dictatorship. In the past, the former so-called "property of the people" was the property of the ruling communist party. Everything from giant industrial companies to

The Kvint Newsletter, 1, No. 7 (April 1994).

small dry cleaning establishments was in the hands of the state. Individuals were powerless.

The process of privatization has given people an understanding of their value as they experience radical political and economic changes in their own countries. Once individuals are granted ownership they will do anything to keep from returning it.

The Evolution of Privatization

In 1986, the transition toward privatization began. Slowly, more and more property continued to move into the hands of the people. Until 1990 in the former Soviet Union, 96% of property was controlled by the government. The mass process of privatization in Russia began in earnest only in 1992. In the other former Soviet republics (especially in Ukraine and Belarus) privatization did not take hold until the last half of 1993.

As of April 1, 1994, almost 26% of all state property in Russia has been privatized. More than 100,000 companies have become either totally or partially privately owned. Approximately 7% of this property has been obtained through purchase, and approximately 30% has been given away. For example, as a form of compensation, employees of many companies received 25% of the shares of formerly state-owned companies for free.

It appears that private owners know how to make these companies operate more profitably than the state does. The value of companies that were privatized in 1992 has already increased by 13%, and those privatized in 1993 have already increased by 8%. The average privatization price of an enterprise depends on previous ownership. Prices average 12 million rubles for properties of the regional government, and 54 million rubles for property of the federal government.

Foreign Opportunity

In January, the new government began encouraging foreign investors to participate in the privatization of major enterprises. I predict that by the end of 1994 at least 10% of all privatized property will be in the hands of foreign companies or in joint ventures with foreign capital.

In June of 1994, privatization will become even more attractive to foreigners. All Russian citizens who were born before September 1, 1992, received one free privatization voucher with a face value of 10,000 rubles. These vouchers are currently very valuable and as of March 31, 1994, had risen in value to 37,000 rubles. However, the vouchers expire on June 1, 1994. Those that have not been used will become worthless. In a meeting last week, the Minister of Finance, Dr. Sergei Dubinin, told me that it is unlikely that the government will extend the redemption date. Therefore, after the vouchers expire, there will be less competition in the privatization process and there will be ways to capitalize on the new Russia.

PRIVATIZATION IN RUSSIA ENTERS PHASE TWO

Before making an economic forecast, one must first look at the past. Economists call this extrapolation. To view the progress and prospects for the privatization process in Russia, it is neither necessary, nor possible, to look before 1991. At that time, only a few initial steps had been made under the very indecisive leadership of Gorbachev. The USSR did not even have regulations for privatization.

Much has changed since then. Statistics on the Russian economy in 1994 show that 62% of the GDP was produced by privately held companies. In 1990, this figure was only 4%. In my mind, this is the real revolution taking place in Russia. While skeptics think that other former Soviet-bloc countries have achieved similar results, they actually pale in comparison. Even in Poland and Hungary, where the process of privatization began ten years earlier than in Russia, the percentage of companies in state hands is now higher than in Russia.

Russia's record on privatization could qualify for the *Guinness Book of World Records*. Before one becomes overly excited about Russia's record, however, keep in mind that many of its past records have had a very negative impact on both Russia and the entire world. Just one example illustrates this point. Remember the socialist revolution in 1917 and the process of "nationalizing" the entire economy? This record was achieved at a price of millions of victims and the Cold War.

Russia on Sale

On July 3, 1991, the Russian Federation parliament created two entities, the State Committee for Federal Property Management, commonly called the Committee for Privatization, and the Fund for Federal Property. These two entities put the largest country in the world on sale. Many think that the privatization process proceeded

The Kvint Newsletter, 2, No. 6 (March 1995).

along a single path. However, there were four separate branches: the voucher system (1992 to June 1994); the Moscow City privatization; Tatar Autonomous Republic privatization, and post-voucher or cash privatization, which started in July 1994.

Not So Equal

In 1992 the Russian government issued privatization vouchers or checks, with a 10,000 ruble face value, to anyone who was born before September 1, 1992. These vouchers could be used at privatization auctions of state-owned properties. Foreigners could participate only in the secondary market. The Russian government made so many mistakes that it decreased the value of the vouchers to approximately the price of one bottle of vodka or less. As a result, hundreds of criminals bought millions of vouchers. During 1992–93, about 10%-12% of the Russian economy was privatized into the hands of 1 percent of the population, composed of high-level executives, former party bosses, and a few hundred crooks.

Millions of Russians who had received the vouchers had practically nothing to show for it. The government failed to guarantee the underlying value, and 10,000 rubles, even at that time, represented a small amount of money. Knowing that the vouchers would expire on December 31, 1993, many tried to sell their vouchers, often receiving next to nothing. Unexpectedly, the government extended the expiration date until June 30, 1994, which was the end of voucher privatization. People referred to the process as "prihkvatizatsia," which roughly translates into "crooks gain control of property for nothing, using their connections, power, and money." It was a process of laundering criminal and communist money.

In my opinion, the voucher system was, from the outset, a primitive idea reflecting the communist goal of making everyone equal. But 74 years of communism in Russia has shown that by trying to make everyone equal, no one is equal.

Moscow Plays It Straight

The mayor of Moscow, Yuri Luzhkov, decided to exclude his city from the corruption related to the voucher system. After a major fight with the chairman of the government committee, Anatoly Chubais, Luzhkov used his influence to induce Yeltsin to issue special regulations for the city of Moscow.

Because of Mayor Luzhkov's strategy, which strictly limited vouchers and utilized competitive bidding, the Russian state received more money from the privatization of Moscow City (8.5 million people) than from the privatization of all other Russian territory (142 million people). Most of the property was purchased by private companies and individuals (foreigners were able to participate indirectly).

Within the borders of the Tatar Republic, there was also a strategy to control the privatization process. Vouchers were limited, and the privatization process was kept mostly to residents. The result, however, was less successful than in the city of Moscow. In Tatar, bureaucrats were able to retain control of much of the property.

On February 6 of this year, President Yeltsin signed an order entitled "About the Second Stage of Privatization in the City of Moscow." From the very first paragraph of that document, it is obvious that the drafters lacked a clear understanding of the privatization process and the economic issues involved. The decree allows the Moscow government to establish the initial price of the companies to be privatized based on their balance sheet. This will cause their stock to be grossly undervalued and will not allow companies to raise sufficient capital. However, this situation presents an invaluable opportunity for Western companies with expertise in appraisal and valuation services to assist the Russian government, increasing a strategy that will maximize the benefits of privatization. The decree allows investors to lease land under privatized property for 49 years. This marks a major breakthrough in the Russian legal system.

Russia Enters Stage Two

Before July 1994, 67% of Russian companies had been privatized, thus successfully destroying the state monopoly. It also created a false impression for a large part of the population who believed foreigners bought large pieces of property for next to nothing.

In this atmosphere, Russia entered the next stage of post-voucher privatization. This stage, with President Yeltsin's decree issued on

July 22, 1994, has new characteristics. As of January 1, 1995, 111,000 companies have been privatized. In 1994 the rate of privatization was approximately 2,000 companies a month, and of those, about 65% were profitable.

Only 33% of all Russian companies now remain in the hands of the government, but, in terms of total revenues, it is 50%. In about 27% of the privatized companies, the Russian Fund of Federal Property holds between 31% and 49% of the voting shares, and they will soon be available. This new stage provides more opportunity for foreigners, because they can participate in the process directly, including bidding and tenders. Better quality companies will be for sale. Many think this process will be slow, because the government does not want to lose control of its best and biggest companies. Privatization did, in fact, slow down in 1994 but is expected to resume its pace this year.

Even the best companies are not highly profitable; they need international connections to market their products. Additionally, these companies need modern management skills, high-tech equipment, and technology, as well as raw materials from abroad. Finally, the companies need money. Sometimes they are not even able to pay employees. Because of these problems, the Yeltsin government faces increasing unemployment, a tremendous shortage of currency, and growing Russian debt. In 1991, before privatization, Russian debt was $80 billion. Currently, the debt tally is approximately $120 billion.

Russian industry also continues to decline. In 1994, it was 15% lower than in 1993 and 40% lower than in 1991. Investment also continues to decline. There was a 28% decrease in direct capital investment from 1993, and a 62% decline from 1991. At the same time, unemployment increased in 1994, up 29% to 5.4 million people.

It is clear from these figures that Russia's only choice is to put the best property up for privatization. There is an urgent need to receive hard currency, service debt, reduce unemployment, stop the decline of industrial production, and ease social tension.

In the future, privatization will be more profitable for foreign investors, and provide easy access to Russian property (without bribes). The government began selling foreign companies voting shares, currently in state hands, in select industries. These include nonferrous gas, telecommunications, and some former military plants.

Process on Track

Based on statements made by the new chairman of the State Property Management Committee, Vladimir Polevanov, in January, some people were afraid that privatization would be delayed. But two weeks later, he was fired. This sent a clear message to the Russian bureaucrats.

Early 1996 will be the last time foreigners can buy property directly from the state for relatively small amounts. As of April 1, 1995, the Russian Federal Property Management Committee established all the necessary legal regulations for conducting interregional and nationwide investment auctions. This will signify the start of a free flow of capital across Russia. After 1996, the government will not be in the position to offer much for privatization, and almost everything of value will already have been sold.

Russia Has Competition

It is very important for foreigners to make it clear to the Russians that they are not the only ones looking for money from the world business community. China, Latin America, Southeast Asia, South Africa, and Russia's neighbors in Eastern Europe all desperately need capital.

Romania, in the five years since the fall of communism, has privatized only 1,000 companies out of 7,000. I met with the speaker of the Romanian parliament, Dr. Adrian Nastase, to discuss the future of privatization in the country. Two weeks later its parliament passed a resolution to privatize 3,000 companies in 1995.

To foreigners, Eastern and Central Europe are more attractive than the former Soviet republics. To Westerners, these appear more politically stable, and the economies have started to mature. For example, in 1994 Poland's GDP expanded by 5%; Slovenia's, by 4.4%;

Hungary's, by 3.5%; Czech's, by 2.5%; and Slovakia's, by 4%. Even Bulgaria and Albania showed small economic growth.

Nonetheless, Russia remains an investor's best option. It is attractive in terms of abundant natural resources, an excellent labor force, and a huge marketplace.

HOW TO ACCESS BUSINESS INFORMATION IN RUSSIA: INFORMATION AND DEMOCRACY GO HAND-IN-HAND

It is impossible for foreigners, operating in a new business environment, to make any business-related decision without access to accurate information. Currently, access to information is one of the major barriers to the development of markets in the former Soviet countries. It is extremely difficult to obtain quality business and economic information for decision-making purposes. As in all things Russian, an historical perspective is useful in understanding the current situation. The lack of democracy is the root cause of Russia's information problems.

For a tyrant to give accurate information to society is tantamount to relinquishing his grasp of power. This was well known and exercised by Stalin. The communists established censorship immediately. At first, it was directed against foreign capitalist enemies. It quickly spread to include everything and everybody.

In the 1970s and 1980s, in order to publish any financial or other information, one had to hand over the document to a special censor. As a result, virtually all information was kept secret, especially economic information. Each year during the Soviet era the Central Statistic Bureau published what came to be known as the "Blue Book" on the USSR National Economy.

Each of the former Soviet republics published its own Blue Book as well. But these books really provided very little information. For example, it was decided to keep even the numbers of trucks produced a secret. The official position was that trucks were very important during wartime, and publishing the production figures could disclose the military power of the Soviet Union.

In the mid-1980s, these books became statistically worthless in

The *Kvint Newsletter*, 1, No. 10 (July 1994).

terms of the data in most industries, businesses, and products. The Blue Book's worthlessness was based on the fact that much of the information it contained was actually misinformation to mislead foreign enemies.

In addition, the information gathered was subject to each bureaucratic level's efforts to look good, so, ultimately, all information was abused. At the end of the 1980s, the major secret of the Soviet Union was that the Soviet Union had no secrets worth keeping. The totalitarian system destroyed the country and almost destroyed its people.

Accurate Information Is Again Difficult to Obtain

After the Soviet and communist failures, by 1992 and 1993, the KGB and the censors had lost their position in society. But gradually they have regained some influence, not to the same degree as before, but in 1994 it is again difficult to publish results of many economic statistical studies. Information has become a valuable commodity. Many of those with access to information have come to realize that they can sell this information, either privately or officially.

Information at a Price

Today many private consulting companies are selling information that can be received directly from government offices for free. They will also provide you with additional unpublished information that is not for foreign eyes. If they have good connections, they can help you sort out information to determine what is accurate.

Between 1991 and 1994, several electronic data banks appeared offering their services. In Russia, Dow Jones and Reuters have opened offices, as well as Dun & Bradstreet and DirectNet. Primarily, foreign companies are using these services, but Russians are getting a taste for the electronic databases, and are beginning to become heavy users. Why have these companies come to Russia? To calm Russian customers and foreign companies already in Russia. People are beginning to access reliable information. Bureaucrats from the highest offices are trying to sell information to anyone. Of course, they are cautious, but are selling it to fill their own private coffers.

In Russia, private information networks have already appeared. One of the owners, Vladimir Gusinski, created a network through the financing of his private banking group called MOST (which means "bridge" in Russian), and also participated in the creation of two other private banks, Stolichniy and National Credit. The information network already includes one of the major television channels and the newspaper Segodnya (which means "today" in Russian). Network management signed an agreement to exchange information with Reuters and CNN. Gusinsky tried to create an American-style news magazine, like *Time*, and negotiated with Time-Warner.

YAR Communications, Inc., headed by Yuri Radzievski, is another company working to provide accurate and up-to-date information to Russian and American clients. Operating since 1975, YAR works through its network of personal and professional contacts, to act as a guide and consult its clients interested in establishing themselves in the Russian marketplace. It also works with the Russian media on ways to receive more attention from the West.

Public Sources of Information

Of course, companies themselves are a source, although the information will be neither complete nor completely reliable. To verify information, of if you are unsure of the type of company and future partner you seek, several places offer information, and should all be utilized. Different federal government ministries and agencies, such as the Central Statistical Bureau, Committee for State Property Management (the State Committee for Privatization), and any ministry or committee responsible for the industry or area in which you are interested, should be contacted.

On the federal level, there is the Russian Federal Social-Economic and Scientific-Technical Forecast. In 1993, the forecast was developed until the year 2010, and is regularly updated. Each ministry has its own program for future development of industries and services, and usually includes a portion on international cooperation for investment and international trade.

One must also consider the regional level, where much information is available. All major regions and autonomous republics have regional programs, which are more strongly oriented toward social programs. A substantial amount of information is included, and you will understand the direction of the regional government and its future plans, and where it will be supportive of your efforts. All this information is free.

TELECOMMUNICATIONS A BOOMING BUSINESS: EVEN SIBERIA IS WITHIN REACH

Before the fall of communism, the Soviet Union was cut off from the world community, not just politically and economically, but also through vital communications links. Telephone connections with the world were the privilege of very few organizations and people. Through 1988, the Soviet Union had only 15 telephone channels available for international use. Furthermore, all operated through one international telephone station in Moscow, built in 1980 before the Olympic Games.

Telecommunications companies wanting to do business in Russia have an ongoing problem: a lack of information about the country's development in this area. This is a residual effect of the Soviet system, when communications were under the tight control of the KGB and the military. As a result, almost all communications information was secret. To cause further confusion, published statistics were deliberately falsified to mislead Soviet "imperialist enemies," most notably the United States.

After 1988, the Economic Relationship Between the USSR and the U.S. Made It Vital for Telecommunications Links Between the Two Regions to Be Built

Establishing a telecommunications infrastructure became a priority of Soviet leaders in 1989, and foreign cooperation began. Because of its lack of capital and investment, as well as the fact that its isolation had left it trailing behind technological advances, the Soviet Union did not have the resources to bring about the necessary changes. Today, more than 80 foreign companies are participating in Russia's telecommunications industry.

The Kvint Newsletter, 1, No. 11 (August 1994).

Competition Is Heating Up

Telecommunications companies immediately recognized the potential, and currently all major worldwide players are participating in the Russian market. Competition is strong especially in Moscow, St. Petersburg, and the Tymen region (the richest oil and gas region in the world).

One of the first successful telecommunications companies to participate was Sprint. It developed a relationship with the telecommunications division of the Russian military-industrial complex and gained access to its former military satellite. Other companies developed ventures with the Soviet monopoly, the USSR Ministry of Communication.

Besides Sprint, other American companies currently working in Russia include: AT&T, Motorola, IDB Communications Group, GTE, US West, MCI, DirectNet Telecommunications, FGI Wireless, IBCS (International Business Communications Systems), Alaskan Pacific Rim Telecommunications, Andrew Corporation, ABD, Axis Communications, Inc., Belcom, Inc., Global One, Midcom, Millicom International Cellular (a subsidiary of Motorola), and Newbridge Networks.

American companies face tremendous competition from foreign companies, like Cable and Wireless, Italtel, Norwegian Telecom, Alcatel, France Telecom, Korea Teleco, Bosch Group, Duetchebundespos Telecom, PTT Telecom of Netherlands, Telecom Denmark, and Ericcson of Sweden, to name a few.

The Current State of Infrastructure

In Russia, telecommunications is divided into two sections: companies that manufacture equipment and companies that provide services. After the disintegration of the Soviet Union, foreign telecommunications companies were faced with the breakdown of the communications systems on a regional basis.

These former Soviet Republics are now trying to work directly with foreign companies to build the infrastructure to permit services, rather than depend on Russia for transmission. But the technological developments have been minimal. Even today, most telecommunications signals from abroad go to Moscow before being transmitted to the Republics.

Most of the Former Soviet Republics Did Not Have Their Own Satellites and Relied on Russia for Transmission

Rural areas are less developed than the metropolitan areas, have fewer telephones per capita, and technology is outdated. A major problem is access to state-of-the-art digital long distance and international connections. Only 5% of long distance telephone stations operate on a digital level, while the remaining operate on the far less sophisticated analog level. According to the plan of the Ministry of Communication, by the year 2000, more than 40% of metropolitan lines, and more than 70% of international long distance lines, will be developed digitally.

Obtaining a License

To receive a telecommunications license, companies must apply to the Ministry of Communication. However, only 70 percent of the established lines are under the control of the ministry. The other 30 percent is controlled by departments such as the military-industrial complex, the railroad and forest ministries, and the department of the sea fleet.

Up to now more than 400 licenses have been issued to domestic and foreign companies. There are different types of licenses: local service, long distance, international, fiber optic, cable, mobile telephone systems, cellular, and even satellite. Still others have licenses for production, or to work on joint ventures with the current major producers of telecommunications equipment, such as Telecom of Moscow. This company works with 270 former state-owned producers.

Conversion of Military Systems

In order to estimate how much money is needed to develop Russia's communications systems, it is necessary to consider the dozens of military satellites that could be converted to civilian use, and the millions of telecommunications channels not under the control of the Ministry of Communications. These include radio-relay systems, Russian-made mobile systems (duplex and simplex-based technologies and fiber optic systems).

Projects in Process

The typical method for participation in the Russian market is a joint venture with Russian partners. A Russian partner is usually a state-owned company, or a local, long distance, or international telephone station (there are only three). At the same time, some companies are creating wholly owned subsidiaries in Russia, joint-venturing with Western partners, or buying out the shares of their Russian partner.

Several Major Projects Currently in Development Will Strengthen International Connections with Russia and the World

One project is called 50/50. It will connect Seoul, South Korea, Tokyo, and the Russian Pacific Coast. In the south, it will connect Italy, Istanbul, and Novorossiysk, on the Russian Black Sea Coast.

Another project connecting Copenhagen with St. Petersburg and Moscow has a fiber-optics line with 15,360 channels. Of this line 1,250 kilometers are underneath the Baltic Sea. This creates three automated international telephone stations, one in St. Petersburg and two in Moscow, with the total capacity for 4,800 channels. Telecom Denmark is active in this project, as is the Great Nordic Telegraph Company (GNTC). The Russian partner of this project is the joint-stock company Intertelecom which spent half a billion rubles. The total expenses of the foreign partners GNTC and US West for these projects have been $123 million.

Business Services Improve

All this activity has a positive effect on businesses in the CIS. Just two years ago, making a telephone call was difficult. Today, the situation is greatly improved not only for telephones but for all communications equipment. From more than 50 cities, including Krasnoyarsk, and Siberia, calls can be placed directly to the United States and Europe.

This situation will continue to improve and will greatly facilitate conducting business throughout the CIS and in the world at large.

WRECK THE INFORMATION FLOW AND THE ECONOMY COLLAPSES

"It is easier to break the Berlin Wall than the wall of mistrust between people."

Leading Soviet economist Vladimir Kvint believes that the economic effects of all government decisions must be considered by politicians—apparently a radical concept in the Soviet Union.

"Economic evaluation of all political decisions must, in the future, be absolutely necessary. Otherwise the politicians are not responsible," he said.

Siberian-born Kvint is one of the reform-minded economists who have emerged during the glasnost period and are intimately connected with the development of perestroika.

A professor of economics, Kvint is vice chairman of the Academy of Sciences Council for Regional Economy and is one the editorial staff of the leading economic journal, *Eco.* He is now devoting all his time to seeking out joint ventures and arranging educational facilities for East–West traders.

He is scathing in his condemnation of the ways in which authoritarianism has distorted information flows and crippled economic development.

"We still have such an archaic institution as the main Bureau for Protection of Secrets in the Media," he said. "It is practically a ministry of censorship—it is that powerful—and it should have been abolished."

Such institutions and a traditional fear of free flows of information have hampered the introduction of new technology. Kvint says the Soviets are not lagging in computer theory but are at least 15 years behind in getting computers into the workplace.

Despite descriptions of far-reaching reform at the top levels, he says that official data, when they are available, are often misleading.

"From many years of tyranny the people learned to think one

thing, say something else, and do another. The state won the secrecy battle. But it was a Pyrrhic victory.

"Society was killing itself; it was stagnating. An absence of true information distorted public opinion and people got used to lying. It is an awful habit, very difficult to do away with.

"To a great extent this problem still exists. One cannot believe basic data provided by the government."

Compounding these problems is an almost complete lack of information hardware. The lack of computers is just an indicator of the underlying problem. There are very few telephones installed and hardly any fax machines.

"We do not make fax machines and, unlike the United States, we do not have the hard cash to buy them."

It is also often difficult or time-consuming to book long-distance or international telephone calls. The most reliable form of communication is telex, but the machines are few, and there is often considerable demand for them.

Professor Kvint says not only have the barriers to communications limited the flow of facts; they have also led to misleading and incorrect theories. The staggering extent of the isolation imposed by the 70 years of authoritarianism is demonstrated by the country's academics.

"There are just 900 full professors of economics in all of the Soviet Union. Ninety percent of them would not know the works of the Nobel prize winners."

Somewhat defensively Kvint points out that Western economists also know little about Soviet economics and says they often make odd comments and forecasts.

While he is confident that Soviet leader Mikhail Gorbachev will survive, he says that the economic crisis evolving in that nation will peak in the first half of this year.

"Economically the next six months are going to be the worst; the coming year is going to be very difficult," he says.

He will not offer an opinion on whether that survival will be achieved through commitment to reform or through a retreat to more traditional Soviet rule.

"He lives in a very complicated time. He continually balances between the wish for reform and the wish for stability," he says. "But, it is impossible to go ahead always looking back. People do not understand that, for a new economy to be born, we must say good-bye to the old."

RED MILITARY TIME MACHINE WORKS FOR CAPITALISM: SECRET DOORS OPEN ONTO PRIVATIZATION OF THE RUSSIAN MILITARY

For 70 years, the largest country in the world spent almost all of its resources on its military industries. Ostensibly, these expenditures were to protect the Soviet Union's communist achievements. In fact, they funded the most potentially dangerous aggression in the history of mankind.

When the military prevailed, the Soviet Union was a country of secrets. Everything was a secret—even the size of cemeteries and the number of military trucks. Road signs were, and still are, frequently misleading to guard this secret world against the intrusion of foreigners.

The Soviet Union's huge, technologically advanced military-industrial complex was known worldwide for its achievements—the first Sputnik, the first human being in space, the first nuclear power station, and the first nuclear icebreaker. Imagine, then, how many less significant secrets are still being kept by this vast, fading complex.

One can compare this military system with that of the United States to get a sense of its scope. However, while the U.S. maintains strong military alliances with Germany, the United Kingdom, France, Italy, and other global powers, the Soviet Union's strongest military alliance was with . . . Poland, despite its acknowledged military parity with the U.S. Now, 85% of this military complex belongs to Russia. And recent legislation in Russia is opening up this military-industrial complex for privatization and investment from the West.

How much was spent on developing this military? The CIA esti-

The Kvint Newsletter, 1, No. 3 (1993).

mated that 7%–11% of the Soviet Union's annual budget was spent on the military, but this figure was far from reality. By my evaluation, Gorbachev, jumping out of his trousers to compete with Reagan's and Bush's military expenditures, actually increased military spending from 35% of the annual budget in 1985 to more than 50% in 1990. Practically speaking, this level of spending would be sufficient for a country in a state of war. Of course, it was one of the factors that destroyed the Soviet Union.

Secret Doors Begin to Open

While the military was cloaked in secrecy, the mounting needs of the people could not be kept secret. Russian leaders are now trying to sell off parts of the military in order to address more immediate problems, such as food shortages. By a lucky chance for mankind, Russia now hopes to convert this vast military-industrial complex to civilian purposes. However, without cooperation from the West, this tremendous potential will not be realized.

To facilitate this, President Boris Yeltsin issued decree #1267 on August 19, 1993: "About Specifies of Privatization and Additional Measures of State Regulation of Enterprises of the Military Production Industry." It was not meant for press disclosure, and was issued with a high level of confidentiality. The highlights of the decree are presented here, exclusively for our readers, because of their importance for Russian and foreign investors. A list of 477 state-owned companies (military production plants and scientific institutes) that are slated for privatization was also issued.

The disruption of old connections between state-owned plants, an early by-product of the transition to a market economy, has increased supply problems and created a surplus of unfinished goods (work in progress). The present government is trying to stabilize the situation, but the development of a new economic mechanism will take time.

Russian officials are clear that in order to maintain the production level of industrial giants and convert military plants for civilian use, they need cooperation from the West. With Western managerial skills and experience, this giant time machine can become the critical instrument in the development of a free market economy.

What Does This Decree Mean for Foreigners?

President Yeltsin decreed that at the end of November, the government of Russia would release the list of companies that will undergo privatization on January 1, 1994. Foreign companies that are interested in investing in particular regions, industries, or companies now have a list of business possibilities. These companies represent the military segments of the following industries: aviation, special chemicals for production, arms, telecommunications, hardware, radio, missiles and space equipment, electronics, and shipbuilding.

1. In point #5, the decree states that the executive government bodies, especially the Committee for Military Industries and the Committee for State Property Management, must give special incentives to encourage foreign investment.

2. This decree also mandates that all military plants undergoing the process of privatization must first be converted to joint-stock companies. The Russian State agrees to take upon itself all responsibility for the debt of these companies. The decree further also mandates that a portion of the shares (approximately 20%) must belong to the state for at least three years. This means that in three years foreigners who initially bought stock could purchase additional shares that belonged to the state.

3. Shares will be sold only at special interregional auctions. The State Committee for Military Industries will publish information regarding auctions in a special newsletter.

4. Even after the transformation of state-owned military plants to joint-stock companies, the executive director of the company (whether Russian or foreign) is the only person who can receive a special registered certificate from the Russian government which attests to his qualifications.

5. Any Russian plant that wants to produce weapons must receive a special license to do so from the Committee for Military Industries.

One of the best examples of military plant conversion has been the creation of the joint-stock company Motek. One of the plants of this company has been producing missiles (known in the United States as Ss-20). Now, this plant manufactures the following civilian products:

- 40-foot refrigeration containers at international quality standards;
- mini-plants for production of fast-frozen vegetables and fruits; and

- mini-plants for initial processing of flax.

Motek expects that its refrigeration containers will be competitive with those of the American company SeaCold. Soon Motek's containers will also be traded in Latin America and the Middle East. Motek is open to cooperation with Western partners. Its telephone number in Moscow is 095–209–5474.

To illustrate the crucial importance of military conversion, the Demidov Award, which had not been awarded in 125 years, was recently reestablished. Named for the famous 18th-century Russian merchant and entrepreneur, it recognizes achievements in economics and entrepreneurship. The last time it was awarded was in 1867.

In November, the Demidov Award was given to Anatoly Karpov (no relation to the chess player), the Director-General of a former military chemical plant. Under his leadership, a conversion strategy was developed and implemented so that it now produces household chemicals. (The head of the committee that issues this award is Dr. Alexander Granberg.)

Here is my conclusion: Military facilities are unusually well-equipped plants with high technology, modern real estate, and highly educated engineers and workers. Cooperation with these plants will give foreign businesses numerous opportunities. In 1994, foreigners will gain new access to the process of privatization and conversion of the military.

INTERNATIONALIZATION OF RUSSIA'S METALLURGY INDUSTRY

The Soviet Union was, and Russia continues to be, the world's largest producer of iron, steel, almost all major heavy nonferrous metals, and platinum, and one of the leading producers of gold. In former days, the entire metallurgy industry, including the black and nonferrous metals, was given special priority because it was a basic necessity of the military industrial complex.

The Soviet Union's totalitarian economic mechanism, however, was not oriented toward the implementation of both scientific and technical advancements even in the lucrative metals area. During the 1980s, industrial technology in the Soviet Union fell far behind modern levels in developed countries throughout the world. Even the many technological achievements of Soviet scientists were not put into practice, except abroad. For example, Russian engineers developed continuous casting methods, but in the Russian black metals industry, it is used in only 25% of production and in the United States in about 80% of production.

With the gradual opening of the Russian market in 1987 and 1988, Russian and foreign investors became interested in working cooperatively. As the first step, Russian companies began utilizing the know-how of Western technologists to produce a wider range and better quality of metals and products.

World Markets Feel the Effect

After the disintegration of the Soviet Union in December 1991, the central authorities started to lose their power over metal producers. As a result, metallurgy plants started searching for cooperation from Western partners to market their metals abroad and generate hard

The Kvint Newsletter, 1, No. 12 (September 1994).

currency flow. Decentralization, along with its positive results, also created many problems in terms of the non-regulated export of Russian metals, very often at prices that bordered on dumping. This had a tremendous influence on world markets for steel (especially technology steel), aluminum, nickel, and many other nonferrous metals. The world was also concerned about Russia's policy on platinum exports. Unlike other countries that have only small reserves, the Russian state owns the world's largest platinum reserve.

Western Technologies Are Adopted

In the last few years, cooperation between major Russian and foreign players has taken on more stable forms, such as joint production and marketing arrangements. Companies throughout the world, such as Alcoa, ASARCO, Engelhard, Gerald Metals, and Sabin of the United States; INCO and Falcombridge of Canada; Outokumpu of Finland, Kwinana of Australia, and many more have become very active in the Russian market, through buying metal products as well as by purchasing shares in Russian companies.

Alcoa, one of the world's largest aluminum companies, has a long-term strategy and several goals with respect to the aluminum market in Russia. The first is to create favorable conditions for buying aluminum products in Russia. The company is currently purchasing at least 30% of the output of the three largest aluminum plants in the world, in Bratsk, Irkutsk, and Krasnoyarsk (all in eastern Siberia).

Alcoa's second priority is to sell alumina to Russia, the raw material required for aluminum production. With very few natural reserves of its own, Russia needs Alcoa to help regulate its market. With the help of companies like Alcoa, Alcan, and Trans-World Metals, Russian aluminum will enter the international market at optimal prices, thus avoiding a flood on the marketplace. Finally, Alcoa is looking to create joint ventures in Russia—through, for example, its Norwegian subsidiary, Elceim.

The heavy metals in Russia, such as nickel, cobalt, and copper are also attracting the attention of the international community. For example, the Norilsk Mining and Metallurgical Company in Russia, the world's largest producer of nickel, cobalt, and platinum, has created a joint venture with Axel Johnson in London for marketing nickel. Meanwhile, Engelhard, the platinum producer, user, and marketer, is also in a position to play an important role in regulating the flow of platinum from Russia.

Platinum Eases the Deficit

Unlike Russia's gold reserves, which Gorbachev depleted in an effort to build up the military complex, Russia has substantial state reserves of platinum. It is in Russia's best interest to sell platinum on the world market, to ease the deficits of its budget and acquire hard currency. Russian executives in the industry know, however, that once they enter the marketplace, world prices will be driven down and the platinum and palladium markets destroyed.

One way to avoid this would be to use this metal as collateral to put in foreign banks; another is to give it to an international bank in exchange for hard currency. In this way, Russia could use its platinum reserves to buttress its economy without upsetting the balance of the marketplace.

The unregulated flow of Russian rare metals into the marketplace decreased their value substantially over the past few years. This is also true with isotopes of osmium, a very expensive metal used in the nuclear industry, as well as lead. After the disintegration of the Soviet Union, Russia's import of lead increased by 80%, mostly on the basis of barter and contract trade (from $3 billion), all of which comes from Kazakstan, which has the good fortune of sitting on one of the world's richest lead reserves.

ASARCO is working with Russia, Kazakstan, and Uzbekistan with regard to copper and lead. In lead there is a net surplus of 120,000 tons (mostly from Kazakstan), and this has had an effect on world prices.

The republic of Kazakstan also produces large amounts of nonferrous metals such as copper, zinc, and precious metals. Kazakstan is exporting these resources to countries like China in exchange for much-needed hard currency. Another republic with major metals is Uzbekistan, which has the world's largest gold mine, Murentau.

A Willing Marketplace

Russia desperately needs foreign investors to supply modern technology and know-how, and escalate it into a world contender in the metals marketplace. Russia boasts inexpensive facilities to produce aluminum, but those will lie fallow without the required raw materials.

Lithuania Sets an Example

Another way to participate is to follow Lithuania's example: In 1992–93 Lithuania was one of the most important exporters of copper, nickel, and rare metals. But Lithuania did not produce any of these metals. Lithuanian entrepreneurs bought metal from Russian companies that had high-quality product but no international contracts, and immediately reexported these metals to the world market at a high price. American entrepreneurs can learn from Lithuania's example and approach Russia's nonferrous metal market.

With the end of privatization's voucher system in the Russian economy in July 1994, Western companies were allowed the chance to privatize Russian state-owned companies for relatively small sums of money. International metals firms now have new opportunities to increase profits and their influence on world metal markets.

WILL RUSSIA BE THE CHIEF OIL SOURCE OF THE FUTURE?

The northern and eastern regions of Russia contain enormous reserves of oil and gas. And they are much closer to the U.S. than the Middle East is.

The Persian Gulf war demonstrated forcefully how dangerous it is for the rest of the world to depend on Middle Eastern oil. But there exists another huge untapped oil reserve that has largely eluded the attention of the West: Siberia produces more oil than Saudi Arabia, Kuwait, and Iraq combined.

Siberia is a treasure trove of resources: gas, coal, nonferrous metals, timber, and hydroenergy resources abound in Siberia and far eastern Russia. Production of these resources will, in the not-so-distant future, lead to the formation of important new economic and business centers. These regions are, in fact, far closer to the U.S. than the Middle East is—oil could be transported in two nights from Siberia to the western U.S.

Siberia is the main producer of Russian oil and gas. Today it produces almost 80% of Russian oil and 90% of Russian natural gas. The European north of Russia, the Urals, and the Volga area produce 11% of Russian oil, while Eastern Siberia and the Far East together yield only 1%.

By the year 2000, however, Eastern Siberia and far eastern Russia will rank second in oil production. By then, the cream will have been skimmed off the west Siberian oil fields, and production will move to virgin lands—the northern regions of Yamal, Gydan, and Tazov peninsulas.

This geographical shift is important because it will change the nature of investment. Over the years, the central and southern regions of Western Siberia were rendered quite habitable. Living in most difficult conditions, Soviet workers built railroads, communications, and cities. There is no such infrastructure in northern Siberia; nearly half the investment made in that area will have to go into transportation and basic services.

"Siberian Hoard," *Institutional Investor* (April 1991).

Western Siberia has different problems, which will necessitate different expenditures. In the 1970s and 1980s, the Soviet administration invested in oil production while completely disregarding the ecological needs of the region. Only 0.5% of the total investment went into conservation. Now, in order to repair some of the damage already done, more than 10% of future investment will have to go to conserve the ecology of the area. An investment in more sophisticated and less ecologically harmful technologies will, however, pay back over the long term. In 1990 each oil well yielded only 20% of its potential production. More sophisticated drilling technologies could improve that recovery significantly.

The rich oil deposits of eastern Siberia are deeper than those of west Siberia, which will mean higher drilling costs. In the north, one-third of all oil reserves are in the seas of the Arctic ocean—another expensive drilling problem.

In spite of all these additional exploration and production expenses, however, according to my calculations, it will be three to five times cheaper to bring oil and condensed gas from these regions to the U.S. than from the Middle East to the U.S.

A gradual relocation of oil production to the North and the East fits in with the overall forecasts for world economic development, which is shifting its center to the Pacific Rim.

The oil fields in the Arctic Ocean should go into production in the years 2000 to 2015, at which time the ocean will become an important transportation artery. Russia will be the only country with experience with this kind of transportation—a year-round cargo delivery system has been operating for ten years from Arkhangel'sk to Dudinka with the help of icebreakers.

By the year 2000, Eastern Siberia and the Russian Far East will be yielding more than 140 million barrels of oil each year, as well as billions of cubic feet of natural gas. These figures presuppose little help from abroad. If countries with modern equipment and technologies, such as the U.S., Japan, Canada, and others, were to participate in the development of these fields, production would proceed at a much greater rate.

PROBLEMS IN THE DEVELOPMENT OF THE NONFERROUS METAL INDUSTRY IN SIBERIA

(with P. K. Vovk and N. F. Orel)

Siberia has vast raw material resources. In addition to huge resources of timber, oil, natural gas, nonferrous metals, and other minerals, 85% of the country's (the USSR) coal deposits, and 60% of all its water resources are concentrated here.

Developing these resources is a key strategic goal of the state's economic policy. In the 10th five-year period alone, Siberia's industrial output is to go up 1.5-fold.

Siberia's development on such a large scale has become possible because of the country's powerful material and technological base, which is capable of ensuring high rates of industrial growth and increased labor productivity.

Areas east of the Urals contain 82% of potential water power and 85% of their technical potential.

Siberia and the Far East have the country's greatest power capacity.

However, the country's historical background is responsible for Siberia's imbalances in the field of developing fuel and raw-material resources, on the one hand, and processing and manufacturing industries, on the other.

Given the current state of geological prospecting, Siberia has the largest areas with promising reserves of mineral wealth. Of national significance here are its resources of coal, nickel, cobalt, copper, lead, rock salt, common mica, graphite, oil, gas, and magnesite.

Siberia's resources of apatite, zinc, phosphorite, alumina. asbestos,

In *Problems in the Development of the Non-Ferrous Metal Industry in Siberia* (Novosibirsk, USSR: Siberian Branch of the USSR Academy of Sciences, 1980), pp. 3–16.

gold, iron ores, antimony, mercury, and rare metals are of significance for the entire area. The existence of large-scale deposits of different minerals is an advantage in Siberia's ore and mineral development, and is the foundation for the emergence of sizable territorial-production complexes, with the power and mining industries playing a major part.

The basic trend in the siting of nonferrous metal industries is to site them even further in the country's eastern regions, with their highly effective raw-materials and power resources. The development of the aluminum industry in Siberia is a key economic endeavor.

The production of alumina and aluminum is centered mainly in Eastern Siberia (at the Bratsk, Irkutsk, and Krasnoyarsk aluminum plants, and the Achinsk alumina plant); the Sayany aluminum plant is under construction; the Novokuznetsk aluminum plant is currently operating in Western Siberia.

The disproportions in the location of alumina and aluminum plants necessitates transporting alumina from the European part of the country to Siberia and the reverse delivery of finished products.

According to VAMI (USSR Aluminum Research Institute) estimates, the production of aluminum in Eastern Siberia reduces the cost of electricity 4.5 times, compared with the same costs in the European part of the country, and 2 to 3 times, compared with the Urals, while the total savings in production costs per ton of aluminum, compared with the average costs for the industry, amounts to 20%. The effectiveness of producing aluminum in Siberia is evident from the falling share of capital investments and the increasing volume of aluminum production, as compared with that of the country in general.

While the share of aluminum production in Siberia in the country's overall volume of production for 1980 increased by 7.3% as against 1970, the share of capital investments in developing aluminum production in Siberia as against those invested throughout the country will decrease by 10%.

Aluminum plants in Siberia are working with delivered raw materials and, to an extent, with Achinsk alumina (at the Krasnoyarsk aluminum plant). The draft plan for 1975–1980 foresees completion of construction at the Achinsk alumina combine, and when full operation begins, it will provide nearly one-third of the needs of aluminum plants.

In the last five-year-plan period, the first unit of the Kiya-Shaltyrsky mine for the strip production of nepheline was put into operation in the Kemerovo region. Its capacities will fully provide the Achinsk alumina combine with raw material.

Three Siberian aluminum plants, the country's latest—Bratsk, Krasnoyarsk, Irkutsk—are equipped with state-of-the-art technology.

The Bratsk and Krasnoyark aluminum plants, now in a stage of initial development, are the world's largest.

Although the region under consideration has only two plants in full operation (Novokuznetsk and Irkutsk), it plays a major part in the country's overall aluminum production.

In the 10th five-year period the final facilities will be put into operation at the Bratsk and Krasnoyarsk aluminum plants, and the Sayany plant will be completed. The Achinsk alumina plant will begin operating, and an additional unit will be completed at the Irkutsk aluminum plant.

These new aluminum plants will take their place as integral elements of the regional production complexes, thus showing the advantages of cooperation.

Along with the Sayany plant now under construction and the Chulym aluminum plant in Achinsk-Nazarov industrial center, a new aluminum plant will go up either in the Angara region in Krasnoyarsk Territory or in the Tomsk region.

With the aim of developing economic integration within the CMEA framework, the consttruction of an aluminum plant near Ust-Ilimsk is now under discussion. The project will be financed by Bulgaria, Hungary, GDR, Poland, and CSSR.

The scope of aluminum production in the region for the 1975–1995 period will require capital investments way above those allocated in the 9th five-year period. This is due, among other reasons, to:

- the need to channel substantial means for construction projects that failed to be started in the 9th five-year period; and
- the growing cost estimates for construction work, with the transition to more capital-consuming production and the setting up at several plants of rolling-stock production.

The size of the workforce at factories of the aluminum sub-industry has been determined by VAMI institute, based on the step-by-step introduction of scientific and technical improvements and the rates of growth in labor productivity, which will are expected to increase 1.7-fold.

The projected growth of aluminum production in the region will be achieved through the renovation and expansion of the plants currently in operation and the construction of new ones.

Siberia's aluminum industry has all the resources for increasing the rates of growth of metal output: economical power sources, redesigned technology, and highly efficient use of metal.

The absence of a reliable raw-material base for the production of aluminum is an unfortunate shortcoming, and this makes the need to find effective aluminum raw materials in Siberia a priority.

There are great prospects in store for the development of the copper-nickel and cobalt industry in the area. The greater part of the country's nickel and cobalt resources and a considerable part of its copper resources are concentrated in the Norilsk mine. With the discovery of the Talnakh deposits, and the October deposits in particular, the country has a unique mining area, rich in copper-nickel ores, cobalt, and platinum metals, whose economic significance can readily be compared with the oil–gas region in Western Siberia. With its reserves of nickel and other metals, the Norilsk region has acquired unique significance and is unmatched on a world scale. The mining is carried on by the large-scale Norilsk mining combine named after Zavenyagin. In its production volume, the combine is the largest complex in the nonferrous metal industry in Siberia and the country as a whole.

The development of Talnakh and October mines, the introduction of more efficient technology at the Norilsk enterprises, and the further development of technology will raise the output in the basic metals while achieving a high return on capital investments.

The economic effect nationally from the expansion of the Norilsk combine will increase substantially with the construction at Abakan of plants for processing nonferrous metals using the products of Norilsk mining combine.

The expediency of locating plants for processing nonferrous metals in Krasnoyarsk is underscored by the need to bring them closer to the consumers: plants in the Sayany territory production complex, which will incorporate a range of plants and industries, as well as in the Western Siberian and Far East economic regions.

Considerable savings in transportation costs for delivering rolled stock to consumers will be achieved through the locating of plants at Abakan, as compared with the cost of rolled-stock deliveries from the European regions to those in Siberia and the Far East, and through the lower electricity cost.

The growth in the volume of nonferrous metals at the combine will be achieved through:

- the comprehensive mechanization and automation of work processes, based on radically new technology and highly efficient machinery adapted to conditions of the North, in open cast mining, technological transportation, and metallurgy;
- the removal and processing of concentrated raw materials in more favorable areas using low-cost electricity.

The combine "Tuvakobalt," located in Tuva ASSR, is Siberia's second nickel-cobalt plant. It has been working since 1970 on nickel-cobalt ores of Khovy-Aksynsky deposits, producing nickel and cobalt in cobalt concentrate which is transported for further processing to the Afaleev combine. Because the deposits at Khovu-Aksyn, which are the sole raw-material base for the combine, have not been confirmed, the combine is no longer under consideration for large-scale development. But if confirmed, the deposits, projected to be first rate, may provide the combine with more material.

Great importance has been attached to the development of the Udokan deposits. Without building the Udokan ore-concentrating combine, it is absolutely impossible to satisfy the country's needs for copper.

Construction work on the Udokan combine will be started only after the railway line Tynda–Chara–BAM begins to operate, even on a temporary basis.

To ensure large-scale construction work on the combine, it would be necessary, beginning in 1985, to lay down every possible prerequisite: to complete detailed prospecting to confirm the existing reserves, study the concentrating properties of the ores, and work out the technological documentation for the project's construction work.

The possibility of attracting foreign capital to finance the Udokan combine has been investigated, with the goal of installing a full mining-metallurgical production cycle. Loans for financing the project may be used to achieve the quickest development of the ore deposits.

The lead and zinc industry in Western Siberia is represented by the Zolotushin and Salair mining boards, and the Belovsky zinc plant; in Eastern Siberia, by the Nerchinsky and Khancheranginsky combines.

The capacities of the lead and zinc ore-concentrating combines of Siberia constitute but a small proportion of the capacities of all the plants in the industry. The lead and zinc industry of Western Siberia is concentrated in the Kemerovo region and is represented by Salair mine, with its ore-concentrating mill, and the Belovsky zinc plant.

The lead concentrates produced at the Salair enterprise are delivered to plants in Kazakstan; the zinc concentrates go to the Belovsky zinc plant; the baryta concentrate, to the oil-processing industry.

Renovation of the Belovsky zinc plant now in operation can be regarded as the first step of the new metallurgical complex for the production of zinc, sulfuric acid, and, eventually, lead.

The existing lead and zinc plants of Eastern Siberia are not too promising because of the poor quality of their ores and their small size.

At present, prospecting for new ore deposits is under way in Siberia, though resources may be increased at the existing deposit sites.

The development of a large-scale raw-material base for lead and zinc is a priority. It calls for extensive prospecting for new deposits in the areas north of Lake Baikal and in the zone of influence near the BAM railway now under construction.

The development of Siberia's lead and zinc industry will be based on the deposits at Gorevsky (Krasnoyarsk Territory), Kyzyl-Tashtyg (Tuva ASSR), Ozerny (Buryat ASSR), Novo-Shirokinsky (Chita region), and Zmeinogorsky (Altai region), and further prospecting will be influenced by the value of these deposits. Though all four will be of interest in the 1980–2000 period, special emphasis will be placed on the Gorevskoye deposits of lead and zinc ores, the largest in the Soviet Union and one of the four largest in the world.

The transport, industrial, and hydroelectric power construction projects planned for the lower reaches of the Angara River will promote the development of these deposits.

Although the deposits are located under the Angara riverbed, studies and estimates show that they are technologically workable and economically expedient. The enterprise built on the basis of Gorevskoye deposits will be distinguished for its high technological and economic results and profitability, the cost of the concentrate being 2.5–3 times above that at the country's operating enterprises.

To provide the Gorevskoye enterprise with the most efficient transportation, the construction of the Abalakovo–Kirgitai–Usovo railway line, with two bridge crossings at the Strelka Andan extension along the Tatarka River valley, is a priority. This variant is more conducive to the task of developing the natural resources along the lower reaches of the Angara River (forests, magnesite, iron ore, talc) and will contribute to the solution of transportation problems at the Gorevskoye deposits.

Among other large deposits of polymetal ores in the Angara–Yenisey area is the Kyzyl–Tashtyg site in Tuva ASSR. Technological and economic estimates testify to the highly beneficial prospects of working this site.

The reserves of ores at the Gorevskoye, Kyzyl-Tashtyg and Ozerny (Buryat ASSR) deposits make it possible to set up in Siberia a huge chemical and metallurgical complex for the production of lead, zinc, and sulfuric acid, and, on this basis, phosphate fertilizer.

Siberia's molybdenum industry will be enhanced by the construction of new facilities on the basis of the deposits proapected at Zhirikensky, Orekitkansky, and Bugdainsky, and by expanding those already in operation: the Sorsky combine, now under renovation and the Dzhidinsky tungsten combine. Though Siberia's molybdenum plants are well provided for by rich ore deposits, they bring in average economic results.

The new tungsten deposits now being developed will be workable for a long period of time and are noted for their economic effect.

The country's tin production is concentrated chiefly in the Far East. In Eastern Siberia (Chita region) only the Sherlovogorsky combine is in operation, based on the Sherlovgorsky tin deposits. Though they can be listed among the country's largest, the practical development of these deposits, has failed to confirm the initially estimated reserves. In the future Siberia's tin industry will not be of much significance for the country's industry as a whole.

The Tuyim plant for the processing of nonferrous metals, going up on the base of the Tuyim mining board in Khakass Autonomous

Region, is the only plant of its kind in Siberia and the Far East. The placing of the plant in this area favors the marketing of the finished product (Siberia and the Far East do not have a single plant for the processing of nonferrous metals), and its convenient location is easily supplied with the initial raw materials.

The large reserves of nickel and copper in Norilsk ensure stable deliveries of raw materials for many years to come.

According to estimates made by specialized institutes, with the placing of plants in Tuva and possibly with time in Abakan, the overall savings in transportation costs for raw materials and finished product will amount annually to 5 million rubles as compared with their siting in the European part of the country.

Siberia has insignificant fluorite resources. Fluorite is mined and dressed at the Kalanguisk mining board (Chita region). The concentrate is transported to metallurgical, cement, chemical, and other enterprises outside the region.

Besides, the Kyakhtin fluorite mine, which has an unsufficient raw-material base, is operated in Buryat ASSR.

For the mine's concentration mill, the basic material is ore imported from the Mongolian People's Republic.

As the outlook for any significant increase in the volume of fluorite production in these regions is poor, prospecting for new deposits will be of special importance.

The projected rates of development for Siberia's nonferrous metal industry will be achieved by building a range of new companies on the basis of developing further the mining facilities in operation and newly prospected deposits.

However, putting new deposits and enterprises into operation is linked with the solution of several industry-related problems; among them are providing transportation and manpower, building industry bases, and supplying specialized repairs, power, and other servicing divisions. Prioity should be given to a solution of the transportation problem which is more critical in Siberia than in other parts of the country, because of the vastness of its territory and the relatively poor state of its transportation network. There are considerably fewer railway lines and roads here per square area unit than in the country in general.

The insufficient development of roads in the more densely populated parts of Siberia hinders economic development in some of the very regions with valuable mineral resources earmarked for development in the upcoming five-year periods. Among them are the areas along the lower and middle reaches of the Angara River and in the areas north of Lake Baikal.

Among Siberia's major transportation projects in the period under discussion is the completion of the Baikal–Amur railway main to ensure year-round transportation links with the Norilsk industrial region.

In the BAM area, the Udokan deposits is earmarked for priority development, and the area around the BAM railway is rich in other large-scale deposits of raw materials useful in the nonferrous metal industry.

Despite the insufficient study of the region's mineral wealth, one can already speak of its prime importance for the future production of copper, polymetals, nickel, tin, molybdenum, titanium, and other metals.

The economic development of the BAM zone will concentrate on setting up territorial production combines (TPC) there as the basis of its economic progress, mainly building enterprises specializing in the production and initial processing of mineral wealth (mining-metallurgical combines), and placing metallurgical and chemical-metallurgical facilities linked with their work outside the zone, in areas more favorable to construction and operation.

The limited navigation season on the Yenisey River necessitates the economic delivery of freight to Norilsk industrial area in one-time volumes covering year-round needs. As a result, storing and overhead costs here are 4 and 1.5-fold higher. The accumulation of additional stocks raises the outlays of the main production processes. Moreover, outlays increase because of losses and the damage to raw and other materials brought about by long-term storage. All this is highly detrimental to the national economy.

For this reason, priority is given to the development of a reliable transportation link with Norilsk.

The successful solution of the transportation problem is the chief requirement for developing Siberia's industry, among them non-ferrous metallurgy. Strict accounting of the transportation factor is a must, along with the placing of production in the territory of the region.

High growth rates in Siberia's nonferrous metallurgy will demand additional manpower. But providing it will be hard, given the constant shortage of workers. Hence, the prime importance of such intensive factors as the mechanization and automation of production, the introduction of highly efficient equipment and new processing technologies, the comprehensive use of raw materials, etc.

In the four years of the 10th five-year period, the mining of ore in nonferrous metallurgy has increased 1.5 fold through the use of self-propelled equipment, four times with the use of high-capacity bulldozers, and 1.6-fold with sand-blowing. Considerable advances in ore processing have been achieved by employing grinding, settling, separation, and other modern technological methods.

These aspects of mining and ore dressing are constantly being improved.

In the metallurgical industry the basic trends of technological progress are:

- introducing autogenous processes using heat and sulfur;
- introducing pressure processes; and
- introducing higher-capacity electrolyzers, etc.

A fine initiative in working out scientifically-grounded technological policy has come from the Krasnoyarsk Territory party committee. Joining efforts with the Siberian branch of the USSR Academy of Sciences, it outlined a promising program to introduce scientific and technical improvements in the region's industry up to 1990.

At nonferrous metal enterprises of Kransoyarsk Territory alone, the introduction of these measures will effect a savings of 250 million rubles, with a concomitant reduction of the labor force by 34,000.

Preservation of nature and a rational use of its resources, including its mineral wealth, has become particularly acute in this time of scientific and technological revolution.

The experiences of a range of enterprises show the existence of large reserves for raising the economic effect of production through the comprehensive use of raw materials.

Extensive work to extract useful minerals from waste water and water circulation supply is making headway.

The experience of Siberia's nonferrous metal enterprises has enabled them to work out measures for the comprehensive use of raw materials in the near future.

They envisage the development of drilling operations, ore concentration schemes, processing of waste from metallurgical and dressing production, improving dust collectors, construction of waste purifiers, automated processes in hydrometallurgy, technology of extracting raw materials from waste gas, etc.

Waste gases and slag often deprive the plants of up to 90% of the heat produced by the burning of fuel. The rising absolute consumption of fuel and heat will go hand in hand with the growing volume of nonferrous metal production. This demands that priority be given to increasing the yield efficiency of technical processes through reducing the losses and the nonproductive expenditure of fuel and heat in pyrometallurgy and alumina production.

Among the extensive measures that have been outlined for nonferrous metallurgy plants is reducing the outlet of secondary power resources. If one considers that the highest yields of secondary resources come from the production of nickel and cobalt, alumina and copper, which are developed in Siberia, it can rightly be assumed that the region's nonferrous metallurgy has great reserves for raising production effectiveness.

Special importance attaches to the economical use of power resources at mining and dressing enterprises in hard-to-reach regions in Northern Siberia. There the costs of fuel and electricity are much higher, presumably because of its rigorous climate, which requires higher fuel consumption than a milder, more temperate zone, but also because of the use of local gas and coal, which turn out to be much more expensive than liquid fuel delivered from other regions.

The high electrical cost is due to the huge consumption of fuel and the relatively small power plants. The costs for electricity in the North are 10 to 12 times above those in the temperate zone.

Advanced Soviet and foreign experience shows that excess production costs in Siberia can be brought down 1.5–2 times by optimizing the location of production sites.

In the main, Northern Siberia's regional policy will amount to all-round economy of manpower and will be based on a comprehensive account of the region's natural and economic conditions.

Protection of the environment is a key factor in raising the social effectiveness of production. Contamination of the atmosphere and water sources reduces the benefits of all the natural resources: it lowers worker productivity, increases capital outlays, and affects the usefulness of natural resources.

Siberia is noted for intensive but irregular, unstable development of geological-geomorphological and biological-climatic processes. The natural restoration of disrupted geosystems moves along at a much slower course than elsewhere, and breakdowns are often irreversible. This irreversibility is more often affected by the following factors:

- poor resistance of the atmosphere to disperse harmful substances (4 times under that in the European part of the country);
- slow self-purification of water surfaces after dumping of sewage (over 10 times);
- slow decomposition of hard waste; and
- poor self-restoring of damaged vegetation.

In designing new nonferrous metallurgy enterprises in Siberia and renovating those in operation, these factors call for additional study and development.

The rapid growth of nonferrous metallurgy in this area calls for the development of auxiliary services, especially those dealing with repairs. At present repair costs have risen to outstanding proportions (up to 10% of the basic production assets), while the proportion of repairmen at some enterprises has reached 40% of the main work force. The high costs of repairs in the industry are due to the low level of specialization and the lack of sufficient mechanization.

The development of specialized repair organizations employing industrial methods is a priority factor in raising the effectiveness of equipment repairs. Specialized repairs-construction trusts have been set up have been set up in the Urals, Siberia, Kazakstan, and Ukraine to improve repairs services in these regions, and the associations "Soyuztsvetmetremont," "Soyuzmashtsvetmet," and "Sibtsvetmet-avtomatika" have also been formed there.

In our opinion the establishing of new, specialized repair organizations must go hand in hand with development of the production base of the existing trusts in order to provide the equipment under repair with the required spare parts, mechanisms, and auxiliary equipment and enhance the quality of repairs.

Similarly, great importance attaches to specializing in the production of spare parts. Today only 30% of all spare parts and units is produced at specialized enterprises and large-scale repair bases. Most of them are produced in small workshops and involve high costs.

This problem should be tackled by concentrating the equipment stock inside the enterprise, setting up large-scale specialized shops and facilities housing repair and construction organizations, and renovating and expanding engineering plants within the association "Soyuzmashtsvetmet."

The introduction of these measures will promote the development of nonferrous metallurgy in Siberia.

ROLE OF AUTOMATION IN DEVELOPING NONFERROUS METALLURGY IN SIBERIA

(with M. E. Tsaregorodtsev)

A considerable share of the country's reserves of nonferrous metals—among them nickel, cobalt, platinum metals, lead, zinc, copper, molybdenum, gold, and aluminum—are located in Siberia, with its rigorous climate and exceptionally diverse natural features, which impede the development of its resources. Here, one feels sharply the shortage of manpower in most industries but especially in nonferrous metallurgy, inasmuch as its enterprises, mainly mines and dressing mills, are located in remote, sparsely populated areas with poorly developed industrial and social infrastructures. Workers are often placed in arduous and harmful conditions, and even such a large enterprise as the Krasnoyarsk aluminum plant has the city's largest labor turnover, though wages there are considerably above those at other enterprises. Apparently, material incentive is no longer a decisive factor if working conditions are hazardous and the work is labor-consuming and monotonous.

As regular deposits in more populated areas dry up, work is switched to deposits located in more remote areas with more complex mining conditions. This transfer necessitates an entire range of projects to ensure safe labor conditions, removing the workforce from hazardous zones, raising labor productivity, reducing the number of workers, and, on the whole, radically changing the content of the work.

A basic way to achieve progress in Siberia's nonferrous metallurgy is to introduce automation.

Automation of production and control systems in nonferrous metallurgy leads to a considerable increase in labor productivity, reduces

* Excerpted from "Problems and Prospects of the Automation of Siberia's Nonferrous Metallurgy," *Problems of the Development of the Nonferrous Metal Industry in Siberia* (Siberia: Siberian Division of the USSR Academy of Sciences, 1980).

the workforce, especially in hazardous and labor-consuming jobs, and raises the return on capital investments and the volume of production.

Automation at all stages of the mining and metallurgical cycle also leads to a more complete use of mineral resources. This is particularly important in Siberia where most of the deposits are of a comprehensive nature and there is an abundance of mineral wealth. Today, for instance, 14 elements are produced from the ores of the Norilsk and Talnakhsko-Oktyabrsky deposits. Enhancing automation can raise this index at least 1.5-fold in the next few years.

A particular benefit from automation is that the investment return is twice that of other technology in a shorter space of time.

On the whole, across the country the return period for investment in the development of Management Information and Control System is within 3 to 3.5 years, and that of Automatic Process Control Systems is 1 to 1.2 years. Within a relatively short period (1966–978), the introduction of Management Information Systems into the national economy has brought in more than over 10 billion rubles.

Automation, it should be underscored, promotes progress in nonferrous metallurgy by combining separate operations, enhancing their interconnection, and turning a multistage process into a nonstop one with fewer operations. It simplifies technology, brings down labor costs, and enhances the quality of the finished product.

Nonferrous metallurgy in Siberia not only makes additional demands for replacing manpower with automation, but has requirements to this effect involving cheaper electricity, relatively new raw materials, etc.

In introducing automation into Siberia, special emphasis must be given to on the training and retraining of the design staff of designers and the operators of automated systems.

Despite the advantages of automation in the tenth five-year period, the level of mechanization and automation in nonferrous metallurgy increased only 4.9%, to constitute 51.9%, including that of the work of the basic workforce to 79% and auxiliary work to 30.9%. The level in mechanizing jobs involving women increased to only 47.3%. Work is performed manually by 78.4% of workers in repair and construction shops and by 50% of workers in transportation and loading jobs.

All in all, 49% of the workers in Siberia's nonferrous metallurgy are engaged in manual work.

By the end of 1980 there will be introduced in the industry 60 ASAK systems, 120 Management Information and Control Systems, and 15 organizational-economy systems for management of enterprises. This will permit cutbacks in both management and service personnel now employed in manual work in hazardous jobs (up to 10,000) and effect an annual saving in materiel of between 6 million and 8 million rubles.

The rates of introducing automation in Siberia have fallen behind those of the country in general. In the 10th five-year period the volume of automation introduced in Siberia's nonferrous metallurgy will increase twofold as compared with the respective indices of the 9th five-year period and will constitute 24% of the total effort to automate the country's nonferrous metal industry (which is expected to grow threefold in the period under review).

One of the basic indices of the level of automation in an industry is the share of capital outlays for it in the overall volume of capital investments in the industry (Table 1).

The above data show that, in the period under review, the share of expenditures for automation in the overall volume of capital in-

Table 1: The Share of Capital Investments for Automation in All Capital Investments Made in the Industry (in percentages)

		Period		
Country		1966–1970	1971–1975	1976–1980
USSR	Industry	3.3	4.3	5.8
	Iron and Steel	2.0	4.0	6.0
	Oil Industry	1.6	4.3	2.0
	Oil processing and oil chemistry	4.0	6.0	8.0
	Nonferrous metallurgy	0.6	1.5	3.0
USA	Industry	18.0	29.2	31.2
	Nonferrous metallurgy	6.8	24.0	30.0

vestments in nonferrous metallurgy is, as a rule, considerably below that for the industry in general, for the separate subindustries of the USSR, and for the U.S. nonferrous metallurgy. At the same time, the rates of growth of this index in the nonferrous metallurgy of the USSR are higher.

Current Level of Automation of Siberia's Nonferrous Metallurgy

In Siberia enterprises and associations of nonferrous metallurgy are located on a very uneven basis. Most of them are concentrated in its eastern areas.

The largest volume of automation work in nonferrous enterprises falls to the scientific and production association "Sibtsvetmetavtomatika."

In the 9th five-year period the expenditures to introduce automation in Eastern Siberia's nonferrous metallurgy will amount to 46,000 thousand rubles, or 70.5% of the general expenditures for automation in this branch of Siberia's industry; the annual economic effect is estimated to be 13,500 thousand rubles, or 67.5%.

Expenses for different administrative units and the respective estimated economic results are distributed unevenly (Table 2) due to specifics of placing and different power capacities of enterprises.

Krasnoyarsk is the location of several nonferrous metal enterprises with unique technological capacities, among them the Norilsk mining and metallurgical combine, the Krasnoyarsk aluminum plant, the Achinsk alumina and Sorsky molybdenum combines, the association "Yeniseizoloto," the Krasnoyarsk nonferrous metal plant, and the Tuyim nonferrous metal processing plant. The volume of nonferrous metal production in the Territory accounts for nearly 25% of the gross output.

Between 1970 and 1979, 140 automated lines were installed in the Territory, among them 4 lines in nonferrous metallurgy.

The Krasnoyarsk nonferrous metal plant has the largest amount of nonline automated and semi-automated equipment (651 units, or 6.8% of total equipment, of which 635 units are automated equipment); on the whole, 763 and 646 units, respectively, have been in-

Table 2: Distribution of Expenditure and Anticipated Economic Effect from the Introduction of Automation as Broken Down by Region in Eastern Siberia Between 1976 and 1980

	Expenditure		Economic Effect	
Location	Thousands of rubles	Percentage	Thousands of rubles	Percentage
Krasmoyarsk Territory	32,500	71.0	10,100	74.8
Tuva ASSR	400	0.9	350	2.6
Irkutsk Region	10,000	21.8	1,500	11.2
Chita Region	2,100	4.5	850	6.2
Buryat ASSR	800	1.8	700	5.2
Total for Eastern Siberia	43,000	100	13,500	100

troduced into nonferrous metallurgy in the area, 148 of them with computer control systems.

Automated control systems are in operation at 9 of the territory's enterprises, among them the following enterprises of nonferrous metallurgy: the Krasnoyarsk aluminum plant, the association "Yeniseizoloto," and the Norilsk mining and metallurgical combine.

Industrial enterprises in the territory have 279 comprehensively mechanized, automated, and comprehensively automated shops, which make up 13.6% of the total number of shops in the Territory's enterprises. The number of workers employed in these shops constitute 15% of the area's workforce.

The introduction of automated and comprehensively automated divisions and shops at enterprises of nonferrous metallurgy, as compared with those of the chemical and oil-chemical industries in Krasnoyarsk Territory, is indicated in Table 3 (as of July 1, 1979).

The data show that the average number of workers employed in a single division shop (Items 2, a, b, c) is higher for nonferrous metallurgy; that is, in the chemical and oil-chemical industries automation has eliminated a sizable number of workers. The largest volume of automated divisions to be introduced in divisions and shops of nonferrous metallurgy occurred occurred between 1971 and 1975; in the 10th five-year period the rates of installation decreased.

Table 3

	Nonferrous Metallurgy		Chemical and Oil Industries	
	Divisions	Shops	Divisions	Shops
1. Total of automated and comprehensively automated systems	16	7	8	11
2. Number of workers	821	612	284	667
Among them, Engineers/technicians	64	87	21	69
Workers	752	525	263	553
Of this number (a) workers operating machines and mechanisms	412	239	167	280
(b) workers servicing machines and mechanisms	312	220	76	222
(c) workers doing manual work	28	66	20	51
3. Number of divisions and shops with no manual labor	12	1	1	3

Analysis of the results of introducing new technology in Krasnoyarsk Territory shows that the automation of production was much more effective than its mechanization. The economic effect per ruble of expenditures for automation amounted to 0.66 rubles; that for mechanization, 0.34 rubles.

A most effective trend in scientific and technological progress for the given period is that of introducing state-of-the-art technology and developing new types of industrial products, which account, respectively, for 0.98 and 1.23 rubles of effect per ruble of expenditure. The relative cost of dispensing with a single worker at enterprises in the area through the introduction of automation is 20,000 rubles, which is far above the cost of introducing mechanization of production and state-of-the-art technology. However, several new technological processes and units already incorporate elements of automation.

The draft of the Comprehensive Regional Program for the Accelerated Introduction of the Achievements of Scientific and Technological Progress in Nonferrous Metallurgy of Krasnoyarsk Territory for 1981–1990 calls for the allocation of 97.0 million rubles for automation, making it possible to eliminate 4,000 workers, with the concomitant annual saving of 40.0 million rubles.

In Tuva ASSR the share of comprehensively mechanized and automated shops constitutes a mere 8%, which is 5.6% less than in Krasnoyarsk Territory. For all this, the introduction of automation and mechanization at its enterprises has resulted in a lower economic benefit due to smaller reductions in manpower than in Krasnoyarsk Territory.

In the Tuva republic's economic development, nonferrous metallurgy is a key industry represented by the combine "Tuvakobalt" and Terlig-Khainsky prospecting and mining enterprise.

The combine "Tuvakobalt" accounts for one-fifth of all the comprehensively mechanized divisions and shops in the republic. In 1980 there were 480 workers, or 57% of the workforce, employed in fully mechanized jobs; by 1985 their number will increase to 65.9%.

In the 10th five-year period, expenditures for automation in the nonferrous metal industry of Western Siberia will make up 29.5% of the overall expenditures for automation in the industry, and the expected annual economic effect will be 6.5 million rubles.

Automation of the Gold-Mining Industry

Throughout the country considerable attention is devoted to the automation of the gold-mining industry. Nevertheless, at most gold-extraction factories labor productivity grows at a slow pace, lagging far behind that of advanced dressing mills of nonferrous metallurgy. This is due to small-scale production capacities, low productivity, and the excessive variety of equipment; numerous labor-intensive and arduous processes operated by hand; a lack of comprehensive automation at enterprises, and insufficient use of per-unit automation; and the low level of design and construction and pilot projects.

In setting up management information systems at gold-mining enterprises, consideration should be given to several aspects of organizational structure and technological development of deposits. Among these peculiarities are:

- considerable territorial dispersion of enterprises dealing with mining and processing of the respective mineral (the distance between mines and management boards can be as great as 500 to 700 kilometers);
- use of several types of mining technology (open-cast dredge, hydraulic, and underground mining);
- use of several types of processing techniques (dredge, hydraulic, dressing mills, factories for finishing processing cycle, roasting plants);
- absence, in most cases, of independent communication links between the combine's management board and the management of mines; and
- low level of automation of technological processes.

At present, considerable investments are being channeled into development of automation for the gold-mining industry.

In the 10th five-year period 20.0 million rubles were earmarked for investment in the automation of this sub-industry, including more than 1 million rubles for Siberian enterprises, with the annual economic effect reaching, respectively, 6 million rubles and 400 thousand roubles. Practical effect, however, is still far from the estimates.

Of the large-scale systems that have brought in effective results, close to the outlined estimates, one can name only the widely introduced system "Draga-1."

Automated dredges are now operating in the associations "Yeniseizoloto," "Zabaikalzoloto," and "Lenzoloto." The average yearly economic effect from a single system amounts to 120.0 thousand rubles.

Nevertheless, the designing and installation of these systems demand huge initial investments, the means of automation, and cable products now in short supply. They also require the development of costly software, algorithms, programs, and special analytical devices, along with other automation means. Given the limited scope of this work, the time needed for developing and installing the systems is protracted. It took nine years (from 1967 to 1975) to develop and install the "Draga-1" system on a mass scale. Today the annual economic effect per ruble spent on its development is 3.60 rubles from each completed project.

At mines and factories the introduction of automatic process control systems (APCS) is slow, because there are as yet no finished systems for the gold-mining industry and no experience with their operation.

In 1978, "Soyuzzoloto" introduced 8 APCS. Plans call for the introduction of 3 more APCS by 1980. Between 1976 and 1980 and 1981 and 1985, the share of planned investments by "Soyuzzoloto" in APCS in the sum total of investments will amount to 1.3%–1.8%, which is 2.6% below the average figures for the USSR Ministry of Nonferrous Metallurgy (3%–5%).

The development of APCS for factories is more costly than for mines. In some factories the cost of research, pilot-construction, and design can exceed one million rubles. Hence, it is more expedient to develop APCS for several factories simultaneously. The number of factories scheduled for priority development of these systems should be reduced. At the same time the amount of local automation and dispatching controls should be increased.

A comparison of the estimated annual economic effect, per ruble of outlays, from the introduction of APCS in the gold-mining industry with the index for APCS operating in the mines of Norilsk mining and metallurgical combine indicates they are almost identical. The estimated annual economic effect per ruble of outlays for automation of North-Yenisey mines amounts to 0.34 rubles; Taseyevsky mine, 0.41 rubles; Darasun and Kochkar mines, 0.50 rubles; "Komsomolsky" mine, 0.43 rubles; "Oktyabrsky" mine, 0.26 rubles, "Zapolyarny" mine, 0.39 rubles. The expense is recoved in 2 to 2.5 years, which is less than the standard rate of 3.1 years.

In the 11th five-year period most of the projects designated for the gold-mining industry will not be ready for the large-scale installation of APCS and Management Information Systems (MIS).

By 1990 APCS are scheduled for introduction at the mine and gold concentration mill at North-Yenisey Mine (costs = 4.0 million rubles; economic effect = 600 thousand rubles). In the 11th five-year period, work will be undertaken to develop APCS for the Darasunsky mine and the Tasev factory.

Introducing an information-dispatching system for the mining shop at Saralinsk mine is envisaged for 1981. Work will be continued to introduce local automation along with the tested system "Draga-1" while updating its separate units and converting to a state-of-the-art element base. The work will be done primarily by the scientific and production association "Sibtsvetmetavtomatika."

The system is to be installed at 15 dredges, 6 of which operate in Siberia, in the 11th five-year period.

The total costs for automation of enterprises of "Zoyuzzoloto" in Siberia for the discussed period will amount to 10 million rubles, or 18% of the cost of automation in this sub-industry for the entire country.

The volume of automation earmarked for installation in the 11th five-year period will be well above that in the previous period. Yet this still falls short of the needs of gold-mining enterprises.

The designing of projects for automation of the gold-mining industry needs further development. Yet there are prerequisites for its expansion and intensification in the next 5 to 10 years. Here, priority should be given to the design and installation of means and systems of local automation, dispatching, automated systems of analytical control, and systems of comprehensive mechanization and automation of "Draga-1" type.

Automation of the Nickel and Cobalt Industry

In the 10th five-year period expenditures for automation in the nickel and cobalt industry were envisaged at 40 million rubles, including 23 million rubles, or 64%, for Siberia. The anticipated total economic effect from automation is expected to reach 15.3 million rubles, including 7.4 million rubles, or 47.9%, for Siberia.

In 1979 the transition from designing and introducing individual technologies, control systems, and local systems of automatic regulation in the nickel and cobalt industry to automated process control systems was still under way. A high level of automation has been achieved in hydrometallurgical processing with the comprehensive introduction of automated technological processing. Automation of the pyrometallurgical industry is lagging far behind due to the imbalance between the bulk of the equipment and the high-efficiency automated working regimes.

The introduction of automation at the Norilsk combine in the 10th five-year period will consume 98.4% of the expenditures for automation of Siberia's nickel and cobalt industry. The total annual economic effect will be 7.0 million rubles. As of July 1, 1979, the combine had 47 mechanized production and automated lines, and 95 comprehensively mechanized, automated divisions and shops.

Nonetheless, automation at the Norilsk mining and metallurgical combine is still a far cry from what it should be.

Due to the absence of a material base and mechanization servicing, 51%–60% of all workers are still engaged in manual work.

Sixty percent of its workforce do indirect work, the direct result of the lag in the rates of automation and mechanization of indirect jobs as compared with the basic operations.

The best achievements in automation at the Norilsk mining and metallurgical combine have been made at the Nadezhdinsk metallurgical plant. Most of the automation devices operating there, along with the basic technological equipment, was installed by Finnish companies. Specialists note the advantages of the Finnish equipment, which is based on integrated circuits, as compared with their domestic counterparts, which are based on relay circuits.

APCS and MIS have been set up at the combine's underground mines. It took six years for the Kiev Institute of Automation to design MIS "Rudnik" for "Komsomolsky" mine.

The projects were to be completed by the end of 1978, but the system failed to prove itself in the conditions of the Norilsk mines. The fixed time limits were disrupted, and the institute failed in its commitments.

The design of MIS for the "Oktyabrsky" mine is envisaged by 1985; for the "Taymyr" mine, by 1990; and for the "Mayak" mine, by 1984.

A project to design APCS for the ore-dressing mill is under way. Preliminary steps have been made in this direction: a mathematical model of regularities for sintering roasting nickel concentrates with high sulfuric properties. Several local automation systems have also been designed and put into operation, among them an automatic device for controlling and regulating the loading of the charge on the sintering machine, the humidifying of the charge in the pelletizer drum, and the regulating of the gas temperature in the kiln.

The introduction of automated control systems equipped with integrating devices linked to the control computer complex M 7000 for the top level APCS at the sintering plant creates the conditions for their efficient operation.

The basic guidelines for developing mechanization and automation of the Norilsk mining and metallurgical combine to the year 1990 envisages the introduction by 1989 of APCS at the nickel plant.

Questions dealing with management of the combine have become a project all by themselves. Such specific features of the combine as its large size, multi-branch character, and its development into the nidus of the territorial and production complex, among others, calls for scientific study by employing up-to-date methods and means of automation.

In this connection the computer center of the Siberian branch of the USSR Academy of Sciences (Krasnoyarsk) is developing a hierarchic automated optimization system for dressing and metallurgical processing at the combine.

In 1977–1978 stage 1 was completed—adaptive models were constructed for the sintering plants and dressing mills, the copper and nickel plants, which makes possible the use of third-generation computers for the timely forecasting of quantitative and qualitative indices of the technological processes.

In 1979 stage 2 was completed. An automated system was designed to calculate the production program of ore dressing and metallurgical processing at the combine, with the view of planning and management of production in the advisory regime. Actual outlays amounted to 360 thousand rubles, and, with the introduction of the results of stage 2, the anticipated annual economic effect fell short by nearly 10 million rubles.

On the whole the work will be completed in 1988–1989. Its full implementation will allow the use of developed models to achieve optimal automatic control in a closed-loop system.

In 1977 the scientific and production association "Sibtsvetmetavtomatika" developed the sub-system MIS, "Repairs servicing of industrial plants," on the basis of the computer system "Minsk-32." Total outlays stood at 260 thousand rubles, giving an economic effect of 113 thousand rubles. At present work is under way to develop programs for the said sub-system for computer system M-4030.

In 1979 a sub-system for calculating the volume, content, and dynamics of the plant was made ready for pilot testing. Outlays stood at 37 thousand rubles; the economic effect was 33 thousand rubles.

The development of an integrated MIS for the Norilsk mining and metallurgical combine is a priority in the designing of automatic control devices.

The combine "Tuvakobalt" is the pioneer of nonferrous metallurgy in Tuva ASSR and its leading enterprise with regard to introduction of scientific and technological results. At present, 1,050 local systems of automatic control and regulation have been introduced at the combine, 160 of which are automatic regulation systems.

In 1970 "Sibtsvetmetavtomatika" developed a project for dispatching (1st unit of APCS) power-supplying units on the basis of teleautomatics "Obzor," and units in the mining shop. The cost of equipment stood at 297 thousand rubles. However, the question of providing all the technological means is still unresolved. The point is that the responsible organization, "Soyuzmetallurguglekomplekt," services only enterprises built from scratch, while the organization "Soyuzsistemkomplekt" delivers equipment only after the installation of the computer. The project, however, envisages its installation only at the second stage.

For the combine "Tuvakobalt" the 10th five-year period envisages the introduction of a chemical analyzer KRF-18 for analytical control, with an outlay of 400 thousand rubles and the anticipated annual economic effect of 350 thousand rubles.

The plan for the development of the combine up to 1985 envisages the installation of the electronic computer M-6000 and the introduction of APCS.

The Krasnoyarsk nonferrous metallurgical plant will get its APCS in 1985, with expenditures totaling 5.0 million rubles. Its economic effect will amount to 2.9 million rubles.

Automation of the Aluminum Industry

According to the 10th five-year plan, 14.5 million rubles will be allocated for automation at enterprises of the aluminum industry, which is 45% of that spent on automation of the industry in general.

The total annual economic effect will be short of 3 million rubles, or, as broken down according to enterprises:

Of late, the introduction of MIS for technological processes with

Outlays in Thousands of Rubles		Annual Economic Effect in Thousands of Rubles
Achinsk alumina combine	800	200
Bratsky aluminum plant	7,000	600
Irkutsk aluminum plant	3,000	900
Krasnoyarsk aluminum plant	2,800	1,000
Novokuznetsky aluminum plant	950	380

the use of control computer complexes has become a priority for the automation of alumina production.

The development of an automated control system for the raw materials shop and the carbonizing process for alumina solutions, with the use of third-generation computers, will be completed in the next five-year period at the Achinsk alumina combine.

Employing an integrated control system at the combine for the sintering of nepheline and lime charge will help regulate the correlation between indices of quality production and cost. The plan of the USSR Ministry of Nonferrous Metallurgy for 1980 calls for the introduction of APCS "Shikhta-3A" at the combine.

According to the long-term plan for 1990, there will be developed and introduced at the Achinsk alumina combine APCS for the sintering shop (overall cost, 700 thousand rubles; economic effect, 300 thousand rubles); MIS for repairs of equipment (outlays for research, 70 thousand rubles; effect, 150 thousand rubles); APCS for calcinating shop (outlays, 220 thousand rubles; effect, 300 thousand rubles); APCS for cement production (outlays, 700 thousand rubles; effect, 250 thousand rubles); APCS for chemical hydrology shop (outlays, 300 thousand rubles; effect, 200 thousand rubles).

Automation of technological processes for the electrolysis of aluminum is performed chiefly by the systems of the "Aluminum" type. The automated capacities for electrolysis of aluminum now in operation account for 90%. The total annual economic effect is 10 million rubles.

The experience of developing and installing "Aluminum" systems, the results of research in the field of MIS, and the development of the equipment and technology for electrolysis and domestic computer technology—all this formed the base for the development of new APCS, "Elektroliz," which are taking the place of "Aluminum" systems. In 1980 "Elektroliz" will be installed at the Bratsk aluminum plant.

Work is expanded on developing and installing integrated MIS, embracing. along with electrolysis, other technological processes, among them casting and rolling, dust suppression, and the processing of fluorides.

The first units of these MIS have already been put into operation at the Krasnoyarsk and Bratsk aluminum plants. The second units are planned to start operating by the end of the 10th five-year period, with the expected economic effect of 1.5 to 2.0 million rubles.

Work is continuing on the comprehensive mechanization and automation of individual labor-consuming processes. For instance, the object of studying the designing and installation of an automatic ingot casting line, carried out by "Sibtsvetmetavtomatika" at the Krasnoyarsk aluminum plant was to free a significant part of the workforce from labor-consuming manual work in hazardous conditions and raise production efficiency. The final index upon implementing the system was the actual eliminating of 144 workers and improving working conditions for 208 workers (with accounts for the removed workers).

From 1981 to 1990 the cost of automation work at the Krasnoyarsk aluminum plant would reach 20 million rubles. The economic effect would be 10 million dollars; the workforce would be reduced by 1,000; and working conditions would be improved.

At the Sayany aluminum plant now under construction, a standard organization and technology MIS will be introduced in 1990, with expenses at 900 thousand rubles and the economic effect at 900 thousand rubles.

Automation of Rare Metals Industry

A total of 16 APCS were installed at enterprises of "Soyuzredmet" of the USSR Ministry of Rare Metals by the end of 1976, among them MIS for power units, repairs, and transportation economies. By the end of the five-year period 7 more APCS will be introduced.

The plan for designing and installing automated control and management systems in the 1976–1980 period under "Soyuzredmet" envisages expenditures in the amount of 24.8 million rubles, including 3.3 million rubles, or 13.2%, for Siberia. The expected total economic effect at "Soyuzredmet" enterprises will amount to 14.6 million rubles, including 1.9 million rubles, or 12.8%, for Siberia.

Among the largest enterprises in the industry is the Sorsky molybdenum combine.

At present, local automation and the automated control system "Karier-2," which has brought in high economic results, are widely used at the combine. With the installation of "Karier-2" MIS, the productivity of operators of dump trucks has grown nearly 1.5-fold.

In the 10th five-year period MIS for dressing processes, including MIS using KRF-18, will be introduced.

In 1982 MIS will be installed at the combine for equipment repairs and an automated system for defect-free work (cost of research work, 130 thousand rubles; economic effect, 220 thousand rubles).

Automation of Polymetallic Industry

Automation at enterprises in the polymetallic industry has not yet reached a high level of development.

Today the enterprises are installed with 5 APCS. In 1980 one more APCS will start operating. The plan for the 10th five-year period calls for the introduction at the Nerchinsk polymetal combine of an automated system of analytical control (ASAC) using the analyzer KRF-18, and a similar system at the Novosibirsk tin combine. The outlays for their introduction come to 400 thousand rubles, with the economic effect projected at 350 thousand rubles.

In 1988 APCS for the dressing plant will be introduced at the Gorevsky mining and dressing combine now under construction (cost, 800 thousand rubles; economic effect, 800 thousand rubles), designed by the "Mekhanobr" institute. In the 12th five-year period APCS will be introduced at the combine (cost of designing and installation, 2.5 million rubles; economic effect, 1.1 million rubles).

Here, too, there is a potential for the introduction of robotics, especially at construction sites of water-conservation development projects and at mining sites.

State and Prospects for Locating of Repair Work Facilities and the Technological Servicing of Automation Means and Systems

The development and installation of automated systems in Siberia is closely linked with the problem of organizing their repairs and technological maintenance.

The location of nonferrous metallurgy enterprises play a decisive part in the siting of facilities for repair services.

Today, repairs are more frequently done by specialists at the enterprise using automated equipment. In most cases repairs are performed in small shops where there is a constant shortage of spare parts and workers are lacking in skills.

Developing a network of facilities dealing with repairs and the technical maintenance of automated means and systems, one that integrates branch and territorial aspects of management in every specific region and the country as a whole, has become an urgent necessity.

The setting up of a wide network of specialized organizations for repairing and technological maintenance of automated means and systems will make it possible to free the maintenance services at industrial enterprises of repair work, thereby concentrating the spare parts in a smaller number of units and setting up an exchange stock of automated devices and units.

The greatest effect in repair work is ensured by specializists serving enterprises of a single industry or all industries located in the same area. An example of this is the specialized pilot plant for repairs of computer technology "SoyuzEVMkompleks."

The scientific production association "Sibtsvetmetavtomatika" is Siberia's only enterprise performing a complex of operations to automate nonferrous metallurgy from "A to Z," including the designing of automated means and systems, repairing and servicing projects in operation, and checking instrumentation. These functions are executed through a network of sub-divisions located throughout the region.

Situating large repair bases in territorial and regional centers with good communication ties with many populated areas is most advisable. Because the weight of automated devices is relatively small, transportation costs will be recovered, and centralized repairs performed at a specialized base will prove to be more profitable than repairs made by amateurs. In areas of industrial concentration (big cities), it is expedient to resort to inter-branch repairs, for the setting up of specialized plants capable of doing repairs along industrial lines, with a high level of automation and mechanization of repair work, will achieve the highest effect.

Forecasting the Automation of Siberia's Nonferrous Metallurgy

The successful development of automation depends on the use of special forecasting methods. Given the growing manpower shortage, the significance of working out forecasts for the development of automation at the pre-plan stage increases as the role of automation increases. Here, special importance attaches to foretelling the socioeconomic consequences of automation.

For such forecasting, using the statistical method of factorial analysis, supplemented with the method of expert evaluation, is possible.

At the first stage of forecasting, the sources of economic effects in the automation process are singled out. All the factors are presented as a hierarchic model, showing their ties from the lowest level, where the automated means and systems to be installed are located, to the general production target located at the highest level.

The specifications and supplements to the model, as well as the determinations of the basic sources of effectiveness, are achieved with the well-known method of expert evaluation "Delfi."

The final variant of the hierarchical model becomes the basis for subsequent analysis.

Within the bounds of a single company, a near-term estimate of the economic effect of automation can be made by determining trends in the changes of factors listed in the hierarchical model, both with and without consideration of the influence of automation in identical conditions. In this case, the latter conditions are discarded and do not affect the "clear effect" of automation.

Subsequent analysis deals with all the production conditions specific to the given enterprise (the state of and prospects for developing the raw material base, basic technological equipment, etc.), diminishing or raising the "clear effect" of automation.

The lack of a sufficiently long-term period showing the particular trend of scientific and technological progress is a significant obstacle to applying regressive methods of forecasting to the development of automation.

For this reason, it is advisable to use factorial analysis, in which each subsequent target is made dependent on the influence of sub-targets in the hierarchical model, and the influence of automation is determined only for the technological and economic factors at the lowest level.

Because it is difficult determine the extent of the effect of auto-mation on technological and economic factors, using recommenda-tions from the literature which determine the correlative dependence between the level of automation and technical and eco-nomic factors of production at an enterprise—an analogue with suf-ficiently developed automation—is likewise advisable. By using specific elasticity factors for each type of dependency curve, it is possible to determine the percentage (within one percent), of changes in the considered factor as a result of changes in the level of automation. Besides, by comparing the elasticity factors, one can determine which factor is most affected by automation. Analysis of the levels of relationship makes it possible to bring out the main trend in the factor's changes as the level of automation rises. One can determine the optimal value of the level of automation esti-mated according to existing methods in regard to each factor.

Scientific and Technological Policy in the Automation of Nonferrous Metallurgy

At the present stage, scientific and technological policy is a major instrument for accelerating scientific and technological progress and raising its effectiveness is scientific and technological policy.

In selecting the trends in automation of nonferrous metallurgy, it is necessary to take into account the regional peculiarities of differ-ent parts of the country. Siberia, for instance, is characterized by complex land forms, climate, and mining conditions. It is far from the country's developed areas and poorly developed economically; it has high power availability per capita in all industries but a shortage of manpower. Under these conditions, the problem of cost-reductions involving workers is an important topic and has unique aspects. Among these are the excessive outlays for replacing of workers, higher wages, more expensive construction work, and improvements to localities. Hence, here technological policy is chiefly concerned with protection of labor.

Its basic lines of development deal with comprehensive mechanization of loading and unloading, transportation and warehouse jobs, accelerated introduction of robotics, automation of hazardous and dangerous jobs, extensive introduction of specialized (suitable to the northern climate) technology, reducing pollution, and a more comprehensive use of mineral wealth.

In the last 5 to 10 years, there has been a typical trend in technological policy in the field of production automation, including that in Siberia, to go from designing and installation of devices and apparatus for the automatic control of different technological parameters, or for managing different production operations, to the designing and introducing of comprehensive automated control systems, and, in the last five-year period, the use of computer technology.

Integrated MIS (IMIS), which combine the solution of organizational-economic problems with technological control of enterprises, are highly promising.

A new trend of technological policy in automation is to set up the servicing of complex automated systems and computers.

In keeping with forecasts for the development of automation in nonferrous metallurgy it is projected that by 1990 automated control systems will have been installed in all technological systems and plants. Automated control systems for technological and production processes with use of computer technology will be operating at 85%–90% of all companies.

The remaining 10%–15% falls to small enterprises using only local automated systems.

It is economically expedient to introduce IMIS at dressing mills and metallurgical plants with comparatively small production cycles. At large combines, encompassing a complex of mining, dressing, and metallurgical operations, as well as at plants processing nonferrous metals and engaged in the production of a wide variety of items for a large number of customers, it is economically profitable to introduce management and information control systems and process control systems.

At small enterprises it is not advisable economically to install centralized automated systems, but in the areas with manpower shortages local automatic systems can bring effective results.

Of late, much attention has been given to designing and installing industrial robots as a major means of achieving the comprehensive automation of production, making it possible to eliminate many labor-consuming jobs and remove workers from harmful and hazardous jobs.

Because of the above-mentioned peculiarities, nonferrous metallurgy is in dire need of industrial robots in all spheres.

At present, the scientific and production association "Sibtsvetmetavtomatika" is conducting studies to determine the best sites for introducing industrial robots at enterprises in the gold-mining, nickel-cobalt, and lead-zinc industries of Siberia.

The emergence of SPA "Sibtsvetmetavtomatika" in Krasnoyarsk was prompted by the high concentration of this industry's enterprises in the area and the availability of the respective scientific and technological base, which is lacking in, for instance, the Chita region. As the hub of the industry, it does an active and timely job, with minimal outlays, in developing enterprises and dealing with research and technological problems with consideration for the specifics of each one. As a progressive form of integrating research and industry, the association promotes the rates of scientific and technological progress not only in its industry but in the area in general.

The progress of mechanization and automation at Siberia's nonferrous metallurgy enterprises is accompanied by a sharp rise in the stock of equipment, devices, precision instruments, and automation systems.

It is now more profitable to have repairs and maintenance services of automated means and systems handled by specialized organizations, among them SPA "Sibtsvetmetavtomatika." Its territorial network of management boards and units ensures high-quality repairs, and its stock of equipment helps save time and money.

Due to the complex character and scope of technological, social, and organizational problems dealing with the automation of Siberia's nonferrous metallurgy, they require a program-target approach.

IT IS NECESSARY TO INCREASE FOOD PRODUCTION IN THE YENISEY NORTH

In the 1950s, I had to sail regularly from Krasnoyarsk to Dudinka. Such Turukhansk piers as Lebed, Vorogovo, and Alinskoye were eagerly awaited by all passengers, both children and adults. At those piers local women sold fresh berries, potatoes, and pickles. Vorogovo was especially famous for sour cream and cottage and farmer's cheese.

Invoices of the 1950s give us a similar picture: these areas supplied beef and vegetables to the North, to Norilsk, and to the South, to Yeniseisk.

In the summer of 1979 I visited those areas again. My ship was greeted by local people, but this time not to sell but to buy potatoes and vegetables. . . .

Of course, the needs of the area have increased, because now there are more consumers. Abundant natural resources were discovered in these areas, and people arrived here to develop them. Supplying such promising areas is a serious problem. Nature, primarily the surrounding woods, which are full of berries and wild animals, could help to resolve it. But there is another problem, caused by the State Committee for Hunting (Glavokhota). In the early 1960s, Glavokhota insisted that prospering collective farms (*kolkhoz*) would be converted into three state industrial farms (*gospromkhoz*) in the local area and that they would be subject to Glavokhota. But Glavokhota was interested only in hunting wild animals. Cattle breeding and grain producing practically stopped. Other agricultural activities, including the picking of wild berries, also began to decrease. However, when the gospromkhozes were originally forming, one of the reasons for their creation was the hope to increase the picking of wild berries.

Dozens of hamlets and villages appeared in the area: Alinskoye, Lebed. . . . In one of them I met Alexandra Denisenko, a hunter. She is 56. We walked together through the village. There are nice houses,

Sovetskaya Torgovly (Soviet Trade), June 17, 1980, p. 2.

and a school building where more generations of children could study. But people had left.

How could they stay in the village: the salary of an employee of the gospromkhoz is less than the one of the sovkhoz. In a sovkhoz, an employee uses the sovkhoz's equipment for fishing, but in a gospromkoz he or she must use his or her own, whatever it is. Gospromkhozes do not have any equipment or funds; nor are they willing to build.

"Before we usually picked 180 centners of potatoes per hectare. Today we don't have either the equipment or the desire to work on the soil," says a local village leader.

That figure, 180 centners per hectare, was confirmed at the Institute of Nature Protection of the Ministry of Agriculture. They said that those lands are very rich and fruitful, a very favorable area for developing agriculture.

Once I had to ride on an airplane from Krasnoyarsk to Evenkiya, a plane that was carrying dried grass. Thousands of miles away! The pilot was very angry because the airplane was too light and, in the air, could easily be tossed by the wind. In the meantime, in the Krasnoyarsk airport products manufactured by local industries went undelivered for several weeks because there were not enough airplanes. Right there, in those areas, whole grass jungles are being wasted.

Recently on Taymyr Peninsula, to the north of Turukhansk, an agro-industrial center "Arktika" was established. Its purpose is to unite in a single complex all the industries that can function in a polar zone. "Arktika" united 13 small kolkhozes and sovkhozes. Its turnover exceeds 10 million rubles.

These are just the first steps. There are some positive changes in Taymyr villages as well. But, here again, the main obstacles are the selfish interests of gospromkhozes. They are designed not to produce but to take from nature. Their ministry, Glavokhota, creates for them privileged conditions for that activity. Hunting is an inseparable part of agriculture in the North. This is why Glavokhota determines the quantities and quotas for gospromkhozes. "Arktika" is granted the least. Despite these obstacles, the center performs effectively.

Thus, we are talking about very promising areas. Geologist-prospectors have already come here, and now it is the turn of construction workers. The local nature is abundant and generous: it can provide for everyone. However, a rational economic approach is needed to use all these resources.

These problems are not just local; they are common for the entire North. Look at the map: the North covers more than half the USSR.

FOOD FOR PEACE?
OR FOR CIVIL WAR?

If we are not careful, the food we send to feed hungry Soviets will serve merely to strengthen the socialist hard-liners against the democratic forces.

Why is the Soviet Union hungry? Why does the biggest and potentially the richest country in the world have empty shelves in the stores?

The hunger is real. In the United States people consume more than 53 pounds of meat per capita per year; in the USSR, if you count the bone and gristle, just 26 pounds. Okay, maybe Americans eat too much meat. But what about fruit? Americans eat three times more fruit than people in the USSR do. Even these figures are for more normal times. These are not normal times. Real hunger looms in the land that was once the breadbasket of Europe.

So, unless Americans and Europeans want to see Soviet children on the nightly TV news, they are going to have to ship food to the Soviet Union. Done the right way, such food aid can help feed the truly hungry. Done the wrong way, it can hasten a civil war.

Russia has an image as a freezing country where nothing really grows. But the Soviet Union's food crisis has nothing to do with resources. The country has vast and fertile lands—470 million acres of rich black earth. (Compare that to the approximately 250 million acres that make up the U.S.'s corn belt.) In the Republic of Georgia, people say that if you drive a stake into Georgian land, tomorrow you will see grapes there.

This year the country again had a blessing of a crop and a curse of a system; 230 million tons of grain were borne by the fields, while the USSR was buying 30 million tons abroad.

This is not a problem of equipment. The USSR has 200,000 more grain harvester combines than the U.S. has. Soviet tractors, the Belarus and the Vlamidirets, are of good quality, but the farmer is not interested in using them. Why bother? The land does not belong to him.

Are Russians lazy? Not by nature. Only by training—goofing off is the only way you can beat the system. In such matters one can't divorce current events from history. The roots of today's food problem in the USSR go back to 1917, when the October Revolution took agriculture from the people and gave it to the state to use for state purposes.

By 1910, well before the revolution, the reformist Prime Minister Piotr Stolypin had pushed through a reform to give land and economic freedom to the peasants. Some peasants used their new freedom wisely; some squandered the fruits. The entrepreneurial peasants got the name "kulaks"—literally, "fists"—meaning that they grasped their households firmly in their hands.

By 1913 the kulaks had created solid, strong farms and even small agro-industrial complexes. Not only did they produce their own grain, they raised cattle, invested in equipment for cattle raising and milk production, and developed transportation networks to get their goods to market. At that time the kulaks, together with well-to-do peasants, constituted 35% of all peasant households. A full one-third of Russia's peasantry was well on its way to middle-class status.

The curtain began to fall on Russian agriculture in the autumn of 1917. Lenin's Bolsheviks ignited the hatred of illiterate, shiftless drunkards against the kulaks. Starting with the October Revolution, whatever the kulaks earned was taken away. They were murdered; their farms, created by long labor, were set on fire. Hard workers were the people's enemies.

Building on Lenin, Stalin sent trainloads of hungry and naked kulaks, along with their exhausted sick babies, and dumped them in the depths of the frozen desert. It was one of the worst genocides in human history—all done in the name of the people. For the Bolsheviks this was sound policy: A prosperous peasant would never make a good communist. A city, well fed by the state, might.

The Bolsheviks took over from the kulaks, and here are some of the results as calculated by the Moscow University agrarian specialist Professor Aleksei Yemelyanov: From 1928 to 1934, cattle and meat production fell 40%, production of eggs more than 70%. In 1929, 5.8 million tons of meat were produced. In 1934, only 2 million. Agriculture in the Soviet Union never recovered.

The Bolsheviks declared this war not only against the kulaks but also against the very idea of private property, and especially private ownership of land. In this regard, the right-wingers around Mikhail Gorbachev are the Bolsheviks' faithful descendants. They may compromise on accepting elements of a market economy, but on private ownership of land, never, unless they are made to do it.

Having eliminated the hardest-working part of the peasantry, the Bolsheviks re-enslaved the rest, and they have remained enslaved in all but name ever since. Slaves and spongers. With nothing to gain by working hard, they worked hardly at all. This year, for example, huge crops of potatoes were left to rot in the fields. Why bother? The farmers had all the potatoes they could eat, and the produce of the state farms did not belong to them, so they didn't bother harvesting it. In the past, a shortage of produce would have been attributed by the officials to bad weather, but now the truth is out.

What development the communists managed went to the military and to the cities. Russian villages are strikingly poor and gloomy. The quality of the roads is such that a Jeep Cherokee would vanish into the mud and never be seen again. The roads are decrepit, partially because of poverty and partially on purpose, to hold the people in the villages. Until Stalin's death the peasants were so enslaved they did not even have I.D. papers and permits to go to the cities. The Stalinist order has long since broken down. With nothing to hold them in the countryside, the peasants flock to the cities. Today many villages are deserted.

What about the food that does get into the Soviet distribution system? The system has a simple feudal character: It is an exchange of goods, services, and favors. I fix your car, you give me good meat. Money, the paper ruble, has no purchasing power. People forage and trade much as they did five centuries ago. A typical example:

Every morning in a Moscow high-level hospital, a nurse takes the ration cards of all the doctors and all the staff and goes food-hunting. By the end of the day she arrives with her trophies. A ruler is applied to a long sausage stick. Everyone gets an equally tiny piece.

Privileged bureaucrats do not measure their sausages in inches. Rubles in the hands of ordinary people are nearly worthless, because people with goods to sell want other goods in return; the rubles buy nothing. But rubles of the regional party boss and rubles of the ordinary peasant in the same region are different rubles. The ruble loses its power if you don't have special permission, in the form of a coupon, to buy specified goods.

Recently in several big cities, such as Leningrad and Chelyabinsk in the hungry Urals, enormous quantities of meat were discovered that had been hidden underground and allowed to rot. Was this sabotage by the right-wingers, who see crisis as their chance to reimpose dictatorship? I cannot prove it, but I certainly suspect this to be the case. And Gorbachev does not do anything to tame these diehard communists.

Back to the question of food aid to the Soviet Union: Western support for Gorbachev is one of the cornerstones of his drive for power. Foreign Minister Eduard Shevardnadze's dramatic, sacrificial resignation is already being forgotten. Roland Dumas, the French foreign minister, said, after Shevardnadze's resignation, that it is even more important to help Gorbachev now.

If the United States and Western Europe send food to Gorbachev's centralized Soviet government, here is what will happen: Distributing the food will fall to the KGB, according to Gorbachev's order. The KGB will distribute the food to its own people, to the army, and to the party bureaucrats. The food will show up in neither the state stores nor the private markets. Rather, part of it will be distributed through the system of stores known as *Raspredilitel*—stores at which only privileged party members are allowed to shop. Very little of the food will reach ordinary people.

With a satisfied army and KGB, Gorbachev will be ready to send troops to the rebellious republics. This will be the beginning of a bloody civil war.

If the West sends food, its distribution should be decentralized. Food should be earmarked to specific republics, cities, villages, hospitals, and orphanages where the need is greatest. It is possible, through the local authorities, to get the addresses of those in greatest need.

Unless the Soviet system is replaced, the country's 300 million people cannot be fed. By its very nature, socialism creates corruption and dishonor. Adam Smith wrote, in effect, that if today a country is without honor, tomorrow it will be without bread. The Soviet system lacks honor and deprives the people of their bread.

Part IV

MANAGEMENT SYSTEMS AND SCIENTIFIC TECHNICAL PROGRESS

BOARD OF DIRECTOR MOTIVATION IN RUSSIA AND THE COMMONWEALTH OF INDEPENDENT STATES

A Western-style corporate board of directors is a very new concept in Russia and the Commonwealth of Independent States (CIS). The events of the last eight years have influenced and altered the motivation or incentive for company directors to become members of these boards. To understand the current motivation of members of boards of directors, one must first consider the previous corporate governance structures in the Soviet Union and the way the present structure has developed.

Before the break-up of the Soviet Union in December 1991, the government structure included approximately 100 ministries, each of which had a "collegium" of about 12 appointed board members. Members of this collegium included the minister, deputy ministers, and heads of major departments of the ministry. This collegium was granted many government privileges, such as a country house, two months' salary for a thirty-day vacation at a free government spa, access to better-quality food at discount prices at special distribution centers, chauffeured limousines, private tailoring, access to books and publications with limited or no public distribution, free tickets to performances of the arts, no waiting in lines, etc.

These privileges were the motivation for reaching high-ranking positions within the ministry. Obviously, the incentives for reaching these high-level positions were different from incentives of board directors in a Western executive structure. In the Western structure, the primary motivations are monetary and the desire for long-term corporate success. Both incentives were missing in the Soviet structure.

Within the former Soviet Union, large companies or consortiums

Directorship, Inc.: Significant Issues Facing Directors, 1996 (Greenwich, Conn: Directorship, Inc., 1996), pp. 10–7 & 8.

had "ruling" boards that acted as advisory groups to the heads of the companies. Unlike members of the collegium of the ministries, board members did not have any special privileges; nor did they have any decision-making power. They simply acted as advisers, and were not given monetary compensation or other incentives.

The company-governing structure in the former Soviet Union changed drastically in January 1987, when the government made it possible to create joint ventures with foreign partners, and a Western-style executive structure was adopted for these ventures. Typically, the German structure was utilized in forming the hierarchy within these companies. The first joint ventures, 23 in total, were established in 1987. Each company had between five and seven directors on its board, who were nominated by the venture's owners. The selection of directors represented a split of company capital, and each director was responsible for his portion of the capital. Between the years 1987 and 1989, board members of these joint ventures did not receive monetary compensation. Again, they were motivated by the privileges associated with the high-level position. The main incentive for becoming a director was the opportunity to travel abroad for business, perhaps two or three times per year. This provided the chance to live in luxury, in a Western lifestyle, and to have contact with Western executives. Because the Soviet lifestyle still lacked the comforts and amenities of Western society, this was a welcome contrast to their lives at home.

With the decentralization of the Soviet Union and the development of the CIS, the economy underwent a transformation. For the most part, Soviet partners of joint ventures privatized their portions of the venture and became owners. (At the collapse of the Soviet Union in December 1991, there were more than 4,800 joint ventures. In comparison, by 1994 there were approximately 47,000 companies with foreign capital in the CIS.) The privatization of state-owned companies in 1991 had a big impact on executive motivation. This period marked a shift in the motivation of members of boards of directors toward monetary compensation and the goal of company success. In 1992, after the disintegration of the Soviet Union, all large companies, including banks, retail stores, manufacturing companies, service companies, etc., established boards of directors. Being only three years old, the history of the board of directors structure in Russia and the CIS is in its infancy.

The current situation in Russia and the CIS with respect to compensation is similar to that in other former Soviet-bloc countries, including Poland, Hungary, Bulgaria, etc. Typically, directors, who are not company employees (except the chairman of the board and the president), are paid annually, at the close of the fiscal year, December 31. Directors' salaries are based on company profits for the year ending. For example, about 15% of Russian companies pay the equivalent of two months of the CEO's salary to their directors. About 27% of Russian companies pay the equivalent of one month of the CEO's salary to their directors. The directors' salaries depend on company profit, because the CEO's salary depends on company profit. The remainder of the companies in Russia and the CIS do not pay their directors; again, the motivation for obtaining these positions is the associated privileges. In addition to a yearly compensation package, it is becoming more and more common for public companies to give their directors common stock for participating on their board.

Currently, there are no regulations for the method or disclosure of payment to executives in the CIS, and this has resulted in unethical activity. In fact, it is typical for directors to be handed an envelope full of money, and the source of the funds is unknown to the recipient. Privileges also remain a strong motivation for directors. Until the lifestyle for executives in Russia and the CIS becomes similar to that of the Western executive, Russian and CIS directors will value the privilege of international business travel.

A change in the typical structure of a large CIS company is currently evolving. As domestic companies strive to operate abroad, they have begun to internationalize their board of directors. Domestic and international executives who contribute to a company's attaining its goal of expanding global operations are selected as board members.

In summary, as a result of current events in the former Soviet Union, the executive structure of Russian and CIS companies has changed dramatically. Generally, the trend is toward the development of boards of directors, assimilating the Western democratic executive business structure. Along with this change in company structure, a change in motivation for the members of the boards of directors of these companies has emerged. Directors' incentives have shifted from strictly special privileges toward monetary compensation and the goal of corporate success. However, for Russian and CIS companies, this newly emerging corporate structure and motivation of directors is in its infancy, and it is expected that change will continue as companies develop further.

CONFRONTING THE SOVIET MANAGEMENT STRUCTURE: BUREAUCRATIC, BUT WORKABLE

The Soviet process of making managerial decisions is unusual for a Western executive to comprehend, because authority often rests in different hands. Consequently, foreign business people often knock on the wrong doors, overestimate the influence of ministries, underestimate the strength of enterprises, and cannot find an appropriate partner for joint ventures.

Now, after the signing of the trade agreement between the United States and the USSR, and in view of the democratization movement in the USSR, it is especially important for executives who would like to do business there to acquaint themselves with the large and complex Soviet management structure.

Lack of Experience

Most firms coming into the USSR have no experience in dealing with Soviet business-people and the Soviet market. For a Western businessperson to understand the Soviet management system, he or she has to be familiar with the various government bodies and the way they constitute the management system. Management methods are totally different from the West's, because for dozens of years these methods were tuned to administrative tasks rather than to economic incentives. Decision making in Soviet government units and business enterprises is drastically different from the West's, as is information gathering, processing, and distribution. Also, Soviet technical equipment lags behind the level of the rest of the world by at least 15 years.

For foreign firms trying to understand the Soviet management system, the first elements to become acquainted with are Soviet or-

The International Executive (November–December 1990), pp. 3–6.

ganizational structures. By understanding them, a firm opens the door to making good strategic decisions and choosing appropriate partners for their operations in the USSR.

Be on Guard

Too often, foreign companies lose a lot of time and money signing contracts or joint-venture agreements with Soviet organizations that are not legal entities and have no legal right to do so.

A legal entity has two special features: one, a stamp with the National Emblem and the name of the enterprise, and, two, a bank account.

If, for example, you receive a document from a Soviet state enterprise on which the director's signature is stamped but the National Emblem does not appear, it is possible that your partner has no right to sign a deal with you. However, even if the Soviet company meets all requirements, it is not enough for it to sign a joint-venture agreement or a barter deal with you. A Soviet firm can engage in foreign business only if it is registered as a "participant in foreign economic activity" with the Ministry for Foreign Economic Ties. This makes it a legal entity entitled to do business with foreign firms. Documentation proving this registration should be available to a foreign firm upon request.

In total, there are more than 1,153,000 legal entities in the USSR, but only about 17,000 companies of these have the right to deal internationally.

Three Stages

In looking for a Soviet partner, the *first* stage of your business research should be to find out whether the firm is a legal entity. The *second* stage is to find out whether this legal entity is permitted to participate in international economic activities.

The same requirements apply to joint ventures. Besides being registered with the Ministry of Finance, joint ventures must have the same certificate for participation in foreign economic activity that is issued by the Ministry for Foreign Economic Ties. Many joint ventures do not have this certificate. This is a harmful restriction that secures a monopoly for the Ministry for Foreign Economic Ties.

In any case, do not ignore the cumbersome bureaucratic procedures because doing so could have grave business consequences for your success in the Soviet market. For example, one of the major Soviet publishing houses, Molodya Gvardia, decided to acquire modern computer equipment for its printing facilities. Because the publishing house had almost no hard currency, it decided to pay for the computers in waste paper that it had in quantity. An Austrian company that sells computers agreed to supply the publishing house with computers and take the waste as barter. The agreement was signed by the director of the publishing house and the chairman of the Austrian company. The trading company, in turn, signed contracts to buy the computers and bought them. But the deal didn't go through.

The problem was that the Austrian businessman did not check on a most important detail: whether the Soviet company had the permission of GOSSNAB, the USSR State Distribution and Supplies Committee, to sell its waste. Permission is needed from this committee, because it regulates all the waste produced by USSR state enterprises. Each enterprise has a certain quota of waste that it must submit to this committee every year—whether it be paper, metal, or food products.

The Austrian businessman's mistake was largely a result of a different mindset. Of course, it is difficult for a Western executive to understand that a firm cannot legally dispose of even waste as it wants.

The *third* stage of research is to make sure the prospective Soviet partner is licensed to sell goods abroad.

License to Sell Abroad

In 1989, the USSR was the only country in the world that licensed exports, not imports. Even if GOSSNAB had allowed the publishing house to dispose of its waste, for example, the company still would have had to get a license from the Ministry for Foreign Ties to sell abroad.

If a foreign firm finds out that its Soviet partner does not have the necessary documents, the company should not wait until the Soviet partner obtains them. Rather, it should look for a strong Soviet partner that already has the necessary documents.

Keep in mind, too, that even if a Soviet partner is armed with all the necessary permissions, it is of the utmost importance whose signature is on the contract. It may be invalid according to Soviet law if it is signed by the wrong person or in the wrong way.

Law of Enterprises

On June 4, 1990, a new Law of Enterprises was adopted. It made the independence of a Soviet enterprise more viable as compared to the law adopted at the beginning of perestroika. The new law, effective in January 1991, has a special section about the management and self-management of enterprises. At last, an enterprise will become completely independent in defining its organizational structure. The new law also refers to joint ventures, defining for the first time the legal and economic notion of a joint venture according to law.

This law clearly defines the proprietor's rights in managing the enterprise independently or through the bodies to which it delegates its rights. The proprietor, for example, now has a clear right to hire a manager. This was out of the question in former years. Only the ministries and the party committees could do it.

In addition, the new Law of Enterprise confirms the rights of the working collectives to define the main direction of the enterprise's development, distribution of profits, and whether it buys or issues shares if a director recommends such action.

Accounting Problems

To fully understand the huge Soviet management machine, it is necessary to have an idea about the breadth and weaknesses of its structure. Consider: Bookkeepers and accountants make up a huge army engaged in routine assignments. Yet the Soviet system does not work, in part because even these people themselves do not know the modern language of business. This is one of the foremost weaknesses of the Soviet management system.

For example, when I became deputy chairman of a major Siberian company, the organization lacked capital, to such an extent that it could not meet payroll. Managers tried solving the problem by reducing the stores of raw materials in the warehouses and trimming salaries, but they still could not make ends meet. Surprisingly, none of the managers thought to check the balance sheet.

After inspecting the balance sheet, I found that the problem stemmed from the fact that a lot of parts were still being manufactured that were no longer used in the final product. As a result, these parts sat idle in storage.

The simple solution was to sell those parts to other organizations that could use them. The point is that 90% of the Soviet managers could not envision this solution because they have engineering educations, not economic ones.

Ronald Weiner, president of Weiner Associates. a well-established New York certified public accounting firm, says that the Soviet Union urgently needs auditing firms that can audit existing companies and advise them on operating in today's changing business environment. American accounting firms can assist in organizing proper cooperation between the State and companies, advising firms on how to maximize after-tax savings, verifying the financial status of foreign companies willing to sign contracts with Soviet partners, and checking the validity of financial commitments made by Soviet organizations. Since the Soviet government no longer guarantees the debts of Soviet companies, it is especially important for a Western company to have information about the ability of the Soviet partner to meet its financial commitments.

I think that the very notion of the USSR will disappear rather soon from the political maps of the world, but organizational problems will remain for a long time in the new confederation of the former republics—and in Russia itself, which constitutes 77% of the USSR's territory.

Shift of Power

Without question, 1990 was a turning point for the Soviet Union. First, the Baltic republic declared its independence, then Moldavia did the same. Finally, on June 12, the Supreme Council of Russia, under the leadership of Boris Yeltsin, approved the Declaration of Sovereignty. The Republic of Uzbekistan went further, saying that it regards the USSR as a foreign state. In July, Ukraine and Byelsrussia followed, as did Armenia in August. Yeltsin now has the task of cutting the tentacles of the ministries and the central party machine from the Russian territory.

Nonetheless, while the critical situations are still ahead, risk-analysis shows a very high reliability and efficiency of investments in some regions of the USSR. The economic and political crisis in the USSR does not argue against the advisability of investing there. Indeed, investments in certain regions within the Russian Federation are no less reliable and efficient than investments in the United States. It is just that the factors of risk are different.

MOSCOW LEARNS THE LANGUAGE OF BUSINESS

Integrating a government-run economy into the global marketplace takes more than exchangeable currency, stock markets, and commercial banks. Much more.

Five years ago, Soviet President Mikhail Gorbachev set in motion the gears of perestroika, the restructuring initiative aimed at increasing Soviet productivity. In September he backed a proposal by Republic of Russia President Boris Yeltsin to implement a free-enterprise economy within 500 days. One of its goals is to integrate the Soviet economy into the global marketplace by adjusting Soviet business practices to mesh with those of the free market. The USSR has made certain strides toward establishing the systems and institutions necessary to expedite its full participation in international commerce. The achievements and shortcomings are explored here.

The focus of the business world has shifted to Moscow. With the advent of perestroika, the Soviet Union's industrial infrastructure, the volume of its products, the extent of its debts, and the inadequacies of its accounting system have fallen under the scrutiny of businesses from Tokyo to New York to Paris. One thing foreign investors and entrepreneurs are finding is confusion. In a country where an accounting profession has never existed, financial numbers tend not to mean much. The valuation of assets, for example, has been so theoretical that it is, for all practical purposes, useless. In fact, Soviet accounting is really no more than a bookkeeping system managed by low-level retired women and inexperienced new graduates of technical schools. In addition, financial and accounting information has, in the past, been distorted by the government in the pseudo-interest of national security. Further complicating the situation, prices have been distorted by the arbitrary introduction into the marketplace of billions of unbacked rubles—18 billion rubles last year alone—by the government, which has run the banks.

The Journal of Accountancy (November 1990), pp. 114–119.

Incorrect or non-existent financial information can mean trouble for both foreign and Soviet companies that want to invest in the Soviet Union. The problem must be solved on several fronts.

Creation of Commercial Banks

First, the Soviet economy needs a new, independent national bank that is subordinate only to the Supreme Soviet (the Soviet parliament) and the law. The current state bank obeys the Council of Ministers formally but, in fact, responds to pressure from the Central Committee of the Communist Party. A phone call from this committee is enough to justify printing more rubles. The lack of backing by any standard or commodity leads inexorably to inflation.

In addition to the circulating of worthless rubles, two other factors doom attempts at economic reform. One is the fact that banks pay interest of only 2% to 3% a year—far less than my estimated inflation rate of 18%. Citizens therefore keep their money at home, ready to spend should an opportunity arise. The other factor is the scarcity of products. When consumers have cash in hand, nothing to buy, and no reason to save, prices will inevitably rise.

Until 1986, there were three Soviet banks, all state-owned. In 1988, three more state banks, also run by the government, were formed for specific financial purposes: construction of housing, schools, and hospitals, agricultural investment, and saving.

In that same year, the first commercial banks were also opened. These cooperative, publicly held banks were not state banks, although industrial ministries were among the founders of some of them. For example, Tehknobank was created at the initiative of the city council of Moscow. Capital of 6.2 million rubles was raised in shares valued at 100,000 rubles. Shareholders received a 5% return at the end of the first year. Tehknobank already has lent money to transportation cooperatives, and to support the growth of consumer goods it plans to lend to military factories that are converting to civilian production.

The second non–state bank, the new Credobank, is licensed to open foreign currency accounts for enterprises doing business abroad. For the first time, hard currency on account in a Russian commercial bank can be given to bank customers in any country in the world or deposited in any foreign bank. This means that Credobank also can pay dividends in foreign currency.

The existence of such banks surprises both Soviet and Western business people. Westerners are surprised to find that commercial banks are only now beginning to operate and that there still are no private banks; Soviets are surprised to see such revolutionary new banking concepts in their country. These banks are totally commercial enterprises, creating their own financial data. Three hundred such commercial banks will facilitate the creation of a modern accounting system.

Formulating New Credit and Budget Policies

In all probability, the specialized state banks will be turned into specialized commercial banks, and the central State Bank eventually will become independent of the prime minister and cease the arbitrary issuance of paper money. This will bring about the second major change needed to correct a fundamental problem with the Soviet economy: a new credit and budget policy. New policies will limit budgetary spending which, in turn, will limit inflation.

The state budget in 1989 allotted 20.24 billion rubles to the military, but, in newspaper accounts two months later, the Soviet minister of defense said military spending had surpassed 70 billion rubles.

Both these figures are wrong. The problem is that the accounting and bookkeeping system of the individual ministries (and of enterprises) does not correlate with the methods of the central government budget calculation. This has led to a budget deficit which I estimate for 1990 at more than 100 billion rubles (the official estimate is 50 billion rubles), which is about 11.5% of the gross national product.

It would seem that, under such conditions, the government would restrict credit, but the interest rate on credit remains only 2%. Even more absurd, credit is granted to enterprises facing bankruptcy. Also, a number of joint ventures involving foreign companies have taken advantage of this inexpensive money to increase their cash position.

Establishing Stock Exchanges

In the near future, foreign enterprises in the Soviet Union can expect higher interest rates. They also can expect some revolutionary new avenues of investment on the Soviet scene: stocks, bonds, and other commercial paper.

In early 1990, a few publicly held companies were created and a few stocks are circulating. In July, the USSR Council of Ministers adopted two regulations dealing with stockholding and shares. In the same month, one of the largest state banks, Zhilsotsbank, was turned into a stockholding commercial bank by the Kremlin, with foreign entities and individuals allowed to buy shares in it.

The decentralization of the banking system was accelerated when the parliament of Russia, the USSR's largest republic, declared on July 13 the creation of a state bank in its territory, independent of the USSR state bank. Such decisions create the necessary elements for a market economy in the Republic of Russia. Preliminary discussions are under way in the Supreme Council to pass laws that will enable foreign business people to be among the founders and shareholders of Soviet enterprises.

The Soviet Union has no experience in this area. Cooperation with the West will be essential in the complex process of issuing, buying, selling, and overseeing stocks, bonds, and other instruments.

The emergence of a stock exchange depends on two conditions. One is an agreement among several state banks concerning the operating rules for trading securities. Also, given the totalitarian history of the Soviet Union, it will be important that exchange operations and share possession be anonymous.

To develop a free-market economy, it will be necessary to establish and operate a stock exchange and privatize at least 50% of state-owned companies. Brokers, who do not yet exist in the Soviet Union, also will be necessary; this means that new training programs will have to be developed.

Expanding Commodities Exchanges

In May 1990, the first Board of Trade, a commodities exchange, was created. In September it became operational. The founders of the Board are a number of Soviet enterprises and cooperatives and a Soviet–Yugoslavian–Italian joint venture. Initially, the Board of Trade mostly will carry out barter operations.

In spite of the current scarcity of goods in the Soviet Union, the

Board of Trade will become the heart pumping blood into the new arteries of the market. Available goods will come not only from the allowed inventory levels worth 500 billion rubles but also from another 200 billion rubles' worth of hoarded goods being stored by enterprises.

Such inventories during times of inflation and scarcity might surprise some Westerners. One reason for the storage tactic is that the ruble is all but worthless. Enterprises have little success trying to use rubles to buy production materials. Domestic bartering proves more effective, though, of course, more awkward. For example, a company would more readily procure bricks by proffering, say, telephones than it would by paying in rubles.

Accounting System

Perhaps one of the most important changes that must take place is in the field of accounting. The current system does not allow for the realistic valuation of products or assets. For example, the concepts of depreciation and current market value do not exist. These gaps lead to disparities between government and commercial financial numbers. The inaccuracies also make it difficult for managers and potential investors to make educated decisions.

Until this summer, there was only one auditing entity in the Soviet Union, IN-AUDIT, which was created by the Ministry of Finance to oversee joint ventures with foreign companies. It did not audit Soviet enterprises. This summer, two foreign accounting firms, Ernst & Young and Arthur Andersen & Co., were licensed to practice in the Soviet Union. More will certainly follow, but, for the time being, the concept of auditing is quite new to Soviet enterprises.

The presence of accounting firms will lead to the creation of a genuine accounting profession in the Soviet Union. Currently, the accountant/bookkeeper has little prestige and earns less than half the salary of an engineer or economist; but accountants are going to prove essential in the shift to a free-market economy with international connections. If accounting is the language of business, Soviet accountants are going to have to learn that language and create a Soviet dialect.

In June, President Gorbachev signed the Law of Enterprises of the

USSR. It will take effect on January 1, 1991. The law states that all companies, whether state-owned or private, have equal rights. (A law governing foreign investment and joint ventures is being drafted now.) The Law of Enterprises also protects commercial secrets. No one—government, union or industrial ministry—can usurp the right to financial information not specifically required by financial reporting law.

Three articles of the new law deal specifically with accounting: Article 32 is devoted to the operational accounting and bookkeeping at enterprises; Article 34 defines the responsibility of enterprises to follow accounting and tax regulations; Article 35 legalizes government audits for tax purposes but specifies that the government may request only relevant information.

The law also allows, for the first time in Soviet history, an enterprise to declare bankruptcy. Previously. there was no such term in Soviet law; enterprises suffering losses got subsidies from the state. When a Soviet or joint-venture enterprise is being closed, a special abolition committee has to be created to assess debts and investigate the creditors' claims. After all claims are satisfied, the employees and foreign investors of the enterprise receive their investment in either currency or securities.

In May 1990, the Soviet Union also adopted its first tax law. It embraces joint ventures and other organizations created with the participation of foreign entities and Soviet and foreign citizens. The law gives official tax inspectors the right to check such an enterprise's monetary documents, bookkeeping records, and other documents relating to the payment of taxes; to fine enterprises; and even to shut down their operations.

By September, 2,060 joint-ventures had been registered in the Soviet Union—1,200 of them in Moscow, where a state tax inspection office is being created with help from the New York City accounting firm of Weiner Associates. Overall, Soviet enterprises involved in foreign economic relations and joint ventures totaled 17,000 as of September 1. Obviously, there exists tremendous interest in foreign trade and, necessarily, international accounting practices.

Moving Forward

The establishment of tax audits, the development of a banking system, and the introduction of auditing firms are beginning to create opportunities for Western business people who want objective information about the financial status of a potential partner in a trade deal or a joint venture. They also make it possible, in some cases, for Soviet organizations to guarantee payment for foreign goods purchased, which has not been possible since the government stopped backing all foreign trading.

As long as Soviet and international accounting practices differ and there is no common language for expressing financial information, Soviet and Western companies will have to be careful when they deal with one another. Western companies need to understand the Soviet tax structure and the lack of a coherent system of accounting for financial transactions. Soviet enterprises, having little or no international business experience, will need the help of auditing firms to interpret financial information.

One thing is clear. The Soviet Union's dramatic progress toward a free-market economy can go only so far before the lack of an adequate accounting system derails all financial dealings. But with private banking controlled by established laws, with financial reporting overseen by independent auditors, and with modern, internationally recognized accounting methods, the Soviet Union will quickly join the world of global commerce.

Executive Summary

- The USSR is poised to enter the global market on a grand scale just five years after President Mikhail Gorbachev announced perestroika, his political reform package.
- In reshaping its economic infrastructure to conform with Western practices, the USSR is creating new and independent commercial banks that deal in hard currencies.
- A non–state-run banking system is the first step in controlling inflation and the indiscriminate issuance of worthless rubles.
- For an accounting system, the Soviets must look to the West for help since neither a reliable system nor knowledgeable accountants are needed in a government-run economy.
- From the West also must come the expertise to establish and maintain stock exchanges and train their traders and brokers.
- New laws protecting the rights of Soviet citizens and foreigners who invest and operate private businesses were adopted in May 1990. Also enacted were the USSR's first tax laws, covering joint ventures and other transactions involving foreign participation.

THE RELATIONSHIP BETWEEN INCREASES IN CAPITAL INVESTMENT AND THE REDUCTION IN THE DURATION OF THE IMPLEMENTATION PHASE

The length of time required to put new technological processes and systems into use can be significantly affected by the application of the latest scientific and technical research. This application will impact both the costs of the new technology and a company's overall expenditures. For this reason, when calculating the effectiveness and annual economic benefit of the new technology (NT), all aspects of the implementation phase should appear as part of the total costs associated with its development and introduction. However, by its nature, the character of these costs is not one-sided. Expenses for NT development appear as expenses in the area of applied research and engineering, that is, as practical expenses associated with scientific and technological development (STD). Installation costs actualize this STD. Outlays for installation significantly affect the length of time between the development phase of the NT and its productive use. Clearly, there is a direct correlation between the level of installation expenditure and the length of time—an increase in expenditure effects a reduction in the length of the implementation phase. Indeed, the costs of putting NT into operation are significant and often are comparable to the cost of the NT itself. Experience shows that the manpower involved in the technical preparation of new production can amount to up to 30% of the overall manpower necessary for STD.

In scientific literature, publications specifically dedicated to questions of determining the economic effectiveness of these processes of implementation are practically nonexistent. Nor in more general

In *Economic Problems of the Implementation of Scientific and Technical Projects* (Moscow: The Institute of the Economy of the USSR Academy of Sciences, Moscow, 1987), pp. 21–25.

works analyzing the economic effectiveness of NT has this problem been satisfactorily addressed.

Defining the economic effectiveness of the installation phase cannot be done outside the framework of the general question of the effectiveness of NT. Therefore, the major criteria in calculating the effectiveness of this initial phase should be the same as that used in calculating the effectiveness of the NT as a whole, that is, increased output and improved quality of the company's product. At the same time, it is clear that the specific nature of the installation (implementation) process requires a different approach in determining cost effectiveness at that stage.

The element of time should be a determining factor in calculating cost effectiveness. In other words, all expenses the company incurs in technical preparation should be directed toward minimizing the time required for installing, adjusting, and launching the NT and achieving planned capacity. Factors preceding preparations—for example, choosing the object of STD, and the like—should function in the same way.

Considering such, in calculating the economic effect of accelerating the preparation and installation phase, the following sequence should be observed.

At the first stage, the annual economic effect of creating and implementing the NT is determined:

$$E_{ann} = \left[\frac{(Y_2 - Y_1)}{Y_1} \times Pl + \frac{(C_1 - C_2)}{100} \times Y_2 \right] - E_c \times C_{di}$$

where:

E_{ann} = the annual economic effect;
Y_1, Y_2 = the volume of goods sold the year before and the year after NT installation ($1,000);
C_1, C_2 = costs per $1.00 of goods sold before and after NT implementation;
P_1 = profits from goods sold before NT implementation ($1,000)

In this case,

$$\left[\frac{(Y_2 - Y_1)}{Y_1} \times P_1 + \frac{(C_1 - C_2)}{100} \times Y_2 \right]$$

is the annual increase in profits $= {}_A P$

where

E_c = standard coefficient of economic effectiveness of capital investments (0.12);

C_{di} = costs of NT development and implementation ($1,000);

$C_{di} = C_d + C_i$, where C_d = costs of development

C_i = costs of implementation

The annual economic effect gives an idea of the extent of NT economic effectiveness, with consideration given to all the costs of NT development and installation.

The effectiveness of these costs may be defined according to the formulas:

$$E_e = \frac{{}_A P}{C_{di}} = \frac{\left[\dfrac{(Y_2 - Y_1)}{-Y_1} \times P_1 + \dfrac{(C_1 - C_2)}{100} \times Y_2\right]}{C_c + C_i} \quad E_e > E_n;$$

where:

E_e = estimated coefficient of cost effectiveness.

At the same time, cost-recovery time will equal:

$$T = C_d + \frac{C_i}{P},$$

where

T = cost-recovery time in terms of years.

If, to reduce the cost-recovery time (T), one minimizes development and implementation costs (C_{di}) as much as possible, thereby making E_e larger than E_i, then the time factor would not be accounted for. The completion time of the cost-recovery (T) period is then postponed to the implementation period. Meanwhile, it is obvious that the time element is a very significant factor in the economy, because it strongly affects the rate of economic growth. The overall economic benefit of NT implementation, which will be realized over a long period of time, is not proportionate to the benefit gained in the initial stages, starting from the beginning of the implementation process.

In our case, this problem becomes one of considering the time factor with varying implementation costs. In considering increasing investment to accelerate the introduction of NT, however, one should not set as obligatory the condition of increasing the absolute sum of costs of this process, but rather increase costs in a time unit of the implementation period that would intensify all operations at this stage of the research and production cycle. But if increasing expenses in the time unit will require an increase of total costs and, therefore, the cost-recovery time, the challenge is to determine the optimal limits that will make increasing implementation costs economically effective.

Let us consider an example. Y_1, Y_2 = \$300,000 and \$400,000, respectively; C_1, C_2 = \$0.90 and \$0.75, respectively; P_1 = \$1,200,000. In this case, the increase in profit after NT implementation will equal:

$$_A P = \frac{(Y_2 - Y_1)}{Y_1} \times P_1 + \frac{(C_1 - C_2)}{100} \times Y_2 = \$406,000.$$

Let us assume that NT development and implementation costs amount to \$1,015,000; concurrently C_{di} = C_d = C_i = \$675,000 + \$340,000. In this case, cost-recovery time will equal:

$$T_1 = \frac{C_{di}}{_A P} = \$1,015,000/\$406,000 = 2.5 \text{ years.}$$

Let us further assume that NT implementation costs (C_i) increase by \$160,000; that is,

$$C_{di} = C_d + C_i I = \$675,000 + \$500,000 = \$1,175,000.$$

Meanwhile, cost-recovery time gets longer:

$$T_2 = \frac{C_{1ai}}{P} = 2.9 \text{ years.}$$

At the same time, NT implementation time decreases to 0.5 years because of intensification of the implementation process at the expense of increasing costs.

By increasing the cost-recovery period, according to the second version, by 0.4 years, we will reduce the economic effectiveness of the implemented NT. However, by increasing the cost-recovery period, we have reduced the implementation period; and at the expense of this, we began to obtain the effect from NT implementation 0.6 years earlier. The sum of the effect equals:

$$E_{add} = P \times T = \$406,000 \times 0.6 = \$243,600,$$

where:

$$T = (T_1 + T_{p1}) - (T_2 + T_{p2}).$$

Despite increasing costs and increasing the cost-recovery period in the second version, additional profits, which will be obtained by the end of the six-year period, equal:

$$P_2 = E_{add} - C_{i'} = \$243,000 - \$160,000 = \$83,600$$

where:

$$C_{i'} = C_{1i} - C_i.$$

Thus, in some instances it is useful to increase implementation costs on the condition that, as the result of this increase, there will be a decrease in the implementation period, and the total amount of this decrease will exceed the decrease of the cost-recovery period.

THE PROCESS OF FORMING A REGIONAL POLICY ON SCIENCE AND TECHNOLOGY

Paramount among the goals of a regional policy on science and technology is the creation of conditions, through advances in research and technology, for bolstering the health of current and future populations. By nature, it is a social goal; its success will be manifested in the sphere of economic policy and measured by the increased efficiency of regional work groups. This goal corresponds with the ultimate goal of socialist production and is perceived, at the regional-complex level, as a subsystem of the overall economic system.

In my opinion, analysis, based on scientific and technological progress, of the ultimate goal of regional-level production also contributes to resolving the issue. First, the most significant potential combinations of socialist advantages and achievements of the scientific and technological revolution are realized; and, second, on a regional level, the practical significance of the most important principle of the whole economic system is fully revealed: democratic centralism's role in the scope of the ultimate goal of production (in its structure) and in reflecting people's interests and demands for greater satisfaction, with consideration of real opportunities at every level of social development.

Specifying regional scientific and technological policy goals in a new period of political forecasting, and creating a hierarchical system of subgoals and subtasks, are linked to conducting a resource analysis of the major factors forming a given policy. At the same time, the collective significance of interregional factors is also being determined, based on the selection of priorities of policy goals, and, further, on the basis of priorities for predicting the scientific and technological development of the labor and production forces in the region.

Excerpt from *The Management of Scientific and Technical Progress: A Regional Aspect* (Moscow: Science Publishing House, 1986).

In analyzing research and development (R&D) problems of the regional program of scientific and technological progress in the Sverdlovsk region, V. Manukhin highlighted the fact that "the question of priorities is one of the most important. Therefore, it is necessary to choose those sectors that should be mechanized first and correlate them with our capabilities."

The basis for forming a regional scientific and technical policy is, by its very definition, to form a comparable national policy on science and technology. The conception of a ranking national institutional policy serves as the launching point for forming the lower levels of a hierarchical policy. A consolidated national policy for advancement in science and technology is reflected in the complex programs for resolving the most important scientific and technological problems, and in the five-year plan's "Scientific and Technological Research and Development" sector. On a regional level, the content of these documents is considered from the vantage point of state specialization, in the light of a region's social and economic orientation, and with consideration of the actual regional resources and opportunities for their inclusion in the state's economic turnover. At higher levels of authority, a scientific and technological policy has a specifying influence on that policy in the given region.

The policy of enterprises that function in, or are destined for, a regional territory in accordance with planning or preliminary R&D significantly influences the regional scientific and technological policy. First, the enterprises' policy on science and technology impacts the regional policy through the complex program of scientific research and development of the district. These programs anticipate increasing the scientific and technological level of operating unions and enterprises in a district, major changes in their technology, and implementation of new production capabilities based on utilization of advances in science and technology. Second, the ministries' influence is carried out through the district's scientific and technological programs for mastering the production of new commodities and through the district's efforts to realize the national goals of the science and technology programs. Third, there should be interaction between planned execution of the regional scientific and technology policy and the ministries' district plans (in the "Scientific and Technological Research and Development" section of the 5-year plan).

Furthermore, factors inherent in the system of the nation's collective science and technology policy, the social and economic policy of the region, and the concept of developing its production capabilities in accordance with the general scheme of developing and allocating production capacity influence regional scientific and technological policy. In other words, in predictive scenarios of the scientific and technological development of the regional economic complex, the main goals of social and economic scenarios are reflected. Such is the beginning of the scientific and technological attainment of the economic and social policy goals. For instance, the strategies of the agrarian regional policy, as a subsystem of an economic policy, may obtain agricultural resources and time characteristics only after specifying the material and technological basis and the scientific aspects of the strategic actions. However, this requires development of the scientific and technological regional policy in order to correlate all district policies on science and technology. Out of such regional and district forecasting scenarios, a major portion of the scientific and technological development scenario of the country's economy gradually develops.

The regional resource opportunities are significant interregional factors of a regional science and technology policy. Also, though located in the regions of pioneering economic development, natural resource factors play a major role in economically mature regions, in the resources of production capability, in the scientific and technological possibilities, etc. Currently the relative deficit in the labor force has significantly increased as a factor in the resource balance of most regions of the country. Even for labor-rich regions of Central Asia, Azerbaijan, and Daghestan, this factor is a defining one, because priorities of the science and technology policy in those regions should contribute to involving the able-bodied population of the region in national production. As such, resource analysis should continually be targeted as a chief goal. Concurrently, the traditional approach to estimating the economic effectiveness of involving regional resources in the economic turnover of the country can be augmented by estimating the impact of this process on the ecology of the natural environment and the population of the region.

As our research shows, the results of the resource analysis should be reflected in the projected scenario of the scientific and technological development of the productive forces of the region and, thus, should influence the setting of priority goals. In the process of resource analysis, there should be considered a defining sense of setting a shared science and technology policy, as well as the social and economic strategy of the region. That is why, at this stage, it is already important to define the scientific and technological opportunities when allocating resource obligations of a given region to other regions of the country in accordance with nationwide planning. Then, the preliminary resource balance of the regional scientific and technological policy goals will indicate the respective perspectives. Thereupon, the resources that need be obtained from other regions in order to realize these goals can be defined. Once priority goals are established, the resource balance should be determined.

The priority goals of a rational scientific and technological policy should be defined in four dimensions: territory, common-district, inter-district, and district.

The territorial dimension permits defining the priorities of regional scientific and technological development as a whole, in connection with the ecology and the complex use of land, water, wood, energy resources, etc. Setting territorial priorities is connected to the participation and obligations of a given region in interregional labor specialization and in interregional cooperation vis-à-vis scientific and technological potentials.

Common-district priorities permit resource concentration in the goals common to the majority or to all districts of the regional economic complex. This might be the development and production of equipment for the execution of regional policy. Thus, to illustrate, practically all enterprises functioning in the north and northeastern parts of the country require equipment designed for use in extremely cold climates (CC). In total, during the 10th 5-year plan, 30,000 pieces of construction machinery and equipment and 17,500 cars were produced for such use. The 11th 5-year plan designates production of 45,000 CC pieces of construction machinery of 30 types. Given projected increases in industry and transport development in the northern regions, this volume of CC equipment is insufficient. For this reason, in several regions of Siberia and the Far East, programs are being developed to design, produce, refurbish, and implement CC machinery. In other words, we are talking about a prioritized common-district task for these regions; executing this task is possible with the use of a common-district program, and a regional program for scientific and technological advancement as well. Common-district, as well as inter-district, priorities include mechanization, automation, robotization of production, utilization of laser technologies, etc.

The inter-district dimension of defining goal priorities shows those trends of scientific and technological development that, in a number of regions, secures an effect that results from the interaction of several regional district complexes. The resources and efforts of scientific and technological potential should be concentrated on these trends. To successfully clarify the priority tasks, regional inter-district programs may be developed, and multi-district regional scientific and technological unions and complementary industrial plants may be created.

An example of such a scientific and technological task may be the various electronic and chemical multi-product technological complexes that are being created in a number of regions. Thus, in connection with the imminent mastering and exploitation of the apatit (a calcium phosphate mineral) fields in Maymecha-Koltuy province, it is possible to extract the chemical- and metallurgy-enriching copper-nickel ores (concentrates) of the Norilsk ore area through the use of phosphorus acid, which is derived from the apatits of the given province, and, thus, realize the simultaneous production, in the common technological cycle, of the nonferrous metals and phosphorus fertilizers as well. Priority realization of such inter-district programs will allow the attainment of economic benefits not only in a few industrial districts, but also in agriculture and the entire agro-industrial complex as well.

In particular, in nonferrous metallurgy, this will allow the avoidance of less productive physical methods of enrichment and secure the production of additional commodity products, with overall costs diminished by 35% to 40%. In agriculture, increased efficiency of farming based on the large-scale use of phosphorus fertilizers is being secured.

On the whole, the described technology is an example of rational technologies developed on the basis of the interconnection of technological links of enterprises in a couple of districts in the region. This interconnection may be (as in this case) a result of solving tasks through a more complex use of regional natural resources. Regional technologies are also being developed for the purpose of the further processing of raw materials and byproducts of enterprises in different regional districts, and organizing technological complexes for collective inter-district use, etc.

Thus, in choosing the priority goals in the scientific and technological development of regional district complexes, the resource aspect of the problem obtains top priority. If there is a labor shortage in the region, then it is necessary to develop new non-human production methods, and reconstruct and modernize the old ones based on implementing labor-saving scientific and technological solutions.

The scientific and technological policy of corresponding economic districts in the country significantly influences the formation of the regional district priorities. However, the district and regional interests may not be consistent.

A narrow-district approach to estimating effectiveness may show that creating new enterprises on the basis of new technologies—powder metallurgy and biotechnological complexes—is more economical in the developed regions, which have a mature social and living infrastructure. However, the regional aspect of a common national scientific and technological policy is oriented, for example, toward building such enterprises in the regions of pioneering mastering with the low total volume of the old main production funds. At the same time, the priorities of the scientific and technological policy of the developed region may show higher effectiveness through the reconstruction of old enterprises on a principally new technological basis.

At the stage of setting the priorities of the scientific and technological policy of the region, the directions of optimization of its industrial structure are defined. For example, the structure of the regional energy balance may be regulated; here the district aspect or the regional scientific and technological policy specifies and adds propositions from the perspective of ministries and administrations of the fuel and energy complex in the country. The regional scientific and technological policy in the end should always be oriented to the regional human population ecology. Setting the priorities of this policy, balanced with the resource potentials of the region, leads to individualization, in various regions, of the cost structure in the sphere of scientific and technological progress. Priorities should implement achievements from scientific and technological progress in those particular regional economic complexes that disturb its balance.

The resource analysis of the goals and prognoses of regional development allows the defining of which resources are correspondent with the level of interregional needs, and which resources are correspondent with the regional goals in the overall state specialization. However, only those resources obtain scientific and technological priority that either are insufficient to allow the region to solve its tasks, or are so significant and multi-complex that a developed technological level does not secure their full and complex utilization.

Forming the strategy of the regional scientific and technological policy on the basis of chosen priorities allows securing the proportionate development of the region in accordance with orientation of the common state policy in this sphere, that is, securing the regional economic balance. This opportunity is reached through the use of a tactical block of the regional scientific and technological policy and effective functioning of the mechanism for its realization. Consistent realization of the strategy and continual orientation toward the main goal free this policy from the entry of elements that reflect subjective interests of separate links in the regional economic system. We are talking about those interests that disturb the economic balance and the regional scientific and technological development as a subsystem of the common economic complex of the country.

Setting the priority goals and prognoses and conducting the resource balance create conditions for the interactive macro-aggregate modeling of the district and territory proportions of scientific and technological contributions to the enlargement of regional reproduction.

At this stage, the first interaction of conceptual modeling is carried out, and it is expedient to use the exponents of modeling in the inter-district and inter-regional optimization of the model. This allows for coordinating more accurately the regional scientific and technological development with the goals of the common state scientific and technological policy, with its district subsystems, and with the scientific and technological policy in the higher hierarchy regions. The problem of modeling the regional scientific and technological policy is not sufficiently developed. With this goal, the utilization of the mechanism of multilevel (depending on the regional hierarchy, the scientific and technological policy of which is being developed) imitation modeling seems effective. It is important to emphasize that the absence of adequate models and their systems for managing regional scientific and technological development on a strategic level decreases the effectiveness of regional and state governance of scientific and technological progress as a whole. In large part, the development of a model level of managing the scientific and technological progress is bogged down by an insufficient level of theoretical understanding of the regional scientific and technological policy as an economic category.

As a result of realizing the described steps in developing the regional scientific and technological policy, its concept is formed. The concept must take into consideration the scientific and technological level of the regional economic complex and the level and perspective trends of the regional scientific and technological development potential. The concept should include the extended estimation of the effectiveness of the accepted version of the scientific and technological policy. By representing the basis for forming the complex regional scientific and technological program, the concept reflects a thesis of a collective national policy in the scientific and technological progress sphere, and the concept, in turn, influences the formation of the schemes for developing and allocating the regional labor force on the basis of directing the regional economic and social development.

The process of forming the strategy for the regional scientific and technological policy concludes by preparing the complex regional scientific and technological program. This document is implemented not only by means of all elements of the tactical block, but also through the subregional levels of science and technology policy (regarding economic regions, these are province, industrial complex, etc.) and the major economic structures, that is, production unions and enterprises.

In previous works, we studied the problem of forming the scientific and technological policy of enterprises and unions; here we will present only the formalized structure of this process (see the scheme below), which is specified in the given study.

It is necessary to begin developing the tactical block of the regional scientific and technological policy on the basis of an analysis of the region.

The resources of the accepted version of the strategy are secured. The especially important question in the tactical block is perfecting the structure of the administrations that govern the scientific and technological progress in the region. First of all, this is the least developed element in the entire organizational structure governing the economy. Second, in connection with the objective necessity of strengthening the combination of state, district, and territory approaches toward governing, the significance of effectively managing the scientific and technological progress in the region increases immensely.

The factual absence of the independent administrations of the state in governing scientific and technological progress in the regional organization structures (first, in the composition of the regional deputy committees) led to forming a broad and differentiated chain of public organizations for managing this sphere in many regions of the country. Therefore, at the stage of forming policy tactics, it is even more important to define those regional public-organizing forms of integrating research projecting the production, and implementing and exploiting new equipment, that showed their effectiveness in the process of experimental use in a few regions during the preceding planned period. On the whole, at this stage, the necessary regional economic experiments are planned, as are those actions of the regional scientific and technological policy which are to be tested in the course of the experiment.

The tactical block has a more developed plan and program dimension than the strategic block. At a given stage, the major regional goal of the scientific and technological program, the list of the most significant regional scientific and technological problems, and actions of the section "The development of science and technology" of the plan for the complex economic and social development of the region are defined. In forming these materials, consideration is given to corresponding state and district programs and plans, the complex regional program of scientific and technological progress for a 20-year period, and the suggestions for scientific and technological development received from regional research and manufacturing organizations. The system of interconnection of the major program and plan documents, which develops on the state, district, and region levels in the process of forming and implementing the regional scientific and technological policy, is presented in scheme 4.

In the process of the tactical development of the policy, the methodical recommendations for organizing and managing regional scientific and technological progress should be viewed and accepted.

The success of the policy in the sphere of scientific and technological progress is defined, in large part, by the speed with which scientific thought passes through every stage of the "science–technology–production" cycle. It is important to secure the clear and reliable interconnection between the organizational economic links that implement each step of the cycle. Here, the impact of such an economic law as the law of the time economy fully manifests itself.

During the years of the 11th 5-year plan in the country, along with the district forms, various regional forms were developed for integrating, constructing, projecting, producing, and implementing organizations, which accelerate the processing of scientific thought to the degree of their broad use in the regional economic complex. In a number of regions in the country, the regional scientific and productive unions, institutions, and constructive and productive organizations of districts are functioning. Also, they are operating not only as public structures (as in the experience of the Lvov region), but also as double- or triple-subjection structures (as with the scientific and productive union of powder metallurgy to the Board of Ministers in Belorussia and others).

The tactical development of the regional scientific and technological policy should take into consideration the progressive experience of the functioning of these unions of scientific, technological, and productive potentials of the regions, should recommend the broad disbursement of their most effective forms, and should contribute to the acceleration of their normative and legal appropriation and formation.

After initially choosing a tactical version of the substantial strategy (during the process of the first interaction of conceptual modeling), it is expedient to conduct the next step of conceptual modeling, which will allow one the selection of a version of the regional scientific and technological policy that will maximize the regional economic benefit and take into account the main goal of the region.

The concrete version of the regional scientific and technological P policy in k region may be implemented by means of numerous strategies and the numerous corresponding tactics. Assume that:

Pk = a multitude of possible scenarios of the regional scientific and technological policy in k region;

$Pkj = j$ scenario of the regional scientific and technological policy in k region;

Qkj = a multitude of scenarios in k region according to j regional scientific and technological policy;

$qikj$ = i strategy in k region according to j policy;

$Zikj$ = a multitude of tactics according to i strategy, j policy in k region;

$zsikj$ = s scenario of tactic according to i strategy, j policy, in k region.

As a result we can write the following hierarchy system of correlation:

$$zsikj \in Zikj <= qikj \in Qikj <= Pkj \in Pk$$

where

k = index of the region;

j = index of the regional scientific and technological policy;

i = index of the strategy of the given policy;

s = index of the tactic of the given policy.

Obviously, every version of the strategy of the regional scientific and technological policy generates its multitude of versions.

On the basis of this scheme, the system of the optimization modes, with the purpose of maximizing the economic effect with the corresponding system of the technology, ecology, and resource limits in the scenario of the policy, with the corresponding versions of the strategy and tactic, may be formed.

The model of choosing the optimal tactic may look like:

$$\max_{s} \sum f(zsikj) N_{sikj}$$

where

$f_{(Zsikj)}$ = the integral social and economic effect from implementation of s scenario of tactic, according to i strategy, j policy, in k region. The effect is oriented to the main goal of the regional scientific and technological policy;

N_{sikj} = Boole variable, value of which describes choice according to tactic: 1 if s tactic was selected, 0 in all other cases.

In the view of interchangeability of the versions, limits are needed:

$$\sum_s n_{sikj} = 1i, j, k.$$

Besides that, various types of additional limits may be needed—for instance, limits:

$$\sum e_{(Zsikj)} n_{sikj} < = Re\ 1$$

where

$e_{(Zsikj)}$ = the resource expenditure of 1 type in implementation s scenario of tactic; Re = the permissible expenditure of the 1-type resource; here, the concept of "resource" may be understood broadly, including the impact of scientific and technological progress on the environment and human ecology of the region.

The analogical choice of the optimal strategy is made according to the following model:

$$\max \sum_i u_{(qikj)} y_{ikj}$$

where

$u_{(qikj)}$ = the integral social and economic effect with the single intensive exploitation of i scenario of strategy with j scenario of the regional scientific and technological policy;
y_{ikj}:1 if i strategy was selected, 0 in all other cases.
$\sum y_{ikj} = 1$
$\sum he_{(qikj)} y_{ikj} < = De$

After that, scientific and technological policy is conducted according to the following model:

$$maz \sum_j c(Pkj) Xkj,$$

where

$c(Pkj)$ = the integral social and economic effect from implementing j scientific and technological policy in k region;
Xkj: 1 if the policy was selected, 0 in all other cases.
$\sum_j xkj = 1;$
$\sum_j m_e(Xkj) Xkj < = Ne.$

The given scheme is accordant to the simplified case when there is a rigid hierarchical order in the scheme "regional scientific and technological policy => strategy => tactic." In other words, one tactic, one strategy, and one scenario of tactic may be implemented simultaneously. Besides that, the same tactic may be accordant only to one strategy, and the same strategy may be accordant only to one scenario of the policy. In reality, more sophisticated cases may take place. Then, the given models should be a corresponding way of modification.

However, even this simplified formulation allows one to proceed to executing the concrete calculations for choosing the most profitable version of the regional scientific and technological policy (after formulating all necessary normative information, describing all versions of the multitudes of scenarios of regional policy tactics and strategies, and defining the type of functions of the effect of f, u, c, functions of e, h, m resource expenditure and of R, D, N limits).

For example, the choice of corresponding scenarios of strategy and tactic for two different regions may be written by means of the following indexes.

The regional indexes:

k = 1—Far East economic region;
k = 2—Ural.

The indexes of the scenarios of the policy:

j = 1—labor-saving scenario of version of the regional scientific and technological policy;
j = 2—fund-saving scenario of the regional scientific and technological policy.

The indexes of strategies of the given policy:

i = 1—the growth of power of equipment per unit;
i = 2—the automatization and robotization of production;
i = 3—increasing the energetic equipment of labor;
i = 4—improving working conditions.

The indexes of tactic:

s = 1—the growth of power of metallurgy equipment per unit;
s = 2—the growth of power of press equipment per unit;
s = 3—the robotization of underground mining works;
s = 4—the robotization of production in the processing industry;
s = x—. . .

Then $Z^{k_1}_{s_3 i_2 j_1}$—the tactic of the robotization of underground mining works with the condition of accepting the automatization and robotization productive strategy while conducting the labor-saving scenario of the scientific and technological policy in the Far East economic region. That is how the development of the optimal tactic model is prepared.

The concrete strategy and regional scientific and technological policy, in general, are modeled analogically.

After choosing the strategy and tactic of the regional scientific and technological policy, its organizing and economic mechanism of implementation is defined. This is the least developed block of the system in the given policy. It falls behind the corresponding mechanisms of the scientific and technological policy of the district and common state policy in the sphere of scientific and technological progress, with regard to the level of development.

In our opinion, the regional administrations do not fully utilize such means of governing scientific and technological development as taxes, amortization, price control, investment in new technologies, and standardization. The implementation of the elements of planned and programmed government of scientific and technological progress in the region is far from sufficient. However, the experience of a number of regions in the country shows the high effectiveness and opportunities of utilizing these organizational and economic means of governing by regional administrations.

In the economic literature, there are suggestions for differentiating the amortization norms in the regions of Russia (at first, areas with high wages and unfavorable climate conditions are being emphasized). However, in our opinion, we should now approach changing the amortization norms in the regions considering not only indicated conditions, but also their impact on the rate of the scientific and technological development of the regional economy and regional social and economic tasks.

The territorial branches of the State bank should play their role in conducting the regional scientific and technological policy as well. It is expedient for them to offer credit on privileged terms upon acquiring or producing new equipment, the absence of which holds back the social and economic development of the region.

If the region is interested in attracting to its territory the powers of a manufacturing enterprise, the region can accept the obligations of training and retraining of the necessary workers and of investment for creating the social and even productive infrastructure.

In our opinion, it is expedient to develop special funds within the regional budget in order to finance the accelerated scientific and technological development of the productive force in the region. The facilities of the fund may be spent to create the regional scientific and technological centers (for collective use of equipment and laboratory facilities) and to conduct for the region the most important projects and research aimed at developing the regional complex, protecting the environment, securing the ecology of the regional human population, etc.

Regions where the top-priority development of the industry is effective may be granted the right of decreased (or full permanent or temporary removal of) fund fees.

Now, in all republics and regions, in many cities and districts, there are territorial branches of the State Committee of the USSR for standardization. These branches conduct the common state scientific and technological policy in the regions. The territorial systems of quality control, which are usually created with the participation of the branches, embrace activities of the largest number of enterprises in the region. The organizing and technological basis of these systems is the standards of the enterprises. At the same time, the regional standards, which are developed on the basis of the state standardization system and on the basis of considering the domestic ecological, social and economic, and natural and climate conditions, should have served this purpose.

The technological basis of the regional scientific and technological policy should be the territorial computing chains of inter-district or directly regional administrations. Such territorial chains are functioning in the system of inter-district administrations in all republics and in a number of regions in the country. For example, in Armenia, the inter-district information and computation system was created, embracing more than 30% of computing centers and stations in the republic. In Armenia, 70% of enterprises and organizations in the different branches of the economy are using the services offered by the system. In 1981, on a contractual basis alone, the computation center and stations in Armenia served 1,419 enterprises, ministries, and administrations in the republic. Such level of development of the territorial computation chains is characteristic of most republics.

In the regions, these chains are less developed, and in some of the regions, they are absent. Orientation of practically all territorial computation systems toward solving problems of the regional scientific and technological development of the regional economy is an important reserve for increasing the effectiveness of the regional policy.

One of the most effective means of governing scientific and technological progress in the region is organizing socialist competition. During the years of the 11th 5-year period, a positive experience in this sphere was accumulated. The competition between adjacent scientific and productive teams participating in the same project, contracts for creative interaction in developing and implementing the regional programs for scientific and technological progress, etc., became the most effective forms of competition. Creative interaction is successfully unfolding among the participants in implementing the scientific and technological programs on the republic, regional, and district scale and in developing large-scale objects of new equipment. This type of competition may be called an engineering version of "Working Relay Race." On the whole, forms and methods of public influence on governing scientific and technological progress in the region necessarily have to be united in the single system of the organizational and economic mechanism of the regional scientific and technological policy.

As was noted, the shared state scientific and technological policy should integrate and define the scientific and technological policy of the economic branches and regions of the country as well. Therefore, the practical success of the policy depends in large part on the place that will be occupied by the complex regional programs of scientific and technological progress and other methods of governing scientific and technological progress within the economic system of planning and governing.

UNIFIED SCIENTIFIC AND TECHNICAL POLICY: WHAT AND WHY

The main aim of the scientific and technical policy is to select the most promising directions and priorities in developing science and technology and apply their achievements to production, both on a large scale and effectively, so as to secure its accelerated progress in order to reach our social goals as soon as possible.

These goals are no secret; they are to satisfy to the greatest extent the Soviet people's material and cultural requirements and achieve the harmonious development of the individual personality.

However, it is much easier to state in general the task facing the scientific and technical policy than to work out its content, structure, and the means of shaping and carrying it out.

What Is the Complexity?

Experience shows that tackling these problems means consolidating the efforts and combining the research of economists, sociologists, process engineers, political scientists, lawyers, and other specialists.

Underestimating, until recently, the importance of this work has left the theoretical basis of scientific and technical policy less developed than that of economic and social policy.

Related to both the economic basis of society and its superstructure, scientific and technical policy is determined, first and foremost, by the level and forms of the development of productive forces and, at the same time, by the goals and principles of the organization of social production and ways of managing it.

Scientific and technical policy is also part and parcel of society's scientific management, because managing society in a scientific way means drafting and implementing a correct, flexible, and realistic policy expressing objective requirements of social development.

Moscow News, No. 45 (1983), 12.

In the USSR the validity of scientific and technical policy is a prerequisite for building an advanced material-technical base.

The state scientific-technical policy, as the accepted economic trend, is of a directive nature. It presupposes that the determination of its principal aims and the means for attaining them should be subordinated, at all territorial and departmental stages, to the tasks of developing the country's economy as a whole, while preserving the initiative of each and every element in social production.

A Must

The capability, built up by Soviet labor, is truly immense.

- The USSR today produces a fifth of the world's industrial output.
- The value of fixed assets has topped 1.7 trillion rubles.
- Our country has one-quarter of all the research workers in the world—more than 3,500.
- Soviet scientists have been awarded honorary titles and degrees from academies, research societies, universities, and institutes in 59 states.
- State budget and other spending on science totals almost 22 billion rubles annually.
- Some 90,000 items, produced in this country, have the State Quality Sign, i.e., are on par with the best international standards.
- On average, some 4,000 types of machines, equipment, devices, and instruments are developed in the USSR every year. And the manufacture of more than 1,500 obsolete items is discontinued.
- The contribution of electric power-engineering, machine-building, metal-working, chemical, and petrochemical industries to gross industrial output and industrial fixed assets is increasing all the time and now equals 50%.

Granted such a scope, a further increase in economic and social effectiveness of the country's production is possible only with a broad-scale application of the most advanced processes and the more important scientific and engineering achievements.

The idea is to combine the advantages of socialism with the possibilities opened up by the scientific and technological revolution. This goal is unattainable without a unified scientific and technical policy.

The Main Directions

Our scientific and technical policy is drafted and implemented under socialist ownership of the means of production. This provides the opportunity, when dealing with the new tasks that emerge at the sharp turns in social, economic and political development, for implementing large-scale maneuvers and reorienting all or part of the state's scientific-technical capability, rather than simply that of separate firms or monopolies, which is a feature of the capitalist world.

During the cold war unleashed by militarists, the USSR, concentrating the necessary forces, secured the quick development of atomic and then thermonuclear weapons. The USSR became, not by chance but strategically, the first power to use nuclear energy for peaceful purposes. The Obninskaya and Sibirskaya atomic power plants, with 500- and 600- megawatt capacity respectively, generated the first commercial electricity nearly 30 years ago. The nuclear-powered icebreaker *Lenin* was launched in 1959. A new era was opened in power engineering and in civil shipbuilding. We have quite a few social, economic, scientific, and engineering achievements.

At the same time, our economy has a number of specific problems.

First of all, our territory comprises, in effect, a sixth of the total land-surface of the earth and offers a broad spectrum of natural-geographic conditions. Of all the climatic zones that exist in the world, the USSR lacks, probably, only the tropics. In Yakutia, where the Northern Hemisphere's Pole of Cold is, machinery must stand up to extreme sub-zero temperatures. In Western Siberia machines must operate on bogland, and in the Caucasus, in the mountains.

We do not as yet have the capability to equip ourselves completely with machinery best adapted to these or other conditions. Both in the north and in the south we have to use standard models. The losses from this are estimated at five billion rubles annually. Estimates indicate that each additional ruble spent on developing regionally adapted machines would save about seven rubles on maintenance.

In the 1980s the situation in the Soviet economy has become considerably more complicated. Its fuel, energy, and raw materials bases are moving to remote, practically deserted areas in Siberia with its harsh climate. And in addition to the developing of new territories, the already developed industrial areas in the European part of the USSR need to be rebuilt. The country has a scarcity of manpower, and greater effort and resources must be devoted to coping with ecological problems.

A unified scientific and technical policy can and must be decisive in overcoming all these difficulties.

The Comprehensive Program for Scientific and Engineering Progress in the USSR is being drafted for the third time, now until 2005. In the next, the 12th Five Year-Plan (1986–1990), similar projects will be drafted for the country's various regions and industries at practically all levels. And the main assignment in the programs for developing science and technology is included in current and long-term economic plans.

As we have already indicated, priority is given to the most promising trends. Today they include, in particular, economizing waste-producing technological processes, flexible systems of comprehensive automation, and the mechanization of production, industrial robots, laser instrument production, and biotechnology.

Siberia Remains the Pioneer

The Soviet economy is relying more and more on Siberia, in spite of the fact that the greater part of the population still lives in the European part of the USSR, and 70% of industrial output is concentrated there. That is how Russia's economy has taken shape historically. Nature, however, thought differently. Nearly three-quarters of the mineral, fuel, and energy resources and more than half the hydroresources, an impressive part of ores of nonferrous metals, a fifth of the agricultural land, and about half of all timber resources are located east of the Urals. This is truly a tremendous wealth, and we started tapping it half a century ago. This work was done most energetically in the postwar years.

The scope of Siberia's present-day development and the varied nature of the challenge the work poses demands a fundamentally new approach to the elaboration of the scientific-technical policy. Nearly all researchers in the region have pooled their efforts to formulate the "Siberia" superprogram. The program is divided into 26 sections dealing either with problems common to the entire region or with more local problems: "Timber resources," "Oil and gas,"

"Kuzbas coal," "Norilsk mining-metallurgical complex," etc. There are also special chapters on "The population's health" and "Baikal's ecology." There is also a chapter on "Synnyrtis"—the mining and processing of the unique potassium-alumina material that can yield, when used in recycling, dozens of items that today are scarce in the chemical industry—and nonferrous metallurgy, agriculture, construction work, etc.

Answering the West's Technological Challenge

The USSR could, in principle, develop its economy without maintaining foreign scientific and technological relations. But the USSR is developing much quicker cooperation with other, above all, socialist states.

The USSR is confronting the technological challenge of the West, which is trying to distort mutually advantageous relations, with an agreed-upon strategy of dealing with long-term and current socioeconomic problems. For example, the pooling together of the scientific and engineering capabilities of the CMEA countries in computer making (300 firms and 350,000 experts) has made it possible to carry out, in the course of five or six years, work equal to that done over the preceding 25 years.

Scientific and engineering cooperation is being implemented between socialist states, with an agreed-upon scientific and engineering policy, taking into account their common national interests, the industrial patterns that have taken shape in each of them, and accumulated research and professional know-how. In Czechoslovakia, for example, a country with a mild Central European climate and superb roads, Tatra Works, which had traditionally specialized in making large-capacity trucks, now produces serially cross-country vehicles adapted for the Arctic, deserts, and tropics. According to experts there, Tatra trucks are second to none in the world.

It has now been suggested that the CMEA countries work out a comprehensive, long-term program for scientific and engineering progress based on the Soviet experience. Its implementation along the line "research technology-production-exploitation" promises an impressive economic benefit.

As we know, pooling our labor internationally, which embraces all these stages, enables each country to cut both its costs and research and development time by half, as compared with doing it all alone.

Many concerns in the industrialized capitalist states are turning cooperation with the Soviet economy into a sort of proving ground to test their latest ideas in production. This is characteristic, for example, of Finland, which delivers equipment to the USSR for deep processing of wood and various types of icebreakers and icebreaker-type ships. Magirus Deutz, a West German firm, considerably strengthened its reputation after many of its trucks were used in Siberia. In its turn, the Soviet Belarus tractors are working very well in countries with different climatic and natural conditions.

Developing the international division of labor and improving scientific and engineering relations continue throughout the world, despite the complexity of the international situation. The shaping of regional and worldwide scientific and technical policies is very much up-to-date and should account far more for the specific natural, economic, and social conditions of separate countries and regions of the world.

Here is a simple example. Western firms deliver to the developing countries costly energy-consuming technology calculated to save manpower. But their partners in many countries in Asia, Africa, and Latin America need exactly the opposite; due to a lack of money and energy resources, they have today a great excess of manpower.

The up-to-dateness of building a worldwide scientific and technical policy is related to a number of global problems now facing mankind. They include: the comprehensive use of resources of the world's oceans, the use of space, and the development of general health programs. Scientific and technical programs, which may be regarded as a serious contribution to worldwide scientific and engineering progress, are already being implemented in the USSR today.

In particular, the systems approach has been made the basis for developing the productive forces of the Pacific coast and tapping the resources of its continental shelf in our country. The "Arktika" project is now being prepared; it is immense in scope and difficulties: it is the drawing of the northern Eurasian areas into the economic turnover based on year-round navigation in the Soviet sector of the Arctic Ocean.

Regional health programs have been drafted for the various climatic zones in the USSR. They are aimed at giving each person scientific recommendations on the natural conditions of his work, rest, and diet and at making the region's environment healthier.

TO ACCURATELY DETERMINE A COURSE OF ACTION: AN ECONOMIST ANALYZES THE RESULTS OF KRASNOYARSK'S PAST DECADE

An extrapolation method that is popular among economists requires taking several steps backward in order to have a better perspective. For example, if you want to understand trends for the next 20 years, analyze the past 20 years first.

By the 1970s, the Krasnoyarsk Territory, the largest in the USSR (covering one-fifth of the earth), had lived through sharp and dramatic changes. The new policy of the Soviet leadership, which was aimed at the accelerated development of the country's East, made us realize that until now we have been quite shy in mastering our vast resources. It is not easy to admit that. Our habit of admiring blindly whatever was done to the east of the Urals has been too strong.

No doubt, we have indeed had something real to admire. By 1970, the major indicators of economic development in Krasnoyarsk Territory were comparable to the indicators for central regions of the USSR. In terms of manufacturing output and cargo turnover per capita, the figures were 1.5 times higher than the central regions. In capital construction, the figures were 1.7 times higher. Profit per employee exceeds the average figure for Russia by 9% to 10%.

Thus, in terms not only of production volume but also of production costs Krasnoyarsk Territory was not behind. As for individual industries, such as nonferrous metallurgy, for example, profit was much higher than the average for the USSR as a whole.

The Yenisei River has generated considerable power: six aggregates of the Krasnoyarskaya hydroelectric power plant are rotated by this

Za Nauku v Sibiry [For Science in Siberia], *Novosibirsk*, 35 (September 11, 1980), 4–5.

powerful river. That power transformed Kiya-Shaltydskiye nephe-lines into aluminum. Sorsky molybdenum, Chernogorsky clothes, and Abaza and Teya ore were also supplied by Khakassiya.

Railroads connecting Abakan and Taishet, Achinsk and Abalakovo, were built through wild woods (taiga).

Since 1960, within 10 years, the gross industrial output produced in Krasnoyarsk Territory increased by 276.9%, which is higher than the average for the USSR. This figure means that 6 times more power was produced in the area, 8 times more pulp, 11 times more paper, and 3 times more reinforced concrete were manufactured in our region than in the USSR at large.

Examples discussed during this period were often introduced with the words "the largest," which occurred by hundreds in the printed media of those years. However, there were other figures, too, which were less often mentioned in the press but talked of and thought of.

Krasnoyarsk Territory has substantial natural resources: 40% of the nation's reserves of brown coal, 13% of hydro resources, 18% of high quality wood pulp. All this wealth is located within easy access. It seems as if nature herself was telling people to use her resources.

Figures for the period demonstrate that this wealth was used in the same way as taking only cream and throwing away the milk. Kras-noyarsk Territory was far behind in terms of the average economic indicators for the USSR. The more natural resources there were, the more difficult it was to master all of them. Krasnoyarsk Territory was trailing the Urals economic region, though it is very similar to it.

Then, for the first time, the idea arose of a long-term program for the production and development of this promising region. Was that indeed the first time?

Since 1925, the State Planning Committee (GOSPLAN) had been developing the project "Angaro-Yeniseistroj." The project involved the Angaro-Yenisei cascade of hydroelectric power plants, the largest in the world, and the formation on their basis of heavy industry in Siberia. The project was led by such prominent Soviet researchers as I. Alexandrov, N. Kolossovsky, and V. Malyshev.

The project was approved at the First Conference for Studies of Industry in Eastern Siberia.

Prior to that, there was another project, a general plan for the economic development of Siberia, which to many at that time seemed too daring. Its authors were making plans for the next 10 to

16 years to develop promising regions in Siberia. They thought that all future economic projects would face the underexploration of natural resources. They created a comprehensive program for exploring Siberia, which was accomplished in pre-war (World War II) years. Today, we can only be amazed by the authors of these daring projects and admire the courage of the pioneers who explored the Siberian wilderness. The fact that we have a comparatively clear vision of the scope of the natural resources to be developed is an achievement in itself.

That was the beginning of a new stage in the development of Krasnoyarsk Territory, the stage of forming its economy on a scientific basis.

1960s—The USSR was experiencing a turbulent stage in its scientific and technical revolution. Not only were new production lines evolving but also new industries. At that time a disproportion became evident: the main industrial potential was concentrated in the European part of the USSR, but the main source of raw materials, fuel, and power was located in Siberia and the Far East.

Then, once again, the idea of a complex long-term program for the development of industry in Krasnoyarsk Territory was raised. At that time, there were numerous discussions related to another idea, the concept of economic geography, its subject matter and methods of research. From today's perspective, we can say that it was the beginning of a new science—regional economics.

The new science was the result of the urgent problem of mastering the vast territories in Siberia. Having generated this science, the same project immediately demanded answers to thousands of questions. A full member of the Soviet Academy of Sciences, Abel Aganbegian, wrote at that time: "Krasnoyarsk Territory is one of the most characteristic areas of Siberia, with all types of climatic and economic zones. It should be considered as very important in terms of research, as a proving ground for scientific and technical innovations. This is particularly true for those scientific programs aimed at creating possibilities for high productivity and favorable living conditions in this area."

The Krasnoyarsk 10-year plan became a new field for such research. An important contribution to the development of the plan's concept was a set of recommendations for a scientific conference on industry in Siberia, which was organized by the USSR Academy of Sciences in Novosibirsk in 1969.

The Krasnoyarsk 10-year plan was part of the general plan for the economic development of the USSR and the Russian Federation in particular. The 10-year plan included programs and concepts elaborated by more than 30 organizations and R & D institutes.

Along with local Krasnoyarsk scholars and economists, research fellows of the Institute of Economics and Organization of Industrial Production, which is affiliated with the Siberian division of the USSR Academy of Sciences, and experts from GOSPLAN and the Central economic R&D institute participated.

By 1971, a strategic plan of an unprecedented 10-year scope was prepared for Krasnoyarsk Territory. Today, we can say that the plan has been accomplished. Krasnoyarsk Territory had never seen such purposeful and intensive economic use of its region.

The following are some economic indicators of the period. Industrial output doubled. The production of nonferrous metals also doubled. Ferrous metallurgy, mechanical engineering, and light industries increased their output by 150%. New industries have evolved such as electrical engineering, machine tool manufacture, and automobiles.

This is the result of a precisely set strategic goal, that goal being the accelerated mastery of natural resources in the region and the development of priority industries on that base. Also, the intricate interweaving of factors, both industrial and territorial, had to be achieved.

The complex development of production forces brought to life new modern cities: Lesosibirsk, Divnogorsk, Sayanogorsk, Sosnovoborsk, and Svetlogorsk. Old cities like Krasnoyarsk have renewed their faces, too.

About 350,000 families moved to new dwellings, including one-fifth of them in rural areas. The important strategic direction of the 10-year plan reached a high level of productivity of labor by introducing achievements of scientific and technical progress.

The accelerated development of industries related to mining and mineral-resources processing requires the enlargement of the raw materials base. Of course, geological exploration in various remote areas demands serious financing. This requires the extensive use of space research related to the exploration of natural resources. Pictures taken from outer space provide data that are very helpful for geological and other purposes.

Introducing the latest achievements of domestic and world science and technology, the automation and mechanization of labor-intensive processes resulted in a 170% increase in labor productivity. Two-thirds of the growth in the gross product was generated by this factor.

However, a question naturally arises. What if the current program had not been adopted 10 years ago? Would the labor techniques have improved anyway and would labor productivity have grown and new industries evolved? Of course, all these processes would have taken place, but not so quickly. However, it is not only a matter of pace. First and foremost, the structure of the regional economy has improved. Krasnoyarsk Territory began to obtain more products needed for its own development and for the country as a whole.

There are also some results and achievements of the Krasnoyarsk 10-year plan which are not easily expressed in numbers and figures. Consider the social and cultural development of the region. Without it, the economic program would not be realized. For example, today the number of people who move to Krasnoyarsk Territory exceeds the number of those who leave it. Ten years ago the picture was reversed.

This new trend has been integrated into plans for social and economic development by 1,440 organizations. Krasnoyarsk Territory became the first area in the country to have each of its towns and counties create its own plan for social development. If under the 9th 6-year plan there were 253 such plans, then under 10-year plan that number increased 6-fold. That 10-year plan made everyone like planning. This is one of its invisible but essential achievements.

The 10-year plan removed the "blinders" from hundreds of offices of top executives of the region. At one time, many of them did not care about their neighboring enterprises, but now they have learned to think in terms of the interests of the entire region.

This was the first time that a country considered in its economic plan the figures of a regional program. The sophistication of the organizational and economic mechanism of management has risen beyond regional borders. Local authorities were given the opportunity to influence the formation and development of all enterprises of their region. The goals to achieve were set not for the whole of

East Siberia but for one of its specific regions—Krasnoyarsk Territory. Another important result of the 10-year plan is that the leadership of Krasnoyarsk Territory gained valuable experience in the issues of complex planning. The hope was born that right there, in Krasnoyarsk Territory, cooperation between local authorities and central agencies could result in the development of plans for their region's future.

This is true not only of officials but also of the general population, ordinary people. For example, Victor Nadezhdin, a worker from "Sibtjazhmash," said that "the 10-year plan taught us to think of a shop, a plant, and a region."

This is how the sense of being "the boss" has evolved. This is another achievement of the 10-year plan.

Under the 10-year plan Krasnoyarsk Territory became a region of territorial and production complexes (TPK). TPK is strengthened by the ties between the enterprises that constitute it. Those ties were becoming stronger all over the region: between TPK, industrial centers, and individual enterprises. That has multiplied the economic feedback, increasing the productivity of the region. Transportation expenses have been substantially reduced because products of one enterprise are becoming the raw materials for neighboring enterprises.

This way, the share of the final product began to increase in the region. If, before, the region was mostly just a supplier of raw materials for the European part of the country, now 40,000 combines, flatcars for carrying containers, light aluminum modules, high-voltage vacuum switches, trailers and other machines, and industrial equipment are sent to the East.

For its part, cooperation between the region's enterprises and a better industrial structure overall strengthen its ability to effectively use natural resources.

This complex approach applied to everything everywhere—that is probably the main lesson of the Krasnoyarsk 10-year plan. Its success is being taken into account in a new 10-year plan for 1980–1990 that is now under consideration.

The new 10-year program stipulates for Krasnoyarsk Territory the further development of existing TPKs, the improvement of their structure, and the intensive mastery of new areas, primarily in Priangariye. According to the new plan, two new cities and several hydroelectric power plants are to be erected there. In Krasnoyarsk a plant for heavy excavators will be built. Its "walking" and rotary excavators will help to mine coal in KATEK and other coal basins in the USSR.

While preparing this new program, its authors took into account that in the past not enough attention was given to regional policy in science and technology. Today, a special complex program for this field has been worked out. It stipulates the accelerated introduction of automatic device engineering, the mechanization of loading works, and the use of equipment adjusted to the northern climate. These factors will help to reduce the labor shortage in the region.

Krasnoyarsk Territory takes off in 1990. It looks further, to the next century, even to the next millennium.

THE INTERMEDIARY ROLE OF SCIENTIFIC/TECHNOLOGICAL COMPANIES: FROM THE EXPERIENCE OF "SIBTSVETMETAVTOMATIKA"

The intensive development of new regions in Siberia, with its mineral wealth, forest, water, and power resources, calls for the large-scale introduction of technology adapted to the conditions of the region, a constant quest for forms and methods that will enhance the connections between science and industry. Among the more progressive forms of this kind are scientific-production associations (SPA).

Having first appeared only a short time ago there are now some 150 SPAs operating in all the branches of the national economy. Like any other organizational form, these associations are going through a development period. Work is still in progress on specific reports regulating their work, defining organizational patterns, determining their place in the country's system of industrial management, and developing their economic mechanism.

How are these problems solved in the conditions in Siberia?

From the Blueprint to Services

Among the country's first scientific-production complexes was the inter-district scientific-technological enterprise "Kraspromavtomatika," set up in 1957 in Krasnoyarsk. In 1965 it was transferred under the authority of the USSR Ministry of Nonferrous Metallurgy, and in 1977 was reorganized as SPA "Sibtsvetmetavtomatika."

It is not by chance that the scientific-technological base of SPA is

Ekonomicheskaya Gazeta [The economic newspaper] (Moscow), no. 38 (1978), p. 16.

located in Krasnoyarsk Territory. This is the site of the giant of heavy industry the Norilsk mining-metallurgical combine, the Krasnoyarsk aluminum plant, and several other industrial facilities. However, the area of SPA activity is not confined to this territory. Its branches have mushroomed in Yakutia, Kuzbass, Buryatia, Kazakstan, the Urals, the Far East, and the republics of Central Asia.

Today, SPA is an organization with a complete scientific-technological cycle. A special design bureau—the head structural unit of the association—is concerned with project research and design; a parts division supplies SPA with all the necessary mass-produced elements for projected automation systems, and an experimental plant responsible for their production transmits them to assembly boards and divisions of SPAs for assembly work and adjustment of the systems. The association's training center provides advanced training for workers and engineers who will be operating the envisaged projected systems. Besides, SPA does its own repair jobs, and provides maintenance service to several systems.

Virtually the entire volume of work at "Sibtsvetmetavtomatika" is accomplished on the basis of direct economic contracts. How is the effectiveness of SPA's work and the quality of its services maintained?

As Applied to Specifics

SPAs began to set up their own permanently operating local branches/boards and sectors that are now functioning virtually in all associations and combines of nonferrous metallurgy in Siberia, the Far East, Urals, and Central Asia.

In these conditions the central SPA apparatus is oriented to the development of new technical systems and their stock production and the training of personnel for future operating staffs.

The conditions in Siberia have a specific effect on logistics. Siberian enterprises, as a rule, have a variety of structural and production units, each one in need of complete sets of plans for the introduction of new technologies.

According to the logistics, the funding for material and technological supplies, including the development of automation, is in the hands of the client. It turns out that although the Ministry is provided with the required amount of plant sets, the latter are actually delivered to warehouses of the different enterprises, which prolongs the introduction of automation. In this respect SPAs have acquired extensive positive experience.

During the development of an automation system for dredges ("Draga-1"), the funds for the required sets of equipment were allocated to our association. Now the plants for this system were delivered to the central SPA warehouse and then distributed to experimental plants and units in strict conformity with the plan and order of priority for their demand. The result: it has been possible to reduce twice the time needed for introducing the system, and the technological level of "Draga-1" has long received the high approval of clients, along with an award of the Exhibition of Economic Achievements.

Due to the specific conditions of Siberia, especially its lack of proper roads, it is often possible to deliver the new equipment to most of the dredges only during the winter. Moreover, assembly work is out of the question during the flushing season. It is typical that the equipment is delivered to the client at the wrong time and because of the lack of proper storage at remote factories and mines, it is left to rust and deteriorate out in the open.

At present, the automatic systems ("Draga-1") are stored in well-equipped premises provided by the association, and the bank provides SPAs with loans for the timely stocking of new equipment. Thus, consideration is given in the interests of both parties.

Our experience will undoubtedly be of use to other scientific-technological associations located in Siberia or delivering its products to the region.

Zone of Attraction

Scientific-technological associations and organizations always specialize in a certain aspect of scientific and technological progress. This, like a magnet, attracts many enterprises regardless of their Departmental jurisdiction. There is actually no possibility of placing several Departments in every SPA industrial center. Consequently, in addition to managing their own branch, SPA is compelled through different boards and social bodies to guide the work of regional automation, promoting its scientific-technological level at enterprises under other Ministries and Departments.

For example, in Krasnoyarsk, the SPA "Sibtsvetmetavtomatika" plays the part of a base organization in the technology and economics board under the Territory's Party Committee, which lends support to the board's sector concerned with scientific and technological progress. The sector coordinates the efforts of all industrial enterprises in the area aimed at introducing new technology and promotes the shaping and implementing of technological policies.

The Territorial Party Committee is engaged in extensive work on popularizing and introducing robotics into industries in the area. Development has begun on an automated line for ingot casting at the Krasnoyarsk aluminum plant. The association makes wide use of technology developed at the Krasnoyarsk Television Plant in the production of electronic appliances. Several SPA developments have been applied not only in nonferrous metallurgy but in other industries as well. Among these are devices for geophysical prospecting (DEMP-3 and AEMM-3) used in prospecting construction work.

Recently, proposals have come in on setting up "go-between organizations" to reduce the time needed to bring the development to the consumer. It is surmised that with the experience of "Sibtsvetmetavtomatika" the functions of such a go-between catalyst could well be performed by the scientific-production associations themselves, though this will certainly require a higher level of comprehensiveness in the system of services to the enterprises/clients.

Such organizations should accept the function of taking charge along regional lines of the respective industrial aspects. There are barriers to overcome, but, on a regional scale, the effect is worthwhile both for the SPA and the industry it represents.

PREPARATION FOR PRODUCTION: A KEY STAGE IN IMPLEMENTING TECHNOLOGICAL POLICY

The Significance of Preparing for Production in the Acceleration of Scientific and Technological Progress

"Preparation for production" (PP) comprises a system of measures aimed at applying the latest scientific and technical research to industry. It is the final stage of technical development and incorporates a number of diverse operations calling for systematization, general purposeful management, and planning. Having created new possibilities for the practical implementation of scientific discoveries which earlier lacked technical solutions, scientific and technological research has set the technology departments of companies the task either of applying new equipment and new, more economical and more effective technological processes, or of automating the systems already in operation. This way companies will be able to bring down costs, improve quality, and increase the volume of production.

The process of preparing for the production of new goods, or introducing new machines and technology, whether automation or mechanization systems, may require the renovation of production shops, changes in the organization of production, and the like.

"Preparing for production" is a link in the "idea–production" cycle. Specifically, it is this link that straddles the border between science and production, and determines in large part the success of the scientific-industrial cycle.

Determining the content of the basic direction of improvement and the role of the preparatory stage in carrying out the technical policy is a key condition both for the intensification of industrial output and for its increased effectiveness.

Excerpt from *The Increase in the Technical Development of Industry* (Moscow: Znanie [Knowledge] Publishing House, 1976).

Throughout Russian economic history, much attention has been focused on the preparation-for-production stage. Before the mid-1930s, PP was conducted on an individual basis and in some cases was purely of a cottage-industry nature, dealing with the specifics of individual products and the conditions of production at each company. By the end of the 1930s, however, the first theoretical works on the subject appeared which scientifically substantiated the need for standardization and unification of technology.

Since the early 1940s, perfecting PP has been the subject of research on the part of many Soviet scientists. During the 5th and 6th five-year plans, industrial enterprises accumulated experience in perfecting PP (for example, Leningrad metallurgical plant, etc.), which then developed into a system of accelerated preparation for production (for example, Yaroslav motor plant, "Severny Press" plant in Leningrad, etc.).

The increasing attention given to PP showed workers in management and technology the importance of speeding up the introduction of know-how into new production processes and mastering the specific technology and equipment. At the same time it revealed the complex nature of managing this process, which involved a significant number of participants: research institutes, design and construction bureaus, and company technology and economic departments. With their static interrelation scheme, the line graphs that were in used at the time in planning and preparation work failed to reflect fully the dynamic character of the jobs and ensure timely control and management.

The search for better planning methods of PP led, in the early 1960s, to the development and implementation abroad, and later in the Soviet Union, of methods of network planning and management (NPM), making it possible to coordinate and determine the organized functioning of large numbers of participants in a project, and define the critical line of development, thus ensuring a speedy and timely fulfillment of the job. Even at that stage of PP, network methods made it possible to reduce production time by 20% to 30% and to lower production costs.

In the Soviet Union, the organizational structure of management had become an obstacle to further improving PP work. It was insufficiently adjusted to the target management of the complex scientific and technological programs that had superseded developments using individual machines and technological processes.

Matrix structures of management organization, which made the most effective use of NPM possible, were a step forward. However, matrix structures put certain restrictions on the potential of network graphs. Though allowing the coordination and organization of the work of a large number of developers dealing with complex technological systems and distributing the available resources, these structures failed to ensure control (in the process of development) of the product's technological parameters and its progressive development.

Combining the latest organizational forms of management—matrix structures and network methods of management—became the preparatory stage in introducing radically new functions in the process of PP (showing both the need for them and the potential for their realization): an industrial-economic *(functional-cost) analysis and configuration management,* allowing analysis from the consumer's position at each stage of the preparatory work of the specific product. There emerges the possibility of making alternative decisions: to go on with the development, to stop at the achieved technological level of the designated product, or to take it off the production line.

At present, based on the wealth of actual and theoretical material, it has become possible to undertake a comprehensive standardization of the elements needed for the preparatory stage, to develop a single interbranch system of technological preparation for production (ISTPP).

In this period of rapid development of scientific and technological progress, the volume and importance of the preparatory stage are steadily on the rise.

First, with the acceleration of scientific and technological progress, the manufactured product is replaced more quickly, its batch production and production time are reduced, and the time needed for PP either equals or exceeds the actual production time. For instance, the process of renewing the manufactured systems and automation circuits for the mining and metallurgical industries has accelerated five to ten times in the last decade. Characteristic of the increasing share of PP work is the growing number of workers involved in the process.

Second, the intensification and expansion of automation in production, and the introduction of fully automated processes, not only relieve man of taking a direct part in production but to a certain extent free him from the functions of control and regulation of production. Equipment, transducers, software for automatic devices, etc., handle all of this, allowing man more time for PP work. As a result, organizational improvements in this type of production offer greater potential for manpower savings.

Third, constant improvement in the quality of new machinery goes hand in hand with its growing complexity and relative increase in the amount of large technological projects (automation systems among them) in total volume. This leads to the growth of research, construction, technological, pilot, and other types of work, labor input, and the cost and time of preparing for production.

Fourth, the improvement in PP, which reduces the time from scientific conception to its practical realization, significantly decreases the process of depreciation of products designated for production, and of the equipment and technologies developed for introduction into the production process. Delays in the PP phase of new products not only lead to excess direct outlays of both financial and labor resources and the waste of machines, mechanisms, and technical equipment, but also result in a product that, having been manufactured with outdated technology, turns out to be technologically obsolete.

A non-comprehensive approach to PP at industrial enterprises may lead to situations in which some equipment is ready to be implemented while other elements of the new technology are only in the preparatory stage. The result: the introduced equipment becomes dated, for although it is ready for operation, it is in disuse; left unattended, it is negatively affected by the environment.

A reduction in depreciation and deterioration ensures economy of materialized labor. However, at the PP stage, economies can be achieved by employing, as much as possible, elements of earlier constructions, as well as technological apparatus and equipment in the development of new constructions and technological processes.

Fifth, while ensuring continuity in determining the types of new products and their manufacturing technologies at the PP stage, a choice is made in favor of more progressive constructions, technologies, and parameters for achieving their optimization, from the best of all possible methods of production organization which support the output of high quality produce.

Elements and Methods of Organizing Preparatory Work for Production

Determining the role and place of PP in the overall effort to increase productivity allows the formulation of its basic tasks:

- the choice of the best economic-management and technological solutions;
- the acceleration of development and learning to handle new products, and progressive technology; reduction in duration of the "idea–production" cycle;
- the reduction of all costs associated with PP.

These tasks can be solved only on the basis of a multi-component and flexible system. The complexity of the PP system is due to the interaction of elements and the number of links between functions, that is, the multi-aspect character of its structure.

Scientific literature gives several definitions of PP. Most often, PP is subdivided into construction, technology, etc. Other publications view PP by its duration in time, place of realization, etc. A scientifically grounded definition of PP would be a uniform system conducive to carrying out all the aspects of technological policies of enterprises. This classification, while stating the concept of this process, can be well realized by using methods of analysis and modeling.

Analysis of the PP system can be based on a variety of principles. Here separate elements have been singled out on the basis of the vertical principle, with consideration for the following peculiarities: time-target, sphere of action, object, and stage of realization. Having broken down this process, one way or another, into elements (to facilitate its survival and management), it is necessary to reduce as much as possible the time span between these elements, to augment their interaction, etc.

Analysis of the single PP process makes it possible to systematize and constantly improve this process. All PP classifications have to be based on, and its realization has to envisage, a certain complexity of the basic PP functions: research, technical, organizational-economic, social-psychological, and material. The more intense the specialization of the elements of the PP system, the more complex the methods of management of the overall system. This approach allows the carrying out of the required decomposition in order to bring out the system's diverse elements for analysis, the optimal methods and forms of their functioning and management, and at the same time present PP as a single complex system.

An expression of this approach is the conceptual model of the PP system which, first, shows how the system is formed, second, gives its structural-functional description, and, third, shows the system's dynamics in time. The description of the given model should reflect, above all, the origins and the formation order of the basic PP functions.

The next PP stage—*the* technical *preparation for production*—is carried out with the close cooperation of the client and producer. For instance, if a company is engaged in construction and technological preparatory work for an automated system, the construction-technological work has to be carried out by the client-center to prepare the unit that is to be automated. Here, owing to the changes made in the technological process, the automation system, new product, etc., one can expect new technological results.

At this stage, the finishing touches are added by the construction division, sets of new technological equipment are selected, and norms of material and labor outlays are determined. This stage, in regard to the character of the work, is broken down into two large divisions—*construction* and *technological preparation.*

Learning to handle the new production mechanism and introducing new technology, automation, and the modernization of technology call for forecasting the effect that can be achieved at the given company through the implementation of the aforementioned measures and the effectiveness of the new product during its utilization at other companies and in export–import operations. The execution of this work will be part of the stage of *organizational-economical* preparation of production.

At this stage, production receives its organizational and economic backup; that is, necessary changes are undertaken in organizing the technological process and other production elements, and costs are analyzed on the basis of the company's estimates to determine the cost of the new product (or to bring down its cost with the use of new technology).

The handling of new technologies calls for training and retraining at the enterprise. Prior to installing the system, the client needs to send its future operators for training. It is obvious that the profile of the classes has to be expanded to train employees for all the systems developed by the trust.

That the work force often meets the introduction of radically new technology with some skepticism calls for certain psychological and social training for workers engaged in the new production process.

To ensure normal functioning, the production process should be furnished with raw materials, the required basic and auxiliary materials, machines, and operational capital. Organizing reserves and determining their norms for different production aspects *constitute* the *material preparation for production*, which completes the PP cycle.

With regard to their organization, these PP stages should by no means be viewed as strictly consecutive. Although each stage lays the foundation for the one that follows, some of the jobs can be conducted simultaneously. Moreover, in practice their diffusion should be maximally supported.

It is surmised that with regard to the structural-functional characteristic of the PP system it is necessary to determine two aspects: first, singling out the elements that constitute the PP system; and second, explaining their relationship, method, and nature of contacts.

As already noted, the formation of the PP system is essential in selection of all implementation methods. These can be classified into six aspects of production preparation, each aspect forming the basic structural unit in the system. To be implemented industrially, each of the selected aspects may demand the execution of some or all of the mentioned PP functions. These functions can be realized within the systems of internal or outside training, depending on the complexity of its character and the length of PP demanded by the project.

The designing of the PP system would be incomplete if the emerging model did not reflect its dynamics. More often than not, the realization of PP requires a considerable period of time.

Preparing for production as an element of technological policy may entail long spans of time needed for planning and organization to utilize the achievements of technological progress in industry. For instance, while introducing into the long-term plan of an enterprise the targets for switching over to new technology, one should simultaneously envisage the carrying out of research in the production organization, retooling of production, and the costs incurred by the customers, etc. While *current* PP is aimed at perfecting technologies and machines in operation by introducing changes and modernization, medium-term PP is aimed at utilizing the results of research for the partial improvement of the production process, and long-term PP is set on preparing for the introduction and exploitation of radically new technologies and organizational solutions. Hence, the specific tasks of each PP stage.

The singling out of PP types according to their time-target aspect is evidence of the PP system's dynamic character; it also shows that by extensive, continuous purposeful work PP is not a one-time campaign. Analysis of the composition of PP makes it possible to:

A. Single out the following elements of the PP system and their classification:

1. *According to the time-target aspect*: long-term; medium-term; current.

2. *According to the sphere of realization*: inter-plant; extra-plant.

3. *According to the object of preparatory work*: preparing for the output of new products; installation of new equipment; introducing new technology, new types of power and materials; introducing automation and mechanization into production processes; management measures; reconstruction of production.

4. *According to types of work (stages of realization)*: research, technical (construction, technological); organizational-economic; social-psychological; material.

B. Express the prevalent idea of the PP system in the form of its conceptual model. The offered model can be the basis for coordinating preparatory work for introducing scientific and technological achievements and carrying out a single technological policy.

More than ever before there is a need for specialization of PP work. However, in the current conditions, differentiation and specialization of this work would be constantly augmented by their integration, single uniform planning, and management. Besides, along with specialization and diffusion (for a more profound study) of PP elements, it is necessary to promote coordination and integration of hands-on work in implementing scientific and technological achievements. This approach has certain advantages over the "traditional" one.

First, it ensures the comprehensive realization at companies of a uniform technology policy, as the model embraces all the areas of its application: machinery, technology, and the final product.

Second, it becomes possible to incorporate in a single comprehensive plan all the preparatory work for implementing technological achievements and carrying out organizational-economic measures. Such a comprehensive plan, uniting the available plans for science and technology and the plan for organization, has been regularly drawn up at enterprises of the association AERO (CzSSR) since 1973. This has made it possible to adjust more precisely the measures for scientific and technological development of the enterprise and to incorporate more intensively new technology.

Third, it becomes possible to systematize all the work conducted at industrial enterprises in preparation for improvement of production and management, and to establish cooperation and proper functioning for parties involved in PP.

Fourth, it is possible to solve to a certain extent a major, extremely complex methodological problem—the development of methods to classify measures for the introduction of new machinery and technology, and improve organization of production and labor.

Conceptual Model of System for Preparing for Production

(1) System to prepare for production—system for management of development
(2) Preparation for output of new product
(3) Preparation for output of new machinery
(4) Preparation for introduction of new technology, new types of power and materials
(5) Preparation for introduction of automation and mechanization systems
(6) Preparation for management changes
(7) Preparation for reconstruction of production
(8) Research preparation
(9) Technical preparation
(10) Organizational-economic preparation

(11) Social-psychological preparation
(12) Material preparation
(13) Construction preparation
(14) Technological preparation
(15) Development of technological documentation
(16) Development of technological processes
(17) Development of technological equipment
(18) Control
(19) Incentive
(20) Regulation
(21) Coordination
(22) Organization
(23) Planning
(24) Current preparation
(25) Medium-term preparation
(26) Long-term preparation
(27) Management functions
(28) Time

Generalization and incorporation of all PP elements into a single system allows the use of standard-type forms and methods in their organization. To achieve the tasks facing an industrial enterprise calls for a precise and clear-cut organization of management of the PP process. In developing an organization structure for managing PP, special research must be carried out to study the technologies and standard production methods for the new product, coordination and control of PP, etc.

Organization of research and implementation at the PP stage is determined by the nature of the tasks (complexity and volume), the structure of the unit of the company responsible for introduction of new technology, and the methods used, which in itself depends on what is to be solved—single-aspect tasks or a diversity of tasks at one and the same time.

Analysis of the existing PP systems at several industrial enterprises shows that considerable losses of diverse resources at this stage of production are due to organizational flaws in PP management.

Of late there has been a trend in industrial development to go over to the production of more complicated products and machinery, to develop more complicated technological systems. The entire company is drawn into preparation work for the production of these systems. This is due to the ever more complex character of machinery and the ongoing industrial specialization and concentration. These trends necessitate the perfection of organization structures for production management, forming services that make it possible, in keeping with the new requirements, to coordinate all the participants in the project (individual workers, services, teams) and its huge technological systems.

In the field the organization structure of an enterprise and its divisions usually turns out to be much less dynamic, less changeable, than the object of their efforts and the product. This results in a certain contradiction between the latest technological systems developed and implemented in industrial production and the dated organizational structures. Hence, the need to search for ways of improving the organizational aspect of PP. Centralization, for instance, may bring positive results either at enterprises with batch production or in conditions where PP is handled by dealing with its separate elements in different functional services without *a* single *management system.*

Yet, even in this case, centralization, with its positive results, will have a certain dampening effect: lengthening of time needed for PP due to despecialization of workers recruited to the PP division from different functional services (Head Constructor, Head Metallurgist, Technologist, etc.).

On the other hand, enterprises involved in rapid switching of products, small serial production, and simultaneous preparation work for several types of products or large-scale technological systems require a different, more flexible organizational structure. It must envisage the organization of management for the entire preparatory cycle of work for each item designated for production. This method of management, however, can diminish the responsibility for the development of the product on the part of the heads of functional services, thereby immediately affecting the rates of incorporating PP. Hence, it is necessary to see that management of PP on the part of the person responsible for the overall process goes hand in hand with management on the part of heads of functional divisions.

The leader responsible for preparatory work in regard to a product (group of items, technological system) stands in charge over specialists engaged in developing the product while retaining them in their respective functional divisions. This gives rise to *matrix organizational structure*, where management of PP is conducted along two lines: "vertically," with each PP stage being the responsibility of the head of the respective functional subdivision; and "horizontally," with the PP of an item or its development becoming fused into an integrated process by the head in charge of preparing or developing the technological scheme as a whole.

In hands-on preparatory work a specialist (or group) in the functional division is singled out for individual tasks. He works immediately under the division head, but is ultimately responsible to the project director. The organization works well when the spheres of work are precisely defined and there is good teamwork.

The head of the project determines *"what"* has to be done and *"when,"* while the heads of functional divisions make decisions in regard to *"how"* and *"who."*

Naturally, conflict is possible between the divisions in the projects and between the heads of divisions in regard to the spheres of activity and the costs and quality involved in different solutions. Nevertheless, this organizational structure of PP management has several advantages over current structures. It provides for a swifter resolution of said conflict in functional divisions, and by performing specifically designated work on a permanent basis, workers are able to acquire excellent professional skills. Moreover, the fact that an individual worker is responsible only for the given project (preparing the designated item for production) helps expedite the introduction of the item into production.

The experience of using matrix structures shows that they promote the observance of a stable production discipline and are conducive to individual incentive and teamwork, and expedite the transition from research stage to production process 3–4 fold.

A study made of organization of PP work and work to introduce automated systems in nonferrous metallurgy shows that matrix structures of two types can be used: (a) in the process of developing and designing automated systems by joint effort of several organizations—in this case it would be expedient to develop a detailed coordinating and planning body either under the head contracting organization or under the leadership of the customer-organization;

and (b) inside separate organizations incorporating the efforts of numerous divisions and subdivisions.

The matrix structure allows the use of more developed methods of controlling the technological level of the designated product (technological system) and, consequently, promotes the fulfillment of one of the basic PP requirements—the choice of the best technological solutions. These methods should be targeted, above all, to achieve the fullest conformity between the characteristics of the product, the requirements for and conditions of its utilization, and raising the quality of individual elements of technology from the point of the final product. They must also bring down production costs by constantly reducing all expenses related to the production of new products and the handling of new technology. The significance of this for raising the effectiveness of production can hardly be overestimated.

The growing volume of work to put new types of products and new technology into production underscores the need to rationalize and develop ways to lower PP costs. This envisages improvement in forecasting methods and long-term planning of development expenditures, thereby making it possible to foresee their volume and work out measures to determine both the optimal level of costs and the time needed to put the product into production. The basic task is to turn planning and forecasting of outlays for development into a means of managing technological progress.

The planning of investment for the development of a new product and its incorporation into production is performed in two ways: by the direct calculations method, using norms and ratios of expenditure of production resources for each type of product, or by the estimation-analytical method, which takes into account the experience of producing similar items. Quicker innovation of products and sharp quality distinctions between their consecutive types (models) accounting for their original and inimitable character make these methods non-effective and even unacceptable for the preliminary estimation of costs of the newly developed systems. In this case, the methods cannot be applied, because they are built along the lines of extrapolating previous experience on the new production process without taking into account the quality distinctions in similar yet technologically different types of product.

The high level of cooperation in present-day production, and the complex character of technology and machinery, make it hard to do away with non-productive excess outlays during the production process, given the limited possibility of changing the operating technology or modifying existing construction. The greater complexity of machinery leaves many things unspecified, leading to the need for more changes later, and this too can hardly be taken into account in the preliminary estimates. The result: planned outlays are consistently overestimated.

The quality of the future product and its volume of production are largely dependent on the preparatory stage. According to a number of specialists, 70% of the volume of costs involved in the production of an item is determined at this stage. It is therefore necessary to use methods that would enable one to *avoid* the unnecessary expenses, *forecast* future outlays, and, consequently, *control production expenses*.

Control of production expenses should go hand in hand with raising the quality of work, analyzing the technological properties and the functional and consumer properties for the future item. *Combining control of production costs with control of its quality from the position of the final product* is a dual task that practical experience sets before researchers and organizers of the PP system in industry.

By generalizing all that has been said, it is possible to formulate the following principles—it is on these principles that the methods for the solution of the set task should be predicated:

- not simply fixing outlays, but containing and forecasting them;
- including within the sphere of control of outlays not only production expenses but also the costs of exploiting the respective product;
- combining control of expenditure with control of product quality;
- controlling outlays and quality of product with regard to consumer requirements as well as the functional task of the product during its utilization.

Product control at all stages of production envisions control of quality from the earliest stages of development. Such a method can be based on the recently developed *configuration control* aimed at organizing, with the help of identification and systematization, control over the base configuration of the product following the introduction of changes into its construction proper and the respective documentation. Each change, as a rule, involves changes in related details, etc. The authors of Russia's first publications on configuration control underline that, to many engineers and technologists, the term still has a mysterious implication. Actually, it defines what remains their regular practical work (even though it is not always organized along the required professional lines). Configuration control, which allows maintaining and controlling the interaction of change, shows at every moment of the PP period the extent to which the product conforms to the required technological norms.

In the event that the product is determined to be non-profitable (at the moment), its PP stage can be checked until technical, technological, or organizational ways are found to bring down its cost.

The provisions of configuration control should be extended to the technology developed for the designed projects, item or circuit, and its operation. The experience of several foreign firms demonstrate the successful and highly effective application of this system. For instance, IBM (USA), which specializes in the production of electronic automated circuits and electronic computers, has extensive experience in using configuration control. IBM not only markets the circuits but also handles the assembly and adjustment work and puts them into operation, and provides consultations and technical support. Hence, the proposal to introduce the system in the trust to similar organizations is quite justified.

Configuration control is applied at the stage when the basic elements accounting for the quality of the product are introduced into the technical and technological aspects of its production process. The realization of subsequent measures of quality control have to adhere to the general stages of development (technical target, draft design, etc.).

The complex and systematic character of the methods of industrial-economic analysis, organizing the interaction of all services employing this method in the process of PP, make it imperative to single out a body that would bear responsibility for the entire work. This function could be vested in a group (bureau) for the planning and coordination of PP work.

Costs are what determine the expediency of organizing the production of any item. It is the task of the industrial-economic analysis service that is part of the aforesaid bureau to assess and provide precise information on costs and check their size by analyzing the pertinent information before the production stage. The work of this service should be *characterized* not only by the number of exposed miscalculations but also by the sum of forestalled expenses, resulting in a permanent improvement of the work of the enterprise.

Methods of network planning and management (NPM) should be employed to optimize the development of new equipment and technology in regard to time and resources, coordinate the work of all PP participants, and ensure the consecutive character of all the operations. The USSR has had extensive experience in the application of NPM methods.

All the described methods of organization and management of PP are sufficiently effective. There is already some experience of their application. However, their analysis shows that under current conditions they should not be used independently but integrated into the work of the enterprise.

Planned work of an enterprise is based on the observance of certain standard requirements. Their scientific justification, high level of authenticity, quality, and near-term introductions are a prime condition for making optimal planned estimates. Most of the standard requirements are established at the PP stage. Hence, the period needed for the handling of a new product stems from the labor-consuming character and time required in developing summary documents for technological procedures.

A single system of technological PP envisages extensive use of computers with centralization of the entire standardization process. Besides, the centralized recording and storage of standardized information on disk makes it possible to use computers for subsequent calculations of industrial-economic planning, accounting, material and technical supplying, etc.

As production becomes more effective, there is an increasing need for the further automation of production processes and their control. Today, planning, dispatching, and control are hardly possible without the use of computers and complex automation means.

General indices reflecting the technological preparation for PP includes: time of development and the labor-consuming character of the new product and its material-consuming properties, cost, reliability, durability, etc. Due to the irregular character of the technological PP (TPP) level, analysis of these and other indices will define the main restructuring needs of production. On the other hand, the growing role of incentive-prompting material factors for bringing down costs and improving the quality indices of the PP period will improve the general indices for industrial production.

It is already obvious that the development and introduction of USTPP is only the starting point of extensive work along new lines of raising the effectiveness of social production.

First, the use of USTPP standards in the work of an enterprise may expose certain inaccuracies—it will be necessary to develop a number of new standards and change the existing ones. On the other hand, it would be wrong to assume that improvement of production starts with the direct introduction of USTPP. This process should be preceded by extensive organization and inculcation work that would draw the attention of managers and engineers to PP problems. This would make it possible to use "easily accessible" reserves and examine the promising trends of perfecting production.

A preliminary analysis of PP systems carried out at separate enterprises has showed the availability of substantial reserves. However, in its present form USTPP fails to embrace all industries and is confined to instrument making and engineering. Besides, from the point of PP it still lacks a comprehensive approach.

At present, questions dealing with PP and its management are applied chiefly to engineering, instrument-making, and metal-processing industries. At these enterprises sufficient attention is devoted to PP, and especially to technological PP, during planning, organization, and execution of the production process. The achievements of technological PP and the attained level of technological standardization in these industries show the need for a systemic approach in developing USTPP.

However, the principles underlying USTPP make it acceptable to other industries—among them, mining and metallurgical enterprises where PP organization is the more complex process.

In perfecting but one stage, that of technological PP (minus design), the single system of technological preparation for production serves as a fine prerequisite for developing a single *engineering* PP, calling for a single system of construction PP and providing it with a reliable base. This approach to perfecting the engineering PP allows one to draw a conclusion on the formation of a single enterprise-wide engineering policy whose direct execution starts at the stage of engineering PP.

The task of working out a single inter-branch system for comprehensive PP has not been set. But the work that is being carried out along these different lines—the introduction of USTPP, the development of problems dealing with economic preparation, the working out of principles and methods of organizational preparation, and the improvement of personnel training and material preparation—demonstrates that in the near future solutions to these and similar tasks will be achieved.

Analysis of USTPP leads to the conclusion that the development of a comprehensive system of measures for improving even a single PP stage will allow for the full and consistent use of progressive methods of organization and implementation, thereby raising the quality of work, expediting its completion, reducing costs for TPP, and increasing production effectiveness.

UNIFORM SYSTEM FOR THE TECHNICAL PREPARATION OF PRODUCTION

Standardization is key to the acceleration of scientific and technological progress. Today, the objects of standardization are not only quality of production, documentation, and terms, but also the designing of systems and the organization and management of production. This calls for complex standardization, that is, the purposeful and planned defining and implementation of a system of interlocked requirements, with the objective of comprehensive standardization as a whole and of its basic elements with the aim of providing for the optimal solution of a specific problem. This approach to standardization calls for the implementation of large-scale statewide systems of standardization.

The government decree, "On Raising the Role of Standards in Improving the Quality of Output," sets the task of elaborating and approving a complex of standards for the Uniform System of Technological Preparation for Industrial Output (USTPIO) of products in the engineering, instrument engineering, and automation industries. The task was assigned to the State Committee for Standards and to several of the ministries for engineering and instrument engineering.

The goal of the Uniform System of Technological Preparation for Industrial Output is to raise the level of typification of technological processes for preparation of production and standardize the design, technological documentation, and equipment needed to reduce the time for designing, preparing, and introducing new products into production while bringing down manpower, material, and financial resources.

The basis for the USTPIO is:

- the Uniform System of Technological Documentation (USTD);
- typification and standardization of technological processes;

From *The Handbook of the Economics of Industrial Enterprise* (Moscow: Ekonomika [Economics] Publishing House, 1974), pp. 267–275.

- standardization and unification of building-block designing of technological equipment and tooling;
- inter-district system of readjusted tooling;
- standardization of the means and methods of automation and mechanization of engineering operations for the technological preparation of production, etc.

The setting up of USTPIO presupposes the practical implementation at industrial enterprises of the previously developed *Uniform System of Design Documentation* (USDD).

The Uniform System of Design Documentation defines uniform stages for developing, storing, registering, and circulating of draft, maintenance, and repair documentation.

The *Uniform System of Documentation* (USTD) envisages the typification, mechanization, and automation of developing technological processes as well as the processes themselves; it provides for their stability and control, microfilming of technological documentation, and the large-scale introduction of computer technology into managing the technological preparation of production.

USTD makes it possible to rework manufactured goods with regard to their technical properties during the process of their designing; it establishes a single system of stages, thoroughness in developing the respective documentation, and a uniform order for its presentation and circulation.

USTPIO is intended to increase the processing time of information more than tenfold and, at the same time, cut in half the nomenclature of technical documentation. The introduction of USTPIO will substantially increase the role of information and the uniform system of its indices. This task is being solved in the USTD.

Although USDD and USTD are independent uniform statewide systems they are subsystems of USTPIO and to a great extent define its development and implementation.

An integral part of USTPIO is *type design and standardization of technological processes* on the basis of previously developed type sizes and parameters for the production of specific items within definite classification groups without any additional technological developments.

With the introduction of USTPIO 50%–60% of all work performed in this cycle will consist of type-designed processes; at present their share stands at 12%–14%.

The classification of processed items and the introduction of type-designed technologies are based on the implementation of state technological classification of parts for the engineering and instrument engineering industries.

The time for preparing and enhancing production mobility is reduced through the *standardization and unification of operations for technological preparation of equipment and tooling,* by introducing devices capable of being retooled, joint processing of type-designed items, and other adjusting fixtures. Each element of the listed adjustments is independent in terms of design and can be quickly removed.

At present, a considerable amount of effort that goes into the technological preparation work falls to designing and constructing special technological tooling. These outlays are being considerably reduced through the development and introduction of an *inter-district system of readjustable and reusable tooling* based on principles of long-term usage, universal properties, and reversibility, and consisting of subsystems, sets, and different type sizes including standardized parts. In developing an inter-district system of adjustable tooling, consideration should be given to the continuity between the tooling in use and the tooling that is developed, the possibility of using existing instruments and equipment, and maximum reduction of the cost of developing and implementing the system.

An important aspect of USTPIO is *standardization of the means and methods of automation and mechanization of engineering work for the technological preparation of production.*

An automated USTPIO (ASTPIO) can include subsystems dealing with: information, control of technological preparation (TPP), norms and technical data, and the design of both technological tooling and TPP processes.

USTPIO contains documents defining the consecutiveness of work dealing with automation and mechanization of TPP, setting up ASTPIO, methods of computerizing TPP, a nationwide reserve of type-designed algorithms, and programs for the preparation of production.

ASTPIO, like other automated systems, requires a technical and economic basis for its implementation.

The base for the informational support for ASTPIO consists of technical and economic classifiers of information, including the nationwide classifier of industrial and agricultural output, technological classifier of parts for the engineering and instrument engineering industries, classifier of operations, etc.

The standard information-forecasting model USTPIO, with the highest level of automated processing of information, serves as the basis of an information-model TPP operating at a specific company. It ensures an optimal level of automation for that company on the basis of which further work is performed on the TPP. The information carriers are chosen for their storing convenience and for the reliability and correctness of the information. In the process of creating the information model, the composition and structure of information are determined and a chart is drawn up of its movement with account for the timely and optimal loading of all the means of automation.

The software should reduce as much as possible the labor-intensive programming by creating and choosing problem-oriented algorithm languages and employing a unified method for solving standardized problems.

The task of reducing the time for the technological preparation of production is effectively solved by computerizing TPP designing. The design process down to receiving technological documentation is automated.

USTPIO is a highly convenient base for developing and designing the automated system for control of technological preparation of production (ASCTPP) as a subsystem of ASCP. The need for designing this subsystem arises out of the increased level of production automation in general and the insufficient automation of control over technological preparation and of the process itself.

The effect of introducing USTPIO is determined for all companies intending to implement the system and for the consumers of their products.

The effect on enterprises (E) is calculated by using the formula

$$E = (O_2P_2 - O_1P_1) - (O_2C_2 - O_1C_1) - E_f (K_2 - K_1).$$

where

O = output of product (program);
P = price of unit of product;
C = cost of unit of product;

K = production assets of enterprise (capital investments and current assets);

E_f = share of allocation to the State budget for production assets (usually 0.06);

index 1 and index 2 = indices, respectively, before and after introduction of USTPIO.

The economic effect is determined in the second year after introduction of USTPIO with account for the volume of output and the respective outlays.

An important prerequisite for calculating the effect of introducing USTPIO is its comprehensive character—selecting initial data embracing indices of the developed objects, labor expenditure, costs, length and characteristics of technological processes, their organization and employed tooling; determining standard technological processes, production operations, control and testing of product.

Effect of standardizing technology is made up of:

(a) reducing cost of developing technology determined by the formula

$$E_1 = B (Z_1 + Z_a) = 0.2 Z_2$$

where

B = average number of processes developed yearly;

Z_1 = average cost of developing a single process;

Z_a = cost of additional work to adjust the standard technological process to specific part (item);

Z_2 = cost of developing standard technological process;

0.2 = factor of reducing costs for the development of standard technological process;

(b) reduction of number of readjustments and time required:

$$E_2 = n (P_w + \frac{Z_y}{F}) \bullet (\alpha_1 T_{r1} - \alpha_2 T_{r2}),$$

where

n = average number of sets of identical parts produced yearly;

P_w = wages per time unit of worker engaged in readjustment with account of additional wages and allocations for social insurance;

Z_y = yearly sum of conditionally permanent costs;

α = number of operations assigned to equipment and requiring readjustment;

T_r = time for readjustment;

here and further index 1 and index 2 = indices, respectively, before and after standardization of technology;

(c) reduction of time for preparation of production depending on effectiveness of equipment earmarked for production:

$$E_3 = N E_t (T_{p1} - T_{p2}),$$

where

N = norm factor of economic effect of capital investments (0.12);

E_t = effect from output of new machinery for financial production year;

T_p = time of preparation for production;

(d) increase of labor productivity:

$$E_4 = B_2 \sum_1^m (T_{r1}P_{w1} - T_{r2}P_{w2}) + (T_{o1}X_{o1} - T_{o2}X_{o2}) + \frac{N}{F} (\frac{X_1T_{o1}}{K_{l1}} - \frac{X_2T^{o2}}{K_{l2}}),$$

where

m = number of operations per unit of output;

T_r = time rate for one operation;

P_w = wages per time unit of work with account for additional wages and allocations for social insurance;

T_o = time of machine load for one operation (distinct from T_r in multi-machine and team servicing, periodical use of equipment);

X_o = cost of one minute or one hour of machine operation;

X_l = cost of equipment;

k_l = factor of equipment load;

(d) reduction of the cycle of production activity due to less labor-consuming control and testing, reducing interruptions and changing the form of production movement:

$$E_5 = \frac{NB_2C (1 + y) \bullet (T_{c1} + T_{c2})}{2F},$$

where

y = specific gravity of materials and purchased items in cost of production;
C = cost of unit of output;
T_c = length of production cycle;
(e) raising quantity production:

$$E_6 = \frac{C_1 (100 - n_c)}{100},$$

where

C_1 = cost of operation (excluding cost of materials and blanks) before type-designing of technology;
n_c = cost of operations after type-designing in percentage.

Effect of unification of technological tooling and its elements is made up of:
(a) reducing designing costs:

$$E_7 = B_o (Z_{p1} - Z_a) - 0.2 Z_{p2},$$

where

B_o = average number of tooling projects for replacement of given unified construction developed in the course of one year;
Z_{p1} = average cost of designing tooling;
Z_a = average cost of additional work for designing separate parts or separate changes in unified tooling, if they are needed for its specific application;
Z_{p2} = cost of development of unified construction;
(b) standardization (unification of adjustments:

$$E_8 = B \left(\frac{C_{a1}}{K_{p1}} - \frac{C_{a2}}{K_{p2}}\right),$$

where C_a = cost of adjustment;

K_p = number of processed items until wear-out of adjustments;
index 1 and index 2 = indices, respectively before and after unification of tooling.

Effect of reduction of nomenclature of operated equipment is achieved by:
(a) reducing the units of equipment:

$$E_9 = (\frac{a}{100} + N) \bullet (X_{11} - X_{12}),$$

where

a = percentage of amortization;
X_{11} and X_{12} = cost of equipment before and after reduction of
  nomenclature of operated equipment;

(b) reducing repair work:

$$E_{10} = T_r P_w (R_1 - \frac{R_2}{K}),$$

where

T_r = labor input into repairs per group of repairs complexity;
P_w = average wages of repairman per time unit with account for
  additional wages and allocations for social insurance;
R = number of groups of repairs complexity;
k = factor of nomenclature of equipment, i.e., the ratio of
  number of equipment trademarks before and after unification;

(c) reduction of specifications of turnover capital

$$E_{11} = N (Z_{z1} - Z_{z2}),$$

where

Z_{z1} and Z_{z2} = cost of spare parts of equipment, excluded from
  nomenclature or newly introduced.

Effect of type designing of means and methods of control and testing
is achieved by:
(a) reduction in the volume of testing and reducing its costs:

$$E_{12} = \frac{b P_w}{100} - (\frac{T_{t1} b_1}{k_{c1}} - \frac{T_{t2} b_2}{k_{c2}}),$$

where

P_w = wages per time unit of tester (controller) with account for
  additional wages and allocations for social insurance;
T_t = testing time;
b = percentage of selectivity of parts for testing;

k_c = number of testing stands (apparatus) serviced by one tester;

here and further index 1 and index 2 = indices, relatively before and after type-designing of means and methods of control;

(b) reduction of missed spoilage (if loss from use of spoiled units is known):

$$E_{13} = BY \frac{b \bullet b_y}{100},$$

where

b_y = percentage of cases when use of spoiled units brings losses;
Y = losses from use of spoiled item;
(c) reduction of output discarded as spoilage:

$$E_{14} = \frac{B \bullet b_g (C - Y_s)}{100},$$

where

b_g = percentage of reduction of cases when good output turns up at spoilage;
Y_s = cost of spoiled unit discarded as waste;

Effect of using USTD in the process of technological preparation of production is determined by the formula

$$E_{15} = KF_w P_w \left(1 - \frac{100}{100 + p}\right),$$

where

K = number of workers;
F_w = yearly time fund of worker;
p = percentage of raising labor productivity.

Effect of using USTD instead of documentation in force is achieved by:

(a) accelerating training of workers;

$$E_{16} = \frac{K_p}{T_c} \Delta T P_w,$$

where

K_p = number of workers in given category;
T_c = average number of years of continuous work;
T = reduction of time for training with use of USTD;
(b) mechanization of filling in technological documentation:

$$E_{17} = [G\,T_g + G_m\,(T_g - T_{gm})]\,P_{wt} - (N + \frac{a}{100})\,K_m,$$

where

G = number of excluded columns in documentation;
G_m = number of columns transferred to mechanical filling in;
T_g = average time for filling in a single column by hand;
T_{gm} = average time for mechanized filling in of one column;
P_{wt} = wages of industrial engineer per time unit;
K_m = capital investments into copying machinery;

Effect from improvement of work organization due to introduction of USTPIO is determined by the formula

$$E_{18} = \sum_{1}^{m_1} \sum_{1}^{n_1} B_u\,T_{p1}\,P_w,$$

where

m_1 = number of types of jobs;
n_1 = number of types of operations in performing jobs, including inspection jobs;
B_u = yearly number of job units;
T_{p1} = labor input into a unit of work.

Effect of measures included in USTPIO to raise effectiveness of production as compared with the elaboration of similar individual plans at enterprise equals

$$E_{19} = N\,(Z_{t1} - Z_t),$$

where

Z_{t1} and Z_{t2} = expenses for transition to USTPIO, respectively, without and with using the typical list of measures to raise the effectiveness of production.

The choice of means is determined by:

(a) expenses for their acquisition for one year:

$$Z_c = \left(N + \frac{a}{100}\right) Z_1,$$

where

Z_1 = cost of equipment;

(b) expenses for exploitation (per unit of output):

$$Z_k = T_c P_3 + Z_c + \frac{Z_3}{n_{oc}},$$

where

T_c = time for treating unit of production;

Z_c = cost of electricity or other power and technological fuel per unit of output;

Z_c = cost of tooling;

n_{oc} = cost of tooling in units of output;

(c) scale of production:

$$Z_g = Z_k B + Z_c,$$

where

Z_g = total expenses for one year's production.

The more general average indices of effectiveness of work on technological preparation of production are: time of developing and labor capacity of new output, its material capacity, cost, reliability, durability, etc. Analysis of these and other indices will expose TPP sections calling for utmost improvement.

BIBLIOGRAPHY

Listed in reverse chronological order

I. Monographs, Books, Articles, and Research Papers

"Is It Time for a Gold Rush?" *Novoye Russkoye Slovo/Russian-American Daily* (New York), October 2, 1998, p. 2 [in Russian].

"Fixing Russia." *Forbes* (New York), September 21, 1998, pp. 70–72.
   Reprinted: *Forbes Global Business and Finance* (New York), September 21, 1998, p. 25.

"The Last Days of Boris Yeltsin." *Forbes* (New York), September 7, 1998, pp. 145–151.
   Reprinted: *Forbes Global Business & Finance* (New York), September 7, 1998, pp. 58–63.
   Translated into Russian: *Novoye Russkoye Slovo/Russian-American Daily* (New York), August 28, 1998, p. 11; *Segodnia* (Today) (Moscow), September 8, 1998, p. 3.

"Economic Problems of Russia Require Political Decisions." *Novoye Russkoye Slovo/Russian-American Daily* (New York), September 2, 1998, p. 2 [in Russian].

"Building Capitalism in Russia Is Impossible Without Expropriation." *Novoye Russkoye Slovo/Russian-American Daily* (New York), July 4–5, 1998, p. 11 [in Russian].

"The Nature of International Joint Ventures and Their Role in Global Business." In *International M&A, Joint Ventures, and Beyond: Doing the Deal.* New York: John Wiley and Sons, 1997. Pp. 295–314.

"Emerging Market of Brazil: Evaluation of the Potential Market for Future Telecommunication Companies." Brazilia, Brazil: Arthur Andersen, 1997. 51 pages.

Emerging Market of Russia: Source Book for Investment and Trade. [Cover editor, author, and co-author]. New York: John Wiley and Sons, 1997. 705 pages.

"Incorporating Global Risk Management in the Strategic Decision Making Process." *World Markets Series.* London: The World Markets Research Centre, DRI/McGraw Hill, 1997. 16 pages.

"Tragic Influence of the Government on the Country." *Rabochaya Tribuna* (Workers' tribune) (Moscow), August 19, 1997, p. 2 [in Russian].

Prepared by Christopher Cox.

"Europe's Six Top Emerging Markets," South and Central Europe, Regional Analysis, *Emerging Markets Investments, World Markets Series, Business Briefing*. London: The World Markets Research Centre, DRI/McGraw Hill, 1996. Pp 34–38.

"Ukraine Without Russian Influence." *Business Information Analytical Journal* (Kharkov, Ukraine), December 1996, pp. 42–44 [in Russian].

"Ukraine: Living in Russia's Shadow." *The Journal of Commerce* (New York), June 25, 1996, p. 7A.

"Russia's Imbalance of Power." *The New York Times*, March 10, 1996, section 3, p. 14.

"Board of Director Motivation in Russia and the Commonwealth of Independent States." In *Directorship: Director Motivation—Incentives, and Disincentives to Board Service*. A Quantitative Research Report. Greenwich, Connecticut: Directorship, Inc., 1996. Pp. 10–7, 10–8.

"Development of International Joint Ventures: Risks and Opportunities." In *Creating and Managing International Joint Ventures*. Edited by Arch G. Woodside and Robert E. Pitts. Westport, Connecticut: Quorum Books, 1996. Pp. 159–175.

"How Emerging Is Emerging?" *Global Investment*, 2, No. 1, December 1995, pp. 43–44.

"A Different Perspective on Emerging Markets." In *The Fourth Annual World Economic Development Congress, Addendum, World Markets in 1996—A Special Summit Briefing of Some of the Speakers' Addresses*, Washington, D.C., October 4–6, 1995, pp. 50–54.

"Russia's Crumbling Infrastructure." *The Journal of Commerce* (New York), September 12, 1995, Editorial/Opinion, p. 8a.

"Russia Is Falling Behind in the Struggle for Investment Capital." *ITAR–TASS–Business World* (Moscow–New York), August 2, 1995, pp. 1–2 [in Russian].

"Foreword." In *The Ross Register of Siberian Industry*. New York: Norman Ross Publishing, Inc., 1995. Pp. vii–viii.

"Russia's Capitalist Institutions." *The Journal of Commerce* (New York), January 25, 1995, Editorial/Opinion, p. 8a.

"The Political-Economic Climate for Investment in Belarus." New York: Arthur Andersen, July 1994, 28 pages.

"Restoring the Romanovs," *Forbes* (New York), December 5, 1994, pp. 145–152.

"Now Is the Time to Do Business in Russia." *Harvard Business Review* (Cambridge, Massachusetts), May/June 1994, pp. 42–43.

"The Russia Investment Dilemma: Perspectives." *Harvard Business Review* (Cambridge, Massachusetts), May/June, 1994, p. 35.

With Dr. Charles J. Cicchetti and Colin M. Long. *Situation Analysis of the Current Telecommunications Sector in the Russian Federation and Forecast*. New York: Arthur Andersen & Co., May 1994. 183 pages.

"Don't Give Up on Russia." *Harvard Business Review* (Cambridge, Massachusetts), March/April 1994, pp. 62–74.

"Reserves, Production, and Utilization of Nickel in Russia." New York: Arthur Andersen & Co., 1993. 23 pages.

"Six Years' Experience of Success and Failure of Joint Ventures in the Former Soviet Union." Scranton, Pennsylvania: Academy of International Business, June 1993. 18 pages.

"A Healthy Realism for the Russians." *The New York Times*, January 24, 1993, Business Section, p. F13.

> Translated into Russian: *The New York Times Biweekly Review*, March 1, 1993, p. A7.

Political Disintegration and Economic Reintegration in Eurasia: Competing in the New World Economy. Pittsburgh, Pennsylvania: Robert Morris College, 1993, 15 pages.

"Insights into Russian Business." *GBA Forum* (Fordham University Graduate School of Business Administration, New York), 10, No. 5, June 1993, pp. 3, 8.

In collaboration with Natalia Darialova. *The Barefoot Shoemaker: Capitalizing on the New Russia*. Boston: Arcade Publishing, 1993, 234 pages.

The Russian Chronicle, March 1, 1993, 1 page.

"Russian Diamonds." *Forbes* (New York), February 15, 1993, pp. 42–43.

"Gorby Takes the Fifth: Is Yeltsin Persecuting the Deposed Leader? Or Is Gorbachev Hiding Something?" *Forbes* (New York), November 9, 1992, p. 48.

"Down the Rat Hole: Doesn't Anyone Remember What Happened to the Loans to Latin America or to Mikhail Gorbachev's Regime?" *Forbes* (New York), August 3, 1992, pp. 40–41.

"Expanding the E.C.'s Communication Links to Diversity Centers of Influence: Opportunities of the Russian Market." *Communication in New Words*, 42nd Annual Conference of the International Communication Association, Miami, Florida, May 1992.

"International Business Curriculum: What Interests Students?" *GBA Forum* (Fordham University Graduate School of Business Administration, New York), 10, no. 11, April 1992, p. 3.

"Russengold" (Russian gold). *Forbes Von Burda* (Munich), February 1992, pp. 29–40 [in German].

"Opportunity in a Shattered Land." *The New York Times*, January 19, 1992, Business Section, Forum, p. F11.

With Natalia Darialova. "Where Are the Diamonds?" *Novoye Vremya* (New times) (Moscow), no. 46, November 1991, p. 14 [in Russian].

> Translated into English, German, Italian, and Polish.

With Natalia Darialova. "Man in the Shadows: The Soviet Union Is Not as Broke as It Pretends; Stolen by the Communist Party, Substantial Assets Exist Both Abroad and at Home." *Forbes* (New York), October 28, 1991, pp. 120–122.
> Translated into Japanese: Kiodo Agency (Tokyo); Jiji Press (Tokyo).
> Translated into Russian: *Mir i Muy* (We and the world), TASS Agency (Moscow) October 15, 1991, p. 16; *Megapolis–Express* (Moscow), 45 (1991).

News Clips: Vladimir Kvint (Collection of Articles). Wellesley, Massachusetts: Babson College, October 1991. 59 pages.

With Natalia Darialova. "Watch Your Wallet: It's Wild West Time in the Emerging Business World of the Old Soviet Union." *Forbes* (New York), September 30, 1991, pp. 60–62.

"Siberia: A Warm Place for Investors: The Soviet Break-up Presents Great Opportunities for Investors." *Forbes* (New York), September 16, 1991, pp. 96–97.

"Gennadi Yanayev, Overachiever." *The New York Times*, August 20, 1991, Op-ed Page, p. A27.
> Reprinted: "Spawn of the Party Machine." *Miami Herald*, August 21, 1991.

"Dead Souls: Workers in the Soviet Union Seem Lazy and Thieving, But the Soviet People Are Fundamentally Honest and Capable of Hard Work. It Is the System That Has Made Them Bad—and the System Is Dying." *Forbes* (New York), May 27, 1991, pp. 96–102.

"United We Fall." *Moscow Magazine*, April 1991, p. 45 [in Russian].

"Siberian Hoard: Will Russia Be the Chief Oil Source of the Future?" *Institutional Investor*, 4 (1991), Energy Forum, 18.

"Political, Economic, and Legal Reform in the Soviet Union." *Whittier Law Review*, 12, no. 2, 1991, pp. 143–146.

"The Myth of Good Czar Gorbachev: Baltic Repression Shows We Could Have Been Together with the Kremlin. *Forbes* (New York), February 4, 1991, pp. 36–37.
> Forecast for 1991 as the last year of the USSR.

"Food Shortages, Now Violence Makes Soviet Investing Dicier." *The New York Times*, January 20, 1991, section 3, p. F5.

"Food for Peace, or for Civil War?" *Forbes* (New York), January 21, 1991, pp. 39–41.

"Confronting the Soviet Management Structure: Bureaucratic, but Workable." *The International Executive*, November/December 1990, pp. 3–6.

"Go East, Young Man: Russian Opportunities in the East." *Forbes* (New York), November 26, 1990, pp. 234–238.

"Moscow Learns the Language of Business: Integrating a Government-Run Economy into the Global Marketplace Takes More Than Exchangeable Currency, Stock Markets, and Commercial Banks—Much More." *The Journal of Accountancy*, November 1990, pp. 114–119.

"Opportunities in Soviet Disintegration: Anticipating the Division of the Soviet Union into Several States and the Opportunities for Foreign Investment That Will Result." *The New York Times*, October 28, 1990, section 3, p. 13.

"Role of International Connections in the Creation of a New Political Structure." *Regional Science Association International* (Urbana, Illinois), 1990. 12 pages.

"Eastern Siberia Could Become Another Saudi Arabia." *Forbes* (New York), September 17, 1990, pp. 130–133 [Cover Story].

"Who's in Charge Around Here?" *Forbes* (New York), September 3, 1990, pp. 54–57.

"The Soviet Market: Crisis of Power and New Economic Opportunities." A Report for the General Electric Co. New York: Kvint Associates, August 1990. 27 pages.

"The Best Way to Help Gorbachev Is to Make Life Difficult for Him." *Forbes* (New York), June 11, 1990, pp. 168–172.

"Free the Ruble! Currency Convertibility in the Soviet Union." *Forbes* (New York), April 2, 1990, pp. 92–95.

Reprinted: *Moscow Magazine* (Moscow) 7 (1990), 37–39.

Translated into Russian: *Moscow Magazine* (Moscow). 7 (1990), pp. 10–11.

"Kapitalismus, Jetzt! (Capitalism, immediately). *Wochenpresse* (Vienna) February 23, 1990, pp. 27–28 [Cover Story] [in German].

"Russia Should Quit the Soviet Union: A Soviet Economist's Revolutionary Proposal." (Russia as Cinderella). *Forbes* (New York), February 19, 1990, pp. 103–108 [cover story].

"Wreck the Information Flow and the Economy Collapses." *Austria Business and Economy* (Vienna), 2, no. 3, January 1990, p. 54.

"Alle könnten alles verlieren" (Everyone could lose everything). *Wochenpresse* (Vienna) January 19, 1990, p. 42 [in German].

The inevitable future disintegration of the USSR.

"Study of the USSR Refrigerator and Freezer Markets: Trends of Production and Operation." For the General Electric Company. Vienna, Austria, January 2, 1990. 86 pages.

"Study of the Tendencies of Production in Washing Machine Market in the USSR." For the General Electric Company, Vienna, Austria, December 20, 1989. 23 pages.

"Crisis and Recovery in Soviet Economy." *East–West Forum* (Vienna), no. 4, December 1989, pp. 76–77 [in German, English].

"Erste Schritte der Sowjetunion auf das glatte Eis der freien Marktwirt-
schaft" (The first steps of the Soviet Union on the slippery ice of a market economy). *Neue Kronen Zeitung* (Vienna), December 2, 1989,
Experten-Forum, pp. 2–3 [in German].

"Ohne Demokratisierung greifen die Reformen nicht" (Without democracy, there is no reform available). *Nordbayerischer Kurier* (North Bavar-
ian Courier) (Bayreuth, West Germany), December 1, 1989, p. 9 [in
German].

"Everything You Always Wanted to Know About Business in the USSR."
Link (Zurich), November 19, 1989.

"Are We Ready for Price Reforms?" *Sovety Narodnych Deputatov* (Soviet
people's deputies) (Moscow) 3 (1989), 53 [in Russian].

"Is It Profitable for a Country to Be Free?" *Nedelya* (The week) (Moscow),
13 (1989), 6–7 [in Russian].
    From a discussion with Nobel Laureate Wassily Leontief.

"Soviet People's Deputies: The Problems of Private Ownership and Regional Self-Sufficiency." In *The Perestroika in the Regulation of Economics: The Second Stage—The All-Union Economics Seminar*. (April 1–3,
1988). Moscow: Institute of National Economics after Plekhanov, 1989.
Pp. 108–116 [in Russian].

"The USSR Exporters Association." Moscow: Chamber of Commerce,
1989. 2 pages.

"Memorandum." Vienna: Austrian Academy of Sciences, December 14,
1988.

"Go For It, You Are Talented!" *Komsomolskaya Pravda*, October 6, 1988, p.
1 [in Russian].
    The creation of the first school for young managers in Moscow, USSR.

With M. Gamzatov and Z. Uzbekov. *The Scientific and Technical Development of the Economy of Daghestan* (in Russian). Mahachkala, Daghestan,
USSR: The Daghestan State Publishing House, 1988. 143 pages [in Rus-
sian].
    Awarded the Daghestan Republic Prize.

"Is Economic Reform Possible Without Perestroika in Government Policy?—A Roundtable Discussion." *Voprosy Ekonomiky* (Problems in economics) (Moscow), no. 6, 1988, 13–14 [in Russian].

"Soviet Peoples Deputies: The Owners of Property." In *The Problems of
Socialist Property Ownership: The Structure and Perestroika of the Models
of Economic Attainment*. Moscow: Institute of Economy, USSR Academy
of Sciences, 1988. Pp. 48–50 [in Russian].

"Österreich nutzt seine Chance als Bindeglied nicht effektiv" (Austria isn't
using its chance to be an effective link). *Neue Kronen Zeitung* (Vienna),

December 17, 1988, Experten-Forum Wirtschafts Magazin, pp. 2–3 [in German].

"Enterprise and Local Government under New Conditions." *Novoye Vremya* (New times) (Moscow), no. 18, 1988, p. 32 [in Russian].

"Perestroika and the Lessons of Economic Reforms: A roundtable discussion." *Voprosy Ekonomiky* (Problems in economics) (Moscow), no. 2, 1988, pp. 62–63.

With T. Dorzh. "Modernization in the Management of Scientific and Technical Progress (STP)." In *The Complex Program of STP in Mongolia Through the Year 2005*, vol. II (Main). Mongolia, Novosibirsk, USSR, and Ulan-Bator, Mongolia: The Academy of Sciences of the USSR and The Academy of Sciences of Mongolia, 1988. Pp. 422–440 [in Russian].
   Translated into Mongolian.

Problems of Inter-Republican Relations in the USSR. Warsaw: Warsaw University Publishing House, 1988. 33 pages [in Polish].

"On Poor Utilization of Industrial Waste in Production of Construction Materials." *Stroitelnaya Gazeta* (The construction newspaper), February 14, 1988, p. 2 [in Russian].

With others. "Price and the Process of Setting It." *New Times* (Moscow), no. 1, 1988, pp. 29–31.
   Translated into Russian, Italian, German, French, Spanish, Portuguese, Czech, and Polish.

With M. Holdakowskiy. "Making Up For Lost Time." *Novoye Vremya* (New times) (Moscow), no. 52, December 29, 1987, pp. 18–19 [in Polish].
   Translated into German, English, Russian.

"On the Possibility of Increasing the Influence of the Daghestan Branch of the USSR Academy of Sciences on the Effectiveness of Scientific-Technical Progress in the Republic" (in Russian). In *Programs and Steps of Scientific-Technical Progress in a Region of High Labor Supply*. Mahachkala, Daghestan, USSR: USSR Academy of Sciences, Daghestan Branch, 1987. Pp. 18–28 [in Russian].

With Z. Uzbekov. "Productivity of Enterprise—Productivity of Region." *Dagestanskaya* [Daghestanian] *Pravda* (Mahachkala, Daghestan, USSR), September 18, 1987, p. 2 [in Russian].

"The Relationship Between the Increase in the Cost of Capital Investment and the Decrease in the Lag from Outlay to Implementation." In *Economic Problems of the Implementation of Scientific and Technical Projects*. Moscow: Institute of the Economy, USSR Academy of Sciences, 1987. Pp. 21–25 [in Russian].

"The Importance of Scientific and Technical Policy in the Development of the Political System in Society." In *Political Science and the Scientific-Technical Revolution: The Annual Edition of the Soviet Political Science*

Association. Moscow: Nauka (Science) Publishing House, 1987. Pp. 84–94 [in Russian].

With B. Rudzitskiy and Z. Uzbekov. *Enterprise–Industry–Region: The Economic and Scientific-Technical Information* (in Russian). Moscow: Finansy i Statistika (Finance and statistics) Publishing House, 1987. 175 pages.

With Z. Uzbekov. "The Role of the Budget in the Intensification of the Economy in the Autonomous Republic." *Ekonomicheskiye Nauki* (Economic sciences) (Moscow), no. 11, 1987, pp. 27–34 [in Russian].

"The Methodological Problems of Targeting Regional Economies." In *The Methodological Problems in the Fundamental Perestroika of Economic Management*. Moscow: Institute of the Economy, USSR Academy of Sciences, 1987. Pp. 157–165 [in Russian].

With Z. Uzbekov. "Daghestan-Mangyshiak: The Effectiveness of Inter-Regional Collaboration." In *Regional Socioeconomic Development on the Basis of Increased Scientific and Technological Progress (STP)*. Moscow: Institute of the Economy, USSR Academy of Sciences, 1987. Pp. 75–82 [in Russian].

With Ataev. "Government of Republic—A Look from the Inside." *Novoye Vremya* (New times) (Moscow), no. 36, September 1987, pp 10–11 [in Russian].

"The Soviet People's Deputies as the Central Organizing Bodies for Management of the Economy." *Voprosy Ekonomiki* (Problems in economics) (Moscow), no. 6, 1987, pp. 23–32 [in Russian].

With L. Abalkin. "Where Are We Going?—Economic Reform in the Light of Facts and Principles." *Novoye Vremya* (New times) (Moscow), no. 28, July 1987, pp. 3–5 [in Russian, English].

Reprinted in *It Depends on Us*. Moscow: Knizhnaya Palata (Book palace) Publishing House, 1988. Pp. 155–162 [in Russian].

"Enterprise Collaboration with the Regional Government: A Discussion of the Proposed Law of the USSR on State Enterprises." *Voprosy Ekonomiky* (Problems in economics) (Moscow), no. 5, 1987, pp. 89–90 [in Russian].

"The Organization of Regional Management of Scientific-Technical Development of the Unified National Economic Complex." In *An Authorized Synopsis of the Dissertation for the Doctorate in Economic Science*. Moscow: Institute of the Economy, USSR Academy of Sciences, 1987. 38 pages [in Russian].

"Regional Scientific-Technical Policy: The Formation Process." *Achievements and Outlooks: Management and Scientific-Technical Progress* (Moscow), no. 10, 1986, pp. 34–45 [in Russian].

With A. Petrov. "The Growth of the Planning and Management System in the Formation of the Kansk-Achinsk Fuel-Energetic Complex

(KATEK)." In *Problems of Theory in Organizational Structures of Management Economics*. Moscow: Institute of the Economy, USSR Academy of Sciences, 1986. Pp. 165–177 [in Russian].

With Z. Mikitishin and L. Radzhievskaya. *The Harmony of Industrial and Territorial Principles in the Management of Scientific-Technical Progress (STP) in the Regions of Ukraine*. Kiev: The Gosplan of the Ukraine (State Committee Plan), 1986. 51 pages [in Russian].

"Factors and Stages in the Formation of Scientific-Technical Policy." In *Scientific-Technological Progress and Intensive Economic Growth*. Moscow: Institute of the Economy, USSR Academy of Sciences, 1986 [in Russian].

With V. Aleksandrova and I. Rakhlin. *Strategic Direction in the Organization of Start-to-Finish Planning in the Scientific-Technical Progress*. Moscow: Institute of the Economy, USSR Academy of Sciences, 1986. 20 pages [in Russian].

"Technicalization and Regionalization as a Tendency of Technological Progress." In *The Management of Scientific-Technical Progress in Soviet Republics*. Tallinn, Estonia, USSR: Valgus Publishing House, 1986 [in Russian].

"The Technological Policy of Enterprises." *Eco Magazine* (Novosibirsk and Moscow), no. 6, 1986, pp. 215–218 [in Russian].

With V. Ivanchenko. "The Analysis and Forecast of Regional Economics." *Voprosy Ekonomiky* (Problems in economics) (Moscow), no. 5, 1986 [in Russian].

"The Economic Problems in Saving Resources: A Roundtable Discussion." *Planovoe Khoziaistvo* (Planned economy) (Moscow), no. 4, 1986 [in Russian].
  Reprinted: *Voprosy Ekonomiky* (Problems in economics) (Moscow), no. 4, 1986.

"The Experience of the Development of the System of Regional Management in the Economy." *Obshestvennye Nauky* (Social sciences) (Moscow), no. 1, 1986 [in Russian].

"The Coming of Age of the Organizational Structure for the Management of the Economy: A Discussion of the Central Directives for the Socioeconomic Development of the USSR for the Years 1986–1990, and for the Period up to the Year 2000." *Voprosy Ekonomiky* (Problems in economics) (Moscow), no. 1, 1986 [in Russian].

The Management of Scientific-Technical Progress: A Regional Aspect. Moscow: Nauka (Science) Publishing House, 1986. 216 pages [in Russian].
  Including:
    Introduction, pp. 3–9.
    Chapter 1, "Regionalization-Legality of Modern Scientific Technical Progress.

1. "Technologicalization and Regionalization of Scientific-Technical Progress," pp. 10–24.
2. "Economics of Regional Technologies: New Direction in Economic Science," pp. 24–43.

Chapter 2, "The Scientific-Technical Policy of the United States—Problems of Methodology."

1. "Scientific Technical Policy as a Subject of Interdisciplinary Studies," pp. 45–50.
2. "The Role of Scientific-Technical Policy in the Functioning of Political Systems of Society," pp. 50–55.
3. "System of United Scientific-Technical Policy," pp. 56–88.

Chapter 3, "Economic Aspect of Regional Scientific Technical Policy."

1. "Regional Scientific-Technical Policy," pp. 89–98.
2. "Methodological Bases of Target Setting of Regional Scientific-Technical Policy," pp. 98–106.
3. "Process of Formation of Scientific-Technical Policy," pp. 106–127.

Chapter 4, "Organizational-Economic Mechanism of Implementation of Regional Scientific-Technical Policy."

1. "Direction of the Evolution of Mutual Dependence: State, Industrial, and Territorial Approaches to Organization of Management of National Economy," pp. 128–142.
2. "Experience and Methodology of the Development of Regional Programs of Scientific-Technical Progress," pp. 142–171.
3. "Creation of the Organizational Mechanism for the Implementation of Regional Programs of Scientific-Technical Progress," pp. 171–185.
4. "Development of Economic-Methodical and Normatively-Legal Support of Regional Scientific-Technical Policy," pp. 185–193.
5. "Organizational Forms of Regional Integration of Science and Production," pp. 193–214.

The Methodic Research Program: "The Theoretical Basis of Organizations of Management in the National Economy and Its Industrial and Regional Economic Subsystems." Moscow: Institute of the Economy, USSR Academy of Sciences, 1985 [in Russian].

With T. Kovriga, G. Mikava, and V. N. Ivanchenko. *Methodic Recommendations for the Evaluation of Economic Efficiency and Organizational Structure in the Use of the Research Fleet of the USSR Academy of Sciences During Sea Research Expeditions.* Moscow: Institute of the Economy, USSR Academy of Science, 1985. 87 pages [in Russian].

With F. Golland. "Scientific-Technical Development in the Siberian Economy" (in Russian). In *Economic Problems of Scientific-Technical Progress in Regions*. Novosibirsk, USSR: Institute of the Economy and Organization of Industry, Siberian Branch, USSR Academy of Sciences, 1985. Pp. 69–81 [in Russian].

"Methodology of Research into Regional Problems of Scientific-Technical Progress and Programs for Its Development." In *Economic Problems of Scientific-Technical Progress in Regions*. Novosibirsk, USSR: Institute of the Economy and Organization of Industry, Siberian Branch, USSR Academy of Sciences, 1985. Pp. 10–21 [in Russian].

"The Problems of the Transportation System of the Norilsk Industrial Region." In *The Problems of the Development of Transportation in Siberia*. Novosibirsk, USSR: Siberian Branch, USSR Academy of Sciences, 1985 [in Russian].

"The Harmony of National, Regional, and Industrial Management in the Economy." *Voprosy Ekonomiky* (Problems in economics) (Moscow), no. 7, 1985, pp. 68–77 [in Russian].

"The Methodology of Research Concerning the Organizational Structure of Management in the National Economy." In *The Complex Evolution of the Management of the National Economy*. Moscow: Institute of the Economy, USSR Academy of Sciences, 1985. Pp. 15–37 [in Russian].

With V. Ivanchenko. "The Coordination of State, Regional, and Industrial Approaches to Management in the National Economy." In *The Role of the Economic Mechanism in the Development of the Socialist Economy*. Moscow: Nauka (Science) Publishing House, 1985. Pp. 318–333 [in Russian].

Recognized as the Best Book of The Institute of the Economy of the USSR Academy of Sciences.

With N. Singur. "A Polar Star Above Us: An Arctic Economic Expedition." Moscow: Sovetskaya Rossiya (Soviet Russia) Publishing House, 1984. 192 pages [in Russian].

Awarded the Best Popular Scientific Book Prize in the All-Union Competition in 1985.

"Methodological Problems in Setting the Target of Regional Scientific-Technical Policy." In *Economic Problems of Acceleration of Implementation of Scientific-Technical Achievements*. Moscow: Institute of the Economy, USSR Academy of Sciences, 1984. Pp. 168–175 [in Russian].

"The Problem of the Coordination of Government, Territorial, and Sectoral Approaches to Improve the Management of National Economy." Moscow: The Institute of the Economy of the USSR Academy of Sciences, 1984. 24 pages [in Russian].

"Problems in the Relationship Between State and Regional Scientific-Technical Policy." In *Problems of Regional Development in the Progress of Scientific-Technical Management*. Donetzk, Ukraine, USSR: Institute of Industrial Economy, Ukraine Academy of Sciences, 1984 [in Russian].

"Region and Industry: The Ways of Cooperation." *Pravda* (Moscow), October 22, 1984, p. 3 [in Russian].

"The Methodology for Setting the Target of State and Regional Scientific-Technical Policy." In *Regional Management of Economic and Social Development*. Donetzk, Ukraine, USSR: Institute of Industrial Economy, Ukraine Academy of Sciences, 1984 [in Russian].

With V. Chichkanov. "The Russian Far East." *Sztandaru Ludu* (Warsaw), March 3, 1984 [in Polish].

With others. "Improvement of Management of the Scientific-Technical Progress in the Regions." *Gosplan of Ukraine*. Kiev: State Planning Committee, 1984. 16 pages [in Russian].

"The Coming of Age in the Management Structure of the National Economy." *Voprosy Ekonomiky* (Problems in economics) (Moscow), no. 7, 1984, p. 25 [in Russian].

"The Economic and Legal Aspects of Regional Scientific-Technical Policy." In *Economic and Organizational Legal Problems in the Management of Scientific-Technical Progress*. Moscow: The All-Union Institute of Patent Information, 1984 [in Russian].

With V. Chichkanov. "The Soviet Far East and the International Division of Labor." *Sovetskaya Panorama* (Soviet outlook) (Moscow), no. 14, 1984 [in Russian].

"The Far East Program, or, Looking to the Year 2000." *Socialism: Theory and Practice* (Moscow), no. 4, 1984, pp. 46–51 [in English, French, German, Spanish].

"Unified Scientific and Technical Policy: What and Why?" *Moscow News*, no. 45 (1983), p. 12 [in Russian].

Translated into English, Arabic, Spanish.

"Regionalization as a Contemporary Trend of Scientific-Technical Progress." In *Economic Problems of Territorial Scientific-Technical Complexes*. Moscow: The Institute of the Economy of the USSR Academy of Science, 1983. Pp. 41–66 [in Russian].

Awarded the All-Union Silver Medal for Achievement in National Economy of the USSR; awarded the Ukrainian Republic Prize after Artem.

With I. Podolev. "Programmed Target Approach for Achieving Regional Aspects of Scientific-Technical Policy" (in Russian). In *Target Programs for the Development of Industries and Regions*. Donetzk, Ukraine, USSR: Institute of Economics of Industry, Ukraine Academy of Sciences, 1983. Pp. 34–50 [in Russian].

"Trend Toward Regionalizing Scientific-Technical Progress and the Policy of Using It." In *Third City Scientific-Practical Conference: Problems of Economic and Social Development of City of Moscow*. Moscow: Institute of Complex Development of Moscow, 1983. Pp. 103–106 [in Russian].

"Government and Industrial Scientific-Technical Policy: The Political-Economic Aspect." In *The Development of the Economic Mechanism with the Increase in Scientific-Technical Progress (STP)*. Moscow: Institute of the Economy, USSR Academy of Sciences, 1983 [in Russian].

"Problems in the Formation of Organizational Mechanisms in Regional Programs for Scientific-Technical Progress." In *Methodological Problems in the Development of Economic Ties in the System of "Scientific Production."* Moscow: The Institute of the Economy of the USSR Academy of Sciences, 1983 [in Russian].

"The Planning of Scientific-Technical Progress in COMECON Countries." *Izvestia AN USSR, Seria Ekonomicheskaya* (News of the Academy of Sciences of the USSR, Economic Section) (Moscow), no. 6, 1983 [in Russian].

"Regional Scientific Potential." *Trud* (Labor) (Moscow), October 4, 1983, p. 2 [in Russian].

"Political and Legal Aspects of Regional Scientific-Technical Policy." *Sovietskoe Gosudarstvo i Pravo* (Soviet state and law) (Moscow), no. 4, 1983, pp. 28–36 [in Russian].

"Siberia: Mechanics on the Construction Site." *Soviet Panorama* (Moscow), March 23, 1983, pp. 1–2 [in Russian].

"Arctic Riches." In *Novosti Press Agency Publishing House Original Manuscripts*. Moscow: APN, 1983. Pp. 6, 46, 83, 124, 163 [in Russian, English, Spanish, German, French].

"Esencia y objetivos de la politica cientifico-technica unificada." *Novedades de Moscu* (Moscow news) (Moscow), November 1983, p. 12 [in Spanish].

"Siberia: To be Developed Not Extensively, But Intensively." *Sovetskaya Panorama* (Soviet outlook) (Moscow), no. 57, 1983 [in Russian].
   Translated into Slavic: "Siberia: To Be Developed Not Extensively, But Intensively." *Delo* (Labor) (Bratislava, Czechoslovakia), April 2, 1983.

"The Key to the Region: Complex Programs." *Pravda* (Moscow), March 22, 1983, p. 2 [in Russian].

With M. Gurtovoy. *The Krasnoyarsk Experiment*. Moscow: Sovetskaya Rossiya (Soviet Russia) Publishing House, 1982. Pp. 192 [in Russian].

"On the Verge of the Arctic" (in Finnish). *Kaleva* (Helsinki) April 6, 1982.

"Siberia: An Experiment Without Counterpart." *Sputnik* (Digest of the Soviet press) (Moscow), no. 11, 1982, pp. 42–51 [in Russian].
   Translated into English, German, French, Spanish, Hungarian, Czech.

Translated into Finnish: "Siberia: An Experiment Without Counterpart." *Maailma Ga Me* (Helsinki), no. 11, 1982.

Translated into Polish: "Siberia: An Experiment Without Analogies" (Polish). *Aktualnosci I Informasue* (Gdansk), no. 3, 1983, and *Gazety Olsztynskiey*, August 23, 1983.

"Regional Problems of Scientific-Technical Progress and Approaches to Their Solutions." In *The Methodological Basis for the Management of Scientific-Technical Progress*. Moscow: Institute of the Economy, USSR Academy of Sciences, 1982. Pp. 113–126 [in Russian].

With S. Kropachev. "The Structural Mathematical Modeling of Business Relationships in the Actualization of Regional Scientific-Technical Programs." In *Problems of Economic Management in a Large Region*. Novosibirsk, USSR: Institute of the Economy and Organization of Industry, Siberian Branch, USSR Academy of Sciences, 1981. Pp. 59–74 [in Russian].

With S. Laikevitch. "Scientific-Technical Progress and the Formation of the Northern Krasnoyarsk Territorial Industrial Complex." In *Problems in the Development of Road Construction Transportation Equipment for Use in Siberia and the North: A Thesis of a Report of the All-Union Scientific-Technical Conference*. Moscow: State Committee of the USSR for Science and Technology, 1981. Pp. 21–23 [in Russian].

"Problems in the Development of Regional Complex Programs in Scientific-Technical Progress" (in Russian). Moscow: Institute of the Economy, USSR Academy of Sciences, 1981. P. 38 [in Russian].

With A. Vaygauskas and V. Nenadystin. *Problems in the Regional Development of Scientific-Technical Progress*. Moscow: Institute of Economics, USSR Academy of Sciences, 1981. 35 pages [in Russian].

With K. Chacktarzhik. "Scientific-Technical Problems in the Development of the Tuva Autonomous Republic's Economy." In *Problems in Complex Development of Industry of Tuva Autonomous Republic*. Kyzyl, Tuva: Central Economic Research Institute and GOSPLAN of Russia, 1981 [in Russian].

The Implementation and Use of Automation Systems (Regional Economic Problems) (in Russian). Moscow: Znaniye (Knowledge) Publishing House, 1981. 64 pages [in Russian].

"Zvezdnyi Chas Sibiri" (Siberia's hour of glory). *Sovetskaya Panorama* (Soviet outlook) (Moscow), no. 206, November 3, 1981, III–108, pp. 1–3 [in Russian].

"The Development of Regional Programs for Scientific-Technical Progress." *Izvestia Sibirskogo Otdelenia AN SSSR, Seria Obshestvennych Nauk* (News of the Siberian Branch of the Academy of Sciences of the USSR, Social sciences section) (Novosibirsk, Siberia), no. 1, 1981, pp. 60–64 [in Russian].

"The Territorial Organization for the Repair of Equipment and Automatization Systems." In *Problems in the Development and Location of Industry*. Moscow: Moscow Institute of National Economy after G. Plekhanov, 1980 [in Russian].

With others. *Complex Regional Program on the Acceleration of the Implementation of Developments of Scientific-Technical Progress in the Economy of the Krasnoyarsk Territory for the Years 1981–1990*. Krasnoyarsk, USSR: Institute of the Economy and Organization of Industry, Siberian Branch, USSR Academy of Sciences, 1980 [in Russian].

With I. Petrov. "The Prospects for Using Industrial Waste from the Krasnoyarsk Territory in the Production of Construction Material." In *Siberian Construction Complex: The Problems and Prospects for Development*, Novosibirsk, USSR: Institute of the Economy and Organization of Industry, Siberian Branch, USSR Academy of Sciences, 1980. Pp. 104–109 [in Russian].

With others. *The Feasibility Findings of Utilizing Industrial Robots in the Gold, Lead-Zink, and Nickel-Cobalt Industries*. Krasnoyarsk, USSR: Scientific-Production Concern—Sib Tsvetmet Automatika [Siberian Automation], 1980 [in Russian].

Fact-Finding Tours of Companies in the Lead-Zink Industry on Automation and Robotization [et al.]. Krasnoyarsk, USSR: Scientific-Production Concern—Sib Tsvetmet Automatika [Siberian Automation], 1980, p. 75 [in Russian].

"Regional Scientific-Technical Policy." *Za Nauky v Sibiry* (On science in Siberia) (Novosibirsk, USSR), no. 8, 1980, pp. 1, 4, 5 [in Russian].

"Methodological Problems in the Development of Programs of Scientific-Technological Progress (Based on a Large Region)" (in Russian and Bulgarian). *Problems of Scientific-Technical Forecasting in States and the Use of Scientific-Technical Forecasting in National Economic Management: Theses of Reports on the Second International Symposium on Scientific-Technical Forecasting*. COMECON Publishing House, 1980, pp. 51–54.

> Translated into Czech: "Metodologicke Otazky Vypracovani Programy Vedeckotechnickeho Rozvoje (Na Prikladu Velkeho Vzemi)." in *Edieni Rada UVTR, Prognozovi Vedeckotechnickeho Rozvoje V Zemich RVHP* (Prague), no. 14, 1981, pp. 109–112.

With P. Vovk and N. Orel. "Improvement in the Planning of Nonferrous Metal Enterprises in the Krasnoyarsk Territory." In *Improvements in Planning and Analysis of Industrial Indices of Nonferrous Metal Enterprises*. Krasnoyarsk, USSR: Territorial Scientific-Technical Association, 1980. Pp. 3–8 [in Russian].

The Problems of the Elaboration of the Scientific and Technical Programs: The Experience of the Krasnoyarsk Territory. Novosibirsk, USSR: Institute of the Economy and Organization of Industry, Siberian Branch, USSR Academy of Sciences, Siberian Branch, 1980. 15 pages [in Russian].

"The Problems in the Formation of Regional Scientific-Technical Policy." *Za Nauky v Sibiry* (On science in Siberia) (Novosibirsk, USSR), no. 46, 1980 [in Russian].

With M. Gurtovoy. "The Krasnoyarsk Experiment." *Znamya* (The banner) (Moscow), no. 11, 1980 [in Russian].

"To Accurately Determine a Course of Action: An Economist Analyzes the Results of Krasnoyarsk's Last Decade." *Za Nauky v Sibiry* (On science in Siberia) (Novosibirsk, USSR), no. 35, 1980, pp. 4–5 [in Russian].

"Regional Scientific-Technical Policy." In *Economic Problems of Regional Scientific-Technical Policy.* Krasnoyarsk, USSR: Institute of the Economy and Organization of Industry, Siberian Brancy, USSR Academy of Sciences, 1980 [in Russian].

With O. Volkov and others. *Methodical Rules for the Development of Complex Programs of Regional Scientific-Technical Progress.* Moscow: Institute of the Economy, USSR Academy of Sciences, 1980. 30 pages [in Russian].

"The Regional Approach." *Krasnoyarskiy Rabochiy* (The Krasnoyarsk worker) (Krasnoyarsk, USSR), July 3, 1980 [in Russian].

"It Is Necessary to Increase Food Production in the Yenisey North." *Sovetskaya Torgovlya* (Soviet trade) (Moscow), June 17, 1980, p. 2 [in Russian].

"Regional Scientific-Technical Policy." *Za Nauky v Sibiry* (On science in Siberia) (Novosibirsk, USSR), no. 8, 1980, pp. 1, 4–5 [in Russian].

"The Key Regional Scientific-Technical Problems." In *Problems in the Complex Development of Industry in the Krasnoyarsk Territory.* Novosibirsk, USSR: Institute of the Economy and Organization of Industry, Siberian Branch, USSR Academy of Sciences, 1980 [in Russian].

"The Problems of Scientific-Technical Progress." In *The Problems in Development of the Angara–Yenisey Region.* Irkutsk and Novosibirsk, USSR: Institute of the Economy and Organization of Industry, Siberian Branch, USSR Academy of Sciences, 1980 [in Russian].

"The Regional Aspects in the Utilization of Automation in the Telecommunication Industry of Siberia." In *Economic Problems of Scientific-Technical Progress in Radio, Electronics, Telecommunication, and Business Machines: Theses.* Krasnoyarsk, USSR: All-Union Scientific Technical Association, 1980. Pp. 65–66 [in Russian].

With P. K. Vovk and N. F. Orel. "Problems in the Development of the Nonferrous Metal Industry in Regions of Siberia." In *Problems in the Development of the Nonferrous Metal Industry in Siberia.* The Publications of the All-Union Conference on the Development of Siberian Industry. Novosibirsk, USSR: Siberian Branch, USSR Academy of Sciences, 1980. Pp. 3–16 [in Russian].

With M. Y. Tsaregorodtsev. "The Problems and Perspectives of Automation in the Nonferrous Metal Industry." In *Problems in the Development of the Nonferrous Metal Industry in Siberia*. The Publications of the All-Union Conference on the Development of Siberian Industry. Novosibirsk, USSR: Siberian Branch, USSR Academy of Sciences, 1980. Pp. 54–76 [in Russian].

"Complex Regional Scientific-Technical Program for the Development of Industry in the Krasnoyarsk Territory, 1981–1990." In *Problems in the Development of Regional Complex Programs and in the Development of Siberian Territorial Industrial Complexes*. Novosibirsk, USSR: Siberian Branch, USSR Academy of Sciences, 1980 [in Russian].

With Z. Tsimdina. "Nonferrous Metals Industry." In *Problems in the Development of Regional Complex Programs and in the Development of Siberian Territorial Industrial Complexes*. Novosibirsk, USSR: Siberian Branch, USSR Academy of Sciences, 1980. Pp. 76–80 [in Russian].

With A. Golland. "Problems and Perspectives of the Scientific-Technical Progress of the Siberian Economy." In *The Problems of Economic and Social Development of Siberia: A Perspective*. Novosibirsk, USSR: Siberian Branch, USSR Academy of Sciences, 1980. Pp. 127–136 [in Russian].

With V. Belenkiy. "The Social Aspects of Robotization in Companies." *Nauchnuy Kommunism* (Scientific communism) (Moscow), no. 5, 1980, pp. 39–47 [in Russian].

With others. *An Economic Expedition into the Northern Regions of the Krasnoyarsk Territory*. Novosibirsk-Krasnoyarsk, USSR: Institute of the Economy and Organization of Industry, Siberian Branch, USSR Academy of Sciences, 1979. 350 pages [in Russian].

    A scientific study directed by Drs. A. Aganbegyan and V. Kvint.

    Chapter 1, "Informational Report," pp. 1–10.

    Chapter 2 (with U. Nestirichin), "Regional Problems of Scientific-Technical Progress in Northern Regions of Krasnoyarsk Territory," pp. 10–44.

    Chapter 8, "The Current State of and Future Perspectives of Oil and Gas Exploration in Northern Regions of Krasnoyarsk Territory," 28 pages.

    Chapter 12, "The Prospects for the Development of the Igarko Industrial Complex," 8 pages.

    Chapter 13 (with Z. Tsimdina), "The Problems of the Norilsk Industrial Complex," 43 pages.

    Chapter 14, "Problems and Effectiveness of the Accelerated Utilization of the Gorevko Lead-Zinc Field," 12 pages.

    Chapter 15, "Problems of the Creation and Operation of Regional Museums," 4 pages.

With A. Aganbegyan. "Program of Economic Expedition," 7 pages.

"Development of a Regional Scientific-Technological Program." In *Problems of Economic Organization and Management in Industry*. Issue no. 2. Moscow: Moscow Institute of National Economy after Plekhanov, 1979. Pp. 31–39 [in Russian].

With others. *Development and Use of Industrial Robots in the Economy of the Krasnoyarsk Territory*. Krasnoyarsk, USSR: Scientific-Technical Association, 1979 [in Russian]

A study directed by V. Kvint and M. Tsaregorodtsev.

With M. Tsaregorodtsev. "A Scientific-Production Concern Responsible For: Development, Manufacturing, Assembly, and Servicing." *ECO* (Monthly business magazine) *Magazine* (Novosibirsk, USSR), no. 10, 1979, pp. 100–114 [in Russian].

Regional Inter-Industrial Scientific-Technical Programs for the Development of the Economy in the Krasnoyarsk Territory Novosibirsk, USSR: Institute of the Economy and Organization of Industry, Siberian Branch, USSR Academy of Sciences, 1979. 24 pages [in Russian].

With U. Benderskiy and V. Semyonov. *Scientific-Technical Progress and the Economy of Krasnoyarsk Territory*. Krasnoyarsk, USSR: Krasnoyarskoye Knizhnoe Izdatelstvo [Krasnoyarsk Publishing House], 1979. 135 pages [in Russian].

With N. Akishin. *Regional Utilization of PERT: Methodical Recommendations*. Krasnoyarsk, USSR: Znanie [Knowledge] Publishing House, 1979. 22 pages [in Russian].

With N. Burmakina. "Forecasting the Development of Automation Systems for the Nonferrous Metal Industry." In *The Economics of Organizational Problems in the Management of Scientific-Technical Progress*. Moscow: Znanie (Knowledge) Publishing House, 1979. Pp. 146–150 [in Russian].

With L. Krasov. "The Robot in the Factory Workshop." *Sotsialisticheskaya Industria* (Socialist industry) (Moscow), January 3, 1979, p. 2 [in Russian].

"The Intermediary Role of Scientific-Technological Companies (from the Experience of Sib Tsvetmet Automatika)." *Ekonomicheskaya Gazeta* (The economic newspaper) (Moscow), no. 38, 1978, p. 16 [in Russian].

"Current Problems of Automation in Siberia: A Time Command." *Yenisei* (Krasnoyarsk, USSR), nos. 2, 5, 1978 [in Russian].

With V. Kuzmenko. *Industrial Robots: Classification, Implementation, Effectiveness*. Krasnoyarsk, USSR: Znanie [Knowledge] Publishing House, 1978, 23 pages.

"Raising the Effectiveness of Research in Scientific-Technical Concerns." In *Raising the Effectiveness of Research: The Link Between Science and*

Production. Krasnoyarsk, USSR: Scientific-Technical Association, 1978. Pp. 225–227 [in Russian].

With others. *Economic Efficiency and Perspectives of the Development of Automation in the Gold Industry.* Krasnoyarsk, USSR: Scientific-Production Concern—Sib Tsvetmet Automatika [Siberian Automation], 1978–80 [in Russian].

A study directed by V. Kvint.

FIRST STAGE

Volume I: *The Economic Problems of Automation of Gold-Industry Companies* (Literature Scan and Review). 1978.

Volume II: *Methodology for the Examination of Companies in the All-Union Gold Concern* [Soyuz Zolota]. 1978.

Volume III: *Examination of the Gold Companies "ZABAIKAL ZOLOTO" and "PRIMOR ZOLOTO."* 1978.

Volume IV: *Examination of the Gold Companies: "Mining after Matrosov," "DUKAT," "ARM ZOLOTO," "URAL ZOLOTO."* 1978.

Volume V: *Examination of the Gold Companies: "MINING COCHCANAR," "YENISEY ZOLOTO," "YAKUT ZOLOTO."* 1978.

Volume VI: *Programs and Methods of Forecasting and Systems of Automation for the Companies of the All-Union Gold Concern* [Soyuz Zolota]. 1978.

Volume VII: *Conclusions of the Examinations.* 1978.

SECOND STAGE

Volume I: *Main Indicators of Scientific Research and Construction Projects Achieved by Sib Tsvetmet Automatika [Siberian Automation] for the Gold Industry in the Years 1966–1977.* 1978.

Volume II: *Organizational and Economic Bases for the Use of Automation and Computer Systems: An Overview.* 1979.
Classification of Automation Systems. 1979.

Volume III:
Development of Norms of Unit Expenditures on Automation of Technological Processes for the Gold Industry for 1982 and 1985–1990. 1979.

Volume IV:
Fact-finding Tours of Companies in the Norilsk Mining-Metallurgical Concern. 1979.

With M. Tsaregorodtsev. "A Path to Production." *Sotsialisticheskaya Industrial* (Socialist industry) (Moscow), May 20, 1978, p. 2 [in Russian].

"The Methodology of Increasing Entrepreneurialism Among Engineers" (in Russian). *Tsvyatnaya Metalurgia* (Nonferrous metal industry) (Moscow), no. 22, 1977 [in Russian].

"The Successes and Problems of Sib Tsvetmet Automatika Concerns." *Krasnoyarskiy Rabochiy* (The Krasnoyarsk worker) (Krasnoyarsk, USSR), October 18, 1977, p. 2 [in Russian].

"The Role of Scientific Production Concern in the Growth of Enterprise Specialization." In *The Development of Methods for Economic Management, Ekonomicheskaya Gazeta* (The economic newsaper) (Krasnoyarsk, USSR), 1977, pp. 51–55 [in Russian].

"The Experience of Management in Scientific-Technical Progress Concerning 'Sib Tsvetmet Automatika.'" In *The Development of a Management System for Scientific-Technical Progress in Industrial Enterprises.* Leningrad, USSR: Leningrad Finance Economic Institute, 1977 [in Russian].

"The Creation of a System of Personnel Training for Effective Use of Automation Systems in Gold Mining Concerns and Economic Stimulation of the Work Force." In *Maintaining Systems of Increasing Development, Implementation, and Centralization of Maintenance of Automated Management Systems of Technology in Underground Mines, Gold-Mining Factories and Gold Draglions.* Krasnoyarsk, USSR: Scientific-Technical Council of the USSR Ministry of Nonferrous Metals Industry, 1977 [in Russian].

"The Relationship of Industrial and Territorial Aspects in the Management of National Assets and Its Evolution." In *The Growth of Progressive Forms of Organization in Territorial Industrial Companies.* Krasnoyarsk, USSR: Krasnoyarsk Polytechnic Institute, 1977 [in Russian].

The Formation and Development of Territorial Industrial Comiplexes in Krasnoyarsk Territory During the 10th Five-Year Plan [1976–1980]. Krasnoyarsk, USSR: Znaniye (Knowledge) Publishing House, 1977, 28 pages [in Russian].
  Second Edition, 1977. 23 pages.

With L. Vid and B. Kazakov. *Organizational Structures of Management of Norilsk Mining-Metallurgical Concern.* Norilsk, USSR: Norilsk Mining-Metallurgical Concern, 1976 [in Russian].

With B. Kazakov. "The Stages of Development in the Organizational Structures of Management in the Norilsk Mining-Metallurgical Production Concern." In *Theses of the Reports from the Scientific-Technical Conference.* Vol. 1. Norilsk, USSR: Norilsk Industrial Institute, 1976 [in Russian].

The Increase in the Technical Development of Industry. Moscow: Znanie (Knowledge) Publishing House, 1976, 68 pages [in Russian].
  Awarded the Best Popular Scientific Book Prize in the All-Union Competition in 1977.

"The Classification of Elements in Systems of Preparation for Production." In *The Evolution of Management and the Planning of Production.* Moscow: Moscow Institute of Management, USSR, 1976 [in Russian].

"Key Principles of Development in the Technological Preparation of the Trust." In *The Development of Methodological Principles for the Establishment of an Automation Management System of the Sib Tsvetmet Automatika Trust*. Moscow: Moscow Institute of National Economy after Plekhanov, 1975 [in Russian].

"United Technical Policy: Entity and Formation." In *The Problems of Management and Organization of Industry Under Current Conditions of Scientific-Technical Revolution*. Moscow: Moscow Institute of National Economy after Plekhanov, 1975, pp. 37–48 [in Russian].

"The Matrix Structure of Management in the Preparation of Production." *Express-Standard* (Moscow), no. 38, 1975 [in Russian].

Organization and Stages of Management in the Technical Development of Production (Based on the Development and Implementation of Automation Systems in the Nonferrous Metals Industry). Authorized Synopsis of Ph.D.. Moscow: Moscow Institute of National Economy after Plekhanov, 1975, 27 pages [in Russian].

Organization and Stages of Management in the Technical Development of Production (Based on the Development and Implementation of Automation Systems in the Nonferrous Metals Industry). Ph.D. Dissertation. Moscow: Moscow Institute of National Economy after Plekhanov, 1975. 190 pages [in Russian].

"Determining the Entity for the Preparation of Production in Mining-Metallurgical Concerns." In *Problems of Evolved Management under Conditions of Scientific-Technical Revolution* (Theoretical Conference Dedicated to the 250th Anniversary of the USSR Academy of Sciences). Vol. 1. Moscow: Moscow Institute of National Economy after Plekhanov, 1975. Pp. 295–299 [in Russian].

"The Control of Operating Expenditures in the Production of Technical Systems." In *The Role of Economics in Increasing Production Efficiency*. Sverdlovsk, USSR: Ural Polytechnical Institute, 1975 [in Russian].

With M. Raihlin. *Methodical Recommendations on the Evolution of Technological Preparation of Production in the Sib Tsvetmet Automatika Trust Under Conditions of Automation Management*. Moscow: Moscow Institute of National Economy after Plekhanov, 1975 [in Russian].

"Organization of Management of Technical Preparation of Production of New Equipment." In *The Evolution of Planning and Management in Socialist Production* (Reports of the Conference Dedicated to the 250th Anniversary of the USSR Academy of Sciences). Vol. 1. Moscow: Moscow Engineering-Economic Institute, 1974 [in Russian].

"United System of Technological Preparation of Production." In *The Handbook of the Economist of Industrial Enterprise*. Moscow: Ekonomika (Economics) Publishing House, 1974. Pp. 267–275 [in Russian].

The Evolution of the Preparation of Production of Products in Industrial Enterprises: Methodical Recommendations. Krasnoyarsk, USSR: Znanie (Knowledge) Publishing House, 1974. 22 pages [in Russian].

"United System of Technological Preparation of Production—Basis of Development of Automation Management System of Technological Preparation of Production." In *Problems in the Evolvement of Management, Organization, and Planning of Socialist Production Under Conditions of Scientific-Technical Revolution.* Moscow: Moscow Institute of National Economy after Plekhanov, 1974 [in Russian].

"The Path of Products to Workshops: Technical Progress—Birth of Innovation." *Krasnoyarskiy Rabochiy* (The Krasnoyarsk worker) (Krasnoyarsk, USSR), January 10, 1974, p. 2 [in Russian].

"On a United Technical Policy." In *Society, Collective, Individual,* Krasnoyarsk, USSR: Krasnoyarsk Institute of Non-Ferrous Metals, 1974. Vol. V, pp. 22–24 [in Russian].

"Upbringing by Labor." *Soviet Student,* Newspaper of Moscow Institute of National Economy after Plekhanov (Moscow), October 10, 1973, p. 2 [in Russian].

With N. Fyodorov. "Work in Students' Construction Units as a Form of Social Development." In *Problems in the Social Activity of Students,* Krasnovarsk, USSR: Krasnoyarsk State University, 1972. Pp. 178–187 [in Russian].

With N. Fyodorov. "Romanticism—A Forbidden Word?" *Krasnoyarskiy Komsomolets* (Krasnoyarsk, USSR), July 27, 1972, p. 2 [in Russian].

"Arctic Semester." *Krasnoyarskiy Komsomolets* (Krasnoyarsk, USSR), January 8, 1972, p. 2 [in Russian].

"Students Are Volunteers, Too." In *Ballad of the Summer Semester.* Krasnoyarsk, USSR: Krasnoyarskoye Knizhnoe Izdatelstvo (Krasnoyarsk publishing house), 1971 [in Russian].

"Exam Passed." *Za Kadry Tsvetnoy Metallurgii* (Personnel of nonferrous metals industry) (Krasnoyarsk, USSR), May 24, 1971, p. 2 [in Russian].

With B. Kazakov. "Preface to the Purchase (On Commercial Advertising)." *Krasnoyarskiy Komsomolets* (Krasnoyarsk, USSR), January 6, 1971, p. 2 [in Russian].

With G. Bogdanovsky. "The Fruits and Roots of the Electric Tree (On Mining Electricity)." *Krasnoyarskiy Komsomolets* (Krasnoyarsk, USSR), December 22, 1970, p. 2 [in Russian].

"Through the Prism of Labor." *Krasnoyarskiy Komsomolets* (Krasnoyarsk, USSR), October 27, 1970, p. 2 [in Russian].

"The Results of the Summer Working Semester." *Yeniseyskaya Pravda* (Yeniseysk, USSR), September 11, 1970, p. 2 [in Russian].

"Under the Northern Sky (Summer Student Labor in the North)." *Krasnoy-*

arskiy Rabochiy (The Krasnoyarsk worker) (Krasnoyarsk, USSR), September 9, 1970 [in Russian].

"Young People Help the Rural School." *Student Meridian* (Krasnoyarsk, USSR), August 5, 1970, p. 3 [in Russian].

"Our Summer Working Semester." *Yeniseyskaya Pravda* (Yeniseysk, USSR), July 17, 1970, p. 2 [in Russian].

"The Third Working Semester." *Krasnoyarskiy Rabochiy* (The Krasnoyarsk worker) (Krasnoyarsk, USSR), July 3, 1970, p. 4 [in Russian].

"Find Us on the Map." *Krasnoyarskiy Rabochiy* (The Krasnoyarsk worker) (Krasnoyarsk, USSR), April 8, 1970, p. 4 [in Russian].

With M. Gurtovoy. "How It Was Finished on the Carousel." *Krasnoyarskiy Komsomolets* (Krasnoyarsk, USSR), January 29, 1970, p. 2 [in Russian].

"Hero of the French Commune: Louis Jean Varlen." *Krasnoyarskiy Komsomolets* (Krasnoyarsk, USSR), October 9, 1969, p. 3 [in Russian].

"Yeniseysk Territory in 1920." In *Student Research Essays*. Krasnoyarsk, USSR: Krasnoyarsk Institute of Nonferrous Metals, 1967. 28 pages [in Russian].

II. Monographs, Books, and Papers Developed and Edited under Dr. Kvint's Direction

Emerging Market of Russia: Source Book for Investment and Trade. [Cover editor, author, and co-author]. New York: John Wiley and Sons, 1997. 705 pages.

Ryvkina, R., and L. Kosals *Socio-Economic Position and Migration Plans of the Jews in Russia: Sociological Analysis.* Results of a survey conducted in July 1995. [with Alexander G. Granberg, co-editor], Moscow and New York: National Conference on Soviet Jewry, United Jewish Appeal, 1995. 86 pages.

ECO (Monthly business magazine). [with other members of the Editorial Board], Novosibirsk, USSR, 1988–1991, 195 pages per issue (29 issues) [in Russian].

Economic and Social Problems in Regional Development. [with L. Abalkin, co-director], Moscow: The Institute of the Economy of the USSR Academy of Sciences, 1989. 150 pages [in Russian].

Soviet People's Deputies: Economic, Legal, Political Problems of Development. Moscow: Scientific Council for Regional Economy, USSR Academy of Sciences, 1989. 169 pages [in Russian].

Problems of Regional Scientific-Technical Policy. Moscow: Scientific Council for Regional Economy, USSR Academy of Sciences 1989, 159 pages [in Russian].

Bulletin of the Scientific Council for Problems of Regional Economy, vol. 2. Moscow and Novosibirsk: USSR Academy of Sciences, 1989, 55 pages [in Russian].

V. I. *Vernadskiy and Problems of Organizational-Economic Studies*. Moscow: Scientific Council for Regional Economy, USSR Academy of Sciences, 1989. 178 pages [in Russian].

Lichtenstein, V. M. *Economics of Preparation of Production of New Technics*. Moscow: Nauka [Knowledge] Publishing House, 1989, 153 pages [in Russian].

Link–Contract Dossier: The Personal Soviet Business Information Service, Zurich: Hoffset Graphische Betriebe, 1989.

Sagidov, U. N. *Evolution of Construction Management (Social-Economic Aspects of Development of Daghestan)*. Mahachkala, USSR: Daghestan Publishing House, 1988. 108 pages [in Russian].

Bulletin of the Scientific Council for Problems of Regional Economy, vol. 1. Moscow and Novosibirsk: USSR Academy of Sciences, 1988. 34 pages [in Russian].

Gamzatov, M. G. *Organization of Management of Scientific-Technical Progress in an Autonomous Republic* (Authorized Synopsis of the Dissertation for the Ph.D. in Economics). Donetzk, USSR: Institute of Industrial Economy, Ukraine Academy of Sciences, 1987. 18 pages [in Russian].

Gamzatov, M. G. *Organization of Management of Scientific-Technical Progress in an Autonomous Republic* (Dissertation for the Ph.D. in Economics). Donetzk, USSR: Institute of Industrial Economy, Ukraine Academy of Sciences, 1987. 150 pages [in Russian].

Social and Economic Development of Regions on the Basis of Acceleration of Scientific-Technical Progress. Moscow: Institute of the Economy, USSR Academy of Sciences, 1987. 170 pages [in Russian].

Methodological Problems in the Theory of Organizational Structures of Management of the National Economy. Moscow: Institute of the Economy, USSR Academy of Sciences, 1987. 236 pages [in Russian].

Economic Problems in the Actualization of Scientific-Technical Research [L. Abalkin and V. Kamayev, co-directors], Moscow: Institute of the Economy, USSR Academy of Sciences, 1987. 215 pages [in Russian].

Scientific-Technical Revolution and Economic Growth of Socialist National Production [L. Abalkin and V. Kamayev, co-directors], Moscow: Institute of the Economy, USSR Academy of Sciences, 1986. 248 pages [in Russian].

Scientific-Technical Progress and the Formation of the Economic Complex of the Republic of Daghestan [Z. Uzbekov, co-director]. USSR Academy of Sciences, Daghestan Branch, 1986. 185 pages [in Russian].

Problems of the Theory of Organizational Management Structure of National

Economy [V. Udovenko, co-director]. Moscow: Institute of the Economy, USSR Academy of Sciences, 1986. 212 pages [in Russian].

The Strategic Direction of the Organization of Start-to-Finish Planning of Scientific-Technological Progress. Moscow: Institute of the Economy, USSR Academy of Sciences, 1986. 20 pages [in Russian].

Methodic Recommendations for the Evaluation of the Economic Efficiency and Organizational Structure of the Use of the Research Fleet of the USSR Academy of Sciences During Sea Research Expeditions [E. S. Kovriga, T. G. Mikava, and V. N. Ivanchenko, co-directors]. Moscow: Institute of the Economy, USSR Academy of Sciences, 1985. 87 pages [in Russian].

Organizational-Economic Problems of Management of Scientific-Technical Development of Regions. Moscow: Institute of the Economy, USSR Academy of Sciences, 1985. 225 pages [in Russian].

The Complex Evolution of National Economic Management [V. Ivanchenko, co-director]. Moscow: Institute of the Economy, USSR Academy of Sciences, 1985. 170 pages [in Russian].

Awarded the Annual Award of the Institute of the Economy, USSR Academy of Sciences.

Economic Problems of Scientific-Technical Progress in Regions.[with U. Benderskiy, co-director]. Novosibirsk, USSR: Institute of the Economy and Organization of Industry, USSR Academy of Sciences, Siberian Branch, 1985 [in Russian].

Economic Mechanism for the Acceleration of Scientific-Technical Progress [with L. Abalkin and V. Kamayev, co-directors]. Moscow: Institute of the Economy, USSR Academy of Sciences, 1984. 185 pages [in Russian].

Management of the Economic and Social Development in Regions [with A. Aganbegian and L. Kantorovich, co-directors]. Donetzk, USSR: Institute of Industrial Economy, Ukraine Academy of Sciences, 1984. 145 pages [in Russian].

Economic Problems of Territorial Scientific-Technical Complexes [with N. Chumachenko and O. Volkov, co-directors]. Moscow: Institute of the Economy, USSR Academy of Sciences, 1983. 218 pages [in Russian].

Awarded the All-Union Silver Medal for Achievement in National Economy of the USSR.

Awarded the Ukranian Republic Prize after Artem.

The *Evolution of the Economic Mechanisms for Scientific-Technical Progress* [with L. Abalkin and V. Kamayev, co-directors]. Moscow: Institute of the Economy, USSR Academy of Sciences, 1983. 218 pages [in Russian].

BAM: Railroad of Creation [with N. Singur and U. Poliykov, co-directors]. Moscow: Sovetskaya Rossiya [Soviet Russia] Publishing House, 1983. 208 pages [in Russian].

Evolution in the Regional Management of Scientific-Technical Progress on the Basis of Perestroika in the Management of the Regional Economy. Moscow–Donetzk: Institute of Industrial Economy, Ukraine Academy of Sciences, 1983. 21 pages [in Russian].

Economic Problems with the Improvement of Renovation of Companies in the Nonferrous Metal Industry [with L. M. Lagutkin]. Moscow: The Institute of Steel and Alloys, 1983. 32 pages [in Russian].

Methodical Rules for the Development of Complex Programs of Regional Scientific-Technical Progress [under the direction of O. Volkov and V. Kvint, et al.]. Moscow: Institute of the Economy, USSR Academy of Sciences, 1980. 30 pages [in Russian].

Economic Problems of Regional Technical Policy [with A. Granberg, co-director]. Novosibirsk, USSR: Institute of the Economy and Organization of Industry, USSR Academy of Sciences, Siberian Branch, 1980. 336 pages [in Russian].

Problems in the Development of the Nonferrous Metal Industry in Siberia [with B. I. Kolesnikov and M. V. Kurlenia, co-directors]. Publications of the All Union Conference on the Development of Siberian Productive Forces. Novosibirsk, USSR: USSR Academy of Sciences, Siberian Branch, 1980. 232 pages [in Russian].

Development and Implementation of Industrial Robots in the Economy of Krasnoyarsk Territory. Krasnoyarsk, USSR: Territorial Scientific-Technical Association, 1979. 160 pages [in Russian].

III. Interviews with Dr. Kvint

Novoye Russkoye Slovo/Russian-American Daily (New York), October 10–11, 1998, p. 13 [in Russian].

Novoye Russkoye Slovo/Russian-American Daily (New York), September 22, 1998, p. 9 [in Russian].

Novoye Russkoye Slovo/Russian-American Daily (New York), September 11, 1998, p. 6 [in Russian].

Russian BAZAAR (New York), March 2, 1998, pp. 14–15 [in Russian].

Novoye Russkoye Slovo/Russian-American Daily (New York), November 19, 1997, p. 7 [in Russian]

Reuters, "Yearend—Bull Run in Russia, East Europe May Slow," by Nailene Chou Wiest, December 12, 1996.

Reuters, "Russian Eurobond Sells on Novelty, Diversification," by Nailene Chou Wiest, November 18, 1996.

The Philadelphia (Pennsylvania) Business Journal, August 30–September 5, 1996, p. 16.

Financial Trader, Innovative Trading Strategies for Global Markets, 3, no. 6, August/September 1996, p. 16.

Securities Operations Letter (New York), International Edition, New York, August 2, 1996, pp. 1, 3, 8.

ITAR-TASS, News from Five Continents (New York), July 24, 1996.

The Journal of Commerce (New York), July 18, 1996, p 6B.

ECHO of the Planet (Moscow), July 13, 1996, p. 8 [in Russian].

The Journal of Commerce (New York), Interview with Robert Selwitz, July 1996.

Council Connect Seminars, On-Line Conference, June 28, 1996.

Los Angeles Times, June 16, 1996, p 1D.

Zerkalo Nedeli (The mirror of the week) (Kiev, Ukraine), June 15, 1996, 3 pages. [in Russian].

Reuters America, Inc., "Yeltsin May Get Some US Investors Off Sideline," Financial Report, June 13, 1996, time: 13:38.

The Guardian (London), June 6, 1996.

The Journal of Commerce (New York), May 31, 1996, p 5A.

ITAR-TASS, News from Five Continents (New York), May 28, 1996.

Novoye Russkoye Slovo (New Russian word) (New York), 87, no. 30,204, May 17, 1996, p. 6 [in Russian].

ITAR-TASS, "US Businessmen Hope That Yeltsin Will Win the Election," May 16, 1996.

Dow Jones Emerging Markets Report, May 15, 1996, 1130 EDT.

V *Novom Svete* (In the new world) (New York), April 15, 1996, p. 22 [in Russian].

Privatization Opportunities, Intelligence Report (New York), 1, no. 5, April 1996, p. 4.

New Jersey Law Journal (Newark), March 25, 1996, p. 40.

Legal Times (Washington, D.C.), 18, no. 44, March 18, 1996, p. 41.

Chemical Marketing Reporter, 249, no. 8, February 19, 1996, p. SR7.

Trud (Labor) (Sofia, Bulgaria), December 14, 1995, pp. 1, 9 [in Bulgarian].

24 Chasa (24 hours) (Sofia, Bulgaria), December 13, 1995, p. 8 [in Bulgarian].

Pirin (Pirin news) (Blagoevgrad, Bulgaria), December 12, 1995 [in Bulgarian].

The Journal of Commerce (New York), November 29, 1995, p. 6A.

The Journal of Commerce (New York), November 8, 1995.

The Journal of Commerce (New York), November 1, 1995.

CNN News, Business, September 23, 1995, 2:32 a.m. ET.

ITAR-TASS (New York), September 8, 1995.

The Journal of Commerce (New York), August 31, 1995, p. 8A.

The Guardian (London), The Guardian City Page, August 26, 1995, p. 36.

ITAR-TASS Business World (New York–Moscow), August 2, 1995, p. 1 [in Russian].

Chemical Week, Turning the Corner in Eastern Europe, Chemical Week Associates, April 26, 1995, p. 28.

The Chemical Reporter, 247, no. 10, March 6, 1995, p. SR18.

The Journal of Commerce (New York), January 27, 1995, p. 8A.

The Journal of Commerce (New York), July 25, 1994, p. 8A.

The Journal of Commerce (New York), May 3, 1994, p. 3A.

The Journal of Commerce (New York), April 20, 1994, p. 2B.

The Wall Street Journal (New York), March 11, 1994, p. A8.

The Journal of Commerce (New York), December 13, 1993.

The Journal of Commerce (New York), December 6, 1993, pp. 1A, 6A.

The Wall Street Journal (New York), October 11, 1993, p. A8.

The Chicago Herald, October 10, 1993.

The Los Angeles Times, October 6, 1993, pp. B5, 7.

The Journal of Commerce (New York), September 23, 1993, p. 3A.

Daily Journal of Commerce (Portland), September 21, 1993, p. 28.

The Journal of Commerce (New York), September 14, 1993, p. 10A.

GBA Forum, Fordham University (New York), June 1993, pp. 3, 8.

The New York Times, February 21, 1993, section 3, p. 15.

The New York Times, December 1992, Business Diary, p. 2.

The New York Times, December 13, 1992, Business Diary, p. F2.

The New York Times, September 13, 1992, Business Diary, p. 2.

The New York Times, April 19, 1992, Business Diary, p. F2.

The Christian Science Monitor (Boston), March 31, 1992, p. 8.

Wellesley (Massachusetts) Townsman, January 2, 1992, pp. 1, 7, 15.

Babson Bulletin (Wellesley, Massachusetts), Winter 1992, pp. 14–17.

The New York Times, December 29, 1991, Business Diary, p. F2.

The New York Times, December 15, 1991, Business Diary, p. F2.

Arguments and Facts (Moscow), No. 45, November 1991, p. 6.

Babson College Happenings (Wellesley, Massachusetts), November 21, 1991, p. 3.

The Spotlight, Washington, D.C., November 4, 1991, p. 3.

The Chicago Tribune, November 3, 1991, Business, section 7, p. 1.

Daily News (Los Angeles), Week in Review, October 20, 1991.

The New York Times, October 20, 1991, Business Diary, p. F2.

The New York Times, October 13, 1991, Business Diary.

The Chicago Tribune, September 29, 1991, section 1, p. 14.

USA Today (New York), August 26, 1991, p. 2A.

The New York Times, August 25, 1991, Business Diary, p. 2.

David Crosson. Hearst News Service, Washington, D.C., June 19, 1991, 2 pages.

The New York Times, April 28, 1991, Business Diary, p. 2.

The Chicago Tribune, April 6, 1991, Business Zone, p. C2.

The West Side TV Shopper (New York), March 15, 1991, p. 15 (Cover Story).

The Chicago Tribune, February 3, 1991, section 7, p. 7.

Neue Kronen Zeitung Wirtschafts Magazin, Vienna, January 26, 1991, pp. 2–3 [in German].

Sheehy, Gail. *The Man Who Changed the World: The Lives of Mikhail S. Gorbachev*. New York: HarperCollins Publishers, 1990. Pp. xiii, 106, 134–135, 137, 242, 263, 289–290.

San Antonio (Texas) Light, September 20, 1990, pp. D1–5.

Midland Reporter-Telegram (San Antonio, Texas), September 20, 1990, p. 8C.

David Crosson. Hearst News Service, Washington, D.C., September 17, 1990, 2 pages.

The Los Angeles Times, September 4, 1990, p. H-4.

The Times (London), August 10, 1990, p. 23.

The New York Times, August 5, 1990, section 3, p. 13.

The Chicago Tribune, August 5, 1990, Perspective, section 4, pp. 1–4.

The Jewish Week (New York), May 18, 1990, p. 7.

Trend (Vienna), no. 4, April 1990, pp. 300–303 [in German].

Schweizer Bank (Zurich), no. 4, 1990, pp. 56–57 [in German].

Quick (Munich), no. 4, January 1990, pp. 52–53 [in German].

Vanity Fair (New York), no. 2, 1990, p. 184.

Kurier (Vienna), January 19, 1990 [in German].

Die Presse (Vienna), January 19, 1990, p. 2 [in German].

AZ Arbeit Zeitung (Vienna), January 19, 1990, p. 55 [in German].

The Philadelphia Inquirer, January 18, 1990.

Frankenpost (Marktredwitz, Germany), January 17, 1990 [in German].

The Chicago Tribune, January 14, 1990, Business Section, pp. 1, 6.

Las Vegas Sun, January 10, 1990.

Victor Valley Daily Press (Victorville, California), January 10, 1990.

Fortune (Rome), no. 1, January 1990, pp. 149–150 [in Italian].

Neue Züricher Zeitung [Wirtschaft] (Zurich), December 12, 1989, p. 16. [in German].

Global Finance (New York), December 1989, p. 63.

Süddeutsche Zeitung (Munich), November 29, 1989 [in German].

Frankenpost (Marktredwitz, Germany), November 28, 1989 [in German].

Marktredwitz Kurier (Marktredwitz, Germany), November 28, 1989 [in German].

Frankenpost (Marktredwitz, Germany), November 27, 1989, p. 3 [in German].

Die Presse (Vienna), November 13, 1989 [in German].

Trud (Labor) (Moscow), TASS Interview, October 25, 1989, pp. 2–3 [in Russian].

The Times (London), October 18, 1989.

The Guardian (London), October 18, 1989, Financial News Section, p. 11.

Daily Mirror (London), October 17, 1989.

The Independent (London), October 12, 1989, Business Section, p. 31.

Cash Flow (Vienna), no. 9, 1989, pp. 82–83 [in German].

The Journal of Commerce (New York), August 30, 1989, section 1, p. 1.

La Repubblica (Rome), August 18, 1989 [in Italian].

NTR: Problemy i Reshenia (Scientific-technical revolution: Problems and decisions), TASS Interview, Moscow, no. 17, 1989, p. 3 (Cover Story) [in Russian].

Corporate Finance (New York), July 1989, pp. 13, 15.

Die Presse (Vienna), June 19, 1989, p. 8 [in German].

De Standaard (Brussels), June 16, 1989 [in Dutch].

The Journal of Commerce (New York), May 16, 1989, p. 1.

Books and Art in the USSR (Moscow), no. 2, April 1989, pp. 12–13 [in Russian].
    Translated into English, German, French, Spanish.

The Journal of Commerce (New York), April 25, 1989, pp. 1–3A.

Knack (Brussels), March 15, 1989, pp. 26–28 [in Dutch].

Le Soir (Brussels), March 10, 1989, p. 26 [in French].

Gazet Van Antwerpen (Antwerp), March 6, 1989, p. 10 [in Dutch].

Neues Volksblatt (Krems, Austria), February 3, 1989 [in German].

Niederösterreichishe Information (Krems, Austria), February 2, 1989 [in German].

Sonntags Zeitung (Zurich), January 8, 1989, Business Section, p. 8 [in German].

Schweizer Illustrierte (Zurich), no. 2, January 9, 1989, pp. 20–22 [in German].

Niederösterreichishe Nachrichten (Vienna), January 1989 [in German].

Niederösterreichishe Kurier, Vienna, December 22, 1988 [in German].

Rigas Balss (Riga, Latvia), September 1, 1988, p. 6 [Latvian].
    Translated into Russian in the Russian edition.

Sotsialisticheskaya Industria (Socialist industry), TASS Interview (Moscow), July 16, 1988, p. 2 [in Russian].

Books and Art in the USSR (Moscow), no. 2, April 1988, pp. 8–9 [in Russian].
    Translated into English, German, French, Spanish.

New Times (Moscow), no. 52, 1987, pp. 18–19.
    Translated into Russian, German, French, Spanish, Italian, Portuguese, Czech, Polish.

New Times (Moscow), no. 46, 1987, pp. 20–21.
   Translated into Russian, German, French, Spanish, Italian, Portuguese, Czech, Polish.
New Times (Moscow), no. 36, 1987, pp. 10–11.
   Translated into Russian, German, French, Spanish, Italian, Portuguese, Czech, Polish.
Izvestia (Moscow) July 31–August 1, 1984, p. 2 [in Russian].
   Reprinted in *Moscow News*, no. 41, October 14, 1984, p. 12 [in Russian].
   Translated into English, Arabic, French, Spanish, Portuguese.
Soviet Union Today (Tokyo), no. 7, 1983, pp. 14–17 [in Japanese].
Vecherniy Donetzk (Donetzk nightly) (Donetzk, Ukraine, USSR), December 16, 1983 [in Russian].
Moscow News (Moscow), no. 1, January 1983, p. 12 [in Russian].
   Translated into English, Spanish, Portuguese, Arabic, French.
Moscow News (Moscow), February 7, 1982, p. 12 [in Russian]
   Translated into English, Spanish, Portuguese, Arabic, French.
Krasnoyarskiy Rabochiy (The Kransnoyarsk worker) (Krasnoyarsk, USSR), July 3, 1980, p. 3. [in Russian].
Krasnoyarskiy Rabochiy (The Krasnoyarsk worker) (Krasnoyarsk, USSR), June 15, 1979, p. 3 [in Russian].
Krasnoyarskiy Komsomolets (Krasnoyarsk, USSR), July 3, 1971 [in Russian].
Zapolyarnaya Pravda (Arctic Pravda) (Norilsk, USSR), June 24, 1971, p. 1 [in Russian].
Krasnoyarskiy Komsomolets (Krasnoyarsk, USSR), February 7, 1970 [in Russian].
Student Meridian (Krasnoyarsk, USSR), August 5, 1970 [in Russian].

IV. Reviews and Opinions about the Publications and Activities of Dr. Kvint

Novoye Russkoye Slovo/Russian-American Daily (New York), October 24–25, 1998, p. 9 [in Russian].
Novoye Russkoye Slovo/Russian-American Daily (New York), October 2, 1998, p. 2 [in Russian].
Moskovskiy Komsomolets (Moscow), September 8, 1989, p. 2 [in Russian].
Tiempos del Mundo (Montevideo, Uruguay), August 26, 1998, p. 4 [in Spanish].
The Global Future Is Here Today: Dean's Report, 1997. New York: Fordham University Graduate School of Business, 1998. P. 16.

New York University Bulletin. New York: New York University, The Leonard N. Stern School of Business, March 1998. P. 156.

ELBIM Bank Annual Report, 1997. Moscow: ELBIM Bank, 1998. Pp. 4–5 [in Russian].

PLD Telecom Inc. . . . Is on Course. New York: PLD Telecom, 1998. P. 102.

The Bretton Woods Committee Newsletter, Washington, D.C.: February 13, 1998. P. 6.

Russian Bazaar (New York), January 26, 1998, p. 15 [in Russian].

Novoye Russkoye Slovo/Russian-American Daily (New York), January 10–11, 1998, p. 14 [in Russian].

ITAR-TASS Express Weekly (New York), no. 1, 1998, p. 2 [in Russian].

ITAR-TASS Express Weekly (New York), no. 50, 1997, p. 30 [in Russian].

International M & A, Joint Ventures, and Beyond: Doing the Deal. New York: John Wiley & Sons, 1997. P. viii.

ITAR-TASS Express Weekly (New York), no. 43, 1997, p. 27 [in Russian].

24 Hours (Sophia, Bulgaria), October 13, 1997, p. 11 [in Bulgarian].

Deresky, Helen. *International Management: Managing Across Borders and Cultures*. 2nd edition. New York: Addison-Wesley Educational Publishers, Inc., 1997. Pp. 165, 168–169.

Banking Journal (New York), December 1996, p. 30.

Emerging Market Investments, World Markets Series, Business Briefing. London: World Markets Research Centre, November 1996, p. 7.

Banking Journal (New York), November 1996, p. 52.

Financial Times (London), November 22, 1996, p. 5.

The Fifth Annual World Economic Development Congress, Program Guide, World Congress, Inc., Washington, D.C., September 25–27, 1996, pp. 33–39, 79.

The Scribe, University of Bridgeport (Bridgeport, Connecticut), N.S., 3, No. 2 (September 12, 1996), p. 1.

Los Angeles Business Journal (Los Angeles, California), August 26, 1996.

Financial Times (London), August 28, 1996.

Financial Times (London), August 20, 1996.

Securities Operations Letter, International Edition (New York), August 2, 1996, p. 3.

ECHO of the Planet (Moscow), July 13, 1996, p. 8 [in Russian].

Voronezh News (Voronezh, Russia), July 19, 1996, pp. 1, 2 [in Russian].

Investing and Building in the Former Soviet Union. London: The Institute for Infrastructure Finance, Institutional Investor, June 5, 1996. Pp. 10, 14, 30.

Inside Fordham, Fordham University (New York), 17, no. 7, April 19, 1996, p. 8.

New York Chapter Newsletter, The American Jewish Committee (New York), Spring 1996, p. 6.

Inside Fordham, Fordham University (New York), 17, no. 6, March 25, 1996, p. 7.

Morozov, Sergey. *Financial Mechanicisms and Social Consequences.* Moscow 1996, p. 14 [translated into Russian].

CBA Newsletter, Fordham University (New York), March 1996, insert.

Inside Fordham, Fordham University (New York), 17, no. 5, February 15, 1996, p.7.

The Hellenic Journal (New York), January 11, 1996.

Who's Who in America, 1996. 50th edition. New Providence, New Jersey: Marquis Who's Who/Reed Elsevier, 1996. Vol. 1, p. 2370.

International Who's Who of Intellectuals. 12th edition. Cambridge, England: International Biography Centre, 1996.

Who's Who Among America's Teachers, 1996.

New England Center for International and Regional Studies Brochure. Bridgeport, Connecticut: New England Center for International and Regional Studies (NEC), 1996.

Who's Who in American Education, 1996–1997. 5th edition. Place: New Providence, New Jersey: Marquis Who's Who/Reed Elsevier, 1995.

Who's Who in the World, 1996. 13th edition. Place: New Providence, New Jersey: Marquis Who's Who/Reed Elsevier, 1995.

Who's Who in Finance and Industry, 1996–1997. 29th edition. Place: New Providence, New Jersey: Marquis Who's Who/Reed Elsevier, 1995. P. 421.

Who's Who in Science and Engineering. 3rd edition. Place: New Providence, New Jersey: Marquis Who's Who/Reed Elsevier, 1995.

Kommersant Daily (Merchant daily), December 26, 1995, p. 15 [in Russian].

Duma (Sofia, Bulgaria), December 14, 1995, p. 1 [in Bulgarian].

Trud (Labor) (Sofia, Bulgaria), December 14, 1995, p. 2 [in Bulgarian].

24 Chasa (24 hours) (Sofia, Bulgaria), December 13, 1995, pp. 6, 8 [in Bulgarian.

Pirin (Pirin news) (Biagoevgrad, Bulgaria), December 13, 1995, p. 3 [in Bulgarian].

Pirin (Pirin news) Biagoevgrad, Bulgaria, December 12, 1995, pp. 1, 3. [in Bulgarian].

Trud (Labor) (Sofia, Bulgaria), December 11, 1995, p. 3 [in Bulgarian].

Standart (Standard) (Sofia, Bulgaria), December 11, 1995, p. 3 [in Bulgarian].

24 Chasa (24 hours) (Sofia, Bulgaria), December 11, 1995, pp. 1, 3 [in Bulgarian].

24 Chasa (24 hours) (Sofia, Bulgaria), December 10, 1995. p. 3 [in Bulgarian].

24 Chasa (24 hours) (Sofia, Bulgaria), December 9, 1995, p. 4 [in Bulgarian].

MBA Forum, Fordham University (New York), 15, no. 14, December 1995, p. 4.

Inside Fordham, Fordham University (New York), 17, no. 2, October 20, 1995, p. 7.

World Economic Development Congress, Program Guide, World Congress, Inc., Washington, D.C., October 4–6, 1995, pp. 22–27, 57, 70.

MBA Forum, Fordham University (New York), 15, no. 8, May 1995, p. 3.

Finansovye i Delovye Novosti (Financial and business news) (Moscow), February 1995, p. 11.

Who's Who in America, 1995. 49th edition Place: New Providence, New Jersey: Marquis Who's Who/Reed Elsevier, 1995. Vol. 1, p. 2113.

Who's Who in the East. 26th edition. Marquis Who's Who, 1995.

International Directory of Business and Management Scholars and Research. Cambridge, Massachusetts: Harvard Business School Press, 1995.

Who's Who in the World, 1995. 12th edition. New Providence, New Jersey: Marquis Who's Who/Reed Elsevier, 1995. P. 777.

International Who's Who of Intellectuals. 11th edition. Cambridge, England: International Biography Centre, 1995.

"Quote of the Day," *The Journal of Commerce*, New York, January 12, 1995, p. 3A.

Who's Who in Finance, 1994–1995. 28th edition. New Providence, New Jersey: Marquis Who's Who/Reed Elsevier, 1994. Pp. 426–427.

Who's Who in Science and Engineering, 1994–1995. 2nd edition. New Providence, New Jersey: Marquis Who's Who/Reed Elsevier, 1994. Pp. 496–497.

The International Directory of Distinguished Leadership. 5th Edition. Raleigh, North Carolina: American Biographical Institute, Inc., 1994.

The New York Academy of Sciences, Directory of Members, 1994, p. 193.

Inside Fordham, Fordham University (New York), 16, no. 4, December 19, 1994, p. 3.

Harvard Business Review (Cambridge, Massachusetts), November/December 1994, p. 191.

GBA Forum, Fordham University (New York), no. 8, December 1994, p. 3.

Inside Fordham, Fordham University (New York), 16, no. 3, November 21, 1994, p. 7.

The International Directory of Distinguished Leadership. Raleigh, North Carolina: American Biographical Institute, 1994. P. 205.

Big/Small Fordham, New York City's Jesuit University. New York: Fordham University, 1994. P. 30.

Bretton Woods: Looking to the Future. Washington, D.C.: Bretton Woods Commission, September 1994.

The Journal of Commerce (New York), July 25, 1994, p. 1.

The American-Jewish Committee Newsletter (New York), Summer 1994, p. 8.

Harvard Business Review (Cambridge, Massachusetts), May/June 1994, pp. 35–44, 168.

Inside Fordham, Fordham University (New York), 15, no. 8, May 20, 1994, p. 7.

The Journal of Commerce (New York), April 20, 1994, p. 2B.

CUBC Bulletin (Toronto), 5, no. 2, March 1994, p. 1.

Who's Who in America, 1994, 48th edition. New Providence, New Jersey: Marquis Who's Who/Reed Elsevier, 1994. Vol. 1, p. 1971.

Fordham, Fordham University (New York), 27, no. 1, Fall/Winter 1993–94, pp. 19–21.

The American Economic Review, American Economic Association, 1993 Survey of Members, December, 1993, p. 273.

Wexner Heritage Review (New York), no. 9, December 1993, p. iv.

"Booknotes," *World Affairs Council*, November 1993, p. 3.

Inside Fordham, Fordham University (New York), November 1993, p. 7.

Journal of International Business Studies, Western Business School, 24, no. 4, 4th Quarter 1993, p. 834.

Wexner Heritage Foundation Directory, New York, 1993.

Daily Journal of Commerce (Portland), September 21, 1993, p. 28.

Inside Fordham, Fordham University (New York), September 17, 1993, p. 7.

Membership Directory, 1993–1994, Academy of International Business (Detroit), 1993, p. 38.

Newsletter, Academy of International Business (Detroit), Fall 1993, p. 39.

Whittier Law School News (Los Angeles, California), 12, no. 1, Fall 1993, p. 13.

Moscow Times, July 31, 1993.

"A Look Inside Russia's Transition to Capitalism." *Financial Post* (Toronto), July 10, 1993.

"New Americans Are Good for America." *NYANA, Inc.* (New York), 1993, p. 6.

Academy of International Business, Northeast USA Regional Meeting Notes, Scranton, Pennsylvania, June 1–3, 1993, p. 3.

Human Systems Management (New York), 12, no. 4, 1993, pp. 303, 309.

Forbes (New York), April 12, 1993, p. 20.

Political Science Quarterly (New York), Spring 1993.

Inside Fordham, Fordham University (New York), March 10, 1993, p. 5.

GBA Forum, Fordham University (New York), February 1993, p. 2.

Inside Fordham, Fordham University (New York), February 1993, p. 7.

GBA Quarterly, Fordham University (New York), February 1993, p. 2.

The New York Times, February 21, 1993, p. F15.

Competing in a Tripolar (EC, Japan, USA) World Economy Pittsburgh, Pennsylvania: Robert Morris College, 1993. Pp. 3, 10.

Inside Fordham, Fordham University (New York), December 11, 1992, p. 4.

Fordham University, GBA—Programs and Perspectives, 1992–1993, Fordham University (New York), 1992, p. 7.

Arcade Publishing, Catalogue, Spring/Summer 1993, p. 3.

GBA Forum, Fordham University (New York), December 1992, p. 2.

GBA Forum, Fordham University (New York), December 1992, pp. 1–2.

Inside Fordham, Fordham University (New York), October 16, 1992, p. 2.

Little, Brown and Company, Catalogue, April–August 1992, p. 66.

Arcade Publishing, Catalogue, Fall/Winter 1991–1992, and Spring 1992 Selected Titles, 1992, p. 18.

Alaska World Affairs Council, Anchorage, May 1992.

The Anchorage (Alaska) Times, April 30, 1992, p. C8.

The Wellesley (Massachusetts) Townsman, January 2, 1992, pp. 1, 7, 15.

Babson Bulletin, Babson College (Wellesley, Massachusetts), Winter 1992, pp. 13, 15–16, 22.

Fordham University Graduate School of Business Administration Bulletin, Fordham University (New York), September 1992, p. 27.

The New York Observer, December 30, 1991–January 6, 1992, p. 12.

Fordham University School of Business, Faculty Resources for the Media, Fordham University (New York), 1992, p. 19.

1991 Media Guide: A Critical Review of the Media. Edited by Jude Wanniski. 6th edition. Morristown, New Jersey: Polyconomics, Inc., 1991. P. 198.

The Needham (Massachusetts) Chronicle, December 18, 1991, p. 2.

The New York Times, December 15, 1991.

Babson College: On Campus (Wellesley, Massachusetts), December 2, 1991, p. 2.

Partial Bibliography of Dr. Vladimir L. Kvint, 1967–November 1991. Prepared by Barbara C. Beyer and Michael J. Frumin. Wellesley, Massachusetts:, Babson College, 1991. 34 pages.

Babson Free Press (Wellesley, Massachusetts), November 21, 1991, p. 4.

Argumente i Fakti (Arguments and Facts) (Moscow), no. 45, 1991, p. 6 [in Russian].

The Spotlight (Washington, D.C.), November 4, 1991, p. 3.

Babson College: On Campus (Wellesley, Massachusetts), October 20, 1991, p. 2.

We and the World, Telegraph Agency of the Soviet Union (TASS), October 15, 1991, p. 16 [in Russian].

Babson College: On Campus (Wellesley, Massachusetts), October 18, 1991, p. 1.

Babson Free Press (Wellesley, Massachusetts), September 26, 1991, pp. 1–2.

The RAM, Fordham University (New York), September 26, 1991.

The Wellesley (Massachusetts) Townsman, September 19, 1991, p. 29.

Babson Free Press (Wellesley, Massachusetts), September 19, 1991, p. 4.

Babson College: On Campus (Wellesley, Massachusetts), September 6, 1991, p. 2.

Forbes, Side Line. New York, September 16, 1991, p. 8.

ELEM (Youth in Distress in Israel), Patron Section. New York, Fall 1991.

USA Today (New York), August 26, 1991, p. 2A.

The New York Times, Op-ed, August 20, 1991.

The New York Times, May 13, 1991, p. D12.

Fordham University Graduate School of Business Administration Bulletin, Fordham University (New York), May 1991, pp. 9, 27, 58.

Whittier Law Review (Los Angeles, California), 12, no. 2, 1991, p. 143.

The New York Times, Business Diary, April 28, 1991.

The West Side TV Shopper (New York), March 15, 1991, p. 15 [Cover Story].

Institutional Investor (New York), April, 1991, p. 97.

The Jewish Week (New York), February 22, 1991, p. 40.

Forbes (New York), Side-Line, February 4, 1991, p. 8.

Chicago Tribune, February 3, 1991.

The Best Business Stories of 1990 [A Bonus Supplement to the TJFR Business News Reporter], TJFR Publishing Co., February 1991, p. S-2.

Morath, Inge. *Russian Journal: 1965–1990*. An Aperture Book, USA, 1991, pp. 52–53.

Sheehy, Gail. *The Man Who Changed the World: The Lives of Mikhail S. Gorbachev*. New York: HarperCollins Publishers, 1990. Pp. xiii, 106, 134–135, 137, 242, 263, 289–290.

Forbes (New York), November 26, 1990, p. 234.

1990 YPO Eastern Area Conference. *Young Presidents' Organization*, New York, 1990.

Bulletin, The Harvard Club of New York, October 1990, p. 9.

International Executive (New York), November/December 1990, pp. 3, 6.

Forbes (New York), Side-Line, September 17, 1990, p. 8.

Harvard Club of New York City, September 1990.

The Times (London), August 10, 1990, p. 23.

Forbes (New York), Side Line, August 6, 1990, p. 8.

RSAI News, Newsletter of the Regional Science Association International (Urbana, Illinois), August 1990, p. 4.

ABA Journal (New York), August, 1990, p. 54.

The Jewish Week (New York), May 18, 1990.

Schweizer Bank (Zurich), April 1990, pp. 56–57 [in German].

*European Trade: European Community and Eastern Europe—1992 and Be-

yond, Whittier College, School of Law (Los Angeles, California), April 1990, p. 1.

Basler Zeitung (Basel, Switzerland), March 20, 1990, p. 1 [in German].

Komsomolskaya Pravda (Moscow), March 7, 1990, p. 3 [in Russian].

International Management (London), March, 1990, pp. 14–15.

Perestroika mit Hindernissen (Austria), March, 1990.

Fortune (New York), February 19, 1990.

The Los Angeles Daily Journal, February 13, 1990, News Update.

Vanity Fair (New York), February, 1990, p. 184.

Law School News, Whittier College (Los Angeles), 8, no. 2, 1990.

Austria Business and Economy (Vienna), January 1990, p. 54.

Fortune (Rome), January 1990, pp. 149–150 [in Italian].

AZ (Vienna), January 19, 1990, p. 55 [in German].

Chicago Tribune, January 14, 1990, Business Section, p. 21.

East–West Forum (Vienna), December 19, 1989, pp. 75–76.

Nord Bayerischer Kurier (Bayreuth, Germany), December 1, 1989 [in German].

International Management (London), December, 1989, p. 54.

Marktredwitzer Kurier (Marktredwitz, Germany), November 30, 1989 [in German].

Der Neue Tag (Bavaria, Germany), November 29, 1989 [in German].

Marktredwitzer Tagblatt (Marktredwitz, Germany), November 29, 1989, p. MAK1 [in German].

Oberpfalzpost (Frankfurt), November 29, 1989, p. 1 [in German].

Frankenpost (Marktredwitz, Germany), November 28, 1989 [in German].

Marktredwitzer Kurier (Marktredwitz, Germany), November 28, 1989 [in German].

Der Neue Tag (Bavaria, Germany), November 28, 1989, p. 1 [in German].

Frankenpost (Marktredwitz, Germany), November 27, 1989, p. 3 [in German].

Frankenpost (Marktredwitz, Germany), November 22–23, 1989, Wirtschaft und Soziales.[in German].

Die Presse (Vienna), November 13, 1989 [in German].

Der Standard (Vienna), November 8, 1989 [in German].

Greenwich (Connecticut) Times, November 5, 1989, p. A17.

Link (Zurich), no. 1, November 1989, p. 2.

The Times (London), October 18, 1989.

Link Assist—Your Guide to the Soviet Business Leaders (Zurich), 1989, p. 6.

The Guardian (London), October 18, 1989, Financial News, p. 11.

Vanity Fair (New York), October, 1989, pp. 152–153.

Cash Flow (Vienna), no. 9, 1989, pp. 82–83 [in German].

Corporate Finance (New York), July 1989, pp. 13, 15.

Greenwich (Connecticut) Times, June 23, 1989.

De Standaard (Brussels) June 16, 1989 [in Dutch].

Schweizer Familie (Zurich), March 1989, p. 71 [in German].

Europees Instituut, Rijksuniversitet Gent (Ghent, Belgium), March 9, 1989 [in Dutch].

Neues Volksblatt (Krems, Austria), February 3, 1989 [in German].

China Economic Information (Beijing), no. 5, 1989, pp. 14–15 [in Chinese].

Knack (Brussels), March 15, 1989, pp. 26–28 [in Dutch].

Book and Arts of the USSR (Moscow), no. 2, 1989, pp. 12–13.
    Translated into Russian, German, Spanish, French.

Schweizer Illustrierte (Zurich) January 9, 1989, pp. 20–21 [in German].

Niederösterreichishe Nachrichten Magazin (Vienna), January 9, 1989 [in German].

New Times (Moscow), no.1, 1989, p. 48 [in Russian].
    Translated into English, French, German, Spanish, Portuguese, Italian, Polish, Czech, Greek.

Lichtenstein, V. M. *Economics of the Preparation of New Techniques*, Moscow: Nauka (Science) Publishing House, 1989. P. 12 [in Russian].

Die Neue (Vienna), December 20, 1988 [in German].

Der Standard (Vienna), December 20, 1988 [in German].

East–West Guide: Common Commercial Communications. Vienna: Signum Verlag, October 1988. P. 138.

Riga Balss (Voice of Riga) (Riga, Latvia), September 1,1988, p. 6 [in Russian and Latvian].

Narodnoye Chosiaystvo Byelorussii (National economy of Byelorussia) (Minsk, Byelorussia, USSR), no. 3, 1988 [in Russian].

ECO (Monthly business magazine) (Novosibirsk and Moscow), no. 12, 1988, cover page [in Russian].

Ost–West Management Aktiv, Niederösterreichische Landesakademie (Wirdim, Austria), 1988 [in German].

Die Presse (Vienna), 1988 [in German].

Bildungspolitik und Forschung (Vienna), 1988, p. 19 [in German].

Kolesov, A. S. *Management of Science in the Region*. Leningrad: Nauka, 1988. Pp. 92, 94, 96–98, 102, 104 [in Russian].

Books and Art in the USSR (Moscow), no. 2, 1988, pp. 8–9.
    Translated into Russian, German, Spanish, French.

All-Union Scientific-Practical Conferences—"Scientific-Technical Progress and Intensification of Industry" (Donetzk, Ukraine), Ukraine Academy of Sciences, 1988, p. 17 [in Russian].

Kuznetsov, G. C. *Flexible Automization of Industry: Socio-Economic Entity and Factors of Efficiency*. Moscow: Academy of Social Sciences, 1988. P. B [in Russian].

Prebore i Systieme Upravleniya (Equipment and control systems) (Moscow), no. 12, 1987 [in Russian].

Vestnik Leningradskovo Universiteta (Courier of the Leningrad State University) (Leningrad), issue 11, series 25, 1987, pp. 127–128 [in Russian].

Planovoe Khoziaistvo (Planned economy) (Moscow), no. 11, 1987, pp. 123–124 [in Russian].

Ekonomika Sovietskoy Ukrainy (Economy of Soviet Ukraine) (Kiev, Ukraine, USSR), no. 6, 1987, pp. 88–89 [in Russian].

Sovietskoe Gosudarstvo i Pravo [Soviet state and law] (Moscow) no. 5, 1987, pp. 142–143 [in Russian].

Izvestia of Estonia Academy of Sciences, Social Sciences Division (Tallinn, Estonia, USSR), no. 36, 1987, pp. 323–324 [in Russian].

Actions, Information, Chronicles, Moscow Chapter of USSR Union of Journalists (Moscow) February, 1987, p. 1 [in Russian].

Slovo Lektora (The lecturer's word) (Moscow), no. 6, 1987 [in Russian].

Tsvetnayae Metallurgiya (Nonferrous metallurgy) (Moscow), no. 2, 1987, p. 92 [in Russian].

Soviety Narodnych Deputatov (Soviet people's deputies) (Moscow), no. 1, 1987, pp. 94–95 [in Russian].

Khoziaystvo i Pravo (Business and law) (Moscow), no. 12, 1986, pp. 87–88 [in Russian].

Sovietskiy Daghestan (Soviet Daghestan) (Mahachkala, Daghestan, USSR), no. 6, 1986, p. 48 [in Russian].

Voprosy Ekonomiky (Problems in Economics) (Moscow), no. 10, 1986, pp. 148–150 [in Russian].

Izvestia of the Georgia Academy of Sciences (Tbilisi, Georgia, USSR), no. 3, 1986, pp. 113–116 [in Russian and Georgian].

Planovoe Khoziaistvo (Planned economy) (Moscow), no. 8, 1986 [in Russian].

Liaudies Ukis (National economy of Lithuania) (Vilnius, Lithuania, USSR), no. 8, 1986, p. 17 [in Lithuanian].

Books and Art in the USSR (Moscow) no. 2, 1986.
    Translated into Russian, German, Spanish, French.

Slovo Lektora (The lecturer's word) (Moscow), no. 6, 1986 [in Russian].

Khosiaystvo i Pravo (Economy and law) (Moscow), no. 12, 1986, pp. 87–88 [in Russian].

Guber, A. A. *Our Economy: Changing Times.* Moscow: Politizdat Publishing House, 1986. Pp. 45–47 [in Russian].

Magadanskaya Pravda (Magadan, USSR), December 26, 1985, p. 3 [in Russian].

Moscow News, August 18, 1985.
    Translated into Russian, Spanish, Arabic, Portuguese.

Daghastanskaya Pravda (Daghestan, USSR), March 6, 1985, p. 2 [in Russian].

Aganbegiyan, A. and A. Ibragimova, Z. *Siberia at the Border of the Centuries*, Moscow: Sovetskaya Rossiya (Soviet Russia) Publishing House, 1984. Pp. 195–196 [in Russian].

Ekonomicheskaya Nauki (Economic sciences) (Moscow), no. 11, 1984, p. 121 [in Russian].

Ekonomicheskaya Gazeta (Economic gazette) (Moscow), no. 11, 1983 [in Russian].

Bibliography of Publications of the Institute of the Economy and Organization of Industry of the Siberian Branch of the USSR Academy of Sciences, 1976–1980 (Novosibirsk, USSR), 1982, pp. 217 and passim [in Russian].

Sovetskaya Rossiya, September 20, 1981, p.2.

Krasnoyarskiy Komsomolets (Krasnoyarsk, USSR), September 12, 1981, pp. 2–3 [in Russian].

Moskovskaya Pravda (Moscow), September 11, 1981, p. 1 [in Russian].

Komsomolets Donbassa (Donetzk, Ukraine, USSR), September 8, 1981, p. 3 [in Russian].

Sovetskaya Rossiya [Soviet Russia] 1982 Plan of Publications (Moscow), 1981, p. 17 [in Russian].

Za Nauku v Sibiry (On science in Siberia) (Novosibirsk, USSR), no. 33, August 20, 1981, p. 2 [in Russian].

Ekonomicheskya Gazeta (Economics newspaper) (Moscow), no. 42, October 1981 [in Russian].

Komsomolskaya Pravda (Moscow), June 23, 1981, p. 2 [in Russian].

Za Nauku v Sibiry (On science in Siberia) (Novosibirsk, USSR), no. 49, December 18, 1980, p. 5 [in Russian].

Krasnoyarskiy Rabochiy (The Krasnoyarsk worker) (Krasnoyarsk, USSR), June 15, 1980, p. 3 [in Russian].

Tuvinskaya Pravda (Kyzyl, USSR), April 15, 1980, p. 1 [in Russian and Tuva].

Gornove Delo (Mining business) (Moscow), no. 1, 1980, p. 26 [in Russian].

Za Nauku v Sibiry (On science in Siberia) (Novosibirsk, USSR), no. 50, December 31, 1979, pp. 4, 5 [in Russian].

Krasnoyarskiy Rabochiy (The Krasnoyarsk worker) (Krasnoyarsk, USSR), August 26, 1979, p. 2 [in Russia].

Angarskiy Rabochiy (The Agarsk worker) (Motygino, USSR), July 7, 1979, p. 1 [in Russian].

Krasnoyarskiy Rabochiy (The Krasnoyarsk worker) (Krasnoyarsk, USSR), January 27, 1979, p. 3 [in Russian].

ECO (Monthly business magazine) (Novosibirsk, USSR), no. 10, 1979, pp. 115–120 [in Russian].

Krasnoyarskiy Rabochiy (The Krasnoyarsk worker) (Krasnoyarsk, USSR), December, 1978, p. 4 [in Russian].

Krasnoyarskiy Rabochiy (The Krasnoyarsk worker) (Krasnoyarsk, USSR), November 8, 1978, p. 4 [in Russian].

Krasnoyarskiy Rabochiy (The Krasnoyarsk worker) (Krasnoyarsk, USSR), September 12, 1978, p. 4 [in Russian].

Ekonomicheskya Gazeta (Economics newspaper) (Moscow), no. 52, 1978, p. 22 [in Russian].

Krasnoyarskiy Komsomolets (Krasnoyarsk, USSR), April 30, 1978, p. 4 [in Russian].

Krasnoyarskiy Komsomolets (Krasnoyarsk, USSR), May 26, 1977, p. 2 [in Russian].

Krasnoyarskiy Rabochiy (The Krasnoyarsk worker) (Krasnoyarsk, USSR), August 10, 1976, p. 2 [in Russian].

Krasnoyarskiy Komsomolets (Krasnoyarsk, USSR), August 10, 1976, p. 3 [in Russian].

Zapolyarnaya Pravda (Arctic Pravda) (Norilsk, USSR), April 1976 [in Russian].

Zapolyarnaya Pravda (Arctic Pravda) (Norilsk, USSR), February 6, 1976 [in Russian].

Krasnoyarskiy Komsomolets (Krasnoyarsk, USSR), February 25, 1975, p. 2 [in Russian].

Krasnoyarskiy Komsomolets (Krasnoyarsk, USSR), August 24, 1974, p. 2 [in Russian].

Krasnoyarskiy Komsomolets (Krasnoyarsk, USSR), June 1, 1972, p. 2 [in Russian].

Za Kadry Tsvetnoy Metallurgii (For employees of the nonferrous metals industry) (Krasnoyarsk, USSR), March 31, 1972, p. 1 [in Russian].

Za Kadry Tsvetnoy Metallurgii (For employees of the nonferrous metals industry) (Krasnoyarsk, USSR), November 5, 1971, p. 2 [in Russian].

Krasnoyarskiy Komsomolets (Krasnoyarsk, USSR), September 14, 1971, p. 2 [in Russian].

Zapolyarnaya Pravda (Arctic Pravda) (Norilsk, USSR), August 6, 1971, p. 3 [in Russian].

Krasnoyarskiy Komsomolets (Krasnoyarsk, USSR), July 30, 1971, p. 2 [in Russian].

Krasnoyarskiy Rabochiy (The Krasnoyarsk worker) (Krasnoyarsk, USSR), May 22, 1971, p. 4 [in Russian].

Za Kadry Tsvetnoy Metallurgii (For employees of the nonferrous metals industry) (Krasnoyarsk, USSR), May 7, 1971, p. 2 [in Russian].

Za Kadry Tsvetnoy Metallurgii (For employees of the nonferrous metals industry) (Krasnoyarsk, USSR), April 30, 1971, p. 2 [in Russian].

Krasnoyarskiy Rabochiy (The Krasnoyarsk worker) (Krasnoyarsk, USSR), April 17, 1971, p. 4 [in Russian].

Krasnoyarskiy Rabochiy (The Krasnoyarsk worker) (Krasnoyarsk, USSR), January 13, 1970, p. 4 [in Russian].

Krasnoyarskiy Komsomolets (Krasnoyarsk, USSR), January 3, 1969, p. 4 [in Russian].

Krasnoyarskiy Komsomolets (Krasnoyarsk, USSR), October 6, 1968, p. 2 [in Russian].

Krasnoyarskiy Komsomolets (Krasnoyarsk, USSR), March 20, 1968, p. 3 [in Russian].

Krasnoyarskiy Rabochiy (The Krasnoyarsk worker) (Krasnoyarsk, USSR), December 5, 1967, p. 4 [in Russian].

ABOUT THE AUTHOR

Born February 21, 1949, in Siberia, Russia. Ph.D. in Managerial Economics; Doctor of Science in Economics, Honorary Doctor of Humane Letters (*honoris causa*). Life Title: Professor of Political Economy, Life Member of Russian Academy of Natural Sciences. Currently, Professor of Management Systems and International Business at Fordham University, Graduate School of Business and College of Business Administration, New York.

Vladimir Kvint graduated from high school in 1966 in the city of Norilsk, which is located in the Arctic part of eastern Siberia. Between 1963 and 1969 he was a dedicated sportsman-boxer and in 1968 won the title of Junior Champion of Russia and USSR Student Games. From 1964 to 1971 he was a worker and team leader. Concurrently, from 1966 to 1972, he was a full-time student at the Krasnoyarsk Graduate Institute of Nonferrous Metals. In 1971 he was deemed the best student in economics in a USSR national competition. He graduated with honors in 1972 and received a Master of Science in Mining/Electrical Engineering, with a thesis entitled "Electrification of the Underground Mine 'Zapolyarnyi' of the Norilsk Concern." In 1972 he worked as an Assistant Professor of Political Economy, and from 1972 to 1975 was a full-time Ph.D. candidate at the Plekhanov Moscow Institute of National Economy, where he prepared his dissertation, "Organization and Stages of Management in the Technological Development of Industry" (e.g., the automation of nonferrous metallurgy). This dissertation was presented in 1975 to unanimous approval, and Mr. Kvint was awarded the title of Ph.D. in Economics (Managerial Economics).

In 1988, Dr. Kvint prepared a dissertation on the "Regional Management of the Scientific-Technological Development of the National Economy." He presented this dissertation to the Research Council of the Institute of Economy, USSR Academy of Sciences in Moscow and received the degree of Doctor of Sciences in Economics.

Dr. Kvint worked as the Chief of the Department of Organization of Management of the Norilsk Mining Metallurgical Concern (1975–

76), the largest Russian enterprise (150,000 employees) and the largest producer of nickel, cobalt, platinum, paladins, and osmium in the world, as well as one of the world's largest producers of copper and gold. As the founder of this department, he prepared the first General Organization Structure of the concern, including all its plants and departments.

From 1976 to 1978 Dr. Kvint worked as the Deputy Director General and Deputy Chairman of "Sib Tsvetmet Automatica" (Sib Auto), a scientific-technological company, which automated the nonferrous metals industry throughout the former USSR. This company now has more than 5,000 employees. Dr. Kvint was responsible for economic policy, organization of compensation systems, business planning, and the financial and accounting departments. At the same time he was Chief of the Economics Laboratory, and prepared strategies and forecasts for the nonferrous, precious metal, and diamond industries.

In 1978, Dr. Kvint was invited to join the USSR Academy of Sciences and was elected Chief of the Department of Regional Problems of Scientific-Technical Progress of the Institute of Economy and Industrial Organization of the Siberian branch of the Academy of Sciences. From 1982 to 1989 he worked in the Institute of Economy, USSR Academy of Sciences, in Moscow, as a Senior Researcher in the Department of Economic Problems of Scientific-Technological Revolution. Following that he became the Chief of Department of Theoretical Problems of Organization of Management of National Economy, and later a leading researcher in the Department of Methodology of Political Economy.

During his time in the Siberian branch of the USSR Academy of Sciences, Dr. Kvint developed methods of studying economic situations, natural resources, and business opportunities through the organizing of complex economic expeditions. In 1979, by the decision of the Siberian branch of the Academy of Sciences, he was appointed to head these expeditions, and he continued in this position until 1982. He organized several major economic expeditions into the Siberian Arctic, including the first economic expedition in history to venture through the entire Arctic Seaway (1980) by ship, helicopter, and jeep. In 1982, one of his expeditions traveled by sea over the entire Pacific Coast of Russia to study its natural resources. Later, he used these methods to study the regional economies in Uzbekistan

(1983), the Donetzk region of Ukraine (1984), Daghestan (1985), Estonia (1986), Georgia (1986), Mongolia (1987), Belarus (1988), and Latvia (1988).

In the years from 1978 to 1986, Dr. Kvint developed the concept of the Economic Mechanism of Organization of Management of Scientific-Technical Development. This study prompted several innovations in the theory of regional and emerging markets, its economy and management, including the concept of the economic mechanism of the organization of regional management of scientific-technical developments. This concept is the discovery of two new trends of scientific-technological progress: regionalization and technologicalization, and the influence of the trends on the national economy. Dr. Kvint developed a system of optimization models of developing strategies of companies in new regional and emerging markets using, among others, Boole's algebra and Pareto's Law. He tried to uncover the nature and form of the correlation between scientific-technological progress and regional complexes. He defined the category of regional scientific-technological policy; the main goal of this policy was to promote the health of people and the ecological system of the region. He also studied the role of this policy in the human factor of the economy.

Dr. Kvint was a leader and member of the team which first prepared "Methods of Preparation of Complex Regional Program of Scientific-Technical Progress" (1980). In 1986, he prepared a report on the Organization of Strategic Development of Scientific-Technical Progress, which he presented to the USSR Council of Ministers. He explained that without activation of these factors the Soviet Union would have no economic future. From 1980 to 1988, Dr. Kvint prepared reports on the methodology for the preparation of Regional Programs of Scientific-Technical Progress, and supervised this program, or parts of it, for the Krasnoyarsk Territory, Siberia, Daghestan, Donbas, and Mongolia. For these reports, Dr. Kvint was awarded the Silver Medal for Achievements in National Economy by the USSR Main National Exhibitions Committee (1986), the Artem Award in Ukraine (1986), the Commendation of the Presidium of the USSR Academy of Sciences (1988), and awards from several other academic institutions. In 1988 and 1989 he prepared a political and economic analysis of the situation in the USSR and forecast that the Soviet Union would cease to exist by the end of 1991 or in 1992. In fact, the Soviet Union disappeared in December 1991. His forecast was published in Austria, the United Kingdom, the U.S., and, in part, in Russia. After the Soviet Union disintegrated and the role of regional governments grew, Dr. Kvint's recommendations found practical implementation in Russia and other former Soviet republics.

From 1989 to1994, he conducted studies in the fields of high-tech international business telecommunications and international cooperation in the production of technological control systems and the metallurgy and mining industry. During that period he studied problems related to the creation and operation of international joint ventures with partners from several countries, the operational processess of special industrial, sea ports and trade and free economic zones in Russia, Belarus, China, Belgium, and the United States. Dr. Kvint has presented the results of these studies at several conferences in Austria, Belgium, Poland, Russia, and Ukraine as well as in the U.S.—at the New York Academy of Sciences, the American Economics Association, the Academy of International Business, and other academies.

As a result of his studies, Dr. Kvint has published books in Russia, Ukraine, Poland, and the U.S., and more than 250 articles, which have appeared in numerous periodicals, magazines, and newspapers in several countries, including the U.S. (*Forbes, Harvard Business Review, Institutional Investor, Journal of Accountancy, International Executive, The New York Times*). Some of his books are: *Acceleration of Technical Industrial Development* (Moscow, 1976; received National Award); *The Introduction and Use of Automation Systems* (Moscow, 1981); *Krasnoyarsk Experiment* (Moscow, 1982); *Regional Scientific-Technological Complexes* (with co-authors; Donetzk, Ukraine, 1983); *Under the Polar Star* (Moscow, 1985; received National Award); *Management of Scientific-Technical Progress: Personal Aspect* (Moscow, 1986); *Enterprise-Industry-Region: The Economic and Scientific-Technical Information* (with co-authors; Moscow, 1987); *Scientific Technological Development of the Economy of Daghestan Republic* (Mahachkala, 1988); *The Inter-Republic Relationship* (Warsaw, 1989); and *The Barefoot Shoemaker: Capitalizing on the New Russia* (New York, 1993); *Creating and Managing International Joint Ventures* (with co-authors; Westport, Connecticut, 1996); *Emerging Market of Russia* (title editor and co-author; New

York, 1997). His cover story for *Forbes*, "Russia Should Quit the Soviet Union" (February 1990), was included in a list of best business
stories in the United States.

Dr. Kvint's career includes elections as Deputy Chairman of the
Research Council for Regional Economy, USSR Academy of Sciences; member of the Science Council of the Commission for Productive Forces and Natural Resources with the Presidium of USSR
Academy of Sciences; member of the Research Council for International Relationships with the Presidium of the USSR Academy of
Sciences; member of the USSR (Russia) Philosophical Society;
member of the Research Council of Plekhanov Moscow Institute of
National Economy, board member of the USSR Exporters Association; and member of the editorial board of the most popular Russian
Business magazine, *ECO*, which had a circulation of 200,000. From
1985 to 1989 Dr. Kvint was adviser to the USSR leadership, government, and parliament.

Dr. Kvint has served as the mentor for several Ph.D. dissertations
in economics and management, and for two Doctorates of Science
in Economics dissertations. In 1989, he received the Life-Title Professor of Political Economy—the highest state academic title in the
former USSR and now in all countries of the former Soviet bloc.

Between 1988 and 1990 he was a creator and deputy chairman of
the board of several joint ventures in the USSR with partners from
Western countries.

Since 1989, Dr. Kvint has had a consulting practice and consults
with several leading industrial and financial companies and banks
from several European countries, the U.S., Russia, Ukraine, and
Latin America. He has been consulting with General Electric since
1989, with Timex Corp., TOSCO Corp., Baker & McKenzie (the
largest law firm in the world), Engelhart, Trans-America Leasing,
Cable and Wireless (U.K.), Petersburg Long Distance Investment
Corporation (Russia), Scandinavian Trading Company (Sweden),
State Investment Corporation (Russia), Fairchild Corporation,
Overseas Private Investment Corporation, and others. He also con-
sults with the governments of several European countries, including
Bulgaria and Romania, as well as with U.S. Senators. From 1992 until
November 1997 Dr. Kvint worked with Arthur Andersen (the largest
professional company in the world, with offices in 358 cities in 78
countries). As a senior consultant, he was then promoted to director

and managing director of emerging markets worldwide. His responsibilities included analyzing economies and the development of commercial environment in emerging markets worldwide, including
Latin America, Southeast Asia, North Africa, and the former Soviet
bloc. He developed comprehensive strategic plans for these markets,
with practical steps for management and implementation, for a wide
variety of industrial, consumer, and financial services firms. He conducted market studies and feasibility studies for the creation and
operation of leading global companies in emerging markets, performed economic forecasts, and consulted on establishment of privatization programs and capital market institutions. During that
period he conducted, among others, the following studies: Influence
of Emerging Markets on Global Risk Management Systems; Political,
Economic, and Business Approaches to Evaluation of Emerging Markets; Top Six European Emerging Markets; Economic Analysis of
MERCOSUR; Situational Analysis of Current Telecom Industry and
Forecasts in the Russian Federation; Nature of International Joint
Ventures and Their Role in Global Business; Reserves, Production,
and Utilization of Nickel in Russia; Privatization of Telebras, Brazil.
Dr. Kvint led organization for high-level meetings, conferences, and
forums focused on emerging markets. He was Chairman of the
World Economic Development Congress Summit for Institution In-
vestors, Washington, D.C., 1995; the World Economic Development
Congress Global Risk Management Summit, Washington, D.C.,
1996; and the International Banking Congress: US–CIS and Baltics,
1997.

Dr. Kvint has lectured at universities in Austria, Belarus, Belgium,
Canada, Georgia, Germany, Great Britain, Latvia, Poland, Russia,
and in the United States, including the Russian Research Center at
Harvard University, Kellogg Business School at Northwestern Univer-
sity, and Fuqua School of Business at Duke University, as well as the
New Jersey Institute of Technology, Whittier College, Kent State
University, University of Southern California, UCLA, and Baruch
College of the City University of New York. In 1989, he was elected
a Visiting Professor at the Vienna Economic University. In 1990, he
became a Distinguished Lecturer at the Fordham University Graduate School of Business Administration (New York) and in 1991 a
Distinguished Professor in Economics at Babson College (Massachusetts). From 1995 Dr. Kvint was also Adjunct Professor of Manage-

ment Strategies, Leonard N. Stern School of Business, New York University. In 1992, Dr. Kvint received a two-year scholarship awarded by the Werner Heritage Foundation, New York, and in 1993 a Faculty Scholarship award by the University of Southern California.

In 1993, he was elected a member of the Research Council for Regional Economy and Inter-Republic Relationships of the Russian Academy of Sciences and the International Committee of Muhlenberg College in Pennsylvania. He was elected a board member of the non-government international non-profit organization "Open Economy of Eastern Europe" (Kiev, Ukraine), and a member of the Bretton Woods Committee (Washington, D.C.).

In 1994, he was elected for life as full member (academician) of the Russian Academy of Natural Sciences. He is listed in *Who's Who in America*, *Who's Who in the World*, *Who's Who in Science and Engineering*, *Who's Who in Finance and Industry*, *Who's Who in American Education*, *Who's Who Among American Teachers*, the *International Who's Who of Intellectuals* (Great Britain), the *International Directory of Distinguished Leadership*, and the *International Directory of Business and Management Scholars and Research*, prepared by Harvard University.

In 1997, he was elected a member of the board of directors of the Newscorp subsidiary PLD Telecom, the only telecommunications company whose business focus is exclusively on Russia, Kazakstan, and Belarus, and which is listed on NASDAQ and the Toronto Stock Exchange. He has consulted on the company's listing on NASDAQ, and advised on the development of corporate strategy for expanding and managing business in the former Soviet Union, on entry into new regions, and on appropriate joint venture partners.

Also in 1997, he was elected a vice chairman of one of the most reliable Russian banks—Elbim Bank (Moscow), as well as a member of the board of the largest private holding company in Bulgaria—Nove-Ad-Holding. In the same year, for his studies on Emerging Markets, he was awarded an Honorary Doctorate (*honoris causa*) by the University of Bridgeport, Connecticut, and received the title Honorary Fellow of the New England Center for International and Regional Studies.

CHRISTOPHER COX
HILDA RUDD